SCARECROW AUTHOR BIBLIOGRAPHIES

1. John Steinbeck—1929–71 (Tetsumaro Hayashi). 1973. *See also nos. 64 and 99.*
2. Joseph Conrad (Theodore G. Ehrsam). 1969.
3. Arthur Miller (Tetsumaro Hayashi). 2nd ed., 1976.
4. Katherine Anne Porter (Waldrip & Bauer). 1969.
5. Philip Freneau (Philip M. Marsh). 1970.
6. Robert Greene (Tetsumaro Hayashi). 1971.
7. Benjamin Disraeli (R. W. Stewart). 1972.
8. John Berryman (Richard W. Kelly). 1972.
9. William Dean Howells (Vito J. Brenni). 1973.
10. Jean Anouilh (Kathleen W. Kelly). 1973.
11. E. M. Forster (Alfred Borrello). 1973.
12. The Marquis de Sade (E. Pierre Chanover). 1973.
13. Alain Robbe-Grillet (Dale W. Frazier). 1973.
14. Northrop Frye (Robert D. Denham). 1974.
15. Federico García Lorca (Laurenti & Siracusa). 1974.
16. Ben Jonson (Brock & Welsh). 1974.
17. Four French Dramatists: Eugène Brieux, François de Curel, Emile Fabre, Paul Hervieu (Edmund F. Santa Vicca). 1974.
18. Ralph Waldo Ellison (Jacqueline Covo). 1974.
19. Philip Roth (Bernard F. Rodgers, Jr.). 2nd ed., 1984.
20. Norman Mailer (Laura Adams). 1974.
21. Sir John Betjeman (Margaret Stapleton). 1974.
22. Elie Wiesel (Molly Abramowitz). 1974.
23. Paul Laurence Dunbar (Eugene W. Metcalf, Jr.). 1975.
24. Henry James (Beatrice Ricks). 1975.
25. Robert Frost (Lentricchia & Lentricchia). 1976.
26. Sherwood Anderson (Douglas G. Rogers). 1976.
27. Iris Murdoch and Muriel Spark (Tominaga & Schneidermeyer). 1976.
28. John Ruskin (Kirk H. Beetz). 1976.
29. Georges Simenon (Trudee Young). 1976.
30. George Gordon, Lord Byron (Oscar José Santucho). 1977.
31. John Barth (Richard Vine). 1977.
32. John Hawkes (Carol A. Hryciw). 1977.
33. William Everson (Bartlett & Campo). 1977.
34. May Sarton (Lenora P. Blouin). 1978.
35. Wilkie Collins (Kirk H. Beetz). 1978.
36. Sylvia Plath (Lane & Stevens). 1978.
37. E. B. White (A. J. Anderson). 1978.

38. Henry Miller (Lawrence J. Shifreen). 1979.
39. Ralph Waldo Emerson (Jeanetta Boswell). 1979.
40. James Dickey (Jim Elledge). 1979.
41. Henry Fielding (H. George Hahn). 1979.
42. Paul Goodman (Tom Nicely). 1979.
43. Christopher Marlowe (Kenneth Friedenreich). 1979.
44. Leo Tolstoy (Egan & Egan). 1979.
45. T. S. Eliot (Beatrice Ricks). 1980.
46. Allen Ginsberg (Michelle P. Kraus). 1980.
47. Anthony Burgess (Jeutonne P. Brewer). 1980.
48. Tennessee Williams (Drewey Wayne Gunn). 1980. Out of print. *See no. 89.*
49. William Faulkner (Beatrice Ricks). 1981. *See also no. 88.*
50. Lillian Hellman (Mary Marguerite Riordan). 1980.
51. Walt Whitman (Jeanetta Boswell). 1980.
52. Jack Kerouac (Robert J. Milewski). 1981.
53. Herman Melville (Jeanetta Boswell). 1981.
54. Horatio Alger, Jr. (Scharnhorst & Bales). 1981.
55. Graham Greene (A. F. Cassis). 1981.
56. Henry David Thoreau (Boswell & Crouch). 1981.
57. Nathaniel Hawthorne—1900–78 (Jeanetta Boswell). 1982. *See also no. 82.*
58. Jean Genet (R. C. Webb). 1982.
59. August Derleth (Alison Morley Wilson). 1983.
60. John Milton (Michael A. Mikolajczak). 1983.
61. Algernon Charles Swinburne (Kirk H. Beetz). 1982.
62. George Washington Cable (William H. Roberson). 1982.
63. Christine de Pizan (Edith Yenal). 2nd ed., 1989.
64. John Steinbeck—1971–81 (Tetsumaro Hayashi). 1983. *See also nos. 1 and 99.*
65. John G. Neihardt (John Thomas Richards). 1983.
66. Yvor Winters (Grosvenor Powell). 1983.
67. Sean O'Casey (E. H. Mikhail). 1985.
68. Tennyson (Kirk H. Beetz). 1984.
69. Floyd Dell (Judith Nierman). 1984.
70. R. C. Hutchinson (Robert Green). 1985.
71. Charlotte Perkins Gilman (Gary Scharnhorst). 1985.
72. Maxwell Anderson (Alfred S. Shivers). 1985.
73. Theodore Dreiser (Jeanetta Boswell). 1986.
74. Ezra Pound (Beatrice Ricks). 1986.
75. Robert Bly (William H. Roberson). 1986.
76. Edward Albee (Richard Tyce). 1986.

77. Robinson Jeffers (Jeanetta Boswell). 1986.

78. Edward Bellamy (Nancy Snell Griffith). 1986.

79. Studies on Clarín (David Torres). 1987.

80. Edwin Arlington Robinson (Jeanetta Boswell). 1988.

81. Antonio Buero Vallejo and Alfonso Sastre (Marsha Forys). 1988.

82. Nathaniel Hawthorne—pre-1900 (Gary Scharnhorst). 1988. *See also no. 57.*

83. V. S. Naipaul (Kelvin Jarvis). 1989.

84. Larry Eigner (Irving P. Leif). 1989.

85. Kenneth Roberts (Jack Bales). 1989.

86. Louise Bogan (Claire Knox). 1990.

87. Ogden Nash (George W. Crandell). 1990.

88. William Faulkner (John E. Bassett). 1991. *See also no. 49.*

89. Tennessee Williams (Drewey Wayne Gunn). 2nd ed., 1991.

90. Lord Dunsany (Joshi & Schweitzer). 1993.

91. Elizabeth Gaskell (Nancy S. Weyant). 1994.

92. Andrew M. Greeley (Elizabeth Harrison). 1994.

93. Barbara Pym (Orphia Jane Allen). 1994.

94. James Wright (William H. Roberson). 1995.

95. Bret Harte (Gary Scharnhorst). 1995.

96. Thomas Wolfe (John Bassett). 1996.

97. William Congreve (Laurence Bartlett). 1996.

98. Esther Forbes (Jack Bales). 1998.

99. The Hayashi Steinbeck Bibliography: 1982–1996 (Meyer). 1998 *See also nos. 1 and 64.*

100. Jessamyn West (Ann Dahlstrom Farmer and Philip M. O'Brien). 1998.

The Hayashi Steinbeck Bibliography

1982–1996

Michael J. Meyer

Scarecrow Author Bibliographies, No. 99

The Scarecrow Press, Inc.
Lanham, Md., & London
1998

SCARECROW PRESS, INC.

Published in the United States of America
by Scarecrow Press, Inc.
4720 Boston Way
Lanham, Maryland 20706

4 Pleydell Gardens
Kent CT20 2DN, England

This book is based on and is intended to update *John Steinbeck: A Concise Bibliography (1930–65)* and *A New Steinbeck Bibliography: 1971–1981* by Tetsumaro Hayashi, copyright The Scarecrow Press.

British Library Cataloguing in Publication Information Available

Library of Congress Cataloging-in-Publication Data

Meyer, Michael J., 1943–
   The Hayashi Steinbeck bibliography, 1982–1996 / Michael J. Meyer.
      p.   cm. — (Scarecrow author bibliographies ; no. 99)
   "Based on and . . . intended to update John Steinbeck: a concise
bibliography (1930–65) and A new Steinbeck bibliography: 1971–1981 by
Tetsumaro Hayashi"—T.p. verso.
   Includes index.
   ISBN 0-8108-3482-0 (cloth : alk. paper)
   1. Steinbeck, John, 1902–1968—Bibliography.   I. Hayashi, Tetsumaro.
John Steinbeck: a concise bibliography, 1930–65. II. Hayashi, Tetsumaro.
A new Steinbeck bibliography. III. Title. IV. Series.
Z8839.4.M491998
[PS3537.T3234]
016.813'52—dc21   98-22003

⊖™ The paper used in this publication meets the minimum requirements of
American National Standard for Information Sciences—Permanence of
Paper for Printed Library Materials, ANSI Z39.48–1984.
Manufactured in the United States of America.

With loving thanks to
Agnes McNeill Donohue,
friend and mentor,
who lovingly nurtured my interest in Steinbeck
and made me the scholar I am today

Contents

Acknowledgments

The work required of any serious bibliographer usually adds up to an enormous task. Assembling an accurate listing of citations and deciding on necessary categories has left me exhilarated and exhausted at the same time. I think the feeling of accomplishment at its publication can be compared with the exultation felt when the final piece is finally placed in an extremely difficult jigsaw puzzle. I am honored to continue in Tetsumaro Hayashi's footsteps and to be able to offer the academic community a second supplement to the original bibliography which was published almost thirty years ago. As I began to place individual pieces in place for this book, I realized how indebted I am to other scholars who have gone before me.

First, I owe thanks to Father Carl Stratman of Loyola University whose insistence on meticulous accuracy in graduate school prepared me well for this assignment. I can still remember he gave my fifty-page bibliography on John Dos Passos an A- because my typewriter ribbon was too light. That onetime flaw can now thankfully be corrected with a laser printer.

Other Steinbeck scholars have also been invaluable sources of information. I owe a great deal to Roy Simmonds who graciously photocopied his over-200-page listing of Steinbeckiana. In addition, Warren French, Robert DeMott, Jackson Benson, John Timmerman, Louis Owens, Chip Hughes, Brian Railsback, Susan Shillinglaw and Mimi Reisel Gladstein provided personal listings of their Steinbeck scholarship. I am especially indebted to John Ditsky who not only provided a list but also offered to loan me his copy of Hayashi's first supplement to the original bibliography when even Scarecrow Press was unable to produce a copy from its archives.

Hayashi himself was typically gracious and encouraging as he has been in the past. From the beginning of my publishing experience, Ted has nurtured my career as a Steinbeck scholar, first by inviting me to contribute to Steinbeck Monograph Series No. 15 on *The Long Valley* in 1990 and then by appointing me as an assistant editor of *The Steinbeck Quarterly* from 1990 to 1993. Without his guidance and support during the past 10 years I would never have developed the self-confidence in my writing skills nor thought myself qualified to provide such a much-needed update for future Steinbeck studies.

Furthermore, I owe a great deal to Kiyoshi Nakayama of the Steinbeck Society of Japan for providing back issues of their newsletter and for his work on the foreign bibliography published by Kansai University Press in Osaka. My Japanese-literate students at Hong Kong International School (Tomo Matsumoto, Nami Asaka, Mari Sasaki, Hiroko Usui, Naoko Kudo, Satchi Hattori and Yuko Matsunaga) provided translation of the Japanese characters into Americanized Japanese. Japanese translations were also provided and checked for accuracy by Naoko MacDonald, an HKIS faculty spouse, and F. Curtis Miles Bobbitt, professor of Japanese at the Chinese University of Hong Kong, Shatin, New Territories; a final check was made by a faithful Advanced Placement English student, Reyko Huang, who is also fluent in Japanese. Translators of other languages included my colleagues, Meg Finnin and Linda Dunoye (French), and staff member, Sabine Schaefer (German). HKIS computer whiz Jonathan Chen, now a university student at Rensselaer Polytechnic Institute, provided the necessary knowledge of technology to create an alphabetization system for the entries while Andrew Chung (HKIS '98) developed a program to number and renumber the listing when necessary without retyping. Other computer assistance was provided by Eleanor Shing (HKIS '99) as my typist/transcriber and by Justin Hardman (HKIS '99) who provided assistance with formatting and final printout. The dedication of these students to such levels of excellence is truly a credit to their desire to achieve academic excellence.

Finally, I am thankful for the help provided through the Internet which enabled me to access public and university catalogs from far away in Hong Kong and very grateful to the reference librarians at Wm. Rainey Harper College in Palatine, Illinois, as well as those at the Arlington Heights, Elk Grove Village, Schaumburg and Mt. Prospect Public Libraries. The librarians and technological staff at HKIS (Pat Alter, Rinda Gillespie, David Elliott, Victor Chan, Lisa Tam and Sylvia Thorpe) also were gracious in seeking out Steinbeck citations and in translating computer disks by scanning and downloading.

Introduction

I, of course, am aware that no bibliography is exhaustive. Even the PMLA bibliographies fail to be all-inclusive, missing many Steinbeck studies cited elsewhere. Just when it seemed as if the research was complete, still another entry would appear from a previously undiscovered source. However, I believe I have conscientiously checked all available indexes and journals so that this volume is not only accurate but thorough as well. The following reference works and journals have been consulted as this listing has been compiled:

Abstracts of English Studies
American Literary Scholarship: An Annual
American Literature
Bibliographic Index
Biography Index
Book Review Digest
Book Review Index
Chicago Tribune Index
Cumulative Book Index
Dissertation Abstracts International
Education Index
Essay and General Literature Index
Humanities Index
Infotrac
Journal of Modern Literature
Modern Drama
Modern Fiction Studies
New York Times Index
MLA Annual Bibliography
Reader's Guide to Periodical Literature
The Steinbeck Newsletter
The Steinbeck Newsletter of Japan (now
*   Steinbeck Studies)*
Steinbeck Quarterly (Annual Index)
Studies in American Fiction
Studies in the Novel

Studies in Short Fiction
Subject Guide to Books in Print
Twentieth Century Literature

The divisions I have decided on for the book include the following categories:

Works by Steinbeck - editions of Steinbeck's appearing since 1981 and anthologies and texts which include works by Steinbeck

Books - biographies, biographical sketches, critical studies and collections of secondary criticism of the Steinbeck canon

Articles - essays and critical analyses appearing in scholarly journals as well as collections in books (A separate entry will be given for the book but a cross reference of individual essays will also be found listing specific page numbers)

Dissertations/ M.A. and B.A. Honors Theses - studies listed in Dissertations Abstracts International and theses held in individual research libraries

Book reviews - Reviews appearing in journals or newspapers regarding evaluation of primary sources and/or secondary criticism of the Steinbeck canon

Newspapers - journalistic studies or commentaries regarding Steinbeck or Steinbeckiana

Other Media - entries related to dramatic production of Steinbeck's works, film adaptations, audio tapes, CD-roms, including reviews of the same

Reference - Selective listings on individual works written by Steinbeck, on the canon in general, on work by an individual critic and on works available in certain research collections

Foreign Translations - editions and collections of Steinbeck's works appearing in translation in a language other than English

Foreign Articles - essays and critical analyses in languages other than English appearing in journals and/or collections in books

Foreign Books - biographies, critical studies and collections of secondary criticism in languages other than English

I have decided not to list the critical studies which have appeared in the Steinbeck monograph and essay series separately but instead to list them under books and articles. Unfortunately, this book does not contain the acquisitions of manuscripts and letters since 1981 at the various libraries who hold Steinbeck collections. Scholars should consult the special collections venues at each library for a complete listing of the holdings of notebooks, typescripts, handwritten manuscripts, letters etc. Users should note that the citations also include some works issued in 1997 and an addendum which lists some previous citations missed in earlier bibliographic works covering Steinbeck.

Chronology

1902   Born John Ernst Steinbeck on February 27, Salinas, California, the third child and only son (sisters are Esther, b. 1892, and Beth, b. 1894) of Olive Hamilton Steinbeck, a former schoolteacher, and John Ernst Steinbeck, manager of a flour mill. (Paternal grandfather, John Adolph Grossteinbeck, a German cabinetmaker from Dusseldorf, moved to Jerusalem with his brother Frederic in 1854. There he married Almira Dickson, daughter of Sarah Eldridge Dickson and evangelist Walter Dickson, Americans who had gone to the Holy Land to convert the Jews. After Arab raiders killed Frederic and raped Sarah Dickson and her daughter, Mary, in 1858, John and Almira came to the United States, where they used the name Steinbeck. They settled in New England and then in Florida, where John Ernst Steinbeck was born, before moving to California after the Civil War. Maternal grandfather, Samuel Hamilton, born in northern Ireland, immigrated to the United States at age 17 and settled in New York City, where he married Elizabeth Fagen, an American of northern Irish ancestry; they soon moved to California, where Hamilton homesteaded a ranch and was a skilled blacksmith.)

1903-09   Spends summers by the sea in Pacific Grove near Monterey and on uncle Tom Hamilton's ranch near King City. Sister Mary is born in 1905. Steinbeck enjoys roaming in fields and along seashore; from father learns to love gardening. Receives a red Shetland pony named Jill from family in 1906, and cares for her himself. Home is full of books; parents and older sisters read out loud to him, and he becomes acquainted at an early age with novels of Robert Louis Stevenson and Walter Scott, the Bible, Greek myths, The Pilgrim's Progress, and Paradise Lost. Begins reading books himself and especially enjoys Sir Thomas Malory's *La Morte d'Arthur* (later writes, "The Bible and Shakespeare and Pilgrim's Progress belonged to everyone. But this was mine — secretly mine. . . perhaps a passionate love for the English language opened to me from this one book"). Attends public schools in Salinas; does well in school and skips fifth grade. Enjoys reading Mark Twain and Jack London. Often cared for by older sisters while mother takes active part in town affairs.

1910   When the mill is closed in Salinas, father decides against taking job offer with a company farther north because it would mean uprooting the family. Father opens a feed and grain store which fails, and works briefly as accountant for sugar refinery before being appointed treasurer of Monterey County (holds position through continual re-election, until shortly before his death).

1918   In junior year of high school Steinbeck develops pleural pneumonia and nearly dies; nursed by mother on ranch farther down in Salinas Valley. Writes stories and reads them out loud to friends.

1919-24 Graduates from Salinas High School. Begins sporadic attendance at Stanford University in October as an English major. Meets Carlton "Dook" Sheffield and Carl Wilhelmson, who become lifelong friends. In spring 1920 undergoes operation for acute appendicitis. After working as a surveyor in mountains above Big Sur, works in the summer as carpenter's helper at Spreckels' sugar mill (continues to work over the next several years at the mill and on its many sugar beet ranches, where his duties include running chemical tests on sugar beets and supervising day laborers). Returns to Stanford full time in January 1923; studies English versification with William Herbert Carruth in Spring 1923 and enrolls for summer study at Stanford-affiliated Hopkins Marine Station in Pacific Grove where he takes courses in English and zoology. Studies creative writing with Edith Mirrielees at Stanford for two terms in 1924. Influenced by philosophy lectures of Harold Chapman Brown. Publishes stories "Finger of Cloud: A Satire on College Protervity" and "Adventures in Arcademy: A Journey into the Ridiculous" in the February and June issues of *The Stanford Spectator*, a student literary magazine.

1925-26   Leaves Stanford without a degree in June 1925, having completed less than three years of course work. After working during the summer as a caretaker of a lodge near Lake Tahoe, sails on a freighter by way of the Panama Canal to New York City. Settles in Brooklyn (moves to Gramercy Park area of Manhattan in 1926). Works as a laborer on the construction of Madison Square Garden and as a reporter for the *New York American*. Submits short stories to Robert M. McBride and Company, New York Publishing firm, which rejects them. Returns to California by freighter in Summer 1926, working as an assistant steward in return for passage. Hired in the fall to work as a caretaker of Lake Tahoe estate of Mrs. Alice Brigham.

1927   Lives alone on the Brigham estate during winter. Story "The Gifts of Iban" appears in *The Smoker's Companion* in March under the pseudonym "John Stern". Works with close friend Webster "Toby" Street on Street's play "The Green Lady" (material becomes the basis for *To a God Unknown*).

1928   Finishes first novel, *Cup of Gold* in January. Leaves caretaker job in May and begins work at fish hatchery in Tahoe City in June. Meets Carol Henning, a tourist visiting the hatchery, during summer. Fired from hatchery job for wrecking superintendent's truck. In September moves to San Francisco, where he lives in a "dark little attic" on Powell Street and gets job as warehouse worker for a company owned by sister Mary's husband, Bill Dekker.

1929   With the help of college acquaintance Amasa (Ted) Miller, *Cup of Gold* is accepted for publication by Robert M. McBride. Gives up warehouse job and with father's financial help spends most of the year writing in Pacific Grove and Palo Alto (father frequently sends money during the next several years). *Cup of Gold* published in August. Moves back to San Francisco in the fall.

1930   Marries Carol Henning in January. In September they move to the family's three-room cottage in Pacific Grove, where they live rent-free and feed themselves in part through fishing and raising vegetables. Manuscript of *To a God Unknown* rejected by Robert M. McBride. Meets marine biologist Edward F. Ricketts, owner of Pacific Biological Laboratory, who becomes close friend and major intellectual influence. Writes experimental novella, *Dissonant Symphony* and, under pseudonym Peter Pym, crime novel *Murder at Full Moon*; neither is accepted for publication, and he later destroys manuscript of *Dissonant Symphony*.

1931   Works on series of related stories, *The Pastures of Heaven*. Begins lifelong association with New York literary agency McIntosh & Otis (agent Elizabeth Otis becomes close friend).

1932   *The Pastures of Heaven* accepted for publication by Cape and Smith in February. Through Ricketts, becomes acquainted with religious scholar Joseph Campbell. Following bankruptcy of Cape and Smith, *The Pastures of Heaven* is published by Brewer, Warren, and Putnam (where Cape and Smith editor Robert O. Ballou had moved)

1933   Despite father's financial help, Steinbeck and Carol are unable to make ends meet and are forced in February to give up their new home. Mother becomes seriously ill in March, and after being hospitalized, suffers massive stroke; Steinbeck and Carol move to family home in Salinas. Steinbeck spends most of his time taking care of his mother at hospital, and, after her release in June, at home. Writes the first of the four stories later joined together as *The Red Pony*. Father collapses in August and remains incapacitated for nearly a year; cared for by Carol at Pacific Grove cottage while Steinbeck spends much time in Salinas caring for mother. *To a God Unknown* published in September by Robert O. Ballou under his own imprint. During summer and fall completes first draft of *Tortilla Flat*, partly based on anecdotes told to him by Susan Gregory, a high school Spanish teacher in Monterey. "The Red Pony" (later titled "The Gift") and "The Great Mountains" appear in *North American Review*, November/December (both later become part of *The Red Pony*).

1934   Mother dies in February. Steinbeck and Carol live with father
        in Pacific Grove cottage until arrangements are made for father
        to move back into Salinas home with caretakers in March.
        Steinbeck meets fugitive labor organizers Cicil McKiddy and
        Carl Williams in Seaside, California; interview them about their
        involvement with 1933 cotton workers' strike in the San
        Joaquin Valley, organized by Communist-led Cannery and
        Agricultural Workers' Industrial Union, and about strike leader
        Pat Chambers. Manuscript of *Tortilla Flat* rejected by Robert
        O. Ballou and by Louis Kronenberger at Knopf. During
        summer completes nine short stories, eight of which are later
        collected in *The Long Valley*. Begins writing *In Dubious Battle*,
        based in part on interviews with McKiddy and Williams, in
        August. *Tortilla Flat* is accepted for publication by Pascal
        Covici of Covici-Friede. Enunciates "aggregation" theory of
        groups in unpublished essay, "Argument of Phalanx": "Men are
        not final individuals but units in the greater beast, the phalanx.
        The nature of the phalanx is not the sum of the natures of unit-
        men, but a new individual having emotions and ends of its own,
        and these are foreign and incomprehensible to unit-men."

1935   *In Dubious Battle* accepted by Covici-Friede. Father dies in
        May. *Tortilla Flat*, published in May, first commercially
        successful book. Meets Pascal Covici for the first time in
        August. Learns that film rights for *Tortilla Flat* have been sold
        to Paramount for $4,000. Returns to United States at year's
        end, traveling to New York to sign Paramount contract and then
        to Pacific Grove before Christmas.

1936   *In Dubious Battle* published by Covici-Friede in January.
        Begins work on children's book (project eventually leads him to
        write *Of Mice and Men*); much of manuscript is destroyed by
        his dog in May. Visited by John O'Hara, who had contracted to
        write a dramatic adaptation (eventually abandoned) of *In
        Dubious Battle*; O'Hara becomes lifelong friend. In May begins
        to build house in Los Gatos, north of Monterey. Goes on six-
        day trip with Ricketts collecting octopuses along Baja
        California coast. Moves into Los Gatos house, completed at
        end of July. Completes *Of Mice and Men* in August.

Commissioned by San Francisco News to write articles on migrant farm workers. After meeting with federal officials at Resettlement Administration in San Francisco, tours San Joaquin Valley in bakery truck accompanied by former preacher Eric H. Thomsen, regional director of federal migrant camp program. At Arvin Sanitary Camp ("Weedpatch") in Kern County, meets camp director Tom Collins, and from his conversation and written reports on migrant workers gathers material later incorporated into *The Grapes of Wrath*. Articles published as "The Harvest Gypsies" in seven installments in October. Begins researching and writing novel about migrants (later referred to as "The Oklahomans"). Limited editions of "Nothing So Monstrous" (excerpt from *The Pastures of Heaven*) and "Saint Katy, the Virgin" published by Covici-Friede.

1937   *Of Mice and Men* published in March; becomes a bestseller and Book-of-the-Month Club selection. Works with director George S. Kaufman on dramatic adaptation of *Of Mice and Men*. Visits Farm Security Administration office in Washington, and talks with deputy administrator Dr. Will Alexander. Stories, "The Promise," "The Gift," and "The Great Mountains" published as *The Red Pony* in a limited edition by Covici-Friede. Travels in California in October doing research on migrants; joined at migrant camp in Gridley by Tom Collins, who accompanies him on rest of trip. *Of Mice and Men* opens on Broadway on November 23, starring Wallace Ford and Broderick Crawford; it runs for 207 performances (Steinbeck never sees the production).

1938   Dramatic adaptation of *Tortilla Flat* by Jack Kirkland opens on Broadway in January (closes after four performances). Meets documentary filmmaker Pare Lorentz. Makes two trips to San Joaquin Valley in February and March, where he joins Tom Collins in investigating conditions of migrant workers in the wake of devastating floods in Visalia. Article based on trips is rejected by Life. Invited by Lorentz, travels to Hollywood where he meets film directors King Vidor, Lewis Milestone, and Mervyn Le Roy and actor James Cagney. Article on floods published in April as "Starvation Under the Orange Trees" in *The Monterey Trader*. *Their Blood Is Strong*, expanded version of *The Harvest Gypsies* published as a pamphlet by Simon J. Lubin Society of California to raise money for migrant workers. In May abandons unfinished satirical novel ("Le Affair Lettuceberg") about vigilantes, suggested by brutal Salinas lettuce strike of September 1936. Learns that *Of Mice and Men* has won the New York Drama Critics' Circle Award as best play of 1937. In late May begins 100 day period of work on novel that becomes *The Grapes of Wrath*. Keeps journal of novel's composition (published posthumously in 1989 as *Working Days*); of the title, suggested by Carol, Steinbeck writes: "I like it because it is a march, and this book is a kind of march because it is in   our own revolutionary tradition and because in reference to this book it has a large meaning." Purchases 47-acre ranch (the "Old Biddle Ranch") outside Los Gatos; begins construction of new house on property in September 4. In July, Covici-Friede goes bankrupt and Pascal Covici joins Viking Press as senior editor; short story collection *The Long Valley* is published by Viking in September and sells well. (Viking becomes the publisher of all of Steinbeck's subsequent books.) Physically exhausted, completes manuscript of *The Grapes of Wrath* in November.

1939   Suffers for most of the year from crippling leg pain. Elizabeth Otis, his agent, urges him to make changes in *The Grapes of Wrath*; during two days of intensive work agrees to some revisions. Later writes to Covici, "This book wasn't written for delicate ladies. If they read it at all they're messing in something not their business. I've never changed a word to fit the prejudices of a group and I never will." Argues further with Covici over proposal to change the novel's ending: "You know that I have never been touchy about changes, but I have too many thousands of hours on this book, every incident has been too carefully chosen and its weight judged and fitted. The balance is there. One other thing — I am not writing a satisfying story. I've done my damnedest to rip a reader's nerves to rags, I don't want him satisfied." In March hears rumor that he is being investigated by the FBI; worries about

possible violence against him by Associated Farmers'
Organization. *The Grapes of Wrath*, published in April by
Viking with large advance sale, becomes the number one
national bestseller; screen rights are sold for $75,000. Novel is
banned or burned in Buffalo, New York, East St. Louis,
Illinois, and Kern County, California, is denounced in Congress
by Oklahoma representative Lyle Boren, and is the subject of a
protest meeting at the Palace Hotel in San Francisco. Steinbeck
is   overwhelmed   by   flood   of   public   attention   and
correspondence. Travels to Chicago in April to work with Pare
Lorentz on *The Fight For Life*, documentary about Chicago
Maternity Center. Rents apartment in Hollywood in June.
Through old friend Max Wagner, now working in Hollywood,
meets singer Gwendolyn ("Gwyn") Conger, and begins affair
with her. Difficulties with Carol lead to temporary separation;
they reconcile and go on car trip in Pacific Northwest, visiting
Vancouver. Travels with Carol in September to Chicago,
visiting Lorentz and science writer Paul de Kruif in connection
with *The Fight For Life*. Plans to devote himself to study of
science and to write science textbooks in collaboration with
Ricketts; spends much time at Ricketts' laboratory, and makes
marine collecting trips with him in San Francisco Bay area. In
December sees previews of John Ford's film version of *The
Grapes of Wrath* ("No punches were pulled — in fact . . . it is a
harsher thing than the book") and Lewis Milestone's film of *Of
Mice and Men* ("Milestone has done a curious lyrical thing. It
hangs together and is underplayed").

1940   In March, embarks with Ricketts, Carol, and small crew on
          marine collecting expedition in Gulf of California on boat
          Western Flyer, returning to Monterey April 20. Wins Pulitzer
          Prize for *The Grapes of Wrath*. Impressed by singer Woody
          Guthrie, who records "The Ballad of Tom Joad," based on *The
          Grapes of Wrath*. Travels with Carol to Mexico in May to work
          on script for *The Forgotten Village*, an independent feature film
          produced and directed by Herbert Kline, about the struggle to
          bring modern medicine to a remote village. Meets with Lewis
          Milestone in Hollywood about film version of *The Red Pony*.
          Disturbed by influence of German propaganda in Latin

America, writes to President Franklin D. Roosevelt, who receives him for a brief visit in which Steinbeck proposes the formation of a propaganda office focusing on the Western hemisphere. Visits Roosevelt again in September and proposes scheme to undermine Axis powers by distributing counterfeit German money in occupied countries of Europe. Returns to Mexico in October to work on *The Forgotten Village*.

1941   Buys small house on Eardley Street in Monterey. Tells Carol in April about affair with Gwyn Conger. Separates from Carol at end of April; lives in Eardley Street house. *The Forgotten Village*, film version of film script, illustrated with stills, published in May. Works on book about Gulf of California trip, describing it to Pascal Covici as "a new kind of writing," and completes manuscript in July. Works on screenplay for *The Red Pony*. In autumn moves to East Coast with Gwyn; they stay in a house on Burgess Meredith's farm in Suffern, New York, before moving in November into Bedford Hotel in Manhattan. Writes radio speeches for Foreign Information Service under direction of Robert E. Sherwood; travels frequently between New York and Washington. *Sea of Cortez: A Leisurely Journal of Travel and Research*, narrative by Steinbeck with a detailed scientific appendix by Ricketts, published in December. Film of *The Forgotten Village* banned for indecency by New York State Board of Censors because of scenes of childbirth and breast-feeding (ban lifted after public hearing).

1942   *The Moon Is Down*, set in occupied Norway, published in March; opens as play on Broadway in April. Moves into rented house at Sneden's Landing in Rockland County New York in April. Sells film rights to *The Moon Is Down*. Appointed special consultant to the Secretary of War and accepts assignment from the Army Air Force to write book about the training of bomber crews. Visits 20 air bases across the United States with photographer John Swope; their work is published in *Bombs Away: The Story of a Bomber Team*. Rents house in Sherman Oaks, California in September to work on film based on *Bombs Away* but production is plagued by difficulties and film is never made. With old friend Jack Wagner (brother of

Max Wagner) writes script for *A Medal for Benny*. Film of
Tortilla Flat, directed by Victor Fleming and starring Spencer
Tracy is released.

1943   Writes novella, (unpublished) as basis for film, *Lifeboat*,
directed by Alfred Hitchcock. Moves into apartment on East
51st Street in New York City with Gwyn. Divorce from Carol
becomes final on March 18. Marries Gwyn on March 29 in
New Orleans. Accredited as a war correspondent for the *New
York Herald Tribune*, following intensive security investigation
by army counter-intelligence. Travels to England on troop ship
in June: Meets photographer Robert Capa. Receives clearance
in early August to go to North Africa; travels in Algeria and
Tunisia, writing reports and doing an army film project. Sails
on PT boat from Tunisia to Sicily as part of a special operations
unit commanded by actor Douglas Fairbanks, Jr. that carries out
coastal raids designed to harass and mislead the Germans.
Participates in operations, including capture of Italian island of
Ventotene. After a few weeks in London, returns to New York
City in early October, suffering from effects of combat,
including burst eardrums and partial amnesia. Begins *Cannery
Row* in November. The Portable Steinbeck edited by Pascal
Covici published by Viking Press. Film of *The Moon is Down*
directed by Irving Pichel, is released.

1944   Sees screening of Hitchcock's *Lifeboat;* angered by changes in
his original story and tries unsuccessfully to have his name
removed from the credits. Travels with Gwyn to Mexico by
way of Chicago and New Orleans in mid-January. Begins to
develop film project, "The Pearl" (based on Mexican folktake
briefly recounted in *Sea of Cortez*, to be directed by Emilio
Fernandez. Returns to New York in March. Discusses plans for
a musical comedy, "The Wizard of Maine," with Frank Loesser.
Receives Academy Award nomination for best original story
for *Lifeboat*. Finishes *Cannery Row* in May, with central
character molded on Ricketts. Writes about the book: "One
thing it never mentions the war — not once .. The crap I wrote
overseas had a profoundly nauseating effect on me. Among
other unpleasant things, modern war is the most dishonest thing

imaginable." Son Thorn born August 2. In October moves back to California, settling in Soto House, large 19th-century adobe house near waterfront in Monterey.

1945   *Cannery Row* published; it sells well despite poor reviews. Completes draft of novella "The Pearl" and goes to Mexico with Gwyn in February to work with Fernandez on the film; they return in mid-March. Troubled by resentment he has experienced in Monterey, writes to Covici: "You remember how happy I was to come back here. It really was a homecoming. Well there is no home coming nor any welcome. What there is is jealousy and hatred and the knife in the back — Our old friends won't have us back... And the town and the region — that is the people of it — just pure poison." Returns to Mexico in April with Jack Wagner, followed by Gwyn and Thom; works on shooting script for "The Pearl" in luxurious rented house in Cuernavaca. Does research in Mexican archives for proposed film about Emiliano Zapata. With Jack Wagner, receives Academy Award nomination for best original story for *A Medal for Benny* (directed by Irving Pichel). Begins to work on *The Wayward Bus*. Gwyn leaves Mexico for New York because of ill health; Steinbeck visits her there for over a month, then returns to Cuernavaca in October for filming of "The Pearl." Having sold Monterey house, Steinbeck and Gwyn buy pair of adjacent brownstones on East 78th Street in New York City; he drives back to New York in early December.

1946   Settles into new home. Son John born June 12. After difficult pregnancy, Gwyn continues to be in poor health. Steinbeck returns to Mexico in August for further work on film of "The Pearl." After finishing *The Wayward Bus*, sails to Europe with Gwyn in October, visiting Sweden, Denmark, Norway, and France. Awarded King Haakon Liberty Cross in Norway for *The Moon Is Down*.

1947   Works on play "The Last Joan" (abandoned by April). *The Wayward Bus* published in February. Amid marital difficulties Gwyn goes to California for a month. With Robert Capa, Steinbeck plans trip to Russia for the *New York Herald Tribune*.

Hospitalized after seriously injuring knee and foot when second
story railing in apartment breaks. Still walking with a cane,
travels to France in June with Gwyn and Capa; after Gwyn
returns home in July, goes on with Capa for brief stay in
Sweden before proceeding to Soviet Union; visits Moscow,
Stalingrad, Ukraine, and Georgia; returns by way of Prague and
Budapest. Begins research for novel *The Salinas Valley* (later
East of Eden). *The Pearl* published in November.

1948   Invests in World Video, television venture which collapses after
a few months. Film of *The Pearl* released in the United States.
Goes to Monterey for several weeks in February mainly to
research *East of Eden*. *A Russian Journal*, with text by
Steinbeck and photographs by Capa, published in April.
Hospitalized in April for removal of varicose veins. Ed Ricketts
is severely injured in automobile accident on May 7 and dies on
May 11; Steinbeck writes to friend Bo Beskow, "There died the
greatest man I have known and the best teacher. It is going to
take a long time to reorganize my thinking and my planning
without him." After returning from funeral in Monterey, is told
by Gwyn that she wants a divorce; moves into Bedford Hotel.
Spends much of summer in Mexico, researching screenplay for
Viva Zapata! to be directed by Elia Kazan. Returns to
California in September, settling again in Pacific Grove house.
Divorce becomes final in October. Devotes himself to
gardening and home repairs; drinks heavily, and suffers from
deep depression. Travels to Mexico in November with Kazan.
Learns in December that he has been elected to the American
Academy of Arts and Letters.

1949   Film of *The Red Pony*, directed by Lewis Milestone and with
screenplay by Steinbeck released. Returns briefly to Mexico in
February. Over Memorial Day weekend, meets Elaine Scott,
wife of actor Zachary Scott; sees her frequently thereafter while
working in Hollywood on *Zapata* screenplay. Sons come to
stay for two months in the summer, first in a series of annual
visits mandated by custody agreement. Begins work on
Everyman (later *Burning Bright*) play in novella form. Finishes
draft of *Viva Zapata!* screenplay. Elaine Scott files for divorce;

Steinbeck moves to New York City and Elaine joins him there with her daughter Waverly; they settle in a large apartment on East 52nd Street.

1950   Finishes *Burning Bright* in January. In February works with Kazan in Los Angeles on *Zapata*. Travels with Elaine to Texas in the spring to meet her family in Fort Worth. *Burning Bright,* produced by Richard Rodgers and Oscar Hammerstein II and starring Kent Smith and Barbara Bel Geddes, opens on Broadway in October to generally poor reviews; novel version published in November. Resumes work on *East of Eden*. Marries Elaine on December 28, and they honeymoon in Bermuda.

1951   Writes in *East of Eden* journal addressed to Pascal Covici: "the form will not be startling, the writing will be spare and lean, the concepts hard, the philosophy old and yet new born. In a sense it will be two books — the story of my country and of me." Steinbeck and Elaine move in February into brownstone on East 72nd Street (their home for the next 13 years). Summers in Nantucket with Elaine and sons. *The Log From The Sea of Cortez*, edition of the narrative portion of *Sea of Cortez* with new introductory memoir "About Ed Ricketts," published in September. Completes draft of *East of Eden* in November.

1952   Renews acquaintance with playwright Arthur Miller. *Viva Zapata!* released. Travels from March to September in Morocco, Algeria, Spain, France, Switzerland, Italy, England, Scotland, and Ireland, writing articles for *Colliers*, with Elaine collaborating as photographer. Attacked by Italian communist newspaper *L'Unita* while in Rome for failure to denounce U. S. policy in Korea, and writes lengthy retort (incident recounted in *Colliers* article ("Duel Without Pistols"). *East of Eden* is published in September; receives mixed reviews but sells well. Writes and delivers on-camera introduction to omnibus film *O. Henry's Full House*. Writes speeches for supporters of Adlai Stevenson's presidential campaign.

1953   Travels with Elaine and writer Barnaby Conrad to the Virgin
            Islands, for first of nine annual Caribbean vacations. Receives
            Academy Award nominations for best story and best screenplay
            for *Viva Zapata!;* collaborates with Cy Feuer and Ernest
            Martin, who are to produce musical *Bear Flag*, a continuation
            of *Cannery Row*; works on a novel derived from idea for the
            musical, later entitled *Sweet Thursday*. In September rents
            cottage in Sag Harbor, Long Island, where he consults with
            neighbor Ernest Martin on progress of musical. Suffers from
            depression and consults psychologist Gertrudis Brenner.

1954   Richard Rodgers and Oscar Hammerstein take over both
            writing and production of *Bear Flag* (now titled *Dream*). Sails
            with Elaine to Europe in March; they travel in Portugal and
            Spain, and in May begin four-month stay in Paris; suffers minor
            stroke on his way to Paris. Shocked by news that Robert Capa
            has been killed by a land mine in Vietnam. *Sweet Thursday*
            published in June. Travels to Munich to visit facilities of Radio
            Free Europe; writes statement of freedom of expression for
            broadcast behind the Iron Curtain. Writes weekly articles for
            literary supplement of *Le Figaro*; honored at dinner given by
            the Academie Francaise. Leaves Paris in September to travel in
            England, southern France, Italy, and Greece; returns with
            Elaine to America in December on the Andrea Doria.

1955   Buys house in Sag Harbor, Long Island. Film of *East of Eden*,
            directed by Elia Kazan, with screenplay by Paul Osborn based
            on the novel's final segment, opens in March. Joins staff of
            Saturday Review as "Editor-at-Large" (contributes 17 articles
            and editorials by 1960). *Pipe Dream* opens on Broadway in
            September.

1956   Covers Democratic and Republican political conventions in
            Chicago and San Francisco for *Louisville Courier-Journal* and
            its syndicated papers. Meets Adlai Stevenson, who becomes
            close friend; again contributes speech material to Stevenson
            campaign. Beginning in November serves on writers'
            committee (chaired by William Faulkner) of government
            sponsored People to People program. Finishes comic novel,

The Short Reign of Pippin IV, in November. Begins version of Sir Thomas Malory's *Morte d'Arthur* in modern English (never completed; it is published posthumously in 1976 as *The Acts of King Arthur and His Noble Knights.* Collection of essays in French written for *Le Figaro Litteraire* and other magazines published in Paris as "Un Americain a New York et a Paris".

1957   Reads Malory intensively; does medieval research in Morgan Library in New York, assisted and advised by book store manager Chase Horton. Writes defense of Arthur Miller then standing trial for contempt of Congress as a result of House Un-American Activities Committee investigation: "The Congress is truly on trial along with Arthur Miller . . . I feel profoundly that our country is safe and public patriotism which Dr. Johnson called 'the better served by individual courage and morals than by the last refuge of scoundrels.'" Sails in March to Italy with Elaine and sister Mary Dekker, partly under auspices of United States Information Agency, staying mostly in Florence and Rome. Continues Arthurian research, including investigation of Thomas Malory's life. Writes about the trip for *Louisville Courier-Journal. The Short Reign of Pippin IV* published in April. Meets leading Malory scholar Eugene Vinaver in Manchester, England. Flies to Tokyo in September with John Hersey and John Dos Passos to attend P.E.N. conference; becomes ill with severe influenza shortly after arrival.

1959   Travels to the Bahamas with Burgess Meredith and others as part of an unsuccessful treasure salvage project. Spends June in England with Elaine. Sees Vinaver again; continues Malory research. Works on novella *Don Keehan,* based on Don Quixote (eventually abandoned). *Once There Was a War,* collection of war dispatches from 1943, published in September. Sails with Elaine to England in February; spends next eight weeks in rented cottage near Groton, Somerset. Works on Malory project. Discouraged by unsympathetic response of Elizabeth Otis and Chase Horton to Malory book. In August goes an motor trip through Wales. Returns to the United States in October. Suffers an undiagnosed attack (possibly from a small stroke) and is briefly hospitalized. Letter to Adlai Stevenson on destructive aspects of American affluence creates controversy when it is published in the press ("If I wanted to destroy a nation, I would give it too much, and I would have it on its knees, miserable, greedy, and sick")

1960   Puts aside Malory book, intending to return to it later. Begins novel eventually titled *The Winter of Our Discontent* in March; completes first draft in mid July. Becomes involved in unsuccessful effort to draft Adlai Stevenson for Democratic presidential nomination. In September sets out on eleven week journey (Operation Windmill) with dog Charley across America, in pick-up truck he names Rocinante. Travels through New England, the Great Lakes region, and the Dakotas to the West Coast where he is joined temporarily by Elaine in Seattle, then to New York by way of California, Texas, and Louisiana.

1961   Attends inauguration of President John F. Kennedy. Continues working on *Travels with Charley*, account of his cross country journey, in February during vacation on Barbados. Sons Thorn and John move in permanently with Steinbeck and Elaine because of difficulties with Gwyn. Accompanies Mohole expedition off the Mexican coast and writes account that appears in *Life* in April (project attempted to drill hole through the oceanic crust into the earth's mantle). *The Winter of Our Discontent* published in spring; Steinbeck is depressed by reviews, "even the favorable ones." In September begins ten-month stay in Europe with wife, sons, and their tutor, future playwright Terrence McNally. In Milan, at end of November, suffers attack (either a small stroke or heart attack). Family spends Christmas in Rome.

1962   Stays on Capri with Elaine, recuperating for several months, while sons travel with McNally. Pays tribute to his Stanford creative writing teacher, Edith Mirrielees, in preface to Viking reissue of her book, *Story Writing*. *Travels with Charley in Search of America* published in midsummer. Learns on October 25 that he has won Nobel Prize for Literature. Writes to Swedish friend Bo Beskow: "I suppose you know of the attack on the award to me not only by *Time* Magazine with which I have had a long-time feud but also from the cutglass critics, that grey priesthood which defines literature and has little to do with reading. They have never liked me and now are really beside themselves with rage." Travels to Stockholm for award ceremonies; makes short visit to London.

1963   Moves with Elaine out of brownstone into high-rise apartment on same block in March. Dog Charley dies in April. Undergoes surgery for detached retina in June. At the suggestion of President Kennedy, makes two-month cultural exchange visit to Eastern Europe; in October travels with Elaine to Finland, the Soviet Union (including visits to Ukraine, Armenia, and Georgia), Poland, Austria, Hungary, Czechoslovakia, and West Germany. Tour joined (as Steinbeck had requested) by Edward Albee in Moscow. Steinbeck publicly protests pirating of Western books in the Soviet Union. Learns in Warsaw of assassination of President Kennedy. In West Berlin meets German writers Gunter Grass and Uwe Johnson. Travels with Elaine to Washington in December for State Department debriefing; they attend private dinner with President Lyndon Johnson and Lady Bird Johnson (Elaine had known Lady Bird at University of Texas), establishing friendship.

1964   Asked by Jacqueline Kennedy to write book about John F. Kennedy; has long correspondence with her, but declines project. Estranged from sons, who return to live with Gwyn and bring suit with her for additional child support (large increase denied by New York Family Court in April). Spends Easter in Rome with Elaine. Begins work on text originally designed to accompany collection of photographs of America (eventually published as an essay collection *America and Americans*). Helps write Lyndon Johnson's speech accepting the Democratic presidential nomination. Receives Presidential Medal of Freedom in September. Resumes work on Malory book. Pascal Covici dies October 14; Steinbeck speaks at memorial service, along with Arthur Miller and Saul Bellow. Works on President Johnson's inaugural address.

1965   Spends several weeks in London and Paris in early January; in
        Paris learns of sister Mary Dekker's death. Asked by President
        Johnson to make trip to Vietnam as special emissary, but
        declines. Writes to Elizabeth Otis proposing publication of
        journal written during the composition of *East of Eden*.
        Begins regular column for *Newsday* (it runs, with some
        interruptions, from November 1965 to May 1967). Travels
        with Elaine to England in December; accompanied by Eugene
        Vinaver and his wife on tour of libraries in northern England.

1966   Travels with Elaine to Israel in February for *Newsday*; visits
        graves of relatives there. Appointed by President Johnson to
        council of the National Endowment for the Arts in   April.
        America and Americans published.   Son John finishes basic
        training and asks father's help in getting assigned to serve with
        American forces in Vietnam; Steinbeck writes: "I was horrified
        when you asked me to get you orders to go out, but I couldn't
        have failed you there . . . But if I had had to request that you
        not be sent, I think I would have been far more unhappy."
        Writes to Lyndon Johnson in May in support of his Vietnam
        policy. After *The New York Times* publishes poem by
        Yevtushenko attacking Steinbeck's failure to oppose the
        Vietnam War, Steinbeck writes public letter describing war as
        "Chinese-inspired" and criticizing the Soviet Union for arming
        North Vietnam. Makes unsuccessful attempt to start new novel,
        A Piece of It Fell on My Tail. In December goes to Southeast
        Asia as reporter for *Newsday* with Elaine; met in Saigon by son
        John. Over six-week period tour wide area of South Vietnam,
        frequently going on combat missions and reporting
        sympathetically on American war effort.

1967   Visits Thailand, Laos, Indonesia, Hong Kong, where he suffers
        slipped disk, and Japan; returns home in April.   Spends
        weekend at White House in May, and at President Johnson's
        request discusses his journey with Vice-President Hubert
        Humphrey, Secretary of State Dean Rusk, and Secretary of
        Defense Robert McNamara.   Suffers debilitating pain as a
        result of back injury, and in October enters hospital for
        surgery. While awaiting operation, learns of son John's arrest

in Washington, D. C. in connection with marijuana found in his apartment; John visits his father in hospital, but rejects offer of legal assistance. (While still in the army, John had written a magazine article about widespread marijuana use among the soldiers in Vietnam; following his arrest, his comments on the subject are given wide press exposure; he is acquitted of the drug charge in mid-December.) Steinbeck undergoes successful back operation and spinal fusion on October 23; released from hospital in early December. Flies to Grenada with Elaine for Christmas.

1968   After a month in Grenada, recuperates in New York apartment. Goes to Sag Harbor in spring. Suffers minor stroke on Memorial Day weekend in Sag Harbor, followed by heart attack later in July. Enters New York Hospital July 17, and suffers another heart attack while there. Leaves the hospital and returns to Sag Harbor in August. Writes to Elizabeth Otis: "I am pretty sure by now that the people running the war have neither conception nor control of it. I know we cannot win this war, nor any war for that matter." Returns to city apartment in November. Dies at home of cardio-respiratory failure at 5:30 P. M. on December 20. Funeral service is held at St. James Episcopal Church on Madison Avenue. Elaine takes ashes to Pacific Grove; after family service at Point Lobes on December 26, they are later buried in the family plot in Garden of Memories Cemetery, Salinas.

Works by Steinbeck

1   DeMott, Robert, ed., and Elaine A. Steinbeck, Special Consultant. *Steinbeck: Novels and Stories, 1932-1937.* New York: The Library of America, 1994. (contains *The Pastures of Heaven, Tortilla Flat, To a God Unknown, In Dubious Battle* and *Of Mice and Men*)

1A   DeMott, Robert, ed., and Elaine A. Steinbeck, Special Consultant. *John Steinbeck: The Grapes of Wrath and Other Writings, 1936-1941.* New York: The Library of America, 1996. (contains *The Grapes of Wrath*)

2   Steinbeck, Elaine, and Robert Walsten, eds. *Steinbeck: A Life in Letters.* New York: Penguin, 1989. (paperback of original 1974 ed.)

3   Steinbeck, John. *The Acts of King Arthur and His Noble Knights, from the Winchester Manuscripts of Thomas Malory and Other Sources.* Ed. Chase Horton. London: Mandarin, 1992.

4   Steinbeck, John. "The Author, on *The Grapes of Wrath*," *New York Times* (August 6, 1990), A13.

5   Steinbeck, John. *Bombs Away: The Story of a Bomber Team: Written for the U.S. Army Air Force.* New York: Paragon House, 1990. (with 60 photographs by John Swope)

6   Steinbeck, John. *Burning Bright: A Play in Story Form.* London: Mandarin, 1990.

7   Steinbeck, John. *Burning Bright: A Play in Story Form.* New York: Penguin, 1986, 1994.

8   Steinbeck, John. *Cannery Row.* New York: Penguin Twentieth Century Classics, 1994. (with an introduction by Susan Shillinglaw, pp. vii-xxx)

9   Steinbeck, John. *Cannery Row*. New York: Penguin, 1986.

10   Steinbeck, John. *Cannery Row*. New York: Penguin, 1992.

11   Steinbeck, John. *Cannery Row*. London: Heinemann, 1989.
       New hardcover edition.

12   Steinbeck, John. "The Chrysanthemums," in *American Short
       Stories* (5th ed.). ed. Eugene Current-Garcia and Bert
       Hitchcock. Glenview, Ill.: Scott, Foresman / Little, Brown,
       1989. (pp. 425-434)

13   Steinbeck, John. "The Chrysanthemums," in *Discovering
       Fiction.* ed. Guth and Rico. Englewood Cliffs, N. J.:
       Prentice Hall, 1993.

14   Steinbeck, John. "The Chrysanthemums," in *Fiction: An
       Introduction to Reading and Writing* (3rd ed.). ed. Roberts
       and Jacobs. Englewood Cliffs, N. J.: Prentice Hall, 1992.

15   Steinbeck, John. "The Chrysanthemums," in *50 Great Short
       Stories.* ed. Milton Crane. New York: Bantam, 1988. (a
       reprint of the 1952 edition)

16   Steinbeck, John. "The Chrysanthemums," in *Garden Tales:
       Classic Stories from Favorite Writers.* New York: Viking
       Studio Books, 1990.

17   Steinbeck, John. "The Chrysanthemums," in *The World of
       Fiction.* ed. Rubenstein and Larson. New York:
       Macmillan, 1993.

18   Steinbeck, John. *The Chrysanthemums and Other Stories.*
       New York: Penguin 60s, 1995. (contains "Flight," "The
       Murder," and "The Chrysanthemums")

19   Steinbeck, John. *Conversations with John Steinbeck.* ed.
       Thomas Fensch. Jackson, Miss.: University ofMississippi
       Press, 1988.

20 Steinbeck, John. "A Correspondence with John Steinbeck," *KPFA Folio* (October 1989), 5, 26.

21 Steinbeck, John. *Cup of Gold.* London: Mandarin, 1994.

22 Steinbeck, John. *Cup of Gold.* London: Penguin, 1995.

23 Steinbeck, John. "The Day the Wolves Ate the Vice-Principal," *Steinbeck Newsletter*, 9:1 (Fall 1995), 10. (excised Ch. VI of the original manuscript of *Cannery Row*)

24 Steinbeck, John. "Dear Mr. Sturz" (the author's letter on *Grapes of Wrath* to Herbert Sturz), *New York Times*, August 6, 1990, A13.

25 Steinbeck, John. "The Death of a Racket," in *The Matusow Affair: Memoir of a Scandal* by Albert E. Kahn. New York: Moyer Bell Ltd., 1987. (pp. 285-287)

26 Steinbeck, John. *East of Eden.* London: Heinemann, 1989. New hardcover edition.

27 Steinbeck, John. *East of Eden.* London: Mandarin, 1990.

28 Steinbeck, John. *East of Eden.* London: Mandarin, 1995.

29 Steinbeck, John. *East of Eden.* New York: Penguin, 1986.

30 Steinbeck, John. *East of Eden.* New York: Penguin Twentieth Century Classics, 1992. (with an introduction by David Wyatt, pp. vii-xxviii)

31 Steinbeck, John. *East of Eden.* New York: Viking, 1986.

32 Steinbeck, John. *Five Bestsellers.* London: Heinemann, 1989. New hardcover edition. (contains *The Grapes of Wrath,*

The Moon Is Down, Cannery Row, East of Eden and *Of Mice and Men*)

33   Steinbeck, John. *Flight.* Covelo, Calif.: Yolla Bolly Press, 1984. (with lithographs by Karen Wickstrom and an afterword by Wallace Stegner)

33A   Steinbeck, John. *'The Gift'.* Mankato, MN.: Creative Education, 1993.

34   Steinbeck, John. "The Gift" in *Great Horse Stories.* comp. Suzanne LeVert. New York: Julian Meisner, 1984.

35   Steinbeck, John. "The God in the Pipes," *Steinbeck Newsletter*, 9:1 (Fall 1995), 4-9. (manuscript fragment from Special Collections at the Stanford University Libraries)

36   Steinbeck, John. *The Grapes of Wrath.* London: Arrow Books, Ltd., 1988. (an Arena Book paperback)

37   Steinbeck, John. *The Grapes of Wrath.* London: Everyman's Library, Random House, 1993. (with an introduction by Brad Leithauser, pp. v-xxvii) (published in New York by Knopf)

38   Steinbeck, John. *The Grapes of Wrath.* London: Heinemann, 1988.

39   Steinbeck, John. *The Grapes of Wrath.* London: Mandarin, 1990.

40   Steinbeck, John. *The Grapes of Wrath.* New York: Penguin, 1986.

41   Steinbeck, John. *The Grapes of Wrath.* New York: Penguin, 1991.

42   Steinbeck, John. *The Grapes of Wrath.* New York: Penguin Twentieth Century Classics, 1992. (with an introduction by Robert DeMott, pp. vii-xliv)

43   Steinbeck, John. *The Grapes of Wrath*. New York: Reader's
        Digest Assn., 1991. (with illustrations by James Hays and
        an afterword by Bernard A. Weisberger)

44   Steinbeck, John. *The Grapes of Wrath*. New York: Viking,
        1986.

45   Steinbeck, John. *The Grapes of Wrath* (Ch. 19) in *Of
        Discovery and Destiny*. ed. Robert C. Baron and Elizabeth
        Darby Junkin. Golden, Colo.: Fulcrum, 1986. (pp. 259-
        268)

46   Steinbeck, John. *The Harvest Gypsies: On the Road to "The
        Grapes of Wrath, "* with an Introduction by Charles
        Wollenberg. Berkeley, Calif.: Heyday Books, 1988. (a
        reprint of the 1936 publication).

46A   Steinbeck, John. "How Six Short Novels Came to Be," in
        Readings on John Steinbeck. ed. Clarice Swisher. San
        Diego: Greenhaven Press, 1996. Literary Companion
        Series. (27-29) (reprinted from *My Short Novels* (Viking,
        1953) by John Steinbeck)

47   Steinbeck, John. *In Dubious Battle*. London: Heinemann,
        1989. New hardcover edition.

48   Steinbeck, John. *In Dubious Battle*. London: Mandarin, 1992.

49   Steinbeck, John. *In Dubious Battle*. New York: Penguin
        Twentieth Century Classics, 1992. (with an introduction by
        Warren French, pp. vii-xxix)

50   Steinbeck, John. "'Introduction' to *Sweet Thursday*," in *The
        Short Novels of John Steinbeck*. ed. Jackson J. Benson.
        Durham, N.C.: Duke University Press, 1990. (quoted in full
        in Louis Owens' essay, "Critics and Common
        Denominators: Steinbeck's *Sweet Thursday*.")

51   Steinbeck, John. "The Invaders," in *World War II Stories: 50th Anniversary Collection*. London: Octopus Group Ltd., 1989. (extracted from *The Moon Is Down*)

52   Steinbeck, John. *John Steinbeck's "The Grapes of Wrath"* adapted for the stage by Frank Galati. Garden City, N.Y.: The Fireside Theater, 1990.

53   Steinbeck, John. *John Steinbeck's "The Grapes of Wrath"* adapted for the stage by Frank Galati. New York: Dramatists Play Service, 1991.

54   Steinbeck, John. *John Steinbeck's 'The Grapes of Wrath'* adapted for the stage by Frank Galati. New York: Penguin, 1991.

55   Steinbeck, John. *The Journal of a Novel.* London: Mandarin, 1991.

56   Steinbeck, John. *The Journal of a Novel: The East of Eden Letters.* New York, Penguin 1990.

57   Steinbeck, John. "The Knight with Two Swords," in *The Pendragon Chronicles: Heroic Fantasy from the Time of King Arthur.* ed. Mike Ashley. New York: P. Bedrick Books, 1990.

58   Steinbeck, John. "The Leader of the People," in *Arbor House Treasury of Nobel Prize Winners.* ed. Martin Greenberg and Charles Waugh. New York: Arbor House, 1983.

59   Steinbeck, John. "The Leader of the People," in *Cowboy Tales: Western Classics from American Masters.* New York: Viking Studio Books, 1990.

60   Steinbeck, John. "The Leader of the People," in *Great California Stories.* ed. A. Grove Day. Lincoln: University of Nebraska Press, 1991.

61   Steinbeck, John. "The Leader of the People," in *Great Short Stories of the 20th Century*. ed. Martin Greenberg and Charles Waugh. New York: Avenel Books, 1987.

62   Steinbeck, John. "The Leader of the People," in *Prose and Poetry of the American West*. ed. James C. Work. Lincoln: University of Nebraska Press, 1990. (pp. 468-482)

63   Steinbeck, John. "Letter to Dorothea Lange; 3 July 1965," *Steinbeck Newsletter*, 2:2 (Summer 1989), 6-7. (The gift of Lange's son, John Dixon to Steinbeck Research Center, San Jose State)

64   Steinbeck, John. "Letter to George Hedley," *Steinbeck Newsletter*, 10:1 (Spring 1996), 16. (with background on Hedley by Susan Shillinglaw)

65   Steinbeck, John. *The Log from the Sea of Cortez: The Narrative Portion of the book, "The Sea of Cortez," with a Profile "About Ed Ricketts."* London: Mandarin, 1990.

66   Steinbeck, John. *The Log from the Sea of Cortez: The Narrative Portion of the book, "The Sea of Cortez," with a profile "About Ed Ricketts."* New York: Penguin, 1986.

67   Steinbeck, John. *The Log from the Sea of Cortez.* New York: Penguin, 1986.

68   Steinbeck, John. *The Log from the Sea of Cortez.* New York: Penguin, 1995. (with an introduction by Richard Astro)

69   Steinbeck, John. *The Log from the Sea of Cortez.* ed. Kenji Inoue (Kenkyuska New Collegiate English Textbooks, 4). Tokyo: Kenkyusha Press, 1983.

70   Steinbeck, John. *The Long Valley.* London: Mandarin, 1990.

71   Steinbeck, John. *The Long Valley.* New York: Penguin, 1986.

72   Steinbeck, John. *The Long Valley*. New York: Penguin
      Twentieth Century Classics, 1995. (with an introduction by
      John Timmerman, pp. vii-xxx)

73   Steinbeck, John. *The Long Valley*. New York: Viking, 1986.

74   Steinbeck, John. "Man, Myth and Moustache," *The
      Independent on Sunday*, March 22, 1992, 10-11.
      (excerpted from *Zapata*)

75   Steinbeck, John. *The Moon Is Down*. London: Mandarin,
      1993.

76   Steinbeck, John. *The Moon Is Down*. New York: Penguin,
      1986.

77   Steinbeck, John. *The Moon Is Down*. New York: Viking
      Penguin edition, 1995. (with an introduction by Donald
      Coers (pp. vii-xxviii))

78   Steinbeck, John. *The Moon Is Down* in *Great World War II
      Stories: A 50th Anniversary Collection*. London: Methuen,
      1989. (Extracts on pp. 585-602.)

79   Steinbeck, John. "The Murder," in *Nobel Crimes: Stories of
      Mystery and Detection by Winners of the Nobel Prize for
      Literature*. ed. Marie Smith. New York: Carroll and Graf
      Publishers, 1992. (formerly published in London: Xanadu,
      1992)

80   Steinbeck, John. *Of Mice and Men*. Hampton, N. H.: Chivers
      North America (Curley), 1989. (large print ed.)

81   Steinbeck, John. *Of Mice and Men*. New York: Penguin
      Twentieth Century Classics, 1994. (with an introduction by
      Susan Shillinglaw, pp. vii-xxv)

82 Steinbeck, John. *Of Mice and Men* in *Famous American Plays of the 1930s.* ed. Harold Clurman. New York: Dell, 1988. (with an introduction by Gordon Davison)

83 Steinbeck, John. *Of Mice and Men.* London: Heinemann, 1989. New hardcover edition.

84 Steinbeck, John. *Of Mice and Men.* London: Mandarin, 1992.

85 Steinbeck, John. *Of Mice and Men.* New York: Penguin, 1992.

86 Steinbeck, John. *Of Mice and Men.* New York: Viking, 1986.

87 Steinbeck, John. "*Of Mice and Men* and Marketing," in *Writer's Digest* (August 1987), 54. (previously unpublished letter to Lloyd Nosler)

88 Steinbeck, John. *Of Mice and Men: A Play.* ed. David Self. Amherst, Mass.: Hutchinson Education, 1990.

89 Steinbeck, John. *Once There Was a War.* London: Mandarin, 1990.

90 Steinbeck, John. *Once There Was a War.* New York: Penguin, 1986.

91 Steinbeck, John. *Once There Was a War.* New York: Penguin, 1994.

92 Steinbeck, John. *The Pastures of Heaven.* London: Arrow Books, Ltd., 1988. (an Arena Book paperback)

93 Steinbeck, John. *The Pastures of Heaven.* New York: Penguin, 1994. (with an introduction by James Nagel)

94 Steinbeck, John. *The Pearl.* Hampton, N. H.: Chivers North America (Curley), 1989. (large print ed.)

95 Steinbeck, John. *The Pearl.* London: Mandarin, 1990

96   Steinbeck, John. *The Pearl*. New York: Penguin, 1992.

97   Steinbeck, John. *The Pearl*. New York: Penguin Twentieth
        Century Classics, 1994. (with an Introduction by Linda
        Wagner-Martin, pp. vii-xxiv and drawings by Jose
        Clemente Orosco)

98   Steinbeck, John. *The Pearl*. New York: Viking, 1986.

99   Steinbeck, John. *The Pearl* (and) *The Red Pony*. New York:
        Penguin, 1986.

100   Steinbeck John. *The Portable Steinbeck*. ed. Pascal Covici, Jr.
        New York: Penguin, 1996. (with an introduction by the
        editor, pp. xi-xxix). Contents: From *The Long Valley:*
        "Flight," "The Snake," "The Harness," "The
        Chrysanthemums." From *Pastures of Heaven*: Ch. IV:
        Tuleracito; Ch VIII: Molly Morgan; Ch. X: Pat Humbert's.
        From *Tortilla Flat*: Ch. I: Danny; Ch. II: Pilon; Ch. VII:
        Pirate; Ch. VIII: The Treasure Hunt; Ch. XIII: Tortillas
        and Beans. From *In Dubious Battle*: Ch. 13 and 15: A
        Future We Can't Foresee. *Of Mice and Men*. *The Red
        Pony*. From *The Grapes of Wrath*: The Turtle, "The Last
        Clear and Definite Function of Man", Migrant People, Life
        and Death, Breakfast and Work, Ma and Tom, The Flood.
        From *The Log from the Sea of Cortez*: Ch. 15: "Is"
        Thinking and "Living Into"; Ch. 11: The Pearl of La Paz;
        Ch. 18: Parable of Laziness; Ch. 26: Differences; Ch. 28:
        "It Might Be So." From "About Ed Ricketts": Knowing Ed
        Ricketts, Speculative Metaphysics. From *Cannery Row*:
        Ch. 15: The Frog Hunt. From *East of Eden*: Ch. 22: Adam
        and His Sons; Ch. 24: Choice and Responsibility; Ch. 29:
        Technology and the Technocrat; Ch. 55: Timshel. From
        Unpublished Stories: "The Affair at 7 Rue de M———,"
        "How Mr. Hogan Robbed a Bank." From *Travels with
        Charley*: Pt. 3: People; Pt. 4: Texan Ostentation; Pt. 4:
        Southern Troubles; Pt. 4: Last Leg. The Language of
        Awareness: from *East of Eden*; Nobel Prize Acceptance
        Speech.

101 Steinbeck, John. *The Red Pony*. New York: G.K. Hall, 1994. (Large print edition)

102 Steinbeck, John. *The Red Pony*. London: Mandarin, 1990.

103 Steinbeck, John. *The Red Pony*. New York: Penguin, 1994. (with an Introduction by John Seelye, pp. vii-xxix)

104 Steinbeck, John. *The Red Pony*. New York: Viking, 1986.

105 Steinbeck, John. "The Red Pony," in *The American Short Story: A Collection of the Best Known and Most Memorable Short Stories by Great American Authors*. ed. Thomas K. Parkes. New York: Galahad Books, 1994.

106 Steinbeck, John. "The Red Pony," in *The Literary Horse: Great Modern Stories about Horses*. ed. Lilly Golden. New York: Atlantic Monthly Press, 1995.

107 Steinbeck, John. *A Russian Journal: With Pictures by Robert Capa*. New York: Paragon House, 1989. (reprint in paperback from the 1948 version)

108 Steinbeck, John. "St. Katy, the Virgin," in *Angels and Awakenings: Stories of the Miraculous by Great Modern Writers*. ed. M. Cameron Gray. Accord, Mass.: Wheeler Publishing, 1995.

109 Steinbeck, John. *The Short Reign of Pippin IV*. London: Mandarin, 1991.

110 Steinbeck, John. *The Short Reign of Pippin IV: A Fabrication*. New York: Penguin, 1994.

111 Steinbeck, John. *The Short Reign of Pippin IV: A Fabrication*. New York: Penguin, 1986.

112 Steinbeck, John. "The Snake," in *Fiction's Many Worlds*. ed. May. New York: D. C. Heath, 1993.

113   Steinbeck, John. "A Snake of One's Own," in *Lust, Violence,
       Sin, Magic: 60 Years of Esquire Fiction*. ed. by Rust Hills,
       Will Blythe, and Erika Mansourian. New York: Atlantic
       Monthly, 1993.

114   Steinbeck, John. "The Summer Before," in "John Steinbeck:
       A Collector's Edition," *Monterey Life: The Magazine of
       California's Spectacular Central Coast*, 7 (July 1987), 45-
       48.

115   Steinbeck, John. *Sweet Thursday*. London: Mandarin, 1992.

116   Steinbeck, John. *Sweet Thursday*. New York: Penguin, 1986.

117   Steinbeck, John. *Sweet Thursday*. New York: Penguin
       Twentieth Century Classics, 1996.

118   Steinbeck, John. *To a God Unknown*. New York: Penguin
       Twentieth Century Classics, 1995. (with an introduction by
       Robert DeMott, pp. vii-xxxvii)

119   Steinbeck, John. *To a God Unknown*. London: Mandarin,
       1990.

120   Steinbeck, John. *To a God Unknown*. New York: Penguin,
       1986.

121   Steinbeck, John. *Tortilla Flat*. New York: G.K. Hall, 1994.
       (Large print edition)

122   Steinbeck, John. *Tortilla Flat*. New York: Penguin, 1986.

123   Steinbeck, John. *Tortilla Flat*. London: Mandarin, 1990.

124   Steinbeck, John. *Travels with Charley in Search of America*.
       New York: Penguin, 1986.

125   Steinbeck, John. *Travels with Charley in Search of America*.
       London: Mandarin, 1990.

126   Steinbeck, John. *Uncollected Stories of John Steinbeck.* ed.
       Kiyoshi Nakayama. Tokyo: Nan'un-do, 1986. Contents:
       "His Father" (1949); "The Summer Before" (1955); "How
       Edith McGillicuddy Met Robert Louis Stevenson" (1941);
       "Reunion at the Quiet Hotel (1958); "The Miracle of
       Tepayac (1948); "The Gifts of Iban" (1927) and "The
       Time Wolves Ate the Vice-Principal" (1947).

127   Steinbeck, John. *The Wayward Bus.* London: Arrow Books,
       Ltd., 1988. (an Arena Book paperback)

128   Steinbeck, John. *The Wayward Bus.* New York: Penguin,
       1986.

129   Steinbeck, John. *The Wayward Bus.* New York: Penguin
       Twentieth Century Classics, 1995.

130   Steinbeck, John. *The Winter of Our Discontent.* New York:
       Penguin, 1986.

131   Steinbeck, John. *The Winter of Our Discontent.* London:
       Mandarin, 1992.

132   Steinbeck, John. *The Winter of Our Discontent.* New York:
       Penguin Twentieth Century Classics, 1996.

133   Steinbeck, John. *Working Days: The Journals of "The Grapes
       of Wrath".* ed. Robert DeMott. New York: Viking, 1989.

134   Steinbeck, John. *Working Days: The Journals of "The Grapes
       of Wrath".* ed. Robert DeMott. New York: Penguin, 1990.
       (paperback ed.)

135   Steinbeck, John. *"Your Only Weapon Is Your Work": A Letter
       by John Steinbeck to Dennis Murphy*, ed. Robert DeMott.
       San Jose, Calif.: Steinbeck Research Center, 1985.

136   Steinbeck, John. *Zapata.* ed. Robert E. Morsberger. New
       York: Viking Penguin, 1991.

136A   Steinbeck, John, and Ed Ricketts. *Sea of Cortez*. Mt. Vernon,
        N. J.: Paul J. Appel, 1993.

Works About Steinbeck

Books

137   Allen, Mary. *Animals in American Literature*. Urbana, Ill.: University of Illinois Press, 1983. (pp. 115-134)

138   Allmendinger, Blake. *The Cowboy: Representations of Labor in American Work Culture*. New York: Oxford University Press, 1992. (pp. 11, 28-29, 129, 134, 142)

139   Ariki, Kyoko, and Kiyohiko Tsuboi, eds. *John Steinbeck "Viva, Zapata!"* Tokyo: Eihosha Press, 1985.

140   Ariss, Bruce. *Inside Cannery Row: Sketches from the Steinbeck Era in Words and Pictures*. San Francisco: Lexikos, 1988.

141   Ashabrenner, Brent. *Dark Harvest: Migrant Farm Workers in America*. New York: Dodd and Mead, 1985.

142   Assouline, Pierre. *Gaston Gallimard: A Half-Century of French Publishing*. New York: Harcourt Brace Jovanovich, 1988. (pp. 133-134, 332-334, 339-340)

142A   Atkin, S. Beth. *Voices from the Field*. Boston: Little Brown, 1993. (Migrant Workers)

143   Bair, Deidre. *Simone de Beauvoir*. New York: Summit Books, 1990. (pp. 238-249)

144   Barber, Richard. *King Arthur: Hero and Legend.* New York:
        St. Martin's, 1986. (p. 198)

145   Barbour, James, and Tom Quirk, eds. *Biographies of Books:
        The Compositional Histories of Notable American
        Writings.* Columbia, Mo.: University of Missouri Press,
        1995. (includes Robert J. DeMott, "A Truly American
        Book: Pressing *The Grapes of Wrath,*" pp. 187-225)

146   Barbour, James, and Tom Quirk, eds. *Writing the American
        Classics.* Chapel Hill: University of North Carolina, 1990.
        (includes Louis Owens, "The Mirror and the Vamp:
        Invention, Reflection and Bad, Bad Cathy Trask in *East of
        Eden,*" pp. 235-257)

147   Baron, Robert C., and Elizabeth Darby Junkin, eds. *Of
        Discovery and Destiny: An Anthology of American Writers
        and the American Land.* Golden, Colo.: Fulcrum, 1986.
        (pp. 259-268)

148   Baughman, Judith S., and Matthew J. Bruccoli, eds. *Modern
        Classic Writers.* New York: Facts on File, 1994.

149   Baxter, John. *Bunuel.* London: Fourth Estate, 1994. (pp. 195-
        196)

150   Beacham, Walton, and Suzanne Niemeyer, eds. *Popular
        World Fiction, 1900-Present.* Vol. IV. Washington, D.C.:
        Beacham Publications, 1987. (contains "John Steinbeck"
        by Lawrence W. Mazzeno on pp. 1465-1475 and
        comments on *The Grapes of Wrath, In Dubious Battle,* and
        Of Mice and Men)

151   Beegel, Susan, Susan Shillinglaw, and Wes Tiffney, eds.
        *Steinbeck and the Environment: Interdisciplinary
        Approaches.* Tuscaloosa: University of Alabama Press,

1997. Contents: Pt. I: Origins. James C. Kelley, "John
Steinbeck and Ed Ricketts: Understanding Life in the
Great Tide Pool"; Richard E. Hart, "Steinbeck on Man and
Nature: A Philosophical Reflection." Pt. II: *The Grapes of
Wrath*. David N. Cassuto, "Turning Wine into Water:
Water As Privileged Signifier in *The Grapes of Wrath*";
Lorelei Cedarstrom, "The 'Great Mother' in *The Grapes of
Wrath*"; Peter Valenti, "Steinbeck's Ecological Polemic:
Human Sympathy and Visual Documentary in the
Intercalary Chapters of *The Grapes of Wrath*"; Marilyn
Chandler McEntyre, "Natural Wisdom: Steinbeck's Men
of Nature As Prophets and Peacemakers." Pt. III: Sea of
Cortez. Brian Railsback, "Searching for 'What Is': Charles
Darwin and John Steinbeck"; Stanley Brodwin, "The
Poetry of Scientific Thinking": Steinbeck's *Log from the
Sea of Cortez* and Scientific Travel Narrative"; Clifford
Eric Gladstein and Mimi Reisel Gladstein, "Revisiting *The
Sea of Cortez* with a Green Perspective"; Peter A. J.
Englert, "Education of Environmental Scientists: Should
We Listen to Steinbeck and Ricketts's Comments?";
Kiyoshi Nakayama, "*The Pearl* in *The Sea of Cortez*:
Steinbeck's Use of Environment." Pt. IV: Later Works.
Robert DeMott, "'Working at the Impossible': *Moby-
Dick*'s Presence in *East of Eden*"; Nathaniel Philbrick, "At
Sea in the Tide Pool: The Whaling Town and America in
Steinbeck's *The Winter of Our Discontent* and *Travels with
Charley*"; H. R. Stoneback, "'The Scars of Our Grasping
Stupidity' and the 'Sucked Orange': John Steinbeck and
the Ecological Legacy of John Burroughs"; Robert E.
Morsberger, "Steinbeck Under the Sea at the Earth's
Core." Pt. V: Overviews. Warren French, "How Green
Was John Steinbeck?"; Joel W. Hedgpeth, "John
Steinbeck: Late-Blooming Environmentalist"; John
Timmerman, "Steinbeck's Environmental Ethic: Humanity
in Harmony with the Land"; Roy Simmonds, "A World to
Be Cherished: Steinbeck As Conservationist and
Ecological Prophet." Bibliography.

152   Beja, Morris. *Epiphany in the Modern Novel.* Seattle:
         University of Washington Press, 1971.

153   Bendixon, Alfred, ed. *Encyclopedia of American Literature.*
         New York: Frederick Ungar, forthcoming. (contains Susan
         Shillinglaw's "John Steinbeck")

154   Bennett, Robert. *The Wrath of John Steinbeck or St. John
         Goes to Church.* Norwood, Pa.: Telegraph Books, 1985. (a
         reprint of the original published in 1939 by Albertson
         Press, Los Angeles)

155   Benson, Jackson J. *John Steinbeck's "Cannery Row": A
         Reconsideration.* Steinbeck Essay Series, No. 4. Muncie,
         Ind.: Steinbeck Research Institute, Ball State University,
         1991.

156   Benson, Jackson J. *Looking For Steinbeck's Ghost.* Norman,
         Okla.: University of Oklahoma Press, 1988. Contents:
         "Prologue: Would You Trust This Man?," 3-19; Ch. 1: "In
         the Big City," 21-34; Ch. 2: "Lost in High Tech," 35-50;
         "The Search for the Early Life," 51-64; Ch. 4: "High
         Anxiety," 65-78; Ch. 5: "Biographer as Detective," 79-94;
         Ch. 6: "Gwyn and Kate: Two Women in His Life," 95-
         115; Ch. 7: "Coping With the Famous," 116-124; Ch. 8:
         "Fear, Envy and Loathing," 125-144; Ch. 9: "Looking For
         Steinbeck's Ghost," 145-160; Ch. 10: "The Joys of Being
         Threatened," 161-181; Ch. 11: "Pride and Prejudice," 182-
         202; "Epilogue: The Spirit of a Writer," 203-226.

157   Benson, Jackson J., ed. *The Short Novels of John Steinbeck.*
         Durham: Duke University Press, 1990. Contents: Jackson
         J. Benson, Introduction; Joseph Fontenrose, "*Tortilla Flat*
         and the Creation of a Legend"; Robert Gentry, "Non-
         teleological Thinking in Steinbeck's *Tortilla Flat*"; Anne
         Loftis, "A Historical Introduction to *Of Mice and Men*;
         William Goldhurst, "*Of Mice and Men*: John Steinbeck's

Parable of the Curse of Cain"; Mark Spilka, "Of George
and Lenny and Curley's Wife: Sweet Violence in
Steinbeck's Eden"; Warren French, "*The Red Pony* as
Story Cycle and Film"; Howard Levant, "John Steinbeck's
The Red Pony: A Study in Dramatic Technique";
Tetsumaro Hayashi, "Dr. Winter's Dramatic Function in
The Moon Is Down"; John Ditsky, "Steinbeck's
'European' Play-Novella: *The Moon Is Down*"; Peter
Lisca, "*Cannery Row*: Escape into the Counterculture";
Robert S. Hughes, Jr., "'Some Philosophers in the Sun':
Steinbeck's *Cannery Row*"; Jackson J. Benson, "*Cannery
Row* and Steinbeck as Spokesman for the 'Folk
Tradition'"; John H. Timmerman, "The Shadow and the
Pearl: Jungian Patterns in *The Pearl*"; Michael J. Meyer,
"Precious Bane: Mining the Fool's Gold of *The Pearl*";
Roy Simmonds, "Steinbeck's *The Pearl*: Legend, Film,
Novel"; Charles Metzger, "Steinbeck's Version of the
Pastoral"; Louis Owens, "Critics and Common
Denominators: Steinbeck's *Sweet Thursday*"; Richard
Astro, "Steinbeck's Bittersweet Thursday"; Carroll Britch
and Clifford Lewis, "*Burning Bright*: The Shining of Joe
Saul"; Mimi Reisel Gladstein, 'Straining for Profundity:
Steinbeck's *Burning Bright* and *Sweet Thursday*"; Louis
Owens, "Steinbeck's 'Deep Dissembler': *The Short Reign
of Pippin IV*"; Howard Levant, "The Narrative Structure of
The Short Reign of Pippin IV"; Robert E. Morsberger,
"Steinbeck and the Stage."

158   Benson, Jackson J., ed. *The Short Novels of John Steinbeck*.
        Durham: Duke University Press, 1991. (paperback ed.)

159   Benson, Jackson J. *The True Adventures of John Steinbeck,
        Writer*. New York: Penguin, 1990. (paperback ed.)

160   Benson, Jackson J. *The True Adventures of John Steinbeck,
        Writer*. New York: Viking Press, 1984. Contents: Preface.
        Prefatory Note. Prologue. Pt. I: The Long Valley. Ch. I-V.
        Pt. II: Apprentice-ship. Ch. VI-IX. Pt. III: Poverty and

Success. Ch. X-XXV. Pt. IV: To New York. Ch. XXVI-
XXXV. Pt. V: The Quest For New Directions. Ch. XXVI-
XLVI. Pt. VI: The Last Battle. Ch. XLVII-LI.
Acknowledgements. Notes and Sources.

161   Berg, A. Scott. *Goldwyn: A Biography.* London: Hamish
        Hamilton, 1989. (pp. 315-316)

162   *The Best from Monterey Life,* 1989 *Collector's Edition: John
        Steinbeck.* (with Steinbeck's color photo on the cover,
        featuring photos and articles in the Steinbeck Country,
        Monterey, Pacific Grove, Carmel, Pebble Beach, Big Sur,
        and Salinas)

163   Beyer, Preston, comp. *Essays on Collecting John Steinbeck
        Books.* Bradenton, Fla.: Opuscula Press, 1989.

164   Bloom, Harold, ed. *John Steinbeck's "The Grapes of Wrath."*
        New York: Chelsea House Publishers, 1988. Contents:
        Harold Bloom, "Introduction"; Frederic I. Carpenter, "The
        Philosophical Joads"; Howard Levant, "The Fully Matured
        Art: *The Grapes of Wrath*"; James D. Brasch, "*The Grapes
        of Wrath* and Old Testament Skepticism"; Floyd C.
        Watkins, "Flat Wine from *The Grapes of Wrath*"; Sylvia
        Jenkins Cook, "Steinbeck, the People and the Party";
        Donald Pizer, "The Enduring Power of the Joads"; John J.
        Conder, "Steinbeck and Nature's Self: *The Grapes of
        Wrath*"; Mimi Reisel Gladstein, "The Indestructible
        Women: Ma Joad and Rose of Sharon."

165   Bloom, Harold, ed. *Modern Critical Views: John Steinbeck.*
        New York: Chelsea House, 1987. Contents: Harold Bloom,
        "Introduction"; Donald Weeks, "Steinbeck against
        Steinbeck"; Richard Astro, "Imitations of a Wasteland";
        Howard Levant, "The Fully Matured Art: *The Grapes of
        Wrath*"; Warren French, "John Steinbeck: A Usable
        Concept of Naturalism"; Arthur F. Kinney, "*Tortilla Flat*

Revisited"; Marilyn L. Mitchell, "Steinbeck's Strong
Women: Feminine Identity in the Short Stories"; Jackson J.
Benson, "John Steinbeck: Novelist as Scientist"; John J.
Conder, "Steinbeck and Nature's Self: *The Grapes of
Wrath*"; Anthony Burgess, "Living for Writing"; Louis
Owens, "*Of Mice and Men*: The Dream of Commitment";
Mimi Reisel Gladstein, "Abra: The Indestructible Woman
in *East of Eden*."

166   Bloom, Harold, ed. *Twentieth Century American Literature*.
         Vol. 6. (The Chelsea House Library of Literary Criticism)
         New York: Chelsea House, 1987. (pp. 3795-3810)
         (contains excerpts from Steinbeck critics, Howard Levant,
         Peter Lisca, Edmund Wilson and Stanley Alexander)

166A   Bloom, Harold. *American Fiction 1914-1945: The Critical
         Cosmos Series*. New Haven, CT.: Chelsea House, 1986.
         (contains Sylvia Jenkins Cook's "Steinbeck, The People
         and The Party" on pp. 347-359)

167   Blotner, Joseph. *Faulkner: A Biography*. (1 Vol. ed.) New
         York: Random House, 1984. (pp. 341, 480, 482-485, 510,
         575, 628-629)

168   Bogardus, Ralph F., and Fred Hobson, eds. *Literature at the
         Barricades: The American Writer in the* 1930s.
         Tuscaloosa: University of Alabama Press, 1982. (contains
         Sylvia Jenkins Cook's "Steinbeck, The People and The
         Party")

168A   Bondi, Victor, ed. *American Decades,* 1930-1939. Detroit:
         Gale, 1995. (Steinbeck references on pp. 34-35, 37, 39, 41,
         43-44, 53, 81, 86, 108, 368, 437)

169   Boyd, Brian. *Vladimir Nabokov: The American Years*.
         Princeton: Princeton University Press, 1991. (p. 23)

170   Boyum, Jay Gould. *Double Exposure: Fiction into Film.* New
        York: Universe Books, 1985. (pp. 13-14, 65)

171   Bradbury, Malcolm. *The Modern American Novel.* New York:
        Oxford University Press, 1983. (pp. 108-113)

172   Bradbury, Malcolm. *The Modern American Novel.* (New ed.)
        Oxford: Oxford University Press, 1992. (pp. 138-142)

173   Bradbury, Malcolm, and Sigmund Ro, eds. *Contemporary
        American Fiction.* London: Edward Arnold, 1987.
        (contains "Fiction vs. Film, 1960-1985," by Warren French
        on pp. 106-121)

174   Brady, Frank. *Citizen Welles.* London: Hodder and Stoughton
        (Coronet Books), 1991. (pp. 136, 203, 231, 249, 258)

175   Braithwaite, Brian, et al., comp. *The Home Front: The Best of
        Good Housekeeping* 1939-1945. London: Ebury Press,
        1987. (contains references to Steinbeck on pp. 110-111,
        113, 115.)

176   Braswell, Mary Flowers, and John Bugge, eds. *The Arthurian
        Tradition: Essays in Convergence.* Tuscaloosa: University
        of Alabama Press, 1988. (contains "Yet Some Men Say . . .
        That Kynge Arthure Ys Nat Ded" by Charles Moorman on
        pp. 188-199)

177   Brennan-Gibson, Margaret. *Clifford Odets: American
        Playwright, the Years From* 1906 *to* 1940. New York:
        Athenaeum, 1982. (pp. 600-601)

178   Brightman, Carol. *Writing Dangerously: Mary McCarthy and
        Her World.* London: Allison Press, 1993. (also published
        in New York: Clarkson Potter, 1992) (pp. 133-134, 135,
        191, 215, 333, 600)

179   Britch, Carroll, and Cliff Lewis, eds. *Rediscovering Steinbeck:
        Revisionist Views of His Art and Politics*. Lewiston, N.Y.:
        Edwin Mellen Press, 1989. Contents: Cliff Lewis and
        Carroll Britch, "Introduction"; Britch and Lewis, "Artist
        as Narrator"; Carroll Britch, "Steinbeck's 'Breakfast':
        Godhead and Reflection"; Britch and Lewis, "Sources and
        Process"; Robert DeMott, "Creative Reading, Creative
        Writing: The Presence of Dr. Gunn's *New Family
        Physician* in Steinbeck's *East of Eden*"; Britch and Lewis,
        "The Fictive Process"; Louis Owens, "The Story of a
        Writing: Narrative Structure in *East of Eden*"; Britch and
        Lewis, "Reinventing the Picaro"; Marcia Yarmus, "The
        Picaresque Novel and John Steinbeck"; Britch and Lewis,
        "Searching for Subjects"; Robert S. Hughes, Jr.,
        "Steinbeck's Uncollected Stories"; Britch and Lewis,
        "Mythmaking"; Carroll Britch and Cliff Lewis, "Shadow
        of the Indian in the Fiction of John Steinbeck"; Britch and
        Lewis, "Revelations"; Bobbie Gonzales and Mimi Reisel
        Gladstein, "*The Wayward Bus*: Steinbeck's Misogynistic
        Manifesto"; Britch and Lewis, "Man and War"; John
        Ditsky, "Steinbeck, Bourne, and the Human Herd: A
        New/Old Gloss on *The Moon Is Down*"; Britch and Lewis,
        "Political Testaments"; Cliff Lewis, "Steinbeck: The
        Author as FDR Speechwriter"; Britch and Lewis, "Cold
        War"; Cliff Lewis, "A Peculiar Air: *Viva Zapata!*"; Britch
        and Lewis, "Observations at Mid-century"; Judith Mulch,
        "The Journalist as Serious Writer: Steinbeck in the
        1950's"; Britch and Lewis, "Exploring America"; Thom
        Tammaro, "Lost in America: Steinbeck's *Travels with
        Charley* and William Least Heat Moon's *Blue Highways*."

180   Brown, Robert L. Jr., and Martin L. Steinmann, Jr., eds.
        *Rhetoric 1978: Proceedings of Theory of Rhetoric: An
        Interdisciplinary Conference*. Minneapolis, Minn.:
        University of Minnesota Center for Advanced Studies in
        Language, Style and Literature, 1979. (contains Robert
        Alain de Beaugrande, "A Rhetorical Theory of Audience
        Response," on pp. 9-20)

181   Bruccoli, Matthew J. *James Gould Cozzens: A Life Apart.*
        New York: Harcourt Brace Jovanovich, 1983. (pp. 137,
        144, 236)

182   Bruccoli, Matthew J., and Judith S. Baughman, eds. *Modern
        Classic Writers.* See #148

183   Bryan III, J. *Merry Gentlemen and One Lady.* New York:
        Athenaeum, 1985. (contains "John Steinbeck 1902-1968:
        Mumbles and Bellows, Scowls and Laughs," pp. 175-197;
        see also pp. 167-169)

184   Bryant, Paul, Mark Busby, and David Mogen. *The Frontier
        Experience and the American Dream.* College Station:
        Texas A & M Press, 1989. (comments on Steinbeck on pp.
        10, 32, 42-43, 58, 136, 144) (*The Grapes of Wrath* and *The
        Red Pony*)

185   Bugge, John, and Mary Flowers Braswell, eds. *The Arthurian
        Tradition: Essays in Convergence.* See #176.

186   Burgess, Anthony. *But Do Blondes Prefer Gentlemen?* New
        York: McGraw-Hill, 1986. (pp. 375-377)

187   Burgess, Anthony. *Enderby's Dark Lady or No End to
        Enderby.* London: Sphere Books, 1985. (pp. 61-62)

188   Burress, Lee, Nicolas Karolides, and John M. Kean. *Censored
        Books: Critical Viewpoints.* Metuchen, N. J.: Scarecrow
        Press, 1993. (contains entries on *Grapes of Wrath* by Lee
        Burress on pp. 278-287, *Of Mice and Men* by Thomas
        Scarseth on pp. 388-394)

189   Busby, Mark, David Mogen, and Paul Bryant. *The Frontier
        Experience and the American Dream.* See #184.

190   Caldwell, Erskine. *With All My Might*. Atlanta: Peachtree
        Publishers, 1987. (pp. 258-259, 274-276)

191   Campbell, Hilbert H., ed. *The Sherwood Anderson Diaries,*
        1936-1941. Athens: University of Georgia Press, 1987.
        (pp. 146, 267)

191A   Cantwell, Robert. *When We Were Good*. Cambridge: Harvard
        University Press, 1997. (pp. 110-112) (references to
        Steinbeck and *The Grapes of Wrath* as well as
        Springsteen's Tom Joad album)

192   Carr, Virginia Spencer. *Dos Passos: A Life*. Garden City:
        Doubleday, 1984. (pp. 513-514)

193   Carruth, Gordon, and Eugene Ehrlich. *The Oxford Illustrated*
        Literary Guide to the United States. New York: Oxford
        University Press, 1982. (numerous references to Steinbeck)

194   Casagrande, Jean. *The Linguistic Connection*. Lanham, Md.:
        University Press of America, 1983. (contains "The Name
        Is the Game" by Kevin M. McCarthy)

195   Castronovo, David. *Edmund Wilson*. New York: Frederick
        Ungar, 1984. (pp. 72-73)

196   Chadha, Rajni. *Social Realism in the Novels of John*
        Steinbeck. New Delhi: Harman, 1990. (republished New
        York: Advent Books, 1990)

197   Clurman, Harold, ed. *Famous American Plays of the* 1930*s*.
        New York: Dell, 1988. (with an introduction by Gordon
        Davison; contains *Of Mice and Men*)

198   Coers, Donald. *John Steinbeck As Propagandist: "The Moon
        Is Down" Goes to War*. Tuscaloosa: University of
        Alabama Press, 1991. Contents: "Preface," ix- xvii; Ch. 1:
        "Publication and American Reception," 3-25; Ch. 2:
        "Norway," 29-53; Ch. 3: "Denmark," 57-83; Ch. 4:
        "Holland," 87-98; Ch. 5: "France," 101-111; Ch. 6: "Other
        Countries," 115-123; Ch. 7: "Conclusion," 127-138.

199   Coers, Donald, Robert DeMott, and Paul Ruffin, eds., *After
        "The Grapes of Wrath": Essays on John Steinbeck in
        Honor of Tetsumaro Hayashi*. Athens: Ohio University
        Press, 1995. Contents: Warren French, "Introduction";
        Cliff Lewis, "Art For Politics: John Steinbeck and FDR";
        Susan Shillinglaw, "Steinbeck and Ethnicity"; Robert .
        Morsberger, "Of Mice and Music: Scoring Steinbeck
        Movies"; Roy Simmonds, "The Metamorphosis of *The
        Moon Is Down*: March 1942-March 1943"; Eiko Shiraga,
        "Three Strong Women in Steinbeck's *The Moon Is Down*";
        Kevin Hearle, "The Boat-Shaped Mind: Steinbeck's Sense
        of Language as Discourse in *Cannery Row* and *Sea of
        Cortez*"; Debra K. S. Barker, "Passages of Descent and
        Initiation: Juana as the "Other" Hero of *The Pearl*"; Brian
        Railsback, "*The Wayward Bus*: Misogyny or Sexual
        Selection?"; John Ditsky, "Work, Blood and *The Wayward
        Bus*"; Robert J. DeMott, "Charting *East of Eden*: A
        Bibliographical Survey"; Robert J. DeMott, "*Sweet
        Thursday* Revisited: An Excursion in Suggestiveness";
        Michael J. Meyer, "Citizen Cain: Ethan Hawley's Double
        Identity in *The Winter of Our Discontent*"; Geralyn
        Strecker, "Reading Steinbeck (Re)-Reading America:
        Travels with Charley and *America and Americans*"; Mimi
        Reisel Gladstein, "*America and Americans*: The Arthurian
        Consummation"; Donald Coers, "'John Believed in Man':
        An Interview with Mrs. John Steinbeck."

200   Comire, Anne, ed. *Something about the Author*. Vol. 9.
        Detroit: Gale Research, 1976. (pp. 176-178)

201   *Concise Dictionary of American Literary Biography: The Age of Maturity,* 1929-1941. Detroit, Mich.: Gale Research Inc., 1987. (contains "John Steinbeck," by Louis Owens on pp. 242-249) Updated entry in 1989 edition of same title (pp. 280-309).

202   Conder, John J. *Naturalism in American Fiction: The Classic Phase.* Lexington: University of Kentucky Press, 1984. (contains "Steinbeck and Nature's Self: *The Grapes of Wrath"*)

203   Conn, Peter. *Literature in America: An Illustrated History.* New York: Guild Publishing, 1990. (pp. 413-417, 444) (also published by Cambridge University Press, 1989)

204   Cooney, Seamus, ed. *John Fante: Selected Letters* 1932-1981. Santa Rosa, Calif.: Black Sparrow Press, 1991. (pp. 12, 166, 175-176, 182, 186-187, 321, 337)

205   Copland, Aaron, and Vivian Perlis. *Copland:* 1900 *Through* 1942. London: Faber and Faber, 1984. (pp. 297-300)

206   Copland, Aaron, and Vivian Perlis. *Copland: Since* 1943. London: Faber and Faber, 1992. (pp. 87-91)

207   Cousineau, Phil, ed. *The Hero's Journey: The World of Joseph Campbell — Joseph Campbell on His Life and Work.* San Francisco: Harper and Row, 1990. (pp. xxvi, 51)

208   Crisler, Jesse S., Susan Shillinglaw, and Joseph R. McElrath, eds. *John Steinbeck: The Contemporary Reviews.* Cambridge: Cambridge University Press, 1995.

209   Crouch, Steve. *Steinbeck Country.* New York: Bonanza Books, 1985. (originally appeared in 1973 from American West Publishing Co.) Contents: "The Land," 13-87; "The

Elements," 89-111; "The People," 114-179; "The View
From The Top," 181-185; "Afterword," 186. (reprinted by
Pilothouse Publishing, Morro Bay, Calif., 1995)

210   Cunliffe, Marcus. *The Literature of the United States*. 4th
         edition. Harmondsworth: Penguin Books, 1986. (pp. 405-
         406)

211   Curley, Dorothy Nyren, Maurice Kramer, and Elaine Fialka
         Kramer, eds. *Modern American Literature*. 4th ed. Vol. 3.
         New York: Frederick Ungar, 1990. (contains "John
         Steinbeck" on pp. 218-224)

212   Cusick, Lee. *John Steinbeck's "The Grapes of Wrath."*
         Picataway, N. J.: Research and Education Assn., 1994.

213   Davidson, Bill. *Spencer Tracy: Tragic Idol*. London:
         Sedgwick and Jackson, 1987. (pp. 7, 92, 102)

214   Davidson, Cathy N. *The Book of Love: Writers and Their Love
         Letters*. New York: Pocket Books, 1992. (pp. 61-62) (a
         letter from Steinbeck to Elaine Anderson Scott)

215   Davis, Robert Con, and Ronald Schliefer, eds. *Contemporary
         Literary Criticism: Literary and Cultural Studies*. New
         York: Longmans, 1989. (contains "Shakespeare and The
         Exorcists" by Stephen J. Greenblatt)

216   Davis, Robert Con, ed. *"The Grapes of Wrath": A Collection
         of Critical Essays*. Englewood Cliffs, N. J.: Prentice Hall,
         1982. Contents: Edwin T. Bowden, "The Commonplace
         and The Grotesque"; Warren French, "From Naturalism to
         the Drama of Consciousness — the Education of the Heart
         in *The Grapes of Wrath*"; J. Paul Hunter, "Steinbeck's
         Wine of Affirmation in *The Grapes of Wrath*"; Peter Lisca,
         "*The Grapes of Wrath*: An Achievement of Genius";

Leonard Lutwack, "*The Grapes of Wrath* as Heroic
Fiction"; George Bluestone, "*The Grapes of Wrath*"; Stuart
L. Burns, "The Turtle or the Gopher: Another Look at the
Ending of *The Grapes of Wrath*"; Mary Ellen Caldwell, "A
New Consideration of the Intercalary Chapters in *The
Grapes of Wrath*"; Robert J. Griffin and William A.
Freedman, "Machines and Animals: Pervasive Motifs in
The Grapes of Wrath"; Horst Groene, "Agrarianism and
Technology in *The Grapes of Wrath*"; Joan Hedrick,
"Mother Earth and Earth Mother: The Recasting of Myth
in Steinbeck's *The Grapes of Wrath*"; R.W.B. Lewis, "The
Picaresque Saint."

217   de Beauvoir, Simone. *Letters to Sartre*. London: Radius, 1991.
        (pp. 399, 434)

218   de St. Jorre, John. *The Good Ship Venus: The Erotic Voyage
        of the Olympia Press*. London: Hutchinson, 1994. (p. 34)

218A   DeMott, Robert, Donald Coers, and Paul Ruffin, eds. *After
        "The Grapes of* Wrath": *Essays on John Steinbeck in
        Honor of Tetsumaro Hayashi*. See #199.

219   DeMott, Robert. *Steinbeck's Reading: A Catalogue of Books
        Owned and Borrowed*. New York: Garland Publishing
        Company, 1983. (Introduction revised and incorporated in
        DeMott's *Steinbeck's Typewriter: Essays On His Art*
        (Troy, N.Y.: Whitston, 1996))

219A   DeMott, Robert. *Steinbeck's Typewriter: A Collection of
        Essays*. Troy, N.Y.: Whitston, 1996. Contents: Preface
        and Acknowledgements; Introduction; Pt. I: Creative
        Reading / Creative Writing. "Things That Happened to
        Me:" Steinbeck's Varieties of Reading Experience, 2-54;
        "A Great Black Book": *East of Eden* and *Gunn's New
        Family Physician,* 55-74; "Working at the Impossible":
        The Presence of *Moby Dick* in *East of Eden,* 75-107; Part
        II: Negotiating Texts. "Writing My Country": Making *To
        A God Unknown*, 108-145; "This Book Is My Life":

Creating *The Grapes of Wrath*, 146-205; "One Book to a
Man": Charting a Bibliographical Preface to *East of Eden*,
206-233; Pt. III: Interior Dimensions. "The Girl of the
Air": A Speculative Essay on Steinbeck's Love Poems,
234-264; "Of Ink and Heart's Blood": Adventures in
Reading Steinbeck, 265-286; "Steinbeck's Typewriter":
An Excursion in Suggestiveness, 287-318. Pt. IV:
Bibliography of Books By and About John Steinbeck, 319-
344; Index.

220   DeMott, Robert, ed. *Working Days: The Journals of "The
Grapes of Wrath,"* 1938-1941. New York: The Viking
Press, 1989. Contents: "Preface," xi-xv; "Introduction,"
xxi-lvii; Pt. I: Prelude (February 1938), with Commentary,
1-6; Pt. II: The Diary of a Book (May - October 1938),
with Commentary, 7-93; Pt. III: Aftermath (1939-1941),
with Commentary, 95-133. (a later version incorporated
into "'This Book is My Life': Creating *The Grapes of
Wrath*" in DeMott's *Steinbeck's Typewriter: Essays On
His Art* (Troy, N.Y.: Whitston, 1996))

221   DeMott, Robert, ed. *Your Only Weapon Is Your Work: A
Letter by John Steinbeck to Dennis Murphy*. San Jose,
Calif.: Steinbeck Research Center, 1985.

222   Dick, Bernard F. *The Star-Spangled Screen: The American
World War II Film.* Lexington: University Press of
Kentucky, 1984. (pp. 154-156, 204-207, 253)

223   *Dictionary of Literary Biography: Documentary Series*. Vol.
2. Detroit: Gale, 1982. (contains "John Steinbeck" on pp.
279-332)

224   Dillard, Annie. *Living by Fiction*. New York: Harper and
Row, 1982. (pp. 81-82)

225   Ditsky, John, ed. *Critical Essays on "The Grapes of Wrath."*
        Boston: G.K. Hall and Co., 1989. Contents: John Ditsky,
        "Introduction"; **Reviews**: Louis Kronenberger, "Hungry
        Caravan"; Burton Rascoe, "But . . . Not . . . Ferdinand";
        Malcolm Cowley, "American Tragedy"; Earle Birney, "A
        Must Book"; Philip Rahv, "Review of *The Grapes of
        Wrath*"; James N. Vaughan, " Review of *The Grapes of
        Wrath*"; Charles Angoff, "In the Great Tradition"; Stanley
        Kunitz, "Wine Out of Those Grapes"; Art Kuhl, "Mostly
        About *The Grapes of Wrath*"; Wilbur L. Schramm,
        "Career at a Crossroads" **Articles and Essays**: Jackson J.
        Benson, "The Background to the Composition of *The
        Grapes of Wrath*"; Roy Simmonds, "The Reception of *The
        Grapes of Wrath* in Britain: A Chronological Survey of
        Contemporary Reviews"; Peter Lisca, "The Dynamics of
        Community in *The Grapes of Wrath*"; Carroll Britch and
        Cliff Lewis, "Growth of the Family in *The Grapes of
        Wrath*"; Louis Owens, "The Culpable Joads:
        Desentimentalizing *The Grapes of Wrath*"; John Ditsky,
        "The Ending of *The Grapes of Wrath*: A Further
        Commentary"; Mimi Reisel Gladstein, "From Heroine to
        Supporting Player: The Diminuation of Ma Joad";
        Christopher L. Salter, "John Steinbeck's *The Grapes of
        Wrath* as a Primer for Cultural Geography"; Warren
        French, "John Steinbeck and Modernism (A Speculation
        on His Contribution to the Development of the Twentieth
        Century American Sensibility)."

226   Ditsky, John. *John Steinbeck: Life, Work and Criticism.*
        Fredericton, New Brunswick, Canada: York Press, 1985.

227   Donald, Miles. *The American Novel in the Twentieth Century.*
        New York: Barnes and Noble, 1978. (references to
        Steinbeck on pp. 8, 16, 59-72, 200)

228   Donaldson, Scott. *John Cheever: A Biography.* New York:
        Delta, 1990. (p. 213)

229   Downs, Robert B., et. al. *More Memorable Americans, 1750-
       1950.* Englewood, Colo.: Libraries Unlimited, 1985. (pp.
       322-325)

230   Eastman, Richard M., and Robert E. Yahnke. *Aging in
       Literature: A Reader's Guide.* Chicago: American Library
       Association, 1990. (comment on "The Leader of the
       People," pp. 65-66)

231   Egusa, Hisashi, et al., eds. *Modern American Masterpieces*
       (Fitzgerald, Hemingway, Steinbeck, and Saroyan). Tokyo:
       Asahi Press, 1984.

232   Egusa, Hisashi, ed. *Steinbeck Studies: On His Short Stories.*
       Tokyo: Yashio Shuppan, 1987. (a collection from the
       symposium entitled "On The Reconsideration of 'The Red
       Pony'" presented during the 5th Conference of the
       Steinbeck Society of Japan in May 1981)

233   Ehrlich, Eugene, and Gordon Carruth. *The Oxford Illustrated
       Literary Guide to The United States.* See #193.

234   Ehrenhaft, George. *John Steinbeck's "The Grapes of Wrath."*
       Woodbury, N.Y.: Barrons, 1984.

235   Eisen, Jonathan, and David Fine, eds. *Unknown California.*
       New York: Macmillan, 1985. (reprint of "Their Blood Is
       Strong")

236   Elliott, Emory, ed. *Columbia Literary History of the United
       States.* New York: Columbia, 1988. (references to
       Steinbeck on pp. 545, 726, 753-754, 805, 859, 864, 868,
       and 1130 and comments on *Tortilla Flat, The Grapes of
       Wrath, In Dubious Battle* and *Of Mice and Men*)

237   Enea, Sparky. *With Steinbeck in The Sea of Cortez: A Memoir
        of the Steinbeck/Ricketts Expedition As Told to Audry
        Lynch.* Los Osos, Calif.: Sand River Press, 1991.

238   Erisman, Fred, and Richard W. Etulain, eds. *Fifty Western
        Writers: A Bio-Bibliographical Source Book.* Westport,
        Conn.: Greenwood Press, 1982. (contains Richard Astro's
        entry on Steinbeck, 477-487.)

239   Etulain, Richard W., and Fred Erisman, eds. *Fifty Western
        Writers: A Bio-Bibliographical Source Book.* See #238.

240   Evory, Anne, ed. *Contemporary Authors. New Revision
        Series.* Vol. 1. Detroit: Gale Research, 1981. (contains
        "John Steinbeck" by Denise Gottis on pp. 627-631)

241   Faber, Doris, and Harold Faber. *Great Lives: American
        Literature.* New York: Atheneum Books For Young
        Readers, 1995. (pp. 259-267)

242   Fabring, Horace W., and Rick Hamman. *Steinbeck Country
        Narrow Gauge.* Boulder: Pruett Publishing Co., 1985.

243   Fensch, Thomas, ed. *Conversations with James Thurber.*
        Jackson: University Press of Mississippi, 1989.
        ("Steinbeck," pp. 60, 110)

244   Fensch, Thomas, ed. *Conversations with John Steinbeck.*
        Jackson: University of Mississippi Press, 1988. Contents:
        Ella Winter, "Sketching the Author of *Tortilla Flat*"; *New
        York World Telegram*, "More a Mouse Than a Man,
        Steinbeck Faces Reporters"; *New York Times*, "Men, Mice
        and Mr. Steinbeck"; Louis Walther, "Oklahomans
        Steinbeck's Theme"; John C. Rice, "John Steinbeck Turns
        His Wrath on *The Grapes of Wrath* Publicity"; Tom
        Cameron, "*The Grapes of Wrath* Author Guards Self from

Threats at Moody Gulch"; Robert DeMott, "Voltaire didn't Like Anything: A 1939 Interview with John Steinbeck"; Lewis Gannett, "John Steinbeck: Novelist at Work"; Robert van Gelder, "Interview with a Best-selling Author: John Steinbeck"; Jack Hollimon, "Country History: Writer to Chronicle Changes Since 1900"; Lewis Nichols, "Talk with John Steinbeck"; Charles Mercer, "Interview at a Barbeque: Writing Gets Harder as You Grow Older, Says Steinbeck"; Sidney Fields, "John Steinbeck: The Sphinx Talks"; Art Buchwald, "John Steinbeck Turns His Hand to Tale of Space Ship, Flying Saucers"; *Books and Bookmen*, "Healthy Anger"; Mike Thomas, "John Steinbeck Back — But Not to Stay"; Curt Gentry, "John Steinbeck: America's King Arthur is Coming"; Hal Boyle, "John Steinbeck Says Changes Put World in Shock"; Associated Press, "Steinbeck Got First Word on TV: Asserts His First Reaction Was One of 'Disbelief'"; Michael Ratcliffe, "Cutting Loose at 60: John Steinbeck"; Caskie Stinnett, "A Talk with John Steinbeck"; John Bainbridge, "Our Man in Helsinki"; Herbert Kretzmer, "London Looks at a Durable Giant"; David Butwin, "Steinbeck Here on Way to Viet"; Ed Sheehan, "Sensitive Writer in a Man-Shell of Gruffness"; Budd Shulberg, "John Steinbeck: A Lion in Winter."

245   Fensch, Thomas. *Steinbeck and Covici: The Story of a Friendship*. Middlebury, Vt.: Paul S. Ericsson, 1984. (paperback edition)

246   Ferguson, Robert. *Henry Miller: A Life*. London: Hutchinson, 1991. (p. 279)

247   Ferrell, Keith. *John Steinbeck: The Voice of the Land*. New York: M. Evans and Co., 1986. (young adult, adolescent biography)

248   Fiedler, Leslie. *What Was Literature? Class Culture and Mass
       Society*. New York: Simon and Schuster, 1984. (pp. 69, 81,
       202)

249   Fine, David, and Jonathan Eisen, ed. *Unknown California*. See
       #235.

250   Foley, Martha F., ed. 200 *Years of Great American Short
       Stories*. New York: Galahad Books, 1982. (contains
       "Steinbeck" on 575)

251   Foner, Eric, and John A. Garraty. *The Reader's Companion to
       American History*. Boston: Houghton Mifflin, 1991.
       (contains "John Steinbeck" by Susan Shillinglaw)

252   Ford, Dan. *The Unquiet Man: The Life of John Ford*. London:
       William Kimber, 1982. (pp. 141-146)

253   Fordin, Hugh. *Getting to Know Him: A Biography of Oscar
       Hammerstein II*. New York: Ungar, 1986. (pp. 287-288,
       304, 323-329)

254   Forman, C. *John Steinbeck's "The Pearl."* New York:
       Barron's, 1985.

255   Franklin, Benjamin, V. *Dictionary of American Literary
       Characters*. New York: Facts on File, 1990. (contains
       entries on *Cannery Row, East of Eden, The Grapes of
       Wrath, In Dubious Battle, Of Mice and Men, The Pearl,
       Tortilla Flat, The Wayward Bus* and *The Winter of Our
       Discontent*)

256   French, Warren, ed. *A Companion to "The Grapes of Wrath."*
       New York: Penguin, 1987. (a reissue of the 1963 original,
       also in a 1989 paperback ed.)

257   French, Warren. *John Steinbeck's Fiction Revisited.* New
        York: Twayne, 1994. Preface. Ch. 1: The Making and
        Unmaking of a Novelist. Ch. 2: John Steinbeck and
        Modernism. Ch. 3: Two False Starts. Ch. 4: The Story
        Cycles. Ch. 5: Travels Through the Long Valley. Ch. 6:
        Dreams into Nightmares. Ch. 7: The Education of the
        Heart. Ch. 8: Wartime Search for a Hero. Ch. 9: Art for
        Art's Sake: Transcendent Man in Cosmic Monterey. Ch.
        10: Searching for a Folk Hero. Ch. 11: The Last Big Push.
        Ch. 12: Ulysses's Final Quest: Cannery Row Revisited,
        Paris, and Long Island. Ch. 13: Steinbeck 2000. Selected
        Bibliography.

258   French, Warren. *John Steinbeck's Non-Fiction Revisited.* New
        York: Twayne, 1996. Contents: Preface, ix-xiv;
        Chronology, xv-xviii. Ch. 1: A Journalist at Heart. Ch. 2:
        Discovering a Mission. Ch. 3: Escape into *The Sea of
        Cortez.* Ch. 4: Artist as Propagandist. Ch. 5: *Once There
        Was a War.* Ch. 6: *A Russian Journal.* Ch. 7: The Quest
        for Zapata. Chapter 8: *Journal of a Novel.* Ch. 9: One
        American in Paris. Ch. 10: *Travels with Charley in Search
        of America.* Ch. 11: *America and Americans.* Ch. 12:
        "Letters to Alicia." Ch. 13: A Legacy in Disarray. Notes
        and References. Selected Bibliography.

259   Fried, Lewis, and Yoshinobu Hakutani, eds. *American
        Literary Naturalism: A Reassessment.* Heidelberg: Carl
        Winter, 1975. (Contains Warren French's "John
        Steinbeck: A Usable Concept of Naturalism," pp. 35-55)

260   Fussell, Paul. *Killing in Verse and Prose and Other Essays.*
        London: Bellew Publishing, 1990. (p. 73)

261   Fussell, Paul. *Wartime: Understanding and Behavior in the
        Second World War.* New York: Oxford University Press,
        1989. (pp. 51, 77, 120-121, 171, 285-286, 288, 303, 305,
        312, 318)

262 Gallup, Donald, ed. *The Journals of Thornton Wilder,* 1939-
     1961. New Haven: Yale University Press, 1985. (pp. 3-5)

263 Garraty, John A., and Eric Foner. *The Reader's Companion to
     American History.* See #251.

264 Gibbons, Kaye. *Charms for the Easy Life.* New York: Putnam,
     1993. (pp. 116-117)

265 Gilmore, Thomas B. *Equivocal Spirits: Alcoholism and
     Drinking in Twentieth Century Literature.* Chapel Hill:
     University of North Carolina Press, 1987.

266 Gladstein, Mimi Reisel. *The Indestructible Woman in
     Faulkner, Hemingway and Steinbeck.* Ann Arbor: UMI
     Research Press, 1986. Contents: "Preface," xi-xii. Ch 1:
     "Introduction," 1-8. Ch. 2: "Faulkner," 9-45. Ch. 3:
     "Hemingway," 47-73. Ch. 4: "Steinbeck," 75-100. Ch. 5:
     "Some Conclusions," 101-111. Bibliography, 127-134.

267 Golding, William. *A Moving Target.* New York: Farrar, Starus
     and Giroux, 1982. (pp. 133-135)

268 Goldman, William. *The Season: A Candid Look at Broadway.*
     New York: Limelight Editions, 1984. (pp. 70-71, 326-337,
     413)

269 Goodin, G. *The Poetics of Protest: Literary Form and
     Political Implication in the Victim of Society.* Charleston,
     Ill.: Southern Illinois University Press, 1985. (contains
     "Permutations and Combinations of Victims," pp. 159-
     189)

270 Goodman, Michael. *John Steinbeck's "Of Mice and Men."*
     Woodbury, N.Y.: Barrons, 1984.

271   Goodwin, Donald W., M.D. *Alcohol and the Writer*. New
       York: Penguin Books, 1988. (pp. 73-92)

272   Goring, Rosemary, ed. *Larousse Dictionary of Literary
       Characters*. New York: Larousse, 1994. (contains
       commentary on characters from *Cannery Row, East of
       Eden, The Grapes of Wrath, In Dubious Battle, Of Mice
       and Men, The Red Pony, Tortilla Flat*)

273   *The Great Writers: Their Lives, Work, and Inspiration*: John
       Steinbeck, "The Grapes of Wrath," Part 44, Vol. 4, 1032-
       1056.

274   Greenfield, A. *Work and the Work Ethic in American Drama,
       1920-1970*. Columbia: University of Missouri Press, 1982.
       (Discussion of *The Moon Is Down*, 88-93)

275   Gregory, James N. *American Exodus: The Dust Bowl
       Migration and Okie Culture in California*. New York:
       Oxford Press, 1989.

276   Greiner, Donald J. *Women Enter the Wilderness: Male
       Bonding and the American Novel of the 1980s*. Columbia,
       S.C.: University of South Carolina Press, 1991. (pp. 9, 18,
       31, 82, 90, 94)

277   Grogg, Sam L., Michael T. Marsden, and John H. Nachbar.
       Movies As Artifacts: Cultural Criticism of Popular Film.
       Chicago: Nelson Hall, 1982. (contains "*Gone with the
       Wind* and *The Grapes of Wrath* as Hollywood Histories of
       the Depression," by Thomas H. Pauly on pp. 164-176)

278   Gunton, Sharon R., ed. *Contemporary Literary Criticism*. Vol.
       21. Detroit: Gale Research, 1982. (pp. 365-393)

279   Guy, Betty. *Surprise for Steinbeck*. San Francisco: Feathered
        Serpent Press, 1992.

280   Hadella, Charlotte Cook. *"Of Mice and Men": A Kinship of
        Powerlessness*. New York: Twayne, 1995. (also available
        from London: Prentice Hall — An entry in Twayne's
        Masterworks Series) Contents: Literary and Historical
        Context. Ch. 1: Historical Context. Ch. 2: Importance of
        the Work. Ch. 3: Critical Reception. A Reading. Ch. 4:
        An Experiment in Form. Ch. 5: Layers of Complexities:
        Reality, Symbol and Myth. Ch. 6: Stage and Screen.

281   Hakutani, Toshinobu, and Lewis Fried. eds. *American
        Literary Naturalism: A Reassessment.* See #259.

282   Hall, Sharon K., ed. *Contemporary Literary Criticism.* Vol.
        34. (Yearbook 1984) Detroit: Gale Research, 1985. (pp.
        404-415 list reviews of Jackson J. Benson's biography,
        The True Adventures of John Steinbeck, Writer)

283   Hamilton, Ian. *Writers in Hollywood* 1915-1951. London:
        Mandarin Paperbacks, 1990. (pp. 180-182, 279-281)

284   Hammalian, Linda. *A Life of Kenneth Rexroth*. New York:
        W.W. Norton, 1991. (pp. 84-85)

285   Hamman, Rick, and Horace W. Fabring. *Steinbeck Country
        Narrow Gauge*. Boulder: Pruett Publishing Co., 1985.

286   Hanson, Robert F. 132 *Central Avenue*. Bradenton, Fla.:
        Opuscula Press, 1985. (This miniature book is on the
        boyhood home of John Steinbeck.)

287   Harmon, R., et. al., eds. *American Cultural Leaders: From
        Colonial Times to the Present.* Santa Barbara: ABC /
        CLIO, 1990. (pp. 461-462)

288   Harmon, Robert B., comp. *The Collectible John Steinbeck: A
        Practical Guide*. Jefferson, N.C.: McFarland and
        Company, 1986.

289   Harmon, Robert B., comp. *A Collector's Guide to the First
        Editions of John Steinbeck*. Bradenton, Fla.: Opuscula
        Press, 1985.

290   Harris, Laurie Lazen. *Characters in 20th Century Literature*.
        Detroit: Gale Research, Inc., 1990. (contains "John
        Steinbeck" pp. 380-383 and discussions of *Tortilla Flat,
        The Grapes of Wrath, Of Mice and Men, East of Eden*)

291   Hart, James D., ed. *The Oxford Companion to American
        Literature*. 6th edition. New York: Oxford, 1995. (contains
        an entry on Steinbeck, pp. 635-636 as well as entries on
        *The Grapes of Wrath, East of Eden, Tortilla Flat, In
        Dubious Battle* and *Of Mice and Men*)

292   Hashiguchi, Yasuo, ed. *The Complete Works of John
        Steinbeck*. Kyoto, Japan: Rinsen Shoten Co., 1985.
        Contents: Vol I: *A Cup of Gold*. Vol. II: *The Pastures of
        Heaven*. Vol. III: *To a God Unknown*. Vol. IV: *Tortilla
        Flat*. Vol. V: *In Dubious Battle*. Vol. VI: "Saint Katy the
        Virgin," "The Red Pony," *The Long Valley*, "How Edith
        McGillicuddy Met Robert L. Stevenson." Vol. VII: *Of
        Mice and Men, Of Mice and Men: A Play in Three Acts*.
        Vol. VIII: *The Grapes of Wrath*. Vol. IX: *The Moon Is
        Down, The Moon Is Down: A Play in Two Parts, Viva
        Zapata!* Vol. X: *Cannery Row, Sweet Thursday*. Vol XI:
        The Wayward Bus, The Pearl. Vol. XII: *Burning Bright: A
        Play in Story Form, Burning Bright, acting edition*. Vol.
        XIII: *East of Eden*. Vol. XIV: *The Short Reign of Pippin
        IV, a Fabrication, The Winter of Our Discontent*. Vol. XV:
        The Acts of King Arthur and His Noble Knights. Vol. XVI:
        *Their Blood Is Strong, Travels with Charley in Search of
        America, America and Americans*. Vol. XVII: *The
        Forgotten Village, The Log from the Sea of Cortez*. Vol.

XVIII: *Bombs Away, Once There Was a War*. Vol. XIX: *A Russian Journal, Positano, Speech Accepting the Nobel Prize, Journal of a Novel*. Vol. XX: Appendix; Unpublished Stories and Non-Fiction, Steinbeck Research Libraries in the U.S.

293   Hashiguchi, Yasuo, and Koichi Kaido, eds. *John Steinbeck, "The Grapes of Wrath."* Tokyo: Eichosha Shinsha Press, 1988.

294   Hashiguchi, Yasuo, and Koichi Kaido. *A Catalogue of the Maurice Dunbar John Steinbeck Collection at Fukuoka University*. Okayama, Japan: Mikado Printing Office, 1992.

295   Hashiguchi, Yasuo, Shigeharo Yano, Tetsumaro Hayashi, and Richard F. Peterson, eds. *John Steinbeck: From Salinas to the World: Proceedings of the Second International Steinbeck Congress* (1984), dedicated to Warren French and Jackson J. Benson. Tokyo, Japan: Gaku Shobo Press, 1986. Contents: "Introduction," xii-xv; Pt. I: Proceedings of the Second Annual Steinbeck Congress (North American Papers). Warren French, "John Steinbeck: From Salinas to the World," 1-12; John Ditsky, "Steinbeck as Dramatist: A Preliminary Account," 13-23; Mimi Reisel Gladstein, "From Lady Brett to Ma Joad," 24-33; Tetsumaro Hayashi, "John Steinbeck: His Concept of Writing," 34-44; Robert E. Morsberger, "Steinbeck's Films," 45-67. Pt. II: Proceedings of the Second Annual Steinbeck Congress (Asian Papers). Kiyoshi Nakayama, "John Steinbeck and Yasumari Kawabata," 68-82; Kiyohiko Tsuboi, "Two Jodys: Steinbeck and Rawlings," 83-96; Kingo Hanamoto, "Steinbeck, Faulkner and Buddism," 97-102; Noburo Shimomura, "Steinbeck and Monterey: Theme and Humor in the 'Monterey Trilogy,'" 102-112; M.R. Satyanarayana, "Indian Thought in Steinbeck's Works," 113-122; Rajul Bhargava, "*Tortilla Flat*: A Re-Evaluation," 123-129; Takahiko Sugiyama,

"Camille Oakes, A Heroine of Nonsense — A
Reassessment of *The Wayward Bus*," 130-136.

296   Haslam, Gerald. *Coming of Age in California: Personal
        Essays.* Walnut Creek, Calif.: Devil Mountain Books,
        1987.

297   Haslam, Gerald, ed. *Many Californias: Literature from the
        Golden State.* Reno: University of Nevada Press, 1992.

298   Haslam, Gerald. *Voices of a Place: Social and Literary Essays
        from the Other California.* Walnut Creek, Calif.: Devil
        Mountain Books, 1990.

299   Haslauer, Wilfried. *A Salzburg Miscellany: English and
        American Studies* 1964-1984. Salzburg: Institute fur
        Anlistik and Amerikanstik Univ., 1984. (contains William
        Oxley, "The Sick Novel," pp. 117-129)

300   Hay, Peter, ed. *Movie Anecdotes*. New York: Oxford
        University Press, 1990. (p. 181)

301   Hayashi, Tetsumaro, ed. *John Steinbeck and the Vietnam War.
        (Pt. I)* Steinbeck Monograph Series. No. 12. Muncie, Ind.:
        Steinbeck Research Institute, Ball State University, 1986.
        Contents: Preface; Epigraph; Reloy Garcia, "Introduction";
        Pt. I: "Introduction"; Pt. II: "Steinbeck As a Moralist and
        His 'Arthurian Quest and Discovery'"; Pt. III: "Steinbeck
        As an Anti-Communist Hawk"; Pt. IV: "The Soviet
        Denunciation of Steinbeck's Involvement"; Pt. V:
        "Steinbeck's Concept of the Vietnam War and His
        Growing Pessimism"; Pt. VI: "Conclusion."

302   Hayashi, Tetsumaro, ed. *John Steinbeck on Writing*. Steinbeck
        Essay Series, No. 2. Muncie, Ind.: Steinbeck Research
        Institute, Ball State University, 1988. Contents: Preface;

Reloy Garcia, "Introduction," Pt. I: "Advice on Writing";
Pt. II: "The Craft of Writing"; Pt. III: "A Novelist as a
Minstrel"; Pt. IV: "Work Habits"; Pt. V: "Censorship"; Pt.
VI: "Literature, Journalism and Criticism"; Appendix I:
"John Steinbeck: The Art and Craft of Writing"; Appendix
II: "Bibliography: A Checklist of Sources Quoted";
Appendix III: "Bibliography: A Checklist of Outstanding
Reference Books."

303   Hayashi, Tetsumaro, ed. *John Steinbeck: The Years of
Greatness,* 1936-1939. Tuscaloosa, Ala.: University of
Alabama Press, 1993. Contents: Preface, xi- xii; John H.
Timmerman, "Introduction — Power and Grace: The
Shape of a Tradition," xv-xxiii. Pt. I: The Years of
Greatness: Steinbeck's Women. John Ditsky, "'Your Own
Mind Coming Out of the Garden': Steinbeck's Elusive
Woman," 3-19; Robert DeMott, "After *The Grapes of
Wrath*: A Speculative Essays on John Steinbeck's Suite of
Love Poems for Gwyn, 'The Girl of The Air,'" 20-45;
Abby H. P. Werlock, "Looking at Lisa: The Function of
the Feminine in Steinbeck's *In Dubious Battle,*" 46-63;
Charlotte Cook Hadella, "The Dialogic Tension in
Steinbeck's Portrait of Curley's Wife," 64-74. Pt. II: The
Years of Greatness: Steinbeck's Worker Trilogy. Louis
Owens, "Writing 'in Costume': The Missing Voices of *In
Dubious Battle,*" 77-94; Thomas M. Tammaro, 'Sharing
Creation: Steinbeck, *In Dubious Battle* and the Working
Class Novel in American Literature," 95-105; Thomas
Fensch, "Reflections of Doc: The Persona of Ed Ricketts
in *Of Mice and Men,*" 106-110; Robert E. Morsberger,
"Tell It Again, George," 111-131; Mimi Reisel Gladstein,
"*The Grapes of Wrath* and the Eternal Emigrant," 132-144;
Susan Shillinglaw, "California Answers *The Grapes of
Wrath,"* 145-164.

304   Hayashi, Tetsumaro, ed. *A New Study Guide to Steinbeck's
Major Works, with Critical Explications.* Metuchen, N. J.:
Scarecrow Press, 1993. Contents: Tetsumaro Hayashi,
Editor's Preface; Reloy Garcia, Introduction; Barbara

Heavilin, *America and Americans*; Michael J. Meyer, *Cannery Row*; Louis Owens, *East of Eden*; Louis Owens, *The Grapes of Wrath*; Helen Lojek, *In Dubious Battle*; Charlotte Hadella, *Of Mice and Men*; Patrick W. Shaw, *The Pearl*; Patrick W. Shaw, *The Red Pony*; Barbara Heavilin, *Travels with Charley*; Michael J. Meyer, *The Winter of Our Discontent*; Tetsumaro Hayashi, "John Steinbeck: The Art and Craft of Writing"; Bibliography.

305   Hayashi, Tetsumaro, ed. *Steinbeck's "The Grapes of Wrath"*: *Essays in Criticism*. Steinbeck Essay Series, No. 3. Muncie, Ind.: Steinbeck Research Institute, Ball State University Press, 1990. Contents: John Timmerman, "Introduction"; A. Carl Bredahl, "The Drinking Metaphor in *The Grapes of Wrath*"; Duane R. Carr, "Steinbeck's Blakean Vision in *The Grapes of Wrath*"; Sylvia J. Cook, "Steinbeck, the People and the Party"; Richard Allan Davison, "Charles G. Norris and John Steinbeck: Two More Tributes to *The Grapes of Wrath*"; Reloy Garcia, "The Rocky Road to Eldorado: The Journey Motif in *The Grapes of Wrath*"; Helen Lojek, "Jim Casy: Politico of the New Jerusalem"; Richard S. Pressman, "'Them's Horses — We're Men': Social Tendency and Counter-Tendency in *The Grapes of Wrath*"; Patrick W. Shaw, "Tom's Other Trip: Psycho-Physical Questing in *The Grapes of Wrath*."

306   Hayashi, Tetsumaro, ed. *Steinbeck's Literary Dimension: A Guide to Comparative Studies*. Series II. Metuchen, N. J.: Scarecrow Press, 1991. Contents: Duane Carr, "Steinbeck's Blakean Vision in *The Grapes of Wrath*"; Richard Peterson, "Homer Was Blind; John Steinbeck on the Character of William Faulkner"; Stanley Renner, "Mary Teller and Sue Bridehead: Birds of a Feather in 'The White Quail' and *Jude the Obscure*"; Richard Astro, "Phlebas Sails the Caribbean: Steinbeck, Hemingway, and the American Waste Land"; Jackson J. Benson, "Hemingway the Hunter and Steinbeck the Farmer"; Richard Allan Davison, "Hemingway, Steinbeck, and the Art of the Short Story"; Edward W. Waldron, "*The Pearl*

and *The Old Man and the Sea*: A Comparative Analysis";
Donal Stone, "Steinbeck, Jung and *The Winter of Our
Discontent*"; Roy S. Simmonds, "Cathy Ames and Rhoda
Penmark: Two Child Monsters"; Richard Allan Davison,
"Charles G. Norris and John Steinbeck: Two More
Tributes to *The Grapes of Wrath*"; Bett Yates Adams, "The
Form of the Narrative Section of *Sea of Cortez*: A
Specimen Collected from Reality"; Bett Yates Adams,
"Steinbeck, Ricketts and *Sea of Cortez*: Partnership or
Exploitation"; Sydney J. Krause, "Steinbeck and Mark
Twain"; Sydney J. Krause, "*The Pearl* and 'Hadleyburg':
From Desire to Renunciation."

307   Hayashi, Tetsumaro, and Thomas J. Moore, eds. *Steinbeck's
Posthumous Work: Essays in Criticism*. Steinbeck
Monograph Series, No. 14. Muncie, Ind.: Steinbeck
Research Institute, Ball State University Press, 1989.
Contents: Reloy Garcia, "Introduction"; Nancy Zane, "The
Romantic Impulse in Steinbeck's *Journal of a Novel: The
East of Eden Letters* (1969)"; John H. Timmerman,
"Steinbeck: *A Life in Letters* (1975): Steinbeck's Place in
the Modern Epistolary Tradition"; Clifford Lewis,
"Outfoxed: Writing *Viva Zapata!* (1975)"; Michael
Sundermeier, "Why Steinbeck didn't Finish His *Arthur —
The Acts of King Arthur and His Noble Knights* (1976)";
Maurice Dunbar, "A Review of *Letters to Elizabeth: A
Selection of Letters from John Steinbeck to Elizabeth Otis*
(1978)".

308   Hayashi, Tetsumaro, and Thomas J. Moore, eds. *Steinbeck's
"The Red Pony": Essays in Criticism*. Steinbeck
Monograph Series, No. 13. Muncie, Ind.: Steinbeck
Research Institute, Ball State University Press, 1988.
Contents: Thomas M. Tammaro, "Erik Ericson Meets John
Steinbeck: Psycho-Social Development in 'The Gift'";
Robert S. Hughes, Jr., "The Black Cypress and the Green
Tub: Death and Procreation in Steinbeck's 'The Promise'";
Roy S. Simmonds, "The Place and Importance of 'The

Great Mountains'"; Mimi Reisel Gladstein, "'The Leader of the People': A Boy Becomes a 'Mensch'".

309   Hayashi, Tetsumaro, ed. *Steinbeck's Short Stories in "The Long Valley": Essays in Criticism*. Steinbeck Monograph Series, No. 15. Muncie, Ind.: Steinbeck Research Institute, Ball State University Press, 1991. Contents: Warren French. "Introduction"; Susan Shillinglaw, "'The Chrysanthemums': Steinbeck's Pygmalion"; Michael J. Meyer, "Pure and Corrupt: Agency and Communion in the Edenic Garden of 'The White Quail'"; Robert M. Benton, "A Search for Meaning in 'Flight'"; Robert M. Benton, "'The Snake' and Its Anomalous Nature"; Michael J. Meyer, "'Symbols for the Wordlessness': Steinbeck's Silent Message in 'Breakfast'"; Michael J. Meyer, "'The Illusion of Eden': Efficacious Commitment and Sacrifice in 'The Raid'; Louis Owens, "'Bottom and Upland': The Balanced Man in Steinbeck's 'The Harness'"; Louis Owens, "'The Little Bit of a Story': Steinbeck's 'The Vigilante'"; Patricia M. Mandia, "Chaos, Evil, and The Dredger Subplot in Steinbeck's 'Johnny Bear'"; Patricia M. Mandia, "Sexism, Racism or Irony?: Steinbeck's 'The Murder'"; Thomas M. Tammaro, "'Saint Katy the Virgin': The Key to Steinbeck's Secret Heart"; Robert S. Hughes, Jr., "Steinbeck the Short Story Writer."

310   Hayashi, Tetsumaro, ed. *Steinbeck's World War II Fiction: "The Moon Is Down" — Three Explications*. Steinbeck Essay Series, No. 1. Muncie, Ind.: Steinbeck Research Institute, Ball State University Press, 1986. Contents: "Introduction," by Reloy Garcia, 1-4; Pt. I: "Steinbeck's Political Vision in *The Moon Is Down*," 1-16; Pt. II; "Steinbeck's *The Moon Is Down*: A Shakespearean Analogy," 17-30; Pt. III: "Dr. Winter's Dramatic Functions in *The Moon Is Down*," 31-41.

311   Hayashi, Tetsumaro, Richard F. Peterson, Shigeharo Yano, and Yasuo Hashiguchi, eds. *John Steinbeck: From Salinas*

to the World: Proceedings of the Second International Steinbeck Congress (1984), dedicated to Warren French and Jackson J. Benson. See #295.

312   Hedgpeth, Joel W. "Ed Ricketts (1897-1948), Marine Biologist," in *Managing Inflows to California's Bays and Estuaries: Proceedings of the Symposium Organized by the Bay Institute*, held at Monterey, California, November 13-15, 1986.

313   Hellman, John. *American Myth and the Legacy of Vietnam*. New York: Columbia University, 1986. (p. 20)

314   Hemp, Michael Kenneth. *Cannery Row: The History of Old Ocean View Avenue*. Monterey: The History Company, 1986.

315   Henderson, Lesley, ed. *Twentieth Century Romantic and Historical Writers*. 2nd ed. Chicago and London: St. James Press, 1990. (contains "John Steinbeck" by Roy Simmonds on pp. 611-613)

316   Hendrick, George, ed. *To Reach Eternity: The Letters of James Jones*. New York: Random House, 1989. (pp. 123, 219)

317   Henson, S. *The Play of John Steinbeck's "The Pearl."* London: Heinemann Educational Books, 1989.

318   Herron, Don. *The Literary World of San Francisco and Its Environs*. San Francisco: City Light Books, 1985. (pp. 214-227)

319   High, Peter B. *An Outline of American Literature*. London: Longman, 1986. (pp. 163-164)

320   Hillyard, Kay, ed. *Steinbeck House Cookbook*. Salinas, Calif.:
           Valley Guild, 1984.

321   Himes, Chester B. *My Life of Absurdity: The Later Years*.
           New York: Athena Books, Paragon House, 1990. (p. 28)
           (*Cannery Row*).

322   Himes, Chester B. *The Quality of Hurt: The Autobiography of
           Chester Himes*. Garden City, N.Y.: Doubleday, 1972. (p.
           62) (*Of Mice and Men*).

323   Hobson, Fred, and Ralph F. Bogardus, eds. *Literature at the
           Barricades: The American Writer in the 1930s*. See #168.

324   Holman-Williams, C. Hugh. *A Handbook to Literature*. New
           York: Macmillan, 1986. (p. 54)

325   Hoopes, Roy. *Cain: The Autobiography of James M. Cain*.
           New York: Holt, Rinehart and Winston, 1982. (p. 287)

326   Hughes, Robert S., Jr. *Beyond "The Red Pony": A Reader's
           Companion to Steinbeck's Complete Short Stories*.
           Metuchen, N. J.: Scarecrow Press, 1987. Contents:
           "Preface," ix-x; Ch. 1: "Introduction and Stories from the
           1920s," 1-8; "Unpublished Stories (1924-26)," 9-25; "The
           Gifts of Iban," 25-28. Ch. 2: "*The Pastures of Heaven*
           (1932)," 29-51. Ch. 3: "*The Long Valley* (1938) and Other
           Short Fiction of the 1930s," 52-90; "*The Red Pony*
           Stories," 90-104. Ch. 4: "Uncollected Stories of the 1940s
           and 1950s," 105-125; "Conclusion," 126-127; 'Selected
           Bibliography," 142-155.

327   Hughes, Robert S., Jr. *John Steinbeck: A Study of the Short
           Fiction*. Boston, Mass.: Twayne, 1989. Contents:
           "Preface," xi-xii. Pt. I: The Short Fiction: A Critical
           Analysis. "Steinbeck, the Short Story Writer," 3-19;

"Scenes from 'Steinbeck Country,'" 20-68; "'From Salinas to the World': Stories of the 1940s and 1950s," 69-89; "A Steinbeck Short Story Cycle: *The Pastures of Heaven*," 90-117; "Conclusion," 118-119; "Notes," 119-132. Pt. II: The Writer: Autobiographical Statements on Short Story Writing. "Introduction," 135; (Letter to Edith Mirrielees,) 136-137; "John Steinbeck: His Concept of Writing," 138-149. Pt. III: The Critics. "Introduction," 153; Marilyn Mitchell, "Steinbeck's Strong Women: Feminine Identity in the Short Stories," 154-166; Charles E. May, "Myth and Mystery in Steinbeck's 'The Snake': A Jungian View," 166-180; M.R. Satyanarayana, "'And Then the Child Becomes a Man': Three Initiation Stories of John Steinbeck," 181-187; Arnold L. Goldsmith, "Thematic Rhythm in *The Red Pony*," 188-193; "Chronology," 195-197; "Bibliography," 198-210.

328   Hunter, Jefferson. *Image and Word: The Interaction of Twentieth Century Photographs and Text.* Cambridge, Mass.: Harvard University Press, 1987.

329   Hurst, Mary Jane. *Voice of the Child in American Literature.* Lexington, Ky.: University of Kentucky Press, 1990.

330   Hurt, R. Douglas. *The Dust Bowl.* Chicago: Nelson-Hall, 1984. (pp. 54, 97-99)

331   Husebow, Arthur R. and Nancy Owen Nelson. *The Selected Letters of Frederick Manfred.* Lincoln: University of Nebraska Press, 1988. (pp. 84-89, 98-108, 126-127, 140-141, 153-161, 170-173, 184, 193, 197, 202-205, 211, 224, 232, 262, 338, 350-352, 354, 357)

332   Inge, M. Thomas, ed. *Handbook of American Popular Literature.* Westport, Conn.: Greenwood Press, 1988. (references to Steinbeck on pp. 16, 324, 332, 342-343)

333   Ito, Tom. *The Importance of John Steinbeck*. San Diego:
         Lucent Books, 1994. (juvenile)

334   Janzel, Bill. *Dust Bowl Descent*. Lincoln: University of
         Nebraska, 1984.

335   Jarrell, Mary, ed. *Randall Jarrell's Letters*. London: Faber and
         Faber, 1986. (pp. 458-460)

336   Jennings, Jan. *Roadside America*. Ames: Iowa State
         University Press, 1990. (contains Arthur Krim's essay
         "Route 66: A Cultural Cartography")

337A   Johnson, Claudia Durst. *Understanding 'Of Mice and Men,'
         'The Red Pony' and 'The Pearl'* Westport, Conn.:
         Greenwood Press, 1997.

337   Johnson, Diane. *The Life of Dashiell Hammett*. London:
         Chatto and Windus, 1984. (pp. 157-158)

338   Jones, James Earl. *Voices and Silences*. New York: Charles
         Scribner's Sons, 1993. (pp. 216-223)

338A   Jones, Margaret C. *Prophets in Babylon: Five California
         Novelists in the 1930's*. New York: Peter Lang, 1992. (*The
         Grapes of Wrath*)

339   Jones, William M. *John Steinbeck: Great American Novelist
         and Playwright*. Outstanding Personality Series #89.
         Charlottesville, New York: SamHar Press, 1982.

340   Jungk, Peter Stephan. *Franz Werfel: A Life in Prague, Vienna
         and Hollywood*. New York: Grove, Weidenfeld, 1990. (p.
         201)

341   Junkin, Elizabeth Darby, and Robert C. Baron, eds. *Of
       Discovery and Destiny: An Anthology of American Writers
       and the American Land.* See #147.

342   Jurak, Mirko, ed. *Literature, Culture, and Ethnicity: Studies
       on Medieval, Renaissance and Modern Literatures.*
       Ljubljana: Author, 1992. (contains "And the Greatest of
       These Is Love: John Steinbeck's *The Grapes of Wrath* as a
       Statement of Moral Humanism; Festschrift for Janez
       Stanonik" by Wilton Eckley on pp. 223-227)

343   Kaido, Koichi, and Yasuo Hashigushi, eds. *John Steinbeck,
       "The Grapes of Wrath."* See #293.

344   Karl, Frederick R. *American Fiction* 1940/1980*: A
       Comprehensive History and Evaluation.* New York:
       Harper and Row, 1983. (pp. xiii, 23, 75-77, 94, 198)

345   Karl, Frederick R. *William Faulkner: American Writer.*
       London: Faber and Faber, 1989. (pp. 908)

346   Karolides, Nicolas J., Lee Burress, and John M. Kean.
       Censored Books: Critical Viewpoints. See #188.

347   Kazan, Elia. *Elia Kazan.* New York: Knopf, 1988. (The last
       chapter of Kazan's autobiography is devoted to the deaths
       of four people, including John Steinbeck. pp. 5, 254, 261,
       273, 331, 373, 377, 393, 394-401, 417-420, 427-431, 433,
       456, 463, 529, 533-539, 545-546, 574, 593-594, 596, 728,
       784-788, 817)

348   Kazin, Alfred. *A Writer's America: Landscape in Literature.*
       New York: Knopf, 1988. (pp. 209-215)

349   Kean, John M., Lee Burress, and Nicolas Karolides. *Censored
       Books: Critical Viewpoints.* See #188.

350   Kelley, Susan Croce and Quinta Scott. *Route 66, A History of the Highway and Its People*. Norman: University of Oklahoma Press, 1988.

351   Kiernan, R. *American Writing since 1945: A Critical Survey*. New York: Frederick Ungar, 1983. (pp. 10-11, 54)

352   Kirkpatric, D. L., ed. *Reference Guide to American Literature*. 2nd ed. Chicago and London: St. James Press, 1987. (pp. 510-513, 637-638)

353   Klehr, Harvey. *The Heyday of American Communism*. New York: Basic Books, 1984.

354   Klein, Joe. *Woody Guthrie: A Life*. New York: Knopf, 1980. (many Steinbeck references).

355   Knight, Stephen. *Arthurian Literature and Society*. New York: St. Martin's, 1983. (pp. 201-207, 214)

356   Kramer, Elaine Fialka, Dorothy Nyren Curley, and Maurice Kramer, eds. *Modern American Literature*. 4th ed. Vol. 3. New York: Frederick Ungar, 1990. (contains "John Steinbeck" on pp. 218-224)

357   Kramer, Maurice, Dorothy Nyren Curley, and Elaine Fialka Kramer, eds. *Modern American Literature*. 4th ed. Vol. 3. See #211.

358   Lacy, Norris, et al., eds. *The Arthurian Encyclopaedia*. New York: Garland, 1988. (contains "John Steinbeck" by Maureen Fries on p. 526)

359   Larsh, Ed B. *Doc's Lab: Myths and Legends of Cannery Row*. Monterey, Calif.: PBL Press, 1995.

360   Larsen, Robin and Stephen Larsen. *A Fire in the Mind: The*
       Life of Joseph Campbell. New York: Doubleday, 1991.
       (pp. 74-77, 160-211, 224-225, 316-317, 330-331, 356-357,
       380-381, 426-427, 436-437, 440-441, 448-449, 458-463,
       512, 594-597, 612-613)

361   Lass, Abraham, et al., eds. *The Facts on File Dictionary of*
       Classical, Biblical and Literary Allusions. New York:
       Facts on File, 1987. (p. 68)

362   Latham, Harold S. *Life in Publishing.* New York: Dutton,
       1965. (mentions Steinbeck in a section entitled "Authors
       I'd Like to Have Known Better," pp. 200-202.)

363   Lawhn, Juanita Luna, ed., et al. *Mexico and the United States:*
       Intercultural Relations in the Humanities. San Antonio,
       Tex.: San Antonio College, 1984. (contains Edward
       Murguia's "The Sociology of Steinbeck's *Tortilla Flat*: A
       Study of Class-Based Rationalizations," pp. 49-56)

364   Lee, Brian. *American Fiction 1865-1940.* London: Longman,
       1987. (pp. 158-169)

365   Leff, Leonard J. *Hitchcock and Selznick*. London: Weidenfeld
       and Nicolson, 1988. (pp. 111-14, 117, 134)

366   Leininger, Philip, Barbara Perkins, George Perkins, eds.
       Benet's Reader's Encyclopaedia of American Literature.
       New York: Harper Collins, 1991. (contains entries on John
       Steinbeck on pp. 1012-1013 and commentary on *The*
       Grapes of Wrath, Of Mice and Men, Cannery Row and *The*
       Pearl)

367   Lesnick, James, ed. *Contemporary Authors. New Revision*
       Series. Vol. 35. Detroit: Gale Research, 1992. (contains
       "John Steinbeck" on pp. 452-458)

368   Levene, Bruce, ed. *James Dean in Mendocino: The Filming of
       "East of Eden."* Mendocino, Calif.: Pacific
       Transcriptions, 1995.

369   Lewis, Clifford, and Carroll Britch, eds. *Rediscovering
       Steinbeck: Revisionist Views of his Art and Politics.* See
       #179.

370   Lisca, Peter. *The Wide World of John Steinbeck.* New York:
       Gordian Press, 1981. (a reprint of Lisca's 1958 study)

371   Long, Elizabeth. *The American Dream and the Popular Novel.*
       Boston: Routledge and Kegan Paul, 1985. (pp. 22, 94, 96-
       98, 192, 218)

372   Lorentz, Pare. *FDR's Moviemaker.* Reno, Nev.: University of
       Nevada Press, 1992. (pp. 105-158)

373   Lottman, Herbert R. *The Left Bank: Writers, Artists, and
       Politics from the Popular Front to the Cold War.* Boston:
       Houghton Mifflin, 1982. (pp. 180-187)

374   Lutwack, Leonard. *Birds in Literature.* Gainesville, Fla.:
       University of Florida Press, 1995. (pp. 203-205) ("The
       White Quail")

375   Lutwack, Leonard. *The Role of Place in American Literature.*
       Syracuse, N.Y.: Syracuse University Press, 1984.

376   MacNicholas, John, ed. *Dictionary of Literary Biography.*
       Vol. 7: *20th Century American Dramatists, Pt. 2: L-Z.*
       Detroit: Gale Research, 1981. (contains "John Steinbeck"
       by William B. Thesing on pp. 271-276)

377   Mailer, Norman. *Pieces and Pontifications*. London: New
        English Library, 1982. (p. 160)

378   Magill, Frank, ed. *Critical Survey of Short Fiction*. Vol. 6.
        Pasedena, Calif.: Salem Press, 1993. (contains "John
        Steinbeck" by Edward Fiorelli on pp. 2205-2210 and
        comments on *The Pastures of Heaven and The Long
        Valley*)

379   Magill, Frank, ed. *Cyclopaedia of Literary Characters II.*
        Pasedena, Calif.: Salem Press, 1990. (contains entries on
        Cannery Row by Donald Noble, Vol. I, pp. 231-233; *The
        Pearl* by Jill Rollins, Vol. III, pp. 1188-1189; *The Red
        Pony* by David Peck, Vol. III, p. 1281; *Tortilla Flat* by
        Donald R. Noble, Vol. IV, pp. 1595-1596)

380   Magill, Frank, ed. *Masterplots. Revised Category Edition.
        American Writer Series.* Pasadena, Calif.: Salem Press,
        1985. (contains *East of Eden,* Vol. I, 326-330; *The Grapes
        of Wrath,* Vol. I. 491-495; *In Dubious Battle,* Vol. II, 588-
        590; *Of Mice and Men,* Vol. II, 861-865)

381   Magill, Frank. *Masterplots II: American Fiction Series.*
        Englewood Cliffs, N. J.: Salem, 1986. (contains *Cannery
        Row* by Edward Fiorelli, Vol. I, 242-246; "The Red Pony"
        by Anthony Bernardo, Vol. 3, 1334-1338; *Tortilla Flat* by
        Anthony Bernardo, Vol. 4, 1688-1691)

382   Magill, Frank, ed. *Masterplots II: Short Story Series.*
        Pasadena, Calif.: Salem Press, 1986. (contains entries in
        Vol. I on "The Chrysanthemums," pp. 392-395; in Vol. II
        on "Flight," pp. 792-794 and on "The Gift," pp. 843-846;
        on *The Pearl* in Volume IV, pp. 1785-1788; on "The
        Leader of the People" in Volume VIII, pp. 3521-3523; and
        on 'The Snake' in Vol. IX, pp. 4039-4041)

383   Magill, Frank, ed. *The Nobel Prize Winners.* Vol. 3. 1962-
          1987. Pasadena, Calif.: Salem Press, 1987. (contains "John
          Steinbeck" by Carl E. Rollyson, Jr. on pp. 691-699)

384   Magill, Frank, ed. *Survey of American Literature.* Vol. 6.
          Pasadena, Calif.: Salem Press, 1991. (pp. 1885-1899)
          (contains entries on *Of Mice and Men, East of Eden, The
          Pearl, The Red Pony, The Grapes of Wrath,* and *Cannery
          Row*)

385   Mahoney, John, and Stewart Martin. *Of Mice and Men:
          Guide.* London: Letts, 1987.

386   Mangelsdorf, Tom. *A History of Steinbeck's Cannery Row.*
          Santa Cruz, Calif: Western Tanager Press, 1986.

387   Mann, Susan Garland. *The Short Story Cycle: A Genre
          Companion and Reference Guide.* Westport, Conn.:
          Greenwood Press, 1989. (contains "John Steinbeck's *The
          Pastures of Heaven,*" pp. 93-106, 204)

388   Marowski, Daniel G., and Roger Matuz, eds. *Contemporary
          Literary Criticism.* Vol. 45. Detroit: Gale Research, 1987.
          (pp. 368-385)

389   Martin, Stewart, and John Mahoney. *Of Mice and Men:
          Guide.* See #385.

390   Martine, James, ed. *Dictionary of Literary Biography. Vol. 9:
          American Novelists, 1910-1945. Pt. 3: Sandoz - Young.*
          Detroit: Gale Research, 1981. (contains "John Steinbeck"
          by Richard Astro on pp. 43-68)

391   Marsden, Michael T., John H. Nachbar, and Sam L. Grogg.
          Movies as Artifacts: Cultural Criticism of Popular Film.
          See #277.

392   Martin, Stoddard. *California Writers: Jack London, John Steinbeck, the Tough Guys*. New York: St. Martin's Press, 1983. (Ch. 3, pp. 67-122)

393   Matuz, Roger, ed. *Contemporary Literary Criticism*. Vol. 59. (Yearbook 1989) Detroit: Gale Research, 1989 (pp. 311-354 regarding the Fiftieth Anniversary of Steinbeck's *The Grapes of Wrath)*

394   Matuz, Roger, and Daniel G. Marowski, eds. *Contemporary Literary Criticism*. Vol. 45. See #388.

395   McElrath, Joseph R., Susan Shillinglaw, and Jesse S. Crisler, eds. *John Steinbeck: The Contemporary Reviews.* See #208.

395A   McKenna, C. W. F. *John Steinbeck: "The Grapes of Wrath."* Harlow, Essex, U.K.: Longman / York Press, 1990. (York Notes Series.

396   McKerns, Joseph. *Biographical Dictionary of American Journalism.* Westport, Conn.: Greenwood Press, 1989. (pp. 669-671)

397   Mead, Shepherd, and Dakin Williams. *Tennessee Williams: An Intimate Biography*. New York: Arbor House, 1983. (pp. 189-191)

398   Meldrum, Barbara Howard. *Under the Sea: Myth and Realism in Western American Literature.* Troy, N.Y.: Whitston, 1985. (references to Steinbeck on pp. 26, 27, 79)

399   Meredith, Burgess. *So Far, So Good: A Memoir*. Boston: Little, Brown and Co., 1994. (pp. 124-139, 242, 244, 248-249)

400   Michaels, Leonard, David Reid, and Racquel Scherr. *West of
       the West: Imagining California*. Berkeley, Calif.: North
       Point Press, 1989. (reprinted New York: Harper Collins,
       1991 and University of California Press, 1995.)

401   Miller, Arthur. *Timebands: A Life*. New York: Grove Press,
       1987. (pp. 284-285)

402   Miller, John, ed. *Voices Against Tyranny: Writing of the
       Spanish Civil War*. New York: Charles Scribner's Sons,
       1986. (pp. 146)

403   Millichap, Joseph R. *Steinbeck and Film*. New York:
       Frederick Ungar, 1983. Contents: "Chronology," xi-xiii. 1:
       John Steinbeck and Film, 1-7. 2: The Depression Decade.
       I: "The Early Works," 8-12; II: "*Of Mice and Men,*" 13-
       26; III: "*The Grapes of Wrath*," 26-50; IV: "*The Forgotten
       Village*," 50-56; V: "The End of an Era," 56-57. 3: The
       War Years. I. "A New Decade," 58-61; II. "*Tortilla Flat*,"
       61-69; III: "*The Moon Is Down*," 69-76; IV: "*Lifeboat*,"
       76-85; V: "*A Medal For Benny*," 85-89; VI: "The War and
       After," 89-92. 4: The Postwar Period. I. "After the War,"
       93-95; II. "*The Pearl*," 96-107; III. "*The Red Pony*," 107-
       121; IV. "*Viva Zapata!,*" 121-137; V: "*East of Eden*," 137-
       152; VI: "*The Wayward Bus*," 152-160; VII: "'Flight' and
       Final Works," 160-164; VIII: "Television," 165-172; IX:
       "*Cannery Row*," 172-178; 'Selected Bibliography," 191-
       194; "Filmography," 195-199.

404   Mills, Nicolaus. *The Crowd in American Literature*. Baton
       Rouge: Louisiana University Press, 1986. (pp. 12, 78, 98-
       111)

405   Milton, John R. *The Novel of the American West*. Lincoln:
       University of Nebraska Press, 1982.

406   Minter, David. *A Cultural History of the American Novel:*
        Henry James to William Faulkner. Cambridge: Cambridge
        University Press, 1994. (pp. 188-190) (*The Grapes of*
        Wrath)

407   Mogen, David, Mark Busby, and Paul Bryant. *The Frontier*
        Experience and the American Dream. See #184.

408   Moore, Thomas J., and Tetsumaro Hayashi, eds. *Steinbeck's*
        Posthumous Work: Essays in Criticism. Steinbeck
        Monograph Series, No. 14. See #307.

409   Moore, Thomas J., and Tetsumaro Hayashi, eds. *Steinbeck's*
        "The Red Pony": Essays in Criticism. Steinbeck
        Monograph Series, No. 13. See #308.

410   Morgan, Dan. *Rising in the West: The True Story of an*
        "Okie" Family from the Great Depression through the
        Reagan Years. New York: Knopf, 1992. (reprinted New
        York: Vintage, 1993)

411   Morgan, Ted. *Literary Outlaw: The Life and Times of William*
        S. Burroughs. New York: Henry Holt and Co., 1988. (pp.
        510-511) (relates to John Steinbeck IV)

412   Morsberger Robert E., ed. *Steinbeck/Zapata.* New York:
        Penguin, 1993.

413   Morsberger, Robert E. "Zapata — The Man, the Myth, and the
        Mexican Revolution," separately bound article issued with
        the limited edition of *Zapata — Steinbeck.* Covelo, Calif.:
        The Yolla Bolly Press, 1991.

414   Morsberger, Robert E. "Zapata Steinbeck," brochure with
        brief article, announcing the book *Zapata — Steinbeck.*
        Covelo, Calif.: The Yolla Bolly Press, 1991.

415   Mosley, Leonard. *Zanuck: The Rise and Fall of Hollywood's
        Last Tycoon*. Boston: Little, Brown and Co., 1984. (pp.
        189-195)

416   Moss, Joyce, and George Wilson, eds. *Profiles in American
        History: Significant Events and People Who Shaped Them.*
        Vol. 7: Great Depression to Cuban Missile Crisis. Detroit:
        UXL, 1995. (pp. 22-33)

417   Nachbar, John H., Michael T. Marsden, and Sam L. Grogg.
        Movies as Artifacts: Cultural Criticism of Popular Film.
        See #277.

418   Nakayama, Kiyoshi, Scott Pugh, and Shigeharu Yano. *John
        Steinbeck: Asian Perspectives*. Osaka: Kyoiku Tosho,
        1992. Contents: Shigeharu Yano, Preface; Kiyoshi
        Nakayama, Acknowledgements; Scott Pugh, Introduction;
        Syed Mashkoor Ali, "Echoes of Indian Thought in
        Steinbeck"; Malithat Promathatavedi, "Bitter Fruit of
        Karma: *The Winter of Our Discontent* in Thailand"; Jin
        Young Choi, "Steinbeck Studies in Korea"; Scott Pugh,
        "Genre Formation and Discourse Processes in Steinbeck's
        Life of Henry Morgan"; Koichi Kaida, "Multi-layered
        Functions of Animal Imagery in *In Dubious Battle* and *The
        Grapes of Wrath*"; Ikuko Kawata, "'Timshel': Steinbeck's
        Message through the Hebrew Original"; Hiromasa
        Takamura, "John Steinbeck's Dramatic World"; Satoru
        Tagaya, "Steinbeck and American Postmodernists";
        Kiyohiko Tsuboi, "*Cannery Row* Reconsidered"; Rajul
        Bhargava, "*In Dubious Battle*: The Emergence of a
        Vision"; Hirotsugu Inoue,"The Weedpatch Camp as a
        Symbol of American Democracy"; Osamu Kusuhashi,
        "R. L. Stevenson's Light and Shadow in Steinbeck's
        Works"; Kozen Nakachi, "Steinbeck and the West:
        Beyond the Disillusionment"; Yuji Nakata, "Thoreauvian
        Characters in Steinbeck's Fiction"; Kiyoshi
        Nakayama,"Steinbeck's Creative Development of an
        Ending: *East of Eden*."

418A   Niemeyer, Suzanne, and Walton Beacham, eds. *Popular
        World Ficition, 1900-present.* Vol. IV. See #150.

419   Nelson, Nancy Owen, and Arthur T. Husebow. *The Selected
        Letters of Frederick Manfred.* See #331.

420   Noble, Donald, ed. *The Steinbeck Question: New Essays in
        Criticism.* Troy, N.Y.: Whitston Publishing Co., 1993.
        Contents: Jackson Benson, "John Steinbeck: The Favorite
        Author We Love to Hate"; Dennis Prindle, "The Pretexts
        of Romance: Steinbeck's Allegorical Naturalism from *Cup
        of Gold* to *Tortilla Flat*"; Robert S. Hughes, "Steinbeck
        and the Art of Story Writing"; Charlotte Hadella,
        "Steinbeck's Cloistered Women"; Paul Hintz, "The Silent
        Woman and the Male Voice in Steinbeck's *Cannery Row*";
        Mimi Reisel Gladstein, "Missing Women: The
        Inexplicable Disparity between Women in Steinbeck's Life
        and Those in His Fiction"; Michael J. Meyer, "Fallen
        Adam: Another Look at Steinbeck's 'The Snake'";
        Michael G. Barry, "Degrees of Moderation and Their
        Political Value in Steinbeck's *The Grapes of Wrath*";
        Sylvia J. Cook, "Steinbeck's Poor in Prosperity and
        Adversity"; H.R. Stoneback, "Rough People ... Are the
        Best Singers: Woody Guthrie, John Steinbeck and
        Folksong"; Louis Owens, "Patterns of Reality, Barrels of
        Worms: From *Western Flyer* to *Rocinante* in Steinbeck's
        Nonfiction"; Robert C. Morsberger, "Steinbeck's War";
        Alan Brown, "From Artist to Craftsman: Steinbeck's
        Bombs Away"; John Ditsky, "I Know It When I Hear It
        Onstage: Theatre and Language in Steinbeck's *Burning
        Bright*" ; Jeremy G. Butler, "*Viva Zapata*! HUAC and the
        Mexican Revolution"; Charles L. Etheridge, Jr., "Changing
        Attitudes Toward Steinbeck's Naturalism and the
        Changing Reputation of *East of Eden*: A Survey of
        Criticism Since 1974"; John Timmerman, "The Shameless
        Magpie: John Steinbeck, Plagiarism and the Eye of the
        Artist."

421   Norkunas, Martha K. *The Politics of Public Memory:
       Tourism, History and Ethnicity in Monterey, California.*
       Albany: State University of New York Press, 1993.

422   Oates, Stephen B. *William Faulkner: The Man and the Artist.*
       New York: Harper and Row, 1987. (pp. 172, 218-219,
       298)

423   O'Connell, Shaun. *Remarkable, Unspeakable New York: A
       Literary History.* Boston: Beacon Press, 1995. (pp. 206,
       208, 307)

424   O'Connor, Flannery. *Collected Works.* New York: Library of
       America, 1991. (Steinbeck, 849, 850, 947).

425   Odets, Clifford. *The Time Is Ripe: 1940 Journals.* New York:
       Grove Press, 1988. (pp. 16, 265, 296, 303, 329)

426   Orr, John. *The Making of the Twentieth Century Novel:
       Lawrence, Joyce, Faulkner and Beyond.* London:
       Macmillan, 1987.

427   Osborne, John. *Almost a Gentleman.* London; Faber and
       Faber, 1991. (p. 101)

428   Owens, Louis. *The Grapes of Wrath: Trouble in the Promised
       Land.* Boston: Twayne, 1989. Contents: 1: "Historical
       Context," 1-5; 2: "The Importance of Work," 7-9; 3:
       "Critical Reception," 10-17; A Reading. 4: "The
       Beginning: The Camera's Eye," 21-26; 5: "Participation
       and Education: The Narrative Structure," 27-38; 6: "The
       Biblical Joads," 39-45; 7: "The American Joads," 46-57; 8:
       "'Grandpa Killed Indians, Pa Killed Snakes' : The
       American Indian and *The Grapes of Wrath*," 58-64; 9:
       "'Manself' in the Promised Land: From Biology to Bible,"
       65-76; 10: "Turtle and Truck: Animal, Machine, and

Controlling Consciousness," 77-81; 11: "Beyond Blame or
Cause: The Non-teleological Joads," 82-88; 12: "From
Genesis to Jalopies: A Tapestry of Styles," 89-95; 13:
"From Oklahoma to Hollywood: *The Grapes of Wrath* on
Film," 96-105; "Selected Bibliography," 111-117.
(translated into Japanese in Kiyoshi Nakayama's *John
Steinbeck. Ikari No Budo O Yomu: Amerika No Eden No
Hate.* Osaka, Japan: Kansai University Press, 1993.)

429   Owens, Louis. *John Steinbeck's Re-vision of America.* Athens,
        Ga.: University of Georgia Press, 1985. Contents:
        "Preface," xi-xii; "Introduction," 3-8. I: The Mountains.
        "*To a God Unknown*: Steinbeck's 'Mystical Outcrying,'"
        12-29; "'Flight': Into the Jaws of Death," 29-35; "*The
        Pearl*: Shapes of Darkness," 35-46; "*The Red Pony*:
        Commitment and Quest," 46-58; "*The Wayward Bus*: A
        Triumph of Nature," 58-69. II: The Valleys. "*The Pastures
        of Heaven*: Illusions of Eden," 74-89; "*In Dubious Battle*:
        The 'Recording Consciousness,'" 89-100; "*Of Mice and
        Men*: The Dream of Commitment," 100-106; "In *The
        Long Valley*," 106-108; "'The Chrysanthemums': Waiting
        for Rain," 108-113; "'The White Quail': Inside the
        Garden," 113-116; "'The Harness': The Good, Fallen
        Man," 116-118; "'Johnny Bear': Artist as Recorder," 118-
        120; "'The Murder': Illusions of Chivalry," 121-126;
        "'The Raid': Commitment and Sacrifice," 126; "'The
        Vigilante': Psychology of the Cell," 127-128; "*The Grapes
        of Wrath*: Eden Exposed," 128-140; "*East of Eden*: The
        New Eye," 140-155. III: The Sea. "'The Snake': The First
        Lonely Doc," 161-163; "*Tortilla Flat*: Camelot East of
        Eden," 164-177; "*Cannery Row*: 'An Essay in
        Loneliness,'" 178-190; "S*weet Thursday*: Farewell to
        Steinbeck Country," 190-196. **Conclusion.** "*The Winter of
        Our Discontent* and the American Conscience," 199-209.

430   Parini, Jay. *John Steinbeck: A Biography*. London:
        Heinemann, 1994. (reissued in America by Henry Holt,
        1995) Contents: Preface. Ch. I: The Fiction of Origins.
        Ch. II: The Stanford Years. Ch. III: In the Wilderness.

Ch. IV: A Young Buccaneer. Ch. V: A True Liking.
Ch.VI: The Heavenly Valley. Ch. VII: The Sorrow of His
House. Ch. VIII: The Front Line of Poverty. Ch. IX:
Writing The Big Book. Ch. X: The Road to Canonization.
Ch. XI: A Very Personal War. Ch. XII: "The Genial
Famous Man." Ch. XIII: An Uncertain Homecoming.
Ch. XIV: A New Life. Ch. XV: "The Pleasure of Design
and Some Despair." Ch. XVI: New Thinking About
Writing. Ch. XVII: The Consolations of a Landscape.
Ch. XVIII: It Must Have Been Good. Ch. XIX: A Time
for Recovery. Ch. XX: "Bright Is the Ring of Words."
Notes.

431   Parker, Peter, ed. *A Reader's Guide to the Twentieth Century
        Novel.* New York: Oxford University Press, 1994.

432   Pauly, Thomas H. *An American Odyssey: Elia Kazan and
        American Culture.* Philadelphia: Temple University Press,
        1983. (pp. 8, 125-126, 145-161, 194-202)

433   Pearson, Michael. *Imagined Places: Journeys into Literary
        America.* Jackson: University of Mississippi Press, 1991.
        (Ch. 6 : "A Strip Angled Against the Pacific —
        Steinbeck's *East of Eden,* pp. 215-263)

434   Peary, Gerald, and Roger Shatzkin. *The Modern American
        Novel and the Movies.* New York: Ungar, 1978. Contains
        "Trampling Out the Vintage: Sour Grapes (*The Grapes of
        Wrath*)," on pp. 107-117 and "Two Planetary Systems," by
        Robert Aldridge pp. 119, 344-345 and 407-409 which
        discusses *Steinbeck on Film — Tortilla Flat, Of Mice and
        Men, The Grapes of Wrath* and *The Moon Is Down.*

435   Peeler, David P. *Hope among Us Yet: Social Criticism and
        Social Solace in Depression America.* Athens: University
        of Georgia Press, 1987. (contains "John Steinbeck's
        Universal Family," pp. 156-165)

436   Perkins, Barbara, George Perkins, and Philip Leininger, eds.
        Benet's Reader's Encyclopaedia of American Literature.
        See #366.

437   Perkins, George, Barabara Perkins, and Philip Leininger, eds.
        Benet's Reader's Encyclopaedia of American Literature.
        See #366.

438   Perlis, Vivian, and Aaron Copland. *Copland: 1900 Through
        1942.* See #205.

439   Perlis, Vivian, and Aaron Copland. *Copland: Since 1943.*
        See #206.

440   Peters, Nancy J., ed. *The Literary World of San Francisco
        and Its Environs, A Guidebook.* San Francisco: City Lights
        Books, 1985. (contains Don Herron's "John Steinbeck" on
        pp. 215-17)

441   Peterson, Richard F., Shigeharo Yano, Tetsumaro Hayashi,
        and Yasuo Hashiguchi, eds., *John Steinbeck: From Salinas
        to the World: Proceedings of the Second International
        Steinbeck Congress* (1984), dedicated to Warren French
        and Jackson J. Benson. See #295.

442   Pettit, Arthur G. *Images of the Mexican American in Fiction
        and Film.* College Station: Texas A & M University, 1980.

443   Phillips, William. *A Partisan View: Five Decades of the
        Literary Life.* New York: Stein and Day, 1983. (p. 125)

444   Piekarski, Vicki, and Jon Tuska, eds. *Cyclopaedia of
        Frontier and Western Fiction.* New York: McGraw Hill,
        1983. (pp. 333-335)

445   Pizer, Donald. *Realism and Naturalism in Nineteenth Century*
           American Literature. Revised ed. Carbondale, Ill.: Sothern
           Illinois University Press, 1984. (from the 1966 original)

446   Pizer, Donald. *The Theory and Practice of American Literary*
           Naturalism: Selected Essays and Reviews. Carbondale, Ill.:
           Southern Illinois University Press, 1993.

447   Pizer, Donald. *Twentieth Century American Literary*
           Naturalism: An Interpretation. Carbondale, Ill.: Southern
           Illinois University Press, 1982. (contains "John Steinbeck:
           The Grapes of Wrath")

448   Pocock, Douglas C.D., ed. *Humanistic Geography and*
           Literature: Essays on the Experience of Place. London:
           Croom Helm, 1981. (includes Christopher L. Salter, "John
           Steinbeck's *The Grapes of Wrath* As a Primer for Cultural
           Geography," pp. 142-158)

449   Pocock, Tom. *Alan Moorehead*. London: Bodley Head, 1990.
           (p. 260)

450   Pollett, Elizabeth. *Portrait of Delmore: Journals and Notes of*
           Delmore Schwartz, 1939-1959. New York: Farrar, Straus
           and Giroux, 1986. (p. 273)

451   Powell, Lawrence Clark. *California Classics*. Santa Barbara,
           Calif.: Capra Press, 1982. (pp. 220-230)

452   Pringle, David. *Imaginary People: A Who's Who of Modern*
           Fictional Characters. New York: Pharos Books, 1977.
           (entries on Tom Joad, Lennie Small and George Milton)

452A   Pugh, Scott, Kiyoshi Nakayama, and Shigeharu Yano. *John*
           Steinbeck: Asian Perspectives. See #418.

453   Quinones, Ricardo. *The Changes of Cain: Violence and the
        Lost Brother in Cain and Abel Literature.* Princeton:
        Princeton University Press, 1991. (contains Chapter 7:
        "The New American Cain: *East of Eden* and Other Works
        of Post World War II America," pp. 135-144, 242-243,
        247, 267-269)

454   Quirk, Tom, and James Barbour, eds. *Biographies of Books:
        The Compositional Histories of Notable American
        Writings.* See #145

455   Quirk, Tom, and James Barbour, eds. *Writing the American
        Classics.* See #146

456   Railsback, Brian, ed. *The John Steinbeck Encyclopaedia.*
        Westport, Conn.: Greenwood Press, forthcoming.

457   Railsback, Brian. *Parallel Expeditions: Charles Darwin and
        the Art of John Steinbeck.* Boise: University of Idaho Press,
        1995. Contents: Ch. 1: Grasping for What Actually 'Is',
        pp. 1-14. Ch. 2: Homage to the "Older Method", pp. 15-
        40. Ch. 3: Beasts at the Door, pp. 41-76. Ch. 4: Misogyny
        or Sexual Selection?, pp. 77-102. Ch. 5: From *Homo
        sapiens* to Human — Evolution of a Hero, pp. 103-127.
        Ch. 6: The Darwinian *Grapes of Wrath*, pp. 129-139.
        Bibliography, pp. 141-147.

457A   Reef, Catherine. *John Steinbeck.* New York: Clarion Books,
        1996. (Young Adult Biography)

458   Reid, David, Leonard Michaels, and Racquel Scherr. *West of
        the West: Imagining California.* See #400.

459   Renner, Beverly Hollett. *A Child Discovers John Steinbeck:
        A Biographical Story for Young Readers.* Steinbeck
        Creative Writing Series, No. 1. Muncie Ind.: Steinbeck

Research Institiute, Ball State University, 1993. Contents: Ch. 1: "The Challenge," 1-3; Ch. 2: "The Checker," 5-9; Ch. 3: "In John's Shoes," 11-18; Ch. 4: "Clumsy Boots," 19-25; Ch. 5: "The Secret," 27-32.

460   Richmond, Don Stanley, ed. *Modern American Fiction: Readings from the Critics*. Richmond, B.C., Canada: Open Learning Institute, 1982. (contains Sandra Falkenberg's "A Study of Female Characterization in Steinbeck's Fiction," (pp. 117-123), a reprint of her article in *Steinbeck Quarterly*, 8 (Spring 1975), 50-56.)

461   Ring, Frances Kroll. *Against the Grain: As I Remember F. Scott Fitzgerald*. New York: Creative Arts Book Co., 1985. (p. 60)

462   Ro, Sigmund, and Malcolm Bradbury, eds. *Contemporary American Fiction*. See #173.

463   Robins, Natalie. *Alien Link: The FBI's War on Freedom of Expression*. New York: William Morrow and Co., 1992. (15, 72, 77, 96-98, 236, 402)

464   Robinson, David. *Chaplin: His Life and Art*. London: Collins, 1985. (pp. 488, 506)

465   Roeder, Jr., George H. *The Censored War: American Visual Experience During World War II*. New Haven:Yale University, 1993. (p. 17)

466   Rood, Karen L. *American Literary Almanac*. New York: Bruccoli, Clark, Layman, 1988. (references to Steinbeck on pp. 97, 99, 174, 197-198, 301-302, 315, 347)

466A Ruffin, Paul, Donald Coers, and Robert DeMott. eds. *After "The Grapes of Wrath": Essays on John Steinbeck in Honor of Tetsumaro Hayashi.* See #199.

467 Ruiz, Vicki L. *Cannery Women, Cannery Lives: Mexican Women, Unionization and the California Food Processing Industry, 1930-1950.* Albequerque, N.M.: University of New Mexico Press, 1987.

468 Ryan, Bryan. *Major 20th Century Writers: A Selection of Sketches from Contemporary Authors.* Detroit: Gale, 1991. (pp. 2828-2833)

469 Sader, Marion, ed. *The Reader's Advisor. Vol. I: The Best of Reference Works, British Literature, and American Literature.* 14th ed. New York: R.R. Bowker, 1994. (pp. 884-886)

470 Sadler, Geoff, ed. *Twentieth-Century Western Writers.* 2nd ed. Chicago and London: St. James Press, 1991. (pp. 653-656)

471 St. John, John. *William Heinemann: A Century of Publishing, 1890-1990.* London: William Heinemann Ltd., 1990. (pp. 291-292, 395, 449-450, 539, 622)

472 St. Pierre, Brian. *John Steinbeck: The California Years.* San Francisco: Chronicle Books, 1983.

473 Salzman, Arthur. *Designs of Darkness in Contemporary American Fiction.* Philadelphia: University of Pennsylvania Press, 1990.

474 Salzman, Jack, and Pamela Wilkinson, eds. *Major Characters in American Literature.* New York: Henry Holt, 1994. (contains entries on *Cannery Row, The Winter of Our*

Discontent, The Pearl, East of Eden, In Dubious Battle, Of Mice and Men, The Moon Is Down, "The Red Pony," 'The Chrysanthemums')

475   Sarkissian, Adele, ed. *Contemporary Authors: Autobiography Series.* Vol. 6. Detroit: Gale, 1988.

476   Sarton, May. *Encore: A Journal of the Eightieth Year.* New York: W.W. Norton and Co., 1993. (p. 263)

477   Scherr, Racquel, Leonard Michaels, and David Reid. *West of the West: Imagining California.* See #400.

478   Schellinger, Paul E., ed. *St. James Guide to Biography.* Chicago: St. James Press, 1991. (contains "John Steinbeck" by John Ditsky on pp. 737-739)

479   Schlicker, Richard. *Brando: A Life in Our Times.* New York: Atheneum, 1991. (pp. 68-77) (*Zapata*)

480   Schliefer, Ronald, and Robert Con Davis, eds. *Contemporary Literary Criticism: Literary and Cultural Studies.* See #215.

481   Schloss, Carol. *In Visible Light: Photography and The American Writer, 1840-1940.* New York: Oxford University Press, 1987. (pp. 200-229, 283-284)

482   Schlueter, Paul, and Jane Schlueter. *Modern American Literature.* Vol. V. 2nd Supp., 4th ed. New York: Frederick Ungar, 1985. (excerpts from Benson and Paul McCarthy on pp. 457-459)

483   Scott, Quinta, and Susan Croce Kelley. *Route 66, a History of the Highway and Its People.* See #350.

484   Segal, David, ed. *Short Story Criticism: Excerpts from
        Criticism of the Works of Short Fiction Writers, Vol. II.*
        Detroit: Gale Research, Inc. 1992. (contains "John
        Steinbeck" on pp. 201-260 with excerpts from such
        Steinbeck critics as Peter Lisca, Marilyn Mitchell, John
        Timmerman, Robert Hughes, Jr., Arnold Goldsmith, Bruce
        Martin, Elizabeth McMahan, and Louis Owens)

485   Sequeira, Isaac, and R. L. Sharma, eds. *Closing of the
        American Frontier: A Centennial Retrospect, 1890-1990.*
        Hyderabad, India: American Studies Research Center,
        1994. (contains "The Frontiers of Imagination: *Cannery
        Row* and *Sweet Thursday*," by Sherine Upot on pp. 31-39)

486   Seymour-Smith, Martin. *Guide to Modern World Literature.*
        London: Peter Bedick Books, 1985. (pp. 100-101)

487   Sharma, R. K., ed. *Indian Response to Steinbeck: Essays
        Presented to Warren French.* Jaipur, India: Rachana
        Prakashan, 1984. (contains "The Novel Dramatized:
        Generic Transformation in *Of Mice and Men*," by Sherine
        Upot on pp. 152-162)

488   Sharma, R. L., and Isaac Sequeira, eds. *Closing of the
        American Frontier: A Centennial Retrospect*, 1890-1990.
        See #485.

489   Shatzkin, Roger, and Gerald Peary. *The Modern American
        Novel and the Movies.* See #434.

490   Sheffield, Carlton A. *Steinbeck: The Good Companion.*
        Portola Valley, Calif.: American Lives Endowment, 1983.

491   Sheffield, Carlton A. *I Never Met an Anapest I didn't Like.*
        Campbell, Calif.: CRS Publishing, 1985.

492   Sheldon, Michael. *Orwell: The Authorized Biography*.
         London: Heinemann, 1991. (p. 468)

493   Shillinglaw, Susan, Susan Beegel, and Wes Tiffney, eds.
         *Steinbeck and the Environment: Interdisciplinary
         Approaches*. See #151.

494   Shillinglaw, Susan, Joseph R. McElrath, and Jesse S. Crisler,
         eds. *John Steinbeck: The Contemporary Reviews*. See
         #208.

495   Shimomuru, Noboru. *A Study of John Steinbeck: Mysticism in
         His Novels*. Tokyo: Hokuseido Press, 1982. (see especially
         pp. 152-185, 252-255) Contents: Preface, vii-viii. Table of
         Contents, ix. General Introduction, xiii-xviii. Abbreviation
         of Titles/ Personal Names, xix-xx. Chronological Table,
         xxi-xxiii. Irony and Curse in *The Pastures of Heaven*
         1-21. Mysticism in *To a God Unknown,* 22-46. Humor
         and Mysticism in *Tortilla Flat,* 47-71. Christianity and
         Communism in *In Dubious Battle* 72-94. Social Concern
         and Mysticism in *The Grapes of Wrath,* 95-116. Humor
         and Eastern Philosophy in *Cannery Row,* 117-134. Guilt
         and Christianity in *The Pearl,* 135-151. Christianity and
         Eastern Philosophy in *East of Eden*, 152-185. Humor and
         Christianity in *Sweet Thursday,* 186-204. Christianity and
         Paganism in *The Winter of Our Discontent*, 205-227.
         General Conclusion, 228-243. Notes, 245-258. Selected
         Bibliography, 259-266. Index, 267-275.

496   Silverman, Al, ed. *The Book of the Month: Sixty Years of
         Books in American Life*. Boston: Little, Brown and Co.,
         1986. (*Of Mice and Men, The Grapes of Wrath*) (pp. xviii,
         49-55)

497   Sim, Norman, ed. *Literary Journalism in the Twentieth
         Century*. Oxford; Oxford University Press, 1990. (contains

"The Mother of Literature: Journalism and *The Grapes of Wrath*" by William Howarth on pp. 53-81)

498   Simmonds, Roy. *John Steinbeck: The War Years,* 1939-1945. Lewisburg: Bucknell University Press, 1996. Contents: Introduction. Ch. 1: The Creation of a Twentieth Century Masterpiece: *The Grapes of Wrath.* Ch. 2: 1939: Into the Public Domain. Ch. 3: 1940: The Search for New Beginnings. Ch. 4: 1941: Conflict and Creativity. Ch. 5: 1942: In Limbo. Ch. 6: 1943: European War Correspondent. Ch. 7: 1944: A New Masterpiece. Ch. 8: More Filmmaking in Mexico. Ch. 9: The Bus That Failed. Afterword. Appendix. Select Bibliography.

499   Simone, Sam P. *Hitchcock as Activist: Politics and the War Films.* Ann Arbor: UMI Research Press, 1985. (pp. 28, 87-119, 180-183)

500   Snyder, Tom. *Route 66: A Traveler's Guide and Roadside Companion.* New York: St. Martin's Press, 1990.

501   Spoto, Donald. *The Kindness of Strangers: The Life of Tennessee Williams.* London: The Bodley Head, 1985. (pp. 230-232)

502   Spoto, Donald. *The Life of Alfred Hitchcock: The Dark Side of Genius.* London: Collins, 1983. (pp. 265-270)

503   Starr, Kevin. *Inventing the Dream: California through the Progressive Era.* New York: Oxford University Press, 1985.

504   Stegner, Wallace. *Where the Bluebird Sings to the Lemonade Springs.* New York: Random House, 1992. (contains "On Steinbeck's Story, 'Flight,'" pp. 143-154)

505   Steinmann, Jr., Martin and Robert L. Brown, Jr., eds.
        *Rhetoric 1978: Proceedings of Theory of Rhetoric: An
        Interdisciplinary Conference*. See #180

506   Stevick, Philip, ed. *The American Short Story 1900-1945: A
        Critical History*. Boston: Twayne Publishers, 1984.
        (contains "The Question of Regionalism: Limitation and
        Transcendence" by Mary Rohrberger, pp. 178-182)

507   Stout, Janis. P. *The Journey Narrative in American Literature:
        Patterns and Departures*. Westport, Conn.: Greenwood,
        1983. (references to *The Grapes of Wrath* on pp. 53-56,
        161, 174; "The Leader of the People," p. 11; *Travels with
        Charley*, p. 30)

508   Strout, C. *The Veracious Imagination*. Middleton, Conn.:
        Wesleyan University Press, 1985. (contains "Radical
        Religion and the American Political Novel" pp. 70-91)

508A   Swisher, Clarice, ed. *Readings on John Steinbeck*. San Diego:
        Greenhaven Press, 1996. Literary Companion Series.
        Contents: John Steinbeck: A Biography, 15-26; John
        Steinbeck, "How Six Short Novels Came to Be," 27-29;
        Joseph Warren Beach, "John Steinbeck's Authentic
        Characters," 30-39; Charles Child Walcutt, "John
        Steinbeck's Naturalism," 40-49; Peter Lisca, "Escape and
        Commitment in John Steinbeck's Heroes," 50-57; R. W. B.
        Lewis, "John Steinbeck: A Successful Failure," 58-64;
        Charles R. Metzger, "John Steinbeck's Paisano Knights,"
        65-72; Dan Vogel, "John Steinbeck's Myth of Manhood,"
        73-76; Harry Thornton Moore, "John Steinbeck's Mature
        Style in *The Red Pony*," 77-79; Arnold L. Goldsmith,
        "Oneness and Mysticism in *The Red Pony*," 80-85; Warren
        French, "Jody's Growing Awareness in *The Red Pony*,"
        86-94; Harry Morris, "The Allegory of *The Pearl*," 93-99;
        Howard Levant, "The Parable of *The Pearl*," 100-108;
        Martha Heasley Cox, "Symbolic Creatures in *The Pearl*,"
        109- 116; Edwin Berry Burgum, "Attitudes Toward the

Poor in *Of Mice and Men*," 117-121; Peter Lisca, "Patterns
That Make Meaning in *Of Mice and Men*," 122-129;
Warren French, "*Of Mice and Men*: A Knight Dismounted
and a Dream Ended," 130-137; Martin Shockley,
"Christian Symbolism in *The Grapes of Wrath*," 138-144;
J. P. Hunter, "Artistic and Thematic Structure in *The
Grapes of Wrath*," 145-155; Mimi Reisel Gladstein,
"Insdestructible Women in *The Grapes of Wrath*," 156-
164; Stephen Railton, "John Steinbeck's Call to
Conversion in *The Grapes of Wrath*," 165-173; Carl E.
Rallyson, Jr., "John Steinbeck Awarded the Nobel Prize in
Literature," 174-177; Chronology, 178-181; For Further
Research, 185-187.

509   Takamura, Hiromasa. *Steinbeck and the Drama*. Kyoto,
        Japan: Apolon Press, 1990.

510   Tanner, William E., ed. *The Arthurian Myth of Quest and
        Magic: A Festschrift in Honor of Lavon B. Fulwiler*.
        Dallas: Caxton's Modern Arts Press, 1993. (contains "A
        Note on John Steinbeck in King Arthur's Court" by Bob
        Dowell)

511   Thompson, Raymond H. *The Return from Avalon: A Study of
        Arthurian Legend in Modern Fiction*. Westport, Conn.:
        Greenwood, 1985.

512   Tiffney, Wes, Susan Shillinglaw, and Susan Beegel, eds.
        *Steinbeck and the Environment: Interdisciplinary
        Approaches*. See #151.

513   Timmerman, John H. *The Dramatic Landscape of Steinbeck's
        Short Stories*. Norman, Okla.: University of Oklahoma
        Press, 1990. Contents: "Introduction," xiii-xv. Ch. 1:
        "Flaming Youth: The 1920s," 3-32; Ch. 2: Sureness of
        Touch: The 1930s," 33-47; Ch. 3: "*The Pastures of
        Heaven*," 48-116; Ch. 4: "*The Red Pony*: 'The Desolation
        of Love,'" 117-139; Ch. 5: "Foothills Around the Long

Valley," 140-166; Ch. 6: *The Long Valley*," 167-244; Ch.
7: "The Later Short Stories," 245-280; Ch. 8: "East of
Salinas," 281-286; "Steinbeck's Notebooks," 287-289;
"Bibliography," 317-329.

514   Timmerman, John H. *John Steinbeck's Fiction: The Aesthetics
of The Road Taken*. Norman, Okla.: University of
Oklahoma Press, 1986. Contents: "Preface," ix-x; Ch. 1:
"Steinbeck as Literary Artist," 3-41. Ch. 2: "Individual
Freedom and Social Constraint: *Cup of Gold*," 42-57. Ch.
3: "Dreams and Dreamers: The Short Stories," 58-72. Ch.
4: "Vintage of the Earth: *In Dubious Battle* and *Of Mice
and Men*," 73-101. Ch. 5: "The Wine of God's Wrath: *The
Grapes of Wrath*," 102-132. Ch. 6: "Angels in Midheaven:
The Cannery Row Novels," 133-182. Ch. 7: "Their Deeds
Follow Them: The Fiction of the Forties," 183-209. Ch. 8:
"Harvest of the Earth: *East of Eden*," 210-247. Ch. 9:
"Voice From Heaven: *The Winter of Our Discontent*," 248-
265. Ch. 10: "'That They May Rest from Their Labors,'"
266-274; "Selected Bibliography," 297-307.

515   Timmerman, John H. *John Steinbeck's Fiction: The Aesthetics
of The Road Taken*. Norman, Okla.: University of
Oklahoma Press, 1991. (paperback ed.)

516   Townsend, Kim. *Sherwood Anderson*. Boston: Houghton
Mifflin, 1987. (p. 309)

517   Tsuboi, Kiyohiko, and Kyoko Ariki, ed. *John Steinbeck's
"Viva, Zapata!"* Tokyo: Eihosha Press, 1985.

518   Turner, Frederick. *Spirit of Place: The Making of an American
Literary Landscape*. San Francisco: Sierra Club Books,
1989. (reprinted Washington, D.C.: Island Books, 1992)
(contains "Valley of the World: John Steinbeck's *East of
Eden*, pp. 249-282)

519   Tuska, Jon, and Vicki Piekarski, eds. *Cyclopaedia of Frontier and Western Fiction.* See # 444.

520   Tuttleton, James W. *Vital Signs: Essays on American Literature and Criticism.* Chicago: Ivan R. Dee, 1996. (pp. 160, 309, 316)

521   Updike, John. *Hugging the Shore.* London: Andre Deutsch, 1984. (p. 183)

522   Van Antwerp, Margaret A., ed. *Dictionary of Literary Biography, Documentary Series, An Illustrated Chronicle,* Volume 2. Detroit, Mich.: Gale Research Co., 1982. (contains a chapter on John Steinbeck supervised by Martha Heasley Cox, pp. 279-332)

523   Vasudevan, Aruna, ed. *Twentieth Century Romance and Historical Writers.* 3rd ed. Chicago: St. James Press, 1994. (pp. 623-624)

524   Verde, Thomas. *Twentieth Century Writers, 1900-1950.* New York: Facts on File, 1993. (juvenile)

525   Votteler, Thomas, et al. *Contemporary Literary Criticism: Excerpts from Criticism of Today's Novelists, Poets, Playwrights, Short Story Writers, Scriptwriters, and Other Creative Writers.* Detroit: Gale, 1993. (pp. 335, 365-366)

526   Wagner-Martin, Linda. *The Modern American Novel, 1914-1945.* New York: Twayne, 1990. (references to Steinbeck on pp. xvi-xviii, 116-121, 126, 130)

527   Walker, Marshall. *The Literature of the United States.* London: Macmillan Press, 1983. (pp. 146-147)

528   Wallis, Michael. *Route 66: The Mother Road.* New York: St. Martin's, 1990.

529   Wasson, Tyler, ed. *Nobel Prize Winners.* New York: H.W. Wilson Co., 1987. (pp. 1009-1012)

530   Watson, Graham. *Book Society,* New York: Atheneum, 1980. (Autobiography of Steinbeck's English literary agent)

531   Watson, Noelle, ed. *Reference Guide to Short Fiction.* Detroit: St. James Press, 1994. (contains articles on "John Steinbeck" by John Ditsky on pp. 511-12 and entries on "The Chrysanthemums" by David Leon Higdon on pp. 667-668 and on "The Red Pony" by Wilton Eckley on pp. 864-865)

532   Watts, Emily Stipes. *The Businessman in American Literature.* Athens: University of Georgia, 1982. (Steinbeck on pp. 92, 102)

533   Weber, Tom. *Cannery Row: A Time to Remember.* Pacific Grove, Calif.: Cowper House, 1984. (originally published by Mill Valley, California: Orenda/Unity Press, 1983).

534   Weinstein, Arnold. *Nobody's Home: Speech, Self and Place in American Fiction from Hawthorne to DeLillo.* Oxford: Oxford University Press, 1993.

535   Western Literature Association. *A Literary History of the American West.* Forth Worth, Tex.: Texas Christian University Press, 1987. (contains "John Steinbeck" by Richard Astro on pp. 424-446)

536   Whelan, Richard. *Robert Capa.* New York: Knopf, 1985. (Capa's biography features references to Steinbeck on pp. 190, 209, 250-251, 254-260, 280, 285, 313, 317.)

537 White, Betty. *Betty White's Pet Love: How Pets Take Care of Us*. New York: William Morrow, 1983. (pp. 47-48) (*Travels*)

538 Whitebrook, Peter. *Staging Steinbeck: Dramatizing "The Grapes of Wrath."* London: Cassell, 1988.

539 Wigoda, Geoffrey. *They Made History: A Biographical Dictionary*. New York: Simon and Schuster, 1993. (pp. 16-17)

540 Wilkinson, Pamela, and Jack Salzman, eds. *Major Characters in American Literature*. See #474.

541 Williams, A. Susan. *John Steinbeck*. Hove, East Sussex, U. K.: Wayland, 1990.

542 Williams, Dakin, and Shepherd Mead. *Tennessee Williams: An Intimate Biography*. See #397.

543 Wilson, George, and Joyce Moss, eds. *Profiles in American History: Significant Events and People Who Shaped Them*. Vol. 7: Great Depression to Cuban Missile Crisis. See #416.

544 Wilson, Edmund. *From the Uncollected Edmund Wilson*. Ed. Janet Groth and David Castronovo. Athens: Ohio University Press, 1995. (contains "John Steinbeck's *Cannery Row*" on pp. 353-355)

545 Windham, Donald. *Lost Friendships: A Memoir of Truman Capote, Tennessee Williams, and Others*. New York: William Morrow, 1987. (p. 43)

546 Wood, Robin. *Hitchcock's Films Revisited.* London: Faber and Faber, 1989. (pp. 75-79, 232-233, 240, 347-348)

547 Wookcock, George, ed. *Twentieth Century Fiction.* London: Macmillan, 1983. (contains "John Steinbeck" by Warren French, pp. 640-44)

548 Workman, Brooke. *Writing Seminars in the Content Areas: In Search of Hemingway, Salinger and Steinbeck.* Urbana, Ill.: National Council of Teachers of English, 1983.

549 Wright, Reginald. *Great Writers of the English Language. Vol. 7: American Classics; Mark Twain, F. Scott Fitzgerald, John Steinbeck, Ernest Hemingway.* New York: Marshall Cavendish, 1991. Contents: The Writer's Life, 53-59; Reader's Guide to *The Grapes of Wrath,* 60-65; The Writer at Work; 'Natural Saints,' 66-68; Works in Outline: *Cannery Row, Of Mice and Men, Tortilla Flat, East of Eden, The Wayward Bus, Travels with Charley,* "The Red Pony," 69-71; Sources and Inspiration: The Depression, 72-76.

550 Wright, Richard. *Uncle Tom's Children.* San Bernadino, California: Borgo Press, 1991. (p. 78) (*The Forgotten Village*).

551 Wu, William F. *The Yellow Peril: Chinese Americans in American Fiction,* 1850-1940. Hamden, Conn.: Archon Books, 1982.

552 Wyatt, David. *The Fall into Eden: Landscape and Imagination in California.* Cambridge: Cambridge University Press, 1986. (contains Ch. 6: Steinbeck's Lost Gardens, p. 124-157)

553 Wyatt, David, ed. *New Essays on "The Grapes of Wrath."* Cambridge: Cambridge University Press, 1990. Contents:

David Wyatt, "Introduction"; Stephen Railton, "Pilgrim's Politics: Steinbeck's Art of Conversion"; Nellie Y. McKay, "Happy (?)-Wife-Motherdom: The Portrayal of Ma Joad in John Steinbeck's *The Grapes of Wrath*"; William Howarth, "The Mother of Literature: Journalism and *The Grapes of Wrath*"; Leslie Gossage, "The Artful Propaganda of Ford's *The Grapes of Wrath*."

554   Yagyu, Nozumu. *Changes in Modern Consciousness and Anglo American Writers.* (a revision of his earlier work, *Literature Without God*)

555   Yahnke, Robert E., and Richard M. Eastman. *Aging in Literature: A Reader's Guide.* Chicago: American Library Association, 1990. (comment on "The Leader of the People," pp. 65-66)

556   Yano, Shigeharu. *The Current of Steinbeck's World.* Vol. 4. Tokyo: Seibido Press, 1982. Love and Death in *Of Mice and Men,* 391-409. A Mechanism of Defense in *In Dubious Battle* 410-449. The Relationship between Fortune and Freedom in *Tortilla Flat,* 450-487. Notes, 489-490.

556A   Yano, Shigeharu. *The Current of Steinbeck's World.* Vol. 5. Tokyo: Seibido Press, 1986. Loneliness and Alienation in *Cup of Gold* I, 491-502. Loneliness and Alienation in *Cup of Gold* II, 503-512. Loneliness and Alienation in *Cup of Gold* III, 512-522. Curses in *The Pastures of Heaven* I, 523-525. Curses in *The Pastures of Heaven* II, 525-541. Curses in *The Pastures of Heaven* III, 541-558. Notes, 559-561.

557   Yano, Shigeharu, Kiyoshi Nakayama, and Scott Pugh. *John Steinbeck: Asian Perspectives.* See #418.

558   Yano, Shigeharo, Tetsumaro Hayashi, Richard F. Peterson,
       and Yasuo Hashiguchi, eds. *John Steinbeck: From Salinas
       to the World: Proceedings of the Second International
       Steinbeck Congress* (1984), dedicated to Warren French
       and Jackson J. Benson. See #295.

Articles

559   Adams, Bett Yates. "The Form of the Narrative Section of
          The Sea of Cortez: A Specimen Collected from Reality,"
          in *Steinbeck's Literary Dimension: A Guide to
          Comparative Studies. Series II.* ed. Tetsumaro Hayashi.
          Metuchen, N. J.: Scarecrow Press, 1991. (pp. 124-134)

560   Adams, Bett Yates. "Steinbeck, Ricketts, and *The Sea of
          Cortez*: Partnership or Exploitation," in *Steinbeck's
          Literary Dimension: A Guide to Comparative Studies.
          Series II.* ed. Tetsumaro Hayashi. Metuchen, N. J.:
          Scarecrow Press, 1991. (pp. 135-143)

561   Adams, Henry. "Thomas Hart Benton's Illustrations for *The
          Grapes of Wrath*," *San Jose Studies*, 16 (Winter 1990),
          6-18.

562   Aksyonov, Vassily. "An Exile in Literary America," *New
          York Times Magazine*, April 14, 1985, 52-54, 61-62, 65.

563   Aldridge, Robert, "Two Planetary Systems," in *The Modern
          American Novel and the Movies.* ed. Gerald Peary and
          Roger Shatzkin. New York: Ungar, 1978. (pp. 119, 344-
          345, 407-409. (discusses Steinbeck on Film — *Tortilla
          Flat, Of Mice and Men, The Grapes of Wrath* and *The
          Moon Is Down*)

564   Amano, Masafumi. "'Literature and Land,' in Steinbeck and
          Faulkner," *John Steinbeck Society of Japan Newsletter*, 9
          (May 1986), 4.

565   Amidon, Stephen. "The Mythic Power of *The Grapes of
          Wrath*," *Sunday Times Books*, April 25, 1993, 9.

566   Angoff, Charles. "In the Great Tradition," in *Critical Essays
        on "The Grapes of Wrath."* ed. John Ditsky. Boston:
        G.K. Hall and Co., 1989. (pp. 33-35) (reprint from *North
        American Review,* 24777 (Summer 1939), 387-89)

567   "Annals of Government," *New Yorker*, 63 (October 7, 1987),
        47-48.

568   Apthorp, Elaine S. "Steinbeck, Guthrie and Popular Culture,"
        San Jose Studies, 16 (Winter 1990), 19-39.

569   Archer, Stanley. "Sea of Cortez," in *Masterplots II: Non-
        Fiction Series. Vol. III.* Pasadena: Salem Press, 1989.
        (pp. 1309-1313)

570   Ariki, Kyoko. "Cathy's Role in *East of Eden*," "Symposium:
        'On Cathy,'" *John Steinbeck Society of Japan
        Newsletter*, 15 (April 1992), 5-6.

571   Ariki, Kyoko. "Current Studies of Steinbeck in Japan," *Chu-
        Shikoku Studies in American Literature,* 27 (June 27,
        1991), 90-99.

572   Ariki, Kyoko. "Elizabeth in *To a God Unknown*," *Persica*
        (The English Literary Society of Okayama University),
        20 (April 1993), 103-111.

573   Ariki, Kyoko. "*The Grapes of Wrath* and *Tobacco Road*: The
        Analysis of Steinbeck's and Caldwell's Anger," *Persica*
        (The English Literary Society of Okayama University),
        11 (March 1984), 111-123.

574   Ariki, Kyoko. "Is Cathy Ames an Enigmatic Monster? A
        Study of Cathy Relating to the Theme of *East of Eden*,"
        Persica (The English Literary Society of Okayama
        University), 12 (March 1985), 51-61.

575   Ariki, Kyoko. "*The Log from The Sea of Cortez* and *The
        Pearl*," *John Steinbeck Society of Japan Newsletter*, 11
        (April 1988), 5-6.

576   Ariki, Kyoko. "Ma Joad: Another Character Who Carries the
          Theme of *The Grapes of Wrath*," *Persica* (The English
          Literary Society of Okayama University), 12 (March
          1985), 37-49.

577   Ariki, Kyoko. "A Reconsideration of Steinbeck's *The
          Wayward Bus*," *Chu-Shikoku Studies in American
          Literature*, 27 (June 1, 1991), 59-68.

578   Ariki, Kyoko. "Steinbeck's 'Travel' in *Travels with
          Charley*," *Chu-Shikoku Studies in American Literature*,
          23 (June 23, 1987), 27-38.

579   Ariki, Kyoko. "Steinbeck's Two Cardinal Themes
          Condensed in *Viva Zapata!*" *Chu-Shikoku Studies in
          American Literature*, 21 (June 21, 1985), 56-67.

580   Ariki, Kyoko. "The Theme of Love Threaded through *East of
          Eden*," *John Steinbeck Society of Japan Newsletter*, 8
          (May 1985), 2.

581   Ariki, Kyoko. "What 'the Talisman' Symbolizes: Believing
          in the Advent of Dawn after the Dark 'Winter,'" *Persica*
          (The English Literary Society of Okayama University),
          13 (March 1986), 21-32.

582   Asano, Toshio. "Steinbeck's Sense for the Real: The
          Bankruptcy of a Romantic Realist," *Bulletin of Ebaraki
          Christian Junior College*, 21 (1981), 11-20.

583   *Associated Press*. "Steinbeck Got First Word on TV: Asserts
          His First Reaction Was One of 'Disbelief,'" in
          Conversations with John Steinbeck. ed. Thomas Fensch.
          Jackson: University of Mississippi Press, 1988. (pp. 78-
          79) (reprint from *Associated Press*, 26 October 1962)

584   Astro, Richard. "Imitations of a Wasteland," in *Modern
          Critical Views: John Steinbeck*. ed. Harold Bloom. New
          York: Chelsea House, 1987. (pp. 19-34) (reprint from

*John Steinbeck and Edward F. Ricketts: The Shaping of
Novelist.*)

585   Astro, Richard. "John Steinbeck," *Dictionary of Literary
        Biography,* Columbia, S.C.: Bruccoli-Clark Books, IX,
        1981. (pp. 43-68)

586   Astro, Richard. "John Steinbeck" in *A Literary History of
        The American West.* ed. Western Literature Association.
        Fort Worth, Tex.: Texas Christian University Press,
        1987. (pp. 424-446)

587   Astro, Richard. "Phlebas Sails the Caribbean: Steinbeck,
        Hemingway and the American Waste Land," in
        *Steinbeck's Literary Dimension: A Guide to
        Comparative Studies. Series II.* ed. Tetsumaro Hayashi.
        Metuchen N. J.: Scarecrow Press, 1991. (pp. 28-44)

588   Astro, Richard. "Steinbeck in Our Time" in "John Steinbeck:
        A Collector's Edition," *Monterey Life: The Magazine of
        California's Spectacular Central Coast,* 7 (July 1987),
        52-54.

589   Astro, Richard. "Steinbeck's Bittersweet Thursday," in *The
        Short Novels of John Steinbeck.* ed. Jackson J. Benson.
        Durham: Duke University Press, 1990. (pp. 204-215)

590   Atkinson, Rebecca L. "Steinbeck's *East of Eden*," *Explicator*,
        48:3 (Spring 1990), 216-217.

591   Baechie, Bea. "Fifty Years after *The Grapes of Wrath*,"
        Silhouette, 1 (May / June 1989), 20-21.

591A   Bain, Robert. "Two Versions of the West: *The Grapes of
        Wrath* and *The Big Rock Candy Mountain*," *Steinbeck
        Newsletter*, 10:1 (Spring 1997), 14-17.

592   Bainbridge, John. "Our Man in Helsinki," in *Conversations
        with John Steinbeck.* ed. Thomas Fensch. Jackson:

University of Mississippi Press, 1988. (pp. 89-93)
(reprint from *The New Yorker*, 9 November 1963, 43-45)

593   Balogun, F. Odun. "Naturalist Proletarian Prose Epics: *Petals of Blood* and *The Grapes of Wrath*," *Journal of English (Sana'a, Yemen),* 11 (September 1983), 80-106.

594   Barriga, Joan B. "Lark on a Barb-Wire Fence: Ruth Comfort Mitchell's *Of Human Kindness*," *Steinbeck Newsletter*, 2:2 (Summer 1989), 3, 4.

595   Barker, Debra K. S. "Passages of Descent and Initiation: Juana as the 'Other' Hero of *The Pearl*," in *After "The Grapes of Wrath"*: *Essays on John Steinbeck in Honor of Tetsumaro Hayashi.* ed. Donald Coers, Robert DeMott, and Paul Ruffin. Athens: Ohio University Press, 1995. (pp. 113-124)

596   Barry, Michael G. "Degrees of Moderation and Their Political Value in Steinbeck's *The Grapes of Wrath*," in *The Steinbeck Question: New Essays in Criticism.* ed. Donald Noble. Troy, N.Y.: Whitston Publishing Co., 1993. (pp. 108-124)

597   Beach, Joseph Warren. "John Steinbeck's Authentic Characters," in *Readings on John Steinbeck.* ed. Clarice Swisher. San Diego: Greenhaven Press, 1996. Literary Companion Series. (30-39) (excerpted from "John Steinbeck: Journeyman Artist," in Beach's *American Fiction* 1920-1940. Also reprinted in Tedlock and Wicker's *Steinbeck and the Critics* (University of New Mexico Press, 1957))

598   Beaugrande, Robert Alain de. "A Rhetorical Theory of Audience Response," in *Rhetoric* 1978: *Proceedings of Theory of Rhetoric: An Interdisciplinary Conference.* ed. Robert L. Brown, Jr. and Martin Steinmann, Jr. Minneapolis: University of Minnesota Center for Advanced Studies in Language, Style and Literature, 1979. (pp. 9-20)

599   Beck, William J., and Edward Erickson. "The Emergence of
        Class Consciousness in *Germinal* and *The Grapes of
        Wrath*," *Comparatist: The Journal of the Southern
        Comparative Literature Assn.*, 12 (1988), 44-57.

600   Bedford, R. C. "Steinbeck's Nonverbal Invention," *Asphodel*
        (*The English Literature Society of Doshisha Women's
        College*), 18 (1984), 242-258.

601   Bedford, R. C. "Steinbeck's Nonverbal Invention," *John
        Steinbeck Society of Japan Newsletter,* 8 (May 1985),
        3-4.

602   Bedford, R. C. "Steinbeck's Nonverbal Invention," *Steinbeck
        Quarterly,* XVIII, 3-4 (Summer/Fall 1985), 70-78.

603   Beegel, Susan, Wesley N. Tiffney, Jr., and Susan Shillinglaw.
        "Introduction," in *Steinbeck and the Environment:
        Interdisciplinary Approaches.* Tuscaloosa, Ala.:
        University of Alabama Press, 1997. (p. 1-23)

604   Benson, Jackson J. "The Background to the Composition of
        The Grapes of Wrath," in *Critical Essays on "The
        Grapes of Wrath*." ed. John Ditsky. Boston: G.K. Hall
        and Co., 1989. (pp. 51-74) (revised from "John
        Steinbeck and Farm Labor Unionization: The
        Background of *In Dubious Battle,*" (with Anne Loftis)
        American Literature, 52 (May 1980), 194-223; "The
        Background of *The Grapes of Wrath,*" *Journal of
        Modern Literature,* 5 (April 1976), 151-232 and
        Chapters 19, 20 and 21 of *The True Adventures of John
        Steinbeck, Writer* (New York: Viking Press, 1984))

605   Benson, Jackson J. "*Cannery Row* and Steinbeck as
        Spokesman for the 'Folk Tradition'," in *The Short
        Novels of John Steinbeck.* ed. Jackson J. Benson.
        Durham: Duke University Press, 1990. (pp. 132-141)

606   Benson, Jackson J. "Hemingway the Hunter and Steinbeck
        the Farmer," in *Steinbeck's Literary Dimension: A Guide
        to Comparative Studies. Series II*. ed. Tetsumaro
        Hayashi. Metuchen, N. J.: Scarecrow Press, 1991. (pp.
        45-64) (a reprint of "Hemingway the Hunter and
        Steinbeck the Farmer: Two Sides of the American
        Character," *Michigan Quarterly Review*, XXIV (Summer
        1985), 441-460).

607   Benson, Jackson J. "Introduction," in *The Short Novels of
        John Steinbeck*. ed. Jackson J. Benson. Durham: Duke
        University Press, 1990. (pp. 1-13)

608   Benson, Jackson J. "John and Kate: A Tale of Two Artists,"
        Stanford Magazine, XIII (Spring 1985), 42-49.

609   Benson, Jackson. "John Steinbeck," in *Dictionary of
        American Biography*. ed. John A. Garraty. New York:
        Charles Scribner's Sons, 1988. (pp. 624-627)

610   Benson, Jackson. "John Steinbeck: The Favorite Author We
        Love to Hate," in *The Steinbeck Question: New Essays in
        Criticism*. ed. Donald Noble. Troy, N.Y.: Whitston
        Publishing Co., 1993. (pp. 8-22)

611   Benson, Jackson J. "John Steinbeck: Novelist as Scientist," in
        Modern Critical Views: John Steinbeck. ed. Harold
        Bloom. New York: Chelsea House, 1987. (pp. 103-123)
        (reprint from *Novel: A Forum on Fiction,* 10 (Spring
        1977), 3.)

612   Benson, Jackson J. "Steinbeck — A Defense of Biographical
        Criticism," *College Literature*, XVI (Spring 1989), 107-
        116.

613   Benson, Jackson J. "Through a Political Glass Darkly: The
        Example of John Steinbeck," *Studies in American
        Fiction*, XII (Spring 1982), 45-59.

614   Benton, Robert M. "A Search for Meaning in 'Flight,'" in
       *Steinbeck's Short Stories in "The Long Valley": Essays
       in Criticism*. ed. Tetsumaro Hayashi. Steinbeck
       Monograph Series, No. 15. Muncie, Ind.: Steinbeck
       Research Institute, Ball State University Press, 1991.
       (pp. 18-25) (translated into Japanese in *Steinbeck
       Kenkyu: Atarashii Tanpen Shosetsushu (Steinbeck
       Studies: New Essays on Short Stories)*. Osaka, Japan:
       Osaka Educational Publishing Co. 1995. (pp. 177-194))

615   Benton, Robert M. "'The Snake' and Its Anomalous Nature,"
       in *Steinbeck's Short Stories in "The Long Valley":
       Essays in Criticism*. ed. Tetsumaro Hayashi. Steinbeck
       Monograph Series, No. 15. Muncie, Ind.: Steinbeck
       Research Institute, Ball State University Press, 1991.
       (pp. 26-31) (translated into Japanese in *Steinbeck
       Kenkyu: Atarashii Tanpen Shosetsushu (Steinbeck
       Studies: New Essays on Short Stories)*. Osaka, Japan:
       Osaka Educational Publishing Co. 1995. (pp. 195-211))

616   Bergman, David, Joseph de Roche, and Daniel M. Epstein.
       "The Chrysanthemums" in Instructor's Manual, *The
       Heath Guide to Literature*. Lexington, Mass.: D. C.
       Heath, 1984. (p. 50)

617   Bernardo, Anthony. "The Red Pony,*"* in *Masterplots II:
       American Fiction Series. Vol. III*. ed. Frank Magill.
       Englewood Cliff, N. J.: Salem Press, 1986. (pp. 134-138)

618   Bernardo, Anthony. "*Tortilla Flat,"* in *Masterplots II:
       American Fiction Series. Vol. IV*. ed. Frank Magill.
       Englewood Cliff, N. J.: Salem Press, 1986. (pp. 1688-
       1691)

619   "Best of The Century," *Writer's Digest* (December 1990),
       36-37, 43.

620   Beyer, Preston. "John Steinbeck and the Armed Services
       Editions," *The Steinbeck Newsletter*, 4:2 (Summer 1991),
       5.

621   Bhargava, Rajul. "*In Dubious Battle*: The Emergence of a
       Vision," in *John Steinbeck: Asian Perspectives*. ed.
       Kiyoshi Nakayama, Scott Pugh, and Shigeharu Yano.
       Osaka: Osaka Kyoiku Tosho, 1992. (pp. 129-141)

622   Bhargava, Rajul. "*Tortilla Flat*: A Re-Evaluation," in *John
       Steinbeck: From Salinas to the World: Proceedings of
       the Second International Steinbeck Congress* (1984). ed.
       Shigeharu Yano, Tetsumaro Hayashi, Richard F.
       Peterson, and Yasuo Hashiguchi. Tokyo, Japan: Gaku
       Shobo Press, 1986. (pp. 123-129)

623   Birney, Earle. "A Must Book," in *Critical Essays on "The
       Grapes of Wrath."* ed. John Ditsky. Boston: G.K. Hall
       and Co., 1989. (pp. 29-30) (reprint from *Canadian
       Forum*, 9 (June 1939), 94-95)

624   Bloom, Harold. "Introduction," in *John Steinbeck's "The
       Grapes of Wrath*," ed. Harold Bloom. New York:
       Chelsea House Publishers, 1988. (pp. 1-5)

625   Bloom, Harold. "Introduction," in *Modern Critical Views:
       John Steinbeck*. ed. Harold Bloom. New York: Chelsea
       House, 1987. (pp. 1-5)

626   Bluestone, George. "*The Grapes of Wrath*," in "*The Grapes
       of Wrath*": *A Collection of Critical Essays*. ed. Robert
       Con Davis. Englewood Cliffs, N. J.: Prentice Hall, 1982.
       (pp. 79-99) (reprint from *Novels into Film* (Baltimore:
       Johns Hopkins Press, 1957))

627   Bohner, Charles H. "Instructor's Manual," in *Classic Short
       Fiction*. Englewood Cliffs, N. J.: Prentice Hall, 1986.
       ("The Chrysanthemums," p. 111-112)

628   *Books and Bookmen*. "Healthy Anger," in *Conversations with
       John Steinbeck*. ed. Thomas Fensch. Jackson: University
       of Mississippi Press, 1988. (pp. 65-68) (reprint from
       Books and Bookmen, England (October 1958))

629   Boston, Jenny. "Every Picture Tells a Story," *The Steinbeck Newsletter*, 6:2 (Summer 1993), 1.

630   Boyle, Hal. "John Steinbeck Says Changes Put World in Shock," in *Conversations with John Steinbeck*. ed. Thomas Fensch. Jackson: University of Mississippi Press, 1988. (pp. 76-77) (reprint from Associated Press 1961 Interview)

631   Bowden, Edwin T. "The Commonplace and the Grotesque," in *"The Grapes of Wrath"*: *A Collection of Critical Essays*. ed. Robert Con Davis. Englewood Cliffs, N. J.: Prentice Hall, 1982. (pp. 15-23) (excerpted from *The Dungeon of The Heart* (New York: Macmillan, 1961))

632   Brasch, James D. "*The Grapes of Wrath* and Old Testament Skepticism," in *John Steinbeck's "The Grapes of Wrath*," ed. Harold Bloom. New York: Chelsea House Publishers, 1988. (pp. 45-56) (reprint from *San Jose Studies*, 3 (May 1977), 2)

633   Bredahl, A. Carl. "The Drinking Metaphor in *The Grapes of Wrath*," in *"The Grapes of Wrath": Essays in Criticism*. ed. Tetsumaro Hayashi. Steinbeck Essay Series, No. 3. Muncie, Ind.: Steinbeck Research Institute, Ball State University Press, 1990. (pp. 9-19)

634   Breiger, Mark. "Steinbeck's Compassion," *California English* (Spring 1994), 19, 23.

635   Brinkley, Alan. "*The Grapes of Wrath*," in Mark C. Carne's *Past Imperfect: History According to the Movies*. ed. Ted Mico, John Miller-Monzon, and David Rubel. New York; Henry Holt, 1995. (pp. 224-227)

636   Bristol, Horace. "John Steinbeck and *The Grapes of Wrath*," *Steinbeck Newletter*, 2:1 (Fall 1988), 6-8.

637   Bristol, Horace. "Travels with Steinbeck," ed. Jack Kelly, *People Weekly*, 31 (May 1, 1989), 66-68+.

638   Britch, Carroll. "*In Dubious Battle*: The Drive to Power," *San Jose Studies*, 18 (Winter 1992), 6-19.

639   Britch, Carroll. "Steinbeck's 'Breakfast': Godhead and Reflection," in *Rediscovering Steinbeck: Revisionist Views of His Art, Politics and Intellect.* ed. Cliff Lewis and Carroll Britch. Lewiston, N.Y.: Edward Mellen Press, 1989. (pp. 7-32)

640   Britch, Carroll, and Cliff Lewis. "Artist As Narrator," in *Rediscovering Steinbeck: Revisionist Views of His Art, Politics and Intellect.* ed. Cliff Lewis and Carroll Britch. Lewiston, N.Y.: Edward Mellen Press, 1989. (pp. 5-6)

641   Britch, Carroll, and Clifford Lewis. "*Burning Bright*: The Shining of Joe Saul," in *The Short Novels of John Steinbeck.* ed. Jackson J. Benson. Durham: Duke University Press, 1989. (pp. 217-234)

642   Britch, Carroll, and Cliff Lewis. "Cold War," in *Rediscovering Steinbeck: Revisionist Views of His Art, Politics and Intellect.* ed. Cliff Lewis and Carroll Britch. Lewiston, N.Y.: Edward Mellen Press, 1989. (pp. 218)

643   Britch, Carroll, and Cliff Lewis. "Exploring America," in *Rediscovering Steinbeck: Revisionist Views of His Art, Politics and Intellect.* ed. Cliff Lewis and Carroll Britch. Lewiston, N.Y.: Edward Mellen Press, 1989. (pp. 258-259)

644   Britch, Carroll, and Cliff Lewis. "The Fictive Process," in *Rediscovering Steinbeck: Revisionist Views of His Art, Politics and Intellect.* ed. Cliff Lewis and Carroll Britch. Lewiston, N.Y.: Edward Mellen Press, 1989. (pp. 58-59)

645   Britch, Carroll, and Clifford Lewis. "The Growth of the Family in *The Grapes of Wrath,*" in *Critical Essays on "The Grapes of Wrath."* ed. John Ditsky. Boston: G.K. Hall and Co., 1989. (pp. 97-108)

646   Britch, Carroll, and Cliff Lewis. "Introduction," in
           *Rediscovering Steinbeck: Revisionist Views of His Art,
           Politics and Intellect.* ed. Cliff Lewis and Carroll Britch.
           Lewiston, N.Y.: Edward Mellen Press, 1989. (pp. 1-4)

647   Britch, Carroll, and Cliff Lewis. "Man and War," in
           *Rediscovering Steinbeck: Revisionist Views of His Art,
           Politics and Intellect.* ed. Cliff Lewis and Carroll Britch.
           Lewiston, N.Y.: Edward Mellen Press, 1989. (pp. 174-
           176)

648   Britch, Carroll, and Cliff Lewis. "Mythmaking," in
           *Rediscovering Steinbeck: Revisionist Views of His Art,
           Politics and Intellect.* ed. Cliff Lewis and Carroll Britch.
           Lewiston, N.Y.: Edward Mellen Press, 1989. (pp. 125-
           126)

649   Britch, Carroll, and Cliff Lewis. "Observations at Mid-
           Century," in *Rediscovering Steinbeck: Revisionist Views
           of His Art, Politics and Intellect.* ed. Cliff Lewis and
           Carroll Britch. Lewiston, N.Y.: Edward Mellen Press,
           1989. (pp. 238-239)

650   Britch, Carroll, and Cliff Lewis. "Political Testaments," in
           *Rediscovering Steinbeck: Revisionist Views of His Art,
           Politics and Intellect.* ed. Cliff Lewis and Carroll Britch.
           Lewiston, N.Y.: Edward Mellen Press, 1989. (pp. 192-
           193)

651   Britch, Carroll, and Cliff Lewis. "Reinventing the Picaro," in
           *Rediscovering Steinbeck: Revisionist Views of His Art,
           Politics and Intellect.* ed. Cliff Lewis and Carroll Britch.
           Lewiston, N.Y.: Edward Mellen Press, 1989. (pp. 77-78)

652   Britch, Carroll, and Cliff Lewis. "Revelations," in
           *Rediscovering Steinbeck: Revisionist Views of His Art,
           Politics and Intellect.* ed. Cliff Lewis and Carroll Britch.
           Lewiston, N.Y.: Edward Mellen Press, 1989. (pp. 155-
           157)

653   Britch, Carroll, and Cliff Lewis. "Searching For Subjects," in
        *Rediscovering Steinbeck: Revisionist Views of His Art,
        Politics and Intellect.* ed. Cliff Lewis and Carroll Britch.
        Lewiston, N.Y.: Edward Mellen Press, 1989. (pp. 104-
        105)

654   Britch, Carroll, and Clifford Lewis. "Steinbeck's Shadow of
        an Indian," *MELUS*, XI:ii (Summer 1984), 39-58.
        (Reprinted in *Rediscovering Steinbeck: Revisionist Views
        of His Art, Politics and Intellect.* ed. Cliff Lewis and
        Carroll Britch. Lewiston, N.Y.: Edward Mellen Press,
        1989. (pp. 127-154))

655   Britch, Carroll, and Cliff Lewis. "Sources and Process," in
        *Rediscovering Steinbeck: Revisionist Views of His Art,
        Politics and Intellect.* ed. Cliff Lewis and Carroll Britch.
        Lewiston, N.Y.: Edward Mellen Press, 1989. (pp. 33-34)

656   Brodwin, Stanley. "'The Poetry of Scientific Thinking':
        Steinbeck's *Log from the Sea of Cortez* and Scientific
        Travel Narrative," in *Steinbeck and the Environment:
        Interdisciplinary Approaches.* ed. Susan Beegel, Susan
        Shillinglaw, and Wes Tiffney. Tuscaloosa: Alabama
        University Press, 1997. (pp. 142-160)

657   Brown, Alan. "From Artist to Craftsman: Steinbeck's *Bombs
        Away*," in *The Steinbeck Question: New Essays in
        Criticism.* ed. Donald Noble. Troy, N.Y.: Whitston
        Publishing Co., 1993. (pp. 213-222)

658   Brown, Ellie. "John Steinbeck," in *Twentieth Century
        Western Writers.* 2nd ed. ed. Geoff Sadler. Chicago: St.
        James Press, 1991.

659   Brown, Joyce Compton. "Steinbeck's *The Grapes of Wrath*,"
        Explicator, 41 (Summer 1983), 49-51.

660   Buchwald, Art. "John Steinbeck Turns His Hand to Tale of
        Space Ship, Flying Saucers," in *Conversations with John
        Steinbeck.* ed. Thomas Fensch. Jackson: University of

Mississippi Press, 1988. (pp. 62-64) (reprint from *The International Herald Tribune*, 29 March 1955)

661   Bur, Suzanne. "Portrait from the Promised Land: *The Grapes of Wrath* Revisited," *Michigan Alumnus,* (September/ October), 1992, 26-45.

662   Burgess, Anthony. "Living for Writing," in *Modern Critical Views: John Steinbeck.* ed. Harold Bloom. New York: Chelsea House, 1987. (pp. 141-143) (reprint from *But Do Blondes Prefer Gentlemen? Homage to Qwert Yuiop and Other Writings* by Liana Burgess)

663   Burgum, Edwin Berry. "Attitudes toward the Poor in *Of Mice and Men*," in *Readings on John Steinbeck.* ed. Clarice Swisher. San Diego: Greenhaven Press, 1996. Literary Companion Series. (117-121) (excerpted from "The Sensibilities of John Steinbeck," *Science and Society*, X (Spring 1946), 132-147)

664   Burningham, Bradd. "Relation, Vision and Tracking the Welsh Rats in *East of Eden* and *Winter of Our Discontent*," *Steinbeck Quarterly,* XV:3-4 (Summer / Fall 1982), 77-90.

665   Burns, Stuart L. "The Turtle or the Gopher: Another Look at the Ending of *The Grapes of Wrath*" in *"The Grapes of Wrath": A Collection of Critical Essays.* ed. Robert Con Davis. Englewood Cliffs, N. J.: Prentice Hall, 1982. (pp. 100-104) (reprint from *Western American Literature*, 9 (1974), 53-57.)

666   Burress, Lee. "*The Grapes of Wrath:* Preserving Its Place in the Classroom," in *Censored Books: Critical Viewpoints* by Nicolas Karolides, Lee Burress and James M. Kean. Metuchen, N. J.: Scarecrow Press, 1993. (pp. 278-287)

667   Busch, Christopher. "*East of Eden* as Metafiction: Views from America," *The John Steinbeck Society of Japan Newsletter*, 18 (May 1995), 10-12.

668 Busch, Christopher. "Longing for the Lost Frontier: Steinbeck's Vision of Cultural Decline in 'The White Quail' and 'The Chrysanthemums,' *Steinbeck Quarterly*, XXVI: 3-4 (Summer/Fall 1993), 81-90.

669 Busch, Christopher. "Research Opportunities," in *John Steinbeck: Dissertation Abstracts and Research Opportunities* ed. Tetsumaro Hayashi and Beverly K. Simpson. Metuchen, N. J.: Scarecrow Press, 1994.

670 Busch, Christopher. "Steinbeck's *The Wayward Bus*: An Affirmation of the Frontier Myth," *Steinbeck Quarterly,* XXV: 3-4 (Summer/Fall 1992), 98-108.

671 Butler, Jeremy G. "Viva Zapata! HUAC and the Mexican Revolution," in *The Steinbeck Question: New Essays in Criticism.* ed. Donald Noble. Troy, N.Y.: Whitston Publishing Co., 1993. (pp. 239-249)

672 Butwin, David. "Steinbeck Here on Way to Viet," in *Conversations with John Steinbeck.* ed. Thomas Fensch. Jackson: University of Mississippi Press, 1988. (pp. 97-99) (reprint from *The Honolulu Advertiser*, 6 December 1966)

673 Byrd, Charlotte. "The First Person Narrator in 'Johnny Bear'; A Writer's Mind and Conscience," *Steinbeck Quarterly*, XXI: 1-2 (Winter/Spring 1988), 6-13.

674 Calabro, John. "Characters from *Cannery Row,"* in *Dictionary of American Literary Characters.* ed. Benjamin Franklin V. New York: Facts on File, 1990.

675 Caldwell, Mary Ellen. "A New Consideration of the Intercalary Chapters in *The Grapes of Wrath,"* in *"The Grapes of Wrath": A Collection of Critical Essays.* ed. Robert Con Davis. Englewood Cliffs, N. J.: Prentice Hall, 1982. (pp. 105-114) (reprint from *Markham Review,* 3 (1973), 115-119.)

676   Cameron, Tom. "*The Grapes of Wrath* Author Guards Self
      from Threats at Moody Gulch," in *Conversations with
      John Steinbeck*. ed. Thomas Fensch. Jackson: University
      of Mississippi Press, 1988. (pp. 18-20) (reprint from *The
      Los Angeles Times*, 9 July 1939)

677   Campbell, Russell. "Trampling out the Vintage: Sour Grapes
      (*The Grapes of Wrath*)," in *The Modern American Novel
      and the Movies*. ed. Gerald Peary and Roger Shatzkin.
      New York: Ungar, 1978. (pp. 107-17)

678   Cardullo, Bert. "The Function of Candy in *Of Mice and
      Men*," *Notes on Contemporary Literature*, 12:2 (1982),
      10.

679   Cardullo, Bert. "On the Road to Tragedy: The Function of
      Candy in *Of Mice and Men*," in *All the World: Drama
      Past and Present*. ed. Karelisa Hartigan. Lanham, Md.:
      University Press of America, 1982. (pp. 1-8)

680   Cardullo, Bert. "The Past and the Present, the End in the
      Beginning: The Mouse as Symbol in *Of Mice and Men*,"
      Notes on Contemporary Literature, 20:2 (March 1990),
      12.

681   Carey, Thomas J., and P. Zimmerman. "Jefferson, Steinbeck
      and *The Grapes of Wrath*: The Failed Quest for Land,"
      Social Education, 56:7 (November 1, 1992), 376-378.

682   Carpenter, Frederic I. "The Philosophical Joads," in *John
      Steinbeck's "The Grapes of Wrath."* ed. Harold Bloom.
      New York: Chelsea House Publishers, 1988. (pp. 7-15)
      (reprint from *College English*, 2:4 (January 1941))

683   Carr, Duane. "Steinbeck's Blakean Vision and *The Grapes of
      Wrath*," in *Steinbeck's Literary Dimension: A Guide to
      Comparative Studies. Series II*. ed. Tetsumaro Hayashi.
      Metuchen, N. J.: Scarecrow Press, 1991. (pp. 1-8)
      (reprinted from *"The Grapes of Wrath": Essays in
      Criticism*. ed. Tetsumaro Hayashi. Steinbeck Essay

Series, No. 3. Muncie, Ind.: Steinbeck Research Institute, Ball State University Press, 1990. (pp. 13-19))

684 Carrington, Ildiko de Papp. "Talking Dirty: Alice Munro's 'Open Secrets' and John Steinbeck's *Of Mice and Men*," *Studies in Short Fiction,* 31:4 (Fall 1994), 595-606.

685 Cassuto, David. "Turning Wine into Water: Water as Privileged Signifier in *The Grapes of Wrath." Papers on Language and Literature*, 29:1 (Winter 1993), 67-95.

686 Cassuto, David N. "Turning Wine into Water: Water as Privileged Signifier in *The Grapes of Wrath*," in *Steinbeck and the Environment: Interdisciplinary Approaches.* ed. Susan Beegel, Susan Shillinglaw, and Wes Tiffney. Tuscaloosa: University of Alabama Press, 1997. (pp. 55-75)

687 Cedarstrom, Lorelei. "The 'Great Mother' in *The Grapes of Wrath*," in *Steinbeck and the Environment: Interdisciplinary Approaches.* ed. Susan Beegel, Susan Shillinglaw, and Wes Tiffney. Tuscaloosa: Alabama University Press, 1997. (pp. 76-91)

688 Chalupova, Eva. "The Thirties and the Artistry of Lewis, Farrell, Dos Passos and Steinbeck: Some Remarks on the Influence of the Social and Ideological Developments of the Times," *Brno Studies in English Issued as Sbornik-Praci-Filozoficte Fakulty Brnenske University*, 14 (1981) 107-116.

689 Chandler, Marilyn. "The Metaphysics of Style," *San Jose Studies*, 16 (Winter 1990), 40-45.

690 Charters, Ann, William E. Sheidley, and Martha Ramsey. "Instructor's Manual" in *The Story and Its Writer: An Introduction to Short Fiction.* See #690.

691   Checketts, Randy K. "John Steinbeck on Honesty," *Akita Keizai Hoka University, Faculty of Economics Bulletin,* 15 (September 1991), 19-30.

692   Checketts, Randy K. "John Steinbeck on Needs: Economic and Psychological Interpretations," *Akita Keizai Hoka University, Faculty of Economics Bulletin,* 12 (March 1990), 17-27.

693   Checketts, Randy K. "John Steinbeck on Value." *Akita Keizai Hoka University, Faculty of Economics Bulletin,* 13 (September 1990), 17-30.

694   Chen, Kai. "Some Features of Steinbeck's Style of Language," *Waiguoyu (Beijing, China),* 22 (November 6, 1982), 36-39.

695   Cheuse, Alan. "Of Steinbeck and Salinas," *Boston Globe Magazine,* January 29, 1984, 11, 44-46, 48, 52-53.

696   Choi, Jin Young. "Steinbeck Studies in Korea," in *John Steinbeck: Asian Perspectives.* ed. Kiyoshi Nakayama, Scott Pugh, and Shigeharu Yano. Osaka: Osaka Kyoiku Tosho, 1992. (pp. 19-25)

697   Coers, Donald. "Introduction," in *The Moon Is Down* by John Steinbeck. New York: Penguin Twentieth Century Classics edition, 1995. (pp. vii-xxviii)

698   Coers, Donald. "John Believed in Man: Interview with Mrs. John Steinbeck," in *After "The Grapes of Wrath": Essays on John Steinbeck in Honor of Tetsumaro Hayashi.* ed. Donald Coers, Paul Ruffin, Robert DeMott. Athens: The Ohio University Press, 1995. (pp. 241-271)

699   Coles, Nicolas. "Democratizing Literature: Issues in Teaching Working Class Literature," *College English,* 48 (November 1986), 64-80.

700   Conder, John J. "Steinbeck and Nature's Self: *The Grapes of Wrath*," in *Modern Critical Views: John Steinbeck*. ed. Harold Bloom. New York: Chelsea House, 1987. (pp. 125-140) (reprint from *Naturalism in American Fiction: The Classic Phase*. (University of Kentucky Press, 1984), pp. 142-159) (Also available in *John Steinbeck's "The Grapes of Wrath."* ed. Harold Bloom. (New York: Chelsea House Publishers, 1988), pp. 99-114.)

701   Cook, Sylvia J. "Steinbeck's Poor in Prosperity and Adversity," in *The Steinbeck Question: New Essays in Criticism*. ed. Donald Noble. Troy, N.Y.: Whitston Publishing Co., 1993. (pp. 125-142)

702   Cook Sylvia J. "Steinbeck, The People and the Party," in *"The Grapes of Wrath": Essays in Criticism*. ed. Tetsumaro Hayashi. Steinbeck Essay Series, No. 3. Muncie, In.: Steinbeck Research Institute, Ball State University Press, 1990. (pp. 19-31) (also available in *John Steinbeck's "The Grapes of Wrath."* ed. Harold Bloom. (New York: Chelsea House Publishers, 1988) pp. 67-81; *Literature at the Barricades: The American Writer in the 1930s*. ed. Bogardus and Hobson (University of Alabama Press, 1982), (reprint from *Steinbeck Quarterly*, XV: 1-2 (Winter/Spring 1982), 11-23; and in *American Fiction 1914-1945: The Critical Cosmos Series*. ed. Harold Bloom. New Haven, Conn.: Chelsea House, 1986)

703   Covici, Jr., Pascal. "Introduction," in *The Portable Steinbeck*. ed. Pascal Covici, Jr. New York: Penguin, 1986. (pp. xi-xxix)

704   Cowley, Malcolm. "American Tragedy," in *Critical Essays on "The Grapes of Wrath."* ed. John Ditsky. Boston: G.K. Hall and Co., 1989. (pp. 27-29) (reprint from *New Republic*, 98 (3 May 1939), 382-83)

705   Cox, Martha Heasley. "Interview with Peter Stackpole,
            photographer, (1975)," *Steinbeck Newsletter*, 9:1 (Fall
            1995), 19-23.

706   Cox, Martha Heasley. "Symbolic Creatures in *The Pearl*," in
            Readings on John Steinbeck. ed. Clarice Swisher. San
            Diego: Greenhaven Press, 1996. Literary Companion
            Series. (109-116) (reprinted from Cox's study of *The
            Pearl* in *A Study Guide to Steinbeck: A Handbook to His
            Major Works*. ed. Tetsumaro Hayashi (Scarecrow Press,
            1976))

707   Crane, John Kenny. "Literary Machismo: Steinbeck,
            Faulkner and Hemingway," *Steinbeck Newsletter*, 6:1
            (Winter 1993), 1-5.

708   Crider, Jesse. "Frank Norris and John Steinbeck: The Critical
            Reception of Naturalistic Art," *Steinbeck Newletter*, 8:1-
            2 (Winter/Spring 1995), 9-12.

709   Daniel, Duane. "The Tactics of Othering in *The Log from the
            Sea of Cortez:* A Look at Steinbeck's Indians," *South
            Dakota Review,* 33:1 (Spring 1995), 103.

710   Darlin, Damon. "Collecting First Editions," *Forbes,* 152:8
            (October 11, 1993), 160.

711   Davis, Robert Con. "Introduction," in *"The Grapes of
            Wrath"*: *A Collection of Critical Essays*. ed. Robert Con
            Davis. Englewood Cliffs, N. J. : Prentice Hall, 1982. (pp.
            1-11)

712   Davis, Robert Murray. "The World of John Steinbeck's
            Joads," *World Literature Today*, 64:3 (Summer 1990),
            401-404.

713   Davison, Gordon. "Introduction," to *Of Mice and Men* by
            John Steinbeck in *Famous American Plays of the 1930s*.
            ed. Harold Clurman. New York: Dell, 1988.

714   Davison, Richard Allan. "Charles G. Norris and John
        Steinbeck: Two More Tributes to *The Grapes of Wrath*,"
        in *"The Grapes of Wrath": Essays in Criticism*. ed.
        Tetsumaro Hayashi. Steinbeck Essay Series, No. 3.
        Muncie, Ind.: Steinbeck Research Institute, Ball State
        University Press, 1990. (pp. 31-38) (also in *Steinbeck's
        Literary Dimension: A Guide to Comparative Studies.
        Series II*. ed. Tetsumaro Hayashi. Metuchen, N. J.:
        Scarecrow Press, 1991. (pp. 114-123) (reprint from
        Steinbeck Quarterly, XV:3-4 (Summer/Fall 1982), 90-
        97.)

715   Davison, Richard Allan. "Hemingway, Steinbeck and the Art
        of the Short Story," *Steinbeck Quarterly*, XXI (3-4
        Summer Fall 1988), 73-84. (reprinted in *Steinbeck's
        Literary Dimension: A Guide to Comparative Studies.
        Series II*. ed. Tetsumaro Hayashi. Metuchen, N. J.:
        Scarecrow Press, 1991. (pp. 65-79))

716   Davison, Richard Allan. "*Of Mice and Men* and *McTeague*:
        Steinbeck, Fitzgerald, and Frank Norris," *Studies in
        American Fiction*, 17:2 (Autumn 1989), 219-226.

717   Davison, Richard Allan. "An Overlooked Musical Version of
        Of Mice and Men," *Steinbeck Quarterly*, XXVI:1-2
        (Winter/Spring 1993), 9-16.

718   Delgado, James P. "The Facts behind John Steinbeck's 'The
        Lonesome Vigilante,'" *Steinbeck Quarterly*, XVI:3-4
        (Summer/Fall 1983), 70-78.

719   DeMott, Robert. "After *The Grapes of Wrath*: A Speculative
        Essay on Steinbeck's Suite of Love Poems," in *John
        Steinbeck: The Years of Greatness*. ed. Tetsumaro
        Hayashi. Tuscaloosa: University of Alabama Press,
        1993. (pp. 20-45) (enlarged into "'The Girl of the Air':
        A Speculative Essay on Steinbeck's Love Poems" in
        DeMott's *Steinbeck's Typewriter: Essays on His Art*.
        Troy, N.Y.: Whitston, 1996)

720   DeMott, Robert. "The Best-Brewed Plans of Malt and Hop:
        Steinbeck's Minimalist Elegy for Ballantine Ale,"
        Steinbeck Newsletter, 3:1 (Winter, 1990), 6-7.

721   DeMott, Robert J. "Charting East of Eden: A Bibliographical
        Survey," in *After "The Grapes of Wrath": Essays on
        John Steinbeck in Honor of Tetsumaro Hayashi.* ed.
        Donald Coers, Robert DeMott and Paul Ruffin. Athens:
        Ohio University Press, 1995. (pp. 148-171) (reprinted
        and updated in "'One Book to a Man': Charting a
        Bibliographical Preface to *East of Eden*" in DeMott's
        Steinbeck's Typewriter: A Collection of Essays. Troy,
        N.Y.: Whitston, 1996)

722   DeMott, Robert J. "Creative Reading/Creative Writing: The
        Presence of *Dr. Gunn's New Family Physician* in
        Steinbeck's *East of Eden,*" in *Rediscovering Steinbeck:
        Revisionist Views of His Art and Politics.* ed. Carroll
        Britch and Clifford Lewis. Lewiston, N.Y.: Edwin
        Mellen Press, 1989. (pp. 35-57) (incorporated into and
        enlarged in "'A Great Black Book': *East of Eden* and
        Gunn's New Family Physician" in *Steinbeck's
        Typewriter: A Collection of Essays.* Troy, N.Y.:
        Whitston, 1996)

723   DeMott, Robert. "Foreward," in *The Steinbeck Research
        Center at San Jose State University: A Descriptive
        Catalogue* by Robert Woodward. *San Jose Studies,* 11
        (Winter, 1985), 5-7.

724   DeMott, Robert. "In Memoriam: Chase Horton (1897-
        1985)," in *Essays on Collecting John Steinbeck's Books.*
        ed. Preston Beyer. Bradenton, Fla.: Opuscula Press,
        1989. (pp. 27-31)

725   DeMott, Robert. "Introduction," in *The Grapes of Wrath,* by
        John Steinbeck. New York: Penguin Books, 1992. (pp.
        vi-xliv) (reprinted as 'Writing My Country': Making *To
        a God Unknown* in DeMott's *Steinbeck's Typewriter: A
        Collection of Essays.* Troy, N.Y.: Whitston, 1996)

726 DeMott, Robert. "Introduction," in *A New Steinbeck Bibliography. Supplement I:* 1978-1981 by Tetsumaro Hayashi, Metuchen, N. J.: Scarecrow Press, 1983. (pp. 1-4)

727 DeMott, Robert. "Introduction," in *To a God Unknown* by John Steinbeck. New York: Penguin Books, 1995. (pp. vii-xxxvii) (reprinted in *Steinbeck's Typewriter: A Collection of Essays.* Troy, N.Y.: Whitston, 1996)

728 DeMott, Robert. "Legacies," *Steinbeck Quarterly*, XXIV:3-4 (Summer/Fall 1991), 81-83.

729 DeMott, Robert. "Of Ink and Heart's Blood: Adventures in Reading *East of Eden*," *Connecticut Review*, 14 (Spring 1992), 9-21. (reprinted as "'Of Ink and Heart's Blood': Adventures in Reading *East of Eden*," in DeMott's *Steinbeck's Typewriter: A Collection of Essays.* Troy, N.Y.: Whitston, 1996)

730 DeMott, Robert. "Special Message for the Twenty-Fifth Anniversary of the Steinbeck Society," *Steinbeck Quarterly*, XXIV:1-2 (Winter/Spring 1991), 6-7.

731 DeMott, Robert. "Steinbeck on the Novel: A 1954 Interview," *Steinbeck Newsletter*, 5:1-2 (Spring 1992), 6-7.

732 DeMott, Robert. "The Steinbeck Research Center: A Checklist of Autographed First Editions," *Steinbeck Newsletter,* 1 (Fall 1987), 1, 3-4.

733 DeMott, Robert. "Steinbeck's *East of Eden* and Gunn's *New Family Physician*," *The Book Club of California Quarterly Newsletter*, 51 (Spring 1986), 31-48. (incorporated into "'A Great Black Book': *East of Eden* and *Gunn's New Family Physician*" in DeMott's *Steinbeck's Typewriter: A Collection of Essays.* Troy, N.Y.: Whitston, 1996)

734   DeMott, Robert. "Steinbeck's Other Family: New Light on
        East of Eden," Steinbeck Newsletter, 7:1 (Winter 1994),
        1-4.

735   DeMott, Robert. "Steinbeck's Reading: First Supplement,*"
        Steinbeck Quarterly*, XVII: 3-4 (Summer/Fall 1984), 94-
        103. (reprinted and enlarged in "'Things That Happened
        to Me': Steinbeck's Varieties of Reading Experience" in
        DeMott's *Steinbeck's Typewriter: A Collection of
        Essays*. Troy, N.Y.: Whitston, 1996)

736   DeMott, Robert. "Steinbeck's Reading: Second
        Supplement,*" Steinbeck Quarterly*, XXII (1-2
        Winter/Spring 1989), 4-8. (reprinted and enlarged in
        "Things That Happened to Me": Steinbeck's Varieties of
        Reading Experience" in DeMott's *Steinbeck's
        Typewriter: A Collection of Essays*. Troy, N.Y.:
        Whitston, 1996)

737   DeMott, Robert. 'S*weet Thursday* Revisited: An Excursion in
        Suggestiveness," in *After "The Grapes of Wrath":
        Essays on John Steinbeck in Honor of Tetsumaro
        Hayashi*. ed. Donald V. Coers, Paul D. Ruffin, and
        Robert J. DeMott. Athens: University of Ohio Press,
        1995. (pp. 172-196) (reprinted as "Steinbeck's
        Typewriter: An Excursion in Suggestiveness," in
        DeMott's *Steinbeck's Typewriter: A Collection of
        Essays*. Troy, N.Y.: Whitston, 1996)

738   DeMott, Robert. "'A Truly American Book': Pressing *The
        Grapes of Wrath,"* in *Biographies of Books: The
        Compositional Histories of Notable American Writings*.
        ed. James Barbour and Tom Quirk. Columbia:
        University of Missouri Press, 1996. (pp. 187-225)

739   DeMott, Robert. "Vintage Steinbeck: It's Been 50 Years
        Since *The Grapes of Wrath* First Stirred the Conscience
        of a Generation of Readers," *TWA Ambassador
        Magazine* (April, 1989), 33-34.

740   DeMott, Robert. "Voltaire didn't Like Anything: A 1939 Interview with John Steinbeck," in *Conversations with John Steinbeck.* ed. Thomas Fensch. Jackson: University Press of Mississippi, 1988. (pp. 21-27) (reprinted from *Steinbeck Quarterly*, XIX: 1-2 (Winter/Spring 1989), 5-11)

741   DeMott, Robert. "What Goes Around, Comes Around," Introduction in Siefker, Hayashi, and Moore, eds. *The Steinbeck Quarterly : A Cumulative Index to Volumes XI-XX (*1978-1987*), Steinbeck Bibliography Series,* No. 2, 1989, 6-9.

742   DeMott, Robert. "'Working at the Impossible': *Moby-Dick*'s Presence in *East of Eden*," in *Steinbeck and the Environment: Interdisciplinary Approaches.* ed. Susan Beegel, Susan Shillinglaw, and Wes Tiffney. Tuscaloosa: Alabama University Press, 1997. (pp. 211-228) (reprinted in a shorter version under the same title in DeMott's *Steinbeck's Typewriter: A Collection of Essays*. Troy, N.Y.: Whitston, 1996)

743   DeMott, Robert. "'Working Days and Hours': Steinbeck's Writing of *The Grapes of Wrath*," *Studies in American Fiction*, 18 (Spring 1990), 3-15. (a later version incorporated into "'This Book is My Life': Creating *The Grapes of Wrath*" in DeMott's *Steinbeck's Typewriter: Essays On His Art*. Troy, N.Y.: Whitston, 1996)

744   DeRoche, Joseph, David Bergman, and Daniel M. Epstein. "The Chrysanthemums" See #616.

745   Detro, Gene. "The Truth about Steinbeck (Carol and John)," *Creative States Quarterly*, 2 (May 1985), 12-13, 16.

746   Dewey, Joseph. "'There Was a Seedy Grandeur about the Man": Rebirth and Recovery in *Travels with Charley*," *Steinbeck Quarterly*, XXIV:1-2 (Winter/Spring 1991), 22-30.

747   Dickson, John. "*The Grapes of Wrath,*" *The American Scholar,* 64 (Summer 1995), 4.

748   Dietrich, R. F. "The Chrysanthemums," in Instructor's Manual. *The Art of Fiction* by R. F. Dietrich and Roger Sundell, 4th ed. New York: Holt, Rinehart, and Winston, 1993. (pp. 80-84)

749   Dircks, Phyllis T. "Steinbeck's Statement in the Inner Chapters of *The Grapes of Wrath,*" *Steinbeck Quarterly,* XXIV:3-4 (Summer/Fall 1991), 86-94.

750   Ditsky, John. "Between Acrobats and Seals: Steinbeck in the U.S.S.R.," *Steinbeck Quarterly,* XV:1-2 (Winter/Spring 1982), 23-29.

751   Ditsky, John. "California Dreaming: Steinbeck and West," *The Steinbeck Newsletter,* 4:2 (Summer 1991), 6-7.

752   Ditsky, John. "The Depression's 'Graveyard Ghosts': A Shared Motif in *Waiting for Nothing* and *The Grapes of Wrath,*" *The International Fiction Review,* 15:1 (Winter 1988), 21-22.

753   Ditsky, John. "The Devil in Music: Unheard Themes in Steinbeck's Fiction," *Steinbeck Quarterly,* XXV:3-4 (Summer/Fall 1992), 80-86.

754   Ditsky, John. "The Devil Quotes Scripture: Biblical Misattribution and *The Winter of Our Discontent,*" *San Jose Studies,* 15:2 (Spring 1989), 19-28.

755   Ditsky, John. "The Ending of *The Grapes of Wrath*: A Further Commentary," in *Critical Essays on "The Grapes of Wrath."* ed. John Ditsky. Boston: G.K. Hall and Co., 1989. (pp. 116-124) (revised from *Agora,* 2 (Fall 1973), 41-50)

756   Ditsky, John. "*The Grapes of Wrath* at 50: The Critical
        Perspective in Motion," *San Jose Studies*, 16:1 (Winter
        1990), 46-53.

757   Ditsky, John. "'I' in *Eden*: The Narrational Voice in
        Steinbeck," *Kyushu American Literature*, 27 (September
        1986), 57-69.

757A   Ditsky, John. "'I Kind of Like Caleb': Naming in *East in
        Eden*," *Steinbeck Newsletter*, 10:1 (Spring 1997), 7-9.

758   Ditsky, John. "'I Know It When I Hear It on Stage': Theatre
        and Language in Steinbeck's *Burning Bright*," in *The
        Steinbeck Question: New Essays in Criticism*. ed. Donald
        Noble. Troy, N.Y.: Whitston, 1993. (pp. 223-38)

759   Ditsky, John. "'In Love with the Whole Darn Bunch': How
        Sweet Thursday Became a *Pipe Dream*," *Kyushu
        American Literature*, 31 (December 22, 1990), 1-10.

760   Ditsky, John. "Introduction," *in Critical Essays on "The
        Grapes of Wrath."* ed. John Ditsky. Boston: G.K. Hall
        and Co., 1989. (pp. 1-21)

761   Ditsky, John. "Jim Casy Goes to Haiti: A Literary Parallel,"
        The Steinbeck Newsletter, 7:1 (Winter 1994), 14.

762   Ditsky, John. "John Steinbeck," in *Reference Guide to Short
        Fiction.* ed. Noelle Watson. Detroit: St. James Press,
        1994. (pp. 511-512)

763   Ditsky, John. "John Steinbeck," in *St. James Guide to
        Biography*. ed. Paul E. Schellinger. Chicago: St. James
        Press, 1991. (pp. 737-739)

764   Ditsky, John. "John Steinbeck, the Interior Landscape, and
        Tragic Depletion," *South Dakota Review*, 32:1 (Spring
        1994), 106-15.

765   Ditsky, John. "John Steinbeck: Yesterday, Today, and
       Tomorrow," *Steinbeck Quarterly*, XXIII:1-2
       (Winter/Spring 1990), 5-16.

766   Ditsky, John. "'Kind of Play': Dramatic Elements in John
       Steinbeck's 'The Chrysanthemums,'" *Wascana Review,*
       21:1 (Spring 1986), 62-72.

767   Ditsky, John. "The Late John Steinbeck: Dissonance in the
       Post "Grapes" Era," *San Jose Studies*, 18:1 (Winter
       1992), 20-32.

768   Ditsky, John. "Mission to Moscow — A Report," *Steinbeck
       Quarterly*, XXIII: 3-4 (Summer/Fall 1990), 75-77.

769   Ditsky, John. "Preview of *Critical Essays on 'The Grapes of
       Wrath,'*" *The Steinbeck Newsletter*, 1:2 (Spring 1988), 6.

770   Ditsky, John. "'Pu-raise Gawd fur Vittory!' Granma as
       Prophet," *The Steinbeck Newsletter*, 6:2 (Summer 1993),
       4-5.

771   Ditsky, John. "The Re-Inventing of Harry Morgan: A Note,"
       University of Windsor Review, 18:1 (Fall/Winter 1984),
       95-96.

772   Ditsky, John. "Rowing from Eden: Closure in the Later
       Steinbeck Fiction," *North Dakota Quarterly*, 60:3
       (Summer 1992), 87-100.

773   Ditsky, John. "Some Second Thoughts about the Ending of
       The Wayward Bus: A Note," *University of Windsor
       Review*, 20: 1 (Fall/Winter, 1987), 85-88.

774   Ditsky, John. "Some Sense of Mission: Steinbeck's *The Short
       Reign of Pippin IV* Reconsidered," *Steinbeck Quarterly*,
       XVI: 3-4 (Summer/Fall 1983), 79-89.

775   Ditsky, John. "Steinbeck and Albee: Affection, Admiration and Affinity," *Steinbeck Quarterly,* XXVI:1-2 (Winter/Spring 1993), 13-23.

776   Ditsky, John. "Steinbeck as Dramatist: A Preliminary Account," in *John Steinbeck: From Salinas to the World.* ed. Shigeharu Yano, Tetsumaro Hayashi, Richard F. Peterson, and Yasuo Hashiguchi. Tokyo, Japan: Gaku Shobo Press, 1986. (pp. 13-23)

777   Ditsky, John. "Steinbeck, Bourne, and the Human Herd: A New/Old Gloss on *The Moon is Down,*" in *Rediscovering Steinbeck: Revisionist Views of His Art, Politics and Intellect.* ed. Cliff Lewis and Carroll Britch. Lewiston, N.Y.: Edward Mellen Press, 1989. (pp. 177-191)

778   Ditsky, John. "Steinbeck's 'European' Play-Novella: *The Moon Is Down,*" *Steinbeck Quarterly,* XX: 1-2 (Winter/Spring 1987), 9-18. (reprinted in *The Short Novels of John Steinbeck.* ed. Jackson J. Benson. Durham: Duke University Press, 1990. (pp. 101-110))

779   Ditsky, John. "Steinbeck's 'Slav-Girl' and the Role of the Narrator in 'The Murder'," *Steinbeck Quarterly,* XXII: 3-4 (Summer/Fall 1989), 68-76.

780   Ditsky, John. "Work, Blood and *The Wayward Bus,*" in *After "The Grapes of Wrath": Essays on John Steinbeck in Honor of Tetsumaro Hayashi.* ed. Donald Coers, Robert DeMott, and Paul Ruffin. Athens: Ohio University Press, 1995. (pp. 136-147)

781   Ditsky, John. "'Your Own Mind Coming out in the Garden,' Steinbeck's Elusive Woman," in *John Steinbeck: The Years of Greatness, 1936-1939.* ed. Tetsumaro Hayashi. Tuscaloosa, Ala.: University of Alabama Press, 1993. (pp. 3-19, 165-167)

782   Douglas, Jack. "Carol Henning Steinbeck," *Steinbeck Newsletter,* 1:2 (Spring 1988), 3.

783 Douglas, John. "John Steinbeck Research Center, San Jose State University," in *Dictionary of Literary Biography Yearbook,* 1985. ed. Jean W. Ross. Detroit: Gale Research, 1986. (pp. 159-161)

784 Dourgarian, Jim. "The Pastures of Heaven — a Film?" *Steinbeck Newletter*, 2:1 (Fall 1988), 4.

785 Dowell, Bob. "A Note on John Steinbeck in King Arthur's Court," in *The Arthurian Myth of Quest and Magic: A Festschrift in Honor of Lavon B. Fulwiler.* ed. William E. Tanner. Dallas: Caxton's Modern Arts Press, 1993. (pp. 71-74)

786 Dunbar, Maurice. "Freemasonry and the Steinbeck Family," *Steinbeck Newsletter,* 10: 1 (Spring 1996), 7-8.

787 Dunbar, Maurice. "Guns in the Fiction of John Steinbeck," *Steinbeck Newsletter*, 6:1 (Winter 1993), 12.

788 Dunbar, Maurice. "A Review of *Letters to Elizabeth: A Selection of Letters from John Steinbeck to Elizabeth Otis* (1978)," in *Steinbeck's Posthumous Work: Essays in Criticism.* ed. Tetsumaro Hayashi and Thomas J. Moore. Steinbeck Monograph Series, No. 14. Muncie, Ind.: Steinbeck Research Institute, Ball State University Press, 1989. (pp. 43-46)

789 "The Dust Bowl Revisited," *Newsweek*, May 1, 1989, 72.

790 Dye, Morris. "Littoral Interpretations (Edward F. Ricketts)," *Great Escapes,* (Fall 1992), 28-34.

791 Eckley, Wilton. "The Red Pony," in *Reference Guide to Short Fiction.* ed. Noelle Watson. Detroit: St. James Press, 1994. (pp. 864-865)

792 Eckley, Wilton. "'And the Greatest of These is Love': John Steinbeck's *The Grapes of Wrath* as a Statement of Moral Humanism," in *Literature, Culture and Ethnicity:*

Studies on Medieval, Renaissance and Modern Literature. A Festschrift for Janez Stanonik. ed. Jurak-Mirko. Ljubljana: Jurak-Mirko, 1992.

793   Egan, John. "John Steinbeck at Birzeit University," *Arab Perspectives*, 4 (January 1984), 12-13.

794   Egusa, Hisashi. "Both Aspects of 'Localness,'" *Steinbeck Studies,* 19 (May 1996), 10-11. (*The Pastures of Heaven*)

795   Egusa, Hisashi. "On 'Breakfast,' an Experimental Work of Steinbeck's Rhetorical Device of Modernity," *John Steinbeck Society of Japan Newsletter*, 14 (April 1991), n.p.

796   Elder, S. "Steinbeck Reborn," *Vogue*, 182 (October 1992), 170+.

797   Emery, Jean M. "Manhood Beset: Misogyny in *Of Mice and Men*," *San Jose Studies*, 18 (Winter 1992), 33-42.

798   Enea, Bob. "A Brief Sketch of the Monterey Sardine Fishing Industry," *Steinbeck Newsletter*, 9:1 (Fall 1995), 25. (Part I of *On Cannery Row*: Four Perspectives)

799   Enea, Bob. "Notes on the 'Western Flyer' Project," *Steinbeck Newletter,* 8:1-2 (Winter/Spring 1995), 22.

800   Englert, Peter A. J. "Education of Environmental Scientists: Should We Listen to Steinbeck and Ricketts's Comments?" in *Steinbeck and the Environment: Interdisciplinary Approaches.* ed. Susan Beegel, Susan Shillinglaw, and Wes Tiffney. Tuscaloosa: Alabama University Press, 1997. (pp. 176-193)

801   Epstein, Daniel M., David Bergman, Joseph de Roche. "The Chrysanthemums," See #616.

802   Epstein, Lawrence J. "Steinbeck in Sag Harbor: A Personal
       Memoir," Steinbeck Newsletter, 6:1 (Winter 1993), 6-7.

803   Erickson, Edward, and William J. Beck. "The Emergence of
       Class Consciousness in Germinal and The Grapes of
       Wrath," See 599.

804   Evans, Thomas G. "Impersonal Dilemmas: The Collision of
       Modernist and Popular Traditions in Two Political
       Novels, The Grapes of Wrath and Ragtime," South
       Atlantic Review, 52:1 (Fall 1987), 71-86.

805   Everest, Beth, and Judy Wedeles. "The Neglected Rib:
       Women in East of Eden," Steinbeck Quarterly, XXI:1-2
       (Winter/Spring 1988), 13-23.

806   Falkenberg, Sandra. "A Study of Female Characterization in
       Steinbeck's Fiction," in Modern American Fiction:
       Readings from the Critics. ed. Don Stanley Richmond.
       Richmond, B.C., Canada: Open Learning Institute, 1982.
       (pp. 117-123) (a reprint of her article in Steinbeck
       Quarterly, 8 (Spring 1975), 50-56)

807   Farrah, David. "'The Form of the New' in Steinbeck's
       Cannery Row," Shoin Literary Review (Shoin Joshi
       Gakuin University), 25 (March 1992), 21-30.

808   Fensch, Thomas. "Reflections of Doc: The Persona of Ed
       Ricketts in Of Mice and Men," in John Steinbeck: The
       Years of Greatness, 1936-1939. ed. Tetsumaro Hayashi.
       Tuscaloosa, Ala.: University of Alabama Press, 1993.
       (pp. 106-110)

809   Fergus, Jim. "The Art of Fiction CIV: Jim Harrison," Paris
       Review, 107 (1988), 84.

810   Fiedler, Leslie. "Looking Back after 50 Years," San Jose
       Studies, 16 (Winter 1990), 54-64. (The Grapes of Wrath)

811   Fields, Sidney. "John Steinbeck: The Sphinx Talks," in
        Conversations with John Steinbeck. ed. Thomas Fensch.
        Jackson: University of Mississippi Press, 1988. (pp. 59-
        61) (reprint from *The New York Sunday Mirror*, 13
        March 1955)

812   Finnegan, L. J. "Celebrate Steinbeck in Salinas," *Sunset*
        (Central West. Ed.), 191 (August 1993), 32.

813   Fiorelli, Edward. "*Cannery Row,*" in *Masterplots II:
        American Fiction Series*. Vol. I. ed. Frank Magill.
        Englewood Cliff, N. J.: Salem Press, 1986. (pp. 242-246)

814   Fiorelli, Edward. "John Steinbeck," in *Critical Survey of
        Short Fiction*. Vol. 6. ed. Frank Magill. Pasadena, Calif.:
        Salem Press, 1993. (pp. 2205-2210) (discusses *The
        Pastures of Heaven and The Long Valley*)

815   Fontenrose, Joseph. "*Tortilla Flat* and the Creation of a
        Legend," in *The Short Novels of John Steinbeck*. ed.
        Jackson J. Benson. Durham: Duke University Press,
        1990. (pp. 19-30)

816   Freedman, William A., and Robert J. Griffin. "Machines and
        Animals: Pervasive Motifs in *The Grapes of Wrath*," in
        "*The Grapes of Wrath*": *A Collection of Critical Essays*.
        ed. Robert Con Davis. Englewood Cliffs, N. J.: Prentice
        Hall, 1982. (pp. 115-127) (reprint from *Journal of
        English and Germanic Philology*, 62 (July 1963), 569-
        580)

817   French Warren. "Fiction vs. Film, 1960-1985," in
        Contemporary American Fiction. ed. Malcolm Bradbury
        and Sigmund Ro. London: Edward Arnold, 1987. (pp.
        106-121)

818   French Warren. "40 Years in the Angry Vineyard," *San Jose
        Studies*, 16 (Winter 1990), 65-75. (*The Grapes of Wrath*)

819   French, Warren. "From Naturalism to the Drama of
        Consciousness — the Education of the Heart in *The
        Grapes of Wrath*," in *"The Grapes of Wrath"*: *A
        Collection of Critical Essays*. ed. Robert Con Davis.
        Englewood Cliffs, N. J.: Prentice Hall, 1982. (pp. 24-35)
        (reprint from *John Steinbeck* (Boston: Twayne
        Publishers, 1975))

820   French, Warren. "How Green Was John Steinbeck?" in
        *Steinbeck and the Environment: Interdisciplinary
        Approaches*. ed. Susan Beegel, Susan Shillinglaw, and
        Wes Tiffney. Tuscaloosa: University of Alabama Press,
        1997. (pp. 283-292)

821   French, Warren. "Introduction," in *In Dubious Battle* by John
        Steinbeck. New York: Penguin, 1992. (pp. vii-xxix)

822   French, Warren. "Introduction," in *After "The Grapes of
        Wrath"*: *Essays on John Steinbeck in Honor of
        Tetsumaro Hayashi*. ed. Donald Coers, Robert DeMott,
        and Paul Ruffin. Athens: Ohio University Press, 1995.
        (pp. 1-19)

823   French, Warren. "Introduction," in *Steinbeck's "The Red
        Pony"*: *Essays in Criticism*. ed. Tetsumaro Hayashi and
        Thomas J. Moore. Steinbeck Monograph Series, No. 13.
        Muncie, Ind.: Steinbeck Research Institute, Ball State
        University Press, 1988. (pp. ix-xiv)

824   French, Warren. "Introduction," in *Steinbeck's Short Stories
        in "The Long Valley"*: *Essays in Criticism*. ed.
        Tetsumaro Hayashi. Steinbeck Monograph Series, No.
        15. Muncie, Ind.: Steinbeck Research Institute, Ball State
        University Press, 1991. (pp. xi-xvii)

825   French, Warren. "Jackson J. Benson," *Dictionary of Literary
        Biography*. Detroit: Gale Research, 1990. (vol. 111, 16-
        24.)

826   French, Warren. "Jody's Growing Awareness in *The Red Pony*," in *Readings on John Steinbeck*. ed. Clarice Swisher. San Diego: Greenhaven Press, 1996. Literary Companion Series. (86-94) (reprinted from French's *John Steinbeck*. (Twayne, 1961) 1st edition)

827   French, Warren. "John Steinbeck," in *Twentieth Century Fiction*. ed. George Woodcock. London: Macmillan, 1983. (pp. 640-644)

828   French, Warren. "John Steinbeck and American Literature," *San Jose Studies*, 13 (Spring 1987), 41-42.

829   French, Warren. "John Steinbeck and Modernism" (A Speculation on His Contribution to the Development of the Twentieth Century American Sensibility), in *Critical Essays on "The Grapes of Wrath."* ed. John Ditsky. Boston: G.K. Hall and Co., 1989. (pp. 152-162) (reprint from *Steinbeck's Prophetic Vision of America.* ed. Tetsumaro Hayashi and Kenneth D. Swan (Upland, Ind.: Taylor University for the John Steinbeck Society of America, 1976.)

830   French, Warren. "John Steinbeck: From Salinas to the World," in *John Steinbeck: From Salinas to the World: Proceedings of the Second International Steinbeck Congress* (1984). ed. Shigeharo Yano, Tetsumaro Hayashi, Richard F. Peterson, and Yasuo Hashiguchi. Tokyo, Japan: Gaku Shobo Press, 1986. (pp. 1-12)

831   French, Warren, "John Steinbeck, the Model T Ford, and the Theory of the Anglo-Saxon Home," *Kansas Quarterly*, 21 (Fall 1989), 7-13.

832   French, Warren. "John Steinbeck: A Usable Concept of Naturalism," in *Modern Critical Views: John Steinbeck*. ed. Harold Bloom. New York: Chelsea House, 1987. (pp. 63-78) (reprint from *American Literary Naturalism: A Reassessment*. ed. Yoshinobu Hakutani and Lewis Fried)

833   French, Warren. "*Of Mice and Men*: A Knight Dismounted
       and a Dream Ended," in *Readings on John Steinbeck*. ed.
       Clarice Swisher. San Diego: Greenhaven Press, 1996.
       Literary Companion Series. (pp. 130-137) (reprinted
       from French's *John Steinbeck*. (Twayne, 1961) 1st
       edition)

834   French, Warren. "*The Red Pony* as Story Cycle and Film," in
       The Short Novels of John Steinbeck. ed. Jackson J.
       Benson. Durham: Duke University Press, 1990. (pp. 71-
       84)

835   Friend, Tod. "Books: Frederick Barthelme Depicts an
       America Gone Sour; T. C. Boyle Recapitulates
       Steinbeck," *New Yorker*, 28:40 (October 9, 1995), 85.

836   Fries, Maureen. "John Steinbeck," in *The Arthurian
       Encyclopaedia*. ed. Norris J. Lacy, et. al. New York:
       Garland, 1986. (p. 526)

837   Fukazawa, Toshio. "Presentation I: Chair," *John Steinbeck
       Society of Japan Newsletter*, 15 (April 1992), 2.

838   Fukazawa, Toshio. "*Tortilla Flat*, Panel Discussion I:
       Steinbeck and His Sense of Humour," *John Steinbeck
       Society of Japan Newsletter*, 10 (April 1987), 3-4.

839   Gaither, Gloria. "John Steinbeck: From Tidal Pool to the
       Stars: Connectedness, Is Thinking, and Breaking
       Through — A Reconsideration," *Steinbeck Quarterly,*
       XXV:1-2 (Winter/Spring 1992), 42-52.

840   Gamble, Mary Jean S. "Recent Acquisitions of the Steinbeck
       Archives at the Salinas Public Library," *Steinbeck
       Newletter*, 5 (Spring 1992), 8-9.

841   Gamble, Mary Jean, and Thom M. Tammaro. "John
       Steinbeck, Hans Namuth, and the Lost Sag Harbor
       Photographs," *Steinbeck Newsletter,* 4:2 (Summer 1991),
       1-4.

842   Gannett, Louis. "John Steinbeck: Novelist at Work," in
       Conversations with John Steinbeck. ed. Thomas Fensch.
       Jackson: University of Mississippi Press, 1988. (pp. 28-
       42) (reprint from *The Atlantic Monthly* (December
       1945): 55-60)

843   Garcia, Reloy. "Introduction," in *Steinbeck's Posthumous
       Work: Essays in Criticism* ed. Tetsumaro Hayashi and
       Thomas J. Moore. Steinbeck Monograph Series, No. 14.
       Muncie, Ind.: Steinbeck Research Institute, Ball State
       University Press, 1989. (pp. ix-xiii)

844   Garcia, Reloy. "The Rocky Road to Eldorado: The Journey
       Motif in John Steinbeck's *The Grapes of Wrath*," in
       "The Grapes of Wrath": Essays in Criticism. ed.
       Tetsumaro Hayashi. Steinbeck Essay Series, No. 3.
       Muncie, Ind.: Steinbeck Research Institute, Ball State
       University Press, 1990. (pp. 38-48)

845   Gartshore, Bonnie. "Red Williams, the Man, Red Williams,
       the Character in *Cannery Row*," *Steinbeck Newsletter*,
       9:1 (Fall 1995), 24.

846   Gentry, Curt. "John Steinbeck: America's King Arthur is
       Coming," in *Conversations with John Steinbeck.* ed.
       Thomas Fensch. Jackson: University of Mississippi
       Press, 1988. (pp. 73-75) (reprint from *The San
       Francisco Chronicle*, 6 November 1960)

847   Gentry, Robert. "Non-teleological Thinking in Steinbeck's
       Tortilla Flat," in *The Short Novels of John Steinbeck.* ed.
       Jackson J. Benson. Durham: Duke University Press,
       1990. (pp. 31-38)

848   Gerber, Philip L. "Day of Doom, Day of Dreams: Malcolm
       Cowley in the 1930s," *Horns of Plenty*, 2 (Summer
       1989), 36-51.

849   Girard, Maureen. "Steinbeck's 'Frightful' Story: The
           Conception and Evolution of 'The Snake,'" *San Jose
           Studies,* 8:2 (Spring 1982), 33-40.

850   Gladstein, Clifford Eric, and Mimi Reisel Gladstein,
           "Revisiting *The Sea of Cortez* with a Green Perspective,"
           in *Steinbeck and the Environment: Interdisciplinary
           Approaches.* ed. Susan Beegel, Susan Shillinglaw, and
           Wes Tiffney. Tuscaloosa: University of Alabama Press,
           1997. (pp. 161-175)

851   Gladstein, Mimi Reisel. "Abra: The Indestructible Woman in
           East of Eden," in *Modern Critical Views: John
           Steinbeck.* ed. Harold Bloom. New York: Chelsea House,
           1987. (pp. 151-153) (reprint from *The Indestructible
           Woman in Faulkner, Hemingway and Steinbeck*)

852   Gladstein, Mimi Reisel. "*America and Americans*: The
           Arthurian Consummation," in *After "The Grapes of
           Wrath": Essays on John Steinbeck in Honor of
           Tetsumaro Hayashi.* eds. Donald V. Coers, Paul D.
           Ruffin, Robert J. DeMott. Athens, Ohio: Ohio University
           Press, 1995. (pp. 228-237)

853   Gladstein, Mimi Reisel. "*Cannery Row*: A Male World and
           the Female Reader," *Steinbeck Quarterly*, XXV:3-4
           (Summer/Fall 1992), 87-97.

854   Gladstein, Mimi Reisel. "Deletions from the *Battle*: Gaps in
           the *Grapes*," *San Jose Studies*, XVIII:1-2 (Winter 1992),
           43-51.

855   Gladstein, Mimi Reisel. "From Heroine to Supporting Player:
           The Diminution of Ma Joad," in *Critical Essays on
           Steinbeck's "The Grapes of Wrath."* ed. John Ditsky.
           Boston: G.K. Hall & Co., 1989. (pp. 124-137)

856   Gladstein, Mimi Reisel. "From Lady Brett to Ma Joad: A
           Singular Scarcity," in *John Steinbeck: From Salinas to*

the World. eds. Shigeharu Yano, Tetsumaro Hayashi,
Richard Peterson, and Yasuo Hashiguchi. Tokyo: Gabu
Shobo Press, 1986. (pp. 24-33)

857   Gladstein, Mimi Reisel. *"The Grapes of Wrath*: Steinbeck
and the Eternal Immigrant," in *John Steinbeck : The
Years of Greatness, 1936-1939.* ed. Tetsumaro Hayashi.
Tuscaloosa, Ala.: University of Alabama Press, 1994.
(pp. 132-144)

858   Gladstein, Mimi R. "In Search of Steinbeck: A Continuing
Journey," *Nova* (University of Texas at El Paso
Magazine), 19 (September 1983), 7-9, 12.

859   Gladstein, Mimi Reisel. "Indestructible Women in *The
Grapes of Wrath*," in *Readings on John Steinbeck.* ed.
Clarice Swisher. San Diego: Greenhaven Press, 1996.
Literary Companion Series. (pp. 156-164) (excerpted
from Gladstein's *The Indestructible Women in Faulkner,
Hemingway and Steinbeck* (UMI Research Press, 1986))

860   Gladstein, Mimi Reisel. "The Indestructible Women: Ma
Joad and Rose of Sharon," in *John Steinbeck's "The
Grapes of Wrath."* ed. Harold Bloom. New York:
Chelsea House Publishers, 1988. (pp. 115-127) (reprint
from *The Indestructible Woman in Faulkner,
Hemingway and Steinbeck*)

861   Gladstein, Mimi Reisel. "'The Leader of the People': A Boy
Becomes a Mench," in *Steinbeck's "The Red Pony":
Essays in Criticism.* eds. Tetsumaro Hayashi and
Thomas J. Moore. Steinbeck Monograph Series No. 13,
Muncie, Ind.: Steinbeck Research Institute, Ball State
University Press, 1988. (pp. 27-37) (translated into
Japanese in *Steinbeck Kenkyu: Atarashii Tanpen
Shosetsushu (Steinbeck Studies: New Essays on Short
Stories).* Osaka, Japan: Osaka Educational Publishing
Co., 1995. (pp. 83-112))

862   Gladstein, Mimi Reisel. "Missing Women: The Inexplicable
           Disparity between Women in Steinbeck's Life and Those
           in His Fiction," in *The Steinbeck Question: New Essays
           in Criticism*. ed. Donald Noble. Troy, N.Y.: Whitston
           Publishing Co., 1993. (pp. 84-98)

863   Gladstein, Mimi Reisel, and Clifford Eric Gladstein,
           "Revisiting *The Sea of Cortez* with a Green Perspective,"
           in *Steinbeck and the Environment: Interdisciplinary
           Approaches*. See #850.

864   Gladstein, Mimi Reisel. "Straining for Profundity:
           Steinbeck's *Burning Bright* and *Sweet Thursday*," in *The
           Short Novels of John Steinbeck*. ed. Jackson J. Benson.
           Durham, N.C.: Duke University Press, 1990. (pp. 234-
           248)

865   Gladstein, Mimi Reisel. "The Strong Female Principle of
           Good — Or Evil: Women in *East of Eden*," *Steinbeck
           Quarterly*, XXIV:1-2 (Winter/Spring 1991) 30-40.

866   Gladstein, Mimi Reisel. "*The Wayward Bus*: Steinbeck's
           Misogynistic Manifesto," in *Rediscovering Steinbeck:
           Revisionist Views of His Art, Politics, and Intellect*. ed.
           Cliff Lewis and Carroll Britch. Lewiston: The Edwin
           Mellen Press, 1989. (pp. 157-173) (with Bobbi
           Gonzales)

867   Goldberg, Peter B. "Poverty and Nutrition: If Steinbeck Were
           Alive Today," *Families in Society: The Journal of
           Contemporary Human Services,* 76:1 (January 1, 1995),
           46.

868   Goldhurst, William. "*Of Mice and Men*: John Steinbeck's
           Parable of the Curse of Cain," in *The Short Novels of
           John Steinbeck*. ed. Jackson J. Benson. Durham: Duke
           University Press, 1990. (pp. 48-59)

869   Goldsmith, Arnold L. "Oneness and Mysticism in *The Red
        Pony*," in *Readings on John Steinbeck*. ed. Clarice
        Swisher. San Diego: Greenhaven Press, 1996. Literary
        Companion Series. (80-85) (excerpted from "Thematic
        Rhythm in 'The Red Pony,'" *College English*, XXVI
        (February 1965), 391-394)

870   Golightly, B. "Steinbeck Country," *Horizon*, 30 (July/August
        1987), 62.

871   Gonzales, Bobbi. *"The Wayward Bus*: Steinbeck's
        Misogynistic Manifesto," in *Rediscovering Steinbeck:
        Revisionist Views of His Art, Politics, and Intellect*. ed.
        Cliff Lewis and Carroll Britch. Lewiston: The Edwin
        Mellen Press, 1989. (pp. 157-173) (with Mimi Reisel
        Gladstein)

872   Goodin, G. "Permutations and Combinations of Victims," in
        The Poetics of Protest by G. Goodin. Charleston:
        Southern Illinois University Press, 1985. (pp. 159-189)

873   Gossage, Leslie. "The Artful Propaganda of Ford's *The
        Grapes of Wrath*," in *New Essays on "The Grapes of
        Wrath."* ed. David Wyatt. Cambridge: Cambridge
        University Press, 1990. (pp. 101-125)

874   Greenblatt, Stephen J. "Steinbeck and the Exorcists," in
        *Contemporary Literary Criticism: Literary and Cultural
        Studies*. ed. Robert Con Davis and Ronald Schleifer.
        New York: Longmans, 1989.

875   Gregory, James N. "Dust Bowl Legacies: The Okie Impact
        on California, 1939-1989," *California History* (Fall
        1989), 74-85.

876   Griffin, Robert J., and William A. Freedman. "Machines and
        Animals: Pervasive Motifs in *The Grapes of Wrath*," in
        "The Grapes of Wrath": *A Collection of Critical Essays*.
        ed. Robert Con Davis. See #816.

877   Griffith, Benjamin. "The Banishing of Caldwell and
          Steinbeck," *Sewanee Review,* 103:2 (Spring 1995), 325.

878   Groene, Horst. "Agrarianism and Technology in *The Grapes
          of Wrath,*" in *"The Grapes of Wrath": A Collection of
          Critical Essays.* ed. Robert Con Davis. Englewood
          Cliffs, N. J.: Prentice Hall, 1982. (pp. 128-133) (reprint
          from *Southern Review,* 9:1 (1976), 27-31.)

879   Gunn, Drewey Wayne. *"The Pearl,"* in *Masterplots II: Short
          Story Series.* Vol. IV. ed. Frank Magill. Pasadena, Calif.:
          Salem Press, 1986. (pp. 1785-1788)

880   Hadella, Charlotte. "The Dialogic Tension in Steinbeck's
          Portrait of Curley's Wife," in *John Steinbeck: The Years
          of Greatness,* 1936-1939. ed. Tetsumaro Hayashi.
          Tuscaloosa, Ala.: University of Alabama Press, 1993.
          (pp. 64-74)

881   Hadella, Charlotte. Ch. 6: *"Of Mice and Men,"* in *A New
          Study Guide to Steinbeck's Major Works, with Critical
          Explications.* ed. Tetsumaro Hayashi. Metuchen, N. J.:
          Scarecrow Press, 1993. (pp. 139-163)

882   Hadella, Charlotte. "Point of View in John Steinbeck's 'The
          Murder'," *Steinbeck Quarterly,* XXII:3-4 (Summer/Fall
          1989), 77-83.

883   Hadella, Charlotte. "Steinbeck's Cloistered Women," in *The
          Steinbeck Question: New Essays in Criticism.* ed. Donald
          Noble. Troy, N.Y.: Whitston Publishing Co., 1993. (pp.
          51-70)

884   Hagiwara, Tsutomu. *"The Short Reign of Pippin IV*: Panel
          Discussion I: Steinbeck and His Sense of Humor," *John
          Steinbeck Society of Japan Newsletter,* 10 (April 1987),
          4.

885   Hamaguchi, Osamu. "Criticism and Theme in *In Dubious Battle*," *John Steinbeck Society of Japan Newsletter*, 6 (May 1983), 3-4.

886   Hamaguchi, Osamu. "The Other Side of the American Dream," *Steinbeck Studies,* 19 (May 1996), 12-13. (*The Pastures of Heaven*)

887   Hamaguchi, Osamu. "Panel Discussion: *The Log from the Sea of Cortez* and Steinbeck Literature," *John Steinbeck Society of Japan Newsletter*, 11 (April 1988), 4.

888   Hamaguchi, Osamu. "Steinbeck's *The Grapes of Wrath*: The Joads" New Westering," *Toyama University Faculty of Liberal Arts Bulletin: Humanities and Social Science*, 16: 2 (March 1983), 63-86.

889   Hamaguchi, Osamu. "A Study of Steinbeck's *In Dubious Battle,"* *Chu-Shikoku Studies in American Literature* (March 20, 1984), 77-87.

890   Hanamoto, Kingo. "*Cannery Row*: Panel Discussion I: Steinbeck and His Sense of Humor," *John Steinbeck Society of Japan Newsletter*, 10 (April 1987), 4.

891   Hanamoto, Kingo. "Steinbeck, Faulkner and Buddhism," in *John Steinbeck: From Salinas to the World: Proceedings of the Second International Steinbeck Congress* (1984). ed. Shigeharo Yano, Tetsumaro Hayashi, Richard F. Peterson, and Yasuo Hashiguchi. Tokyo, Japan: Gaku Shobo Press, 1986. (pp. 97-102)

892   Harmon, Robert B. "Thomas Hart Benton and John Steinbeck," *Steinbeck Newsletter*, 1:2 (Spring 1988), 1, 2.

893   Harris, Laurie Lazen. "John Steinbeck," in *Characters in 20th Century Literature.* Detroit: Gale Research, Inc., 1990. (pp. 380-383) (discusses characters in *Tortilla*

Flat, *The Grapes of Wrath, Of Mice and Men,* and *East of Eden*)

894   Harris, Mark Edward. "Horace Bristol," *Camera and Darkroom*, 15:8 (August 1, 1993), 22.

895   Hart, Richard E. "Steinbeck on Man and Nature: A Philosophical Reflection," in *Steinbeck and the Environment: Interdisciplinary Approaches.* ed. Susan Beegel, Susan Shillinglaw, and Wes Tiffney. Tuscaloosa: University of Alabama Press, 1997. (pp. 43-52)

896   Hashiguchi, Yasuo. "Fifth Meeting of the Steinbeck Society of Japan," *Steinbeck Quarterly*, XV: 3-4 (Summer/Fall 1982), 118.

897   Hashiguchi, Yasuo. "I Was Privileged to Preside over Mr. Sharma's Presentation," *John Steinbeck Society of Japan Newsletter*, 6 (May 1983), 2.

898   Hashiguchi, Yasuo. "Internationalization of Steinbeck Studies," *Kyushu American Literature,* 28 (October 1987), 65-67.

899   Hashiguchi, Yasuo. "My Ten Years with the Steinbeck Society of Japan," *Steinbeck Quarterly*, XX: 1-2 (Winter/Spring 1987) 26-28.

900   Hashiguchi, Yasuo. "Preface," *The Complete Works of John Steinbeck.* 20 Volumes. ed. Yasuo Hashiguchi. Kyoto: Rinsen Book Co., 1985. (pp. i-v)

901   Hashiguchi, Yasuo. "Report on the Eighth Meeting of the Steinbeck Society of Japan," *Steinbeck Quarterly*, XVIII: 1-2 (Winter/Spring 1985), 49.

902   Hashiguchi, Yasuo. "Report on the Fifth Steinbeck Festival and the Second International Steinbeck Congress," *Steinbeck Quarterly*, XVIII: 1-2 (Winter/Spring 1985), 10-11.

903   Hashiguchi, Yasuo. "Report of the Ninth Conference of the
        Steinbeck Society of Japan — May 20, 1985," *Steinbeck
        Quarterly*, XIX: 3-4 (Summer/Fall 1986), 104.

904   Hashiguchi, Yasuo. "Report of the Seventh Meeting of the
        Steinbeck Society of Japan," *Steinbeck Quarterly*, XVII:
        1-2 (Winter/Spring 1984), 51.

905   Hashiguchi, Yasuo. "Report of the Sixth Meeting of the
        Steinbeck Society of Japan," *Steinbeck Quarterly*,
        XVI:1-2 (Winter/Spring 1983), 57.

906   Hashiguchi, Yasuo. "Report of the Tenth Anniversary
        Conference of the Steinbeck Society of Japan (1986),"
        Steinbeck Quarterly, XX:1-2 (Winter/Spring 1987), 35-
        36.

907   Hashiguchi, Yasuo. "Special Message," *John Steinbeck
        Society of Japan Newsletter*, 10 (April 1987), 1.

908   Hashiguchi, Yasuo. "Special Message," *John Steinbeck
        Society of Japan Newsletter*, 12 (April 1989), 1.

909   Hashiguchi, Yasuo. "Special Message," *John Steinbeck
        Society of Japan Newsletter*, 13 (April 1990), 1.

910   Hashiguchi, Yasuo. "Special Message," *John Steinbeck
        Society of Japan Newsletter*, 14 (April 1991), 1.

911   Hashiguchi, Yasuo. "A Special Message," *Steinbeck
        Quarterly*, XIX:1-2 (Winter/Spring 1986), 35-36.

912   Hashiguchi, Yasuo. "Special Message: The Twentieth
        Anniversary of The Steinbeck Quarterly (1968-1987),"
        Steinbeck Quarterly, XX: 3-4 (Summer/Fall 1987), 73.

913   Hashiguchi, Yasuo. "Special Messages in Honor of the
        Twenty-Fifth Anniversary of the International John
        Steinbeck Society," *Steinbeck Quarterly*, XXIV:1-2
        (Winter/Spring 1991), 10-11.

914   Hashiguchi, Yasuo. "Steinbeck," *Eigo Seinen (The Rising Generation)*, (September 1982), 354-355.

915   Hashiguchi, Yasuo. "The Steinbeck Festival V (1984) and the Second International Steinbeck Congress," *John Steinbeck Society of Japan Newsletter*, 7 (May 1984), 1-2.

916   Hashiguchi, Yasuo. "Steinbeck Studies in Japan," *Bulletin in Commemoration of the Foundation of the Graduate School, Yasuda Women's University,* March 31, 1995, 49-56.

917   Hashiguchi, Yasuo. "Thought upon Retirement," *John Steinbeck Society of Japan Newsletter*, 15 (April 1992), 1-2.

918   Hattenhauer, Daryll. "The Frog as Metaphor in *Cannery Row,"* *Notes on Contemporary Literature,* 21:4 (1991), 7-8.

919   Haupt, Edward J., and Peggy McCardle. "Case Order in Sentences: Newer and More Varied," in *Language and Style: An International Journal,* 16:4 (Fall 1983), 420-432.

920   Havens, R. Larry. "The Computer and John Steinbeck: *Of Mice and Men,"* *Jissen Eibungaku* (English Literature Society, Jissen Women's University), 42 (February 20, 1993), 1-5.

921   Havens, R. Larry. "Evolution of John Steinbeck and *The Grapes of Wrath,"* *Jissen Eibungaku* (English Literature Society, Jissen Women's University), 25 (March 25, 1983), 57-81.

922   Havens, R. Larry. "*Of Mice and Men,"* *Jissen Eibungaku* (English Literature Society, Jissen Women's University), 28 (1986), 128-133.

923   Hayashi, Tetsumaro. "A Checklist of Steinbeck's Title
        Changes," *Steinbeck Newsletter* (Japan), 8 (May 1985),
        7-8.

924   Hayashi, Tetsumaro. "The 'Chinese Servant' in *East of
        Eden*," *San Jose Studies*, 18 (Winter 1992), 43-51.

925   Hayashi, Tetsumaro. "Dr. Winter's Dramatic Function in *The
        Moon Is Down*," in *The Short Novels of John Steinbeck.*
        ed. Jackson J. Benson. Durham: Duke University Press,
        1990. (pp. 95-101) (reprinted from *Reitaku University
        Journal,* 38 (December 1984), 29-40)

926   Hayashi, Tetsumaro. "John Steinbeck and Adlai Stevenson:
        Their Moral and Political Vision," *Steinbeck Quarterly,*
        XXIV:3-4 (Summer/Fall 1991), 94-107.

927   Hayashi, Tetsumaro. "John Steinbeck: The Art and Craft of
        Writing," in *A New Study Guide to Steinbeck's Major
        Works, with Critical Explications*. ed. Tetsumaro
        Hayashi. Metuchen, N. J.: Scarecrow Press, 1993. (pp.
        274-284)

928   Hayashi, Tetsumaro. "John Steinbeck: The Art and Craft of
        Writing," *The Torch*, 64 (Spring/Summer 1992), 9-12.

929   Hayashi, Tetsumaro. "John Steinbeck: His Concept of
        Writing," in *John Steinbeck: From Salinas to the World:
        Proceedings of the Second International Steinbeck
        Congress* (1984). ed. Shigeharo Yano, Tetsumaro
        Hayashi, Richard F. Peterson, and Yasuo Hashiguchi.
        Tokyo, Japan: Gaku Shobo Press, 1986. (pp. 34-44)

930   Hayashi, Tetsumaro. "A Memorial Tribute to Dr. Carol Ann
        (Kendrick) Kasparek," *John Steinbeck Society of Japan
        Newsletter*, 7 (May 1984), 12-13.

931   Hayashi, Tetsumaro. "A Second Look at John Steinbeck's
        Travels with Charley in Search of America," *Reitaku
        University Journal*, 41 (March 1986), 1-13.

932   Hayashi, Tetsumaro. "The Seventh Conference of the
         Steinbeck Society of Japan: Special Message," *John
         Steinbeck Society of Japan Newsletter*, 7 (May 1984),
         2-3.

933   Hayashi, Tetsumaro. "Special Message," *John Steinbeck
         Society of Japan Newsletter*, 9 (May 1986), 1-2.

934   Hayashi, Tetsumaro. "Standards for Publishable Writing:
         What Kind of Article Do We Accept for Publication?"
         John Steinbeck Society of Japan Newsletter, 6 (May
         1983), 4-6.

935   Hayashi, Tetsumaro. "Steinbeck and the Old Testament: Free
         Will in the Fallen World," *Anglo-American Studies*, 6
         (November 1986), 149-59.

936   Hayashi, Tetsumaro. "Steinbeck's America in *Travels with
         Charley*," *Steinbeck Quarterly*, XXIII:3-4 (Summer/Fall
         1990), 88-96.

937   Hayashi, Tetsumaro. "Steinbeck's 'Chinese Servant' in *East
         of Eden*," *Sino American Relations,* 19:2 (Summer
         1993), 29-42.

938   Hayashi, Tetsumaro. "Steinbeck's Concept of Creating
         Writing," *Persica* (The English Literary Society of
         Okayama), 17 (March 1990), 105-113.

939   Hayashi, Tetsumaro. "Steinbeck's Literature: Its Reputation
         and Uniqueness — a Second Survey," *Persica* (The
         English Literary Society of Okayama), 16 (March 1989),
         141-147.

940   Hayashi, Tetsumaro. "Steinbeck's Literature Viewed from
         Archetypal Perspectives," *Reitaku University Journal,* 39
         (July 1985), 125-133.

941   Hayashi, Tetsumaro. "Steinbeck's *The Moon Is Down*: A
       Shakespearean Explication," *Reitaku University Journal*,
       36 (December 1983), 1-13.

942   Hayashi, Tetsumaro. "Steinbeck's Moral Vision in *East of
       Eden*," *Studies in Foreign Language and Literature*
       (Aichi University of Education), 25 (March 25, 1989),
       87-104.

943   Hayashi, Tetsumaro. "Steinbeck's Political Vision in *The
       Moon Is Down*: A Shakespearean Interpretation,"
       Kyushu American Literature, 24 (July 28, 1983), 1-10.

944   Hayashi, Tetsumaro. "Steinbeck's Use of Old Testament in
       The Grapes of Wrath," *Kyushu American Literature*, 29
       (July 1988), 1-11.

945   Hayashi, Tetsumaro. "Teaching Steinbeck in the U.S.A.: A
       Pedagogical Reflection," *Persica* (The English Literary
       Society of Okayama), 21(March 25, 1994), 47-52.

946   Hayashida, Eiji. "The Meanings of Abel and Cain Characters
       in *East of Eden*," *John Steinbeck Society of Japan
       Newsletter*, 13 (April 1990), 2.

947   Hayashida, Eiji. "A Study of *The Pastures of Heaven*: Its
       Naturalistic Aspect — Movement and Destruction of
       Design," *John Steinbeck Society of Japan Newsletter*, 14
       (April 1991), 3.

948   Hays, Peter L. "The *Grapes of Wrath* and *Ironweed*," *The
       Steinbeck Newsletter*, 6:2 (Summer 1993), 5.

949   Hearle, Kevin. "The Boat-Shaped Mind: Steinbeck's Sense of
       Language as Discourse in *Cannery Row* and *Sea of
       Cortez*," in *After "The Grapes of Wrath"*: *Essays on
       John Steinbeck in Honor of Tetsumaro Hayashi*. ed.
       Donald Coers, Robert DeMott, and Paul Ruffin. Athens:
       Ohio University Press, 1995. (pp. 101-112)

950   Hearle, Kevin. "The Pastures of Contested Pastoral
            Discourse," *Steinbeck Quarterly,* XXVI:1-2
            (Winter/Spring 1993), 38-45.

951   Hearle, Kevin. "Sturges and *The Grapes of Wrath*: *Sullivan's
            Travels* as Documentary Comedy," *The Steinbeck
            Newsletter,* 7:2 (Summer 1994), 5-7.

952   Heavilin, Barbara. "Ch. 1: *America and Americans,*" in *A
            New Study Guide to Steinbeck's Major Works, with
            Critical Explications.* ed. Tetsumaro Hayashi.
            Metuchen, N. J.: Scarecrow Press, 1993. (pp. 3-33)

953   Heavilin, Barbara. "The Invisible Woman: Ma Joad as Epic
            Heroine in John Steinbeck's *The Grapes of Wrath,*"
            Kyushu American Literature (Summer 1991), 51-61.

954   Heavilin, Barbara. "Ma Joad, Rose of Sharon, and the
            Stranger Motif: Structural Symmetry in Steinbeck's *The
            Grapes of Wrath,*" *South Dakota Review* (Summer
            1991), 142-52.

955   Heavilin, Barbara A. "Steinbeck's Exploration of Good and
            Evil: Structural and Thematic Unity in *East of Eden,*"
            Steinbeck Quarterly, XXVI:3-4 (Summer/Fall 1993), 90-
            100.

956   Heavilin, Barbara. " Ch. 9: *Travels with Charley*" in *A New
            Study Guide to Steinbeck's Major Works, with Critical
            Explications.* ed. Tetsumaro Hayashi. Metuchen, N. J.:
            Scarecrow Press, 1993. (pp. 211-239)

957   Hedgpeth, Joel W. "Ed Ricketts (1897-1948), Marine
            Biologist," *Steinbeck Newsletter*, 9:1 (Fall 1995), 17-18.
            (Part IV of Edward Flanders Ricketts: Four Perspectives)

958   Hedgpeth, Joel W. "John Steinbeck: Late-Blooming
            Environmentalist," in *Steinbeck and the Environment:
            Interdisciplinary Approaches.* ed. Susan Beegel, Susan

Shillinglaw, and Wes Tiffney. Tuscaloosa: University of
Alabama Press, 1997. (pp. 293-309)

959   Hedrick, Joan. "Mother Earth and Earth Mother: The
Recasting of Myth in Steinbeck's *The Grapes of Wrath*,"
in *"The Grapes of Wrath": A Collection of Critical
Essays.* ed. Robert Con Davis. Englewood Cliffs, N. J.:
Prentice Hall, 1982. (pp. 134-143)

960   Henderson, George. "John Steinbeck's Spatial Imagination in
The Grapes of Wrath," *California History,* 68:4 (Winter
1989/1990), 210-223.

961   Herron, Don. "John Steinbeck" in *The Literary World of San
Francisco and Its Environs, A Guidebook.* ed. Nancy J.
Peters. San Francisco: City Lights Books, 1985. (pp.
215-17)

962   Higdon, David Leon. "The Chrysanthemums" in *Reference
Guide to Short Fiction.* ed. Noelle Watson. Detroit: St.
James Press, 1994. (pp. 667-668)

963   Higdon, David Leon. "Dionysian Madness in Steinbeck's
'The Chrysanthemums,'" *Classical and Modern
Literature,* 11:1 (February 1990), 59-65.

964   Hintz, Paul. "The Silent Woman and the Male Voice in
Steinbeck's *Cannery Row*," in *The Steinbeck Question:
New Essays in Criticism.* ed. Donald Noble. Troy, N.Y.:
Whitston Publishing Co., 1993. (pp. 71-83)

965   Hirose, Hidekazu. "Noboru Shimomura: *Requiescat in
Pace."* *Steinbeck Quarterly,* XXIII:3-4 (Summer-Fall
1990), 73-74.

966   Hirose, Hidekazu. "Panel Discussion: Comparing Steinbeck,"
John Steinbeck Society of Japan Newsletter, 9 (May
1986), 3.

967   Hochenauer, K. "The Rhetoric of American Protest: Thomas
         Paine and the Education of Tom Joad," *Midwest
         Quarterly,* 35 (Summer 1994), 392-404.

968   Hodges, Laura. "Steinbeck's Adaptation of Malory's
         Launcelot: A Triumph of Realism over
         Supernaturalism," *Quondam and Futurus,* 2:1 (Spring
         1992), 69-81.

969   Hodges, Laura. "Steinbeck's Dream Sequence in *The Acts of
         Arthur and His Noble Knights,*" *Arthurian
         Interpretations,* 4:2 (Spring 1990), 35-49.

970   Hoffstedt, Richard. "Steinbeck and Censorship," *The
         Steinbeck Newsletter,* 4:1 (Winter 1991), 8.

971   Hollimon, Jack. "Country History: Writer to Chronicle
         Changes Since 1900," in *Conversations with John
         Steinbeck.* ed. Thomas Fensch. Jackson: University of
         Mississippi Press, 1988. (pp. 49-51) (reprint from *The
         Salinas Californian,* Rodeo Edition (June, 1948))

972   Howarth, William. "The Mother of Literature: Journalism
         and *The Grapes of Wrath,*" in *New Essays on "The
         Grapes of Wrath."* ed. David Wyatt. Cambridge:
         Cambridge University Press, 1990. (pp. 71-99) (also in
         Literary Journalism in the 20th Century. ed. Norman
         Sim. Oxford: Oxford University Press, 1990. (pp. 53-
         81))

973   Howarth, William. "The Okies: Beyond the Dust Bowl,"
         National Geographic, 166 (September 1984), 322-49.

974   Hudson, Theodore R. 'Suite Thursday: Duke Ellington's
         Transformation of John Steinbeck's *Cannery Row,*"
         Popular Culture Review (December 2, 1990), 37-48.

975   Hughes, Robert S., Jr. "The Black Cypress and the Green
         Tub: Death and Procreation in Steinbeck's 'The
         Promise,'" in *Steinbeck's "The Red Pony": Essays in*

Criticism. ed. Tetsumaro Hayashi and Thomas J. Moore.
Steinbeck Monograph Series, No. 13. Muncie, Ind.:
Steinbeck Research Institute, Ball State University Press,
1988. (pp. 9-16) (translated into Japanese in *Steinbeck
Kenkyu: Atarashii Tanpen Shosetsushu (Steinbeck
Studies: New Essays on Short Stories)*. Osaka, Japan:
Osaka Educational Publishing Co., 1995. (pp. 43-60))

976   Hughes, Robert S., Jr. "Searching for Subjects: Steinbeck's
Uncollected Stories," in *Rediscovering Steinbeck:
Revisionist Views of His Art, Politics, and Intellect*. ed.
Cliff Lewis and Carroll Britch. Lewiston: The Edwin
Mellen Press, 1989. (pp. 104-124)

977   Hughes, Robert S., Jr. "'Some Philosophers in the Sun'":
Steinbeck's *Cannery Row*," in *The Short Novels of John
Steinbeck*. ed. Jackson J. Benson. Durham: Duke
University Press, 1990. (pp. 119-131)

978   Hughes, Robert S., Jr. "Steinbeck and the Art of Story
Writing," in *The Steinbeck Question: New Essays in
Criticism*. ed. Donald Noble. Troy, N.Y.: Whitston
Publishing Co., 1993. (pp. 37-50)

979   Hughes, Robert S., Jr. "Steinbeck, the Short Story Writer," in
*Steinbeck's Short Stories in "The Long Valley": Essays
in Criticism*. ed. Tetsumaro Hayashi. Steinbeck
Monograph Series, No. 15. Muncie, Ind.: Steinbeck
Research Institute, Ball State University Press, 1991.
(pp. 78-89) (translated into Japanese in *Steinbeck
Kenkyu: Atarashii Tanpen Shosetsushu (Steinbeck
Studies: New Essays on Short Stories)*. Osaka, Japan:
Osaka Educational Publishing Co. 1995. (pp. 319-344))

980   Hughes, Robert S., Jr. "Steinbeck's Stories at the Houghton
Library: A Case for Authenticity of Four Unpublished
Texts," *Harvard Literary Bulletin*, XXX (February
1982), 87-95.

981   Hughes, Robert S., Jr. "Steinbeck's *Travels with Charley* and
           America and Americans," *Steinbeck Quarterly*, XX:3-4
           (Summer/Fall 1987), 76-88.

982   Hughes, Robert S., Jr. "Steinbeck's Uncollected Stories,"
           Steinbeck Quarterly, XVIII:3-4 (Summer/Fall 1985), 79-
           92.

983   Hughes, Robert S., Jr. "What Went Wrong? How a 'Vintage'
           Steinbeck Short Story Became the Flawed *Winter of Our
           Discontent*," *Steinbeck Quarterly*, XXVI:1-2
           (Winter/Spring 1993), 7-12.

984   Hunter, J. P. "Artistic and Thematic Structure in *The Grapes
           of Wrath*," in *Readings on John Steinbeck*. ed. Clarice
           Swisher. San Diego: Greenhaven Press, 1996. Literary
           Companion Series. (145-155) (excerpted from
           "Steinbeck's Wine of Affirmation in *The Grapes of
           Wrath* in *Essays in Modern American Literature*. ed.
           Richard F. Langford, Guy Owen, and William E. Taylor.
           (Stetson University Press, 1965))

985   Hunter, J. Paul. "Steinbeck's Wine of Affirmation in *The
           Grapes of Wrath*," in *"The Grapes of Wrath"*: *A
           Collection of Critical Essays*. ed. Robert Con Davis.
           Englewood Cliffs, N. J. : Prentice Hall, 1982. (pp. 36-
           47) (reprint from *Essays in Modern American Literature*
           (DeLand, Fla.: Stetson University Press, 1963))

986   Ingram, Laura. "Characters from *East of Eden*," in
           Dictionary of American Literary Characters. ed.
           Benjamin Franklin V. New York: Facts on File, 1990.

987   Ingram, Laura. "Characters from *In Dubious Battle*," in
           Dictionary of American Literary Characters. ed.
           Benjamin Franklin V. New York: Facts on File, 1990.

988   Inoue, Hirotsugu. "'The Snake': Centering on the Figure of
           Dr. Phillips," *John Steinbeck Society of Japan
           Newsletter*, 13 (April 1990), 3-4.

989   Inoue, Hirotsugu. "The Weedpatch Camp as a Symbol of
       American Democracy," in *John Steinbeck: Asian
       Perspectives*. ed. Kiyoshi Nakayama, Scott Pugh, and
       Shigeharu Yano. Osaka: Osaka Kyoiku Tosho, 1992.
       (pp. 143-153)

990   Inoue, Kenji. "Congratulations: Special Twenty-Fifth
       Anniversary of Messages," *Steinbeck Quarterly*,
       XXIV:3-4 (Summer/Fall 1991), 78-79.

991   Inoue, Kenji. "The Reception of *The Grapes of Wrath* in
       Japan," *John Steinbeck Society of Japan Newsletter*, 13
       (April 1990), 4-5.

992   Inoue, Kenji. "The Reception of American Literature since
       1945," in *The Traditional and the Anti-Traditional:
       Studies in Contemporary American Literature*. ed.
       Kenzaburo Ohashi. Tokyo: The Tokyo Chapter of the
       American Literature Society of Japan, 1980. (pp. 219-
       31)

993   Inoue, Toshihiro. "*Cannery Row*: An Ecological View of a
       City," *Philologia* (Society of English, Mie University),
       26 (December 20, 1994), 83-100.

994   Inoue, Toshihiro. "*Tortilla Flat*: The Urbanization of Paisano
       Society," *John Steinbeck Society of Japan Newsletter*, 15
       (April 1992), 2-3.

995   Iwase, Tsuneko. "Steinbeck's Approach to Sin in Shin
       Buddhism Speculation," *Toyo University Junior College
       Bulletin*, 20 (December 1988), 41-52.

996   Iwase, Tsuneko. "Steinbeck's Concepts on Original Sin,"
       Toyo University Junior College Bulletin, 18 (March
       1987), 23-31.

997   Iwase, Tsuneko. "Steinbeck's Failure in *Burning Bright*,"
       Toyo University Junior College Bulletin, 16 (March
       1985), 47-54.

998   Iwase, Tsuneko. "Steinbeck's Parable Elements of *The*
        Pearl," *Toyo University Junior College Bulletin*, 15
        (1984), 65-70.

999   Iwase, Tsuneko. "The Thematic Structure in *The Pearl*,"
        John Steinbeck Society of Japan Newsletter, 12 (April
        1989), 3-4.

1000   "Jalopies I Cursed and Loved," (Reprint of a 1954 article in
        Holiday) *Travel Holiday*, 173 (August 1990), 102.

1001   Jayne, Edward. "Me, Steinbeck and Rose of Sharon's Baby,"
        Amerikastudien (American Studies), Munich, Germany,
        20:2 (1975), 281-305.

1002   Jeon, Jo-Yong. "On the Relationship between John
        Steinbeck's *In Dubious Battle* and John Milton's
        Mythology in *Paradise Lost,"* *Journal of English
        Language and Literature Assn. of Korea* (May 30, 1989),
        129-151.

1003   "John Steinbeck: A Collector's Edition," *Monterey Life: The
        Magazine of California's Spectacular Central Coast*, 7
        (July 1987). (This edition of the magazine features John
        Steinbeck, "The Summer Before"; Richard Astro,
        "Steinbeck in Our Time"; Kiyoshi Nakayama,
        "Steinbeck in Japan"; and Ray A. March, "Salinas' Son:
        Nearly 20 Years after His Death, Salinas Takes Another
        Look at Steinbeck.")

1004   "John Steinbeck in the Ukraine: What the Secret Soviet
        Archives Reveal," *The Ukranian Quarterly,* 51:1 (Spring
        1995), 62.

1005   Johnson, Linck C. "Compositional History and the
        Composition of the Canon," *Resources for American
        Literary Study*, 19 (1993), 301-308.

1006 Johnson, Ronald C. "Flight" in *Masterplots II: Short Story Series. Vol. II.* ed. Frank Magill. Pasadena, Calif.: Salem Press, 1986. (pp. 792-794)

1007 Johnston, Kenneth G. "'The Butterfly and the Tank': Casualties of War," *Studies in Short Fiction,* 26 (Spring 1989), 183-186.

1008 Jones, Robert. "Report from Steinbeck Country," *Theology Today,* 46:3 (October 1, 1989), 277-282.

1009 Kaida, Koichi. "About the Rough Words Signifying a Person in *In Dubious Battle,*" *Yatsushiro National College of Technology Bulletin,* 4 (March 1982), 61-66.

1010 Kaida, Koichi. "The Cave Experience in *The Grapes of Wrath,*" *Kyushu American Literature,* 28 (October 1987), 67-69.

1011 Kaida, Koichi. "The Cave Symbolism in *The Grapes of Wrath,*" *Shujitsu English Studies* (Shujitsu Women's University, English Literature Society), 11 (March 1993), 1-17.

1012 Kaida, Kochi. "'Crawl' and 'Move' in *The Grapes of Wrath,*" *John Steinbeck Society of Japan Newsletter,* 13 (April 1990), 6-7.

1013 Kaida, Koichi. "Irishism in *Cup of Gold,*" *John Steinbeck Society of Japan Newsletter,* 7 (May 1984), 3.

1014 Kaida, Koichi. "Multi-layered Functions of Animal Imagery in *In Dubious Battle* and *The Grapes of Wrath,*" in *John Steinbeck: Asian Perspectives.* ed. Kiyoshi Nakayama, Scott Pugh, and Shigeharu Yano. Osaka: Osaka Kyoiku Tosho, 1992. (pp. 49-71)

1015 Kaida, Koichi. "A Stylistic Approach to *The Pearl,*" *Shujitsu English Studies* (Shujitsu Women's University), 10 (March 20, 1992), 1-32.

1016   Kalogeras, Yiorgos. "Narrative and Interpretation in *The Grapes of Wrath,*" *Diavazo,* 173 (September 2, 1987), 29-31.

1017   Kakegawa, Wakako. "The Humour of *Cannery Row,*" *John Steinbeck Society of Japan Newsletter,* 8 (May 1985), 5.

1018   Kakegawa, Wakako. "*The Log from the Sea of Cortez* and *Cannery Row,*" *John Steinbeck Society of Japan Newsletter,* 11 (May 1988), 4-5.

1019   Kakegawa, Wakako. "A Weak Cathy," Symposium: "On Cathy," *John Steinbeck Society of Japan Newsletter,* 15 (April 1992), 6.

1020   Kami, Yuji. "John Steinbeck's View of Life and Death," *English Language and Literature Studies* (Soka University), 28 (March 1991), 147-49.

1021   Kami, Yuji. "Life and Death in *The Grapes of Wrath,*" *Shoka University English Language and Literature Studies* (Japan), 31 (December 1992), 111-27.

1022   Kami, Yuji. "On Steinbeck's Non-Teleology," *Eigo Eibungaku Kenkyu* (*English Language and Literature Studies,* Soka University), 27 (December 1990), 73-74.

1023   Kamins, Mort. "Leon Uris," *Writer's Digest,* 67 (August 1987), 39-41. (Includes "Of Steinbeck, O'Neill, and the Rest.")

1024   Kaname, Hiroshi. "A Study of John Steinbeck's *Of Mice and Men,*" *John Steinbeck Society of Japan Newsletter,* 6 (May 1983), 1-2.

1025   Kanoza, Theresa. "Steinbeck's *The Grapes of Wrath,*" *Explicator,* 51:3 (Summer 1993), 187-189.

1026   Kappel, Tim. "Trampling out the Vineyards: Kern County's
        Ban on *The Grapes of Wrath*," *California History*, 61
        (Fall 1982), 210-220.

1027   Kasparek, Carol A. "*The Winter of Our Discontent*: A
        Critical Survey," ed. John Ditsky, *Steinbeck Quarterly*,
        XVIII: 1-2 (Winter/Spring 1985), 20-34.

1028   Kato, Mitsuo. "Forming California Myths or Legends,"
        Steinbeck Studies, 19 (May 1996), 8-9. (*POH*)

1029   Kato, Mitsuo. "The Locations of Steinbeck's Manuscripts
        and Letters," *John Steinbeck Society of Japan
        Newsletter*, 12 (April 1989), 4.

1030   Kato, Tunehiko. "'The American Dream' and Its Failure: A
        Comparative Study of *The Grapes of Wrath* and *An
        American Tragedy*," (Dreiser) *John Steinbeck Society of
        Japan Newsletter*, 9 (May 1986), 4.

1031   Kato, Yoshifumi. "*In Dubious Battle*: Characterization,"
        John Steinbeck Society of Japan Newsletter, 6 (May
        1983), 3.

1032   Kato, Yoshifumi. "*The Log from the Sea of Cortez* and *The
        Winter of Our Discontent*," *John Steinbeck Society of
        Japan Newsletter*, 11 (April 1988), 6-7.

1033   Kato, Yoshifumi. "The Search for Radical Humanities in
        East of Eden," *Oita University Keizai, Faculty of
        Economics Bulletin*, 36:5 (January 1985), 275-297.

1034   Kawata, Ikuko. "A Study of 'Timshel' and Its Significance in
        Steinbeck's *East of Eden*," *Tabard* (The English
        Literary Society of Kobe Women's University), 4
        (December 20, 1988), 31-43.

1035   Kawata, Ikuko. "A Study of 'Timshel' in *East of Eden* (I, II,
        and III)," *Bulletin of Kobe Women's University*, 18
        (1985), I, 19-39; II, 1-4; and III, 1-20.

1036   Kawata, Ikuko. "A Study of 'Timshel': Some Aspects of the
        Hebrew Original," *John Steinbeck Society of Japan
        Newsletter*, 11 (April 1988), 2-3.

1037   Kawata, Ikuko. "'Timshel': Steinbeck's Message through the
        Hebrew Original," in *John Steinbeck: Asian
        Perspectives*. ed. Kiyoshi Nakayama, Scott Pugh, and
        Shigeharu Yano. Osaka: Osaka Kyoiku Tosho, 1992.
        (pp. 73-87)

1038   Kawata, Ikuko. "*To a God Unknown* in Steinbeck (2)," *Kobe
        Jyoshi Daigaku (Bungaku-Bu) Kiyo (Kobe Women's
        University, Faculty of Literature Bulletin)*, 13 (February
        1982), 47-78.

1039   Kazan, Elia. "Kazan: Maker of Legends," *Sunday Times
        Magazine*, May 22, 1988, 62-66.

1040   Kelley, James C. "Ed Ricketts, Ecologist," *Steinbeck
        Newsletter*, 9:1 (Fall 1995), 15-16. (Part III of Edward
        Flanders Ricketts: Four Perspectives)

1040A   Kelley, James. "The Geoecology of Steinbeck Country,"
        Steinbeck Newsletter, 10:1 (Spring 1997), 1-6.

1041   Kelley, James C. "John Steinbeck and Ed Ricketts:
        Understanding Life in the Great Tide Pool," in *Steinbeck
        and the Environment: Interdisciplinary Approaches*. ed.
        Susan Beegel, Susan Shillinglaw, and Wes Tiffney.
        Tuscaloosa: University of Alabama Press, 1997. (pp. 27-
        42)

1042   Kennedy, Dorothy, and X. J. Kennedy. "The
        Chrysanthemums," in Instructor's Manual, *Introduction
        to Fiction,* 3rd ed. New York: Little Brown, 1983. (pp.
        39-41)

1043   Kennedy, X. J., and Dorothy Kennedy. "The
        Chrysanthemums," See #1042.

1044   Kenyon, Karen. "Remembrance for John Steinbeck IV," *The Steinbeck Newsletter*, 4:2 (Summer 1991), 10.

1045   Kimball, Margaret J. "Steinbeck Archives: Pt. III," (Stanford's Steinbeck Collection — Recent Acquisitions) *The Steinbeck Newsletter*, 6:2 (Summer 1993), 10-11.

1046   Kinney, Arthur F. "*Tortilla Flat* Revisited," in *Modern Critical Views: John Steinbeck*. ed. Harold Bloom. New York: Chelsea House, 1987. (pp. 79-90) (reprint from *Steinbeck and the Arthurian Theme*. ed. Tetsumaro Hayashi. Steinbeck Monograph Series #5)

1047   Kleine, Ted. "Books: Steinbeck Country," *In These Times,* 19:10 (April 3, 1995), 32.

1048   Knapp, John, and Cheryl Weston. "Profiles of the Scientific Personality: John Steinbeck's 'The Snake,'" *Mosaic,* 22:1 (Winter 1989), 87-99.

1049   Kocela, Chris. "The Redefining of Self in the 'Gradual Flux': An Existentialist Reading of *In Dubious Battle*," *Steinbeck Newsletter,* 10:1 (Spring 1996), 1-6.

1050   Koenig, Jacqueline. "Steinbeck Festival XIV: A Report," *The Steinbeck Newsletter*, 6:2 (Summer 1993), 11.

1051   Krause, Sydney J. "*The Pearl* and 'Hadleyburg': From Desire to Renunciation," *Steinbeck's Literary Dimension: A Guide to Comparative Studies. Series II*. ed. Tetsumaro Hayashi. Metuchen, N. J.: Scarecrow Press, 1991. (pp. 154-171)

1052   Krause, Sydney J. "Steinbeck and Mark Twain," *Steinbeck's Literary Dimension: A Guide to Comparative Studies. Series II*. ed. Tetsumaro Hayashi. Metuchen, N. J.: Scarecrow Press, 1991. (pp. 144-153)

1053   Krim, Arthur. "Elmer Hader and *The Grapes of Wrath* Book
        Jacket," *The Steinbeck Newsletter*, 4:1 (Winter 1991),
        1-3.

1054   Krim, Arthur. "*Fruchte Des Zorns*: The Grapes of Wrath in
        Wartime Germany," *The Steinbeck Newsletter*, 7:2
        (Summer 1994), 1-4.

1055   Krim, Arthur. "John Steinbeck and Highway 66," *The
        Steinbeck Newsletter*, 4:2 (Summer 1991), 8-9.

1056   Krim, Arthur. "Steinbeck, Lorentz and Lange in 1941," *The
        Steinbeck Newsletter*, 6:2 (Summer 1993), 8-9.

1057   Kretzmer, Herbert. "London Looks at a Durable Giant," in
        Conversations with John Steinbeck. ed. Thomas Fensch.
        Jackson: University of Mississippi Press, 1988. (pp. 94-
        96) (reprint from *The New York World Telegram and
        Sun*, 25 January 1965)

1058   Kronenberger, Louis. "Hungry Caravan," in *Critical Essays
        on "The Grapes of Wrath."* ed. John Ditsky. Boston:
        G.K. Hall and Co., 1989. (pp. 23-25) (reprint from
        Nation, 148 (15 April 1939), 440-41)

1059   Kruger, Herbert B. "Letters: Ecological Steinbeck,"
        Alternatives, 19 (January/February 1993), 45.

1060   Kuhl, Art. "Mostly about *The Grapes of Wrath,"* in *Critical
        Essays on "The Grapes of Wrath."* ed. John Ditsky.
        Boston: G.K. Hall and Co., 1989. (pp. 36-42) (reprint
        from *Catholic World,* 150 (November 1939), 160-65)

1061   Kunitz, Stanley. "Wine Out of Those Grapes," in *Critical
        Essays on "The Grapes of Wrath."* ed. John Ditsky.
        Boston: G.K. Hall and Co., 1989. (pp. 35-36) (reprint
        from *Wilson Library Bulletin,* 14 (October 1939), 165)

1062   Kusuhashi, Osamu. "R. L. Stevenson's Light and Shadow in
        Steinbeck's Works," in *John Steinbeck: Asian*

Perspectives. ed. Kiyoshi Nakayama, Scott Pugh, and Shigeharu Yano. Osaka: Osaka Kyoiku Tosho, 1992. (pp. 155-172)

1063   Kusuhashi, Osamu. "R. L. Stevenson's Light and Shadow in Steinbeck's Works," *John Steinbeck Society of Japan Newsletter*, 13 (April 1990), 2-3.

1064   Lambert, Tim, and Matthew Lee. "UFW Renews Boycott" (*Grapes of Wrath* rally), *Catholic Worker* (June/July 1986), n.p.

1065   Lee, Matthew, and Tim Lambert. "UFW Renews Boycott," See #1064.

1066   Leithauser, Brad. "The Flare of Want," *(The Grapes of Wrath)*, *New Yorker*, 65 (August 21, 1989), 90-93.

1067   Leithauser, Brad. "Introduction," in Steinbeck's *The Grapes of Wrath*. London: Everyman's Library, Random House, 1993. (pp. v-xxvii)

1068   Levant, Howard. "The Fully Matured Art: *The Grapes of Wrath*," in *Modern Critical Views: John Steinbeck*. ed. Harold Bloom. New York: Chelsea House, 1987. (pp. 35-62) (reprint from *The Novels of John Steinbeck: A Critical Study*.) (Also available in Bloom, ed. *John Steinbeck's "The Grapes of Wrath."* New York: Chelsea House, 1988. (pp. 17-44))

1069   Levant, Howard. "John Steinbeck's *The Red Pony*: A Study in Dramatic Technique," in *The Short Novels of John Steinbeck*. ed. Jackson J. Benson. Durham: Duke University Press, 1990. (pp. 83-94)

1070   Levant, Howard. "The Narrative Structure of *The Short Reign of Pippin IV*," in *The Short Novels of John Steinbeck*. ed. Jackson J. Benson. Durham: Duke University Press, 1990. (pp. 257-269)

1071   Levant, Howard. "The Parable of *The Pearl*," in *Readings on
        John Steinbeck*. ed. Clarice Swisher. San Diego:
        Greenhaven Press, 1996. Literary Companion Series.
        (100-108) (reprinted from Levant's *The Novels of John
        Steinbeck: A Critical Study* (University of Missouri
        Press, 1974))

1072   Levy, Josephine. "Biological and Animal Imagery in John
        Steinbeck's Migrant Agricultural Novels: A Re-
        Evaluation," *Between the Species,* 10:1-2 (Winter 1994),
        66.

1073   Lewis, Clifford. "Art for Politics: John Steinbeck and FDR,"
        in *After "The Grapes of Wrath": Essays on John
        Steinbeck*. ed. Donald Coers, Robert DeMott, and Paul
        Ruffin. Athens: Ohio University Press, 1995. (pp. 23-
        39)

1074   Lewis, Clifford. "HUAC's Influence on *Viva Zapata!*"
        American Examiner (Fall 1982), 1-11.

1075   Lewis, Clifford. "Introduction to John Steinbeck," *Heath
        Anthology of American Literature II*. Lexington, Mass.:
        D. C. Heath, 1994. (pp. 1872-1873)

1076   Lewis, Clifford. "John Steinbeck's Alternative to Internment
        Camps: A Policy for the President, December 14, 1941,"
        Journal of the West (January 1995), 55-61.

1077   Lewis, Clifford. "Outfoxed: Writing *Viva Zapata!*" in
        Steinbeck's Posthumous Work: Essays in Criticism. ed.
        Tetsumaro Hayashi and Thomas J. Moore. Steinbeck
        Monograph Series, No. 14. Muncie, Ind.: Steinbeck
        Research Institute, Ball State University Press, 1989. (pp.
        22-34)

1078   Lewis, Clifford. "A Peculiar Air: *Viva Zapata!*" in
        *Rediscovering Steinbeck: Revisionist Views of His Art
        and Politics*. ed. Clifford Lewis and Carroll Britch.

Lewiston, N.Y.: Edwin Mellen Press, 1989. (pp. 218-237)

1079 Lewis, Clifford. "Steinbeck: The Artist as FDR Speechwriter," in *Rediscovering Steinbeck: Revisionist Views of His Art and Politics.* ed. Clifford Lewis and Carroll Britch. Lewiston, N.Y.: Edwin Mellen Press, 1989. (pp. 194-217)

1080 Lewis, Cliff, and Carroll Britch. "Artist as Narrator," in *Rediscovering Steinbeck: Revisionist Views of His Art, Politics and Intellect.* See #640.

1081 Lewis, Cliff, and Carroll Britch. "*Burning Bright*: The Shining of Joe Saul," in *The Short Novels of John Steinbeck.* ed. Jackson J. Benson. See #641.

1082 Lewis, Cliff, and Carroll Britch. "Cold War," in *Rediscovering Steinbeck: Revisionist Views of His Art, Politics and Intellect.* See #642.

1083 Lewis, Cliff, and Carroll Britch. "Exploring America," in *Rediscovering Steinbeck: Revisionist Views of His Art, Politics and Intellect.* See #643.

1084 Lewis, Cliff, and Carroll Britch. "The Fictive Process," in *Rediscovering Steinbeck: Revisionist Views of His Art, Politics and Intellect.* See #644.

1085 Lewis, Cliff, and Carroll Britch. "The Growth of the Family in *The Grapes of Wrath,*" in *Critical Essays on "The Grapes of Wrath."* See #645.

1086 Lewis, Cliff, and Carroll Britch. "Introduction," in *Rediscovering Steinbeck: Revisionist Views of His Art, Politics and Intellect.* See #646.

1087 Lewis, Cliff, and Carroll Britch. "Man and War," in *Rediscovering Steinbeck: Revisionist Views of His Art, Politics and Intellect.* See #647.

1088   Lewis, Cliff, and Carroll Britch. "Mythmaking," in
        Rediscovering Steinbeck: Revisionist Views of His Art,
        Politics and Intellect. See #648.

1089   Lewis, Cliff, and Carroll Britch. "Observations at Mid-
        Century," in *Rediscovering Steinbeck: Revisionist Views*
        of His Art, Politics and Intellect. See #649.

1090   Lewis, Cliff, and Carroll Britch. "Political Testaments," in
        Rediscovering Steinbeck: Revisionist Views of His Art,
        Politics and Intellect. See #650.

1091   Lewis, Cliff, and Carroll Britch. "Reinventing the Picaro," in
        Rediscovering Steinbeck: Revisionist Views of His Art,
        Politics and Intellect. See #651.

1092   Lewis, Cliff, and Carroll Britch. "Revelations," in
        Rediscovering Steinbeck: Revisionist Views of His Art,
        Politics and Intellect. See #652.

1093   Lewis, Cliff, and Carroll Britch. "Searching for Subjects," in
        Rediscovering Steinbeck: Revisionist Views of His Art,
        Politics and Intellect. See #653.

1094   Lewis, Cliff, and Carroll Britch. "Steinbeck's Shadow of an
        Indian," See #654.

1095   Lewis, Cliff, and Carroll Britch. "Sources and Process," in
        Rediscovering Steinbeck: Revisionist Views of His Art,
        Politics and Intellect. See #655.

1096   Lewis, Leon. "The Chrysanthemums," in *Masterplots II:*
        Short Story Series. Vol. I. ed. Frank Magill. Pasadena,
        Calif.: Salem Press, 1986. (pp. 392-395)

1097   Lewis, R. W. B. "John Steinbeck: A Successful Failure," in
        Readings on John Steinbeck. ed. Clarice Swisher. San
        Diego: Greenhaven Press, 1996. Literary Companion
        Series. (58-64) (excerpted from "John Steinbeck: The

Fitful Daemon" in Lewis's *The Young Rebel in American Literature*, ed. Carl Bode, 1959)

1098   Lewis, R.W.B. "The Picaresque Saint," in *"The Grapes of Wrath": A Collection of Critical Essays*. ed. Robert Con Davis. Englewood Cliffs, N. J.: Prentice Hall, 1982. (pp. 144-149) (reprint from *The Picaresque Saint* (New York: Lippincott, 1958))

1099   "Librarians Respond to the Banning of *The Grapes of Wrath*: Green County, Ohio and Kern County, California," *Steinbeck Newsletter*, 6:1 (Winter 1993), 10-11.

1100   Lisca, Peter. *"Cannery Row*: Escape into the Counterculture," in *The Short Novels of John Steinbeck*. ed. Jackson J. Benson. Durham: Duke University Press, 1990. (pp. 111-119)

1101   Lisca, Peter. "The Dynamics of Community in *The Grapes of Wrath*," in *Critical Essays on "The Grapes of Wrath."* ed. John Ditsky. Boston: G.K. Hall and Co., 1989. (pp. 87-97) (reprint from *From Irving to Steinbeck: Studies in American Literature in Honor of Henry R. Warfel*. (Gainesville: University of Florida Press, 1972) pp. 127-140)

1102   Lisca, Peter. "Escape and Commitment in John Steinbeck's Heroes," in *Readings on John Steinbeck*. ed. Clarice Swisher. San Diego: Greenhaven Press, 1996. Literary Companion Series. (50-57) (excerpted from "Escape and Commitment: Two Poles of the Steinbeck Hero" in Astro and Hayashi's *Steinbeck: The Man and His Work*. (Corvallis, Ore.: Oregon State University Press, 1971))

1103   Lisca, Peter. *"The Grapes of Wrath*: An Achievement of Genius," in *"The Grapes of Wrath": A Collection of Critical Essays*. ed. Robert Con Davis. Englewood Cliffs, N. J.: Prentice Hall, 1982. (pp. 48-62) (reprint from *John Steinbeck: Nature and Myth*)

1104   Lisca, Peter. "Patterns That Make Meaning in *Of Mice and Men*," in *Readings on John Steinbeck*. ed. Clarice Swisher. San Diego: Greenhaven Press, 1996. Literary Companion Series. (122-129) (excerpted from Lisca's *The Wide World of John Steinbeck*. (New Brunswick, N. J.: Rutgers, 1958, 1986))

1105   Liu, May Harn. "Characters from *The Pearl*," in *Dictionary of American Literary Characters*. ed. Benjamin Franklin V. New York: Facts on File, 1990.

1106   Liu, May Harn. "Characters from *Tortilla Flat*," in *Dictionary of American Literary Characters*. ed. Benjamin Franklin V. New York: Facts on File, 1990.

1107   Liu, May Harn. "Characters from *Wayward Bus*," in *Dictionary of American Literary Characters*. ed. Benjamin Franklin V. New York: Facts on File, 1990.

1108   "Living with Hard Times," *Esquire*, 99 (June 1983), 27-30. (reprint from June 1960 issue)

1109   Loftis, Anne. "Celestial Gatherings," *Steinbeck Newsletter*, 8:1-2 (Winter/Spring 1995), 5-8.

1110   Loftis, Anne. "A Historical Introduction to *Of Mice and Men*," in *The Short Novels of John Steinbeck*. ed. Jackson J. Benson. Durham: Duke University Press, 1990. (pp. 39-47)

1111   Loftis, Anne. "A Juvenile Classic Follows *The Grapes of Wrath*," *The Steinbeck Newsletter*, 6:2 (Summer 1993), 2-3.

1112   Loftis, Anne. "Literary California: John Steinbeck's 30's Odyssey," *The Californians: The Magazine of California*, 7:1 (January 1, 1989), 48.

1113   Loftis, Anne. "The Media and the Migrants: Steinbeck's
        Contemporary Impact," *The Steinbeck Newsletter*, 2:2
        (Summer 1989), 5, 9.

1114   Loftis, Anne. "The Origins and Impact of *The Grapes of
        Wrath*," *The Steinbeck Newsletter*, 1:2 (Spring 1988),
        4, 5.

1115   Loftis, Anne. "Steinbeck and the Federal Migrant Camps,"
        San Jose Studies, 16 (Winter 1990), 76-90.

1116   Lojek, Helen. "Ch. 5: *In Dubious Battle*," in *A New Study
        Guide to Steinbeck's Major Works, with Critical
        Explications*. ed. Tetsumaro Hayashi. Metuchen, N. J.:
        Scarecrow Press, 1993. (pp. 115-138)

1117   Lojek, Helen. "Jim Casy: Politico of the New Jerusalem," in
        "The Grapes of Wrath": Essays in Criticism. ed.
        Tetsumaro Hayashi. Steinbeck Essay Series, No. 3.
        Muncie, Ind.: Steinbeck Research Institute, Ball State
        University Press, 1990. (pp. 48-56) (reprint from
        Steinbeck Quarterly, XV:1-2 (Winter/Spring 1982), 30-
        37.

1118   Long, Elizabeth. "Ch. 4: Best-Selling Novels 1956-1968: The
        Varieties of Self-Fulfillment — the Goal Achieved," in
        The American Dream and the Popular Novel. Boston:
        Routledge and Kegan Paul, 1985. (pp. 94-98) (*Winter*)

1118A   Lore, Craig. "Abracadabra in Steinbeck's *East of Eden*,"
        Steinbeck Newsletter, 10:1 (Spring 1997), 10.

1119   Lucius, Ramona. "Let There Be Darkness: Reversed Symbols
        of Light and Dark in *The Grapes of Wrath*," *Pleiades*
        (Warrensburg, Mo.) 12:1 (Fall Winter 1991), 50-58.

1120   Lundy, Scrap. "The Unknown Heroes of Cannery Row,"
        Steinbeck Newsletter, 9:1 (Fall 1995), 29. (Part III of On
        Cannery Row: Four Perspectives)

1121   Lutwack, Leonard. "*The Grapes of Wrath* as Heroic Fiction,"
        in *"The Grapes of Wrath"*: *A Collection of Critical
        Essays*. ed. Robert Con Davis. Englewood Cliffs, N. J.:
        Prentice Hall, 1982. (pp. 63-75) (reprint from *Heroic
        Fiction: The Epic Tradition and American Novels of the
        Twentieth Century* (Carbondale, Ill.: Southern Illinois
        University Press, 1971))

1121A   Lynch, Audry L. "'They Knew Steinbeck': Louis
        Archdeacon Travis, Lake Havasu, Arizona," *Steinbeck
        Newsletter*, 10:1 (Spring 1997), 28-29.

1122   Lynch, Audry L. "Two Views of the Trip to the Sea of
        Cortez: Steinbeck vs. Sparky," *Humanities Forum*, 95,
        (n.d.) 3-11. (Mission College, Calif.)

1123   Lytle, Mark Hamilton. "Hollywood Realism and the
        Depression Era," *Book Forum*, 6 (1982), 117-184.

1124   Maeda, Johji. "Some Peculiarities of Character Presentation
        in *Of Mice and Men*," *Kyushu American Literature*, 31
        (1990), 11-22.

1125   Maggiano, Ronald. "Scratching the Mirror: John Steinbeck
        and the Cadbury Legend," *Steinbeck Newletter*, 5:1-2
        (Spring 1992), 1-5.

1126   Maguire, James H. "Western American Drama to 1960," in
        The Reference Guide to American Literature. 2nd ed. ed.
        D. L. Kirkpatrick. Chicago: St. James, 1987. (pp. 204-
        220)

1127   Maine, Barry. "Steinbeck's Debt to Dos Passos," *Steinbeck
        Quarterly*, XXIII:1-2 (Winter/Spring 1990), 17-26.

1128   Makino, Keiko. "*In Dubious Battle* vs. *The Grapes of Wrath*:
        Two Battles," *John Steinbeck Society of Japan
        Newsletter*, 14 (April 1991), 3-4.

1129   Mandia, Patricia M. "Chaos, Evil, and the Dredger Subplot in
        Steinbeck's 'Johnny Bear,'" in *Steinbeck's Short Stories
        in "The Long Valley": Essays in Criticism*. ed.
        Tetsumaro Hayashi. Steinbeck Monograph Series, No.
        15. Muncie, Ind.: Steinbeck Research Institute, Ball State
        University Press, 1991. (pp. 54-62) (translated into
        Japanese in *Steinbeck Kenkyu: Atarashii Tanpen
        Shosetsushu (Steinbeck Studies: New Essays on Short
        Stories)*. Osaka, Japan: Osaka Educational Publishing
        Co. 1995. (pp. 263-282))

1130   Mandia, Patricia M. "Sexism, Racism or Irony? Steinbeck's
        'The Murder,'" in *Steinbeck's Short Stories in "The
        Long Valley": Essays in Criticism*. ed. Tetsumaro
        Hayashi. Steinbeck Monograph Series, No. 15. Muncie,
        Ind.: Steinbeck Research Institute, Ball State University
        Press, 1991. (pp. 62-69) (translated into Japanese in
        *Steinbeck Kenkyu: Atarashii Tanpen Shosetsushu
        (Steinbeck Studies: New Essays on Short Stories)*. Osaka,
        Japan: Osaka Educational Publishing Co. 1995. (pp. 283-
        298))

1131   Mann, Susan Garland. "John Steinbeck's *The Pastures of
        Heaven*," in *The Short Story Cycle: A Genre Companion
        and Reference Guide*. New York: Greenwood Press,
        1989. (pp. 93-106, 204)

1132   March, R. A. "Ed Ricketts and John Steinbeck's Doc,"
        Oceans, 19 (August 1986), 22-25.

1133   March, Ray A. "Salinas' Son: Nearly 20 Years after His
        Death, Salinas Takes Another Look at Steinbeck," in
        "John Steinbeck: A Collector's Edition," *Monterey Life:
        The Magazine of California's Spectacular Central Coast*,
        7 (July 1987), 49-50.

1134   Marks, Lawrence. "The Bitter Harvest," *The Observer
        Magazine* (January 1, 1989), 42.

1135   Marsden, John L. "California Dreamin': The Significance of
        'A Couple Acres' in Steinbeck's *Of Mice and Men*,"
        Western American Literature, 29:4 (Winter 1995), 291-
        297.

1136   Marshall, Kathryn. "A Quality of Light," *American Way*
        (October 1, 1988), 70, 72-73, 76, 105-106, 108-109.

1137   Martin, Stoddard. "John Steinbeck," chapter 3 in *California
        Writers*. New York: St. Martin's Press, 1983. (pp. 67-
        122)

1138   Matsuo, Yumiko. "The World of John Steinbeck: A Human
        Being and His Nature in *East of Eden*," *Minerva*,
        (English Literature Society, Shinna Women's University,
        7 (January 24, 1983), 76-92.

1139   Mazzeno, Lawrence W. "John Steinbeck," in *Popular World
        Fiction: 1900-Present.* Vol. 4. ed. Walter Beacham and
        Suzanne Niemeyer. Washington, D. C. : Beacham
        Publishing, 1987. (pp. 1465-1475) (discusses *The
        Grapes of Wrath, In Dubious Battle* and *Of Mice and
        Men)*

1140   McCardle, Peggy, and Edward J. Haupt. "Case Order in
        Sentences: Newer and More Varied," See #919.

1141   McCarthy, Kevin M. "The Name Is the Game," in *The
        Linguistic Connection.* ed. Jean Casagrande. Lanham,
        Md.: University Press of America, 1983. (pp. 161-170)

1142   McCosker, John E. "Ed Ricketts: A Role Model for Marine
        Biologists," *Steinbeck Newsletter*, 9:1 (Fall 1995), 14-16.
        (Part II of Edward Flanders Ricketts: Four Perspectives)

1143   McEntyre, Marilyn Chandler. "Natural Wisdom: Steinbeck's
        Men of Nature as Prophets and Peacemakers," in
        *Steinbeck and the Environment: Interdisciplinary
        Approaches.* ed. Susan Beegel, Susan Shillinglaw, and

Wes Tiffney. Tuscaloosa: Alabama University Press, 1997. (pp. 113-124)

1144   McGinty, Brian. "American Landmarks: Steinbeck Country," *American History Illustrated*, 24 (September/October 1989), 18, 72.

1145   McKay, Nellie Y. "Happy (?)-Wife-Motherdom: The Portrayal of Ma Joad in John Steinbeck's *The Grapes of Wrath,*" in *New Essays on "The Grapes of Wrath."* ed. David Wyatt. Cambridge: Cambridge University Press, 1990. (pp. 47-69)

1146   McKibben, Carol. "Monterey's Cannery Women," *Steinbeck Newsletter*, 9:1 (Fall 1995), 26-29. (Part II of On *Cannery Row*: Four Perspectives)

1147   Mendelson, Lee. "'*America and Americans*': Opening Address of the 1994 Steinbeck Festival, Salinas," *Steinbeck Newletter,* 8:1-2 (Winter/Spring 1995), 13-15.

1148   Mercer, Charles. "Interview at a Barbeque: Writing Gets Harder as You Grow Older, Says Steinbeck," in *Conversations with John Steinbeck.* ed. Thomas Fensch. Jackson: University of Mississippi Press, 1988. (pp. 55-58) (reprint from *The Oakland Tribune*, 18 October 1953)

1149   Metzger, Charles R. "John Steinbeck's Paisano Knights," in *Readings on John Steinbeck.* ed. Clarice Swisher. San Diego: Greenhaven Press, 1996. Literary Companion Series. (65-72) (excerpted from "Steinbeck's Mexican-Americans" in Astro and Hayashi's *Steinbeck: The Man and His Work.* (Corvallis, Ore.: Oregon State University Press, 1971))

1150   Metzger, Charles. "Steinbeck's Version of the Pastoral," in *The Short Novels of John Steinbeck.* ed. Jackson J. Benson. Durham: Duke University Press, 1990. (pp. 185-195)

1151   Meyer, Michael J. "Ch. 2: *Cannery Row*," in *A New Study
        Guide to Steinbeck's Major Works, with Critical
        Explications*. ed. Tetsumaro Hayashi. Metuchen, N. J.:
        Scarecrow Press, 1993. (pp. 34-65)

1152   Meyer, Michael J. "Citizen Cain: Ethan Hawley's Double
        Identity in *The Winter of Our Discontent*," in *After "The
        Grapes of Wrath": Essays on John Steinbeck in Honor of
        Tetsumaro Hayashi*. ed. Donald Coers, Robert DeMott,
        and Paul Ruffin. Athens: Ohio University Press, 1995.
        (pp. 197-213)

1153   Meyer, Michael J. "Fallen Adam: Another Look at
        Steinbeck's 'The Snake,'" in *The Steinbeck Question:
        New Essays in Criticism*. ed. Donald Noble. Troy, N.Y.:
        Whitston Publishing Co., 1993. (pp. 99-107)

1154   Meyer, Michael J. "Finding a New Jerusalem: The Edenic
        Myth in John Steinbeck," in *Literature and the Bible*. ed.
        David Bevan. Amsterdam/Atlanta: Rodopi, 1993. (pp.
        95-117)

1155   Meyer, Michael J. "'The Illusion of Eden': Efficacious
        Commitment and Sacrifice in 'The Raid,'" in *Steinbeck's
        Short Stories in "The Long Valley": Essays in Criticism*.
        ed. Tetsumaro Hayashi. Steinbeck Monograph Series,
        No. 15. Muncie, Ind.: Steinbeck Research Institute, Ball
        State University Press, 1991. (pp. 38- 44) (reprinted in
        Japanese in *Steinbeku Kenkyu: Atarashii Tanpen
        Shosetsushu (Steinbeck Studies: New Essays on Short
        Stories)*. trans. Kyoko Ariki, Ikuko Kawata, and Wakako
        Kakegawa. Osaka: Osaka Educational Publishing, 1995.
        (pp. 225-240)

1156   Meyer, Michael J. "Precious Bane: Mining the Fool's Gold of
        The Pearl," in *The Short Novels of John Steinbeck*. ed.
        Jackson J. Benson. Durham: Duke University Press,
        1990. (pp. 161-172)

1157   Meyer, Michael J. "Pure and Corrupt: Agency and
        Communion in the Edenic Garden of 'The White
        Quail,'" in *Steinbeck's Short Stories* in *"The Long
        Valley": Essays in Criticism.* ed. Tetsumaro Hayashi.
        Steinbeck Monograph Series, No. 15. Muncie, Ind.:
        Steinbeck Research Institute, Ball State University Press,
        1991. (pp. 10-17) (reprinted in Japanese in *Steinbeku
        Kenkyu: Atarashii Tanpen Shosetsushu. (Steinbeck
        Studies: New Essays on Short Stories).* trans. Kyoko
        Ariki, Ikuko Kawata, and Wakako Kakegawa. Osaka:
        Osaka Educational Publishing, 1995. (pp. 157-176)

1158   Meyer, Michael J. "The Search for King Arthur: John
        Steinbeck's Continuing Preoccupation with the Grail
        Legend," in *Modern Myth.* ed. David Bevan.
        Amsterdam/Atlanta: Rodopi, 1993. (pp. 7-22)

1159   Meyer, Michael J. "'Symbols for The Wordlessness":
        Steinbeck's Silent Message in 'Breakfast,'" in
        *Steinbeck's Short Stories in "The Long Valley": Essays
        in Criticism.* ed. Tetsumaro Hayashi. Steinbeck
        Monograph Series, No. 15. Muncie, Ind.: Steinbeck
        Research Institute, Ball State University Press, 1991. (pp.
        32-37) (reprinted in Japanese in *Steinbeku Kenkyu:
        Atarashii Tanpen Shosetsushu (Steinbeck Studies: New
        Essays on Short Stories).* trans. Kyoko Ariki, Ikuko
        Kawata, and Wakako Kakegawa. Osaka: Osaka
        Educational Publishing, 1995. (pp. 211-224)

1160   Meyer, Michael J. "Transforming Good to Evil: The Image
        of Iscariot in *The Winter of Our Discontent,*" *Steinbeck
        Quarterly,* XXVI:3-4 (Summer/Fall 1993), 101-111.

1161   Meyer, Michael J. "Ch. 10: *The Winter of Our Discontent,*"
        in *A New Study Guide to Steinbeck's Major Works, with
        Critical Explications.* ed. Tetsumaro Hayashi. Metuchen,
        N. J.: Scarecrow Press, 1993. (pp. 240-273)

1162   Mieno, Kenichi. "On the Concept of the 'Individual' vs.
        'Group' or 'Collective Subjectivity': An Essay on *In*

Dubious Battle," *John Steinbeck Society of Japan Newsletter*, 9 (May 1986), 2.

1163   Minor, Barbara. "Instructional Resources: Grapevine: An Excursion into Steinbeck Country," *Tech Trends*, 36 (1991), 53.

1164   Mitchell, Marilyn L. "Steinbeck's Strong Women: Feminine Identity in the Short Stories," in *Modern Critical Views: John Steinbeck*. ed. Harold Bloom. New York: Chelsea House, 1987. (pp. 91-101) (reprint from *Southwest Review*, 61:3 (Summer 1976))

1165   Mitgang, Herbert. "Annals of Government: Policing America's Writers," *New Yorker*, 63 (October 5, 1987), 47-48, 51, 54-56, 58-60, 62-64, 69-70, 72, 74, 76-90.

1166   Miyagawa, Hiroyuki. "On Steinbeck's *Tortilla Flat*," *Chu-Shikoku Studies in American Literature*, 20 (1984), 88-100.

1167   Momose, Fumio. "Forum: *The Grapes of Wrath*: New Perspectives," *John Steinbeck Society of Japan Newsletter*, 13 (April 1990), 4.

1168   Momose, Fumio. "Christian Humanism in *The Grapes of Wrath*," *John Steinbeck Society of Japan Newsletter*, 10 (April 1988), 3.

1169   Momose, Fumio. "Special Lecture: Ohashi, Kenzaburo. 'A Sensation of Liberation after World War II in Japan and John Steinbeck,'" *John Steinbeck Society of Japan Newsletter*, 14 (April 1991), 5.

1170   "Monterey: In Search of Cannery Row," *Soldiers,* 46:10 (October 1, 1991), 40.

1171   "*The Moon is Down*" in *Work and the Work Ethic in American Drama*, 1920-1970 by A. Greenfield.

Columbia, Mo.: University ofMissouri Press, 1982. (pp. 88-93)

1172   Moore, Harry Thornton. "John Steinbeck's Mature Style in *The Red Pony*," in *Readings on John Steinbeck*. ed. Clarice Swisher. San Diego: Greenhaven Press, 1996. Literary Companion Series. (77-79) (excerpted from Moore's *The Novels of John Steinbeck: A First Critical Study*. (Normandie House, 1959))

1173   Moorman, Charles. "Yet Some Men Say . . . That Kynge Arthure Ys Nat Ded" in *The Arthurian Tradition: Essays in Convergence*. ed. Mary Flowers Braswell and John Bugge. Tuscaloosa: University of Alabama Press, 1988. (pp. 188-199)

1174   Morita, Shoji. *"Tortilla Flat," John Steinbeck Society of Japan Newsletter*, 8 (May 1985), 4-5.

1175   Morris, Harry. "The Allegory of *The Pearl*," in *Readings on John Steinbeck*. ed. Clarice Swisher. San Diego: Greenhaven Press, 1996. Literary Companion Series. (93-99) (excerpted from Morris's *"The Pearl*: Realism and Allegory," *English Journal*, LII (October 1963), 487-495, 503)

1176   Morsberger, Robert E. *"Cannery Row* Revisited," *Steinbeck Quarterly*, XVI:3-4 (Summer/Fall 1983), 89-95.

1177   Morsberger, Robert E. "Moscow Journal: The Soviet Steinbeck Festival of 1989," *The Texas Review*, 133 (Fall/Winter 1992), 46-70.

1178   Morsberger, Robert. *"Pipe Dream* or Not So Sweet Thursday," *Steinbeck Quarterly*, XXI:3-4 (Summer/Fall 1988), 85-96.

1179   Morsberger, Robert E. "Play It Again, Lennie and George," *Steinbeck Quarterly*, XV:3-4 (Summer/Fall 1982), 123-126.

1180   Morsberger, Robert E. "Steinbeck and the Stage," in *The Short Novels of John Steinbeck*. ed. Jackson J. Benson. Durham, N.C.: Duke University Press, 1990. (pp. 271-293)

1181   Morsberger, Robert E. "The Steinbeck Quarterly: In Honor of the Twenty-Fifth Anniversary," *Steinbeck Quarterly*, XXV:1-2 (Winter/Spring 1992), 12-14.

1182   Morsberger, Robert E. "Steinbeck under the Sea at the Earth's Core," in *Steinbeck and the Environment: Interdisciplinary Approaches*. ed. Susan Beegel, Susan Shillinglaw, and Wes Tiffney. Tuscaloosa: University of Alabama Press, 1997. (pp. 266-277)

1183   Morsberger, Robert E. "Steinbeck's War," in *The Steinbeck Question: New Essays in Criticism*. ed. Donald Noble. Troy, N.Y.: Whitston Publishing Co., 1993. (pp. 183-212)

1184   Morsberger, Robert E. "Tell Again, George," in *John Steinbeck: The Years of Greatness*. ed. Tetsumaro Hayashi. Tuscaloosa: University of Alabama Press, 1994. (pp. 111-131)

1185   Morsberger, Robert E. "Zapata: The Man, the Myth and the Mexican Revolution," in *Zapata*. Covelo, Calif.: Yolla Bolly Press, 1992.

1186   Motley, Warren. "From Patriarchy to Matriarchy: Ma Joad's Role in *The Grapes of Wrath*," *American Literature*, 54:3 (October 1982), 397-412.

1187   Mulcahy, Judith. "The Journalist as Serious Writer: Steinbeck in the 1950's," in *Rediscovering Steinbeck: Revisionist Views of His Art, Politics and Intellect*. ed. Cliff Lewis and Carroll Britch. Lewiston, N.Y.: Edward Mellen Press, 1989. (pp. 240-257)

1188 Mulder, Steven. "The Reader's Story: *East of Eden* as Postmodernist Metafiction," *Steinbeck Quarterly,* XXV:3-4 (Summer/Fall 1992), 109-118.

1189 Murao, Atsuko. "Four Handicapped Characters in Steinbeck's *Of Mice and Men,*" *Steinbeck Studies,* 19 (May 1996), 6.

1190 Murguia, Edward. "The Sociology of Steinbeck's *Tortilla Flat*: A Study of Class-Based Rationalizations," in *Mexico and the United States: Intercultural Relations in the Humanities*. ed. Juanita Luna Lawhn, et al. (San Antonio, Texas: San Antonio College, 1984), 49-56.

1191 Murphy, Cullen. "Dr. Bennett's Two-Foot Shelf (and Mine)," *Atlantic*, 254 (October 1984), 26, 28-29. (Reports that Steinbeck's *The Grapes of Wrath* is included in a list of ten important works in the humanities that every student in the United States might reasonably be expected to have studied before he or she graduates from high school, the list from a survey by the National Endowment for the Humanities chaired by William J. Bennett.)

1192 Mutter, John. "The First Amendment: *The Grapes of Wrath* Survives Banning Attempt in Vermont Town," *Publishers Weekly* (December 11, 1981), 9.

1193 Nakachi, Akira. "*To a God Unknown*, Reconsidered," *John Steinbeck Society of Japan Newsletter*, 9 (May 1986), 2-3.

1194 Nakachi, Kozen. "*East of Eden*: The Theme and Structure," *Ryudai Review of Language of Literature,* 30 (December 1985), 129-55.

1195 Nakachi, Kozen. "Steinbeck and the West: Beyond the Disillusionment," in *John Steinbeck: Asian Perspectives*. ed. Kiyoshi Nakayama, Scott Pugh, and Shigeharu Yano. Osaka: Osaka Kyoiku Tosho, 1992. (pp. 173-182)

1196   Nakachi, Kozen. "Steinbeck Study — 1930s and *The Grapes of Wrath*," *Ryudai Review of Language of Literature*, 26 (December 1981), 29-53.

1197   Nakachi, Kozen. "The Theme and Structure of *East of Eden*,"*John Steinbeck Society of Japan Newsletter*, 10 (April 1987), 2-3.

1198   Nakamura, Maso. "On John Steinbeck's 'The Chrysanthemums,'" *Kyushu American Literature*, 24 (July 28, 1983), 87-88.

1199   Nakane, Sadayuki. "Steinbeck's 'The Chrysanthemums' — A Study in Language and Literature," *Fukui University, Faculty of Education Bulletin: Humanities Foreign Language and Literature*, 37 (1987), 1-22.

1200   Nakashima, Saikichi. "On Some Novelistic Inevitabilities in *The Red Pony*," *John Steinbeck Society of Japan Newsletter*, 11 (May 1988), 1-2.

1201   Nakashima, Saikichi. "*The Pearl*," *John Steinbeck Society of Japan Newsletter*, 12 (April 1989), 6.

1202   Nakashima, Saikichi. "Steinbeck and Mexico," *John Steinbeck Society of Japan Newsletter*, 12 (April 1989), 5.

1203   Nakata, Yuji. "Thoreauvian Characters in Steinbeck's Fiction," in *John Steinbeck: Asian Perspectives*. ed. Kiyoshi Nakayama, Scott Pugh, and Shigeharu Yano. Osaka: Osaka Kyoiku Tosho, 1992. (pp. 183-192) (reprinted from *English Literature Studies* (Konan Gakuin Women's University), 27 (March 1991), 91-101)

1204   Nakata, Yuji. "Thoreauvian Characters in Steinbeck's Fiction," *Konan Women's University Studies in English Literature Bulletin*, 8 (January 10, 1991), 11-21.

1205 Nakayama, Kiyoshi. "The Artistic Design of *The Grapes of Wrath*: Five Layers of Symbolism," *Studies and Essays, Kansai University*, 31:3-4 (March 1982), 117-125.

1206 Nakayama, Kiyoshi. "Carol Henning Died," *John Steinbeck Society of Japan Newsletter*, 6 (May 1983), 9.

1207 Nakayama, Kiyoshi. *"The Grapes* Transplanted to Japan," *San Jose Studies, The Grapes of Wrath, A Special Issue*, 16:1 (Winter 1990), 91-97.

1208 Nakayama, Kiyoshi. *"In Dubious Battle*: Biographical Notes," *John Steinbeck Society of Japan Newsletter*, 6 (May 1983), 8.

1209 Nakayama, Kiyoshi. "John Steinbeck: A Wayward Journey," *John Steinbeck Society of Japan Newsletter*, 6 (May 1983), 9.

1210 Nakayama, Kiyoshi. "John Steinbeck and Yasumari Kawabata," in *John Steinbeck: From Salinas to the World: Proceedings of the Second International Steinbeck Congress* (1984). ed. Shigeharo Yano, Tetsumaro Hayashi, Richard F. Peterson, and Yasuo Hashiguchi. Tokyo, Japan: Gaku Shobo Press, 1986. (pp. 68-82)

1211 Nakayama, Kiyoshi. "Michael Hemp," *John Steinbeck Society of Japan Newsletter*, 11 (April 1988), 9.

1212 Nakayama, Kiyoshi. "Panel Discussion: *In Dubious Battle*," *John Steinbeck Society of Japan Newsletter*, 6 (May 1983), 2.

1213 Nakayama, Kiyoshi. "Panel Discussion II: The Art of Steinbeck and Its Form," *John Steinbeck Society of Japan Newsletter*, 10 (April 1987), 5.

1214 Nakayama, Kiyoshi. *"The Pearl* in *The Sea of Cortez*: Steinbeck's Use of Environment," in *Steinbeck and the*

Environment: Interdisciplinary Approaches. ed. Susan
Beegel, Susan Shillinglaw, and Wes Tiffney. Tuscaloosa:
Alabama University Press, 1997. (pp. 194-208)

1215   Nakayama, Kiyoshi. "Preface," in *Uncollected Stories of
John Steinbeck.* ed. Kiyoshi Nakayama. Tokyo:
Nan'undo, 1986. (pp. iii-v)

1216   Nakayama, Kiyoshi. "Recent Publications in Japan," *The
Steinbeck Newsletter,* 6:2 (Summer 1993), 12.

1217   Nakayama, Kiyoshi. "Steinbeck Criticism in Japan: 1980-
81," *Steinbeck Quarterly,* XVI:3-4 (Summer/Fall 1983),
96-104.

1218   Nakayama, Kiyoshi. "Steinbeck Criticism in Japan: 1982-
1983," *Steinbeck Quarterly,* XIX:1-2 (Winter/Spring
1986), 12-19.

1219   Nakayama, Kiyoshi. "Steinbeck Criticism in Japan: 1984-
1985," *Steinbeck Quarterly,* XX:3-4 (Summer/Fall
1987), 89-96.

1220   Nakayama, Kiyoshi. "Steinbeck Criticism in Japan: 1986 -
1987," *Steinbeck Quarterly,* XXII:3-4 (Summer/Fall
1989), 83-91.

1221   Nakayama, Kiyoshi. "Steinbeck in Japan: The International
Writer," in "John Steinbeck: A Collector's Edition,"
*Monterey Life: The Magazine of California's
Spectacular Central Coast,* 7 (July 1987), 55-56, 60-61.

1222   Nakayama, Kiyoshi. "Steinbeck's Bitter/Sweet Holidays in
Japan," in *Essays on Collecting John Steinbeck Books,*
Preston Beyer, comp. (Bradenton, Fla. : Opuscula Press,
1989), 15-17.

1223   Nakayama, Kiyoshi. "Steinbeck's Bitter/Sweet Holidays in
Japan," *Fine Literary Property Catalogue,* 35 (February
1986), 3-4.

1224   Nakayama, Kiyoshi. "Steinbeck's Creative Development of
        an Ending: *East of Eden*," in *John Steinbeck: Asian
        Perspectives*. ed. Kiyoshi Nakayama, Scott Pugh, and
        Shigeharu Yano. Osaka: Osaka Kyoiku Tosho, 1992.
        (pp. 193-208) (reprinted from *Kansai University English
        Literature Bulletin*, 30 (December 20, 1990), 73-84)

1225   Nakayama, Kiyoshi. "Steinbeck's Letters to Wanda Van
        Brunt Sold at $47,575," *John Steinbeck Society of Japan
        Newsletter*, 9 (May 1986), 6.

1226   Nakayama, Kiyoshi. "Steinbeck's Love Poems," *John
        Steinbeck Society of Japan Newsletter*, 7 (May 1984), 13.

1227   Nakayama, Kiyoshi. "The Third International Steinbeck
        Conference: A Reminiscence," *John Steinbeck Society of
        Japan Newsletter*, 14 (April 1991), 1-2.

1228   Nakayama, Kiyoshi. "The Video Report of the Second
        International Steinbeck Congress at Salinas," *John
        Steinbeck Society of Japan Newsletter*, 9 (May 1986), 3.

1229   Nakayama, Kiyoshi. "'What Happened in Between':
        Steinbeck's *Sweet Thursday* as a Sequel to *Cannery
        Row*," *Steinbeck Newsletter,* 10:1 (Spring 1996), 27-29.

1230   "The New Ford," *The UNESCO Courier*, 43 (October
        1990), 20.

1231   *New York Times*. "Men, Mice and Mr. Steinbeck," in
        Conversations with John Steinbeck. ed. Thomas Fensch.
        Jackson: University of Mississippi Press, 1988. (pp. 8-
        10) (reprint from *New York Times*, 5 December 1937)

1232   *New York World Telegram*. "More a Mouse Than a Man,
        Steinbeck Faces Reporters," in *Conversations with John
        Steinbeck*. ed. Thomas Fensch. Jackson: University of
        Mississippi Press, 1988. (pp. 6-7) (reprint from *New
        York World Telegram*, Friday, 23 April 1937)

1233   Newman, Wayne. "John Steinbeck: A Biographical Sketch
        and Brief Analysis," *Journal of Kyiritsu Women's Junior
        College*, 35 (February 1992), 51-59.

1234   Nichols, Lewis. "Talk with John Steinbeck," in
        Conversations with John Steinbeck. ed. Thomas Fensch.
        Jackson: University of Mississippi Press, 1988. (pp. 52-
        54) (reprint from *The New York Times Book Review*, 28
        September 1952)

1235   Nishimura, Chitoshi. "Consciousness of Sin," *Steinbeck
        Studies,* 19 (May 1996), 11-12. (*The Pastures of
        Heaven*)

1236   Noble, Donald R. "*Cannery Row,*" in *Cyclopaedia of Literary
        Characters II*. Vol. I. ed. Frank Magill. Pasadena, Calif.:
        Salem Press, 1990. (pp. 231-233)

1237   Noble, Donald R. "*Tortilla Flat,*" in *Cyclopaedia of Literary
        Characters II*. Vol. IV. ed. Frank Magill. Pasadena,
        Calif.: Salem Press, 1990. (pp. 1595-1596)

1238   "Notes: Forthcoming in May: *Viva Zapata!* Penguin,"
        Publishers' Weekly, April 19, 1993, 57.

1239   "*Of Mice and Men*, and Men and Women Who Would Ban
        It," *Brochure, People for the American Way*, 1984.

1240   Ohnishi, Katsue. "'Why Must Lennie Be Killed?'" *Kyushu
        American Literature* (May 22, 1981), 85-87.

1241   Ohta, Hideo. "The Tree of Life in *East of Eden*," *Journal of
        the Faculty of Letters, Aichi Prefectural University*, 33
        (December 1983), 31-37.

1242   Okoshi, Takashi. "Timshel as a Symbol of American
        Identity: The Search of Self in *East of Eden*," *John
        Steinbeck Society of Japan Newsletter*, 8 (May 1985),
        2-3.

1243   Orr, Kevin Hunter. "Characters from *The Grapes of Wrath*,"
        in *Dictionary of American Literary Characters*. ed.
        Benjamin Franklin V. New York: Facts on File, 1990.

1244   Orr, Kevin Hunter. "Characters from *Of Mice and Men*," in
        Dictionary of American Literary Characters. ed.
        Benjamin Franklin V. New York: Facts on File, 1990.

1245   Otomo, Yoshiro. "Cathy in *East of Eden*," *Miyagi University
        of Education, Department of Foreign Languages
        Bulletin*, 9 (March 18, 1993), 1-13.

1246   Orey, Cal. "*Travels with Charley* (and Omar, Bruga, Tillie,
        Toby Dog, Judy, Willie and Angel)," *Dog World*
        (December 1987), 22, 54-60.

1247   Owens, Louis. "'Bottom and Upland': The Balanced Man in
        Steinbeck's 'The Harness,'" in *Steinbeck's Short Stories
        in "The Long Valley": Essays in Criticism*. ed.
        Tetsumaro Hayashi. Steinbeck Monograph Series, No.
        15. Muncie, Ind.: Steinbeck Research Institute, Ball State
        University Press, 1991. (pp. 44-48) (translated into
        Japanese in *Steinbeck Kenkyu: Atarashii Tanpen
        Shosetsushu (Steinbeck Studies: New Essays on Short
        Stories)*. Osaka, Japan: Osaka Educational Publishing
        Co. 1995. (pp. 241-250))

1248   Owens, Louis D. "Camelot, East of Eden: John Steinbeck's
        Tortilla Flat," *Perspective* 1 (Spring 1984), 1-5. (re-
        printed in condensed form from the same title in *Arizona
        Quarterly*, 38 (Autumn 1982), 203-16)

1249   Owens, Louis. "Critics and Common Denominators:
        Steinbeck's *Sweet Thursday*," in *The Short Novels of
        John Steinbeck*. ed. Jackson J. Benson. Durham: Duke
        University Press, 1990. (pp. 195-203)

1250   Owens, Louis. "The Culpable Joads: Desentimentalizing *The
        Grapes of Wrath*," in *Critical Essays on "The Grapes of*

Wrath." ed. John Ditsky. Boston: G.K. Hall and Co., 1989. (pp. 108-116)

1251   Owens, Louis. "Ch. 3: *East of Eden,*" in *A New Study Guide to Steinbeck's Major Works, with Critical Explications.* ed. Tetsumaro Hayashi. Metuchen, N. J.: Scarecrow Press, 1993. (pp. 66-89)

1252   Owens, Louis. "A Garden of My Land: Landscape and Dreamscape in John Steinbeck's Fiction," *Steinbeck Quarterly,* XXIII:3-4 (Summer/Fall 1990), 78-88.

1253   Owens, Louis. *"Grapes* Goes Marching On," *Resources For American Literary Study,* 18:2 (1992), 165-170.

1254   Owens, Louis. "Ch. 4: *The Grapes of Wrath,*" in *A New Study Guide to Steinbeck's Major Works, with Critical Explications.* ed. Tetsumaro Hayashi. Metuchen, N. J.: Scarecrow Press, 1993. (pp. 90-114)

1255   Owens, Louis. *"The Grapes of Wrath*: Looking Back," *USA Today,* 117 (May 1989), 92-93.

1256   Owens, Louis. "John Steinbeck," in *Book of Days.* Ann Arbor, Mich.: Pierian Press, 1987. (pp. 91-93)

1257   Owens, Louis. "John Steinbeck," in *Concise Dictionary of American Literary Biography: The Age of Maturity, 1929-1941.* Detroit, Mich.: Gale Research Inc., 1987. (pp. 242-249) Updated entry in 1989 edition of same title (pp. 280-309)

1258   Owens, Louis. "John Steinbeck's *The Pastures of Heaven*: Illusions of Eden," *Arizona Quarterly,* 41:3 (1985), 197-214.

1259   Owens, Louis. "'The Little Bit of a Story': Steinbeck's 'The Vigilante,'" in *Steinbeck's Short Stories in "The Long Valley": Essays in Criticism.* ed. Tetsumaro Hayashi. Steinbeck Monograph Series, No. 15. Muncie, Ind.:

Steinbeck Research Institute, Ball State University Press, 1991. (pp. 49-53) (translated into Japanese in *Steinbeck Kenkyu: Atarashii Tanpen Shosetsushu (Steinbeck Studies: New Essays on Short Stories).* Osaka, Japan: Osaka Educational Publishing Co. 1995. (pp. 252-262))

1260   Owens, Louis. "*Of Mice and Men*: The Dream of Commitment," in *Modern Critical Views: John Steinbeck.* ed. Harold Bloom. New York: Chelsea House, 1987. (pp. 145-149) (reprint from *John Steinbeck's Re-Vision of America*)

1261   Owens, Louis. "The Mirror and The Vamp: Invention, Reflection and Bad, Bad Cathy Trask in *East of Eden*," in *Writing the American Classics.* ed. James Barbour and Tom Quirk. Chapel Hill: University of North Carolina, 1990. (pp. 235-257)

1262   Owens, Louis. "Patterns of Reality, Barrels of Worms: From *Western Flyer* to *Rocinante* in Steinbeck's Nonfiction," in *The Steinbeck Question: New Essays in Criticism.* ed. Donald Noble. Troy, N.Y.: Whitston Publishing Co., 1993. (pp. 171-182)

1263   Owens, Louis. "Reconsideration: 'Granpa Killed Indians, Pa Killed Snakes': Steinbeck and the American Indian," MELUS, 15:2 (Summer 1988), 85-92.

1264   Owens, Louis. "'The Road away from Her': Writers and Route 66," *Steinbeck Newsletter*, 1:1 (Fall 1987), 1,2.

1265   Owens, Louis. "Steinbeck's 'Deep Dissembler': *The Short Reign of Pippin IV*," in *The Short Novels of John Steinbeck.* ed. Jackson J. Benson. Durham: Duke University Press, 1990. (pp. 249-257)

1266   Owens, Louis D. "Steinbeck's 'The Murder': Illusions of Chivalry," *Steinbeck Quarterly,* XVII:1-2 (Winter/Spring 1984), 10-14.

1267   Owens, Louis D. "The Story of a Writing: Narrative Structure
        in *East of Eden*," in *Rediscovering Steinbeck: Revisionist
        Views of His Art, Politics and Intellect.* ed. Cliff Lewis
        and Carroll Britch. Lewiston, N.Y.: Edward Mellen
        Press, 1989. (pp. 60-76)

1268   Owens, Louis D. "Winter in Paris: John Steinbeck's *Pippin
        IV*," *Steinbeck Quarterly*, XX:1-2 (Winter/Spring 1987),
        18-25.

1269   Owens, Louis. "Writing 'in Costume': The Missing Voices in
        In Dubious Battle," in *John Steinbeck: The Years of
        Greatness*, ed. Tetsumaro Hayashi. Tuscaloosa:
        University of Alabama Press, 1993. (pp. 77-94)

1270   Owens, Louis, and Hector Torres. "Dialogic Structure and
        Levels of Discourse in *The Grapes of Wrath*," *Arizona
        Quarterly*, 45:4 (Winter 1989), 75-94.

1271   Oxley, William. "The Sick Novel," in *A Salzburg Miscellany:
        English and American Studies,* 1964-1984. ed. Wilfried
        Haslauer. Salzburg: Institut for Angliistik and
        Amerikanstik, Univ. Salzburg, 1984.

1272   Ozawa, Akiko. "Concerning the Relationship between Men
        and Women as Seen in *The Grapes of Wrath*," *John
        Steinbeck Society of Japan Newsletter*, 13 (April 1990),
        5-6.

1273   Ozawa, Akiko. "Some Comments as a Moderator," *John
        Steinbeck Society of Japan Newsletter*, 15 (April 1992),
        3-4.

1274   Ozawa, Akiko. "Some Comments on *The Pearl*," *John
        Steinbeck Society of Japan Newsletter*, 7 (May 1984), 5.

1275   Ozawa, Akiko. "The Tragedy to Be Seen in 'The
        Chrysanthemums': Through Images of Fertility and
        Barrenness," *Gakuen (Campus): Bulletin of English*

and *American Literature* (Modern Culture Institute, Showa Women's University), 544 (April 1989), 1-15.

1276   Parks, Robert. "John Steinbeck in the Pierpont Morgan Library," *Steinbeck Newletter,* 8:1-2 (Winter/Spring 1995), 19-21.

1277   Pasold, Bernadete. "*Grapes of Wrath* and *Canaa:* Two Perspectives of the Man and the Land," *Ilha-do-Desterro: A Journal of Language and Literature (Florianapolis, Brazil),* 15-16:1-2 (1986), 108-115.

1278   Pearson, Michael. "A Strip Angled against the Pacific — Steinbeck's California," Ch. 6 in his *Imagined Places: Journeys into Literary America.* Jackson: University of Mississippi Press, 1991. (pp. 215-263)

1279   Peck, David. "*The Red Pony,*" in *Cyclopaedia of Literary Characters II.* Vol. III. ed. Frank Magill. Pasadena, Calif.: Salem Press, 1990. (p. 1281)

1280   Peckham, Irvin. "Thank You, John (Steinbeck)," *English Journal,* 75 (November 1986), 31-32.

1281   Peeler, David. "John Steinbeck's Universal Human Family," in *Hope among Us Yet: Social Criticism and Social Solace in Depression America.* Athens: University of Georgia Press, 1987. (pp. 156-165)

1282   Pellow, C. Kenneth. "'The Chrysanthemums' Revisited," *Steinbeck Quarterly,* XXII:1-2 (Winter/Spring 1989), 8-16.

1283   Perkin, J. R. C. "Exodus Imagery in *The Grapes of Wrath,*" in *Literature and the Bible.* ed. David Bevan. Amsterdam/ Atlanta: Rodopi, 1993. (pp. 79 - 93)

1284   Person, Leland S., Jr. "*Of Mice and Men*: Steinbeck's Speculation in Manhood," *Steinbeck Newletter,* 8:1-2 (Winter/Spring 1995), 1-4.

1285   Peterson, Richard. "Homer Was Blind: John Steinbeck on the
        Character of William Faulkner," in *Steinbeck's Literary
        Dimension: A Guide to Comparatives Studies. Series II.*
        ed. Tetsumaro Hayashi. Metuchen, N. J.: Scarecrow
        Press, 1991. (pp. 9-14)

1286   Philbrick, Nathaniel. "At Sea in the Tide Pool: The Whaling
        Town and America in Steinbeck's *The Winter of Our
        Discontent* and *Travels with Charley,*" in *Steinbeck and
        the Environment: Interdisciplinary Approaches.* ed.
        Susan Beegel, Susan Shillinglaw, and Wes Tiffney.
        Tuscaloosa: University of Alabama Press, 1997. (pp.
        229-242)

1287   Piper, William Bowman. "The Whole Book of *King Arthur
        and His Noble Knights,*" *Modern Language Quarterly,*
        47:3 (September 1986), 219-234.

1288   Pizer, Donald. "The Enduring Power of The Joads," in *John
        Steinbeck's "The Grapes of Wrath."* ed. Harold Bloom.
        New York: Chelsea House Publishers, 1988. (pp. 83-98)
        (reprint from *Twentieth Century American Literary
        Naturalism: An Interpretation* (Carbondale, Ill.:
        Southern Illinois University Press, 1982)).(Originally
        entitled "John Steinbeck: *The Grapes of Wrath.*")

1289   Plimpton, George. "Tom Wolfe: The Art of Fiction CXXIII,"
        Paris Review, (Spring 1991), 118.

1290   Pomeroy, Charles. "'Realizm i romantika prozy Dshona
        Steinbeka': Alexander Muliarchik's Most Recent
        Introduction," *The Steinbeck Newsletter,* 3:1 (Winter
        1990), 11.

1291   Pressman, Richard S. "Individualists or Collectivists?:
        Steinbeck's *In Dubious Battle* and Hemingway's *To
        Have and Have Not,*" *Steinbeck Quarterly,* XXV:3-4
        (Summer/Fall 1992), 119-133.

1292   Pressman, Richard. "'Them's Horses — We're Men': Social
          Tendency and Counter-Tendency in *The Grapes of
          Wrath*," in *"The Grapes of Wrath": Essays in Criticism*.
          ed. Tetsumaro Hayashi. Steinbeck Essay Series, No. 3.
          Muncie, Ind.: Steinbeck Research Institute, Ball State
          University Press, 1990. (pp. 56-65) (reprint from
          Steinbeck Quarterly, XIX:3-4 (Summer/Fall 1986),
          71-79.

1293   Price, Victoria. "The Leader of the People," in *Masterplots
          II: Short Story Series. Vol. VIII.* ed. Frank Magill.
          Pasadena, Calif.: Salem Press, 1986. (pp. 3521-3523)

1294   Prindle, Dennis. "The Pretexts of Romance: Steinbeck's
          Allegorical Naturalism from *Cup of Gold* to *Tortilla
          Flat*," in *The Steinbeck Question: New Essays in
          Criticism*. ed. Donald Noble. Troy, N.Y.: Whitston
          Publishing Co., 1993. (pp. 23-36)

1295   Promathatavedi, Malithat. "Bitter Fruit of Karma: *The Winter
          of Our Discontent* in Thailand," in *John Steinbeck: Asian
          Perspectives*. ed. Kiyoshi Nakayama, Scott Pugh, and
          Shigeharu Yano. Osaka: Osaka Kyoiku Tosho, 1992.
          (pp. 13-17)

1296   Pugh, Scott. "Genre Formation and Discourse Processes in
          Steinbeck's Life of Henry Morgan," in *John Steinbeck:
          Asian Perspectives*. ed. Kiyoshi Nakayama, Scott Pugh,
          and Shigeharu Yano. Osaka: Osaka Kyoiku Tosho,
          1992. (pp. 29-48) (*Cup Of Gold*)

1297   Pugh, Scott. "Ideals and Inversions in *The Pastures of
          Heaven*," *Kyushu American Literature*, 28 (October
          1987), 70-72.

1298   Pugh, Scott. "Introduction: Looking West from Asia," in
          John Steinbeck: Asian Perspectives. ed. Kiyoshi
          Nakayama, Scott Pugh, and Shigeharu Yano. Osaka:
          Osaka Kyoiku Tosho, 1992. (pp. xi-xvi)

1299   Pugh, Scott. "John Steinbeck: Antibiography, Autobiography
        and the Stuff Legends Are Made Of," *Studies in the
        Humanities,* 59 (February 25, 1995), 51-65. (summarized
        in *Steinbeck Studies,* 19 (May 1996), 4-5)

1300   Quigley, Michael. "For Book Lovers and Collectors: Notes
        from a Steinbeck Scholar," *Volusia* (January 30, 1983),
        13.

1301   Quinones, Ricardo. "Chapter 7: The New American Cain:
        East of Eden and Other Works of Post World War II
        America," in *The Changes of Cain: Violence and the
        Lost Brother in Cain and Abel Literature.* Princeton:
        Princeton University Press, 1991.

1302   Rahv, Philip. "Review of *The Grapes of Wrath,*" in *Critical
        Essays on "The Grapes of Wrath."* ed. John Ditsky.
        Boston: G.K. Hall and Co., 1989. (pp. 30-31) (reprint
        from *Partisan Review,* 6 (Spring 1939), 111-12)

1303   Railsback, Brian. "Darwin and Steinbeck: The 'Older
        Method' and *The Sea of Cortez,*" *Steinbeck Quarterly,*
        XXIII:1-2 (Winter/Spring 1990), 27-34.

1304   Railsback, Brian. "A Frog, a Bear, a Snake and the Human
        Species: Uncomfortable Reflections in John Steinbeck's
        Fiction," in *Literature and the Grotesque.* ed. Michael J.
        Meyer. Amsterdam: Rodopi, 1995. (pp. 53-65)

1305   Railsback, Brian. "Searching for 'What Is': Charles Darwin
        and John Steinbeck," in *Steinbeck and the Environment:
        Interdisciplinary Approaches.* ed. Susan Beegel, Susan
        Shillinglaw, and Wes Tiffney. Tuscaloosa: Alabama
        University Press, 1997. (pp. 127-141)

1306   Railsback, Brian. "Selectivity, Sympathy and Charles
        Darwin," *San Jose Studies*, 16:1 (Winter 1990), 98-106.

1307   Railsback, Brian. "*The Wayward Bus*: Misogyny or Sexual
        Selection?" in *After "The Grapes of Wrath"*: *Essays on*

John Steinbeck in Honor of Tetsumaro Hayashi. ed.
Donald Coers, Robert DeMott, and Paul Ruffin. Athens:
Ohio University Press, 1995. (pp. 125-135)

1308   Railton, Stephen. "John Steinbeck's Call to Conversion in
        The Grapes of Wrath," in *Readings on John Steinbeck*.
        ed. Clarice Swisher. San Diego: Greenhaven Press, 1996.
        Literary Companion Series. (165-173) (abridged from
        Railton's "Pilgrim's Politics: Steinbeck's Art of
        Conversion," in *New Essays on "The Grapes of Wrath."*
        ed. David Wyatt (Cambridge, 1990))

1309   Railton, Stephen. "Pilgrim's Politics: Steinbeck's Art of
        Conversion," in *New Essays on "The Grapes of Wrath"*
        ed. David Wyatt. Cambridge: Cambridge University
        Press, 1990. (pp. 27-46)

1310   Rallyson, Carl E., Jr. "John Steinbeck," in *The Nobel Prize
        Winners*. Vol. III. (1962-1987) ed. Frank Magill.
        Pasadena, Calif.: Salem Press, 1987. (pp. 691-699)

1311   Rallyson, Carl E., Jr. "John Steinbeck Awarded the Nobel
        Prize in Literature," in *Readings on John Steinbeck*. ed.
        Clarice Swisher. San Diego: Greenhaven Press, 1996.
        Literary Companion Series. (174-177) (reprinted from
        Salem Press's *The Nobel Prize Winners*, Vol. III, 691-99
        by Rallyson)

1312   Ramsey, Martha, Ann Charters, and William E. Sheidley.
        "Instructor's Manual," in *The Story and Its Writer: An
        Introduction to Short Fiction*. See #690.

1313   Rao, S. S. Prabhakar. "A Report on the National Seminar on
        John Steinbeck's *The Grapes of Wrath*," *John Steinbeck
        Society of Japan Newsletter*, 13 (April 1990), 2-3.

1314   Rascoe, Burton. "But . . . Not . . . Ferdinand," in *Critical
        Essays on "The Grapes of Wrath."* ed. John Ditsky.
        Boston: G.K. Hall and Co., 1989. (pp. 25-26) (reprint
        from *Newsweek,* 13 (17 April 1939), 46)

1315   Ratcliffe, Michael. "Cutting Loose at 60: John Steinbeck," in
        Conversations with John Steinbeck. ed. Thomas Fensch.
        Jackson: University of Mississippi Press, 1988. (pp. 80-
        84) (reprint from *The Sunday Times of London*, 16
        December 1962, 20.

1316   Rathgeb, Douglas L. "The Four Faces of Cal Trask:
        Steinbeck's Troubled Hero and James Dean," *Steinbeck
        Newsletter*, 6:1 (Winter 1993), 8-9.

1317   Rathgeb, Douglas L. "Kazan as Auteur: The Undiscovered
        East of Eden," *Literature/Film Quarterly*, 16 (1988), 31-
        38.

1318   Renner, Stanley. "Mary Teller and Sue Bridehead: Birds of a
        Feather in 'The White Quail' and *Jude the Obscure*," in
        *Steinbeck's Literary Dimension: A Guide to
        Comparative Studies. Series II.* ed. Tetsumaro Hayashi.
        Metuchen, N. J.: Scarecrow Press, 1991. (p. 15-27)
        (reprint from *Steinbeck Quarterly,* XVIII:1-2
        (Winter/Spring 1985), 35-45)

1319   Renner, Stanley. "The Real Woman inside the Fence in 'The
        Chrysanthemums,'" *Modern Fiction Studies*, 31
        (Summer 1985), 305-17.

1320   Renner, Stanley. "Sexual Idealism and Violence in 'The
        White Quail,'" *Steinbeck Quarterly,* XVII:1-2
        (Winter/Spring 1984), 76-87.

1321   Rice, John C. "John Steinbeck Turns His Wrath on *The
        Grapes of Wrath* Publicity," in *Conversations with John
        Steinbeck.* ed. Thomas Fensch. Jackson: University of
        Mississippi Press, 1988. (pp. 15-17) (reprint from
        Newspaper Enterprise Association (June 1939))

1322   Ricketts, Nancy. "In the sense that . . .," *Steinbeck
        Newsletter*, 9:1 (Fall 1995), 11. (Part I of Edward
        Flanders Ricketts: Four Perspectives)

1323   Rivers, William. "The Peripatetic Poodle: *Travels with Charley in Search of America*," *Saturday Review*, September 1, 1992, n.p.

1324   Roberts, David. "Travels with Steinbeck: Surprisingly No Sour Grapes," *American Photographer*, 22:3 (March 1, 1989), 44-51. (Horace Bristol)

1325   Robins, Natalie. "The Defiling of Writers: Hoover and American Lit," *Nation*, 245 (October 10, 1987), 367-370, 372.

1326   Roggenkamp, K. S. H. "Long Live the Queen: Literature and Life Philosophy," *English Journal,* 83 (December 1994), 33-35. (discusses strategies for using *The Red Pony* in the classroom)

1327   Rohrberger, Mary. "The Question of Regionalism: Limitation and Transcendence," in *The American Short Story* 1900-1945. ed. Philip Stevick. Boston: Twayne Publishers, 1984. (pp. 178-182)

1328   Rollins, J. Barton. "John Steinbeck's Tragicomic Sense," *Journal of English,* 16 (September 1988), 42-56.

1329   Rollins, Jill. "*The Pearl*," in *Cyclopaedia of Literary Characters II.* Vol. III. ed. Frank Magill. Pasadena, Calif.: Salem Press, 1990. (pp. 1188-1189)

1330   Rombold, Tamara. "Biblical Inversion in *The Grapes of Wrath*," *College Literature*, 14:2 (Spring 1987), 146-166.

1330A   Rucklin-Banderier, Christine. "Steinbeck and the Philosophical Joads," *Steinbeck Newsletter*, 10:1 (Spring 1997), 11-13.

1331   Safire, William. "On Language: Get It?" *New York Times Magazine*, October 27, 1991, n.p. (*The Grapes of Wrath*)

1332   Saima, Yumiko. "On the Curses in *The Pastures of Heaven*," *Jissen English Literature* (Jissen Women's University), 41 (July 20, 1992), 145-155.

1333   Sakai, Yasuhiro. "*The Red Pony*: A Psychological Approach," *John Steinbeck Society of Japan Newsletter*, 15 (April 1992), 4.

1334   Sakai, Yasuhiro. "The Steinbeck Country Tour: A *Wayward Bus* Tour," *Steinbeck Studies,* 19 (May 1996), 7.

1335   Sakai, Yasuhiro. "Steinbeck's 'The Chrysanthemums' — Conscious and Unconscious — What Elisa Knows," *Chu-Shikoku Studies in American Literature,* 26 (June 12, 1990), 54-66.

1336   Sakai, Yasuhiro. "Steinbeck's *The Red Pony*: A Study from the Viewpoint of Developmental Psychology," *Chu-Shikoku Studies in American Literature*, 28 (June 1, 1992), 32-41.

1337   Sakai, Yasuhiro. "The Structure of the Unconscious in Tuleracito," *Chu-Shikoku Studies in American Literature* (June 23, 1987), 39-48.

1338   "Salinas to Carmel to Cannery Row . . . Steinbeck Country," *Sunset* (Central West Edition), 175 (July 1985), 46+.

1339   Salter, Christopher L. "John Steinbeck's *The Grapes of Wrath* as a Primer for Cultural Geography," in *Critical Essays on "The Grapes of Wrath."* ed. John Ditsky. Boston: G.K. Hall and Co., 1989. (pp. 138-152) (reprint from *Humanistic Geography and Literature: Essays on the Experience of Place.* ed. Douglas C. D. Pocock (London: Croom Helm, 1981). pp. 142-158)

1340   "Sardines and Sentiment," *Asahi Evening News*, June 17, 1983, n.p.

1341   Sasakura, Hiroko. "The Women's Function in *The Winter of Our Discontent*," *John Steinbeck Society of Japan Newsletter*, 15 (April 1992), 3.

1342   Satyanarayana, M. R. "Indian Thought in Steinbeck's Works," in *John Steinbeck: From Salinas to the World: Proceedings of the Second International Steinbeck Congress* (1984), ed. Shigeharo Yano, Tetsumaro Hayashi, Richard F. Peterson, and Yasuo Hashiguchi. Tokyo, Japan: Gaku Shobo Press, 1986. *(*pp. 113-122)

1343   Satyanarayana, M. R. "Novelist at Crossroads: John Steinbeck During the 1950s and 1960s," *Indian Journal of American Studies*, 14:2 (July 1984), 111-24.

1344   Scarseth, Thomas. "A Teachable Good Book: *Of Mice and Men*," in *Censored Books: Critical Viewpoints* by Nicolas Karolides, Lee Burress, and James M. Kean. Metuchen, N. J.: Scarecrow Press, 1993. (pp. 388-394)

1345   Schmidt, Gary D. "Steinbeck's 'Breakfast': A Reconsideration," *Western American Literature,* 26: 4 (Winter 1992), 303-311.

1346   Schmitt-von Muhlenfels, Astrid. "Theological Continuity and Change: The Ending of Steinbeck's *The Grapes of Wrath*," *Literatur-in-Wissenschaft-und-Unterricht, Wurzburg, Germany,* 24:1 (1991), 17-26.

1347   Schmitz, Edwin F. "The Joy of Collecting Steinbeck," *Steinbeck Quarterly,* XIX:3-4 (Summer /Fall 1986), 83-86.

1348   Schneer, Deborah. "A Psychoanalytic Reading," *San Jose Studies*, 16 (Winter 1990), 107-116.

1349   Schneiderman, Leo. "Steinbeck: The Search for Identity," *San Jose Studies*, 18:2 (Spring 1992), 74.

1350   Schramm, Wilbur L. "Career at a Crossroads," in *Critical Essays on "The Grapes of Wrath."* ed. John Ditsky. Boston: G.K. Hall and Co., 1989. (pp. 42-43) (reprint from *Virginia Quarterly Review,* 15 (Autumn 1939), 630-32)

1351   Schwab, Helvetia. (as told to Bonnie Gartshore) "Growing Up on Cannery Row: Pt. I," *Steinbeck Newsletter*, 9:1 (Fall 1995), 31-33. (Part IV of On *Cannery Row*: Four Perspectives)

1352   Schwab, Helvetia. (as told to Bonnie Gartshore) "Growing Up on Cannery Row: Pt. II — 'Those $%! Schwab Kids,'" *Steinbeck Newsletter,* 10:1 (Spring 1996), 9-11.

1353   "Second Steinbeck International Congress, Salinas, California, August 1-8, 1984," *ASRC Newsletter* (December 1984), 43-46.

1354   Seelye, John. "Introduction," in *The Red Pony* by John Steinbeck. New York: Penguin, 1994. (pp. vii-xxix)

1355   Sharma, Ram Krishna. "John Steinbeck's Burden of Blackness," *John Steinbeck Society of Japan Newsletter*, 6 (May 1983), 2.

1356   Shaw, Patrick W. "Ch. 7: *The Pearl,*" in *A New Study Guide to Steinbeck's Major Works, with Critical Explications.* ed. Tetsumaro Hayashi. Metuchen, N. J.: Scarecrow Press, 1993.

1357   Shaw, Patrick W. "Ch. 8: *The Red Pony,*" in *A New Study Guide to Steinbeck's Major Works, with Critical Explications.* ed. Tetsumaro Hayashi. Metuchen, N. J.: Scarecrow Press, 1993.

1358   Shaw, Patrick W. "Tom's Other Trip: Psycho-Physical Questing in *The Grapes of Wrath,*" in *"The Grapes of Wrath": Essays in Criticism.* ed. Tetsumaro Hayashi. Steinbeck Essay Series, No. 3. Muncie, Ind.: Steinbeck

Research Institute, Ball State University Press, 1990. (pp. 65-73) (reprint from *Steinbeck Quarterly,* XVI:1-2 (Winter/Spring 1983), 17-25) (reprinted in *The Grapes of Wrath.* critical ed. ed. Peter Lisca and Kevin Hearle. New York: Viking, 1997)

1359   Sheehan, Ed. "Sensitive Writer in a Man-Shell of Gruffness," in *Conversations with John Steinbeck.* ed. Thomas Fensch. Jackson: University of Mississippi Press, 1988. (pp. 100-104) [reprint from *The San Francisco Examiner and Chronicle,* "This World" section, 26 January 1969]

1360   Sheff, David. "John Steinbeck's *The Grapes of Wrath*: 1939-1989 — The People Who Lived His Story and Are Living It Now," *California Magazine,* 14:10 (October 1989), 89-93, 95, 172-173.

1361   Sheffield, Carlton A. "Controversy and Steinbeck," *Preston C. Beyer Catalogue No.* 31 (1984), i-ii.

1362   Sheidley, William E., Ann Charters, and Martha Ramsey. "Instructor's Manual," in *The Story and Its Writer: An Introduction to Short Fiction.* 2nd ed. New York: St. Martin's Press, 1987. (pp. 120-121)

1363   Shigematsu, Soiku. "150 Zen Sayings from *The Grapes of Wrath,*" *Journal of the Faculty of Humanities, Shizuoka University,* 34 (January 1984), 47-69.

1364   Shillinglaw, Susan. "California Answers *The Grapes of Wrath,*" in *Steinbeck: The Years of Greatness.* 1936-1939. ed. Tetsumaro Hayashi. Tuscaloosa: University of Alabama Press, 1993. (pp. 145-164)

1365   Shillinglaw, Susan. "'The Chrysanthemums': Steinbeck's Pygmalion," in *Steinbeck's Short Stories in "The Long Valley": Essays in Criticism.* ed. Tetsumaro Hayashi. Steinbeck Monograph Series, No. 15. Muncie, Ind.: Steinbeck Research Institute, Ball State University Press, 1991. (pp. 1-9) (translated into Japanese in *Steinbeck*

Kenkyu: Atarashii Tanpen Shosetsushu (Steinbeck Studies: New Essays on Short Stories). Osaka, Japan: Osaka Educational Publishing Co. 1995. (pp. 135-157))

1366   Shillinglaw, Susan. "Editorial," *San Jose Studies*, 16 (Winter 1990), 5.

1367   Shillinglaw, Susan. "Five Steinbeck Specialists Visit the USSR," *The Steinbeck Newsletter*, 3:1 (Winter 1990), 1-3.

1368   Shillinglaw, Susan. "Introduction," in *Cannery Row* by John Steinbeck. New York: Penguin, 1994. (pp. vii-xxv)

1369   Shillinglaw, Susan. "Introduction," *San Jose Studies*, 18 (Winter 1992), 4-5.

1370   Shillinglaw, Susan. "Introduction," in *Of Mice and Men* by John Steinbeck. New York: Penguin, 1994. (pp. vii-xxvii)

1371   Shillinglaw, Susan, Wesley N. Tiffney, Jr. and Susan Beegel. "Introduction," in *Steinbeck and the Environment: Interdisciplinary Approaches*. See #603.

1372   Shillinglaw, Susan. "John Steinbeck," in *American National Biography*. Oxford: Oxford University Press, 1995.

1373   Shillinglaw, Susan. "John Steinbeck," in *Encyclopedia of American Literature*. ed. Alfred Bendixon. New York: Frederick Ungar, forthcoming.

1374   Shillinglaw, Susan. "John Steinbeck," in *The Reader's Companion to American History*. ed. Eric Foner and John A. Garraty. Boston: Houghton Mifflin, 1991. (pp. 1030-31)

1375   Shillinglaw, Susan. "Local Newspapers Report on *The Oklahomans*," *Steinbeck Newsletter*, 2:2 (Summer 1989), 4, 5.

1376   Shillinglaw, Susan. "Los Gatos: 'Gem City of the Foothills,'"
        Steinbeck Newsletter, 2:2 (Summer 1989), 1, 2.

1377   Shillinglaw, Susan. "Mac and Ava Motion Picture
        Production," *The Steinbeck Newsletter*, 4:1 (Winter
        1991), 6-7.

1378   Shillinglaw, Susan. "Professor Martha Heasley Cox Gives the
        Steinbeck Research Center $50,000 Matching Grant,"
        Steinbeck Newsletter, 10:1 (Spring 1996), 17, 19.

1379   Shillinglaw, Susan. "Steinbeck and Ethnicity," in *After "The
        Grapes of Wrath"*: *Essays on John Steinbeck in Honor of
        Tetsumaro Hayashi*. ed. Donald Coers, Robert DeMott,
        and Paul Ruffin. Athens: Ohio University Press, 1995.
        (pp. 40-57)

1380   Shillinglaw, Susan. "Tetsumaro Hayashi, an Interview on His
        Retirement," *The Steinbeck Newsletter*, 6:2 (Summer
        1993), 6.

1381   Shillinglaw, Susan. "Why is Steinbeck 'Almost Great' and
        'Always Read?': Some Reflections," *Steinbeck
        Newsletter,* 10:1 (Spring 1996), 18-19.

1382   Shimada, Saburo. "Plant Description in Willa Cather and
        John Steinbeck's Works (1)," *Beacon* (Kenmei Women's
        Junior College), 19 (1984), 1-105.

1383   Shimada, Saburo. "Plant Description in Willa Cather and
        John Steinbeck's Works (2)," *Beacon* (Kenmei Women's
        Junior College), 20 (1985), 106-189.

1384   Shimizu, Hiromu. "The Bible and *Of Mice and Men*," *John
        Steinbeck Society of Japan Newsletter*, 11 (April 1988),
        2.

1385   Shimomura, Noburo. "Steinbeck and Monterey: Theme and
        Humor in the 'Monterey Trilogy,'" in *John Steinbeck:
        From Salinas to the World: Proceedings of the Second*

International Steinbeck Congress (1984). ed. Shigeharo
Yano, Tetsumaro Hayashi, Richard F. Peterson, and
Yasuo Hashiguchi. Tokyo, Japan: Gaku Shobo Press,
1986. (pp. 102-112)

1386   Shimura, Masao. "Books in American Literature: 1945-50,"
in *The Traditional and the Anti-Traditional: Studies in
Contemporary American Literature*. ed. Kenzaburo
Ohashi. Tokyo: The Tokyo Chapter of the American
Literature Society of Japan, 1980. (pp. 232-45)

1387   Shimuzu, Hiromu. "Steinbeck's Sweet Maundy Thursday,"
John Steinbeck Society of Japan Newsletter, 8 (May
1985), 5.

1388   Shimomura, Noburu. "Panel Discussion: Monterey Trilogy,"
John Steinbeck Society of Japan Newsletter, 8 (May
1985), 4.

1389   Shinmura, Akio. "The Old 'American Dream' in *Of Mice and
Men*," *Kitakyushu University, Faculty of Literature
Bulletin, A Commemorative Issue of the Fortieth
Anniversary* (February 1987), 217-232.

1390   Shinmura, Akio. "On the Play-Novelette Form of *Of Mice
and Men*," *Kyushu American Literature*, 28 (October
1987), 72-75.

1391   Shiraga, Eiko. "Agape and Courage to Be in Steinbeck's *The
Grapes of Wrath*," *John Steinbeck Society of Japan
Newsletter*, 14 (April 1991), 4.

1392   Shiraga, Eiko. "Curley's Wife: Her Fictional Functions in
Steinbeck's *Of Mice and Men*," *Persica (The English
Literature Society of Okayama)*, 20 (March 25, 1993),
113-21.

1393   Shiraga, Eiko. "The Dramatic Functions of Three Women in
Steinbeck's *The Moon Is Down*," *Shujitsu English*

Studies (Shujitsu Women's University), 11 (March 1992), 19-35.

1394   Shiraga, Eiko. "Steinbeck's *The Pearl* and Hemingway's *The Old Man and the Sea*: A Comparative Study," *Persica* (*The English Literature Society of Okayama*), 18 (April 1991), 101-105.

1395   Shiraga, Eiko. "Three Strong Women in Steinbeck's *The Moon Is Down*" in *After "The Grapes of Wrath": Essays on John Steinbeck in Honor of Tetsumaro Hayashi*. ed. Donald Coers, Robert DeMott, and Paul Ruffin. Athens: Ohio University Press, 1995. (pp. 95-100)

1396   Shockley, Martin. "Christian Symbolism in *The Grapes of Wrath*," in *Readings on John Steinbeck*. ed. Clarice Swisher. San Diego: Greenhaven Press, 1996. Literary Companion Series. (138-144) (reprinted from Shockley's original article in *College English*, XVIII (November 1956), 87-90)

1397   Shulberg, Budd. "John Steinbeck: A Lion in Winter," in *Conversations with John Steinbeck*. ed. Thomas Fensch. Jackson: University of Mississippi Press, 1988. (pp. 105-112) (reprint from *The Four Seasons of Success* (Garden City, N.Y.: Doubleday, 1972), 187-197)

1398   Shuman, R. Baird. "John Steinbeck," in *Magill's Survey of American Literature*. Vol. 6. Pasadena, Calif.: Salem Press, 1991. (pp. 1885-1899) (contains commentary on *Of Mice and Men, East of Eden, The Pearl, The Red Pony, The Grapes of Wrath* and *Cannery Row*)

1399   Shuman, R. Baird. "The Snake," in *Masterplots II: Short Story Series*. Vol. IX. ed. Frank Magill. Pasadena, Calif.: Salem Press, 1986. (pp. 4039-4041)

1400   Shurgot, Michael W. "A Game of Cards in Steinbeck's *Of Mice and Men*," *Steinbeck Quarterly,* XV:1-2 (Winter/Spring 1982), 38-43.

1401   Siefker, Donald L., and Nancy K. Turner. "The John
        Steinbeck Collection in the Alexander M. Bracken
        Library, Ball State University — 1980-1990, A Decade
        in Review," *Steinbeck Newletter* 5 (Spring 1992) 9.

1402   Simmonds, Roy S. "'And Still the Box Is Not Full': *East of
        Eden*," *San Jose Studies*, 18 (Fall 1992), 56-71.

1403   Simmonds, Roy S. "Another Message from England,"
        Steinbeck Quarterly, XXIV:1-2 (Winter/Spring 1991),
        18-21.

1404   Simmonds, Roy S. "Cathy Ames and Rhoda Penmark: Two
        Child Monsters," *Mississippi Quarterly*, 39 (Spring
        1986), 91-101. (reprinted in *Steinbeck's Literary
        Dimension: A Guide to Comparative Studies. Series II.*
        ed. Tetsumaro Hayashi. Metuchen, N. J.: Scarecrow
        Press, 1991) (pp. 102-113)

1405   Simmonds, Roy. "'The God in the Pipes': An Early Version
        of *Cannery Row*," *Steinbeck Newsletter*, 9:1 (Fall 1995),
        1-3.

1406   Simmonds, Roy S. "Interview," *Steinbeck Quarterly*, XVI:1-
        2 (Winter/Spring 1983), 27-32.

1407   Simmonds, Roy S. "John Steinbeck," in *Twentieth Century
        Romantic and Historical Writers* (2nd ed.). ed. Lesley
        Henderson. Chicago and London: St. James Press, 1990.
        (pp. 611-613)

1408   Simmonds, Roy S. "The Metamorphosis of *The Moon is
        Down*: March 1942-March 1943," in *After "The Grapes
        of Wrath"*: *Essays on John Steinbeck in Honor of
        Tetsumaro Hayashi*. ed. Donald Coers, Robert DeMott,
        and Paul Ruffin. Athens: Ohio University Press, 1995.
        (pp. 77-94)

1409   Simmonds, Roy S. "The Original Manuscript," *San Jose Studies*, 16 (Winter 1990), 117-132. (*The Grapes of Wrath*)

1410   Simmonds, Roy, S. "The Place and Importance of 'The Great Mountains' in *The Red Pony* Cycle," in *Steinbeck's "The Red Pony": Essays in Criticism*, ed. Tetsumaro Hayashi and Thomas J. Moore. Steinbeck Monograph Series, No. 13. Muncie, Ind.: Steinbeck Research Institute, Ball State University Press, 1988. (pp. 17-26) (translated into Japanese in *Steinbeck Kenkyu: Atarashii Tanpen Shosetsushu (Steinbeck Studies: New Essays on Short Stories)*. Osaka, Japan: Osaka Educational Publishing Co. 1995. (pp. 61-82))

1411   Simmonds, Roy S. "The Reception of *The Grapes of Wrath* in Britain: A Chronological Survey of Contemporary Reviews," in *Critical Essays on "The Grapes of Wrath."* ed. John Ditsky. Boston: G.K. Hall, 1989. (pp. 74-86)

1412   Simmonds, Roy S. "A Sense of Belonging: John Steinbeck in England," *London Magazine*, 32 (December/January 1993), 77-90. (Arthurian research)

1413   Simmonds, Roy S. "Steinbeck and World War II: *The Moon Goes Down*," *Steinbeck Quarterly*, XVII:1-2 (Winter/Spring 1984), 14-34.

1414   Simmonds, Roy S. "Steinbeck's *The Pearl*: Legend, Film, Novel," in *The Short Novels of John Steinbeck*. ed. Jackson J. Benson. Durham: Duke University Press, 1990. (pp. 173-184)

1415   Simmonds, Roy S. "Steinbeck's *The Pearl*: A Preliminary Textual Study," *Steinbeck Quarterly*, XXII:1-2 (Winter/Spring 1989), 16-34.

1416   Simmonds, Roy S. "The Twentieth Anniversary of the Steinbeck Society," *Steinbeck Quarterly*, XIX:1-2 (Winter/Spring 1986), 36-39.

1417   Simmonds, Roy. "A World to Be Cherished: Steinbeck as
        Conservationist and Ecological Prophet," in *Steinbeck
        and the Environment: Interdisciplinary Approaches*. ed.
        Susan Beegel, Susan Shillinglaw, and Wes Tiffney.
        Tuscaloosa: University of Alabama Press, 1997. (pp.
        323-334)

1418   Simpson, Hassell A. "Steinbeck's Anglo-Saxon 'Wonder-
        Words' and the American Paradox," *American
        Literature*, 62 (June 1990), 310-317. (*The Winter of Our
        Discontent*)

1419   Skinner, P. "Return to *The Sea of Cortez:* Following in the
        Wake of John Steinbeck," *Peterson's Photography
        Magazine*, 15 (February 1987), 36-40.

1420   Smith, Murray. "Steinbeck on Politics," *Steinbeck Newletter*,
        5:1-2 (Spring 1992), 12.

1421   Smith, Murray. "Steinbeck on Politics, Part 2," *Steinbeck
        Newletter*, 7:1 (Winter 1994), 5.

1422   Sosna, Marvin. "Steinbeck's Tender Touch," *Senior
        Magazine* (May 1994), 35. (*The Wayward Bus*)

1423   Spilka, Mark. "Of George and Lenny and Curley's Wife:
        Sweet Violence in Steinbeck's Eden," in *The Short
        Novels of John Steinbeck*. ed. Jackson J. Benson.
        Durham: Duke University Press, 1990. (pp. 59-70)

1424   Stegner, Wallace. "Afterword," in John Steinbeck's *Flight*.
        Covelo, Calif.: Yolla Bolly Press, 1984. (with
        lithographs by Karen Wickstrom)

1425   Stegner, Wallace. "John Steinbeck's 'Flight,'" in *Where the
        Bluebird Sings to the Lemonade Springs*. New York:
        Random House, 1992. (pp. 143-154)

1426   "Steinbeck," in 200 *Years of Great American Short Stories.*
        ed. Martha Foley. New York: Galahad Books, 1982.
        (p. 575)

1427   Steinbeck, Elaine. "A Message from Elaine Steinbeck," Play
        Programme, *East of Eden* and *Dandyism,* Takarazuka
        Grand Theater, June 30, 1995, 52.

1428   Steinbeck, John, IV. "Predisposed and Stuck with It," *Lear's*
        (December 1990), 56-57.

1429   Stinnett, Caskie. "A Talk with John Steinbeck," in
        Conversations with John Steinbeck. ed. Thomas Fensch.
        Jackson: University of Mississippi Press, 1988. (pp. 85-
        88) (reprint from *Back to Abnormal* (New York: Bernard
        Geis Associates, 1963), pp. 92-96)

1430   Stone, Donal. "Steinbeck, Jung, and *The Winter of Our
        Discontent,*" in *Steinbeck's Literary Dimension: A Guide
        to Comparative Studies. Series II.* ed. Tetsumaro
        Hayashi. Metuchen N. J.: Scarecrow Press, 1991. (pp.
        91-101)

1431   Stoneback, H.R. "Rough People . . . Are the Best Singers:
        Woody Guthrie, John Steinbeck and Folksong," in *The
        Steinbeck Question: New Essays in Criticism.* ed. Donald
        Noble. Troy, N.Y.: Whitston Publishing Co., 1993. (pp.
        143-170)

1432   Stoneback, H. R. "'The Scars of Our Grasping Stupidity' and
        the 'Sucked Orange': John Steinbeck and the Ecological
        Legacy of John Burroughs," in *Steinbeck and the
        Environment: Interdisciplinary Approaches.* ed. Susan
        Beegel, Susan Shillinglaw, and Wes Tiffney. Tuscaloosa:
        Alabama University Press, 1997. (pp. 243-265)

1433   Stoneback, H.R. "Songs of 'Anger and Survival': John
        Steinbeck on Woody Guthrie," *Steinbeck Quarterly,*
        XXIII:1-2 (Winter/Spring 1990), 34-42.

1434   Stoneback, H.R. "Woody Sez: Woody Guthrie and *The Grapes of Wrath*," *Steinbeck Newsletter*, 2:2 (Summer 1989), 8-9.

1435   Strecker, Geralyn. "Reading Steinbeck (Re)-Reading America: *Travels with Charley* and *America and Americans*," in *After "The Grapes of Wrath"*: *Essays on John Steinbeck in Honor of Tetsumaro Hayashi*. ed. Donald Coers, Robert DeMott, and Paul Ruffin. Athens: Ohio University Press, 1995. (pp. 214-227)

1436   "Strolling Steinbeck's Salinas," *Sunset* (Central West Ed.), 183 (August 1989), 14.

1437   Strout, C. "Radical Religion and the American Political Novel," in *The Veracious Imagination: Essays on American History, Literature and Biography,* by C. Strout. Middleton, Conn.: Wesleyan University Press, 1985. (pp. 70-91)

1438   Sugiyama, Takahiko. "Camille Oakes, A Heroine of Nonsense — A Reassessment of *The Wayward Bus*," in *John Steinbeck: From Salinas to the World: Proceedings of the Second International Steinbeck Congress* (1984). ed. Shigeharo Yano, Tetsumaro Hayashi, Richard F. Peterson, and Yasuo Hashiguchi. Tokyo, Japan: Gaku Shobo Press, 1986. (pp. 130-136)

1439   Sugiyama, Takahiko. "An Important Aspect of *The Grapes of Wrath*: Symposium: Steinbeck as Modernist," *John Steinbeck Society of Japan Newsletter*, 14 (April 1991), 14, 16.

1440   Sugiyama, Takahiko. "Keynote Lecture by Tetsumaro Hayashi, 'John Steinbeck and Ernest Hemingway: Comparative Notes,'" *John Steinbeck Society of Japan Newsletter*, 15 (April 1992), 4

1441   Sugiyama, Takahiko. "Modernist Steinbeck — Grotesque
        and Nonsense," *Seijo Hogaku Kyoyo Ronshu* (Tokyo), 3
        (March 1982), 31-41.

1442   Sugiyama, Takahiko. "My Ten Years with the Steinbeck
        Society of Japan," *Steinbeck Quarterly*, XX:1-2
        (Winter/Spring 1987) 28-30.

1443   Sugiyama, Takahiko. "Panel Discussion II: Steinbeck and His
        Sense of Humor," *John Steinbeck Society of Japan
        Newsletter*, 10 (April 1987), 3.

1444   Sugiyama, Takahiko. "Papers and Discussion (II):
        Chairman," *John Steinbeck Society of Japan Newsletter*,
        8 (May 1985), 3.

1445   Sugiyama, Takahiko. "Steinbeck Festival IV," *John
        Steinbeck Society of Japan Newsletter*, 7 (May 1984), 10.

1446   Sundermeier, Michael. "Why Steinbeck Didn't Finish His
        *Arthur — The Acts of King Arthur and His Noble
        Knights* (1976)," in *Steinbeck's Posthumous Work:
        Essays in Criticism.* ed. Tetsumaro Hayashi and Thomas
        J. Moore. Steinbeck Monograph Series, No. 14. Muncie,
        Ind.: Steinbeck Research Institute, Ball State University
        Press, 1989. (pp. 34-42)

1447   Suzue, Akiko. "In Defense of Cathy: Her Longing for
        Escape," "Symposium: On Cathy," *John Steinbeck
        Society of Japan Newsletter*, 15 (April 1992), 5, 6-7.

1448   Suzue, Akiko. "On Cathy: Symposium on Cathy Ames,"
        John Steinbeck Society of Japan Newsletter, 15 (April
        1992), 5.

1449   Sweeney, James W. "The Joads Go Home: In the Late 1930s
        John Steinbeck Wrote about Desperate People Seeking a
        Better Life in California," *California Journal,* 23:3
        (March 1, 1992), 131.

1450   Swisher, Clarice. "John Steinbeck: A Biography," in
        Readings on John Steinbeck. ed. Clarice Swisher. San
        Diego: Greenhaven Press, 1996. Literary Companion
        Series. (13-26)

1451   Syed, Mashkoor Ali. "Echoes of Indian Thought in
        Steinbeck," in *John Steinbeck: Asian Perspectives*. ed.
        Kiyoshi Nakayama, Scott Pugh, and Shigeharu Yano.
        Osaka: Osaka Kyoiku Tosho, 1992. (pp. 3-11)

1452   Syed, Mashkoor Ali. "John Steinbeck: Nonfiction Writings
        and Southwestern Humor," *Indian Journal of American
        Studies*, 16 (Summer 1985), 93-98.

1453   "Synopses of the Reports of the Annual Seminar 1986:
        General Subject: John Steinbeck," *Kyushu American
        Literature* (October 28, 1987), 65-75.

1454   Tagaya, Satoru. "Is *East of Eden* a 'Postmodern
        Metafiction,'" *Steinbeck Studies,* 19 (May 1996), 14-20.

1455   Tagaya, Satoru. "Steinbeck and American Postmodernists,"
        in *John Steinbeck: Asian Perspectives*. ed. Kiyoshi
        Nakayama, Scott Pugh, and Shigeharu Yano. Osaka:
        Osaka Kyoiku Tosho, 1992. (pp. 103-112)

1456   Tagaya, Satoru. "Steinbeck and Contemporary Writers,"
        John Steinbeck Society of Japan Newsletter, 13 (April
        1990), 7.

1457   Tagaya, Satoru. "Steinbeck and Vonnegut: From Fable to
        Fabulation," *John Steinbeck Society of Japan Newsletter*,
        9 (May 1986), 4.

1458   Tagaya, Satoru. "Success or Failure? Steinbeck's *The Acts of
        King Arthur and His Noble Knights*," *John Steinbeck
        Society of Japan Newsletter*, 10 (April 1987), 1-2.

1459   Takamura, Hiromasa. " A and C in *Cannery Row*," *Steinbeck
        Quarterly*, XV:3-4 (Summer/Fall 1982), 116.

1460   Takamura, Hiromasa. "John Steinbeck's Dramatic World," in
        John Steinbeck: Asian Perspectives. ed. Kiyoshi
        Nakayama, Scott Pugh, and Shigeharu Yano. Osaka:
        Osaka Kyoiku Tosho, 1992. (pp. 91-101)

1461   Takamura, Hiromasa. "Serving as MC," *John Steinbeck
        Society of Japan Newsletter*, 14 (April 1991), 2-3.

1462   Takamura, Hiromasa. "Steinbeck's Heroes in New
        Perspectives," in *Ogoshi Kazuzo Sensei Taishoku Kinen
        Ronshu (A Collection of Essays in Honor of Kazuzo
        Ogoshi)*, Kyoto: Apolon-sha Press, 1990. (pp. 133-158)

1463   Takamura, Hiromasa. "Steinbeck's Heroes in New
        Perspectives: George Milton and Tom Joad," *John
        Steinbeck Society of Japan Newsletter*, 12 (April 1989),
        2-3.

1464   Takamura, Hiromasa. "The Structure and Language of *Of
        Mice and Men*," *John Steinbeck Society of Japan
        Newsletter*, 8 (May 1985), 2.

1465   "The Talk of the Town: Notes and Comment," *New Yorker*,
        April 8, 1991, 31-32. (on Nobel Winners)

1466   Tammaro, Thom M. "Erik Ericson Meets John Steinbeck:
        Psycho-Social Development in 'The Gift,'" in
        Steinbeck's "The Red Pony": Essays in Criticism. ed.
        Tetsumaro Hayashi and Thomas J. Moore. Steinbeck
        Monograph Series, No. 13. Muncie, Ind.: Steinbeck
        Research Institute, Ball State University Press, 1988. (pp.
        1-9) (translated into Japanese in *Steinbeck Kenkyu:
        Atarashii Tanpen Shosetsushu (Steinbeck Studies: New
        Essays on Short Stories)*. Osaka, Japan: Osaka
        Educational Publishing Co. 1995. (pp. 21-42))

1467   Tammaro, Thom M. "Lost in America: Steinbeck's *Travels
        with Charley* and William Least Heat Moon's *Blue
        Highways*," in *Rediscovering Steinbeck: Revisionist
        Views of His Art, Politics and Intellect*. ed. Cliff Lewis

and Carroll Britch. New York: Edwin Mellen Press, 1989. (pp. 260-275)

1468   Tammaro, Thom M. "'Saint Katy the Virgin': The Key to Steinbeck's Secret Heart," in *Steinbeck's Short Stories in "The Long Valley": Essays in Criticism.* ed. Tetsumaro Hayashi. Steinbeck Monograph Series, No. 15. Muncie, Ind.: Steinbeck Research Institute, Ball State University Press, 1991. (pp. 70-78) (translated into Japanese in *Steinbeck Kenkyu: Atarashii Tanpen Shosetsushu (Steinbeck Studies: New Essays on Short Stories).* Osaka, Japan: Osaka Educational Publishing Co. 1995. (pp. 299-318))

1469   Tammaro, Thom M. "Sharing Creation: Steinbeck, *In Dubious Battle*, and the Working Class Novel," in *John Steinbeck: The Years of Greatness.* ed. Tetsumaro Hayashi. Tuscaloosa: University of Alabama Press, 1993. (pp. 95-105)

1470   Tammaro, Thom M. "Special Message to the International Steinbeck Society," *Steinbeck Quarterly*, XIX:1-2 (Winter/Spring 1986), 39-40.

1471   Tammaro, Thom M. "Thinking of Steinbeck and Charley," in his *Minnesota Suite*. Peoria, Illinois: Spoon River Poetry Press, 1986), pp. 18-19. (dedicated to Tetsumaro Hayashi).

1472   Tammaro, Thom M. "Travels with Steinbeck in North Dakota," *North Dakota Horizons*, 22:3 (Summer 1992), 20-27.

1473   Tammaro, Thom M., and Mary Jean Gamble. "John Steinbeck, Hans Namuth, and the Lost Sag Harbor Photographs," See #841.

1474   Terkel, Studs. "'We Still See Their Faces,'" *San Francisco Review of Books*, 13 (Spring 1989), 24, 29.

1475   Terkel, Studs. "'We Still See Their Faces,'" *New Statesman and Society*, 2 (June 30, 1989), 28-31.

1476   Thomas, Leroy. "Steinbeck's 'The Chrysanthemums,'" *Explicator*, 45 (Spring 1987), 50-51.

1477   Thomas, Mike. "John Steinbeck Back — But Not to Stay," in *Conversations with John Steinbeck*. ed. Thomas Fensch. Jackson: University of Mississippi Press, 1988. (pp. 69-72) (reprint from *The Monterey Peninsula Herald*, 4 November 1960)

1478   Thompson, C. Patrick. "John Steinbeck," *Good Housekeeping*, 44 (December 1943), 4-5, 64-65, 67. (See *Steinbeck Quarterly*, 21 (Summer/Fall 1988), 116, for the report on the reprinting in the British wartime volume entitled *The Home Front*).

1479   Thomsen, Alice Barnard. "Eric H. Thomsen and John Steinbeck," *The Steinbeck Newsletter*, 3:2 (Winter 1990),1-3.

1480   Tibbetts, J. "It Happened in Monterey: Steinbeck's *Cannery Row*," *Literature/Film Quarterly*, 10:2 (1982), 82-84.

1481   Tiffney, Wesley N., Jr., Susan Shillinglaw, and Susan Beegel. "Introduction," in *Steinbeck and the Environment: Interdisciplinary Approaches.* See #603.

1482   Timmerman, John H. "Comic Vision in *The Grapes of Wrath*," *San Jose Studies*, 16 (Winter 1990), 133-141.

1483   Timmerman, John. "*The Grapes of Wrath 50* Years Later," *The Christian Century*, 106:11 (April 5, 1989), 341-43.

1484   Timmerman, John H. "Introduction," in *"The Grapes of Wrath": Essays in Criticism*. ed. Tetsumaro Hayashi. Steinbeck Essay Series, No. 3. Muncie, Ind.: Ball State University Press, 1990.

1485   Timmerman, John H. "Introduction," in *John Steinbeck: The
        Years of Greatness*, 1936-1939. ed. Tetsumaro Hayashi.
        Tuscaloosa, Ala.: University of Alabama Press, 1993.

1486   Timmerman, John H. "Introduction," in *The Long Valley* by
        John Steinbeck. New York: Penguin, 1995. (pp. vii-xxx)

1487   Timmerman, John H. "John Steinbeck, Language, and
        Profanity," *Christian Home and School*, 64:3 (March
        1986), 12-15. [reprinted in *The Western Michigan
        Catholic*, 48:13,14 (March 27, April 31, 1986)]

1488   Timmerman, John H. "On The Trail of Steinbeck's Okies,"
        The Reformed Journal, 33:11 (November 1983), 19-22.
        (*The Grapes of Wrath*)

1489   Timmerman, John H. "The Shadow and the Pearl: Jungian
        Patterns in *The Pearl*," in *The Short Novels of John
        Steinbeck*. ed. Jackson J. Benson. Durham: Duke
        University Press, 1990. (pp. 143-160)

1490   Timmerman, John H. "The Shameless Magpie: John
        Steinbeck, Plagiarism and the Ear of the Artist," in *The
        Steinbeck Question: New Essays in Criticism*. ed. Donald
        R. Noble. Troy, N.Y.: Whitston Publishing Co., 1993.
        (pp. 260-278)

1491   Timmerman, John H. "The Squatter's Circle in *The Grapes of
        Wrath*," *Studies in Short Fiction,* 17:2 (Autumn 1989),
        203-211.

1492   Timmerman, John. "Steinbeck's Environmental Ethic:
        Humanity in Harmony with the Land," in *Steinbeck and
        the Environment: Interdisciplinary Approaches*. ed.
        Susan Beegel, Susan Shillinglaw, and Wes Tiffney.
        Tuscaloosa: University of Alabama Press, 1997. (pp.
        310-322)

1493   Timmerman, John H. "Steinbeck's Place in the Modern
        Epistolary Tradition," in *Steinbeck's Posthumous
        Works: Essays in Criticism.* ed. Tetsumaro Hayashi and
        Thomas J. Moore. Steinbeck Monograph Series, no. 14.
        Muncie, Ind.: Ball State University Press, 1989. (pp. 12-
        22)

1494   Timmerman, John H. "Vintage Wine: Steinbeck's Comic
        Vision in *The Grapes of Wrath*," *San Jose Studies,* 16:1
        (Winter 1990), 133-141.

1495   Tornell, Glenn. "30 Years Ago Steinbeck Traveled through
        Fargo with Charley," *Alumnews* (Moorhead State
        University), 90 (Fall 1990), 16.

1496   Torres, Hector, and Louis Owens. "Dialogic Structure and
        Levels of Discourse in *The Grapes of Wrath*," See
        #1270.

1497   "The Trial of Arthur Miller," *Esquire*, 99 (June 1983), 134-
        36. (reprint from the June 1957 issue)

1498   Tsuboi, Kiyohiko. "The Birth of the Steinbeck Society of
        Japan," *Steinbeck Quarterly*, XX:1-2 (Winter/Spring
        1987) 32-34.

1499   Tsuboi, Kiyohiko. "*Cannery Row* Reconsidered," *Persica*
        (The English Literary Society of Okayama), 19 (March
        25, 1992), 15-22.

1500   Tsuboi, Kiyohiko. "*Cannery Row* Reconsidered," in *John
        Steinbeck: Asian Perspectives.* ed. Kiyoshi Nakayama,
        Scott Pugh, and Shigeharu Yano. Osaka: Osaka Kyoiku
        Tosho, 1992. (pp. 113-125)

1501   Tsuboi, Kiyohiko. "*Cannery Row*: Steinbeck's Carollian
        Fantasy," *John Steinbeck Society of Japan Newsletter*, 7
        (May 1984), 4-5.

1502   Tsuboi, Kiyohiko. "*Cannery Row*: 'Symposium: Steinbeck as
        a Modernist,'" *John Steinbeck Society of Japan
        Newsletter*, 14 (April 1991), 6-7.

1503   Tsuboi, Kiyohiko. "Special Message," *John Steinbeck
        Society of Japan Newsletter*, 15 (April 1992), 1.

1504   Tsuboi, Kiyohiko. "Steinbeck as a Modernist: 'Symposium:
        Steinbeck as a Modernist,'" *John Steinbeck Society of
        Japan Newsletter*, 14 (April 1991), 5-6.

1505   Tsuboi, Kiyohiko. "Two Jodys: Steinbeck and Rawlings," in
        *John Steinbeck: From Salinas to the World: Proceedings
        of the Second International Steinbeck Congress* (1984),
        ed. Shigeharo Yano, Tetsumaro Hayashi, Richard F.
        Peterson, and Yasuo Hashiguchi. Tokyo, Japan: Gaku
        Shobo Press, 1986. (pp. 83-96)

1506   Tsuboi, Kiyohiko. "Viva Zapata!" *John Steinbeck Society of
        Japan Newsletter*, 12 (May 1989), 6.

1507   Tsuji, Takeo. "Mary Teller's Sterile Garden: A Study of
        Steinbeck's 'The White Quail,'"*John Steinbeck Society
        of Japan Newsletter*, 6 (May 1983), 1.

1508   Turner, Frederick. "The Valley of the World: John
        Steinbeck's *East of Eden*," in *Spirit of Place: The
        Making of an American Literary Landscape* by F.
        Turner. Washington, D.C.: Island Books, 1992. (pp. 247-
        282) (also published by Sierra Club in San Francisco in
        1989)

1509   Turner, Nancy K., and Donald L. Siefker. "The John
        Steinbeck Collection in the Alexander M. Bracken
        Library, Ball State University — 1980-1990, A Decade
        in Review." See #1401.

1510   Tuttleton, James. "Steinbeck Remembered," *The New
        Criterion,* 13:7 (March 1, 1995), 22-28.

1511   Uchida, Shigeharu. "Camille in *The Wayward Bus*,"
        Kokushikan University Liberal Arts Bulletin, 19
        (September 1984), 1-5.

1512   Uchiyama, Catherine J. "Report: Steinbeck Festival VIII,
        Salinas, California (July 30-August 3, 1987)," *Steinbeck
        Quarterly*, XXI:3-4 (Summer Fall 1988), 104-107.

1513   Upot, Sherine. "From the Narrative to the Dramatic: Generic
        Problems in *The Moon Is Down*," *Littcrit*, 20:2 (1994),
        40-47.

1514   Upot, Sherine. "The Frontiers of the Imagination: *Cannery
        Row* and *Sweet Thursday*," in *Closing of the American
        Frontier: A Centennial Retrospect*, 1890-1990. ed. R. S.
        Sharma and Isaac Sequeira. Hyderabad, India: American
        Studies Research Centre, 1994. (pp. 31-39)

1515   Upot, Sherine. "The Novel Dramatized: Generic
        Transformation in *Of Mice and Men*," in *Indian
        Responseto Steinbeck: Essays in Honor of Warren
        French*. ed. R. K. Sharma. Jaipur, India: Rachana
        Prakashan, 1984.

1516   Uza, Tokumitsu. "John Steinbeck's *In Dubious Battle* and
        Takiji Kobayashi's *A Crab-Packing Vessel*: A
        Comparative Study," *John Steinbeck Society of Japan
        Newsletter*, 10 (April 1987), 2.

1517   Valenti, Peter. "Steinbeck's Ecological Polemic: Human
        Sympathy and Visual Documentary in the Intercalary
        Chapters of *The Grapes of Wrath*," in *Steinbeck and the
        Environment: Interdisciplinary Approaches*. ed. Susan
        Beegel, Susan Shillinglaw, and Wes Tiffney. Tuscaloosa:
        University of Alabama Press, 1997. (pp. 92- 112)

1518   Valenti, Peter. "Steinbeck's Geographical Seasons: *The
        Winter of Our Discontent*," *Steinbeck Quarterly*,
        XXVI:3-4 (Summer/Fall 1993), 111- 117.

1519   Van Gelder, Robert. "Interview with a Best-Selling Author:
         John Steinbeck," in *Conversations with John Steinbeck*.
         ed. Thomas Fensch. Jackson: University of Mississippi
         Press, 1988. (pp. 43-48) (reprint from *Cosmopolitan*
         (April 1947), 18, 123-25)

1520   Vaughan, James N. "Review of *The Grapes of Wrath*," in
         Critical Essays on "The Grapes of Wrath." ed. John
         Ditsky. Boston: G.K. Hall and Co., 1989. (pp. 32-33)
         (reprint from *Commonweal,* 30 (28 July 1939), 341-42)

1521   Verdier, Douglas L. "Ethan Allen Hawley and the Hanged
         Man: Free Will and Fate in *The Winter of Our
         Discontent*," *Steinbeck Quarterly,* XV:1-2
         (Winter/Spring 1982), 44-50.

1522   Visser, Nicholas. "Audience and Closure in *The Grapes of
         Wrath*," *Studies in American Fiction*, 22 (Spring 1994),
         19-36.

1523   Vogel, Dan. "John Steinbeck's Myth of Manhood," in
         Readings on John Steinbeck. ed. Clarice Swisher. San
         Diego: Greenhaven Press, 1996. Literary Companion
         Series. (73-76) (reprinted from "Steinbeck's "Flight":
         The Myth of Manhood," *College English,* XXIII
         (December 1961), 225-226)

1524   Wada, Tetsuya. "Sociological Features of *In Dubious Battle*,"
         John Steinbeck Society of Japan Newsletter, 6 (May
         1983), 3.

1525   Wagner-Martin, Linda. "Introduction," in *The Pearl* by John
         Steinbeck. New York: Penguin, 1994. (pp. vii-xxiv,
         with drawings by Jose Clemente Orosco)

1526   Walcutt, Charles Child. "John Steinbeck's Naturalism," in
         Readings on John Steinbeck. ed. Clarice Swisher. San
         Diego: Greenhaven Press, 1996. Literary Companion
         Series. (40-49) (reprinted from Walcutt's *American*

Literary Naturalism: A Divided Stream. (Minneapolis/St. Paul: University of Minnesota Press, 1954))

1527   Waldron, Edward E. "*The Pearl* and *The Old Man and the Sea*," in *Steinbeck's Literary Dimension: A Guide to Comparative Studies. Series II.* ed. Tetsumaro Hayashi. Metuchen N. J.: Scarecrow Press, 1991. (p. 80-90)

1528   Waldron, Edward E. "Using Literature to Teach Ethical Principles in Medicine: *Of Mice and Men* and the Concept of Duty," *Literature and Medicine,* 7 (1988), 170-176.

1529   Walther, Louis. "Oklahomans Steinbeck's Theme," in *Conversations with John Steinbeck.* ed. Thomas Fensch. Jackson: University of Mississippi Press, 1988. (pp. 11-14) (reprint from *The San Jose Mercury News*, 8 January 1938)

1530   Wantanabe, Nancy Ann. "*Of Mice and Men*," Ch. 23 in *Beloved Image: The Drama of W. B. Yeats 1865-1939.* Lanham, Md.: University Press of America, 1995. (pp. 302-309)

1531   Ward, Jerry W., Jr. "Lance Jeffers and the Art and Act of Fiction," *Black American Literature Forum*, 18 (Winter 1984), 172.

1532   Ware, Elaine. 'Struggle for Survival: Parallel Themes of Techniques in Steinbeck's 'Flight' and Norris's *McTeague*," *Steinbeck Quarterly*, XXI:3-4 (Summer/Fall 1988), 96-103.

1533   Watkins, Floyd C. "Flat Wine from *The Grapes of Wrath*," in *John Steinbeck's "The Grapes of Wrath,"* ed. Harold Bloom. New York: Chelsea House Publishers, 1988. (pp. 57-66) (reprint from *In Time and Place: Some Origins of American Fiction* (University of Georgia Press, 1977))

1534   Weathers, Virginia. "Characters from *Winter of Our Discontent*," in *Dictionary of American Literary Characters*. ed. Benjamin Franklin V. New York: Facts on File, 1990.

1535   Wedeles, Judy, and Beth Everest. "The Neglected Rib: Women in *East of Eden*." See #805.

1536   Weeks, Donald. "Steinbeck against Steinbeck," in *Modern Critical Views: John Steinbeck*. ed. Harold Bloom. New York: Chelsea House, 1987. (pp. 7-17) (reprint from *The Pacific Spectator*, 1 #4 (Autumn 1947))

1537   Weisberger, Bernard A. "Afterword," in *The Grapes of Wrath*. New York: Reader's Digest Association, 1991.

1538   Weisinger, Marsha. "*The Grapes of Wrath* Reappraised," *Chronicles of Oklahoma*, 70:4 (Winter 1992), 391.

1539   Welsh, Andrew. "Lancelot at the Crossroads in Malory and Steinbeck," *Philological Quarterly*, 70:4 (1991), 485-502.

1540   Wendel, Thomas. "John Steinbeck: Finland's Favorite Author," *The Steinbeck Newsletter*, 3:1 (Winter 1990), 4-5.

1541   Werlock, Abby H. P. "Poor Whites: Joads and Snopeses," *San Jose Studies*, 18 (Winter 1992), 61-71.

1542   Werlock, Abby. "Looking at Lisa: The Function of the Feminine in Steinbeck's *In Dubious Battle*," in *John Steinbeck: The Years of Greatness, 1936-1939*. ed. Tetsumaro Hayashi. Tuscaloosa, Ala.: University of Alabama Press, 1993. (pp. 47-63)

1543   Weston, Cheryl, and John Knapp. "Profiles of the Scientific Personality: John Steinbeck's 'The Snake,'" *Mosaic*, 22:1 (Winter 1989), 87-99.

1544   "What Cannery Row Was," *This Month on Monterey Peninsula*, 27:2 (February 1989), 38.

1545   Wheen, Francis. "The Green Shirts," *Independent Magazine* (October 5, 1991), 34-38, 40. (Story of John Hargrave and the Kibbo Kift movement)

1546   White, Ray Lewis. "The Two *Grapes of Wrath*," *Notes on Modern American Literature*, 9:2 (Fall 1885), 1-3.

1547   White, Ray Lewis. "*The Grapes of Wrath* and the Critics of 1939," *Resources for American Literary Study*, 13:2 (Autumn 1983), 134-164.

1548   Williams, Donald Mace. "*Grapes of Wrath* Note Bears Fruit for Long Island University," *Newsday*, 4 May 1989, 6, 48.

1549   Williams, Mary C. "Lessons from Ladies in Steinbeck's 'Gawain, Ewain and Marhalt,'" *Avalon to Camelot,* 1 (Summer 1984), 40-41.

1549A   Willoughby, James W. "My Father and John Steinbeck," *Steinbeck Newsletter*, 10:1 (Spring 1997), 30-31.

1550   Wilson, Edmund. "John Steinbeck's *Cannery Row*," in *The Uncollected Edmund Wilson*. ed. Janet Groth and David Castronovo. Athens: Ohio University Press, 1995. (pp. 353-355)

1551   Wilson, Jerry W. "The Gift" in *Masterplots II: Short Story Series*. Vol. II. ed. Frank Magill. Pasadena, Calif.: Salem Press, 1986. (pp. 843-846)

1552   Wilson, J. W. "Steinbeck, Fuentes and the Mexican Revolution," *Southwest Review,* 67 (Autumn 1982), 430-440.

1553   Winn, Harbour. "The Unity in Steinbeck's *Pastures*
        Community," *Steinbeck Quarterly*, XXII:3-4
        (Summer/Fall 1989), 91-103.

1554   Winter, Ella. "Sketching the Author of *Tortilla Flat*," in
        Conversations with John Steinbeck. ed. Thomas Fensch.
        Jackson: University of Mississippi Press, 1988. (pp. 3-
        5) (reprint from *San Francisco Chronicle*, 1 June 1935)

1555   Wollenberg, Charles. "Introduction," to *The Harvest Gypsies:
        On the Road to "The Grapes of Wrath."* Berkeley,
        California: Heyday Books, 1988. (a reprint of the 1936
        publication) (pp. v-viii)

1556   Work, James C. "Coordinate Forces in 'The Leader of the
        People,'" *Western American Literature*, 16:4 (February
        1982), 279-289.

1557   Wyatt, David. "Introduction," in *East of Eden* by John
        Steinbeck. New York: Penguin Books, 1992. (pp. vii-
        xxviii)

1558   Wyatt, David. "Introduction," in *New Essays on "The Grapes
        of Wrath."* ed. David Wyatt. Cambridge: Cambridge
        University Press, 1990. (pp. 1-26)

1559   Wyatt, David. "Ch. 6: Steinbeck's Lost Gardens," in *The Fall
        into Eden: Landscape and Imagination in California*.
        Cambridge: Cambridge University Press, 1986. (pp. 124-
        157)

1560   Yamashita, Iwao. "An Interpretation of *East of Eden* from an
        Oriental Viewpoint," *Sei-Ei-Ken Bulletin* (Shizuoka
        Koto Gakko Eigo Kenkyukai (High School English
        Study Society)), 25 (1987), 54-66.

1561   Yanagi, Masami. "Love for Humanity in John Steinbeck's
        The Grapes of Wrath," *Evergreen* (The Society of
        English Literature, Aichi Shukutoku College) 8 (March
        23, 1986), 53-65.

1562   Yano, Shigeharu. "Curses in *The Pastures of Heaven* (1),"
        Reitaku University Journal, 39 (June 1985), 135-150.

1563   Yano, Shigeharu. "Curses in *The Pastures of Heaven* (2),"
        Reitaku University Journal, 40 (December 1985), 183-
        198.

1564   Yano, Shigeharu. "Editor's Postscript," *John Steinbeck
        Society of Japan Newsletter*, 6 (May 1983), 12.

1565   Yano, Shigeharu. "Editor's Postscript," *John Steinbeck
        Society of Japan Newsletter*, 7 (May 1984), 14.

1566   Yano, Shigeharu. "Editor's Postscript," *John Steinbeck
        Society of Japan Newsletter*, 8 (May 1985), 11.

1567   Yano, Shigeharu. "Editor's Postscript," *John Steinbeck
        Society of Japan Newsletter*, 9 (May 1986), 7.

1568   Yano, Shigeharu. "Illusion and Alienation in *Cup of Gold*,"
        Reitaku University Journal, 35 (July 1983), 51-60.

1569   Yano, Shigeharu. "Impressions of the Steinbeck Festival III,
        Salinas, California, 1982," *Reitaku University Journal*,
        34 (December 1982), 11-31.

1570   Yano, Shigeharu. "Impressions of the Steinbeck Festival III,
        Salinas, California, 1982," *Eigo Seinen (The Rising
        Generation)*, (December 1982), n.p.

1571   Yano, Shigeharu. "Impressions of the Second International
        Steinbeck Congress," *Reitaku University Journal*, 38
        (December 1984), 187-91.

1572   Yano, Shigeharu. "Interview with Tetsumaro Hayashi," *John
        Steinbeck Society of Japan Newsletter*, 7 (May 1984), 5-
        8.

1573   Yano, Shigeharu. "Introduction," to Hayashi article, *Reitaku
        University Journal*, 36 (December 1984), 175-78.

1574   Yano, Shigeharu. "Loneliness and Alienation in *Cup of Gold*
        (II)," *Reitaku University Journal*, 36 (December 1983),
        9-27.

1575   Yano, Shigeharu. "Loneliness and Alienation in *Cup of Gold*
        (III)," *Reitaku University Journal*, 37 (July 1984), 15-24.

1576   Yano, Shigeharu. "A Meeting of East and West: The Fifth
        Annual Steinbeck Festival and the Second International
        Steinbeck Congress: 'From Salinas to the World,'"
        Steinbeck Quarterly, XVIII:1-2 (Winter/Spring 1985),
        13-15.

1577   Yano, Shigeharu. "My Ten Years with the Steinbeck Society
        of Japan," *Steinbeck Quarterly*, XX:1-2 (Winter/Spring
        1987) 30-32.

1578   Yano, Shigeharu. "Panel Discussion: Steinbeck's Trilogy
        after World War II," *John Steinbeck Society of Japan
        Newsletter*, 7 (May 1984), 4.

1579   Yano, Shigeharu. "Papers and Discussion (I); Chairman,"
        John Steinbeck Society of Japan Newsletter, 8 (May
        1985), 1.

1580   Yano, Shigeharu. "Participating in the Steinbeck Festival
        (I)," *Kyoiku Gakujutsu Shimbun* (Tokyo), (October 5,
        1983), 3.

1581   Yano, Shigeharu. "Participating in the Steinbeck Festival
        (II)," *Kyoiku Gakujutsu Shimbun* (Tokyo), (October 12,
        1983), 4.

1582   Yano, Shigeharu. "Preface: A Flavor of the East," in *John
        Steinbeck: Asian Perspectives*. ed. Kiyoshi Nakayama,
        Scott Pugh, and Shigeharu Yano. Osaka: Osaka Kyoiku
        Tosho, 1992. (pp. v-vi)

1583   Yano, Shigeharu. "The Quest for God in *To a God
        Unknown*," *Tokoha Gakuen University Review, Faculty
        of Foreign Languages Review,* 6 (1989), 61-74.

1584   Yano, Shigeharu. "A Special Message," *Steinbeck Quarterly,*
        XIX:1-2 (Winter/Spring 1986), 40-42.

1585   Yano, Shigeharu. "The Twenty-Fifth Anniversary of the
        International John Steinbeck Society," *Steinbeck
        Quarterly,* XXIV:3-4 (Summer/Fall 1991), 79-80.

1586   Yarmus, Marcia D. "Federico Garcia Lorca's *Yerma* and
        John Steinbeck's *Burning Bright*: A Comparative
        Study," *Garcia Lorca Review,* 11:1-2 (Spring 1983), 75-
        86.

1587   Yarmus, Marcia D. "John Steinbeck's Hispanic Character
        Names," *Literary Onomastic Studies,* 13 (1986), 193-
        204.

1588   Yarmus, Marcia D. "John Steinbeck's Hispanic Onomastic
        Interests in *The Log from the Sea of Cortez* and *East of
        Eden*," *Literary Onomastic Studies,* 12 (1985), 195-207.

1589   Yarmus, Marcia D. "John Steinbeck's Toponymic
        Preferences in *From Oz to the Onion Patch,*" Publication
        #1 of The North Central Name Society. DeKalb, Ill.:
        Northern Illinois University, 1986. (pp. 147-160)

1590   Yarmus, Marcia. "The Picaresque Novel and John
        Steinbeck," in *Rediscovering Steinbeck: Revisionist
        Views of His Art, Politics and Intellect.* ed. Cliff Lewis
        and Carroll Britch. Lewiston, N.Y.: Edward Mellen
        Press, 1989. (pp. 79-103)

1591   Yoshizawa, Eijiro. "'Flight': A Tragedy of Honor,"
        Komazawa Junior College Bulletin, 17 (March 1989),
        29-34.

1592   Yoshizawa, Eijiro. "*Of Mice and Men:* As the Supplement
        and Preface to 'The White Quail,'"*Komazawa Junior
        College Bulletin*, 14 (March 1986), 15-29.

1593   Yoshizawa, Eijiro. "A Sketch of John Steinbeck's World:
        Focusing on 'The Chrysanthemums,'" *Komazawa Junior
        College Bulletin*, 12 (March 1984), 33-40.

1594   Yoshizawa, Eijiro. "'The Snake': A Study in Paranoia,"
        Komazawa Junior College Bulletin, 16 (March 1988),
        31-43.

1595   Young, Robert, Jr. "*Of Mice and Men* and Marketing,"
        Writer's Digest, 67 (August 1987), 54.

1596   Zane, Nancy. "The Romantic Impulse in Steinbeck's *Journal
        of a Novel: The East of Eden Letters* (1969)," in
        Steinbeck's Posthumous Work: Essays in Criticism. ed.
        Tetsumaro Hayashi and Thomas J. Moore. Steinbeck
        Monograph Series, No. 14. Muncie, Ind.: Steinbeck
        Research Institute, Ball State University Press, 1989. (pp.
        1-12)

1597   Zimmerman, P., and Thomas J. Carey. "Jefferson, Steinbeck
        and *The Grapes of Wrath*: The Failed Quest For Land."
        See #681.

Dissertations and Theses

1598   Anderson, David Louis. "The American Dream in Twentieth-Century California Fiction," Carnegie-Mellon University, 1983. (D.A.) (*Of Mice and Men* and *The Grapes of Wrath*)
DAI, 44/04A (October 1983), 1083-84. #DA8315867

1599   Armstrong, Diane P. "The Effect of Interlocking and Non-interlocking Reading Guides on Text Comprehension of Eleventh Grade English Students," University of Toledo, 1982. (Ph.D.) (*The Grapes of Wrath*)
DAI, 43/11A (May 1983), 3558. #DA8307708

1600   Baines, Laurence Arthur. "Aspects of Language in Literature and Film," University of Texas at Austin, 1993. (Ph. D.)
DAI, 54/4 (October 1993), 1268A. #DA9323324

1601   Barry, Michael Gordon. "Recovering Meaning from the Irony of History: American Political Fiction in Transition," (Steinbeck, Wright, Warren and Trilling) State University of New York at Buffalo, 1987. (Ph.D.)
DAI, 50/12A (June 1990), 3949. #DA 9013031

1602   Balaswamy, P. "Allegory in John Steinbeck's Early Novels," University of Madras, India, 1984. (Ph.D.)

1603   Busch, Christopher Scott. "John Steinbeck and the Frontier West," University of Notre Dame, 1993. (Ph.D.)
DAI, 53/11A (May 1993), 3905. #DA9308221

1604   Campman, M. Sue. "What We Must Love: Marriage in the
        Best-Sellers by Women during the 1930s," University of
        Texas at Austin, 1987. (Ph.D.) (*The Grapes of Wrath*)
        DAI, 48/10A (April 1988), 2627.   #DA8728529

1605   Caputi, Natalino. "A Typological Study of the Unconscious,"
        Drew University, 1982. (Ph.D.) (Steinbeck's Phalanx
        Theory)
        DAI, 44/04B (October 1983), 1220.   #DA8317847

1606   Carlson, Julia Lowell. "American Women of the Thirties:
        Images of Women in American Fiction of the 1930s,"
        University of North Carolina at Chapel Hill, 1985.
        (Ph.D.) (*The Grapes of Wrath*)
        DAI, 46/11A (May 1986), 3350.   #DA8527263

1607   Casey, Roger Neal. "The Driving Machine: Automobility and
        American Literature," Florida State University, 1991.
        (Ph.D.)
        DAI, 52/08A (February 1992), 2923.   #DA9202293

1608   Castanier, Chris. "'Roadworks': The Open Frontier in
        American Literature of Travel," Wayne State University,
        1992. (Ph.D.) (Travels with Charley)
        DAI, 53/12A (June 1992), 4318.   #DA9310633

1609   Christensen, Steven Eric. "An Application of Kohlberg's
        Cognitive-Developmental Theory of Moralization to
        Ninth Grade Student Responses to the Novel,"
        University of Massachusetts, 1982. (Ed. D.) (*Of Mice
        and Men*)   *DAI*, 43/08A (February 1983), 2601
        #DA8229532

1610   Collins, Maurice Joseph. "Aesthetics and Respect or, Look
        What They've Done to My Leftists: Jack London, Upton
        Sinclair, John Steinbeck and Working People," Brown

University, 1992. (Ph.D.)
DAI, 54/4 (October 1993), 1361A.   #DA9308793

1611   DeVasto, Carl H. "The Poet of Demos: John Steinbeck's *The Grapes of Wrath* and Other Major Later Fiction*,*" University of Rhode Island, 1982. (Ph.D.)
DAI, 44/07A (January 1984), 2147.   #DA8326476

1612   Dillman, Mary Alice. "Contexts of Development in John Steinbeck's *The Journals of 'The Grapes of Wrath'* and *Journal of a Novel*," Ohio State University, 1992. (Ph.D.)
DAI, 53/05A (November 1992), 1517.   #DA9219712

1613   Etheridge, Charles Larimore, Jr. "Dos Passos, Steinbeck, Faulkner and the Narrative Aesthetic of the Thirties," Texas Christian University, 1989. (Ph.D.)
DAI, 50/09A (March 1990), 2895.   #DA9004642

1614   Franklin, Elizabeth. "The Popularity of Jack London and John Steinbeck," B.A. Honors, English and American Literature, Harvard University. Harvard Archives, 1983.

1615   Gentry, Robert Wayne. "John Steinbeck's Use of Non-teleological Thinking in His Mexican-American Characters," Baylor University, 1985. (Ph.D.)
DAI, 46/10A (April 1986), 3033.   #DA8528152

1615A   George, Stephen Keith. "Of Vice and Men: A Virtue Ethics Study of John Steinbeck's *The Pearl*, *East of Eden*, and *The Winter of Our Discontent*," Ball State University, 1995. (Ph.D.)
DAI, 56/07A (January 1996), 2716   #DA9538187

1616   Gidding, Joan Colleen. "Steinbeck's Use of the 'Quest' Motif," University of Maryland, 1984. (Thesis, M.A.)

1617   Gilman, Irene Patricia. "Student Responses to Two Literary
        Passages and Two Paintings as They Relate to the
        Perception of Stylistic Complexity and the Dimension of
        Introversion-Extroversion," New York University, 1986.
        (Ph.D.)
        DAI, 47/04A (October 1986), 1223.   #DA8614325

1618   Green, David Leslie. "The Modernist American Landscape,"
        Brown University, 1982. (Ph.D.)
        DAI, 43/11A (May 1983), 3595.   #DA8228259

1619   Hadella, Charlotte Cook. "Women in Gardens in American
        Short Fiction," University of New Mexico, 1989. (Ph.D.)
        DAI, 50/11A (May 1990), 3588.   #DA9008391

1620   Hearle, Kevin James. "Regions of Discourse: Steinbeck,
        Cather, Jewett, and the Pastoral Tradition of American
        Regionalism," University of California at Santa Cruz,
        1991. (Ph.D.)
        DAI, 52/12A (August 1992), 4328.   #DA9213349

1621   Hecker, David Alan. "John Steinbeck: America's Isaiah,"
        Washington State University, 1983. (Ph.D.)
        DAI, 44/11A (May 1984), 3422.   #DA8404592

1622   Hurst, Mary Jane Gaines. "The Voice of the Child in
        American Literature: Linguistic Approaches to Fictional
        Child Language," University of Maryland, 1986. (Ph.D.)
        (*The Grapes of Wrath*)
        DAI, 47/06A (December 1986), 2158.   #DA860793

1623   Jones, Grace McEntee. "The American Epic," University of
        Alabama, 1987. (Ph.D.) (*The Grapes of Wrath*)
        DAI, 48/11A (May 1988), 2873-74.   #DA8801917

1624   Jones, Margaret Catherine. "Prophets in Babylon: Four
        California Novelists in the 1930s," Purdue University,
        1989. (Ph.D.) (Jim Casy in *The Grapes of Wrath*)
        DAI, 50/11A (May 1990), 3589-90   #DA9008635

1625   Kasparek, Carol Ann. "Ethan's Quest Within: A Mythic
        Interpretation of John Steinbeck's *The Winter of Our
        Discontent*," Ball State University, 1983. (Ph.D.)
        DAI, 44/09A (March 1984), 2766.   #DA8401282

1626   LaPresto, Brigitte Loos. "Agricultural Promise and
        Disillusionment in the California Novel: Frank Norris,
        John Steinbeck, Raymond Barrio," Bowling Green State
        University, 1987. (Ph.D.)
        DAI, 48/06A (December 1987), 1455.   #DA 8720073

1627   Lee, Cremilda Toledo. "John Steinbeck, Graciliano Ramos
        and Jorge Amado: A Comparative Study," Texas Tech
        University, 1980. (Ph.D.)
        DAI, 41/12 (June 1981), 5091A-5092A. #DA 8111953

1628   Levy, Josephine. "Biological and Animal Imagery in John
        Steinbeck's Migrant Agricultural Novels," Arizona State
        University, 1991. (M.A. Thesis)

1628A   Li, Luchen. "Between Society and Nature: A Rhetoric of
        John Steinbeck's Aesthetics," University of Oregon,
        1997. (Ph.D.)

1629   Lieberman, Jonathan Aron. "John Steinbeck's Vision of
        Community: An Intellectual Portrait of a Philosophical
        Conservative," B.A. Honors, English and American
        Literature, Harvard University. Harvard Archives, 1985.

1630   Mann, Susan Garland. "A Bibliographic and Generic Study
            of the Short Story Cycle: Essays on *Dubliners,
            Winesburg, Ohio, In Our Time, The Pastures of Heaven,
            The Unvanquished* and *Go Down, Moses,*" Miami
            University, 1984. (Ph.D.)
            DAI, 45/06A (December 1984), 1748.   #DA8416485

1631   Melichar, Donald P. "Censorship in Arizona Public High
            Schools: A Survey of English Department Chairs,"
            Arizona State University, 1987. (Ph.D.) (*Of Mice and
            Men*)
            DAI, 48/12A, Part I (June 1988), 3087.   #DA8802792

1632   Meyer, Michael J. "Darkness Visible: The Moral Dilemma of
            Americans as Portrayed in the Early Short Fiction and
            the Later Novels of John Steinbeck," Loyola University
            of Chicago, 1986. (Ph.D.)
            DAI, 47/01A (July 1986), 179.   #DA8605550

1633   Mulcahy, Judith M. "John Steinbeck's Non-Fiction,"
            University of Delaware, 1988. (Ph.D.)
            DAI, 49/08A (February 1989), 2221.   #DA8824196

1634   Norkunas, Martha Kathleen. "Tourism, History and
            Ethnicity: The Politics of Public Culture in Monterey,
            California," Indiana University, 1990. (Ph.D.)
            DAI, 52/02A (August 1991), 579.   #DA9119749

1635   Ouderkirk, Bruce J. "Children in Steinbeck: Barometers of
            the Social Condition," University of Nebraska —
            Lincoln, 1990. (Ph.D.)
            DAI, 51/06A (December 1990), 2020.   #DA9030141

1636   Pollard, Leslie Thomas. "*The Grapes of Wrath* and *Native
            Son*: Literary Criticism as Social Definition," University
            of Kansas, 1983. (Ph.D.)
            DAI, 44/04A (October 1983), 1136.   #DA8317916

1637   Post, Connie. "History's Myth: John Steinbeck and the
       Twilight of Western Culture," Texas Tech University,
       1993. (Ph.D.)
       DAI, 54/4 (October 1993), 1368A.   #DA9325764

1638   Procter-Murphy, Jeffrey Michael. "John Steinbeck's Use of
       Biblical Imagery in *The Grapes of Wrath*: American
       Dreams and Realities Examined," School of Theology at
       Claremont, California, 1989. (Ph.D.)
       DAI, 50/07A (January 1990), 2099   #DA8925006

1639   Railsback, Brian. "Searching for 'What Is': The Parallel
       Expeditions of Charles Darwin and John Steinbeck,"
       Ohio University, 1990. (Ph.D.)
       DAI, 51/11A (May 1991), 3746.   #DA9111456

1640   Renfro, Robert Bruce. "Three American Novelists at War:
       The World War II Journalism of Steinbeck, Caldwell and
       Hemingway," University of Texas at Austin, 1984.
       (Ph.D.)
       DAI, 46/02A (August 1985), 289.   #DA8508332

1641   Ripley, Jonathan Grant. "The Treatment of Burial Rituals in
       the Modern American Novel," St. John's University,
       1985. (Ph.D.) (*The Grapes of Wrath*)
       DAI, 46/09A (March 1986), 2694.   #DA8526108

1642   Rosenthal, Sherry Lynne. "Four Essays on the Nostalgic
       Appeal of Popular Fiction, Film, and Television: *Hard
       Times, The Birth of a Nation, The Grapes of Wrath*, and
       All in the Family." University of California at San Diego,
       1983. (Ph.D.)
       DAI, 44/05A (November 1983), 1446.   #DA8319138

1643   Sargent, Raymond Matthews. "Social Criticism in the Fiction
        of John Steinbeck," Arizona State University, 1981.
        (Ph.D.)
        DAI, 42/2 (August 1981), 706A.   #DA8117184

1644   Schneer, Deborah Lee. "Splitting in the Thirties: A
        Psychoanalytic Study of Roth, Steinbeck, Hemingway
        and Slesinger," University of Massachusetts, 1990.
        (Ph.D.)
        DAI, 51/08A (February 1991), 2741.   #DA9100541

1645   Shende, Dharamdas Maroti. "A Critical Study of the Problem
        of Evil in the Novels of John Steinbeck," Amvarati
        University, Amvarati, India, 1995. (Ph.D.)

1646   Shindo, Charles Jogi. "Voices of the Migrant: Democracy
        and Culture in the Dust Bowl Works of John Steinbeck,
        John Ford, and Woody Guthrie." University of
        Rochester, 1992. (Ph.D.)
        DAI, 53/02A (August 1992), 502.   #DA9218558

1647   Smith, Steven. "Honest Retailers of Truth: Popular Thinkers
        and the American Response to Modernity, 1912-1939,"
        Brown University, 1990. (Ph.D.) (Steinbeck)
        DAI, 51/11A (May 1991), 3795-96.   #DA9101834

1648   Soloway, Jeff. "Politics and Perspective: A Comparative
        Analysis of *The Grapes of Wrath* and *The Remains of
        The Day,*" B.A. Honors, English and American
        Literature, Harvard University. Harvard Archives, 1994.

1649   Staub, Michael Eric. "From Speech to Text: The 1930s
        Narratives of John Neihardt, Tillie Olsen and James
        Agee," Brown University, 1987.(Ph.D.)
        DAI, 48/04A (October 1987), 965.   #DA8715566

1650   Steinberg, Irene J. "John Steinbeck's Use of Biblical
            Allusions and Parables in 'Breakfast,' 'The Raid,' 'The
            Snake,' *To a God Unknown*, and *The Grapes of Wrath*,"
            Montclair State College, New Jersey, 1987. (Thesis,
            Master of Arts)

1651   Thomas, Jimmie Elaine. "The Once and Present King: A
            Study of the World View Revealed in Contemporary
            Arthurian Adaptations," University of Arkansas, 1982.
            (Ph.D.) (Steinbeck's *Acts of King Arthur*.)
            DAI, 43/10A (April 1983), 3316.   #DA8305079

1652   Upot, Sherine. "Dramatic Adaptations of Narrative Fiction: A
            Study of Selected Works of Henry James and John
            Steinbeck," University of Calicut, Kerala, India, 1990.
            (Ph. D.)

1653   Wilhelm, Arthur Wayne. "Maurice-Edgar Coindreau:
            America's Literary Ambassador to France," Georgia
            State University, 1992. (Ph.D.)
            DAI, 53/08A (February 1993), 2819.   #DA9235326

1654   Wright, Stephen Reginald. "The French Face of Henry
            Miller: An Inquiry into the Comparison of Miller to
            Celine," Harvard University, 1984. (Ph.D.)
            DAI, 45/07A (January 1985), 2095.   #DA8419426

1655   Yarmus, Marcia Dorothy. "The Hispanic World of John
            Steinbeck," New York University, 1984. (Ph.D.)
            DAI, 46/01A (July 1985), 146.   #DA8505541

1656   Zane, Nancy Elizabeth. "Steinbeck's Heroes: 'The Individual
            Mind and Spirit of Man,'" Ohio University, 1982.
            (Ph.D.)
            DAI, 43/05A (November 1982), 1549.   #DA8223282

1657   Zida, Jean. "Commitment as an Aesthetic Form: Ngugi Wa
         Thiong'O and John Steinbeck," University of Iowa,
         1991. (Ph.D.)
         DAI, 52/07A (January 1992), 2546.   #AAC9137016

Book Reviews

1658   Ackroyd, Peter. "Trampling Out the Lord's Vintage: A
        Review of *John Steinbeck: A Biography* by Jay Parini,"
        London Times, March 17, 1994, 36.

1659   Ariki, Kyoko. "Review of *The Indestructible Woman in
        Faulkner, Hemingway and Steinbeck* by Mimi Reisel
        Gladstein," in *Nihon Steinbekku Kyokai Jimukyoku Dayori*
        (*The Steinbeck Society of Japan Newsletter in Japanese*), 4
        (November 11, 1987), 4-5.

1660   Ariki, Kyoko. "Review of *Zapata*. ed. Robert E. Morsberger,"
        John Steinbeck Society of Japan Newsletter, 17 (May,
        1994), 15-17.

1661   Baker, Bill. "Review of *Working Days: The Journals of 'The
        Grapes of Wrath,'* ed. Robert De Mott," *Antioch Review*,
        47 (Summer, 1989), 365.

1662   Barbour, Bryan. "Review of *Steinbeck's 'The Red Pony':
        Essays in Criticism*," ed. Tetsumaro Hayashi and Thomas
        Moore." *Steinbeck Quarterly,* XXII:1-2 (Winter/Spring
        1989), 34-36.

1663   Baskett, Samuel. "Review of *Animals in American Literature*
        by Mary Allen," *Modern Fiction Studies,* 29 (Winter
        1983), 715.

1664   Battersby, Eileen. "The Life and the Work: A Review of *John
        Steinbeck: A Biography* by Jay Parini," *Irish Times*, April
        12, 1994, 13.

1665   Bellman, Samuel Irving. "Review of *The American Short
         Story. 1900-1945: A Critical History* by Philip Stevick," in
         Studies in Short Fiction, 23 (1986), 124.

1666   Benson, Jackson J. "Review of *The Dramatic Landscape of
         John Steinbeck's Short Stories* by John Timmerman,"
         Steinbeck Newsletter, 3:2 (Winter 1990), 5.

1667   Berthold, Dennis. "Review of *The Role of Place in American
         Literature* by Leonard Lutwack," *American Literature,*
         57:1 (March 1985), 178-179.

1668   Binding, Paul. "Review of *John Steinbeck: A Biography* by
         Jay Parini," *New Statesman and Society,* 7 (May 6, 1994),
         37.

1669   Bold, Alan. "Sour Grapes: A Review of *John Steinbeck: A
         Biography* by Jay Parini," *The Herald* (Glasgow), April 9,
         1994, 8.

1670   "Books for Vacation Reading," (Review of *Working Days:
         The Journals of "The Grapes of Wrath"* by Robert
         DeMott) *New York Times Book Review,* June 11, 1989, 37.

1671   Boyes, Kate. "Review of *The Grapes of Wrath: A Fifty Year
         Bibliographic Survey* by Robert B. Harmon and John
         Early," *Western American Literature,* 26 (1991), 151.

1672   Braun, Janice. "Review of *John Steinbeck: A Biography* by
         Jay Parini," *Library Journal,* 120 (January 1995), 102-103.

1673   Breines, Ron. "Steinbeck's Great Depressions: A Review of
         John Steinbeck: A Biography by Jay Parini," *Daily
         Yomiuri,* May 15, 1994, 8A.

1674   Brennan, Stephen C. "Review of *Twentieth Century Literary Naturalism: An Interpretation* by Donald Pizer," *Studies in the Novel,* 15 (1983), 166.

1675   Broyard, Anatole. "Review of *The True Adventures of John Steinbeck, Writer* by Jackson J. Benson," *New York Times,* January 6, 1984, C21, 19.

1676   Bryer, Jackson R. "Review of *The True Adventures of John Steinbeck, Writer* (1984)," *American Literature,* 57:3 (October 1985), 513-15.

1677   Burgess, Anthony. "Plain Man of Letters," *Observer* (April 22, 1984), 23. (a review of *The True Adventures of John Steinbeck, Writer* by Jackson J. Benson)

1678   Burgess, Anthony. "Bottled Demons and Spirits of Invention," *Independent,* March 9, 1990, 17.

1679   Busch, Christopher. "Review of *John Steinbeck's Fiction: The Aesthetics of the Road Taken* by John Timmerman," *Studies in the Novel,* 24 (1992), 463-464.

1680   Busch, Christopher S. "Review of *New Essays on 'The Grapes of Wrath,'* ed. David Wyatt." *Steinbeck Quarterly,* XXIV:3-4 (Summer/Fall 1991), 111-113.

1681   Busch, Christopher S. "Review of *The Short Novels of John Steinbeck: Critical Essays with a Checklist of Steinbeck Criticism,*" ed. Jackson J. Benson, *Steinbeck Quarterly,* XXIV:3-4 (Summer/Fall 1991), 108-111.

1682   Carey, John. "Down and Out in the Dustbowl: A Review of *John Steinbeck: A Biography* by Jay Parini," *Sunday Times (London),* March 27, 1994, Books sec., 3.

1683   Cartier, Francis. "Sardines, Steinbeck as They Really Were,"
         Monterey Sunday Herald, October 23, 1988, 4D. (a review
         of Bruce Ariss's *Inside Cannery Row: Sketches from the
         Steinbeck Era*)

1684   Cawley, Marianne. "Review of *Zapata* by John Steinbeck
         with an intro by Robert E. Morsberger," *Library Journal,*
         118:7 (April 15, 1993), 92.

1685   Checketts, Randy. "Review of *John Steinbeck: Dissertation
         Abstracts and Research Opportunities,* ed. Tetsumaro
         Hayashi and Beverly K. Simpson," *Steinbeck Studies,* 19
         (May 1996), 32-34.

1686   "Fame's Cost," *New Statesman and Society,* 107 (April 20,
         1984), 27-28. (a review of *The True Adventures of John
         Steinbeck, Writer* by Jackson J. Benson)

1687   Clark, Thomas. "Review of *Working Days: The Journals of
         'The Grapes of Wrath'* by Robert DeMott," *Writer's
         Digest* (November 1989), 40-41.

1688   Clemons, Walter. "Cursed by Success," *Newsweek,* 103: 6
         (February 6, 1984) 80. (a review of *The True Adventures
         of John Steinbeck, Writer* by Jackson J. Benson)

1689   Cohn, Jan. "Review of *The Yellow Peril: Chinese Americans
         in American Fiction* by William F. Wu," *Modern Fiction
         Studies,* 28 (Winter 1982), 658-660.

1690   Collins, Geneva. "At 50 Grapes of Wrath Thrives on the
         Vine," (Review of *Working Days: The Journals of "The
         Grapes of Wrath"* by Robert DeMott) *Cincinnati
         Enquirer,* April 17, 1989, n.p. (with *The Grapes of Wrath*)

1691   Collins, Geneva. "Dustbowl Legend Turns Fifty (*The Grapes of Wrath*)," *Daily News* (Halifax, Nova Scotia), April 15, 1989, 23.

1692   Cortese, Vince. "Review of *Many Californias: Literature from the Golden State*, ed. Gerald Haslam," *The Steinbeck Newsletter,* 6:2 (Summer 1993), 4-5.

1693   Covici, Pascal, Jr. "Struggling to a Classic: Review of *Working Days: The Journals of 'The Grapes of Wrath'* by Robert DeMott," *Dallas Morning News Books Magazine,* May 14, 1989, 10C-11C.

1694   Crow, Charles. "Review of *Coming of Age in California: Personal Essays* by Gerald Haslam," *The Steinbeck Newsletter*, 4:2 (Summer 1991), 11.

1695   Crow, Charles. "Review of *Voices of a Place: Social and Literary Essays from the Other California* by Gerald Haslam," *The Steinbeck Newsletter*, 4:2 (Summer 1991), 11.

1696   Cunningham, John. "John Steinbeck: Review of *Working Days: The Journals of 'The Grapes of Wrath'* by Robert DeMott," *Bloomsbury Review,* 9 (July 1989), 13. (with *The Grapes of Wrath, The Harvest Gypsies*, and *The Grapes of Wrath: Trouble in the Promised Land*)

1697   Davis, Charles. "A Biography of Famous Cannery Row," *Monterey Herald,* July 27, 1986, 5D.

1698   Davis, Robert Con. "Review of *John Steinbeck's Re-Vision of America* by Louis Owens," *Studies in the Novel,* 17 (Fall 1985), 326-328.

1699   Davis, Robert Murray. "Review of *John Steinbeck: A
         Biography* by Jay Parini," *World Literature Today*, 69
         (Summer 1995), 592.

1700   Davis, Robert Murray. "Review of *The True Adventures of
         John Steinbeck, Writer* by Jackson J. Benson," *World
         Literature Today*, 58 (Summer 1984), 420.

1701   Davis, Robert Murray. "Review of *Working Days: The
         Journals of 'The Grapes of Wrath'* by Robert DeMott,"
         World Literature Today, 64 (Winter 1990), 120.

1702   Davies, David. "A Literary Giant Who Refused to Conform,"
         Newcastle Herald, November 3, 1984, n.p. (a review of
         The True Adventures of John Steinbeck, Writer by Jackson
         J. Benson)

1703   DeMott, Robert. "Review of *The Collectible John Steinbeck:
         A Practical Guide* by Robert B. Harmon," *The Steinbeck
         Newsletter,* 2:1 (Fall 1988), 10-11.

1704   DeMott, Robert. "Review of *FDR's Moviemaker: Memoirs
         and Scripts* by Pare Lorentz," *Steinbeck Newsletter,* 5:1-2
         (Spring 1992), 13.

1705   DeMott, Robert. "Review of *The Grapes of Wrath: Trouble in
         the Promised Land* by Louis Owens," *Western American
         Literature*, 25 (Spring 1990), 91-92.

1706   DeMott, Robert. "Review of *John Steinbeck's Re-Vision of
         America* by Louis Owens," *Journal of English and
         Germanic Philology*, 87 (Summer, 1988), 464-467.

1707   DeMott, Robert. "Review of *The Short Novels of John
         Steinbeck: Critical Essays with a Checklist to Steinbeck*

Criticism by Jackson J. Benson," *Southern Humanities Review*, XXVI (Summer, 1992), 295-297, 501+.

1708   DeMott, Robert. "Review of *The Short Novels of John Steinbeck: Critical Essays with a Checklist to Steinbeck Criticism* by Jackson J. Benson," *The Steinbeck Newsletter*, 4:1 (Winter 1991),11.

1709   DeMott, Robert. "Review of *Steinbeck Bibliographies: An Annotated Guide* by Robert B. Harmon." *Bulletin of Bibliography*, 44 (December, 1987), 294-297.

1710   DeMott, Robert. "Review of *Steinbeck's Literary Dimension: A Guide to Comparative Studies, Series II* by Tetsumaro Hayashi," *Western American Literature*, 27 (November, 1992), 237-238.

1711   DeMott, Robert. "Review of *A Study Guide to Steinbeck. Part II,* ed. Tetsumaro Hayashi," *Steinbeck Quarterly,* XV:1-2 (Winter/Spring 1982), 51-56.

1712   Detro, Gene. "Focusing on the Cinematic Side: A Review of Joseph R. Millichap's *Steinbeck and Film*," *Houston Post*, January 22, 1984, n.p.

1713   Detro, Gene. "Review of *Steinbeck and Film* by Joseph Millichap," *Christian Science Monitor* (Eastern Ed.), 26 (January 16, 1984), 20.

1714   Detro, Gene. "Review of *The True Adventures of John Steinbeck, Writer* by Jackson J. Benson," *San Francisco Sunday Examiner and Chronicle*, January 22, 1984, 11-12.

1715   Detro, Gene. "Steinbeck Biography — Most Comprehensive Yet, but Marred by Bias: A Review of *The True Adventures of John Steinbeck, Writer* by Jackson J.

Benson," *Christian Science Monitor*, 26 (March 6, 1984), 22.

1716   Deutelbaum, Marshall. "Review of *Images of the Mexican American in Fiction and Film* by Arthur G. Pettit," *Modern Fiction Studies,* 28 (Summer 1982), 367-369.

1717   Dewey, Joseph. "Review of *The American Dream and the Popular Novel* by Elizabeth Long," *Modern Fiction Studies,* 32 (Summer 1986), 292-293.

1718   Dewey, Joseph. "Review of *American Exodus: The Dust Bowl Migration and Okie Culture in California* by James N. Gregory," *Steinbeck Quarterly,* XXIII:3-4 (Summer/Fall 1990), 102-104.

1719   Dewey, Joseph. "Review of *Rediscovering Steinbeck: Revisionist Views of His Art, Politics and Intellect*, ed. Carroll Britch and Cliff Lewis," *Steinbeck Quarterly,* XXIV:1-2 (Winter/Spring 1991), 46-48.

1720   Ditsky, John. "Review of Jackson J. Benson's *Looking for Steinbeck's Ghost*," *Choice*, 26 (June 1989), 1679.

1721   Ditsky, John. "Review of Jackson J. Benson's *Looking for Steinbeck's Ghost*," *University of Windsor Review*, 22 (1989), 116-118.

1722   Ditsky, John. "Review of Jackson J. Benson's *The True Adventures of John Steinbeck, Writer* (1984)," *University of Windsor Review*, 18 (Spring/Summer 1985), 90-92.

1723   Ditsky, John. "Review of *John Steinbeck As Propagandist: 'The Moon is Down' Goes to War* by Donald Coers," *Choice*, 29 (March 1992), 1072.

1724   Ditsky, John. "Review of *John Steinbeck As Propagandist: 'The Moon Is Down' Goes to War* by Donald V. Coers," *Steinbeck Quarterly,* XXV:1-2 (Winter/Spring 1992), 52-53.

1725   Ditsky, John. "Review of *John Steinbeck's Fiction: The Aesthetics of the Road Taken* by John H. Timmerman," *Choice,* 24 (February 1987), 885.

1726   Ditsky, John. "Review of John Timmerman's *John Steinbeck's Fiction: The Aesthetics of the Road Taken* (1986)," *International Fiction Review,* 14 (Summer 1987), 109-10.

1727   Ditsky, John. "Review of Joseph Fontenrose's *Steinbeck's Unhappy Valley* (1981)," *Fine Literary Property* (Catalogue #27, 1983), 33-34.

1728   Ditsky, John. "A Masterpiece Relevant 50 Years Later," (Review of *Working Days: The Journals of "The Grapes of Wrath"* by Robert DeMott) *Toronto Star,* May 27, 1989, M3. (with *The Grapes of Wrath*)

1729   Ditsky, John. "Review of Robert DeMott's *Steinbeck's Reading: A Catalogue of Books Owned and Borrowed* (1984)," *University of Windsor Review,* 18 (Spring/Summer 1985), 90-92.

1730   Ditsky, John. "Review of *Working Days: The Journals of 'The Grapes of Wrath,'* ed. Robert DeMott," *Choice,* 26 (July/August 1989), 1840.

1731   Doniger, Wendy. "A Very Strange Enchanted Mind: A Review of *A Fire in the Mind: The Life of Joseph Campbell,*" *The New York Times Book Review,* February 2, 1992, 7-8.

1732 Dunbar, Maurice. "Review of *The Crowd in American Literature* by Nicolaus Mills," *Steinbeck Quarterly,* XXIII: 3-4 (Summer/Fall 1990), 104-105.

1733 Dunbar, Maurice. "Review of *With Steinbeck in the Sea of Cortez: A Memoir of The Steinbeck/Ricketts Expedition As Told to Audry Lynch* by Sparky Enea," *Steinbeck Quarterly,* XXV:1-2 (Winter/Spring 1992), 53-54.

1734 Dunford, Judith. "Steinbeck Surveyed: Jay Parini Takes a Respectful Look at the Author of *The Grapes of Wrath,*" *Chicago Tribune,* March 5, 1995, Books, 3. (a review of Parini's *John Steinbeck: A Biography*)

1735 Edwards, Thomas R. "The Innocent: A Review of *The True Adventures of John Steinbeck, Writer* by Jackson J. Benson," *New York Review of Books,* 31 (February 16, 1984), 25-27.

1736 Elliott, Jenni. "Review of *Working Days: The Journals of 'The Grapes of Wrath,'* ed. Robert DeMott," *School Library Journal,* 35 (October 1989), 146.

1737 Fender, Stephen. "Keeping Close with the Earth," *Times Literary Supplement* (April 13, 1984), 391-92. (a review of *The True Adventures of John Steinbeck, Writer* by Jackson J. Benson)

1738 Fensch, Thomas. "A Review of *Critical Essays on Steinbeck's 'The Grapes of Wrath,'* ed. John Ditsky," *Steinbeck Quarterly,* XXIII:3-4 (Summer/Fall 1990), 105-107.

1739 Fensch, Thomas. "Review of *John Steinbeck: Asian Perspectives,* ed. Kiyoshi Nakayama, Scott Pugh, and Shigeharu Yano and of *Uncollected Stories of John*

Steinbeck, ed. Kiyoshi Nakayama," *Texas Review,* 13, No. 3-4 (Fall/Winter 1992), 98-100.

1740   Fischer, Jack. *"The Grapes of Wrath,* a 50 Year Vintage," *The Seattle Times/Seattle Post-Intelligencer,* April 9, 1989, A5.

1741   "Footnotes for the Week (Bruce Ariss, *Inside Cannery Row* (1988)," *Monterey Sunday Herald,* August 7, 1988, n.p.

1742   Fradkin, Philip L. "Review of *A History of Steinbeck's Cannery Row* by Tom Mangelsdorf (1986)," *Los Angeles Times Book Review,* September 7, 1986, n.p.

1743   French, Warren. "Review of *A Literary History of the American West,*" in *Resources for American Literary Study,* 17 (1991), 308-311.

1744   French, Warren. "Review of *Literature at the Barricades: The American Writer in the Thirties,* ed. Ralph Bogardus and Fred Hobson," *Modern Fiction Studies,* 30 (Summer 1984), 330-331.

1745   Fukazawa, Toshio. "Review of *Of Mice and Men: A Play in Three Acts,* ed Kiyoshi Nakayama and Hiromasa Takamura," *Jimkyoku Dayori (Japan Steinbeck Society Bulletin),* 15 (June 30, 1993), 4-5.

1746   Fultz, Norma J. "Review of *Cannery Row: A Time to Remember* by Tom Weber," *Steinbeck Quarterly,* XVII:3-4 (Summer/Fall 1984), 107-108.

1747   Fultz, Norma J. "Review of *The Collectible John Steinbeck: A Practical Guide* by Robert B. Harmon," *Steinbeck Quarterly,* XX:3-4 (Summer/Fall 1987), 97-98.

1748   Fultz, Norma J. "Review of *A Collector's Guide to the First
        Editions of John Steinbeck* by Robert B. Harmon,"
        Steinbeck Quarterly, XX:1-2 (Winter/Spring 1987), 41-42.

1749   Fultz, Norma. "Review of *John Steinbeck: A Checklist of
        Books By and About,* comp. Robert DeMott," *Steinbeck
        Quarterly,* XXII:1-2 (Winter/Spring 1989), 26-37.

1750   Fultz, Norma. "A Review of *The Steinbeck Research Center
        at San Jose State University: A Descriptive Catalogue* by
        Robert Woodward," *Steinbeck Quarterly,* XIX:3-4
        (Summer/Fall 1986), 88-89.

1751   Fultz, Norma. "Review of *'Your Only Weapon Is Your Work':
        A Letter from John Steinbeck to Dennis Murphy,* ed.
        Robert De Mott," *Steinbeck Quarterly,* XIX:3-4
        (Winter/Spring 1986), 43-45.

1752   Gaither, Gloria. "Review of *Steinbeck's Literary Dimension:
        A Guide to Comparative Studies* (Series II) (1991), ed.
        Tetsumaro Hayashi," *Steinbeck Quarterly,* XXV:3-4
        (Summer/Fall 1992), 133-134.

1753   Galligan, Edward. "Review of *Working Days: The Journals of
        'The Grapes of Wrath,'* ed. Robert DeMott," *Sewanee
        Review,* 97 (Fall 1989), cxxii.

1754   George, Stephen K. "Review of *A New Study Guide to
        Steinbeck's Major Works with Critical Explications,* ed.
        Tetsumaro Hayashi," *The Steinbeck Newsletter,* 7:2
        (Summer 1994), 12-13.

1755   Gervais, Marty. "Working Days Shed Light on a Tortured
        Writer," (Review of *Working Days: The Journals of "The
        Grapes of Wrath"* by Robert DeMott) *Windsor Star,*

(Windsor, Ontario) June 17, 1989, E5. (with *The Grapes of Wrath*)

1756 Gibson, Charles G. "Review of *A History of Steinbeck's Cannery Row*, by Tom Mangelsdorf (1986)," *Salinas Californian*, (n.v.) (May/June 1988), 60.

1757 Gladstein, Mimi Reisel. "Review of *American Exodus: The Dust Bowl and Okie Culture in California* by James N. Gregory," *Steinbeck Newsletter,* 3:2 (Winter 1990), 6.

1758 Gladstein, Mimi Reisel. "Review of *The Dramatic Landscape of Steinbeck's Short Stories* by John Timmerman," *American Literature*, 63 (September 1991), 558-560.

1759 Gleckner, Robert F. "Review of *The Fall into Eden: The Dramatic Landscape and Imagination in California* by David Wyatt," *American Literature,* 61:3 (October 1989), 508-510.

1760 Gould, Tony. "Cain, Abel, and the Gripes of Wrath: A Review of *John Steinbeck: A Biography* by Jay Parini," *Independent on Sunday*, 20 (March 1994), 36.

1761 Graves, Phyllis. "Review of *John Steinbeck* by Tom Ito," *School Library Journal,* 40 (June 1994), 155.

1762 Grigg, Q. "Review of *Critical Essays on 'The Grapes of Wrath'* by John Ditsky," *Choice* (September 1989), 120-121.

1763 Gullason, Thomas A. "Review of *John Steinbeck's Re-Vision of America* by Louis Owens," *Modern Fiction Studies,* 31 (Winter 1985), 745-748.

1764   Gullason, Thomas A. "Review of *Naturalism in American
        Fiction: The Classic Phase* by John Conder," *Modern
        Fiction Studies,* 31 (Winter 1985), 745-748.

1765   Gullason, Thomas A. "Review of *The True Adventures of
        John Steinbeck, Writer* by Jackson J. Benson." *Studies in
        Short Fiction,* 21:4 (Fall 1984), 415-416.

1766   Gutman, Judith Mara. "'We Made It . . . She and I': A Review
        of *Fruit Tramps*," *New York Times Book Review*, May 13,
        1990, 11.

1767   Hakutani, Yoshinobu. "Review of *John Steinbeck's Re-Vision
        of America* by Louis Owens," *American Literature*, 58:2
        (May 1986), 303-305.

1768   Hakutani, Yoshinobu. "Review of *Realism and Naturalism in
        Nineteenth Century American Literature* (Revised Ed.) by
        Donald Pizer," *Steinbeck Quarterly,* XIX:1-2
        (Winter/Spring 1986), 45-48.

1769   Hakutani, Yoshinobu. "Review of *Twentieth Century
        American Literary Naturalism* by Donald Pizer,"
        Steinbeck Quarterly, XVI:1-2 (Winter/Spring 1983), 46-
        49.

1770   Halloway, David. "Not an Inventor — a Finder: A Review of
        John Steinbeck: A Biography by Jay Parini," *Daily
        Telegraph* (London) March 26, 1994, Arts and Books sec.,
        5.

1771   Hamaguchi, Osamu. "Review of *A Study of John Steinbeck*,
        ed. Masaru Otake and Yukio Rizawa," *Steinbeck
        Quarterly,* XV:1-2 (Winter/Spring 1982), 56-57.

1772   Hamaguchi, Osamu. "Review of *The Current of Steinbeck's World* by Shigeharu Yano," *Steinbeck Quarterly,* XX:3-4 (Summer/Fall 1987), 99-100.

1773   Hamilton, Ian. "The Grapes of Wrath: A Review of *The Thirsty Muse,*" *Sunday Times* (London) February 18, 1990, H4.

1774   Hamilton, Ian. "Not Mad Enough to Be a Genius: A Review of *John Steinbeck: A Biography* by Jay Parini," *Sunday Telegraph* (London) April 3, 1994, Review sec., 10.

1775   Hamilton, Ian. "Steinbeck, the Celebrity," *Sunday Times,* April 6, 1984, 43. (a review of *The True Adventures of John Steinbeck, Writer* by Jackson J. Benson)

1776   Hamilton, John Maxwell. "A Review of *The Way We Warred: How America's Journalists Covered World War II,*" *Chicago Tribune,* September 17, 1995, Books, 1.

1777   Harmon, Robert. "Review of Frank Galati's Three Editions of John Steinbeck's "The Grapes of Wrath" (play adaptations)," *Steinbeck Quarterly,* XXV:3-4 (Summer/Fall 1992), 135-137.

1778   Harmon, Robert. "Review of *John Steinbeck* by A. Susan Williams," *Steinbeck Quarterly,* XXIV:3-4 (Summer/Fall 1991), 113-114.

1779   Harmon, Robert. "Review of *John Steinbeck: Dissertation Abstracts and Research Opportunities.* ed. Tetsumaro Hayashi and Beverly K. Simpson," *Steinbeck Newletter,* 8:1-2 (Winter/Spring 1995), 27.

1780   Hashiguchi, Yasuo. "Review of *After "The Grapes of Wrath": Essays on John Steinbeck in Honor of Tetsumaro Hayashi.*

ed. Donald Coers, Robert DeMott and Paul Ruffin,"
Steinbeck Studies, 19 (May 1996), 30-31.

1781   Hashiguchi, Yasuo. "Review of *A New Study Guide to
        Steinbeck's Major Works*. ed. Tetsumaro Hayashi," *The
        John Steinbeck Society of Japan Newsletter*, 17 (May
        1994), 12-13.

1782   Hashiguchi, Yasuo. "Review of *Steinbeck's Travel Literature:
        Essays in Criticism*, ed. Tetsumaro Hayshi. trans. Mikio
        Inui (Tokyo: Kaibynsha, 1985)," *Kyushu American
        Literature*, 27 (September 25, 1986), 126-127.

1783   Hayashi, Tetsumaro. "Review of *Dictionary of Literary
        Biography, Documentary Series, An Illustrated Chronicle*,
        Volume 2, ed. Margaret A. Van Antwert," *Steinbeck
        Quarterly,* XVI:3-4 (Summer/Fall 1983), 112-115.
        (chapter on John Steinbeck is found on pages 279-332)

1784   Hayashi, Tetsumaro. "Review of *Literature at the Barricades:
        The American Writer in the 1930s,* ed. Bogardus and
        Hobson," *Southern Humanities Review,* 18 (Spring 1984),
        191-192.

1785   Hayashi, Tetsumaro. "Review of *Steinbeck's Reading: A
        Catalogue of Books Owned and Borrowed* by Robert
        DeMott," *Southern Humanities Review*, 20 (Summer
        1986), 292-293.

1786   Hayman, Lee Richard. "Biographer Lays Out a Steinbeck
        Banquet," *Monterey Herald* (Calif.), March 13, 1989, 5D.
        (A review of Jackson J. Benson's *Looking for Steinbeck's
        Ghost.*)

1787   Hayman, Lee Richard. "An Interpretation of Steinbeck:
        Evaluation of *The Grapes of Wrath*," and "A Review *of*

"The Grapes of Wrath": Trouble in the Promised Land by Louis Owens," *Monterey Herald* (Calif.), June 18, 1989, 4D.

1788   Hayman, Lee Richard. "Review of *Beyond "The Red Pony": A Reader's Companion to Steinbeck's Complete Short Stories* by Robert Hughes, Jr. (1987)," *Monterey Herald* (Calif.), March 20, 1988, 5D.

1789   Hayman, Lee Richard. "Review of *Cannery Row: A Time to Remember* by Tom Weber," *Steinbeck Quarterly,* XVII:3-4 (Summer/Fall 1984), 108-109.

1790   Hayman, Lee Richard. "Review of *Collecting Steinbeck* by Maurice Dunbar." *Steinbeck Quarterly,* XVII:3-4 (Summer/Fall 1984), 110—111.

1791   Hayman, Lee Richard. "A Review of *The Grapes of Wrath* (50th Anniversary Edition)," *Steinbeck Quarterly,* XXIII: 3-4 (Summer/Fall 1990), 110-111.

1792   Hayman, Lee Richard. "Review of *A History of Steinbeck's Cannery Row* by Tom Mangelsdorf," *Steinbeck Quarterly,* XXI:1-2 (Winter Spring 1988), 39-40.

1793   Hayman, Lee Richard. "Review of *Inside Cannery Row: Sketches from the Steinbeck Era in Words and Pictures (sic)* by Bruce Ariss," *Steinbeck Newletter*, 2:1 (Fall 1988), 9.

1794   Hayman, Lee Richard. "Review of *John Steinbeck: The California Years* by Brian St. Pierre," *Steinbeck Quarterly,* XIX:1-2 (Winter/Spring 1986), 48-49.

1795   Hayman, Lee Richard. "Review of *John Steinbeck: Great American Novelist and Playwright* by William M. Jones," *Steinbeck Quarterly,* XIX (3-4 Summer/Fall 1986), 89-90.

1796   Hayman, Lee Richard. "Review of *John Steinbeck on Writing,* ed. Tetsumaro Hayashi," *Steinbeck Quarterly,* XXII:3-4 (Summer/Fall 1989), 103-104.

1797   Hayman, Lee Richard. "Review of *Looking for Steinbeck's Ghost* by Jackson J. Benson," *Steinbeck Newsletter,* 2:2 (Summer 1989), 11.

1798   Hayman, Lee Richard. "Review of *Staging Steinbeck: Dramatizing 'The Grapes of Wrath'* by Peter Whitebrook," *Steinbeck Newsletter,* 3:2 (Winter 1990), 4.

1799   Hayman, Lee Richard. "Review of *The True Adventures of John Steinbeck, Writer* by Jackson J. Benson," *Peninsula Herald* (Monterey, Calif.), January 22, 1984, n.p.

1800   Haynes, Michael A. "Review of *A Handbook for Steinbeck Collectors, Librarians, and Scholars,* ed. Tetsumaro Hayashi," *Steinbeck Quarterly,* XV:3-4 (Summer/Fall 1982), 126-127.

1801   Hearle, Kevin. "Review of *John Steinbeck: A Biography* by Jay Parini," *American Literature,* 67:4 (December 1995), 881-882.

1802   Hearle, Kevin. "Review of *John Steinbeck as Propagandist: 'The Moon is Down' Goes to War* by Donald Coers," *American Literature,* 64 (September 1992), 617-618.

1803   Hearle, Kevin. "Review of *The Other California: The Great Central Valley in Life and Letters,* by Gerald Haslam," *Steinbeck Newletter,* 8:1-2 (Winter/Spring 1995), 23.

1804   Hearle, Kevin. "Review of *Steinbeck's Short Stories in 'The Long Valley': Essays in Criticism*, ed. Tetsumaro Hayashi," *Steinbeck Newsletter*, 4:2 (Summer 1991), 12.

1805   Heavilin, Barbara. "Review of *Conversations with John Steinbeck*, by Thomas Fensch," *Steinbeck Quarterly*, XXII:3-4 (Summer/Fall 1989), 104-106.

1806   Heavilin, Barbara. "Review of *Hope among Us Yet: Social Criticism and Social Solace in Depression America* by David P. Peeler," *Steinbeck Quarterly*, XXII:1-2 (Winter/Spring 1989), 37-39.

1807   Heavilin, Barbara. "Review of 'John Steinbeck' by Warren French in Volume 2 of *Sixteen Modern American Authors*: *A Survey of Research and Criticism since 1972*. ed. Jackson R. Bryer," *Steinbeck Quarterly*, XXIV:3-4 (Summer/Fall 1991), 115-118.

1808   Heavilin, Barbara. "Review of *Modern Critical Interpretations: John Steinbeck's 'The Grapes of Wrath,'* ed. Harold Bloom," *Steinbeck Quarterly*, XXIII:3-4 (Summer/Fall 1990), 96-102.

1809   Heavilin, Barbara. "Review of *Steinbeck's Short Stories in 'The Long Valley': Essays in Criticism*. ed. Tetsumaro Hayashi," (1991) *Steinbeck Quarterly*, XXV:1-2 (Winter/Spring 1992), 54-58.

1810   Heavilin, Barbara. "Review of *Working Days: The Journals of 'The Grapes of Wrath'* by Robert De Mott," *Steinbeck Quarterly*, XXIII:1-2 (Winter/Spring 1990), 42-44.

1811   Hennessey, Val. "He Celebrated America's Winos, Hobos and Whores: A Review of *John Steinbeck: A Biography* by Jay Parini," *Daily Mail* (London), April 2, 1994, 33.

1812   Hirose, Hidekazu. "Review of *The Collectible John Steinbeck: A Practical Guide.* comp. Robert B. Harmon and *Steinbeck Bibliographies: An Annotated Guide* by Robert B. Harmon," *The John Steinbeck Society of Japan Newsletter,* 11 (April 1988), 7-8.

1813   Hirose, Hidekazu. "Review of *Steinbeck Sakuhin Ron (II)* (*A Study Guide to Steinbeck. Pt. II.*) ed. Tetsumaro Hayashi. trans. Kenji Inoue, Kiyoshi Nakayama, and Fumio Momose," *Steinbeck Quarterly,* XVII:1-2 (Winter Spring 1984), 44-45.

1814   Hoagland, Edward. "The Making of a Writer: The Job is Pour Out Your Heart" (Steinbeck and Saul Bellow), *New York Times Book Review,* October 4, 1981, 3, 36, 37.

1815   Hogan, William. "A Ramble through Steinbeck Territory: A Review of *John Steinbeck: A Biography* by Jay Parini," *Times Union* (Albany, N.Y.), Life and Leisure Sec., H12.

1816   Holloway, David. "Not an Inventor — a Finder: A Review of *John Steinbeck: A Biography* by Jay Parini," *Daily Telegraph* (London), March 26, 1994, Arts and Books sec., 5.

1817   Horvath, Brooke. "Review of *The American Dream and The Popular Novel* by Elizabeth Long," *American Literature,* 58:1 (March 1986), 130-132.

1818   Horvath, Brooke. "Review of *The Contemporary American Novel,* ed. Bradbury and Ro," *Modern Fiction Studies,* 34 (Winter 1988), 649-659.

1819   Horwitt, Sanford D. "Review of *Rising in the West: The True Story of an 'Okie' Family from the Great Depression through the Reagan Years* by Dan Morgan," *Washington Post*, September 20, 1992, 1, 10.

1820 Hotelling, Neal. "Review of *John Steinbeck: Novels and Stories, 1932-1937,* with notes by Robert De Mott," *Steinbeck Newletter,* 8:1-2 (Winter/Spring 1995), 25.

1821 Houston, James D. "Steinbeck's Obsession: A Novel Born in Pain," (Review of *Working Days: The Journals of "The Grapes of Wrath"* by Robert DeMott) *San Francisco Review of Books,* 13 (Spring 1989), 25-26. (with *The Harvest Gypsies*)

1822 Howarth, William. "The Writer of Our Discontent: A Review of *The True Adventures of John Steinbeck, Writer* by Jackson J. Benson," *Manchester Gaurdian Weekly*, January 22, 1984, 18.

1823 Hughes, Robert S., Jr. "Review of *Critical Essays on Steinbeck's 'The Grapes of Wrath'* by John Ditsky," *Western American Literature*, XXV (August 1990), 188-189.

1824 Hughes, Robert S., Jr. "Review of *The Dramatic Landscape of Steinbeck's Short Stories* by John H. Timmerman," *Texas Review*, 12 (Spring/Summer 1991), 131-32.

1825 Hughes, Robert S., Jr. "Review of *John Steinbeck's Concept of Man: A Critical Study of His Novels* by Sunita Jain," *Steinbeck Quarterly,* XVII:1-2 (Winter/Spring 1984), 46-47.

1826 Hughes, Robert S., Jr. "Review of *John Steinbeck: From Salinas to the World.* ed. Shigeharu Yano, Tetsumaro Hayashi, Richard F. Peterson and Yasuo Hashiguchi,"

Steinbeck Quarterly, XXI:3-4 (Summer/Fall 1988), 108-110.

1827   Hughes, Robert S., Jr. "Review of *Looking for Steinbeck's Ghost* by Jackson J. Benson," *Biography,* XIV (Winter 1991), 65-66.

1828   Hughes, Robert S., Jr. "Review of *Looking for Steinbeck's Ghost* by Jackson J. Benson," *Western American Literature,* XXV (August 1990), 190.

1829   Hughes, Robert S., Jr. "Review of *The Short Novels of John Steinbeck* by Jackson J. Benson," *Texas Review,* XI (Spring/Summer 1990), 98-99.

1830   Hughes, Robert S., Jr. "Review of *Steinbeck and Covici: The Story of a Friendship* by Thomas Fensch," *Steinbeck Quarterly,* XIX:3-4 (Summer/Fall 1986), 90-92.

1831   Hughes, Robert S., Jr. "Review of *West of the West: Imagining California,*" *Western American Literature,* XXVII (August 1992), 363-364.

1832   Hughes, Robert S., Jr. "Review of *The Wide World of John Steinbeck* by Peter Lisca," *Steinbeck Quarterly,* XVI:3-4 (Summer/Fall 1983), 115-116. (a reprint by Gordian Press in 1981 of Lisca's original 1958 text)

1833   Inoue, Hirotsugu. "Review of *John Steinbeck: From Salinas to the World.* (1986) ed. Shigeharu Yano, et al., trans. Osamu Hamaguchi, Kyoko Ariki, and Yoshifumi Kato," *Steinbeck Quarterly,* XXVI:1-2 (Winter/Spring 1993), 46-48.

1834   Inoue, Hirotsugu. "Review of *Sutainbekku Kenkyu: Nagai Tanima Ron (A Study of Steinbeck: Essays on 'The Long*

Valley'). trans. Hiromasa Takamura, T.J. O'Brien, and Tatsuo Narita," (A translation of *A Study Guide to Steinbeck's "The Long Valley*," ed. Tetsumaro Hayashi) *John Steinbeck Society of Japan Newsletter,* 16 (April 1993), 10-11.

1835 Inoue, Kenji. "Review of *Ikari no Budo o Yomu: Amerika no Eden no Hate (A Reading of The Grapes of Wrath: Beyond America's Eden),* trans. Kiyoshi Nakayama and Yoshimitsu Nakayama." (A translation of Louis Owens, *The Grapes of Wrath: Trouble in the Promised Land*) *Jimkyoku Dayori (Japan Steinbeck Society Bulletin),* 15 (June 30, 1993), 6-7.

1836 Inoue, Toshihiro. "Review of *A New Study Guide to Steinbeck's Major Works,* ed. Tetsumaro Hayashi," in *Jimkyoku Dayori (Japan Steinbeck Society Bulletin),* 16 (November 1, 1993), 3-4.

1837 Italie, Hillel. "The Legacy of John Steinbeck: A Review of *John Steinbeck: A Biography* by Jay Parini," *Norwalk* (Connecticut) *Hour,* February 1995, n.p.

1838 Jaehne, Karen. "Review of *Lewis Milestone* by Joseph R. Millichap," *Film Quarterly,* 36 (Winter 1982/1983), 56-58.

1839 Jaehne, Karen. "Review of *Steinbeck and Film* by Joseph R. Millichap," *Film Quarterly,* 38 (Spring 1985), 54-55.

1840 "*John Steinbeck: A Life in Letters,*" *Sunday Times* (London), April 10, 1994, Bookssec. 14.

1841 Johnston, Judy R. "Review of *John Steinbeck* by Catherine Reef," *School Library Journal,* 42 (March 1996), 229.

1842   Jones, J. D. F. "Quality Outshines Fame and Fortune: A
         Review of *John Steinbeck: A Biography* by Jay Parini,"
         Financial Times Weekend, April 2/3, 1994, xv.

1843   Kaida, Koichi. "Review of *A Child Discovers John Steinbeck:
         A Biographical Story for Young Readers* by Beverly
         Hollett Renner," *Steinbeck Quarterly,* XXVI:3-4
         (Summer/Fall 1993), 127-29.

1844   Kaida, Koichi. "Review of *Critical Essays on John
         Steinbeck's 'The Grapes of Wrath,'* ed. John Ditsky." *John
         Steinbeck Society of Japan Newsletter,* 14 (April 1991), 8.

1845   Kami, Yuji. "Review of *Ikari no Budo o Yornu: Amerika no
         Eden no Hate* (A Japanese translation of Louis Owens's
         The Grapes of Wrath: Trouble in the Promised Land).
         trans. Kiyoshi Nakayama and Yoshimitsu Nakayama,"
         John Steinbeck Society of Japan Newsletter, 17 (May,
         1994), 17-18.

1846   Kamiya, Gary. "John Steinbeck: A Review of *John Steinbeck:
         A Biography* by Jay Parini," *San Francisco Examiner*,
         March 12, 1995, C13-C14.

1847   Kaname, Hiroshi. "Review of *Sutainbekku no Sosaku-Ron*,
         trans. Toshio Asano. (A translation of *John Steinbeck: On
         Writing.* Steinbeck Essay Series #2)" in *Jimkyoku Dayori
         (Japan Steinbeck Society Bulletin),* 15 (June 30, 1993), 3-
         4.

1848   Kaneko, Toshio. "Review of *Modern American Masterpieces,*
         ed. Hisashi Egusa et al.," *Steinbeck Quarterly,* XX:3-4
         (Summer/Fall 1987), 100-102.

1849   Kaneko, Toshio. "Review of *Uncollected Stories of John Steinbeck*, ed. Kiyoshi Nakayama," *Steinbeck Quarterly*, XXI:3-4 (Summer/Fall 1988), 110-111.

1850   Kato, Mitsuo. "Review of *Conversations with John Steinbeck* by Thomas Fensch," *John Steinbeck Society of Japan Newsletter*, 13 (April, 1990), 7-8.

1851   Kato, Mitsuo. "Review of *John Steinbeck, 'Viva Zapata!'* ed. Kiyohiko Tsuboi and Kyoko Ariki," *Steinbeck Quarterly*, XX (3-4 Summer/Fall 1987), 102-104.

1852   Kato, Mitsuo. "Review of *Sweet Thursday* by John Steinbeck. trans. Kiyoshi Nakayama, Hiromu Shimizu and Hiroyuki Kobayashi," *Steinbeck Quarterly*, XIX:3-4 (Summer/Fall 1986), 92-94.

1853   Kato, Yoshifumi. "Review of *A Study Guide to Steinbeck's 'The Long Valley,'* (1976) ed. Tetsumaro Hayashi, trans. Hiromasa Takamura, T.J. O'Brien, and Tatsuo Narita," *Steinbeck Quarterly*, XXVI:1-2 (Winter/Spring 1993), 49.

1854   Katz, Joseph. "Review of *American Literary Naturalism* by Donald Pizer," *American Literature*, 56:2 (May 1984), 285-286.

1855   Kawata, Ikuko. "Review of *Amerika Bungaku to Kyuyaku Seisho: Sutainbekku, Heminguuei, Fokuna, Forusuto, Meruviru"* (*American Literature and the Old Testament: Steinbeck, Hemingway, Faulkner, Frost, Melville*) in *Jimkyoku Dayori (Japan Steinbeck Society Bulletin)*, 16 (November 1, 1993), 1-3.

1856   Kellaway, Kate. "Ripeness Is All: *The Grapes of Wrath*," *Observer*, June 25, 1989, n.p.

1857   Keller, Dean H. "Review of *'The Grapes of Wrath': A Fifty-*
         Year Bibliographic Survey, comp. Robert B. Harmon,"
         Steinbeck Quarterly, XXIV:1-2 (Winter/Spring 1991), 50.

1858   Keller, Dean H. "Review of *A New Steinbeck Bibliography*
         1971-1981 by Tetsumaro Hayashi," *Steinbeck Quarterly,*
         XVII:3-4 (Summer/Fall 1984), 111-112.

1859   Keller, Dean H. "Review of *'The Steinbeck Quarterly': A*
         Cumulative Index to Volumes XI - XX (1978-1987). ed.
         Donald Siefker, Tetsumaro Hayashi, and Thomas Y.
         Moore," *Steinbeck Quarterly,* XXIV:1-2 (Winter/Spring
         1991), 50-51.

1860   Keller, Dean H. "Review of *A Student's Guide to Steinbeck's*
         Literature: Primary and Secondary Sources, by Tetsumaro
         Hayashi," *Steinbeck Quarterly,* XXI:3-4 (Summer/Fall
         1988), 111.

1860   Kelley James C. "Review of *Parallel Expeditions: Charles*
         Darwin and The Art of John Steinbeck by Brian
         Railsback," *Steinbeck Newsletter,* 10:1 (Spring 1997), 33.

1861   Kennedy, William. "'My Work Is No Good,'" (Review of
         Working Days: The Journals of "The Grapes of Wrath" by
         Robert DeMott) *New York Times Book Review,* April 9,
         1989, 1, 44-45. (with *The Grapes of Wrath*)

1862   Kisor, Henry. "*The Grapes of Wrath*: Steinbeck's Depression
         Classic Marks Golden Anniversary," (Review of *Working*
         Days: The Journals of "The Grapes of Wrath" by Robert
         DeMott) *Chicago Sun Times Book Week,* March 26, 1989,
         14. (with *The Grapes of Wrath*)

1863   King, Florence. "Review of *John Steinbeck: A Biography* by
         Jay Parini," *The American Spectator,* 28 (June 1995), 65.

1864   Klein, Marcus. "Review of John H. Timmerman's *John Steinbeck's Fiction: The Aesthetics of the Road Taken* (1986)," *American Literature*, 59 (December 1987), 685-87.

1865   Kohn, Martin F. "Wandering in the West: A Review of Wallace Stegner's Memoirs," *Detroit Free Press*, March 29, 1992, 8H.

1866   Koontz, Thomas W. "A Review of *'The Grapes of Wrath'*: *Trouble in the Promised Land* by Louis Owens," *Steinbeck Quarterly*, XXII:3-4 (Summer/Fall 1990), 111-113.

1867   Koontz, Thomas W. "A Review of *Steinbeck's 'The Grapes of Wrath'*: *Essays in Criticism*. ed. Tetsumaro Hayashi," *Steinbeck Quarterly*, XXIV:1-2 (Winter/Spring 1991), 51-52.

1868   Koontz, Thomas. "Review of *San Jose Studies*, 14 (Winter 1990) Special issue: *'The Grapes of Wrath,'* ed. Susan Shillinglaw," *Steinbeck Quarterly*, XXIV:3-4 (Summer/Fall 1991), 119-123.

1869   Krieger, Elliot. "50 Years Later, *The Grapes of Wrath* Remains a Vintage Work," *Seattle Times/Seattle Post-Intelligencer*, April 16, 1989, L8.

1870   Labor, Earle. "Review of *Twentieth Century Literary Naturalism* by Donald Pizer," *Modern Fiction Studies*, 28 (Winter 1982), 665-671.

1871   Leader, Zachary. "Simple, Clear, Generous and Lucky: A Review of *John Steinbeck: A Biography* by Jay Parini," *Times Literary Supplement*, 4750 (April 15, 1994), 25.

1872   Lehmann-Haupt, Christopher. "Steinbeck's *'Grapes,'* with His Diary of Writing It." (review of *The Grapes of Wrath* and *Working Days: The Journals of The Grapes of Wrath 1938-1941*), *New York Times*, March 30, 1989, 12, C23.

1873   Lehmann-Haupt, Christopher. "Steinbeck's Journal Breathes New Life into Epic," (Review of *Working Days: The Journals of "The Grapes of Wrath"* by Robert DeMott) *Sacramento Bee,* April 9, 1989, n.p. (with *The Grapes of Wrath*)

1874   Leithauser, Brad. "The Flare of Want," (Review of *Working Days: The Journals of "The Grapes of Wrath"* by Robert DeMott) *New Yorker*, 65 (August 21, 1989), 90-93. (with *The Grapes of Wrath*)

1875   Leyde, Tom. "Review of *The True Adventures of John Steinbeck, Writer*, a Biography by Jackson J. Benson," *Salinas Californian*, December 31, 1983, 26.

1876   Lisca, Peter. "Review of *John Steinbeck's Fiction: The Aesthetics of the Road Taken* by John Timmerman," *Modern Fiction Studies,* 33 (1987), 322-323.

1877   Lister, David. "Steinbeck, Not So Saintly: A Review of *John Steinbeck: A Biography* by Jay Parini," *Independent on Sunday*, March 27, 1994, 8.

1878   Livingston, Julie A. "Review of *A Child Discovers John Steinbeck: A Biographical Story for Young Readers* by Beverly Hollett Renner," *Steinbeck Quarterly,* XXVI:3-4 (Summer/Fall 1993), 129-31.

1879   Loftis, Anne. "Review of *Steinbeck's 'The Grapes of Wrath':* Essays in Criticism*, ed. Tetsumaro Hayashi," *Steinbeck Newsletter,* 3:2 (Winter 1990), 7.

1880   Long, Fern. "Of Steinbeck and Intricate Music," *Cleveland Press*, November 1, 1979, D18. (Reviews of *The Intricate Music* by Thomas Kiernan and *Steinbeck and Covici* by Thomas Fensch)

1881   No Entry

1882   Ludington, Townsend. "Review of *The True Adventures of John Steinbeck, Writer* by Jackson J. Benson," *Resources for American Literary Study*, 13 (Spring 1983), 105-108.

1883   Lukacs, Paul. "Review of *Nobody's Home: Speech, Self and Place in American Fiction from Hawthorne to DeLillo* by Arnold Weinstein,*"* *Studies in Short Fiction*, 31 (1994), 275.

1884   Lynn, Kenneth S. "Review of *Working Days: The Journals of 'The Grapes of Wrath'* by Robert DeMott," *American Spectator* (August 1989), 41-42. (with *The Grapes of Wrath*)

1885   MacKendrick, L. K. "Review of *The Dramatic Landscape of John Steinbeck's Short Fiction* by John Timmerman," *Choice*, 28 (March 1991), 1138.

1886   Maddocks, Melvin. "The Man Who Belonged Nowhere: Review of *The True Adventures of John Steinbeck, Writer* by Jackson J. Benson," *Time*, 123 (January 23, 1984), 69-70.

1887   "The Man Who Lived Too Long: A Review of *John Steinbeck: A Biography* by Jay Parini," *Economist*, 331 (April 16, 1994), 96.

1888   Marovitz, Sanford E. "Review of Joseph Fontenrose's *Steinbeck's Unhappy Valley: A Study of 'The Pastures of*

Heaven' (1981*),"* *Western American Literature*, 12 (1982),
167.

1889   Marsden, John. "Review of *John Steinbeck's Fiction Revisited*
by Warren French." *Steinbeck Newletter,* 8:1-2
(Winter/Spring 1995), 24-25.

1890   McConnell, Frank. "*In Dubious Battle*: John Steinbeck's
Struggle for Acceptance," (Review of Jay Parini's *John
Steinbeck: A Biography*) *San Jose Mercury News*,
February 5, 1995, 1-2.

1891   McElrath, Joseph R. "Review of *Naturalism in American
Fiction: The Classic Phase* by John J. Conder," *American
Literature,* 57:4 (December 1985), 681-83.

1892   McGrath, Patrick. "Go West, Old Man: A Review of *John
Steinbeck: A Biography* by Jay Parini," *Night and Day*,
April 10, 1994, 36.

1893   McLynn, Frank. "Is George Bush a Mexican," (Review of
Zapata! by John Steinbeck) *Literary Review* (April 1992),
51-52.

1894   McLynn, Frank. "Pregnant Woman with an Abnormally Small
Heart: A Review of *John Steinbeck: A Biography* by Jay
Parini," *Literary Review*, 190 (April 1994), 16-17.

1894   Mesher, David. "Review of John Steinbeck: The War
Years, 1939-1945 by Roy Simmonds," *Steinbeck
Newsletter*, 10:1 (Spring 1997), 34-35.

1895   Meyer, Michael J. "Review of *John Steinbeck: The Voice of
The Land* by Keith Ferrell," *Steinbeck Quarterly,* XXII:1-2
(Winter/Spring 1989), 39-42.

1896   Meyer, Michael J. "Review of *Modern Critical Views: John Steinbeck*, ed. Harold Bloom," *Steinbeck Quarterly*, XXII:3-4 (Summer/Fall 1989), 107-109.

1897   Meyer, Michael J. "Review of *The Changes of Cain: Violence and the Lost Brother in Cain and Abel Literature* by Ricardo Quinones," *The Cresset*, LV:6 (April 1992), 29-30.

1898   Meyer, Michael J. "Review of *The Changes of Cain: Violence and the Lost Brother in Cain and Abel Literature* by Ricardo Quinones," *Steinbeck Newletter*, 5 (Spring 1992) 16.

1899   Meyer, Michael J. "Review of *The Changes of Cain: Violence and the Lost Brother in Cain and Abel Literature* by Ricardo Quinones," *Steinbeck Quarterly*, XXV:1-2 (Winter/Spring 1992), 59-61.

1900   Miller, Roger. "His Book Is Marching On," (Review of *Working Days: The Journals of "The Grapes of Wrath"* by Robert DeMott) *Milwaukee Journal*, April 9, 1989, 1E, 10E. (with *The Grapes of Wrath*)

1901   Millichap, Joseph R. "Review of *California Writers: Jack London, John Steinbeck and the Tough Guys* by Stoddard Martin," *Modern Fiction Studies*, 30 (Winter 1984), 826-828.

1902   Millichap, Joseph R. "Review of *The Dramatic Landscape of Steinbeck's Short Stories* by John Timmerman," *Modern Fiction Studies*, 37 (Summer 1991), 256-258.

1903   Millichap, Joseph R. "Review of *Inside Cannery Row: Sketches from the Steinbeck Era* by Bruce Ariss," *Modern Fiction Studies*, 37 (Summer 1991), 256-258.

1904   Millichap, Joseph R. "Review of *John Steinbeck: The Voice
          of the Land* by Keith Ferrell," *Modern Fiction Studies*, 33
          (Winter 1987), 683-84.

1905   Millichap, Joseph R. "Review of *John Steinbeck as
          Propagandist: "The Moon Is Down" Goes to War* by
          Donald Coers," *Modern Fiction Studies*, 38:2 (Summer
          1992), 483-485

1906   Millichap, Joseph R. "Review of *Looking for Steinbeck's
          Ghost* by Jackson J. Benson," *Modern Fiction Studies*, 35
          (Winter 1989), 753-756.

1907   Millichap, Joseph R. "Review of *New Essays on 'The Grapes
          of Wrath'* by David Wyatt," *Modern Fiction Studies*, 37
          (Summer 1991), 256-258.

1908   Millichap, Joseph R. "Review of *The Short Novels of John
          Steinbeck* by Jackson J. Benson," *Modern Fiction Studies*,
          37 (Summer 1991), 256-258.

1909   Millichap, Joseph R. "Review of *Steinbeck's Reading: A
          Catalogue of Books Owned and Borrowed* by Robert
          DeMott," *Modern Fiction Studies*, 30 (Winter 1984), 826-
          828.

1910   Millichap, Joseph R. "Review of *The True Adventures of John
          Steinbeck, Writer* by Jackson J. Benson," *Modern Fiction
          Studies*, 30 (Winter 1984), 826-828.

1911   Millichap, Joseph R. "Review of *Working Days: The Journals
          of 'The Grapes of Wrath'* by Robert DeMott," *Modern
          Fiction Studies*, 35 (Winter 1989), 753-756.

1912   Mills, Nicolaus. "Book Notes," (Review of *The Harvest
        Gypsies: On The Road to "The Grapes of Wrath"*) *Nation*,
        248 (March 20, 1989), 388-390.

1913   Mitchell, Eleanor R. "Review of *John Steinbeck as
        Propagandist: 'The Moon Is Down' Goes to War* by
        Donald V. Coers," *Texas Review*, 12 (Spring/Summer
        1991), 138-39.

1914   Mitgang, Herbert. "Almost Authorized: A Review of *The True
        Adventures of John Steinbeck, Writer* by Jackson J.
        Benson," *New York Times Book Review*, January 22, 1984,
        1.

1915   Momosi, Fumio. "Review of *Selected Essays of John
        Steinbeck*, ed. Kiyoshi Nakayama and Hidekazu Hirose,"
        Steinbeck Quarterly, XV:3-4 (Summer/Fall 1982), 128-
        129.

1916   Moore, Thomas. "Review of *A Catalogue of the John
        Steinbeck Collection at Stanford University,* ed. Susan F.
        Riggs and *John Steinbeck: A Collection of Books and
        Manuscripts*, Bradford Morrow Bookseller," *Steinbeck
        Quarterly*, XV:1-2 (Winter Spring 1982), 58-60.

1917   Morita, Shoji. "A Review of Tetsumaro Hayashi's *A New
        Steinbeck Bibliography, 1971-1981*." *Chu-Shikoku Studies
        in American Literature*, 20 (June 20, 1984), 101-03.

1918   Morita, Shoji. "Review of *Sutainbekku Kenkyu — Tanpen
        Shosetsu Ron (A Study of Steinbeck: Essays on the Short
        Stories),* ed. Hisashi Egusa," *Nihon Steinbekku Kyokai
        Jimukyoku Dayori (The Steinbeck Society of Japan
        Newsletter in Japanese)*, 4 (November 11, 1987), 2-3.

1919   Morsberger, Robert E. "Review of Tom Mangelsdorf's *A History of Steinbeck's 'Cannery Row'* (1986)," *Western American Literature*, 23 (May 1988), 71.

1920   Morsberger, Robert. "Review of Jackson J. Benson's *The True Adventures of John Steinbeck, Writer* (1984)," *Western American Literature*, 19:3 (November 1984), 231-33.

1921   Mulcahy, Judith M. "Review of *The Indestructible Woman in Faulkner, Hemingway and Steinbeck* by Mimi Reisel Gladstein," *Steinbeck Quarterly*, XXI:1-2 (Winter Spring 1988), 40-43.

1922   Mulder, Stephen L. "Review of 'The Mirror and the Vamp: Invention, Reflection, and Bad, Bad, Cathy Trask in *East of Eden*' by Louis Owens in *Writing the American Classics*, ed. James Barbour and Tom Quirk," *The Steinbeck Newsletter*, 4:2 (Summer 1991), 13.

1923   Nakachi, Kozen. "Review of *San Jose Studies*, Vol. XVI. No. 1 (Winter 1990): *The Grapes of Wrath*, a Special Issue," *John Steinbeck Society of Japan Newsletter*, 14 (April 1991), 8-9.

1924   Nakachi, Kozen. "Review of *Nihon Niokeru Sutainbekku Bunkenshoshi. (Steinbeck in Japan: A Bibliography)*. comp. Kiyoshi Nakayama," *Steinbeck Quarterly*, XXVI:3-4 (Summer/Fall 1993), 131-33.

1925   Nakamura, Masao. "Review of *A Child Discovers John Steinbeck* by Beverly Renner," in *Jimkyoku Dayori (Japan Steinbeck Society Bulletin)*, 16 (November 1, 1993), 6-7.

1926   Nakata, Yuji. "Review of *The Log from the Sea of Cortez*: 'About Ed Ricketts' by John Steinbeck. trans. Kenji

Inoue," *Steinbeck Quarterly,* XIX:3-4 (Summer/Fall 1986), 94-95.

1927   Nakatani, Masami. "Review of *John Steinbeck: Ikari No Budo O Yomu: Amerika No Eden No Hate* (Louis Owens's *The Grapes of Wrath: Trouble in the Promised Land),* trans. Kiyoshi Nakayama and Yoshimitsu Nakayama," *Steinbeck Quarterly,* XXVI:3-4 (Summer/Fall 1993), 133-34.

1928   Nakayama, Kiyoshi. "Review of *The Harvest Gypsies: On the Road to 'The Grapes of Wrath,'* ed. Takahiko Sugiyama." *Jimukyoku Dayori (Steinbeck Newsletter in Japanese),* 14 (November 10, 1992), 4-5.

1929   Nakayama, Kiyoshi. "Review of *Korutesu no Umi.* trans. Noriko Yoshimura and Mioko Nishida," (a translation of *The Log from the Sea of Cortez* by John Steinbeck) *Jimkyoku Dayori (Japan Steinbeck Society Bulletin),* 15 (June 30, 1993), 7-8.

1930   Nakayama, Kiyoshi. "Review of *The Complete Works of John Steinbeck,* ed. Yasuo Hashiguchi," *Steinbeck Quarterly,* XX:1-2 (Winter/Spring 1987), 42-45.

1930   Noble, Donald. "Review of *'Of Mice and Men': A Kinship of Powerlessness* by Charlotte Cook Hadella," in *Steinbeck Newsletter,* 10:1 (Spring 1997), 32.

1931   Noto, Sal. "Capsule Biography of Steinbeck's California Years," *San Jose Mercury News,* July 8, 1984, 27. (Review of Brian St. Pierre's *John Steinbeck: The California Years.* San Francisco, Calif.: Chronicle Books, 1983.)

1932   O'Leary, Timothy M. "*Grapes* at 50 Still Packs a Punch," (Review of *Working Days: The Journals of "The Grapes of Wrath"* by Robert DeMott) *Kansas City Star* (May 14, 1989), 1E, 10E. (with *The Grapes of Wrath*)

1933   Ono, Michio. "Review of *Nihon ni Okeru Suttainbekku Shoshi (Steinbeck in Japan: A Bibliography)*," in *Jimkyoku Dayori (Japan Steinbeck Society Bulletin),* 15 (June 30, 1993), 2-3.

1934   Osawa, Akiko. "Review of *John Steinbeck, 'The Grapes of Wrath,'* ed. Yasuo Hashiguchi and Koichi Kaida," *Steinbeck Quarterly,* XXII:3-4 (Summer/Fall 1989), 109-110.

1935   Osawa, Akiko. "Review of *Steinbeck Studies: On His Short Stories.* ed. Hisashi Egusa," *Steinbeck Quarterly,* XXI:3-4 (Summer/Fall 1988), 111-112.

1936   Osawa, Akiko. "Review of *Steinbeck's Travel Literature: Essays in Criticism.* ed. Tetsumaro Hayashi, trans. Mikio Inui," *Steinbeck Quarterly,* XIX:3-4 (Summer/Fall 1986), 96.

1937   Otomo, Yoshiro. "Review of *Steinbeck, the Man and His Work: Essays in Honor of Tetsumaro Hayashi.* ed. Yasuo Hashiguchi and Eiko Shiraga," *Steinbeck Studies,* 19 (May 1996), 31-32.

1938   Otomo, Yoshiro. "Review of *Steinbeck's Short Stories in 'The Long Valle,'* ed. Tetsumaro Hayashi. (Steinbeck Monograph Series #15)," *John Steinbeck Society of Japan Newsletter,* 15 (May 1992), 6-7.

1939   Owens, Louis D. "Reviews of *The Grapes of Wrath, The Harvest Gypsies, Working Days: The Journals of 'The Grapes of Wrath'* and *Looking for Steinbeck's Ghost,"*

Resources for American Literary Study, 18 (1992), 165-169.

1940   Owens, Louis D. "Review of *Literature at the Barricades: The American Writer in the 1930s,* ed. Ralph F. Bogardus and Fred Hobson," *Steinbeck Quarterly,* XVII:1-2 (Winter Spring 1984), 48-50.

1941   Owens, Louis D. "Review of *Twentieth Century Interpretations of 'The Grapes of Wrath,'* ed. Robert Con Davis," *Steinbeck Quarterly,* XVI:3-4 (Summer/Fall 1983), 118-120.

1942   Ozawa, Akiko. "Review of *John Steinbeck: 'The Grapes of Wrath.'* (Eihosha Commentary Booklet) ed. Yasuo Hashiguchi and Koichi Kaida. Tokyo: Eichosha Shinsha Press, 1988," *Steinbeck Quarterly,* XXII:3-4 (Summer/Fall 1989), 109-110.

1943   Ozawa, Akiko. "Review of *Steinbeck's Studies: On His Short Stories.* ed. Hisashi Egusa. Tokyo: Yasio Shuppan, 1987," *Steinbeck Quarterly,* XXI:3-4 (Summer/Fall 1988), 111-112.

1944   Ozawa, Akiko. "Review of *Steinbeck's Travel Literature: Essays in Criticism.* ed. Tetsumaro Hayashi. trans. Mikio Inui." *Steinbeck Quarterly,* XIX:3-4 (Summer/Fall 1986), 96-97.

1945   Pellow, C. Kenneth. "Review of *Beyond 'The Red Pony': A Reader's Companion to Steinbeck's Complete Short Stories* by Robert S. Hughes, Jr.," *Steinbeck Quarterly,* XXII:3-4 (Summer/Fall 1989), 110-111.

1946   Pellow, C. Kenneth. "Review of *The Fall into Eden: Landscape and Imagination in California* by David

Wyatt," *Steinbeck Quarterly,* XXII:1-2 (Winter/Spring 1989), 42-44.

1947   Pettit, Arthur G. "Review of *Image of the Mexican American in Fiction and Film,*" *Modern Fiction Studies,* 28 (Summer 1982), 367-369.

1948   Phillips, Gary. "Review of *John Steinbeck: Life, Work and Criticism* by John Ditsky," *Steinbeck Quarterly,* XIX:3-4 (Summer/Fall 1986), 96-97.

1949   Powell, David S. "Review of *The True Adventures of John Steinbeck, Writer* by Jackson J. Benson," *Indianapolis Star*, February 5, 1984, 4F.

1950   Pugh, Scott. "Review of *John Steinbeck: A Biography* by Jay Parini," *The John Steinbeck Society of Japan Newsletter*, 18 (May 1995), 9-10

1951   Pugh, Scott. "Review of *A New Study Guide to Steinbeck's Major Works, with Critical Explications*, ed. Tetsumaro Hayashi," *Kyushu American Literature*, 35 (1994), 73-77.

1952   Pugh, Scott. "Review of *Of Mice and Men: A Play in Three Acts*, ed. Kiyoshi Nakayama and Hiromasa Takamura," in *Jimkyoku Dayori (Japan Steinbeck Society Bulletin)* 17 (May 1994), 18-19.

1953   Pugh, Scott. "Review of *Of Mice and Men: A Play in Three Acts*, ed. Kiyoshi Nakayama and Hiromasa Takamura," Steinbeck Newsletter, 6:2 (Summer 1993), 13.

1954   Pugh, Scott. "Review of *Steinbeck's Literary Dimension: A Guide to Comparative Studies (Series II)*, ed. Tetsumaro Hayashi," *Kyushu American Literature* (Kyushu American Literature Society), 33 (1992), 77-81.

1955　Quigley, Michael. "For Book Lovers and Collectors: Notes from a Steinbeck Scholar," *Volusia* (January 30, 1983), 13. (reports on Maurice Dunbar's *Books and Collectors*)

1956　Quirk, Tom. "Review of *The Crowd in American Literature* by Nicolaus Mills," *American Literature*, 59:4 (December 1987), 647-649.

1957　Railsback, Brian. "Review of *The Dramatic Landscape of Steinbeck's Short Stories* by John H. Timmerman," *Steinbeck Quarterly*, XXIV:3-4 (Summer/Fall 1991), 123-125.

1958　Railsback, Brian. "Review of *Rediscovering Steinbeck — Revisionist Views of His Art, Politics and Intellect* by Cliff Lewis and Carroll Britch (1989)," *The Steinbeck Newsletter*, 4:1 (Winter 1991), 10.

1959　Randel, William. "Review of *California Writers* by Stoddard Martin," *American Literature*, 56:4 (December 1984), 608-609.

1960　Reinkin, Charles. "Review of *The True Adventures of John Steinbeck, Writer* by Jackson J. Benson," *Houston Post*, January 22, 1984, 11F.

1961　Reti, Ingrid. "Review of *Working Days: The Journals of 'The Grapes of Wrath'* by Robert DeMott," *Steinbeck Newsletter*, 2:2 (Summer 1989), 10.

1962　"Review of *After The Grapes of Wrath: Essays on John Steinbeck*. ed. Donald Coers, Paul Ruffin, and Robert DeMott," *AB Bookman's Weekly*, April 10, 1995, 1596.

1963　"Review of *Bombs Away* by John Steinbeck," *American Literature*, 63 (June 1991), 384.

1964   "Review of *Bombs Away* by John Steinbeck," *Reference and Research Book News*, 5 (December 1990), 27.

1965   "Review of *Cua Chuot Va Nguoi* by John Steinbeck," *Booklist*, 90 (June 1, 1994), 1782.

1966   "Review of *Cannery Row* (Audio Version) by John Steinbeck," *Booklist*, 86 (September 15, 1989), 200.

1967   "Review of *Cannery Row* (Audio Version) by John Steinbeck," *Library Journal*, 114 (October 1, 1989), 134.

1968   "Review of *Cannery Row* (Audio Version) by John Steinbeck," *Publishers Weekly*, 236 (August 4, 1989), 59.

1969   "Review of *Cannery Row* (Audio Version by Farden) by John Steinbeck," *Kliatt,* 28 (January 1994), 43+.

1970   "Review of *Cannery Row* (Audio Version) by John Steinbeck," *Wilson Library Bulletin*, 65 (November 1990), 76.

1971   "Review of *Conversations with John Steinbeck* by Thomas Fensch," *American Literature*, 61 (March 1989), 155.

1972   "Review of *Conversations with John Steinbeck* by Thomas Fensch," *Village Voice*, 34 (August 29, 1989), 59.

1973   "Review of *The Dramatic Landscape of John Steinbeck's Short Fiction* by John Timmerman," *Journal of American Studies*, 27 (August 1993), 270, 501+.

1974   "Review of *The Dramatic Landscape of John Steinbeck's Short Fiction* by John Timmerman," *University Press Book News*, 2 (December 1990), 36.

1975   "Review of *East of Eden*," *San Francisco Review of Books,* 20 (July 1995), 3.

1976   "Review of 'Flight' by John Steinbeck," *San Francisco Review of Books*, 9 (September 1984), 17.

1977   "Review of 'The Gift' by John Steinbeck," *Horn Book Guide*, 4 (Fall 1993), 307.

1978   "Review of *The Grapes of Wrath* by John Steinbeck," *American Heritage*, 43 (October 1992), 86.

1979   "Review of *The Grapes of Wrath* by John Steinbeck," *American Literature*, 61 (October 1989), 534.

1980   "Review of *The Grapes of Wrath* by John Steinbeck," *American Spectator*, 20 (December 1987), 44.

1981   "Review of *The Grapes of Wrath* by John Steinbeck," *Bloomsbury Review*, 9 (May 1989), 6.

1982   "Review of *The Grapes of Wrath* by John Steinbeck," *Book Week*, 19 (April 16, 1989), 3.

1983   "Review of *The Grapes of Wrath* by John Steinbeck," *College Literature*, 14 (Spring 1987), 146.

1984   "Review of *The Grapes of Wrath* by John Steinbeck," *English Journal*, 79 (October 1990), 67.

1985   "Review of *The Grapes of Wrath* by John Steinbeck," *Guardian Weekly*, 140 (May 21, 1989), 20.

1986   "Review of *The Grapes of Wrath* by John Steinbeck," *Inc.,* 13 (April 1991), 107.

1987   "Review of *The Grapes of Wrath* by John Steinbeck," *Los Angeles Times Book Review* (April 9, 1989), 15.

1988   "Review of *The Grapes of Wrath* by John Steinbeck," *Modern Fiction Studies*, 35 (Winter 1989), 753.

1989   "Review of *The Grapes of Wrath* by John Steinbeck," *New Statesman and Society*, 2 (June 30, 1989), 28.

1990   "Review of *The Grapes of Wrath* by John Steinbeck," *Newsweek*, 113 (May 1, 1989), 72.

1991   "Review of *The Grapes of Wrath* by John Steinbeck," *Reprint Bulletin Book Review*, 33:#4 (1988), 49.

1992   "Review of *The Grapes of Wrath* by John Steinbeck," *Sewanee Review*, 97 (October 1989), R122.

1993   "Review of *The Grapes of Wrath* by John Steinbeck," *Social Education*, 56 (November 1992), 376, 501+.

1994   "Review of *The Grapes of Wrath* by John Steinbeck," *Threepenny Review*, 11 (Spring 1990), 29.

1995   "Review of *The Grapes of Wrath* by John Steinbeck," *Village Voice*, 34 (August 29, 1989), 59.

1996   "Review of '*The Grapes of Wrath*': *Trouble in the Promised Land* by Louis Owens," *Bloomsbury Review*, 9 (July 1989), 13.

1997   "Review of '*The Grapes of Wrath*': *Trouble in the Promised Land* by Louis Owens," *Book Report*, 8 (March 1990), 47.

1998   "Review of '*The Grapes of Wrath*': *Trouble in the Promised Land* by Louis Owens," *Western American Literature*, 25 (Spring 1990), 91.

1999   "Review of *The Harvest Gypsies* by John Steinbeck," *American West*, 26 (June 1989), S12.

2000   "Review of *The Harvest Gypsies* by John Steinbeck," *Bloomsbury Review*, 9 (July 1989), 13.

2001   "Review of *The Harvest Gypsies* by John Steinbeck," *Choice*, 26 (March 1989), 1163.

2002   "Review of *The Harvest Gypsies* by John Steinbeck,"
       Publishers Weekly, 234 (October 14, 1988), 62.

2003   "Review of *The Harvest Gypsies* by John Steinbeck," *Village
       Voice*, 34 (August 29, 1989), 59.

2004   "Review of *The Harvest Gypsies* by John Steinbeck," *Western
       American Literature*, 24 (Summer 1989), 153.

2005   "Review of *A History of Steinbeck's 'Cannery Row'* by Tom
       Mangelsdorf," *Monterey Sunday Herald*, July 27, 1986,
       n.p.

2006   "Review of *John Steinbeck: A Biography* by Jay Parini,"
       American History, 30 (July 1995), 54.

2007   "Review of *John Steinbeck: A Biography* by Jay Parini,"
       Bibliophile, Catalogue 137, 2.

2008   "Review of *John Steinbeck: A Biography* by Jay Parini,"
       Kirkus Reviews, November 15, 1994, n.p.

2009   "Review of *John Steinbeck: A Biography* by Jay Parini,"
       Publishers' Weekly, 241 (December 12, 1994), 54.

2010   "Review of *John Steinbeck: A Life in Letters,* ed. Elaine
       Steinbeck and Robert Wallsten," *Observer* (March 27,
       1994), 18, 501+.

2011   "Review of *John Steinbeck's Fiction: The Aesthetics of the
       Road Taken* by John H. Timmerman," *Western American
       Literature*, 22 (Fall 1987), 228.

2012   "Review of *John Steinbeck's Fiction: The Aesthetics of the
       Road Taken* by John H. Timmerman," *University Press
       Book News*, 3 (December 1991), 40.

2013   "Review of *John Steinbeck's Fiction: The Aesthetics of the
        Road Taken* by John H. Timmerman," *Western Review of
        Books*, 13 (January 1987), 34.

2014   "Review of *John Steinbeck's Fiction: The Aesthetics of the
        Road Taken* by John H. Timmerman," *AB Bookman's
        Weekly*, 63 (October 14, 1991), 1453.

2015   "Review of *John Steinbeck's Fiction: The Aesthetics of the
        Road Taken* by John H. Timmerman," *Reference and
        Research Book News*, 6 (December 1991), 31.

2016   "Review of *John Steinbeck's Re-Vision of America* by Louis
        Owens," *Western American Literature*, 21 (Summer 1986),
        148.

2017   "Review of *John Steinbeck's Re-Vision of America* by Louis
        Owens," *SA Quarterly*, 86 (Winter 1987), 89.

2018   "Review of 'Johnny Bear' and 'The Snake' by John
        Steinbeck," (Audio Version) *Book List*, 82 (April 13,
        1986), 1248.

2019   "Review of *Journal of a Novel: The 'East of Eden' Letters* by
        John Steinbeck," *New York Times Book Review*, 95
        (December 16, 1990), 32.

2020   "Review of *The Long Valley* by John Steinbeck," *Book Week*,
        16 (May 4, 1986), 12.

2021   "Review of *The Long Valley* by John Steinbeck," *Washington
        Post Book World*, 16 (May 4, 1986), 12.

2022   "Review of *Looking for Steinbeck's Ghost* by Jackson J.
        Benson," *Los Angeles Times Book Review* (April 9, 1989),
        15.

2023   "Review of *Looking for Steinbeck's Ghost* by Jackson J.
        Benson," *Publishers Weekly*, 234 (October 21, 1988), 43.

2024   "Review of *Looking for Steinbeck's Ghost* by Jackson J.
        Benson," *University Press Book News*, 1 (June 1989), 22.

2024A   "Review of *Novels and Short Stories 1932-1937*," *American
        Literature*, 67 (June 1995), 428.

2025   "Review of *Novels and Short Stories 1932-1937*," *Book Week*,
        24 (October 9, 1994), 3.

2026   "Review of *Novels and Short Stories 1932-1937*," *Christian
        Century*, 112 (July 19, 1995), 723.

2027   "Review of *Of Mice and Men* (Audio Version)," *Kliatt*, 27
        (May 1993), 46.

2028   "Review of *Of Mice and Men* (Audio Version by Gary
        Sinise)," *Books and Bookmen* (March 1994), 15.

2029   "Review of *Of Mice and Men* (Audio Version)," *Library
        Journal*, 118 (January 1993), 186.

2030   "Review of *Of Mice and Men*," *Studies in Short Fiction*, 31
        (Fall 1994), 595.

2031   "Review of *Of Mice and Men*," *Western American Literature*,
        29 (Winter 1995), 291.

2032   "Review of *The Pearl* (Audio Version by Hector Elizondo) by
        John Steinbeck," *Library Journal*, 119 (June 1, 1994), 186.

2033   "Review of *The Pearl* (Audio Version by Hector Elizondo),"
        Kliatt, 28 (November 1994) 59.

2034   "Review of *The Red Pony* (illustrated by Wesley Dennis) by
        John Steinbeck," *Horn Book Guide*, 1 (July 1989), 69.

2035   "Review of *The Red Pony* by John Steinbeck," (Audio
        Version) *Book List*, 87 (May 15, 1991), 1827.

2036   "Review of *The Red Pony* by John Steinbeck," *Emergent
          Library*, 15 (September 1987), 47.

2037   "Review of *A Russian Journal* (illustrated by Robert Capa) by
          John Steinbeck," *Hungry Mind Review* (May 1990), 3.

2038   "Review of *A Russian Journal* (Photographs by Robert Capa)
          by John Steinbeck," *Los Angeles Times Book Review*
          (November 19, 1989), 14.

2039   "Review of *The Short Novels of John Steinbeck* by Jackson J.
          Benson," *American Literature*, 63 (June 1991), 378.

2040   "Review of *The Short Novels of John Steinbeck* by Jackson J.
          Benson," *Choice*, 28 (February 1991), 934.

2041   "Review of *The Short Novels of John Steinbeck* by Jackson J.
          Benson," *College Literature*, 18 (February 1991), 107.

2042   "Review of 'The Snake' and 'Johnny Bear' by John
          Steinbeck," (Audio Version) *Book List*, 82 (April 13,
          1986), 1248.

2043   "Review of *Steinbeck and Film* by Joseph Millichap," *Choice,*
          21 (February 1984), 829.

2043A   "Review of *Steinbeck's Reading* by Robert DeMott," *Choice*,
          21 (June 1984), 1441.

2043B   "Review of *Steinbeck's Reading* by Robert DeMott,"
          American Literature, 56 (October 1984), 465.

2043C   "Review of *Steinbeck's Reading* by Robert DeMott," *Western
          American Literature*, 19 (Winter 1985), 331.

2043D   "Review of *Steinbeck's Reading* by Robert DeMott,"
          Resources for American Literary Study, 13 (Spring 1983),
          105-108.

2043E "Review of *Steinbeck's Reading* by Robert DeMott," *American Book Collector*, 5 (Fall 1984), 21.

2044 "Review of *To a God Unknown*, (Audio Version) *Kliatt*, 26 (September 1992), 64.

2045 "Review of *To a God Unknown* by John Steinbeck," (Audio Version) *Library Journal*, 117 (April 1, 1992), 172.

2046 "Review of *Travels with Charley in Search of America* by John Steinbeck," *English Journal*, 78 (April 1989), 24.

2047 "Review of *Travels with Charley*," *Observer*, (July 16, 1995), 13.

2048 "Review of *Travels with Charley*, (Audio Version by Sinise)," *Kliatt*, 29 (May 1995), 57.

2049 "Review of *Travels with Charley*, (Audio Version by Sinise)," *Library Journal*, 119 (November 15, 1994), 108.

2050 "Review of *Travels with Charley*, (Audio Version by Sinise)," *Times Educational Supplement*, (April 14, 1995), 32.

2051 "Review of *The True Adventures of John Steinbeck, Writer* by Jackson J. Benson," *America*, 151 (July 21, 1984), 37.

2052 "Review of *The True Adventures of John Steinbeck, Writer* by Jackson J. Benson," *Antioch Review*, 42 (Summer 1984), 385.

2053 "Review of *The True Adventures of John Steinbeck, Writer* by Jackson J. Benson," *Best Sellers*, 43 (March 1984), 447.

2054 "Review of *The True Adventures of John Steinbeck, Writer* by Jackson J. Benson," *Book List*, 79 (July 1983), 1382.

2055 "Review of *The True Adventures of John Steinbeck, Writer* by Jackson J. Benson," *Economist*, 291 (April 21, 1984), 85.

2056   "Review of *The True Adventures of John Steinbeck, Writer* by
        Jackson J. Benson," *Kirkus Review*, 51 (June 1, 1983),
        642.

2057   "Review of *The True Adventures of John Steinbeck, Writer* by
        Jackson J. Benson," *Kliatt*, 25 (April 1991), 29.

2058   "Review of *The True Adventures of John Steinbeck, Writer* by
        Jackson J. Benson," *Macleans*, 97 (February 20, 1984), 58.

2059   "Review of *The True Adventures of John Steinbeck, Writer* by
        Jackson J. Benson," *New Yorker*, 59 (February 6, 1984),
        127.

2060   "Review of *The True Adventures of John Steinbeck, Writer* by
        Jackson J. Benson," *Publishers Weekly*, 224 (July 1, 1983),
        92.

2061   "Review of *The True Adventures of John Steinbeck, Writer* by
        Jackson J. Benson," *Virginia Quarterly Review*, 60
        (Summer 1984), 87.

2062   "Review of *The True Adventures of John Steinbeck, Writer* by
        Jackson J. Benson," *Los Angeles Times Book Review*
        (April 9, 1989), 15

2063   "Review of *The True Adventures of John Steinbeck, Writer* by
        Jackson J. Benson," *Southern Humanities Review*, 19 (Fall
        1985), 380.

2064   "Review of *Working Days: The Journals of 'The Grapes of
        Wrath,'* ed. Robert De Mott," *American Literature,* 61
        (October 1989), 519.

2065   "Review of *Working Days: The Journals of 'The Grapes of
        Wrath,'* ed. Robert De Mott," *Book List*, 85 (January, 15,
        1989), 831.

2066 "Review of *Working Days: The Journals of "The Grapes of Wrath."* ed. Robert De Mott," *Threepenny Review*, 11 (Spring 1990), 29.

2067 "Review of *Working Days: The Journals of 'The Grapes of Wrath,'* ed. Robert De Mott," *Guardian Weekly*, 140 (May 21, 1989), 20.

2068 "Review of *Working Days: The Journals of 'The Grapes of Wrath,'* ed. Robert De Mott," *Los Angeles Times Book Review* (April 9, 1989), 15.

2069 "Review of *Working Days: The Journals of 'The Grapes of Wrath,'* ed. Robert DeMott," *Kirkus Reviews*, 57 (March 1, 1989), 367.

2070 "Review of *Working Days: The Journals of 'The Grapes of Wrath,'* ed. Robert DeMott," *Newsweek*, 113 (May 1, 1989), 72.

2071 "Review of *Working Days: The Journals of 'The Grapes of Wrath,'* ed. Robert DeMott," *New York Times Book Review*, December 16, 1990, 32.

2072 "Review of *Working Days: The Journals of 'The Grapes of Wrath,'* ed. Robert De Mott," *Publishers Weekly*, 235 (January 27, 1989), 462.

2073 "Review of *Working Days: The Journals of 'The Grapes of Wrath,'* ed. Robert De Mott," *Reprint Bulletin Book Review*, 33:4 (1988), 50.

2074 "Review of *Working Days: The Journals of 'The Grapes of Wrath,'* ed. Robert DeMott," *Time,* 133 (April 24, 1989), 87-88.

2075   "Review of *Working Days: The Journals of 'The Grapes of Wrath,'* ed. Robert De Mott," *Village Voice*, 24 (August 29, 1989), 59.

2076   "Review of *Working Days: The Journals of 'The Grapes of Wrath,'* ed. Robert De Mott," *Voice of Youth Advocates* (VOYA), 12 (December 1989), 307.

2077   "Review of *Working Days: The Journals of 'The Grapes of Wrath,'* ed. Robert De Mott," *Western American Literature*, 24 (Summer 1989), 153.

2078   "Review of *Zapata: The Little Tiger* by John Steinbeck," *Sight and Sound*, 2 (May 1992), 42.

2079   "Review of *Zapata!* by John Steinbeck," *Publishers Weekly*, 240 (April 19, 1993), 57.

2080   Rodgers, Lawrence. "Review of *The Dramatic Landscape of Steinbeck's Short Stories* by John Timmerman," *Studies in Short Fiction*, 27 (Summer 1990), 423-25.

2081   Rogers, Michael. "Review of *Novels and Stories, 1932-1937,*" *Library Journal,* 119:18 (November 1, 1994), 116.

2082   Rohrberger, Mary. "Review of *The Modern American Novel* by Malcolm Bradbury," *Modern Fiction Studies,* 30 (Summer 1984), 335-336.

2083   Rooke, Leon. "100 Days in the Creation of a Great Novel — Review of *Working Days: The Journal of 'The Grapes of Wrath,'* ed. Robert DeMott and *The Grapes of Wrath* (an anniversary edition)," *Globe and Mail* (Toronto), April 22, 1989, C7.

2084   Rovit, Earl. "Review of *The True Adventures of John Steinbeck, Writer* by Jackson J. Benson," *Library Journal*, 108 (July 1983), 1363.

2085   Rovit, Earl. "Review of *Working Days: The Journals of 'The Grapes of Wrath,'* ed. Robert De Mott," *Library Journal*, 114 (February 1, 1989), 65.

2086   Ryan, Alan. "50 Years Later, Steinbeck's Works Reflect Agony, Beauty of Writing," (Review of *Working Days: The Journals of "The Grapes of Wrath"* ed. Robert DeMott) *Salinas Californian,* April 29, 1989, 2C. (with *The Grapes of Wrath*)

2087   Sage, Lorna. "A Vagrant in the Limbo House of Fiction: A Review of *John Steinbeck: A Biography* by Jay Parini," *Observer,* March 27, 1994, 18.

2088   St. Pierre, Brian. "Placing John Steinbeck in His Time: A Review of *John Steinbeck: A Biography* by Jay Parini," *San Francisco Chronicle*, February 19, 1995, n.p.

2089   Sakai, Yasuhiro. "Review of *Steinbeck's Literary Dimension: A Guide to Comparative Studies, Series II,* ed. Tetsumaro Hayashi," *John Steinbeck Society of Japan Newsletter,* 16 (April 1993), 14-15.

2090   Sakamoto, Yukio. "Review of *Ikari no Budo o Yomu: Amerika no Eden no Hate (A Reading of 'The Grapes of Wrath': Beyond America's Eden).* trans. Kiyoshi Nakayama and Yoshimitsu Nakayama." (A translation of Louis Owens, *"The Grapes of Wrath": Trouble in the Promised Land*) in *Kansai University Newsletter* (Kansai University Publicity Committee), 220 (July 5, 1993), 7.

2091   "Salinas Revisited," *San Francisco Review of Books*, (September/October 1984), n.p.

2092   Samway, Patrick. "Review of *John Steinbeck: A Biography* by Jay Parini," *America*, 172 (March 18, 1995), 29.

2093   Sanborn, Robert. "Review of *Staging Steinbeck: Dramatizing
          'The Grapes of Wrath'* by Peter Whitebrook," *Steinbeck
          Quarterly,* XXIII:1-2 (Winter/Spring 1990), 44-46.

2094   Sano, Minoru. "Review of *Beyond 'The Red Pony': A
          Reader's Guide to Steinbeck's Complete Short Stories* by
          R.S. Hughes Jr.," *Steinbeck Quarterly,* XXV (1-2
          Winter/Spring 1992), 61-62.

2095   Sano, Minoru. "Review of Louis D. Owens' *John Steinbeck's
          Re-Vision of America* (1985)," *Report of the Steinbeck
          Society of Japan — Executive Director's Office.* ed.
          Kiyoshi Nakayama, 3 (July 1, 1987), 1-6.

2096   Sano, Minoru. "Review of Louis Owens' *John Steinbeck's Re-
          Vision of America,*" in *Nihon Steinbekku Kyokai
          Jimukyoku Dayori* (*The Steinbeck Society of Japan
          Newsletter in Japanese*), 3 (July 1, 1987), 2-3.

2097   Schmitz, Edwin F. "Review of *I Never Met an Anapest I
          Didn't Like* by Carlton Sheffield," in *Steinbeck Quarterly,*
          XIX (3-4 Summer/Fall 1986), 99.

2098   Seaman, Donna. "Review of *John Steinbeck: A Biography* by
          Jay Parini," *Book List,* 91 (January 15, 1995), 892.

2099   Shechner, Mark. "Laureate of the Underdog: A Review of
          John Steinbeck: A Biography by Jay Parini," *Washington
          Post Book World,* February 12, 1995, 4-5.

2100   Shillinglaw, Susan. "Review of *Beyond 'The Red Pony': A
          Reader's Companion to Steinbeck's Complete Short
          Stories* by Robert S. Hughes, Jr.," *Steinbeck Newsletter,*
          1:2 (Spring 1988), 7.

2101   Shillinglaw, Susan. "Review of *The Dramatic Landscape of Steinbeck's Short Stories* by John H. Timmerman," *Western American Literature,* 26 (November 1991), 245-47.

2102   Shillinglaw, Susan. "Review of *'The Harvest Gypsies': On the Road to 'The Grapes of Wrath,'* by John Steinbeck," *The Steinbeck Newsletter,* 2:1 (Fall 1988), 11.

2103   Shillinglaw, Susan. "Review of *John Steinbeck* by A. Susan Williams," *Steinbeck Newletter,* 5 (Spring 1992), 15.

2104   Shillinglaw, Susan. "Review of *The Short Novels of John Steinbeck: Critical Essays with a Checklist to Steinbeck Criticism.* ed. Jackson J. Benson," *Western American Literature,* 26 (November 1991), 245-47.

2105   Shimomura, Noboru. "Review of Steinbeck and Hemingway." ed. Tetsumaro Hayashi, *Chu-Shikoku Studies in American Literature,* 18 (March 1982), 65-67.

2106   Shimuzu, Hiromu. "Review of *John Steinbeck: The Errant Knight* by Nelson Valjean, trans. Minoru Sano," *Steinbeck Quarterly,* XVI:1-2 (Winter/Spring 1983), 49-51.

2107   Shiraga, Eiko. "Review of *Amerikabungaku to Kyuyakuseisho: Sutainbekku, Heminguuei, Fokuna, Forosuto, Merubiru* (American Literature and the Old Testament: Steinbeck, Hemingway, Faulkner, Frost and Melville) by Suketaro Sawada," *The John Steinbeck Society of Japan Newsletter,* 17 (May 1994), 13-15.

2108   Shiraga, Eiko. "Review of *Sutainbekku to Engeki,* (Steinbeck and Drama) by Hiromasa Takamura," *Steinbeck Quarterly,* XXIV:1-2 (Winter/Spring 1991), 52-54.

2109   Siefker, Donald L., and Beverly K. Simpson. "Review of *The Politics of Public Memory: Tourism, History and Ethnicity in Monterey, California* by Martha K. Norkunas," *Steinbeck Quarterly,* XXVI (3-4, Summer/Fall 1993), 135-37.

2110   Siefker, Donald. "Review of *Essays on Collecting John Steinbeck Books,* comp. Preston Beyer," *Steinbeck Quarterly,* XXIII:3-4 (Summer/Fall 1990), 113-114.

2111   Siefker, Donald. "Review of *Steinbeck Bibliographies: An Annotated Guide* by Robert B. Harmon," *Steinbeck Quarterly,* XXI:3-4 (Summer/Fall 1988), 112-113.

2112   Sigal, Clancy. "Great American Novelists Who Lost out to the Bitch Goddess," *Guardian* (April 19, 1984), 10. (Review of *The True Adventures of John Steinbeck, Writer* by Jackson J. Benson)

2113   Sigal, Clancy. "Review of *The True Adventures of John Steinbeck, Writer* by Jackson J. Benson," *Book World (Chicago Tribune),* January 15, 1984, XIV, 23.

2114   Simmonds, Roy S. "The New Steinbeck Biography: A Review of *John Steinbeck: A Biography* by Jay Parini, *Steinbeck Newsletter,* 7:2 (Spring 1994), 14-15.

2115   Simmonds, Roy. "Review of *John Steinbeck As Propagandist*: '*The Moon Is Down' Goes to War* by Donald V. Coers," *Beat Scene,* January 15, 1993, 37.

2116   Simmonds, Roy S. "Review of *John Steinbeck As Propagandist: 'The Moon is Down' Goes to War* by Donald V. Coers," *Steinbeck Newsletter,* 5:1-2 (Spring 1992), 14-15.

2117   Simmonds, Roy. "Review of *John Steinbeck: The Years of Greatness, 1936-1939,* ed. Tetsumaro Hayashi," *Steinbeck Newletter,* 8:1-2 (Winter/Spring 1995), 26-27.

2118   Simmonds, Roy S. "Review of *Steinbeck's Reading: A Catalogue of Books Owned and Borrowed* by Robert DeMott," *Western American Literature*, 19 (February 1985), 331.

2119   Simpson, Beverly K. "Review of *Inside 'Cannery Row': Sketches from the Steinbeck Era in Words and Pictures* by Bruce Ariss," *Steinbeck Quarterly,* XXIII (1-2 Winter/Spring 1990), 46-49

2120   Simpson, Beverly K. "Review of *John Steinbeck: Asian Perspectives,* ed. Kiyoshi Nakayama, Scott Pugh, and Shigeharu Yano," *Steinbeck Quarterly,* XXVI (3-4 Summer/Fall 1993), 137-40.

2121   Simpson, Beverly K. "Review of *A Russian Journal: With Pictures by Robert Capa* by John Steinbeck," *Steinbeck Quarterly,* XXIV (1-2 Winter/Spring 1991), 41-43.

2122   Smith, Juanita. "Review of *The First Editions of John Steinbeck,* ed. Robert B. Harmon," XV (1-2 Winter/Spring 1982), 61-62.

2123   Spies, George H. "Review of *Steinbeck's World War II Fiction: 'The Moon Is Down' — Three Explications*, ed. Tetsumaro Hayashi," *Steinbeck Quarterly,* XX (3-4, Summer/Fall 1987), 104-105.

2124   Spies, George H. "Review of *John Steinbeck: A Study of the Short Fiction* by Robert S. Hughes, Jr.," *Steinbeck Quarterly,* XXIII (3-4 Summer/Fall 1990), 115-116.

2125   Starr, Kevin. "A Life of Dubious Battle," *New York Times
        Book Review,* 89 (January 22, 1984), 1, 32-33. (a review of
        The True Adventures of John Steinbeck, Writer by Jackson
        J. Benson)

2126   Steele, Charles R. "Review of *John Steinbeck: Life, Work,
        and Criticism* (1985) by John Ditsky," *Canadian Book
        Review Annual* (1985), 235.

2127   Stegner, Page. "Review of Jackson Benson's *The True
        Adventures of John Steinbeck, Writer,*" *Salīnas Californian*
        (August 1983), n.p.

2128   Stegner, Wallace. "Review of *The True Adventures of John
        Steinbeck, Writer* by Jackson J. Benson," *Los Angeles
        Times Book Review,* January 1, 1984, 1.

2129   "Steinbeck Classic Turns 50," *Chronicle-Herald/Mail-Star*
        (Halifax, Nova Scoita), April 12, 1989, 4WB. *(The Grapes
        of Wrath)*

2130   Stetler, Charles. "Review of *The Short Novels of John
        Steinbeck* by Jackson J. Benson," *Studies in Short Fiction*
        (Summer 1990), 423-25.

2131   Sugiyama, Takahiko. "Review of *John Steinbeck: Asian
        Perspectives,* ed. Kiyoshi Nakayama, Scott Pugh and
        Shigeharu Yano," *John Steinbeck Society of Japan
        Newsletter,* 16 (April 1993), 11-13.

2132   Sugiyama, Takahiko. "Review of John Steinbeck*: 'Of Mice
        and Men: A Play in Three Acts,'* trans. Kiyoshi Nakayama
        and Hiromasa Takamura," *Steinbeck Quarterly,* XXVI (3-
        4, Summer/Fall 1993), 141-42.

2133   Sugiyama, Takahiko. "Review of *Steinbeck's Writings: The California Years* by Kiyoshi Nakayama," *John Steinbeck Society of Japan Newsletter,* 13 (April, 1990), 8-9.

2134   Sugiyama, Takahiko. "Review of *Sutainbekku Kenkyu — Tanpen Shosetsu Ron, (A Study of Steinbeck: Essays on the Short Stories),* ed. Hisashi Egusa" in *Eigo Seinen (The Rising Generation),* 133:7 (October 1987), 351.

2135   Sundermeier, Michael W. "Review of *'The Harvest Gypsies': On the Road to "The Grapes of Wrath"* by John Steinbeck," *Steinbeck Quarterly,* XXIII:1-2 (Winter/Spring 1990), 49-51.

2136   Sundquist, Eric. "Review of *The True Adventures of John Steinbeck, Writer* by Jackson J. Benson," *National Review,* 36 (April 6, 1984), 55.

2137   Sutherland, John. "Review of *John Steinbeck: A Biography* by Jay Parini," *London Review of Books,* 16 (May 12, 1994), 23.

2138   Sweet, Timothy. "Reviews of *Image and Word: The Interaction of Twentieth Century Photographs and Text* and *In Visible Light: Photography and the American Writer,*" *Resources for American Literary Study,* 18 (1992), 275-279.

2139   Takamura, Hiromasa. "Review of *'The Harvest Gypsies': On The Road To 'The Grapes of Wrath,'* ed. Takahiko Sugiyama," *Steinbeck Quarterly,* XXVI:1-2 (Winter/Spring 1993), 50-52.

2140   Takamura, Hiromasa. "Review of *John Steinbeck: East and West,* ed. Tetsumaro Hayashi, et. al., trans. Shigeharu

Yano," *Steinbeck Quarterly,* XVI:1-2 (Winter/Spring
1983), 52-53.

2141   Takamura, Hiromasa. "Review of *John Steinbeck: From
        Salinas to the World,* ed. Shigeharu Yano, Yasuo
        Hashiguchi, Tetsumaro Hayashi and Richard F. Peterson,"
        in *Nihon Steinbekku Kyokai Jimukyoku Dayori* (*The
        Steinbeck Society of Japan Newsletter in Japanese*), 3 (July
        1, 1987), 2-3.

2142   Takamura, Hiromasa. "Review of *John Steinbeck on Writing*
        by Tetsumaro Hayshi (Steinbeck Essay Series, No. 2),"
        The John Steinbeck Society of Japan Newsletter, 12 (April
        1989), 8-9.

2143   Takamura, Hiromasa. "Review of Shigeharu Yano, et al.
        (eds.), *John Steinbeck: From Salinas to the World* (1986),"
        in *Report of the Steinbeck Society of Japan — Executive
        Director's Office.* ed. Kiyoshi Nakayama, 3 (July 1, 1987),
        1-6.

2144   Takamura, Hiromasa. "Review of *Sutainbekku Bungaku No
        Kenkyu: Kariforunia Jidai.* (Steinbeck's Writings: The
        California Years) by Kiyoshi Nakayama," *Steinbeck
        Quarterly,* XXIV:1-2 (Winter/Spring 1991), 54-56.

2145   Tammaro, Thom. "Review of *Indian Response to Steinbeck:
        Essays Presented to Warren French,* ed. R. K. Sharma,"
        Steinbeck Quarterly, XIX:3-4 (Summer/Fall 1986), 100-
        102.

2146   Tammaro, Thom. "Review of *John Steinbeck's Re-Vision of
        America* by Louis Owens," *Steinbeck Quarterly,* XX:1-2
        (Winter/Spring 1987), 45-47.

2147   Tammaro, Thom. "Review of *The Novel of the American West* by John R. Milton," *Steinbeck Quarterly,* XV:1-2 (Winter/Spring 1982), 62-63.

2148   Tammaro, Thom. "Review of *Steinbeck and Film* by Joseph Millichap," *Steinbeck Quarterly,* XVII:3-4 (Summer/Fall 1984), 112-115.

2149   Tammaro, Thom. "Review of *Steinbeck's Reading: A Catalogue of Books Owned and Borrowed* by Robert DeMott," *Steinbeck Quarterly,* XVIII:3-4 (Summer/Fall 1985), 109-112.

2150   Tanner, Tony. "Boor with a Big Heart: A Review of *John Steinbeck: A Biography* by Jay Parini," *Guardian,* April 12, 1994, 9.

2151   Teachout, Terry. "I'll Be Ever'Where: A Review of *John Steinbeck: A Biography* by Jay Parini," *New York Times Book Review,* February 26, 1995, 25.

2152   Timmerman, John H. "Review of *John Steinbeck and the Vietnam War. (Pt. I)* ed. Tetsumaro Hayashi," *Steinbeck Quarterly,* XX:3-4 (Summer/Fall 1987), 106-108.

2153   Timmerman, John H. "Review of *Looking for Steinbeck's Ghost* by Jackson Benson," *Steinbeck Quarterly,* XXIII: 1-2 (Winter/Spring 1990), 51-53.

2154   Timmerman, John H. "Review of *Steinbeck's 'Cannery Row': A Reconsideration* by Jackson J. Benson," *Steinbeck Quarterly,* XXV:1-2 (Winter/Spring 1992), 62-63.

2155   Traxel, David. "Review of *Alien Link: The FBI's War on Freedom of Expression* by Natalie Robins," *New York Times Book Review,* April 12, 1992, 14.

2156   Tsuboi, Kiyohiko, and Mitsuaki Yamashita. "Review of *Jon
        Sutainbekku No Shousetku: Sono Shudai to Kousatu.
        (Thematic Design in the Novels of John Steinbeck* by
        Lester Jay Marks), trans. Takanori Kinoshita and Haruki
        Kobe," *Steinbeck Quarterly,* XVIII:3-4 (Summer/Fall
        1985), 113-114.

2157   Tsuboi, Kiyohiko. "Review of *A Study of John Steinbeck:
        Mysticism in His Novels* by Noboru Shimomura,"
        Steinbeck Quarterly, XVI:3-4 (Summer/Fall 1983), 120-
        121.

2158   Tsuji, Takeo. "Review of *Steinbeck's 'The Red Pony': Essays
        in Criticism.* ed. Tetsumaro Hayashi and Thomas Y.
        Moore, (Steinbeck Monograph Series, no. 13)," *The John
        Steinbeck Society of Japan Newsletter,* 12 (April 1989), 7-
        8.

2159   Turner, Frederick. "The Wrath, the Discontent, the Grapes,"
        (Review of *Working Days: The Journals of "The Grapes
        of Wrath"* by Robert DeMott) *New York Post,* April 16,
        1989, 10. (with *The Grapes of Wrath*)

2160   Verdier, Douglas L. "Review of *Steinbeck's Unhappy Valley:
        A Study of 'The Pastures of Heaven'* by Joseph
        Fontenrose," *Steinbeck Quarterly,* XVI:1-2 (Winter/Spring
        1983), 54-56.

2161   Vogel, Mark. "Review of *Swift Justice* by Harry Farrell,"
        Steinbeck Newsletter, 6:1 (Winter 1993), 18. (Non-fiction
        account of the murder that inspired Steinbeck's "The
        Vigilante" in *The Long Valley.*)

2162   Waldmeier, Joseph J. "Review of *The True Adventures of
        John Steinbeck, Writer* by Jackson J. Benson," *Centennial
        Review,* 28:3 (Summer 1984) 252-253.

2163   W.C. "Review of *The True Adventures of John Steinbeck, Writer* by Jackson J. Benson," *Newsweek*, 103 (February 6, 1984), 80.

2164   Wender, Abigail. "*The Grapes of Wrath* at 50," *Diversion* (June 1989), 291, 296-302.

2165   Werner, C. "Review of *John Steinbeck's Re-Vision of America* by Louis Owens," *American Literature*, 56:1 (March 1984), 132-133.

2166   Werner, C. "Review of *John Steinbeck's Re-Vision of America* by Louis Owens," *Choice*, 23 (October 1985), 298.

2167   Wilson, Jerry W. "Review of *Humanistic Geography and Literature*, ed. Douglas C. D. Pocock," *Steinbeck Quarterly*, XV (1-2 Winter/Spring 1982), 64-65.

2168   Wolfe, Ron. "Steinbeck and His Depression," (Review of *Working Days: The Journals of "The Grapes of Wrath"* by Robert DeMott) *Tulsa Tribune*, (April 14, 1989), B-1.

2169   Yamashita, Mitsuaki, and Kiyohiko Tsuboi. "Review of *Jon Sutainbekku No Shousetku: Sono Shudai to Kousatu, (Thematic Design in the Novels of John Steinbeck* by Lester Jay Marks) trans. Takanori Kinoshita and Haruki Kobe," *Steinbeck Quarterly*, XVIII (3-4 Summer/Fall 1985),113-114.

2170   Yamashita, Mitsuaki. "Review of *Nihon ni okeru Sutainbekku Bunken Shoshi. (Steinbeck in Japan: A Bibliography)* comp. Kiyoshi Nakayama," *John Steinbeck Society of Japan Newsletter,* 16 (April 1993), 15-16.

2171   Yamauchi, Kiyoshi. "Review of Frank Galati's Playscript of *John Steinbeck's 'The Grapes of Wrath,'* ed. Kiyoshi

Nakayama and Hiromasa Takamura," *Steinbeck Studies,* 19 (May 1996), 35-36.

2172   Yardley, Jonathan. "Dregs of Wrath," (Review of *The Library of America Volume) Washington Post (Book World),* October 9, 1994, 3.

2173   Yardley, Jonathan. "A New Pressing of *The Grapes of Wrath*," (Review of *Working Days: The Journals of "The Grapes of Wrath"* by Robert DeMott) *Washington Post (Book World),* April 16, 1989, 3. (with *The Grapes of Wrath*)

2174   Zabytko, Irene. "Anguish, Doubt Led to Greatness," (Review of *Working Days: The Journals of "The Grapes of Wrath"* by Robert DeMott) *Orlando Sentinel,* April 23, 1989, F-7.

2175   Zane, Nancy. "Review of *California Writers: Jack London, John Steinbeck, the Tough Guys* by Stoddard Martin," *Steinbeck Quarterly,* XVIII:1-2 (Winter Spring 1985), 46-47.

2176   Zane, Nancy. "Review of *John Steinbeck's Fiction: The Aesthetics of The Road Taken* by John Timmerman," *Steinbeck Quarterly,* XXI (3-4 Summer/Fall 1988), 113-114.

2177   Zane, Nancy. "Review of *Looking for Steinbeck's Ghost* by Jackson J. Benson," *American Literature,* 61 (December 1989), 707-708.

2178   Zane, Nancy. "Review of *Steinbeck: The Good Companion* by Carlton A. Sheffield," *Steinbeck Quarterly,* XVII (3-4 Summer/Fall 1984), 115-117.

Newspapers

2179   "A Look at Cannery Row as It Was Yesterday . . .," *Coasting (Monterey, Carmel)*, January 14, 1987, 43.

2180   "A Look Back at Cannery Row," *Coasting (Monterey, Carmel)*, May 14, 1986, 33.

2181   Abrams, Jim. "Report: Attempts to Censor School Material Increasing," *Muncie Star*, August 29, 1991, 8.

2182   Adair, Lara, "A Clean, Well-Lighted Cafe in Montparnasse," *San Francisco Chronicle*, August 20, 1991, E10.

2183   Akeman, Thom. "Honorary Artist Bruce Ariss Dies," *Monterey Herald*, September 12, 1994, n.p.

2184   Akeman, Thom. "Narrow P. G. Street May Get New Name," *Monterey Herald*, June 15, 1994, n.p.

2185   Alberge, Dalya. "Still Deep in Love with Steinbeck," *Times* (London), April 24, 1995, 17. (about Elaine)

2186   Aldrich, Bob. "Literary Lore," *Los Gatos Weekly*, April 3, 1991, 1, 8-9.

2187   Aldrich, Bob. "Moscow to Have Glimpse of Los Gatos," *Los Gatos Weekly*, August 9, 1989, n.p.

2188   Alexander, Ludmilla. "John Steinbeck: The Los Gatos Years," *Los Gatos Weekly* (California), October 17, 1984, 1, 15-16.

2189   Alexander, Paul. "How James Dean, New York Actor, Became James Dean, Hollywood Star," *San Jose Mercury News*, August 20, 1994, 1C, 5C.

2190   Alvarez, Fred. "Burgess Meredith Renews Kindred Ties to John Steinbeck," *Salinas Californian*, February 7, 1987, 1.

2191   Amidon, Stephen. "On the Shelf: The Mythic Power of *The Grapes of Wrath*," *Sunday Times Books*, April 25, 1993, vi, 9.

2192   "Amnesty International Will Benefit from Shows of Steinbeck's Works," *Salinas Californian,* January 7, 1987, 1C.

2193   Andresen, Judy. "Salinas Tour Revisits Sites That Colored Steinbeck's Life," *Salinas Californian*, August 4, 1993, 1E, 3E.

2194   Andresen, Judy. "Steinbeck's Writings Preserve Monterey For Millions of Readers," *Salinas Californian*, August 4, 1993, 3E.

2195   Andrews, LaVonne Rae. "'Steinbeck: A Quest of Genius' Captures Author's Brilliance," *Salinas Californian,* January 15, 1987, 8C.

2196   Andrews, Susan. "Literary Societies: For Facts and Fun," *Nob Hill Gazette*, June 1986, 30-31.

2197   "*Angels, Grapes* Top Tonys," *San Francisco Chronicle*, June 4, 1990, n.p.

2198   Angeloni, Richard. " ——— in Soviet Union, Scholars Say," *Salinas Californian*, August 7, 1989, 1C.

2199   "Aquarium's Tourist Appeal Puts Strain on Cannery Row," Los Angeles Times, May 13, 1985, n.p. See entry #2258

2200   "AT&T Plants Seed for Steinbeck Center," *Salinas Californian,* March 13, 1987, 3A.

2201   Ayers, Anne. "Steinbeck a la Springsteen: New Album a Literary Travelogue," *USA Today*, (International ed.) Section I, 9A. (discusses new album, *The Ghost of Tom Joad*)

2202   Azcarte, Marcos. "Center Offers Glimpses of Author,"
        Spartan Daily, San Jose State University, September 19,
        1990, 5.

2203   Baechle, Bea. "Fifty Years after *The Grapes of Wrath,*"
        (unidentified) 2 (May/June 1989), 20-21.

2204   Baggerly, John S. "Neighborhoods: Pictures from the Past:
        Another Name for the Town's Changeable Old Street,"
        (unidentified), c. March/April 1990, n.p.

2205   Baker, Russell. "That Ma's A Killer," *New York Times,* June
        2, 1992, A21.

2206   Barrett, Elizabeth. "Valley of the Dead Oaks — Jolon," *Coast
        Weekly,* July 4, 1990, 12. (Steinbeck's House)

2207   Basch, Harry, and Shirley Slater. "John Steinbeck's *Cannery
        Row*: More Than a Literary Pilgrimage," *Los Angeles
        Times,* February 2, 1986, VII, 1.

2208   Bateman, Judith. "John Steinbeck: Best-Selling Novelist Who
        Is Also Very Collectible in This Country," *Book and
        Magazine Collector,* 27 (June 1986), 4-13.

2209   Bateson, John. "A Steinbeck Treasure," *San Francisco
        Chronicle,* January 15, 1984, 2.

2210   Beaufort, John. "*Of Mice and Men*: Powerful 50 Years
        Later," *Monterey Herald,* October 28, 1987, n.p.

2211   Beck, Karen. "Hometown Finally Warms Up to Steinbeck,"
        Austin (Texas) American Statesman, February 28, 1988,
        F10.

2212   Beck, Marilyn and Stacy Jenel. "Costner Being Touted for
        Role in 'Charlie' Film," *San Jose Mercury,* January 31,
        1994, n.p.

2213   Begovich, Ray. "He's Ball State University's Steinbeck
        Hotline," *Muncie Star*, December 1, 1991, n.p.

2213A   Belcaming, Kristi. "The Heyday of Cannery Row: Panelists
        Say Steinbeck's Book Accurate," *Monterey County
        Herald*, March 23, 1997, A1.

2214   Belli, Hope. "Steinbeck Style Spawns Popularity," *Salinas
        Californian*, August 8, 1988, 1, 8A.

2215   "Best Books Listed for High School Students," *New York
        Times*, August 13, 1984, n.p.

2216   "Best Sellers," *New York Times Book Review,* April 16, 1989,
        32.

2217   Bishop, Jerry E. "The Demise of Cannery Row," *Wall Street
        Journal* (Eastern ed.), April 4, 1975, 10.

2218   Blades, John. "Bibliolater's Bash: 20 Years after His Death,
        Steinbeck Will Be a Hot Ticket at Rare Book Convention,"
        Chicago Tribune, May 8, 1989, V, 2.

2219   Blades, John. "The New Steinbeck Novel You Won't Be
        Reading: Widow Scuttles Publication of *Lifeboat* Script,"
        Muncie Star, August 16, 1990, B5.

2220   "Boat Steinbeck Used Located, May Come Back to
        Monterey," *Monterey Peninsula Herald,* March 20, 1984,
        17.

2221   Bolas, Alyce. "Steinbeck Works Helped Form Views,"
        Salinas Californian, April 21, 1989, 8A.

2222   Boomershine, April M. "Soviet Scholars Participate in
        Steinbeck Celebration," *Indianapolis Star*, July 30, 1989,
        C16.

2223   Boyd, Denny. "*Of Mice and Men* and Miracles and Marsh,"
        Vancouver Sun, December 29, 1985, n.p.

2224   Bramcamp, Claudia. "Steinbeck's Santa Cruz Fantasy," *Santa Cruz Sentinel*, August 3, 1991, D1, D2.

2225   Brazil, Eric. "Soviet Crash Course in Steinbeck Era: *The Grapes of Wrath* Survivors Relate Times to Editor," *San Francisco Examiner*, December 13, 1988, A1.

2226   Bristol, Horace. "Documenting *The Grapes of Wrath*," *The Californians, The Magazine of California History*, 6 (January/February 1988), 7, 41-47.

2227   Bristol, Horace. "Steinbeck's Faces: The Real People Behind His Characters — Photographs of Depression," *San Francisco Sunday Examiner and Chronicle*, October 25, 1987, 11-14.

2228   "Brown, Carol Henning," *San Francisco Chronicle*, February 10, 1983, 40.

2229   "Brown, Carol Janella," *New York Times*, February 11, 1983, B5.

2230   Bruce, David. "No Wrath with *Working Days*: OU Professor Edits Journals That Depict Writing of *The Grapes of Wrath*," *Athens (Ohio) News*, April 10, 1989, 16.

2231   Burke, Margo. "Author's Works Excluded Women," *Monterey Peninsula Herald*, August 3, 1984, 4.

2232   Burleson, Marty. "Festival Fans a Diverse Group," *Salinas Californian*, August 11, 1992, 3E.

2233   "Busman's Retirement," *Monterey Life*, 11 (July 1990), 31.

2234   Buursma, Bruce. "No More Sour Grapes: Steinbeck Country Celebrates Author," *Orange Country Register,* c. Summer /Fall 1989, n.p.

2235   Caen, Herb. "The Galloping Gamut," *San Francisco Chronicle,* October 16, 1981, n.p.

2236   Caen, Herb. "Belated Scooplet on Censorship," *San Francisco Chronicle,* March 30, 1993, B1.

2237   "California's Oranges of Wrath" (Editorial) , *Los Angeles Times*, December 23, 1992, B6.

2238   Cantrell, Susan. "Steinbeck Festival XIII about to Blossom," *Salinas Californian,* August 1, 1992, n.p.

2239   Cantrell, Susan. "(Steinbeck Memories) Artist's Sketches Recall Heyday of Cannery Row (Bruce Ariss)," *Salinas Californian*, August 8, 1988, 1C, 8A.

2240   Carpenter, Richard P. "Cannery Row: No Sardines, Just Tourists," *Boston Sunday Globe*, July 25, 1993, n.p.

2241   Carroll, Jon. "Another Casualty East of Eden," *San Francisco Chronicle*, February 25, 1991, n.p.

2242   Castro, Peter. "Chatter; Complimentary Admission," *People* (July 9, 1990), 82.

2243   Cathro, Morton. "Steinbeck Country Honors Its Wayward Sons," *Los Angeles Times*, July 17, 1983, IV, 1-2, 18.

2244   Cathro, Morton. *"Travels with Charley* Leads Pilgrims to Steinbeck's Hometown," *Chicago Tribune*, July 17, 1983, XI, 12-13.

2244A   "Celebrate Steinbeck in Salinas," *Sunset,* 191:2 (August 1993), 32.

2245   "Censorship Row (Steinbeck)," *International Herald Tribune*, August 6-7, 1983, n.p.

2246   "Chase Horton Bequest for Conservation Includes Steinbeck Materials," *New York Public Library News*, March/April 1987, n.p.

2247   "The Child in John Steinbeck," *Coasting (Monterey, Carmel),* December 17, 1986, 51. (This article, in a publication from the University of Windsor, speaks about Steinbeck as a voracious reader.)

2248   Chira, Susan. "Helping Migrant Students Beat the Odds in School," *New York Times,* April 25, 1990, Education sec., n.p.

2249   Christ, Carl. "*Cannery Row*: The Party Never Stopped," *Coasting* (Monterey, Carmel, California)*,* January 28, 1987, 54.

2250   Cobb, Mark Hughes. "Biographer: Steinbeck Simply a Storyteller," *The Tuscaloosa News,* February 16, 1989, Life and Leisure sec., 10.

2251   Cole, Jim. "Pearson's Account; Woman Helps Preserve Salinas History," *Salinas Californian,* February 25, 1993, 10, 11.

2252   Cole, Jim. "Salinas Commemorates Steinbeck's 91st Birthday," *Salinas Californian,* February 25, 1993, 3.

2253   Cole, Jim. "Student of Steinbeck," *Salinas Californian,* February 25, 1993, 2, 5.

2254   Cole, Jim. "Valley Guild Brings Down the House," *Salinas Californian,* February 25, 1993, 6, 8.

2255   Colvin, Richard Lee. "Okies" (*The Grapes of Wrath), Austin (Texas) American Statesman,* June 25, 1989, D2, 31; Books sec., 1, D1, D4, D6.

2256   Cone, Tracie. "Monterey Swallows Its *Grapes of Wrath,*" *San Jose Mercury News,* February 27, 1994, 1A, 19A.

2257   Conner, Patrick K. "The Two Lives of Horace Bristol," *San Francisco Chronicle* (*This World*), September 2, 1990, 11-14 (*The Grapes of Wrath*).

2258   Corwin, Miles. "Aquarium's Tourist Appeal Puts Strain on
        Cannery Row," *Los Angeles Times*, May 13, 1985, I, 3, 15.

2259   Corwin, Miles. "Steinbeck Name Pops Up All Over: Salinas
        Growing to Like Author It Once Spurned," *Los Angeles
        Times*, December 6, 1987, 1, 28-30.

2260   "Council OKs Drive for Steinbeck Center," *Monterey Herald*,
        October 29, 1986, 23.

2261   "Czech Editor Samples Steinbeck: Tours Salinas, Monterey,"
        Monterey Herald, May 20, 1986, 15.

2262   Dart, Bob. "Steinbeck's *Of Mice and Men* Top Target of
        Book-Ban Activists," *Star-Bulletin*, September 1988, D-1.

2263   Davis, Charles. "In Search of Steinbeck," *Monterey Sunday
        Herald*, August 5, 1990, 1D.

2264   Davis, Charles. "The Spirit of Steinbeck," *Monterey Sunday
        Herald*, August 5, 1990, 1D, 4D.

2265   Davis, Charles. "Tour of Steinbeck Country," *Monterey
        Herald*, August 3, 1990, 1C, 8C.

2266   Davis, Lee. "A Ritual of Celebrity and Culture,"
        Southhampton Press (England), May 17, 1990, n.p.

2267   "A Day Like This," *Independent*, March 29, 1994, 17.

2268   "Day of the Sardine Celebrated at the Cannery Row Reunion,"
        Coasting, (Monterey, Carmel, California) May 15, 1985,
        42.

2269   "Deadline Has Been Set for the John Steinbeck Writing
        Contest," *Monterey Herald,* March 1, 1987, 5D.

2270   Dean, Paul. "Still Getting Kicks on Route 66," *Los Angeles
        Times*, September 27, 1992, EL, 8.

2271   "Deaths Elsewhere: John Steinbeck IV," *Detroit Free Press*,
       February 12, 1991, B4.

2272   Debowski, Gloria J. "Center Buys Letters of Nobel Winner,"
       Spartan Daily (San Jose University), 85 (November 4,
       1985), 3.

2273   Deck, Martin. "Well Read," *The Lance*, November 24, 1983,
       11.

2274   Detro, Gene. "Author's Pacific Grove House 'Goes Public'"
       Monterey Peninsula Herald Magazine, June 19, 1983, 11-
       14.

2275   Detro, Gene. "Carol Steinbeck: Victor of a Dubious Battle,"
       Monterey Life, January 1985, 83-84. 86-87.

2276   Detro, Gene. "Gripes of Wrath: Why the Steinbeck Inner-
       Circle Is Trashing the New Biography," *San Francisco
       Sunday Examiner and Chronicle,* January 22, 1984, 12.

2277   Detro, Gene. "Loneliness and Professional Writer," *Monterey
       Peninsula Herald,* April 28, 1985, 14.

2278   Detro, John. "Carol Steinbeck and the Round Table," *Sunday
       Herald* (Monterey, California), July 31, 1988, 16, 18.

2279   Detro, John. "The Wild Bunch: Charting the Loh's Place in
       Jazz History," (Steinbeck's *Cannery Row*), *Our Town,*
       (special features) (August 1986), 37-8, 46.

2280   DeVine, Lawrence. "Obituaries: Actor (Jesse Newton}
       Brought Steinbeck's Lennie to Life," *Detroit Free Press,*
       September 17, 1992, 2B.

2281   "Did Steinbeck Know Yaddo," *New York Times* (Letter to
       Editor), September 26, 1993, Sec. 9, 5.

2282   "Doc's Place," *Monterey Herald*, April 1, 1986, 17.

2283   "Doc Ricketts and Friends Live on in John Steinbeck's
        Popular Novels about Monterey," *Coasting* (Monterey,
        Carmel, California*)*, January 7, 1987, 41.

2284   Donald, Colin James. "Thirst for Words," *Weekend Telegraph*
        (London), November 4, 1989, xii.

2285   Donnelly, Kathleen. "Travels with Steinbeck," *San Jose
        Mercury News,* August 12, 1992, ID, 8D.

2286   Donohue, Deidre. "The Photographic Seeds of Steinbeck's
        Grapes," *USA Today*, February 17, 1988, 7D.

2287   Doty, Betty Farrell. "Life with Steinbeck: John IV Sidesteps
        Dad's Shadow," *Salinas Californian,* August 4, 1990, 1F,
        7F.

2288   Doty, Betty Farrell. "Steinbeck Festival Opens Aug. 1,"
        Salinas Californian, July 25, 1986, 9.

2289   Douglas, Jack. "San Jose, Steinbeck Country?" *San Jose
        Historical Museum Association News*, 4 (May 1984), 3.

2290   Drown, Stuart. "Speaker Compares Steinbeck Novels to
        Bible," *Monterey Herald,* August 2, 1986, 38. (Tetsumaro
        Hayashi, keynote speaker)

2291   Drummond, William. "Multi-ethnic Recognition for
        Steinbeck," *San Jose Mercury News*, June 4, 1995, 8H.

2291A   Duman, Jill. "Drawing Conclusions: Opposition to Steinbeck
        Center Design May Indicate a Need for Better PR," *Coast
        Weekly*, March 20, 1997, 11.

2292   Duman, Jill. 'Searching for Steinbeck," *Coast Weekly*, August
        4-10, 1994, 10, 12-13, 14-15.

2293   Duman, Jill. "Steinbeck Birthday," *Coast Weekly*, February
        25, 1993, 52-53.

2294   Dunne, Mike. "Travels with Steinbeck," *Sacramento Bee*,
        April 5, 1989, D-1, 7.

2295   "Ed Ricketts, a Cannery Row Naturalist," *Coasting*
        (Monterey, Carmel, California), November 19, 1986, 49.

2296   "Ed Ricketts: Friend and Philosopher," *Coasting* (Monterey,
        Carmel, California), July 31, 1986, 46-47.

2297   Edelman, Mel. "Steinbeck," *Our Town*, special features
        (August 1986), 28-29, 42.

2298   "Elizabeth Steinbeck Ainsworth, John Steinbeck's Sister,
        Dies," *Monterey County Herald,* October 22, 1992, 4A.

2299   Ellin, Harlene. "Still Getting Her Kicks: Waitress Effie Marks
        Has Become One of Route 66's Most Famous Fixtures,"
        Chicago Tribune, April 10, 1995, Tempo sec.

2300   "End of a Drought (Not This One): From *The Grapes of
        Wrath*," *San Francisco Examiner*, January 10, 1993, A14.

2301   Engstrom, Paul. "'He Bares Human Souls': Steinbeck Touch
        Reaches to India," *Salinas Californian* (January 25, 1982),
        13.

2302   Engstrom, Paul. "Letters Portray a Lonely Steinbeck," *San
        Jose Mercury News*, November 28, 1984, 2.

2303   Engstrom, Paul. "Letters, Story Tell of Steinbeck's Youth,"
        San Jose Mercury News, November 26, 1984, 1B.

2304   Engstrom, Paul. "Steinbeck Letters Shed Light on His Lonely
        New York Years," *San Jose Mercury News*, December 25,
        26, 1984, 4.

2305   "Environment the Focus of Island Weekend Steinbeck
        Conference," *Nantucket Inquirer and Mirror*, May 14,
        1992, 1C.

2306   "Ernest Hemingway and John Steinbeck," *U.S.A. Today*,
        September 4, 1985, 7D. (An ad by Famous Faces of Key
        Biscayne, Florida, of pen and ink portraits by Terry
        Carroll.)

2307   "Essential Steinbeck," *New York Times*, February 26, 1984,
        n.p. (Letter to the Editor)

2308   Evens, Harold. "Five of the Best," *Northern Echo*, June 10,
        1983, n.p.

2309   Evenson, Laura. "Big Sur to Get First Resort in 20 Years,"
        San Francisco Chronicle, April 9, 1991. C1, C12.

2310   "Extensive List of Approved Authors Issued (Steinbeck),"
        Independent, April 16, 1993, (n.p.).

2310A   Eyman, Scott. "Steinbeck Classic *Of Mice and Men* Now on
        CD Rom," *Palm Beach Post*, March 24, 1996, n.p.

2310B   "Facing His Hardest Lesson," *Newsday*, February 5, 1996,
        A6, A22-A23. (*The Pearl*)

2311   Farrell, John, "John Steinbeck IV, 1947-1991: An
        Unforgettable Legacy," *Pen Center USA West*, Spring
        1991, 22.

2312   "FBI Kept Massive Files of US Writers," *Guardian*, October
        1, 1987, n.p.

2313   "FBI Spied on 50 of America's Famous Authors (including
        Steinbeck)," *San Francisco Chronicle*, September 30,
        1987, A2.

2314   Ferriss, Susan. "Suffering of Dust Bowl Era Recalled,"
        Monterey Herald, August 4, 1989, 4.

2315   "Festival Honors Steinbeck," *Carmel Pine Cone,* August 1,
        1985, 31.

2316   Field. Michele. "Living with Steinbeck," *South China Morning Post/Hong Kong*, The Review, April 23, 1994, 9.

2317   Fischer, Jeanne. "Multi-Media Festival Recalls Steinbeck," *Carmel Pine Cone,* July 31, 1986, 34.

2318   Fischer, Jeanne. "Scholars, Locals Remember John Steinbeck," *Monterey Peninsula Review,* July 31, 1986, 1.

2319   Fisher, David. "Last Steinbeck Sister Dies at 98," *Salinas Californian,* October 22, 1992, 1.

2320   Fisher, David. "$3.5 Million Center Will Honor Author," *Salinas Californian,* August 11, 1992, 3E.

2321   Flinn, John. "Monterey Bay: 'Doc' and 'Dave' Packard," *San Francisco Chronicle*, July 28, 1996, T3.

2322   "Follow the Fun at Steinbeck's Historic Cannery Row," *Coasting*, January 7, 1987, 41.

2323   "Follow the Fun at Steinbeck's Historic Cannery Row," *Coasting*, January 14, 1987, 42-43.

2324   "Fonda Photo (as Tom Joad) on the Block for Forest Theater Benefit," *Carmel Pine Cone,* May 17, 1992, n.p.

2325   "Footnotes" (June 15 Deadline for the John Steinbeck Writing Contest), *Monterey Sunday Herald*, March 1, 1987, n.p.

2326   "Forgiving a Classic," *Arkansas Gazette*, October 17, 1990, n.p.

2327   Franklin, Patrick. "Words of Steinbeck: One-Man Show Has Its Debut," *Monterey Herald,* January 10, 1987, 7.

2328   Freedman, Julius. "Classy Trivia (Emiliano Zapata)," *Monterey Herald*, May 19, 1991, 2E.

2328A   Freedman, Mitchell. "Wildrid Sheed Wins Steinbeck Award,"
        Newsday, May 12, 1996, A20.

2329   French, Philip. "Blighted Love Triumphs over All," *Observer*,
        May 24, 1992, 57.

2330   Gartshore, Bonnie. "An Interview with Everett 'Red'
        Williams," *Monterey County Herald*, August 3, 1993, n.p.

2331   Gartshore, Bonnie. "What's a Tom Wallager Party?,"
        Monterey County Herald, May 23, 1991, n.p.

2332   George, Mary. "Fans Find a Bonanza of Steinbeck Items,"
        Denver Post, May 20, 1988, 2B.

2333   "Getting Kicks on Route 66," *New York Times*, June 3, 1990,
        n.p.

2334   "Go Weston Young Man: Fonda Photo on Block for Forest
        Theater Benefit," *Carmel Pine Cone*, May 7, 1992, 25.

2335   Gold, Herbert. "Return to Cannery Row," *New York Times,*
        February 28, 1982, Sec. 20, 43.

2336   Golden, Marita. "Writers Bring Their Own Lives to Life in
        Stories Worth Telling," *Boston Sunday Globe*, January 31,
        1993, B40.

2337   Goodman, Al. "Old Friends Get Together Again: Former
        Cannery Workers Will Relive Row's Halcyon Times,"
        Monterey Peninsula Herald, May 12, 1985, ID.

2338   Goodman, Walter. "'New Harvest, Old Shame,' About Farm
        Workers," *New York Times*, April 17, 1990, n.p.

2339   *"Grapes* Bitter Taste,*"* *Sunday Times,* June 25, 1989, B16.

2340   *"The Grapes of Wrath* II," *Vancouver Sun*, August 8, 1983,
        n.p.

2341   *"Grapes of Wrath* to Be Honored," *Monterey Herald*, April 6, 1989, 5.

2342   Green, Larry. "Monterey Sardine Makes a Comeback: Fishery Must Be Protected — This Time," *San Jose Mercury News*, February 27, 1986, 10G.

2343   Green, Linda. "Salinas Is Definitely Steinbeck Country," *Salinas Californian,* July 7, 1986, 7D.

2344   Green, Richard. "Walk: Stride for Peace," *The Salinas Californian*, July 13, 1988, 2A. (Tankel Golenpolski, a Soviet journalist, said "Steinbeck is a very popular writer in the Soviet Union, with nearly everything he wrote currently translated into Russian.")

2345   Greenberg, Paul. "The Sin of Being Told Not to Read and Learn," *The Commercial Appeal* (Memphis, Tennessee), November 2, 1989, n.p. (*Of Mice and Men*).

2346   Grelen, Jay. "Steinbeck Sale So Successful, Second Slated," *Denver Post*, May 23, 1988, 3B.

2347   Grimm, Michele, and Tom Grimm. "Monterey Has Rebirth: Trip of the Week," *Los Angeles Times*, February 24, 1985, IV, 8.

2348   Grimm, Michele, and Tom Grimm, "Steinbeck Is Celebrated in Salinas," *Los Angeles Times* (Travel Section), April 19, 1987, 11, 23.

2349   "Guild Publishes a Cookbook: Salinas Women Unveil Steinbeck House Restaurant Recipes," *Salinas Californian,* July 4, 1984, 28.

2350   Gunderson, Edna. "Music Review: Springsteen's Stark Vision of Tom Joad," *USA Today*, International ed. November 21, 1995, 7A.

2351   Hahn, Bob. "*Wrath* Turns Fifty," *Cincinnati Post*, April 6,
         1989, n.p.

2352   Hammond, Judy. "Cannery Row Shacks to Show Fishermen's
         Life," *Monterey County Herald*, March 3, 1993, 7A.

2353   Hammond, Judy. "Cannery Row to Party for Steinbeck,"
         Monterey County Herald, February 14, 1995, 1C, 2C.

2354   Hammond, Judy. "Group Saved Ricketts' Lab on Cannery
         Row," *Monterey County Herald*, February 24, 1995, 1A,
         6A.

2355   Hammond, Judy. "Steinbeck 'Absorbs' S. J. Scholar,"
         Monterey County Herald, Feburary 24, 1995, 1C, 2C.

2356   Hampton, Wilborn. "Destitution in the 1930's (No, It's Not
         the *Grapes*)," *New York Times*, February 25, 1991, n.p.

2357   Hanner, Richard. "Arvin Was Steinbeck's Inspiration,"
         Salinas Californian, December 31, 1986, 1. (Part of a five-
         part series entitled "*The Grapes of Wrath* Re-Visited.")

2358   Hanner, Richard. "Black-Tide of Dirt Engulfed Oklahoma
         Panhandle," *Salinas Californian,* December 29, 1986, 1.
         (Part of a five-part series entitled "*The Grapes of Wrath*
         Re-Visited.")

2359   Hanner, Richard. "The Grapes of Wrath Revisited," *Stockton
         Record*, November 16-20, 1986. (A series of five articles:
         November 16, resentment of citizens of Sallisaw, site of
         the start of *The Grapes of Wrath*, at Steinbeck for his
         misrepresentation of the town, which had a drought but no
         dust storm problems, bank takeovers, or other alleged
         disasters; November 17, description of the dust problems
         in the Oklahoma Panhandle, where such disasters did
         develop; November 18, Route 66, replaced by a new road
         and abandoned; November 19, the Arvin (Weedpatch)
         Camp; November 20, "Okieville" in East Stockton.)

2360   Hanner, Richard. "Mother Road: Migrants Followed Route 66 Trail to Promised Land," *Salinas Californian,* December 30, 1986, 1. (Part of a five-part series entitled *"The Grapes of Wrath* Re-Visited.")

2361   Hanner, Richard. "'Real-life Joads' Find a Home," *Salinas Californian,* January 1, 1987, 1. (Part of a five-part series entitled *"The Grapes of Wrath* Re-Visited.")

2362   Hanner, Richard. "Sallisaw Won't Forgive Steinbeck," *Salinas Californian,* December 27, 1986, 1. (Part of a five-part series entitled *"The Grapes of Wrath* Re-Visited.")

2363   "Hard Work Due for Steinbeck Fund," *Salinas Californian,* August 17, 1992, 4A.

2364   Harmetz, Aljean. "His Hometown Now Likes John Steinbeck Better," *New York Times* (February 9, 1982), n.p.

2365   Harmetz, Aljean. "Steinbeck Row: Salinas Loves Lettuce and Author," *Asahi Evening News* (Tokyo), February 27, 1981, 8.

2366   Haslam, Gerald W. "That 'Fifty' Book: 1952 *The Grapes of Wrath* Was Off Limits for a Boy in Kern County," *San Francisco Chronicle, This World,* April 9, 1989, 10-12.

2367   Hauk, Steve. "Cannery Row's Ed Ricketts Topic of Symposium," *Monterey Herald, (Go!)* February 23- March 1, 1995, 7.

2368   Hauk, Steve. "Doc and Ed," *Monterey Herald,* September 11, 1986, 19.

2369   Hauk, Steve. "One-Man Show on Steinbeck," *Monterey Herald,* January 7, 1987, 9.

2370   Hauk, Steve. "Steinbeck Hooked on King Arthur," *Monterey Herald,* August 4, 1986, 1.

2371 Hayman, Lee Richard. "Editorial Contained Some Errors," *Salinas Californian*, August 17, 1987, 6A.

2372 Hayman, Lee Richard. "For John Steinbeck," *El Gabilan*, July 1986, 40.

2373 Hayman, Lee Richard. "Ghost of a Chance (Poem)," *Sunday Peninsula Herald*, September 29, 1985, 5D.

2374 Hayman, Lee Richard. "In the Land of Steinbeck and Jeffers," *Antiquarian Bookman*, February 13, 1984, n.p.

2375 Hayman, Lee Richard. "Local Color Authentic in Novel by Former Peninsula Resident," *Monterey Peninsula Herald*, April 7, 1985, 5D

2376 Hayman, Lee Richard. "Useful Handbook on Steinbeck," *Monterey Peninsula Herald*, June 17, 1984, 20B.

2377 Hayman, Lee Richard. "'SHS' Most Famous Graduate," *Salinas Californian*, October 19, 1983, n.p.

2378 Haynes, Jim. "Houses Where Great Literature Was Born," *Sacramento Bee*, July 19, 1985, 6-7. (Includes a discussion of the Steinbeck House)

2379 Heredia, Rich. "What Wrath Had Wrought," (*The Grapes of Wrath* Censorship), *Bakersfield Californian*, April 23, 1989, E1-2.

2380 Heubel, Robert W. "House Hunting," *Alta Vista Magazine*, April 5, 1992, 6-9.

2381 "A Highway That Spells 'Mother,'" *New York Times*, May 17, 1990, n.p.

2382 Hill, Randy. "Teacher Puts Some Life in Literature (*The Grapes of Wrath*)," *Mail Tribune*, January 1992, 1A, 3A.

2383   Hills, Nancy. "Steinbeck by Karsh," *Carmel Pine Cone,* July
        24, 1986, 1.

2384   Hodgen, Joanne. "*Cannery Row* Revisited: A Fishy Tale in a
        Writer's Dream Come True," *Coasting (Monterey,
        Carmel),* February 4, 1987, 29, 42-45.

2385   Hoggart, Simon. "A Real Sob Story," *Observer Magazine,*
        November 21, 1993, 38.

2386   Holt, Patricia. "Booksellers' Convention — Hype and Hope,"
        San Francisco Chronicle, June 4, 1990, F4. (*Lifeboat*)

2387   "Honoring Steinbeck," *Monterey Peninsula Herald,* July 23,
        1985, 13.

2388   "Honoring Steinbeck," *Salinas Californian,* August 3, 1991,
        3C.

2389   "Hostility to Writer Lingers in Salinas," *New York Times,*
        August 4, 1983, C13.

2390   "Houses Where Great Literature Was Born," *Sacramento
        Bee,* July 19, 1985, 1.

2391   Howard, Gerald. "Let This Be a Lesson to You: The Snakebit
        Life of Nathaneal West (reference to prepublication of *The
        Grapes of Wrath*)," *New York Times Book Review,*
        December 23, 1990, 3, 17.

2392   Howard, Gerald. "Let This Be a Lesson To You: The Snakebit
        Life of Nathaneal West," *New York Times Book Review,*
        December 30, 1990, 3, 17 (*The Grapes of Wrath*).

2393   Howe, Kevin. "'Critics Misread Steinbeck's *East of Eden,*'
        Speaker (Robert DeMott) Says," *Monterey Peninsula
        Herald,* August 4, 1985, 8A.

2394   Huber, Jeanne. "Red Tape Snags Bid to Save Steinbeck Haunt," *San Jose Mercury News*, January 30, 1992, 1B, 2B.

2395   Hughes, Bill. "Mature Traveler: Sentimental Journey Traces Legendary Route 66," *Los Angeles Times*, January 27, 1991, L9.

2396   Hulaniki, Alex. "Sparky Enea, Steinbeck Cohort, Storyteller, Dies," *Monterey Herald,* January 11, 1994, n.p.

2397   Hulse, Jerry. "A Tale of Painters, Butterflies, and Memories," (Pacific Grove, CA), *Los Angeles Times*, February 24, 1985, IV, 1, 23.

2398   "Images of Life's Realities: Photo by Horace Bristol," *Vista* (February 21, 1982), 16-17.

2399   "Investigators Search for Clues to Fire at Steinbeck Museum," *Monterey Herald*, September 4, 1990, 8.

2400   Italie, Hillel. "Steinbeck Writes of Passage," Express Extra, *Eastern Express/Hong Kong*, January 30 - February 1, 1995, 19.

2401   Jenel, Stacy, and Marilyn Beck. "Costner Being Touted For Role in 'Charlie' Film," *San Jose Mercury News*, January 31, 1994, n.p.

2401A   Jenkins, Holman W., Jr. "Cannery Row: An Epilogue," *Wall Street Journal*, March 19, 1996, 1.

2402   Jerram, Elise. "Kalisa: Living Legend of Cannery Row," *Monterey Peninsula Herald,* August 12, 1985, 16.

2403   Jerram, Elise. "Memories Haunt Cannery Row," *Monterey Peninsula Herald,* October 21, 1984, ID.

2404   "John Steinbeck," *Book and Magazine Collector*, 75 (June 1990), 42-47.

2405   "John Steinbeck Festival Schedule," *Salinas Californian*,
          August 11, 1992, 6E.

2406   "John Steinbeck IV Dies of Surgery Complications,"
          Monterey Sunday Herald, February 10, 1991, A4.

2407   "John Steinbeck: Man, Myth, and Moustache," *The
          Independent on Sunday*, March 22, 1992, 10-11.

2408   "John Steinbeck Paid Tribute in His Hometown," *Monterey
          Peninsula*, August 4-10, 1988, 1.

2409   "John Steinbeck's Life and Works Celebrated at Salinas
          Festival," *Coasting,* (Monterey, Carmel, California) July
          31, 1985, 33.

2410   Johnson, Claudia. "*Of Mice and Men,* Censors and Civil
          Libertarians," *AWP Chronicle,* 25 (October/November
          1992), 1.

2411   Johnson, Rhetta Grimsley. "Baptists Wail into the Night Over
          "Filth"," *Commercial Appeal* (Memphis), February 27,
          1984, C14. (Included in this report from Brandon,
          Mississippi, is *The Red Pony* on the "filth list.")

2412   Johnson, Rhetta Grimsley. "Ignorance Goes on Display
          Again," *Commercial Appeal* (Memphis), December 18,
          1994, n.p. (discusses censorship and Steinbeck classics *Of
          Mice and Men* and *The Red Pony*)

2413   Jones, Clarisse. "Epic Celebration: Steinbeck's Timeless *The
          Grapes of Wrath* Is 50 Years Old," *Los Angeles Times*
          (Metro ed.), May 1, 1989, 6.

2414   Jones, Malcolm. "The Real Cannery Row," *St. Petersburg
          Times* (Florida), July 17, 1988, 1D-7D.

2415   Judd, Judith. "The National Curriculum: Authors (Steinbeck)
          and Texts Selected for Study: Accent Put on Standard
          English," *Independent*, February 3, 1993, 3.

2416 Judd, Judith. "Schools' Modern Book List Cut to 12 Authors," *Independent*, October 8, 1994, 6.

2417 Kanter, Lawrence. "A Little Tour of California: The Steinbeck Map of America," *Image (San Francisco Examiner Chronicle Magazine)*, October 11, 1987, 30-31.

2418 Kaplan, Tracy. "Steinbeck Sketch Donated to SJSU Research Center," *Spartan Daily*, San Jose State University, January 24, 1985, n.p.

2419 Kemp, Peter. "Real Nephews of Their Uncle Sam," *Independent*, July 21, 1987, 12. (This includes a reference to Steinbeck and *The Grapes of Wrath.)*

2420 Kessler, Julia Braun. "A New Definition of Family in *Home Free*," *Book Page* (February 1991), n.p.

2421 Kestler, Frances. "Reflections: Steinbeck's Sag Harbor," *Sag Harbor Herald*, July 16, 1992, n.p.

2422 Kestler, Frances. "Reflections: Steinbeck's Sag Harbor, Part II," *Sag Harbor Herald*, July 23, 1992, n.p.

2423 Killeen, Jacqueline. "Lunch and Literature at the Steinbeck House," *PG & E Progress* (April 1990), 6-7.

2424 Kinsley, David. "Baxter Road's Literary Side," *Nantucket Beacon*, May 15, 1991, 4.

2425 Kinsley, David. "Forty Years Later, It's Still *East of Eden*," *Nantucket Beacon*, May 15, 1991, 4, 11.

2426 Kinsock, John, "Steinbeck Country," *California*, 2 (October/November 1991), 24-29.

2427 Knebel, Fletcher. "Carmel: Beyond the Tourist Tides," *New York Times*, August 15, 1982, Sec. 20, 16, 17.

2428   Knott, John. *"The Winter of Our Discontent* Comes out as Morality Play," *Commercial Appeal* (Memphis), December 6, 1983, B7.

2429   Kohn, F. Martin. "Stegner Ruminates on Favorite Places: *Where the Bluebird Sings to the Lemonade Springs: Living and Writing in the West*," *Detroit Free Press*, March 29, 1992, 8H.

2430   Kot, Greg. "Ghost Stories: Bruce Springsteen's Muted Approach Dulls Bewitching 'Tom Joad,' *Chicago Tribune,* November 21, 1995, Tempo, 1.

2431   Kress, Nancy. "Dictus Interruptus: You May Be Tempted to Let Your Characters Tell the Whole Story, But Sometimes You Must Interrupt," *Writer's Digest*, February 1995, 8, 10-12.

2432   Krieger, Elliot. *"Grapes of Wrath* at 50: Steinbeck's Okie Epic Endures," *Providence Sunday Journal*, April 9, 1989, n.p.

2433   Kruger, Herbert B. "Ecological Steinbeck," *Alternatives*, 19 (1993), 45.

2434   "Kurt Vonnegut, Recipient of the John Steinbeck Award," *Sag Harbor Express*, May 14, 1992, n.p.

2435   Lachman, Andrew. "Powerful Tale Lives on in Steinbeck Country," *Monterey County Herald*, August 3, 1993, D1.

2436   Lachman, Andrew. "Steinbeck Grave Place for Reflection, " *Monterey County Herald*, August 6, 1993, 1A, 4A.

2437   Lajeunesse, George. "Elevated into Serenity: SJS Steinbeck Scholars Get a Little Peace," *San Jose Mercury-News*, May 22, 1984 (5), 1B, 4B.

2438   Lajeunesse, George. "A Quiet Time with the Works of Steinbeck," *San Jose Mercury News,* May 21, 1984, 1B.

2439   Larimer, Timothy. "Hustle and Bustle on Cannery Row: The
        Sardines Are History, But Developers Hope Tourists Will
        Be Next Big Catch," *San Jose Mercury News*, March 7,
        1985, 1F, 10F.

2440   Larimer, Timothy. "Sardines Return, but Cannery Row
        Doesn't Care," *San Jose Mercury News,* December 16,
        1984, 1B.

2441   Larimer, Timothy. "Site of Steinbeck's *Tortilla Flat* Subject to
        Debate," *San Jose Mercury News,* May 29, 1985, 2A.

2442   Larimer, Timothy. "A Steinbeck Riddle: Where Is, or Was
        Tortilla Flat?" *San Jose Mercury News,* May 28, 1985, 1A,
        9A.

2443   Larimer, Timothy. "Steinbeck Story Languishes in Vault (at
        the John Steinbeck Library, Salinas, California)," *San Jose
        Mercury News*, August 1, 1986, B1.

2444   Laubach, David. "Controversial Book Argued before Board,"
        Tuscaloosa News, March 28, 1989, 1, 4.

2445   Lauderale, Beverly. "Steinbeck Still Controversial in Salinas,"
        The Press-Enterprise, August 4, 1991, F1, 3.

2446   LeDuc, Daniel. "Still a Kick: The Legendary Route 66 Finds
        New Life As a Nostalgia Trip," *Chicago Tribune,* January
        21, 1996, Transportation, 5.

2447   Lehmann-Haupt, Christopher. "A Good Title Does Not Make
        a Book, But It Certainly Helps," *San Jose Mercury News*,
        January 29, 1994, n.p.

2448   "Letters: Steinbeck Ticky-Tacks," *Los Angeles Times Book
        Review*, April 30, 1989, 15.

2449   Leyde, Tom. "International Congress to Celebrate Steinbeck,"
        Salinas Californian, July 14, 1984, 33.

2450   Leyde, Tom. "John Steinbeck Chose Him for 'Flight,'"
        Salinas Californian, August 11, 1984, 32.

2451   Leyde, Tom. "John Steinbeck Chose Him for 'Flight,'"
        Salinas Californian, May 2, 1985, 20A.

2452   Leyde, Tom. "Steinbeck Letters on Loan from Arthurian
        Expert," *Salinas Californian,* October 27, 1984, 2.

2453   "Librarians Say *Go Ask Alice* Is Censored Most in Schools,"
        New York Times, November 28, 1982, n.p.

2454   Lindsey, Robert. "Family Members' Objections Delay
        Publications of Steinbeck Biography" (by Jackson J.
        Benson), *New York Times,* August 4, 1983, Y, 20. (C13)

2455   Lindsey, Robert. "Glow of Green Begins to Fade in California
        Valley," *New York Times,* February 19, 1986, 9.

2456   Lindsey, Robert. "Gripes of Wrath: Some Go to Salinas to
        Honor John Steinbeck but Many of the Residents Hate
        Him," *International Herald Tribune,* August 6-7, 1983,
        n.p.

2457   Lindsey, Robert. "High Ocean-Front Aquarium to Open in
        Steinbeck's Monterey," *New York Times,* October 20,
        1984, n.p.

2458   Lindsey, Robert. "The Lure of the Trees and the Pacific," *New
        York Times,* August 15, 1982, Sec. 20, 16, 17.

2459   Lindsey, Robert. "What's Doing around Monterey," *New York
        Times,* September 30, 1990, Sec. 20, 10.

2460   Lipson, Eden Ross. "Otters and Sea Lions in Steinbeck
        Country: Monterey's Aquarium Changes the Face of
        Cannery Row," *New York Times,* Sec. 20, May 25, 1986, 9,
        24.

2461   "A Literary Garage Sale," *San Francisco Chronicle*, May 24, 1988, n.p.

2462   Livernois, Joe. "School Named for Steinbeck," *Monterey County Herald*, October 16, 1992, 1A.

2463   Livernois, Joe. "Two Local Collectors Adore Steinbeck," *Monterey County Herald*, February 27, 1995, 1A, 8A.

2464   Loftis, Anne. "The Steinbeck-Steffens Connection," *The Californians Magazine*, (January-February 1987), n.p.

2465   Loh, Jules. "Steinbeck Would Have to Do Some Rewriting Today: Okies Have Left Their Mark on California," *Muncie Star,* September 6, 1992, 12B.

2466   Lopez, Eddie. "Festival Celebrates Steinbeck, Man and Country," *Sacramento Bee*, June 28, 1989, 1D.

2467   Lopez, Hortensia M. "Steinbeck's Widow, Friends Share Memories at Festival," *Monterey County Sunday Herald*, August 16, 1992, 1A, 16A.

2468   Lordan, Betsy. "Ed Ricketts' Real Life Distorted Say His Children," *Monterey County Herald*, February 27, 1995. 1C, 2C.

2469   Lucero, John. "Steinbeck Center Looks Like a Winner," *Monterey Herald*, December 9, 1993, n.p.

2470   Machuca, Ana. "Foundation Lays Cultural Groundwork," *Salinas Californian*, February 25, 1993, 4, 12.

2471   Machuca, Ana. "Steinbeck's Life in Salinas," *Salinas Californian*, February 25, 1993, 5, 9, 12.

2472   MacIntyre, Ben. "Spirit of America," *Times Weekend* (London), March 19,1994, 16.

2473 Magill, John. "The Last Frontier of Bohemia," *Gambit*, March 14, 1989, 15-18.

2474 Malanczuk, Kim. "Voyage to *The Sea of Cortez*," Saratoga News, December 18, 1991, 22-23.

2475 Manglesdorf, Tom. "The Way We Were: Pilon of *Tortilla Flat*," *Monterey Life* (September 1981), 71-72.

2476 March, Ray A. "Ed Ricketts and John Steinbeck's 'Doc'," *Oceans*, 19 (July/August 1986), 22-25.

2477 Marek, Tony. "Remembering Steinbeck," *Spartan Daily* (San Jose State University), September 20, 1991, 4.

2478 Marksman, Pamela Marsh. "A Correspondence with John Steinbeck: Dear Avuncle John," *KPFA Folio*, October 1989, 5, 26.

2479 Mauro, Tony. "Groups Trying to Ban Books Shift Strategies," *USA Today*, September 1, 1988. (Most frequently challenged author: John Steinbeck; Most frequently challenged book: *Of Mice and Men*.)

2480 "Mavis Macintosh," *Publisher's Weekly*, 230 (August 22, 1986), 18.

2481 McCabe, Michael. "John Steinbeck's Kindred Spirits Still Whoop It Up on Cannery Row," *San Francisco Chronicle*, February 24, 1995, A1, A7.

2482 McDowell, Edwin. "Articles Assert FBI Often Watched Writers," *New York Times*, October 1, 1987, n.p.

2483 McDowell, Edwin. "Eastern Europe Pays," *New York Times*, June 13, 1990, C16. (discusses royalties on Steinbeck's work received from sales on the continent)

2484 McDowell, Edwin. "Unpublished Steinbeck That May Stay That Way," *New York Times*, May 9, 1990, C19.

2485   McKelvey, Bob. "Steinbeck Townsfolk Are Proud of Their
        Winner," *Detroit Free Press*, May 26, 1985, 7C.

2486   McLeish, Kenneth. "Educating Anthea: Classic Fiction for the
        Filofax," *Sunday Times*, July 9, 1989, G8, G9.

2487   McLennan, Gerald. "An Unlikely Pair: 'Tom' and Steinbeck,"
        San Francisco Chronicle, April 26, 1990, E 1-2.

2488   McQuay, David. "Steinbeck Possessions Going on Sale to the
        Public," *Denver Post*, May 20, 1988, 1F.

2489   Medina, Dina. "Steinbeck Chronicler's Reflections," *Spartan
        Daily,* San Jose State University, February 24, 1993, 1, 6.

2490   Medina, Dina. "Steinbeck Writer Chanced on to Job," *Spartan
        Daily,* San Jose State University, March 1, 1993, 6.

2491   Meek, Jim. "No Strings Attached: A Woman's Game,"
        Chronicle-Herald/Mail-Star (Halifax, Nova Scotia), July
        28, 1988. (Meek refers to *Cannery Row* in his discussion
        of a theory on male-female relationships.)

2492   "Meet Laura Hubbard, New Principal of John Steinbeck
        School," *Creekbridge Gazette*, Fall 1990, 1.

2493   Messick, Everett. "Plans for John Steinbeck Center Unveiled
        at Festival in Salinas," *Monterey Herald*, August 3, 1991,
        4A.

2494   Messick, Everett. "Steinbeck Pilgrims Find Simple Shrine,"
        Monterey Herald, August 4, 1989, 1, 4.

2495   Meurer, Phyllis. "Multiplying Like Rabbits," *Coast Weekly*,
        August 4-10, 1994, 7.

2496   Milich, Melissa. "Steinbeck: A Very Public Celebration of a
        Private Man's Work," *Sacramento Bee*, August 11, 1983,
        E3.

2497   Mill, Kay. "New Wars, Old Politics: An Activist Reviews Hollywood Then and Now," *Los Angeles Times*, February 16, 1986, 3. (Makes reference to the right wing attacking *The Grapes of Wrath*.)

2498   Miller, Bryan. "Dusk's Magic: As Day Ends, The Fun Begins," *New York Times Weekend*, May 21, 1993, C1.

2499   Minor, Barbara. "Instructional Resources: Grapevine: An Excursion into Steinbeck Country," *Tech Trends*, 36 (1991), 53.

2500   Mitgang, Herbert. "Making Documentaries for Roosevelt," *New York Times,* May 21, 1992, n.p.

2501   *Monterey Cannery Row (50th Anniversary Edition)* Vol. 2 (1994) "This is Why We Call It 'Steinbeck's' Cannery Row," 1, 2; "Celebrating the Fiftieth Anniversary of John Steinbeck's Cannery Row," 1, 12; "Ed 'Doc' Ricketts, Steinbeck's Best Friend," 3, 6; "Flora Woods, Monterey Madam: 'One Hell of a Woman,'" 4; "Steinbeck Called It Lee Chong's Heavenly Flower Grocery," 5; "Events and People Who Shaped the Monterey Area," 6, 12; "Chinese Were the First Settlers on Cannery Row," 11, 13; "Fire on the Row! Smoke Filled Disasters Helped Shape Today's Cannery Row," 13, 15; "Development of Fishing Industry Was Driven by New Technology," 14; "Rise and Fall of the Sardine Industry," 16; "Salinas Basks in Premiere's Publicity Glare," *Salinas Californian*, January 6, 1982, n.p.

2502   Moore, Judith. "Destiny Manifest," *San Diego Reader*, March 7, 1991, 5, 9, 10. (on John Steinbeck IV)

2503   Moore, Judith, Abe Opincar, and Bob Shabrom. "Where The Grapes of Wrath Are Stored: John Steinbeck Was My Father," *San Diego Leader Weekly*, March 30, 1989, 26-29. (on John Steinbeck IV)

2504   Moore, Kerry. "Steinbeck Given Voice," *The Province*
        (Vancouver, British Columbia), March 25, 1988, 61.
        (Actor James Nisbet Clark's 90-minute program)

2505   Moores, Lew. "Steinbeck's Message Echoes after 50 Years,"
        Cincinnati Post, April 14, 1989, 1A, 6A.

2506   Muchnic, Suzanne. "Travels with Steinbeck: Horace Bristol's
        Remarkable Depression-Era Photographs Are on Display
        for the First Time," *Los Angeles Times*, January 22, 1989,
        8, 89.

2507   Murray, Joe. "Steinbeck's Dangerous Words Make a Gem of a
        Gift," *Minneapolis Star Tribune*, July 11, 1991, n.p.

2508   Mydans, Seth. "In a Small Town, a Battle Over a Book: Book
        Ban in California School Strikes Down Familiar Target
        (*The Catcher in the Rye*)," *New York Times*, September 3,
        1989, 1, 11. (*Of Mice and Men* and *Ther Grapes of Warth*).

2509   Myers, George, Jr. "The Industry: Report on Non-Publication
        of *Lifeboat*," *Columbus Dispatch*, September 9, 1990, n.p.

2510   Nakayama, Kiyoshi. "Steinbeck in Japan, the International
        Writer," *Monterey Life* (July 1987), 55-56, 60-61.

2511   "Names and Notes," *Boulder Colorado Sunday Camera*, May
        22, 1988, 2A.

2512   Nathan, Paul. "Short Subjects," *Publisher's Weekly*, April 8,
        1988, 19.

2513   Neary, Walter. "Appeal International in Scope," *Salinas
        Californian*, August 11, 1992, 3E.

2514   Neary, Walter. "Celebrating Steinbeck," *Salinas Californian*,
        August 4, 1993, 1E, 3E.

2515   Neary, Walter. "A Man, a Dog and Rocinante," *Salinas
        Californian*, August 1, 1991, 1E.

2516   Neary, Walter. "Memories That Fill Volumes: Salinas
        Embraces Native It Once Scorned," *Salinas Californian*,
        August 11, 1992, 1E.

2517   Neary, Walter. "Son Shares Insight on Steinbeck Novel,"
        Salinas Californian, August 6, 1990, 1B.

2518   Neary, Walter. "Soviets Rediscover American Author,"
        Salinas Californian, August 6, 1990, 1B, 3B.

2519   Neary, Walter. "Steinbeck's Son Helps Kick Off Fund Drive
        for Salinas Center," *Salinas Californian*, August 1, 1991,
        1C.

2520   "Steinbeck's Son Wings It on a Dare," *Salinas Californian
        Extra*, August 6, 1991, n.p.

2521   Neswitz, Margye. "Fairbanks and Steinbeck," *Carmel Pine
        Cone*, May 18, 1989, 14, 15, 16.

2522   Neswitz, Margye. "Steinbeck Maquette Unveiled," *Monterey
        Herald*, October 5, 1993, n.p.

2523   "New School is a Lesson for Students," (John Steinbeck
        School in Salinas), *Monterey Sunday Herald*, September 8,
        1991, 9A.

2524   "New Steinbeck Guide," *Stanford Observer*, May 1981, n.p.

2525   Nickerson, Roy. "Following in the Wake of *The Log*,
        Steinbeck and Ricketts Journey Blazed a Trail for Others
        to Follow," *Monterey Peninsula Herald*, May 12, 1985,
        10-15.

2526   Nickerson, Roy. "Row's Favorite Son," *Monterey Peninsula
        Herald*, May 26, 1985, 3D.

2527   Nordstrand, Dave. "Celebrating Steinbeck," *Salinas
        Californian Weekend*, February 26-27, 1994, 1A, 8A.

2528   Nordstrand, Dave. "Dates of Wrath (1939-1989)," *Salinas Californian*, March 31, 1989, 1B, 8B.

2529   Nordstrand, Dave. "Hitting Its Stride: Steinbeck Fest Strives for Balance," *Salinas Californian*, August 5, 1993, n.p.

2530   Nordstrand, Dave. "Steinbeck's Novel Rattled Bones in Valley Closets," *Salinas Californian*, March 31, 1989, 1B.

2531   "Notable & Quotable," *Wall Street Journal*, May 24, 1984, 28. (The notable quote is from Steinbeck's *The Acts of King Arthur and His Noble Knights.*)

2532   O'Connell, Mary E. "Steinbeck Country," *Salinas Californian*, February 28, 1987, 64.

2533   "Obituary: Carol J. H. Brown, 76, Was Married to John Steinbeck Early in His Career," *San Jose Mercury News*, February 10, 1983, 5B.

2534   "Obituary: Horace 'Sparky' Enea," *Monterey County Herald*, January 11, 1994, n.p.

2535   "Obituaries: John Steinbeck IV, Author, Reporter," *Los Angeles Times*, February 12, 1991, A24.

2536   "Obituary: John Steinbeck 4th, Freelance Writer, 44," *New York Times*, February 11, 1991, D10.

2537   "Obituary: John Steinbeck IV, Son of Famed Writer," *San Jose Mercury News*, February 11, 1991, 4B.

2538   "Obituary: John Steinbeck IV, Writer," *Independent*, February 19, 1991, 27.

2539   "Obituary: John Steinbeck IV, Writer," *Monterey Sunday Herald*, February 10, 1991, n.p.

2540   "Obituary: John Steinbeck IV, Writer," *Washington Post*, February 11, 1991, n.p.

2541 "Obituary: John Steinbeck IV, Writer," *San Francisco Examiner*, February 10, 1991, B7.

2542 *"Of Mice and Men* Gets Solid Reading," *Monterey Peninsula Herald,* January 20, 1985, 13A.

2543 "Of Steinbeck and O'Neill and The Rest," *Writer's Digest*, August 1987, 40.

2544 "Old Fashioned Doctor H.T. Stotler Dies at 72," *Monterey County Herald,* April 28, 1992, n.p.

2545 Opincar, Abe, Judith Moore, and Bob Shabrom. "Where The Grapes of Wrath Are Stored: John Steinbeck Was My Father," *San Diego Leader Weekly*, March 30, 1989, 26-29. (on John Steinbeck IV)

2546 Orr, John. "No Sour Grapes for Salinas: Town Venerates Its Native Son, John Steinbeck," *Anaheim Bulletin*, July 22, 1988, B3.

2547 Orr, John. "Salinas Embraces Its Prodigal Son with Yearly Event," *San Jose Mercury News*, July 24, 1988, 7T. (1T, 6T)

2548 Oshita, Lori. "Steinbeck Festival Bus Trip Draws Variety of Tourists," *Salinas Californian*, August 6, 1985, 11.

2549 Owens, Louis. *"The Grapes of Wrath*: Looking Back," *USA Today*, 17 (May 1989), 92-93.

2550 Palazzo, Tracy. "Monte Sereno Compromises on Steinbeck House Changes," *Los Gatos Weekly News*, 114 (May 31, 1995), n.p.

2551 Palazzo, Tracy. "The Preservation Ordinance of Monte Sereno Faces a Challenge," *Los Gatos Weekly News*, 115 (November 1, 1995), 1, 12.

2551A   Parker, Ian. "Making Advances (An Interview with Harold
        Robbins)," *New Yorker*, April 1, 1996, 72, 76.

2552   Parry, Richard Lloyd. "Seen This, Read That? (*The Grapes of
        Wrath*)," *Sunday Times: The Culture,* November 15, 1992,
        4.

2553   Parsons, Larry. "A Fountain of Resources for Steinbeck's
        Works, Legacy," *Salinas Californian*, February 25, 1993,
        9.

2554   Parsons, Larry. "It's Ambitious but Do-able," *Salinas
        Californian*, February 25, 1993, 7, 8.

2555   Parsons, Larry. "Oral Histories of Steinbeck to Go Public,"
        Salinas Californian, February 19, 1994, n.p.

2556   Parsons, Larry. "Site Proposed for Showcase of Steinbeck,"
        Salinas Californian, January 4, 1988, 1A.

2557   "Past Mingles with a Thriving Present," *Coasting* (Monterey,
        Carmel, California), November 5, 1986, 47.

2558   Pate, Nancy. "Writer's First Magic Words," *Detroit Free
        Press*, January 24, 1990, 3B.

2559   Patterson, Arnie. "Don't Despair. Read Steinbeck," *Daily
        News* (Halifax, Nova Scotia), April 15, 1989, 2.

2560   Penney, Beth. "Steinbeck Fans, Take Note! Plethora of Events
        Honoring Famed Author Begin This Month," *Carmel Pine
        Cone*, February 9, 1995, n.p.

2561   "Personalities," *Washington Post*, May 2, 1989, D3. (PEN
        Center USA West-sponsored *The Grapes of Wrath* event)

2562   "Photographs an Inspiration to John Steinbeck's *Grapes of
        Wrath*," *This Month on Monterey Peninsula*, 28 (February
        1990), 17.

2563 "The Pinnacles Monument," *New York Times*, February 24, 1991, n.p.

2564 "Preserving Cannery Row's Past," *Coasting* (Monterey, Carmel, California), November 26, 1986, 49.

2565 Pringle, Peter. "Where's Waldo? Not on the Shelf (*EOE*)," *Independent,* April 12, 1993, 17.

2566 Pulig, Claudia. "*Wrath* Marathon: Lest We Forget," *Calendar* (California) November 23, 1989, F 1.

2567 Quarnstrom, Lee. "Breathing the 'Poem' Back into Cannery Row," *San Jose Mercury-News*, May 15, 1983, 1B, 3B.

2568 Quarnstrom, Lee. "Travels with Steinbeck," *San Jose Mercury-News*, (West) May 20, 1993, 12-15, 16-17.

2569 Rader, Eddy. "*Cannery Row* Goof: Buttlestars Really Brittlestars," *Salinas Californian*, January 25, 1982, n.p.

2570 Randall, Sharon. "Remembering a Native Son," *Monterey Herald*, August 11, 1991, 1D, 3D.

2571 Rasco, Judith. "A Cautionary Tale for Reviewers," *New York Times Book Review*, May 14, 1989, n.p.

2572 Ratliff, William. "Steinbeck's Peninsula Roots: Memories of Stanford in Writings: Letters to a Coed Fill a Gap," *Palo Alto Times Tribune*, November 2, 1984, B-1, B-6.

2573 Raymo, Chet. "On a Voyage 50 Years Ago, Steinbeck Saw Nature's Unity," *Boston Globe*, May 10, 1993, n.p. (*The Log from the Sea of Cortez*)

2574 Rayner, Jay. "On the Road with the American Dream," *Guardian*, September 17, 1992, 27.

2575   "Recognition for Humanitarianism (Peter Matthiessen,
         recipient of the John Steinbeck Award)." *Sag Harbor
         Express*, May 16, 1991 n.p.

2576   Reeves, Phil. "After 66 Years You Can Still Get Kicks En
         Route," *Independent*, October 8, 1992, 13.

2577   Reeves, Richard. "The Numbing of America's Heart and
         Mind," *Monterey Herald*, c. March 1990, n.p.

2578   Reeves, Richard. "Real-Life Joads Still out on the Street," *San
         Francisco Chronicle*, June 7, 1990, E4.

2579   Reeves, Richard. "Thirty-One Years Later, Steinbeck's Story
         Is Still Vital," *Detroit Free Press*, June 7, 1990, n.p.

2580   Renshaw, Patrick. "Pare Lorentz," *Independent*, March 20,
         1992, 21.

2581   Richards, Jane. "Dilys Powell Picks Her Top 14,"
         Independent, April 22, 1988, 28.

2582   Risser, James V. "First-Class Biking in Baja California," *New
         York Times*, March 27, 1988, Sec. XX, 14.

2583   Ritnick, Richard. "Steinbeck Festival," *Coast Weekly*, August
         5-11, 1993, 41-42.

2584   Robertson, Michael. "Looking Back at Steinbeck: Salinas
         Reconciles with Its Naughty Son," *San Francisco
         Chronicle*, March 22, 1989, B3-4.

2585   Robertson, Nan. "Who Was I to Tinker with John Steinbeck?"
         New York Times, December 4, 1983, H37.

2586   Rodriguez, Mary. "Monterey's Heritage," *This Month on
         Monterey Peninsula*, 28 (February 1990), 16.

2587   Roggeman, Buck. "City Offered Doc Ricketts' Lab for
         $170,000," *Monterey Herald*, May 13, 1994, n.p.

2588 Roggeman, Buck. "Salinas Ceremony Honors 'Local Boy,'"
     Monterey Sunday Herald, August 16, 1993, 16A.

2589 Rubin, Dana. "SJS Buys 31 Steinbeck Letters," *San Jose
     Mercury News*, October 26, 1985, 1B-2B.

2589A Rumsey, Spencer. "High Expectations — How to Keep Your
     Hopes for Your Children from Crossing the Line into
     Unhealthy Pleasure," *Newsday*, May 11, 1996, B-1, B-2.
     (*East of Eden*)

2590 Ryan, Carol. "French Students Seek Steinbeck Data," *Salinas
     Californian,* February 18, 1986, 15.

2591 Ryan, Carol. "University Buys Steinbeck's 'Dark Night'
     Letters," *Salinas Californian,* October 26, 1985, 1.

2592 Saffire, William, "On Language: Get It?" *New York Times
     Magazine*, October 27, 1991, n.p. (*The Grapes of Wrath*)

2593 "Salinas-Born Nobel Laureate's Life and Works Are
     Remembered," *Coasting* (Monterey, Carmel, California),
     July 30 - August 6, 1986, 48.

2594 "Salinas Center Will Honor Author: Developers Hope
     Steinbeck Plaza Will Help Town That Hated Him," *Los
     Angeles Times*, December 6, 1987, pt. 1, 29-30.

2595 "Salinas Recalls Native Son Steinbeck with Wrath, Awe," *St.
     Paul Pioneer Press Dispatch*, August 13, 1988, 12B.

2596 Sanchez, Edgar. "Steinbeck's Valley, the Hatred Is Slowly
     Turning to Love," *San Francisco Examiner*, July 5, 1987,
     B1, 4.

2597 "Sardines — Boom and Bust," *Coasting (Monterey, Carmel),*
     December 24, 1986, 43.

2598   "Sardines: Fish That Made Cannery Row Famous Are
        Beginning to Make a Comeback," *Salinas Californian,*
        August 13, 1985, 1A.

2599   Scanlon, Bill. "Steinbeck IV Deals with '80s," *Daily Camera*
        (Boulder, Colorado), October 21, 1985, 1C, 3C.

2600   Scanlon, Tom. "Did Steinbeck Have Sour Grapes about Los
        Gatos," *Palo Alto Times Tribune*, August 4, 1989, n.p.

2601   "Schedule of Steinbeck Events," *Salinas Californian*, August
        4, 1993, 3E.

2602   Schilling, Elizabeth. "John Steinbeck's Salinas: A Guide to
        the Place and the People," *Image, the Magazine of
        Northern California, San Francisco Examiner*, July 27,
        1986, 34-35.

2603   Schilling, Elizabeth. "John Steinbeck's Salinas: A Guide to
        the Place and People," *The New York Post*, July 27, 1986,
        34.

2604   "School Censorship Attacks Intensify Nationwide: Attacked in
        1990-1991, *The Red Pony, The Grapes of Wrath*," *Forum:
        A Bulletin for People of the American Way*, September 20,
        1991, E7.

2605   Schultz, Ken. "Leading Steinbeck Dealer Started Young, "
        Monterey Herald, August 1, 1989, Sec. 2, 17.

2606   Schultz, Ken. "Publishing Flourishing, Reports Soviet
        Official," *Monterey Herald*, August 4, 1989, 4.

2607   Schultz, Ken. "'Rocinante' to Travel to Salinas," *Monterey
        Herald*, March 30, 1990, n.p.

2608   Schultz, Ken. "Son of Famous Author Would Like to See
        Contest for Aspiring Writers," *Monterey Herald*, August 1,
        1991, 1C-2C.

2609   Schultz, Ken. "Steinbeck Festival to Open Thursday: Films,
        Tours, Talks Planned," *Monterey Herald*, July 30, 1991,
        3C.

2610   Schultz, Ken. "Walkers See Steinbeck Country on Guided
        Tour," *Monterey Herald*, August 2, 1991, 1C-2C.

2611   Scott, Nancy. "Steinbeck in Salinas: From Pariah to Tourist
        Attraction," *San Francisco Examiner* (February 11, 1982),
        E1, E4.

2612   "Secret Steinbeck Letters Sold," *Monterey Peninsula Herald,*
        October 25, 1985, 1.

2613   Shabrom, Bob, Judith Moore, and Abe Opincar. "Where the
        Grapes of Wrath Are Stored: John Steinbeck Was My
        Father," *San Diego Leader Weekly*, March 30, 1989, 26-
        29. (on John Steinbeck IV)

2614   "Shakespeare Then, Shakespeare Now: What They Read in
        High School," *New York Times* (Education), May 20,
        1992, n.p.

2615   Shuler, Barbara Rose. "Steinbeck's Words Come to Life,"
        Coasting (Monterey, Carmel, California), January 14,
        1987, 22.

2616   Silverstein, Michael. "In Bunkhouse, They're Laughin' at
        IRA," *Los Angeles Times*, January 12, 1986, IV, 3.

2617   Simon, Jim. "Porn Bill Worries Librarians (*The Grapes of
        Wrath*)." *Seattle Times*, February 27, 1991, A1, 2.

2618   Sirica, Jack. "FBI Dogged Steinbeck," *San Jose Mercury
        News,* June 4, 1984, 1F.

2619   Sirica, Jack. "FBI Tracked Steinbeck's Travels and
        Friendships for Nearly 30 Years," *San Jose Mercury News*,
        June 14, 1984, 1A, 12A.

2620 Sirica, Jack. "The Fourth Chapter of Steinbeck Festival to Close," *San Jose Mercury News*, August 10, 1983, n.p.

2621 Sirica, Jack. "The U.S. Army vs. John Steinbeck," *San Jose Mercury-News*, June 2, 1984, 1A, 12A;

2622 "Sixth Annual Steinbeck Festival Scheduled for August 2-6," *Salinas Californian,* July 27, 1985, 35.

2623 Skipitares, Connie. "'Garlic Gulch': Steinbeck's Spirit Lives in His House," *San Jose Mercury News*, March 12, 1986, 1-2.

2624 Skipitares, Connie. "'Garlic Gulch': Steinbeck's Spirit Lives in Cottage Where He Wrote *The Grapes of Wrath*," *San Jose Mercury News*, March 19, 1986, 1-2.

2625 Skipitares, Connie. "Steinbeck House Owner Blocked in Plans," *San Jose Mercury News*, April 19, 1995, 1-2.

2626 Skipitares, Connie. "Steinbeck's Mountain Retreat Is Now Expanded Family Home," *The New York Post*, March 17, 1986, 1B.

2627 Skipitares, Connie. "Work on Home Incites Wrath," *San Jose Mercury News*, October 20, 1995, 1B-2B.

2628 Slater, Shirley, and Harry Basch, "John Steinbeck's *Cannery Row*: More Than a Literary Pilgrimage," *Los Angeles Times,* February 2, 1986, VII, 1.

2629 Smith, Jack. "View: On the Road Again — Or, Some Folks Are Still out There Getting Their Kicks on Route 66," *Los Angeles Times*, August 20, 1986, n.p.

2630 "Son Fights 'Curse' of Famous Father," *Denver Post,* October 8, 1984, 2A.

2631 "Sources of Information about Steinbeck," *Salinas Californian*, August 11, 1992, 4E.

2632   "Soviets Help Celebrate *The Grapes of Wrath*," *San Francisco Chronicle*, August 2, 1989, A2.

2633   "Springsteen Makes Music out of *Grapes,*" *Chicago Tribune*, October 17, 1995, 2.

2634   Stanton, Mike. "Steinbeck's 'Folks' Come to Find a Bit of Eden," *Chicago Tribune*, August 15, 1982, Sec. 1, 13-14.

2635   Stanton, Mike. "Steinbeck's 'Folks' Come to Find a Bit of Eden," *Chicago Tribune*, August 25, 1982, Sec. 3, 1, 4.

2636   Starr, John R. "Steinbeck's *Cannery Row* Can't Be Found," *Arkansas Democrat*, January 30, 1987, 5D.

2637   Starrett, Kathleen Wagner. "A Young Steinbeck and His Teacher," *Herald Weekend Magazine*, April 24, 1988, 3-4.

2638   "Steinbeck Account One-Sided," *Salinas Californian*, April 11, 1989, 6A.

2639   "Steinbeck Archives Housed in Salinas," *Monterey Herald*, June 22, 1986, 29E.

2640   "Steinbeck Award," *Monterey Sunday Herald*, May 27, 1990, 6A.

2640A   "Steinbeck Award," *Tulsa World*, October 20, 1996, n.p.

2641   "Steinbeck Bequest One of Obstacles for *Cannery Row*," *Variety*, 306 (February 17, 1982), 4, 38.

2642   "Steinbeck Birthday Celebration," *Coast Weekly*, February 2, 1993, 20.

2643   "Steinbeck Center Foundation," *Carmel Pine Cone*, August 5, 1993, 33.

2644   "Steinbeck Country: Markham Ranch/Palm Grove Ranch Homes," *San Jose Mercury News*, July 13, 1991, E12.

2645   "Steinbeck Course," January 29, 1987, *San Luis Obispo Sun-Bulletin*, 25.

2646   "Steinbeck Course," *Salinas Californian,* January 28, 1987, 2B.

2647   "Steinbeck Edition for Anniversary," *San Francisco Chronicle*, June 30, 1988, n.p.

2648   "Steinbeck Fan Brings Expertise to UTEP," *The El Paso (Texas) Times*, March 6, 1983, n.p.

2649   "Steinbeck Festival," *Coast Weekly*, August 3, 1989, 9.

2650   "Steinbeck Festival," *Monterey Life*, 11 (July 1990), 70.

2651   "Steinbeck Festival," *Salinas Californian*, August 2, 1990, 30.

2652   "Steinbeck Festival Opens Run Today in Salinas," *Monterey Herald,* August 1, 1986, 15.

2653   "Steinbeck Festival to Open Friday," *Salinas Californian,* August 1, 1985, 13.

2654   "Steinbeck Festival XIII About to Blossom," *Salinas Californian,* August 1, 1992, 3F.

2655   "Steinbeck in Eden," *Western State*/SummerFest '90, August 1990, 10-11.

2656   "Steinbeck Letters," *Monterey Herald*, August 25, 1988, 23.

2657   "Steinbeck Letters Tell of His New York Years," *San Jose Mercury News*, November 28, 1984, n.p.

2658   "Steinbeck Letters Reveal His Winter of Discontent." *San Francisco Examiner & Chronicle*, October 27, 1985, B-7.

2659   "Steinbeck Novel Banned in Maine Classroom," *Muncie Evening Press* April 15, 1982, 8.

2660   "Steinbeck Observed Life through His Writing," *Prologue*, 6
       (April 1992), (n.p).

2661   "Steinbeck Park Dedication Party on Saturday, December 8,"
       Creekbridge Gazette, Fall 1990, 1.

2662   "Steinbeck Projects Top Library Agenda," *Salinas
       Californian,* January 21, 1987, 2A.

2663   "Steinbeck Recipes Fill Pages of Book," *Salinas Californian,*
       June 5, 1985, 13.

2664   "Steinbeck Scholars to Convene," *Monterey Peninsula
       Herald,* July 30, 1984, 17.

2665   "Steinbeck Society," *Book and Magazine Collector*, 43
       (October 1987), 46. (Letter to the Editor)

2666   "Steinbeck through the Years," *Salinas Californian,* August
       11, 1992, 4E.

2667   "Steinbeck Treasure: Well-Traveled Truck," *Salinas
       Californian*, November 20, 1990, 1B.

2668   "Steinbeck Works Eyed as Sources for New Films," *San
       Francisco Chroncicle*, July 23, 1993, C3.

2669   "Steinbeck's Camper Truck is Back Home For Good,"
       Monterey Herald, November 29, 1990, n.p.

2670   "Steinbeck's Genius to Be Celebrated in One-Man Show,"
       Coasting (Monterey, Carmel, California), January 7, 1987,
       9.

2671   "Steinbeck's Letter," *Salinas Californian,* September 6, 1986,
       10.

2672   "Steinbeck Locales on *Cannery Row*," *This Month on
       Monterey Peninsula*, 28 (February 1990), 29-30.

2673   "Steinbeck's Mountain Retreat Is Now Expanded Family
        Home," *San Jose Mercury News*, March 17, 1986, 1B.

2674   "Steinbeck's Saga of Salinas Valley Farmers Will Play in
        Santa Cruz," *Carmel Pine Cone*, November 18, 1993, n.p.
        (*The Grapes of Wrath*)

2675   "Steinbeck's Son Files for Bankruptcy," *San Francisco
        Chronicle*, May 24, 1988, n.p.

2676   "Steinbeck's Son John to Attend Salinas Festival," *Salinas
        Californian*, July 11, 1990, n.p.

2677   "Steinbeck's Words Come to Life," *Coasting* (Monterey,
        Carmel, California), January 14, 1987, 22.

2678   Stone, Dave. "Life on the Edge: Ojai Photojournalist
        Achieved World Fame," *Vista* (February 21, 1982), 4-6.
        (article on Horace Bristol)

2679   Stone, Judy. "Salinas Recalls Steinbeck and *Cannery Row*,"
        San Francisco Chronicle (February 2, 1982).

2680   Stout, Kate. "Back in the Footlights," *Nantucket Map and
        Legend*, 7 (April/May 1992), 1, 12.

2681   "Strolling Steinbeck's Salinas," *Sunset*, (August 1989), 14.

2682   Sturz, Herbert. "Dear Mr. Sturz: The Author on *The Grapes of
        Wrath*," (a letter from John Steinbeck in reply to Mr.
        Sturz's complimentary letters about *Grapes of Wrath*) *New
        York Times*, August 6, 1990, A13.

2683   Sutton, Joseph. "My Accidental Mentor," *Writer's Digest*,
        December 1994, 6.

2684   Sylvester, T. O., "Grapes of Wrath, $.99 lb., Less Irate
        Grapes, $1.29 lb." (Cartoon), *San Francisco Chronicle
        Review*, July 21, 1991, 2.

2685   Taylor, D. J. "John Steinbeck," *Sunday Times Magazine*,
        November 3, 1991, n.p. (Entry in a series "1,000 Makers
        of the Twentieth Century — Week 7")

2686   Taylor, Robert. "Sweet Grapes But No Wrath," *Observer*
        (London), January 25, 1987, 55.

2687   Taylor, Ted M. "Steinbeck and the Dook: Tales from a
        College Roommate," *Monterey Life*, 18 (July 1988), 53-54.

2688   "Teaching Self Image Stirs Furor," *New York Times*, October
        13, 1993, n.p.

2689   Tenenbaum, Joanne. "John Steinbeck: A Quest of Genius,"
        Carmel Pine Cone, January 15, 1987, 28.

2690   "Terrance McNally Honored at Bookfair (John Steinbeck
        Award)," *Sag Harbour Express*, April 29 1993, 10.

2691   Tessler, Ray. "Salinas Losing Landmark: Steinbeck Era Hotel
        to Be Razed," *San Francisco Chronicle*, April 24, 1989,
        A2.

2692   Tessler, Ray. "Steinbeck's Hotel Faces Bulldozer," *Denver
        Post*, April 25, 1989, n.p.

2693   Thompson, John. "John and Carol," *Coast Weekly*, March 22,
        1990, n.p.

2694   Thompson, John. "Forest Whitaker," *Coast Weekly*, August 2,
        1990, 30.

2695   Thompson, John. "Susan Gregory," *Coast Weekly*, March 29,
        1990, 30.

2696   Thompson, John, "Wild Cherries," *Coast Weekly*, July 19-29,
        1990, 32. (Ed Ricketts)

2697   Thurman, Chuck. "From the Editorial Desk," *Coast Weekly*,
        August 4-10, 1994, 2.

2698   "Tong Wars," *Coast Weekly*, July 12-18, 1990, 32
        (Steinbeck).

2699   Toro, Prof. "Lore Galore," *Monterey Peninsula Herald*,
        November 12, 1985, 15.

2699A   Trotter, Jim. "California's Ambassador to the World," *San
        Jose Mercury News*, March 30, 1997, Sec. B, (n.p.).

2700   Truheart, Charles. "Documents Show FBI Kept Files on
        Leading US Writers," *Washington Post*, September 30,
        1987, A1, A7

2701   Turner, Paul. "All We Ask: Give Gilbert a Chance (Books
        most frequently targeted by would-be censors of school
        libraries during 1991-1992)," *Spokane Spokesman Review*,
        October 31, 1992, E1.

2702   "Twain, Steinbeck Stay on District's Must-Read List,"
        Salinas Californian, May 13, 1992, 17A.

2703   "Two Students Disappointed," *Monterey Herald* (Letter to
        Editor), March 27, 1994, n.p.

2704   Updike, Kelly. "Steinbeck Scholars/Japanese Researchers
        Complete Month Long Visit to Ball State," *The Muncie
        Star*, August 14, 1983), n.p.

2705   Uzelac, Ellen. "Salinas' Not So Favorite Son: Devotees
        Gather to Discuss Legacy of John Steinbeck," *Baltimore
        Sun (Today)*, August 9, 1988, 1C, 2C.

2706   Uzelac, Ellen. "Salinas Recalls Native Son Steinbeck with
        Wrath, Awe," *St. Paul Pioneer Press Dispatch*, August 13,
        1991, 12B.

2707   Van Asselt, Karl A. "No Kidding? John Steinbeck's Jobs
        before Becoming an Author," "Something about the
        Author," *Muncie Evening Press*, December 14, 1990, 12.

2708   Villagren, Nora. "The Essential Steinbeck and Beyond," *San Jose Mercury News*, March 15, 1989, 5D.

2709   Vinocur, John. "The Politics of the Nobel for Literature," *New York Times*, December 7, 1983, C25.

2710   Volpe, Nicole. "Creating a Scene," *Coast Weekly*, August 4-10, 1994, 32-33.

2711   Walsh, John. "The Write Stuff," *Independent Magazine Supplement*, December 4, 1993, 6-10.

2712   Warren, Howard. "Route 66, Immortalized in Saga and Song, to Vanish from Maps," *Los Angeles Times*, December 20, 1985, VIII, 4.

2713   Waters, Christina. "Return of the Native," *Pacific*, August 1989, 24-25.

2714   Weatherby, W. J. "The Days Before the Dream Died," *Guardian* (London), August 8, 1986, 15.

2715   Weatherby, W. J. "Obituary: John Steinbeck IV: Father and Son," *Guardian*, February 15, 1991, n.p.

2716   Weatherby, W. J. "Of Knights and Men," *In Britain*, January 1984, 20-21.

2717   Weatherby, W. J. "Of Knights and Men: John Steinbeck: The Poet Laureate of Camelot," *Monterey Life*, 18 (July 1988), 48-50.

2718   Weatherby, W. J. "The Somerset of Love," *Guardian*, April 16, 1992, 28.

2719   Weingarten, Paul. "Dust Bowl Image Haunts Oklahoma/ Memories of Dust Bowl Recalled," *Daily News* (Reseda, California), July 3, 1988, 1, 16.

2720   Wennergren, Mike. "Salinas Libraries May Be Fund-Raising
            Target," *Salinas Californian,* September 6, 1986, 1.

2721   Wennergren, Mike. "Sardines Making a Comeback in
            Monterey Bay," *Salinas Californian,* July 7, 1986, 14C.

2722   Wennergren, Mike. "Site, Fund-Raiser Selected for Steinbeck
            Center," *Salinas Californian,* October 29, 1986, 1.

2723   Wennergren, Mike. "Steinbeck Center Fund-Raising Drive Is
            Called Feasible," *Salinas Californian,* October 15, 1986, 1.

2724   Wennergren, Mike. "A Walk on the Wild Side of Salinas,"
            Salinas Californian, December 13, 1986, 1.

2725   Werner, Irma. "Steinbeck's Words Still Have Value Today,"
            Salinas Californian, February 24, 1992, 4A.

2726   "What Makes A Story Work?" *Cornell Alumni News*,
            November 1990, 6.

2727   "What's Ahead: Steinbeck Festival*,"* *Watsonville (CA)*
            Register-Pajaronian, June 12, 1981, 11.

2728   "What's Your Favorite Steinbeck Novel," *Coast Weekly*,
            August 4-10, 1994, 4.

2728A   "Where Fact and Fiction Intertwine," *New York Times*,
            November 1, 1996, C1, 30. (Horace Bristol and
            Photography)

2729   "Where is the Head of John Steinbeck?" *Monterey Herald*,
            October 10, 1991, 1A, 16A.

2730   "While He Expected the Worst, Nobel Hoped for the Best,"
            Smithsonian, November 1988, n.p.

2731   Whitmore, Jeffrey. "*Sweet Thursday*: John Steinbeck Was on
            to Something," *Pacific*, 6 (August 1990), 17-26.

2732   "Who Made the Best Unabridged Book Recording in 1989?"
        Forthcoming Books, 25 (July 1990), n.p.

2733   Wickers, David. "Cruising the Pacific Highway," *Sunday
        Times*, March 19, 1989, H7.

2734   Wigglesworth, Zeke. "Many Writers Had a Word for
        California: They Called It Home," *San Jose Mercury
        News*, January 15, 1994, n.p.

2735   Wigglesworth, Zeke. "When Riding into Salinas Just Skip
        That Rodeo Road," *San Jose Mercury News*, July 17, 1994,
        1G, 8G.

2736   "William B. Brown," *San Francisco Chronicle*, April 3,
        1987, 30. (Reports the death of Mr. Brown, who was
        married for thirty-two years to Carol Henning Brown, the
        first wife of Steinbeck.)

2737   "William Beresford Brown Dies at C.V. Home at 74,"
        Monterey Herald, March 26, 1987, 4. (Mr. Brown was
        married for more than thirty-two years to Carol Henning
        Brown, the first wife of Steinbeck.)

2738   Williams, Donald Mace. "*The Grapes of Wrath* Note Bears
        Fruit for LIU (Long Island University)," *Newsday*, May 4,
        1989, 6, 48.

2738A   Willoughby, James. "My Father and John Steinbeck," *The
        Sunday Herald* (Monterey), March 31, 1996, n.p.

2739   Winston, Elston. "John Steinbeck, Knight of Monterey," *This
        Month on the Monterey Peninsula*, 25 (December 1987),
        44-45.

2740   Witt, Linda. "Nation Still Caught in the Maw of Steinbeck's
        'Monster,'" *Salinas Californian*, May 13, 1989, 6A.

2741   Woodward, Hobson. "John Steinbeck's East Coast Eden,"
        Nantucket Inquirer and Mirror, May 14, 1992, C1.

2742   Woodward, Lillian. "Moss Landing Footnotes: Boat Blood
        Runs Deep," *Monterey Herald,* August 2, 1986, 8.
        (reference to *Of Mice and Men*).

2743   Woolsey, David. "LRSD Has No Banned Book List,"
        Arkansas Gazette, December 14, 1989, 1B, 2B.

2744   "World Deaths: John Steinbeck IV," *Austin (TX.) American
        Statesman*, February 12, 1991, B4.

2745   "Wrestling with Steinbeck's Wrath," *San Jose Mercury News,*
        January 29, 1984, 22.

2746   "You Can't Judge a Book by the Price on Its Cover," *New
        York Times*, December 20, 1990, C3.

2747   Young, Gavin. "The Quest for Queequeg," *Observer Review*,
        January 17, 1993, 41.

2748   Zambo, Marianna. "New Vision Expected for Steinbeck
        Works (by John Ditsky)," *Monterey Herald*, August 5,
        1988, 26.

2749   Zambo, Marianna. "Soviet Journalist Listens to Yarns about
        Steinbeck, Depression Era," *Monterey Herald*, December
        13, 1988, 18.

2750   Zambo, Marianna. "Steinbeck Son Tells Memories,"
        Monterey Herald, August 4, 1990, 1, 4.

2751   Zoticas, Robert. "John Steinbeck Arthurian Society Presents a
        Photo Exhibit of the Works of Robert Capa," *This Month
        on the Monterey Peninsula*, 26 (June 1988), 28.

Other Media:
Films, Plays, Operas
CDs, Audio Recordings

2752   Abarbanel, Jonathan. "Steppenwolf in Steinbeck Country: The Chicago Troupe Shoulders an American Epic," *American Theatre,* 6:3 (June 1, 1989), 22.

2753   Adams, David. "*Of Mice and Men,*" *Guardian,* March 9, 1993, Sec. 2, 6. (review of Sherman Theater's Production of the play)

2754   Adler, Anthony. "Big Budget: *The Grapes of Wrath,*" *Chicago Reader,* September 23, 1988, 42.

2755   Argas, Rick. "Forget the Exterminator! The Mice (and Men) in the Attic Are Entertaining and Welcome Guests," *The Varsity News:* University of Detroit Campus Newspaper, March 5, 1986, 6.

2756   Asquith, Ros. "A One Way Ticket to Hades," *Observer,* November 25, 1984, n.p.

2757   Bahnemann, David. "*The Grapes of Wrath,*" in *Magill's American Film Guide.* Englewood Cliffs, N. J.: Salem Press, 1983. (pp. 1307-1309)

2758   "Baldwin Going into *Battle,*" *Los Angeles Times,* February 28, 1996, 2F. (*In Dubious Battle*)

2759   Barnes, Hugh. "The Grass Is Seedier on the Other Side (*The Grapes of Wrath*)," *Glasgow Herald,* August 25, 1987, n.p.

2760   Bassett. Kate. "Depressed Men from the Dust Up," *Times*,
        March 3, 1994, 36. (*Of Mice and Men*)

2761   Bassett, Kate. "More Anger from the Vineyard," *Times*, April
        28, 1994, 36. (*The Grapes of Wrath*)

2762   Bauers, Sandy. "Good Things Large and Small for the
        Discerning Listener," *Chicago Tribune,* December 22,
        1994, Tempo, 9. (reviews *Travels with Charley* read by
        Gary Sinise, cassette produced by Penguin HighBridge)

2763   Benson, Jackson J. *An Introduction to John Steinbeck's
        Fiction.* Detroit: Omnigraphics, 1988. (a videotape
        production in the Eminent Scholar/Teacher Series)

2764   Bernheimer, Martin. "Hidden Valley Ensemble Stages *Of
        Mice and Men*, Steinbeck Opera in Steinbeck Country,"
        Los Angeles Times, February 13, 1985 (Calendar), 1, 5.

2765   Bernstein, Sharon. "Well, the Last One (*The Grapes of Wrath*)
        Was Made in 1939," *Los Angeles Times Calendar*, August
        4, 1991, 30.

2766   Billington, Michael. "A Moving Migration" (*The Grapes of
        Wrath*), *Guardian* (England), June 24, 1989, 21.

2767   Billson, Anne. "Caring and Correct: *Of Mice and Men*,"
        Sunday Telegraph, November 29, 1992, 15.

2768   Bindi, Jim. "Strong Cast Carries UCSC's *Grapes of Wrath*,"
        Santa Cruz Sentinel, December 31, 1993, n.p.

2769   Blades, John. "A Timely Trail of Tears: Steppenwolf Breathes
        New Life into John Steinbeck's *The Grapes of Wrath*"

(Theater Review), *Chicago Tribune*, September 11, 1988, xiii, 4-5.

2770   Borgman, Beverly. "Is *Sweet Thursday* a *Pipe Dream*?" *Coasting (*Monterey, Carmel, California*),* July 30, 1986, 23.

2771   Borgman, Beverly. "Steinbeck Stories Often Made Their Way to Silver Screen," *Coasting,* (Monterey, Carmel, California) September 18, 1985, 5.

2772   Brinkley, Alan. "Why Steinbeck's Okies Speak to Us Today," *New York Times*, March 18, 1990, 1, 12, 13. (*The Grapes of Wrath*)

2773   Brooks, Lee. "Steinbeck Story Adapted into Moving, Poignant Opera," *Coasting,* (Monterey-Carmel, California) January 30, 1985, 70.

2774   Brown, Geoff. "Heroes Who Turn Up in Unlikely Places," *Times*, November 26, 1992, 29. *(Of Mice and Men)*

2775   Brozan, Nadine. "An Opera Has Special Meaning for John Steinbeck's Widow," *New York Times*, November 1, 1993, n.p. (*Burning Bright*)

2776   Brustein, Robert. "End of the Season Notes," *The New Republic*, 203 (July 9, 1990), 33. (*The Grapes of Wrath*)

2777   Brustein, Robert. "What Makes a Play Live," *The New Republic*, 202 (May 7, 1990), 30. (*The Grapes of Wrath*)

2778   Buchan, David. "Superb Steinbeck Saga Makes UK Premiere," *Wimbledon Comet*, September 30, 1994, n.p. (*Burning Bright*)

2779   "Burning Bright," *The Issue,* 97 (September 20-26, 1994), n.p.

2780   Caen, Herb. "Belated Scooplet," *San Francisco Chronicle*,
       March 30, 1993, B1. (Reference to *The Grapes of Wrath*
       movie and President Hoover and "Hoovervilles.")

2781   Cagin, Seth. 'Shorn Cannery," *Sun News*, February 1982, n.p.

2782   Campbell, James. "The Best-Laid Plans (*Of Mice and Men*),"
       Times Literary Supplement, December 11, 1992, 18.

2783   Canby, Vincent. "Cannery Row," *New York Times*, February
       21, 1982, n.p.

2784   Canby, Vincent. "Life by the Shacks," *New York Times*,
       February 12, 1982, n.p.

2785   Canby, Vincent. "New Facets Heightened in a Classic," *New
       York Times*, October 10, 1992, C5. (*Of Mice and Men*)

2786   Canby, Vincent. "*Of Mice and Men*," *New York Times*, March
       4, 1993, C5.

2787   Canby, Vincent. "Screen: The Fanciful Dropouts on *Cannery
       Row*," *New York Times,* February 12, 1982, C10.

2788   Cantrell, Susan. "Steinbeck Stories: Film Company Will
       Produce Three in Valley," *Salinas Californian*, June 7,
       1989, 1B.

2789   Carson, Linda. "Forest Theatre Musical Gives Nod to
       Steinbeck," *Carmel Pine Cone*, August 7, 1986, 34.

2790   Carson, Linda. "Forest Theatre Musical Gives a Nod to
        Steinbeck," *Monterey Peninsula Review,* August 7, 1986,
        5.

2791   Cashman, Dennis. "Steinbeck Opera Shows Promise but
        Needs Work," *New Haven Register*, November 7, 1993,
        n.p. (*Burning Bright*)

2792   Chanko, Kenneth M. "Review of *Of Mice and Men* (video
        recording with Gary Sinise and John Malkovich),"
        Parenting, 8:1 (February 1994), 98.

2793   "Channel 4: *Tortilla Flat*," *Observer*, February 12, 1989, 60.

2794   Chollet, Lawrence. "The Joads Ride Again: *The Grapes of
        Wrath*," *The Record* (Northern N. J.), March 18, 1990,
        E3-5.

2795   Christiansen, Richard. "Sluggish Road Spoils *Grapes*,"
        Chicago Tribune, September 19, 1988, 1-2.

2796   "The Chrysanthemeums," (videocassette) Santa Monica:
        Pyramid Films, 1990.

2797   Churnin, Nancy. "*The Grapes of Wrath*: It's Mother's Milk to
        Steppenwolf," *Los Angeles Times*, May 11, 1989, VI, 12.

2798   Clark, James Nisbet. "Old Cannery Row Comes Alive at
        Carmel's Forest Theatre," *Salinas Californian,* August 9,
        1986, 36.

2799   "Classic Opera, Steinbeck Tale Open 10th Hidden Valley
        Year," *Carmel Pine Cone,* January 17, 1985, 19.

2800   Collins, Glenn. "Staging a *Grapes* of Dust, Fog, Fire, and
        Blood," *New York Times*, April 3, 1990, C19, 20.

2801   Conn, Steward. "Theatre: *The Grapes of Wrath*," *The Listener*,
        August 20, 1987, n.p.

2802   Cooper, Brian. "*The Grapes of Wrath*," *The Stage and
        Television Today*, August 27, 1987, 24.

2803   Costanzo, William V. *Reading the Movies: Twelve Great
        Films on Video and How to Teach Them*. Urbana, IL.:
        NCTE, 1992. (Chapter 12: '*The Grapes of Wrath*', pp.
        129-135)

2804   "Critic's Choice," *Chicago Sun Times*, September 25, 1988,
        n.p. (Steppenwolf's *Grapes Of Wrath*)

2805   "Critics' Choice: *The Moon Is Down*," *Independent*, April 24,
        1993, 27; April 25, 1993, 31; April 26, 1993, 24.

2806   Cronen, Michele. 'Staged *Of Mice and Men* Is a Novel Idea,"
        Tri-Valley Herald, c. April 1991, C4.

2807   Cunningham, Kim. "Chatter: Food for Thought (Gary Sinise,
        Of Mice and Men)," *People*, October 19, 1992, 170.

2808   Curco, Chris. "Acting, Direction Are Strong in PLT's *Of Mice
        and Men*," *Arizona Republic*, February 21, 1992, D6.

2809   Cushman, R. "Review of *Of Mice and Men*," *Plays/Players*,
        376 (January 1985), 32-33.

2810   Davies, Pete. "Hopes Turn to Dust (*Of Mice and Men*),"
        Guardian, November 26, 1992, Sec. 2, 2, 3.

2811   Delacoma, Wynne, and Hedy Weiss. "Steppenwolf Gathers
        Support for *The Grapes of Wrath* Staging," *Chicago Sun-
        Times*, August 9, 1988, 2, 30, 34.

2812   Denision, Paul. "New *Cannery Row* Movie Is a Hybrid Drawn
        from Two Steinbeck Novels," *Monterey Penisula Herald,*
        January 18, 1982, 14.

2813   DeVine, Lawrence. "*Grapes of Wrath* Reels with Painful
        Beauty," *Detroit Free Press*, April 28, 1992 , 3D.

2814   DeVine, Lawrence. "*Of Mice and Men* and the Attic Make a
        Good Match," *Detroit Free Press*, March 3, 1986, 4E.

2815   Dillon, John. "The Paradoxical Professor," *American Theater,*
        12:8 (October 1, 1995), 20. (Frank Galati of Northwestern
        University and his adaptations of Steinbeck, Faulkner and
        Stein)

2816   "Dilys Powell's Film of the Week (*Grapes Of Wrath*),"
        Sunday Times, April 4, 1993, ix, 28.

2817   Disch, Thomas. "Theater," *The Nation*, 250 (April 30, 1990),
        610-611. (*Grapes of Wrath*)

2818   Ditsky, John. "Review of *Cannery Row,* the Play in Two
        Acts," *Steinbeck Newsletter,* 10:1 (Spring 1996), 20-21.

2819   Donnelly, Kathleen. "Steinbeck Narrative for *Zapata*
        Uncovered," *Mercury News*, November 18, 1991, n.p.

2820   Drake, Sylvie. "La Jolla's Rich Harvest of *Grapes*," *Los
        Angeles Times Calendar,* May 16, 1989, 1.

2821   Durrant, Sabine. "Suburban Cowboy," *Independent*,
         November 19, 1992, 15. (*Of Mice and Men*)

2822   "The Early Birds Home In on the Fringe (*The Grapes of
         Wrath*)," *Evening News*, April 25, 1987, n.p.

2823   *"East of Eden,"* *New Yorker*, 65 (March 27, 1989), 28.

2824   *"East of Eden,"* *New Yorker*, 68 (September 28, 1992), 21.

2825   Ebert, Roger. "Amen to *Mice*: Malkovich and Sinise Render a
         Steinbeck Pearl," *New York Daily News* (Entertainment
         section), October 2, 1992, 1, 49.

2826   Eckert, Thor, Jr. "Steppenwolf Stages a Steinbeck Epic:
         Commitment Shines in Adaptation of *The Grapes of
         Wrath*," *Christian Science Monitor*, November 3, 1988, 19.

2827   Edwards, Christopher. "Pilgrim's Regress: *The Grapes of
         Wrath* at Lyttelton," *Spectator*, 263 (July 1, 1989), 30-31.

2828   Edwards, Owen Dudley. *"The Grapes of Wrath*: American
         Festival Theatre," *Scotsman*, August 13, 1987, n.p.

2829   Elder, Sean. "Steinbeck Reborn," *Vogue*, 182 (October 1992),
         170, 185-186. (*Of Mice and Men*)

2830   Espe, Erick. "Of Mice, Men and Diversity," *Santa Cruz Good
         Times,* February 20, 1992, 8.

2831   Faberson, Paul. "For All Its Glory *The Grapes* Lacks
         Emotional Intensity," *Skyline (Chicago's People
         Newspaper),* September 22, 1988, n.p.

2832   "Fall Movie Preview: *Of Mice and Men,*" *Entertainment
        Weekly,* August 12, 1992, 24-26.

2833   Fender, Stephen. "Communal Values John Steinbeck, *The
        Grapes of Wrath* at the Lyttelton Theatre," *Times Literary
        Supplement*, June 30 - July 6, 1989, 720.

2834   "Film Check: *Of Mice and Men,*" *Sunday Times*, November
        29, 1992, Sec. 8, 25.

2835   "Film on the Square: *Of Mice and Men,*" Official Programme
        of the 36th London Film Festival. London: British Film
        Institute, 1992.

2836   "First Batch of 'Protected' Films" (*Grapes of Wrath*), *San
        Francisco Chronicle*, September 20, 1989, E1.

2837   "First XI: *The Grapes of Wrath,*" *Festival Times*, No. 2,
        August 19-25, 1989, n.p.

2838   "Footlight Parade: Tough Love, Strong Memory," *Chicago
        Tribune*, September 30, 1988, Sec. 7, 16. (Steppenwolf's
        Grapes of Wrath)

2839   "Forest Theatre Reveals 1992 Summer Season (*The Grapes of
        Wrath*)," *Carmel Pine Cone/CV Outlook*, January 23,
        1992, 25.

2840   Franklin, Patrick. "*Cannery Row* Play Opens in Carmel,"
        Monterey Peninsula Herald, August 1, 1986, 24.

2841   Franklin, Patrick. "'Chrysanthemums' Latest Steinbeck Story
        to Be Filmed," *Monterey Sunday Herald*, March 25, 1990,
        19A.

2842 Franklin, Patrick. "Hidden Valley to Offer Two Versions of *Of Mice and Men*," *Monterey Peninsula Herald,* January 13, 1985, 12B.

2843 Franklin, Patrick. "*Of Mice and Men* Opera Gains Intensity," *Monterey Peninsula Herald,* January 26, 1985, 9.

2844 French, Phillip. "Dancing through the Tragedies of Disability (*Of Mice and Men*)," *Observer*, November 29, 1992, 15. (Arts Section, 60),

2845 "Fringe First Awards (*The Grapes of Wrath*)," *Scotsman*, August 14, 1987, n.p.

2846 "Fringe First Awards (*The Grapes of Wrath*)," *Scotsman*, August 15, 1987, n.p.

2847 Frymer, Murry. "Capra Sold Us on Ourselves, but It Was a Bill of Goods," *San Jose Mercury News*, September 5, 1991, n.p.

2848 Garofolo, Denise A. "Review of *The Pearl* (sound recording by Hector Elizondo)," *Library Journal,* 119:10 (June 1, 1994), 186.

2849 "Gary Sinise Wears 3 Hats for *Of Mice and Men* Film," *Salinas Californian*, January 18, 1992, 6F.

2850 Georgakas, Dan. "Don't Call Him Gadget: A Reconsideration of Elia Kazan," *Cineaste*, 16 (1988), 4-7.

2851 Gerstel, Judy. "*Mice and Men* Costar Is a Big Steinbeck Fan," *Detroit Free Press,* November 8, 1992, 8P.

2852   "Getting Kicks on Route 66," *New York Times*, June 3, 1990, n.p.

2853   Gilbert, W. Stephen. "Networked Films: *The Grapes of Wrath*," *The Independent*, January 28, 1989, 46.

2854   Gilbert, W. Stephen. "Networked Films: *Tortilla Flat*," *The Independent*, February 11, 1989, 46.

2855   Gilbert, W. Stephen. "Television and Radio: *The Grapes of Wrath* Revisited," *The Independent*, January 25, 1989, 29.

2856   Gladstein, Mimi Reisel. "Still *Burning Bright*," *Steinbeck Newsletter*, 10:1 (Spring 1996), 21.

2857   Gold, Sylvane. "Steppenwolf Tries to Be True to Steinbeck," *Wall Street Journal*, September 22, 1988, 32.

2858   Goldstein, P. "Gary Sinise Goes to Hollywood," (adaptation of John Steinbeck's *Of Mice and Men*) *Esquire*, 118 (November 1992), 138-40.

2859   Gossage, Leslie. "The Artful Propaganda of Ford's *The Grapes of Wrath*," in *New Essays on "The Grapes of Wrath"* ed. David Wyatt. Cambridge: Cambridge University Press, 1990. (pp. 101-125)

2860   *"The Grapes of Wrath,"* New Yorker, 64 (December 5, 1988), 31.

2861   *"The Grapes of Wrath,"* New Yorker, 64 (July 2, 1990), 18.

2862   *"The Grapes of Wrath,"* Reader, September 23, 1988, 42, 44.

2863   *"The Grapes of Wrath," The Observer,* January 29, 1989, 52.

2864   *"The Grapes of Wrath,"* (Stage West Theatre) *Park Press*
        (Windsor, Ontario, Canada), 2.

2865   *"The Grapes of Wrath*: An American Classic Coming to
        Broadway on March 13, 1990," *New York Times,*
        November 26, 1989, II, 3.

2866   *"Grapes of Wrath* at the Netherbow Arts Centre,"
        Independent, August 19, 1987, n.p.

2867   *"Grapes of Wrath* at the Netherbow Arts Centre," *Festival
        Scotsman,* August 10, 1987, n.p.

2868   *"The Grapes of Wrath": CD-rom.* New York: Penguin
        Electronic, 1996. (multi-media, including the complete text
        of the novel and excerpts from Jackson Benson's *The True
        Adventures of John Steinbeck, Writer,* film footage from
        the John Ford movie, pictures, and the text of "The Harvest
        Gypsies," a series of newspaper articles Steinbeck wrote
        that prefigured his novel. Interviews with Elaine
        Steinbeck and Benson, and critical commentary by leading
        Steinbeck scholars are also included as are retrieval links
        that connect the historical and fictional aspects of the
        work)

2869   *"The Grapes of Wrath*: Journey Begins April 24 at Hilbery
        Theater," *Prologue,* 6 (April 1992), n.p.

2870   Green, Judith. "Cannery Now: A Review of Western Stage
        Production of *Cannery Row* 2," *San Jose Mercury News,*
        August 11, 1995, 43-44.

2871   Green, Judith. "Singing Steinbeck: *Of Mice and Men* Opera Deserves an Audience," *San Jose Mercury News,* February 13, 1985, 1D.

2872   Hackett, Larry. "Movies, Men and Myths (*Of Mice and Men*), *Province Showcase*, October 15, 1992, C1, C3.

2873   Hanks, Robert. "Take a Hint," *Independent*, April 28, 1994, 23. (*Grapes of Wrath*)

2874   Hanshew, Dennis. "Writer Says Steinbeck Novel Not Easy to Adapt to Film: Internal Conflict Poses Problem," *Indianapolis Star*, November 29, 1983, 14.

2875   Harmetz, Aljean. "25 U.S. Films 'Treasures' to Be Picked, Protected," *Muncie Star,* July 17, 1989, 6. (The leader in preliminary balloting was the 1939 movie made from Steinbeck's *The Grapes of Wrath*)

2876   Hartigan, Karelisa., ed. *All the World: Drama Past and Present II.* Lanham, Md.: University Press of America, 1982. (contains "On the Road to Tragedy: The Function of Candy in *Of Mice and Men,"* by Robert Cardullo, pp. 1-8)

2877   Hart, John. "The American Nightmare (*The Grapes of Wrath*)," *The Times Educational Supplement/Scotland*, August 21, 1987, n.p.

2878   Harvey, Dennis. "Review of Hartnell Theater's production of *East of Eden*," *Variety,* 336:7 (September 12, 1994), 53.

2879   Haskell, Molly. "Is it Time to Trust Hollywood?" *New York Times Book Review*, January 28, 1990, 1, 36-37.

2880   Haun, Harry. "Gossip," *San Francisco Chronicle*, December
        30, 1986, 32. ("Add Steinbeck's Novel *In Dubious Battle*
        to Producer Jerry Tokofsky's Film Slate.")

2881   Hauk, Steve. "Work-in-Progress (*East Of Eden*) Staged at
        Hartnell," *Monterey Herald,* March 22, 1990 n.p.

2882   Hayashi, Tetsumaro. "Steinbeck on Broadway: The
        Steppenwolf Theater Company Production of *The Grapes
        of Wrath* at the Cort Theater in New York City," *Newletter
        of John Steinbeck Society of Japan*, 14 (April 1991), 7.
        (*The Grapes of Wrath*)

2883   Hayashi, Tetsumaro. "Steinbeck's *East of Eden:* A Musical
        Triumph at the Takarazuka Theater — A Review Article,"
        Steinbeck Studies, 19 (May 1996), 27-29.

2884   Hayden, Bill. "Robert Blake Stars in Steinbeck Classic,"
        Salinas Californian, August 27, 1985, 20.

2885   Hayman, Lee Richard. "Steinbeck Corner: '*Cannery Row*,'"
        Lariat, February 3, 1982, 2.

2886   Hayman, Lee Richard. "Steinbeck Wrote It (play version *Of
        Mice and Men*)," *Good Times*, March 5, 1992, 5.

2887   Hearle, Kevin. "Review: The Wooden-O Theatre Presents
        'Robert Viharo's adaptation of John Steinbeck's stories
        from *The Long Valley:* A Work in Progress,'" *Steinbeck
        Newsletter,* 10:1 (Spring 1996), 26.

2888   Henahan, Donal. "Music: *Of Mice and Men* in City Opera
        Premiere," *New York Times*, October 15, 1983, 12.

2889   Hendrickson, Val. "Of Writers and Directors (*Of Mice and Men*)," *Good Times,* March 19, 1992, 5.

2890   Henk, Dianne. "Adapting John Steinbeck's Stories into Feature Films," (Thom Steinbeck's Film Project), *South Bend Tribune*, March 27, 1988, n.p.

2891   Henk, Dianne. "His (Steinbeck's) Sons Plan Film Library of Steinbeck's Books," *Monterey Herald*, March 27, 1988, 15A.

2892   Henk, Dianne. "Sons to Ensure Steinbeck Legacy through Film," *Philadelphia Inquirer*, February 2, 1988, n.p.

2893   Henry, William A., III. "Just What the Doctor Ordered: Broadway Looks Robust with Three Powerful Dramas," *Time*, April 2, 1990, 11. (*The Grapes of Wrath*)

2894   "(Wayne State's) Hilbery, Bonstelle Set Their Stages," (*The Grapes of Wrath*, April 1992), *Detroit Free Press*, February 18, 1991, 8F.

2895   Hill, Rodney. "Small Things Considered: *Raising Arizona* and *Of Mice and Men,*" *Post-Script: Essays in Film and the Humanities, Commerce TX.,* 8:3 (Summer 1989), 18-27.

2896   Hoekstra, Dave. "Composer Squeezes Songs from *Grapes*: Michael Smith Puts Steinbeck to Music," *Chicago Sun-Times*, October 2, 1988, E2.

2897   Horn, John. "*Of Mice and Men* Filmed in Santa Ynez," *Salinas Californian*, February 21, 1992, 3E.

2898   Hornby, Richard. "The Blind Leading the Blind," *Hudson Review*, 43 (Autumn 1990), 467-474. (*The Grapes of Wrath*)

2899   Howe, Kevin. "*Whipping Boy* Novel Likened to *Moby-Dick*," *San Jose Mercury News*, c. August 1985, n.p.

2900   Hoyle, Martin. "American Groups Carry the Day (*The Grapes of Wrath*)," *The Mail*, August 23, 1987, n.p.

2901   Hubbard, Kim. "A Powerful Staging of Steinbeck's *The Grapes of Wrath* Puts the Spotlight on a Company Named Steppenwolf," *People Weekly*, 30 (October 3, 1988), 55-56.

2902   Hurren, Kenneth. "At the Edinburgh Festival," *Mail on Sunday*, August 23, 1987, n.p.

2903   "*In Dubious Battle* Coming to Screen," *Salinas Californian*, March 1, 1989, 3B.

2904   An Introduction to John Steinbeck. (videocassette) N.A.: Manley, 1988.

2905   "The Industry Eye: The Big-Screen Adaptation of John Steinbeck's *In Dubious Battle*," *San Francisco Examiner*, February 16, 1989, C2.

2906   Jenner, Andrew. "London Premiere of *Burning Bright*," *Steinbeck Newletter,* 8:1-2 (Winter/Spring 1995), 25.

2907   "John Steinbeck," *West Coast Review of Books*, 14 (July/August 1989), 18. (New Steinbeck Movies)

2908   *The John Steinbeck Map of America.* Los Angeles: Aaron
        Blake Publishers, 1987.

2909   Johnson, Kevin. "*Grapes* Completes Its Journey to the Stage,"
        Shows, *USA Today*, October 3, 1988, 6D.

2910   Johnston, Sheila. "Phony Depression and Real Uplift (*Of Mice
        and Men*)," *Independent*, November 27, 1992, 20.

2911   Jones, Alan. "Devoted Wife's Loving Sacrifice," *Wimbledon
        Guardian*, October 6, 1994, n.p. (*Burning Bright*)

2912   Jordan, June. "A Chance at Grace," *The Progressive*, 54
        (October 1990), 10. (*The Grapes of Wrath*)

2913   Kael, Pauline, "*East of Eden*," *New Yorker*, 66 (May 7, 1990),
        31.

2914   Kaplan, Sherman. "*The Grapes of Wrath*: A WBBM Theater
        Review, Broadcast, September 26, 1988," *WBBM* News
        Radio 78: In Touch with Chicago.

2915   Kauffmann, Stanley. "On Film: My Brother's Keeper," *New
        Republic,* 207:19 (November 2, 1992), 24. (*Of Mice and
        Men)*

2916   Kazin, Alfred. "*Of Mice and Men,*" *TV Guide,* 29 (November
        28, 1981), 12-13.

2917   Kellaway, Kate. "Ripeness Is All" (*The Grapes of Wrath)
        Observer*, June 25, 1989, 41.

2918   Kemp, Peter. "Review of Steppenwolf's *The Grapes of Wrath*
        at the National — A Company of Wolves," *Independent*,
        June 24, 1989, 32.

2919   King, Francis. "Theatre (*The Grapes of Wrath*)," *Sunday Telegraph*, August 30, 1987, n.p.

2920   King, Susan. "Depression-Era Harmon: NBC Movie About Hard Times Lifts Actors' Spirits," *TV Times* (*Los Angeles Times*), February 24 - March 2, 1991, C3.

2921   Kingston, Jeremy. "Grace and Balance of Rare Quality: *The Grapes of Wrath* at the Lyttelton Theatre," *Times* (London), June 24, 1989, 39.

2922   Kobayashi, Hiroyuki. "Musical: *Pipe Dream*": "Panel Discussion II: The Art of Steinbeck and Its Form," *John Steinbeck Society of Japan Newsletter*, 10 (April 1987), 5-6.

2923   Koehler, Robert. "Teamwork Pays Off in *Grapes*," *Los Angeles Times,* May 14, 1992, n.p.

2924   Koenig, Rhoda. "Hokey Okies," (*The Grapes of Wrath*), *Punch*, 297 (July 7, 1989), 48.

2925   Kramer, Mimi. "The Theatre: Tender Grapes," *New Yorker*, 23 (April 2, 1990), 87-88.

2926   Kroll, Jack. "Of the People: Steinbeck's Okie Classic," (*The Grapes of Wrath*), *Newsweek*, 115 (April 2, 1990), 55.

2927   Kuchwara, Michael. "*The Grapes of Wrath* Presented on Broadway," *Monterey Herald*, March 24, 1990, 10.

2928   Kuchwara, Michael. "Ten Shows to Watch That Aren't on Broadway," *St. Petersburg Times,* September 18, 1988, 3F.

2929   Kupcinet, Irv. "Kup on Sunday," *Chicago Sun Times*,
            September 25, 1988, 11.

2930   Lachtman, Howard. "Steinbeck Classic Takes 'Flight' Again,"
            San Jose Mercury News, August 14, 1984, 3C.

2931   Lane, Anthony. "Depression Ralph Lauren (*Of Mice and
            Men*)," *Independent on Sunday*, November 29, 1992, 21.

2932   Law, Graham. "Trek of Hope: *The Grapes of Wrath*,
            Netherbow," *Evening News*, August 26, 1987, n.p.

2933   Lazare, Lewis. "Editor's Choice: Steppenwolf Takes You to
            California with the Joads," *Crain's Chicago Business*,
            September 26, 1988, 57.

2934   "Lennie and George Hit the Square," *Commercial Appeal*,
            October 14, 1985, n.p.

2935   LeSourd, Jacques. "*Grapes of Wrath* Achieves Grandeur of
            Greek Tragedy," *The Californian*, March 30, 1990, B.

2936   Letts, Vanessa. "Cinema: *Of Mice and Men*, Softening the
            Blow," *Spectator,* 269 (December 5, 1992), 62.

2937   Leyde, Tom. "Hidden Valley Opera Ensemble ip and
            Running," *Salinas Californian,* January 26, 1985, 34.

2938   Leyde, Tom. "*Of Mice and Men* Opera a Rare Treat," *Salinas
            Californian,* January 29, 1985, 24.

2939   Lipson, Eden Ross. "Otters and Sea Lions in Steinbeck
            Country," *New York Times*, May 25, 1986, Sec. XX, 9, 24.

2940   Livernois, Joe. "Actor Revisits Steinbeck Land as Monterey
        Film Festival Continues," *Monterey Herald,* February 7,
        1986, 6.

2941   "Looks: *Of Mice and Men,*" *Los Angeles Times Magazine,*
        July 19, 1992, 29.

2942   Loomis, George W. "Review of *Burning Bright* (the opera, as
        performed by Frank Lewin and the Philharmonic Orchestra
        of Yale)," *American Record Guide,* 57:1
        (January/February 1994), 39.

2943   Lovell, Glen. "*Of Mice and Men* Reviving a Real American
        Dream," *San Jose Mercury News,* October 1, 1992, 1D,
        3D.

2944   Lovell, Glenn. "A Festival of Movie Endings That You Never
        Got to See (*The Grapes of Wrath*)," *San Jose Mercury
        News,* June 28, 1992, 12.

2945   Loynd, Ray. "TV Preview: A Searing *Grapes of Wrath,*" *Los
        Angeles Times*, March 22, 1991, F1, 25. (1991 TV
        Presentation of *The Grapes of Wrath* by Steppenwolf)

2946   Loynd, Ray. "TV Review: Grit, Passion Power Drama of
        'Long Road,'" *Los Angeles Times,* February 25, 1991, F1,
        9.

2947   Lukas, Betty. "Audiocassettes: *The Grapes of Wrath,*" *Los
        Angeles Times Calendar*, January 7, 1986, n.p.

2948   Lyons, Donald. "Underdogs and Underwear," *New Criterion*,
        8 (May 1990), 47-51. (*The Grapes of Wrath*)

2949   Madgwick, Donald. *"Burning Bright,"* *Croyden Advertiser*,
        September 30, 1994, n.p.

2950   Malcolm, Derek. *"Of Mice and Men,"* *Guardian,* November
        26, 1992, Sec. 2, 2.

2951   Markham-Smith, Ian. "Raquel: A Lion's Share," *Today*, June
        26, 1986, 3. (Film: *Cannery Row*)

2952   Marks, Lawrence. "Bitter Harvest: *The Grapes of Wrath*
        Revisited," *Observer Magazine* (London), January 15,
        1989, 42-43, 45, 47, 49.

2953   Matuszek, Chris. "Steinbeck Play Hits the Fringe,"
        Wimbledon Guardian, September 29, 1994, n.p. (*Burning
        Bright*)

2954   McCarthy, Todd. *"Of Mice and Men,"* *Official Programme of
        36th London Film Festival* (1992), 30.

2955   McCleland, Jack. *"Of Mice and Men*: The Official Movie Tie-
        In Edition," *Library Journal*, 118 (January 1993), 186-
        187.

2956   McKinnon, Arlo J., Jr. "At Last — Frank Lewin's *Burning
        Bright*," *Opera News,* 58 (October 1993), 62.

2957   Miller, Jeff. *"Mice and Men* Still Packs Punch," *Houston
        Chronicle*, October 16, 1992, D1.

2958   "Molly Morgan," (videocassette) Santa Monica: Pyramid
        Films, 1991.

2959   Molotsky, Irvin. "Twenty-Five Films Chosen for National
        Registry," *New York Times*, September 20, 1989, C19.

2960   Mooney, Michael G. "Salinas Basks in Premiere's Publicity
        Glare," *Salinas Californian,* January 6, 1982, n.p.

2961   Morgenstein, Joe. "Vintage Hollywood/50 Years Ago: *The
        Grapes of Wrath* Shines on the Screen," in *Memories:
        Magazine of Then and Now,* 2 (December 1989/January
        1990), 44-48.

2962   Morsberger, Robert E. "*Burning Bright* Burns Brightly as an
        Opera," *The Steinbeck Newsletter,* 7:2 (Summer 1994), 8-
        11.

2963   Morsberger, Robert E. "'The Chrysanthemums' and 'The
        Raid' on Film" *Steinbeck Quarterly,* XXIV:3-4
        (Summer/Fall, 1991), 125-130.

2964   Morsberger, Robert E. "*East of Eden* on Film," *Steinbeck
        Quarterly,* XXV:1-2 (Winter/Spring 1992), 28-42.

2965   Morsberger, Robert E. "Of Mice and Music: Scoring
        Steinbeck Movies," in *After "The Grapes of Wrath":
        Essays on John Steinbeck in Honor of Tetsumaro Hayashi.*
        ed. Donald Coers, Paul Ruffin, and Robert DeMott.
        Athens: Ohio University Press, 1995. (pp. 58-73)

2966   Morsberger, Robert E. "Play It Again, Lennie and George,"
        Steinbeck Quarterly, XV:3-4 (Summer/Fall, 1982), 123-
        126.

2967   Morsberger, Robert E. "Review of Steinbeck's 'Molly
        Morgan' (from *Pastures of Heaven*) Video," (Santa
        Monica: Pyramid Film and Video) *Steinbeck Quarterly,*
        XXV:3-4 (Summer/Fall 1992), 137-139.

2968   Morsberger, Robert E. "Steinbeck and Steppenwolf: The
        Enduring Rage for Justice," *The Steinbeck Newsletter*, 7:1
        (Winter, 1994), 6-11.

2969   Morsberger, Robert E. "Steinbeck's Films," in *John
        Steinbeck: from Salinas to the World.* ed. Shigeharu Yano
        and others. Tokyo: Gaku Shobo Press, 1986. (pp. 45-67)

2970   Nachman, Gerald. "Actors' Theatre's Familiar *Mice and
        Men*," *San Francisco Chronicle,* July 10, 1992, E3.

2971   Nakata, Yuji. "*The Grapes of Wrath*: Film from Fiction," *John
        Steinbeck Society of Japan Newsletter*, 7 (May 1984), 1-2.

2972   Nakata, Yuji. "Movies,": "Panel Discussion II: The Art of
        Steinbeck and Its Form," *John Steinbeck Society of Japan
        Newsletter*, 10 (April 1987), 5.

2973   Nemy, Enid. "On Stage: *The Grapes of Wrath*," *New York
        Times*, July 8, 1988, n.p.

2974   Nemy, Enid. "Sinise on Celebrity," *New York Times*, July 27,
        1990, B2.

2975   "New Movies: *Of Mice and Men,*" *San Francisco Chronicle,*
        October 12, 1992, E1.

2976   "New Version of Steinbeck's Classic Is the Best Yet," *Ottawa
        Citizen*, October 16, 1992, E3.

2977   Nightingale, Benedict. "Steppenwolf Plays Together, Stays
        Together," *New York Times*, October 23, 1988, H5, 8.

2978   Nightingale, Benedict. "The Wolf at the Door," (*The Grapes of Wrath* play at Chicago's Steppenwolf Theatre), *Independent*, June 19, 1989, 14.

2979   Nordstrand, David. "Festival Guest Robert Blake Shares Spotlight with Author," *Salinas Californian*, August 6, 1989, 1C.

2980   Norman, Phillip. "*Of Mice and Men*: TV Review, Film 92," BBC1, November 23, 1992.

2981   Novak, Ralph. "*Of Mice and Men*," *People,* October 12, 1992, 19.

2982   O'Connor, John J. "Steppenwolf's *Grapes* as It Was on Broadway," *New York Times*, March 22, 1991, C32. (1991 TV Presentation of *The Grapes of Wrath* by Steppenwolf)

2983   O'Haire, Patricia. "*Grapes of Wrath* Finally on Stage," *San Jose Mercury News*, March 22, 1990, 7D.

2984   O'Malley, Thomas P. "Theatre," *America*, 162 (April 1990), 382. (*The Grapes of Wrath*)

2985   O'Mahoney, John. "*Burning Bright*," *Time Out*, October 12-19, 1994, n.p.

2986   O'Rourke, Donny. "Why the Yanks Are Coming (*The Grapes of Wrath*)," *Glasgow Herald*, August 26, 1987, 4.

2987   "*Of Mice and Men*," *New Yorker,* 68 (October 19, 1992), 33.

2988   "*Of Mice and Men*," *Sunday Times,* November 29, 1992, Sec. 8, 25.

2989   "*Of Mice and Men*": *CD-rom.* New York: Penguin Electronic,
        1995. (multi-media, including the complete text of *Of Mice
        and Men* and Jackson Benson's *The True Adventures of
        John Steinbeck, Writer,* video clips from the movies,
        interviews with Elaine Steinbeck and Benson, and critical
        commentary by leading Steinbeck scholars)

2990   "*Of Mice and Men:* Coming in October to Select Theatres
        (advertisement)," U: *The National College Magazine,*
        October 1992, 21.

2991   "*Of Mice and Men* Continues Valley Run," *Carmel Pine
        Cone,* January 31, 1985, 21.

2992   "*Of Mice and Men*: Drama Adapted from Steinbeck's Classic
        Novel," *Muncie Star: Television* (November 29-December
        5, 1981), T-1.

2993   "*Of Mice and Men* Opera Gains Intensity," *Monterey
        Peninsula Herald,* January 26, 1985, 9.

2994   "Of Special Interest," *New York Times,* December 6, 1983,
        n.p. (TV adaptation of *The Winter of Our Discontent*)

2995   "Offstage Duo Enhances Play by Steinbeck," *Commercial
        Appeal,* October 26, 1985, C5.

2996   Oliver, Edith. "The Theatre" (*Of Mice and Men*), *New Yorker,*
        63 (November 2, 1987), 146.

2997   "On Stage: 1991 Monterey Bay Theatrefest, *Of Mice and
        Men*," *Carmel Pine Cone,* June 27, 1991, 37, 39.

2998   "On Staging Steinbeck," *Scotsman,* July 27, 1987, n.p.

2999   Osborne, Charles. "Rich Pickings from a Steinbeck Novel,"
        (*The Grapes of Wrath), Weekly Telegraph*, June 24, 1989,
        ix. (repeated in *Sunday Telegraph*, June 25, 1989, 41.)

3000   Oshita, Lori. "Rip Torn to Play John Steinbeck in KGO
        Television's Fall Special," *Salinas Californian,* July 27,
        1985, 35.

3001   Pacheo, Patrick. "Tonys: Battles of the Ages," *Los Angeles
        Times*, June 5, 1993, F7. (*The Grapes of Wrath*)

3002   Papineau, Anne. "Play Gives New Voice to John Steinbeck,"
        Carmel Pine Cone, January 8, 1987, 25.

3003   Papineau, Anne. "*Pipe Dream* Recalls the *Cannery Row* of
        Old," *Monterey Peninsula Review,* August 14, 1986, 7.

3004   Papineau, Anne. "*Pipe Dream* Summons Mixed Memories of
        the *Cannery Row* of Old," *Carmel Pine Cone,* August 14,
        1986, 21.

3005   Parini, Jay. "A Constant Dream," *Times Literary Supplement*,
        March 11, 1994, 20. (*Of Mice and Men* at the Nottingham
        Playhouse)

3006   Parini, Jay. "Film Preview: *Of Mice and Men* a Timely
        Remake," *Indianapolis Star,* October 12, 1992, D1, 2.

3007   Parini, Jay. "Of Bindlestiffs, Bad Times, *Mice and Men,*" *New
        York Times,* September 27, 1992, 24H.

3008   Parsons, Larry. "Homecoming for Steinbeck: Moviegoers
        Praise *Of Mice and Men*," *Salinas Californian*, October 17,
        1992, 1B.

3009   Paul, Nancy. "Review of *Travels with Charley* (a sound
           recording by Gary Sinise," *Library Journal,* 119:19
           (November 15, 1994), 108.

3010   Pauly, Thomas H. "*Gone with the Wind* and *The Grapes of
           Wrath* as Hollywood Histories of the Depression," in
           Movies as Artifacts: Cultural Criticism of Popular Film.
           ed. Michael T. Marsden, John H. Nachbar, and Sam L.
           Grogg Chicago: Nelson Hall, 1982. (pp. 164-176)

3011   "*The Pearl*" & "*The Red Pony*": *CD-rom.* New York: Penguin
           Electronic, 1996. (multi-media, including the complete text
           of the novels and Jackson Benson's *The True Adventures
           of John Steinbeck, Writer*, video clips from the movies,
           interviews with Elaine Steinbeck and Benson, and critical
           commentary by leading Steinbeck scholars)

3012   Perry, George. "Films: *Tortilla Flat*," *Sunday Times*, February
           12, 1989, Screen IV.

3013   Peter, John. "Chicago Shows How to Distill a Potent Brew,"
           (*Grapes Of Wrath* play) *Sunday Times*, June 25, 1989, C7.

3014   Peter, John. "Phedra Joins the Middle-Class Brits," *Sunday
           Times*, November 25, 1984, n.p.

3015   Pixler, Joe. "Galati Bottles *Grapes* for Stage," *Chicago Sun-
           Times*, September 9, 1988, 25.

3016   Powell, Dilys. "Films on TV: *The Grapes of Wrath*," *Sunday
           Times*, January 29, 1989, C24.

3017   "Preview (*The Grapes of Wrath*)," *Time Out*, August 12-19,
           1987, n.p.

3018   Price, Michael H. "Heartbreaking Story (*Of Mice and Men*)
         Powerfully Retold," *Spokesman-Review,* October 31, 1992,
         E1.

3019   Pugh, Scott. "Review of *Of Mice and Men: A Play in 3 Acts,*
         ed. Kiyoshi Nakayama and Hiromasa Takamura," *The
         Steinbeck Newsletter,* 6:2 (Summer 1993), 13.

3020   Quinn, Michael. "People: Of Mice and Fenn," (John
         Malkovich/Sherilyn Fenn in *Of Mice and Men*), *Time,* 139
         (March 16, 1992), 57.

3021   Quinnell, Richard A. "Steinbeck's Tale of Loneliness," *Santa
         Cruz Good Times,* June 25, 1992, 22. (1991 TV
         Presentation of GOW by Steppenwolf)

3022   Raeburn, Paul. "A Troubadour for Troubled Folk: Michael
         Smith's Score for *The Grapes of Wrath* Has Made the
         Song Writer a Sudden Success," *New York Times,* May 20,
         1990, II, 7, 12.

3023   "The Raid," (videocassette) Santa Monica: Pyramid Films,
         1990.

3024   Rainier, Peter. "*Mice and Men*: 92 Edition, Squeaks By," *Los
         Angeles Times,* October 2, 1992, F-12.

3025   "Raquel Case: Casting Director's View," *San Francisco
         Chronicle,* June 14, 1986, 36. (*Cannery Row*).

3026   "Raquel Welch vs. MGM for Millions of Dollars," *San
         Francisco Chronicle,* May 23, 1986, 84. (*Cannery Row*).

3027   Rathgeb, Douglas L. "Kazan as Auteur: The Undiscovered
        East of Eden," Literature /Film Quarterly, 16:1 (1988),
        31-38.

3028   Rechshaffen, Michael. "*Of Mice and Men* Tenderly
        Reinterpreted," *Financial Post,* October 5, 1992, S6.

3029   Reeves, Richard. "The Joads' Tale Echoes on Broadway —
        On All Our Streets," *Los Angeles Times,* June 6, 1990, B7.

3030   Renton, Alex. "All the World's a Stage (Frank Galati's
        adaptation of *The Grapes of Wrath*)," *Independent,* March
        22, 1989, 28.

3031   Resnikova, Eva. "Sentimental Journey," *National Review,* 42
        (June 11, 1990), 58-59. (*The Grapes of Wrath*)

3032   "Review of *Of Mice and Men*," *New Yorker,* 68 (October 19,
        1992), 33.

3033   "Review of the Salt Lake City Walk-Ons Production of *Of
        Mice and Men*," *Utah Holiday,* April 1983, n.p.

3034   Rich, Frank. "Broadway's Bounty: Dramas Bursting with
        Life," *New York Times,* June 3, 1990, Sec. 2, 1, 8.

3035   Rich, Frank, "Chicago Steppenwolf Group Adapts *The Grapes
        of Wrath*," *New York Times,* October 6, 1988, n.p.

3036   Rich, Frank. "Hoping Again for Generosity of Spirit in a
        Brutal Land — *The Grapes of Wrath* Lives for a New
        Generation in Steppenwolf Adaptation," *New York Times,*
        March 23, 1990, B1.

3037   Rich, Frank. "New Era for *Grapes of Wrath*," *New York Times
        Weekend*, March 23, 1990, C1, C5.

3038   Rich, Frank, "Reality Nearly Upstaged a Paradoxical Year,"
        New York Times, December 30, 1990, H5, 12. (*The Grapes
        of Wrath*, Steppenwolf Theatre's adaptation).

3039   Rickey, Carsse. "*Cannery Row*," *Voice*, March 16, 1982, n.p.

3040   "Rip Torn to Play Steinbeck in KGO-TV Special on Author,"
        Salinas Californian, July 12 (13), 1985, 9.

3041   Rodebaugh, Dale. "Movie Makers Scout South Bay for Two
        Locations," *San Jose Mercury News*, July 8, 1991, n.p.

3042   Rogers, Caroline. "New Wrath from Old Grapes," *East Bay
        Express*, April 28, 1989, n.p.

3043   Rosenberg, Scott. "The Great Broadway Diaspora: Regional
        Theater Pours Its Lifeblood into New York," *San
        Francisco Examiner*, June 3, 1990, E-3. (Steppenwolf's
        adaptation of Steinbeck's *The Grapes of Wrath*)

3044   Rosser, Maxine. "Steppenwolf Company's *The Grapes of
        Wrath*," *The Steinbeck Newsletter,* 3:1 (Winter 1990), 10.

3045   Rothstein, Mervyn. "A Box Office Record for the Third
        Season in a Row," *New York Times*, June 6, 1990, C15.

3046   Rothstein, Mervyn. "Broadway: Expect Orphans and Cats,
        Spring Rush Will Follow Winter Lull," *San Francisco
        Chronicle*, January 1, 1990, E2.

3047   Rothstein, Mervyn. "*Grand Hotel* and *City of Angels* Lead the
        Nominations For Tonys," *New York Times*, May 8, 1990,
        C15, 18.

3048   Rothstein, Mervyn. "Tony Winner's Journey from Rock
        Bottom to Top," *New York Times*, June 5, 1990, C13, 15.

3049   Russell, Joan. "Hartford Stage Company: Steinbeck's *Of Mice
        and Men* Expertly Produced," *Stratford Bard*, January 18,
        1984, 12.

3050   Salamon, Julie. "New Movies Worth Seeing: *Of Mice and
        Men*," *Wall Street Journal*, November 17, 1992, A14.

3051   Sanderson, Jim, "American Romanticism in John Ford's *The
        Grapes of Wrath*: Horizontalness, Darkness, Christ, and
        F.D.R.," *Literature/Film Quarterly*, 17 (October 1989),
        231-44.

3052   Sarris, Andrew. "Henry Fonda: An Appreciation," *American
        Film* (January/February 1982), 8, 12, 70.

3053   Scheer, Ronald D. "Steinbeck into Film: The Making of
        Tortilla Flat," *West Virginia University Philological
        Papers, Morganstown, WV*, August 26, 1980, 30-35.

3054   Shillinglaw, Susan. "Carmel's Forest Theater Presents *Of
        Mice and Men*," *The Steinbeck Newsletter*, 4:1 (Winter
        1991), 9.

3055   Shillinglaw, Susan. "Review of *East of Eden*, the Play in
        Three Parts: 'The Chain is Forged,' 'The Unrelenting
        Past,' 'The Chain is Broken,' adapted for the stage by Alan
        Cook and Directed by Tom Humphrey," *Steinbeck
        Newletter,* 8:1-2 (Winter/Spring 1995), 28-29.

3056   Shillinglaw, Susan. "Review of 42nd Street Moon's *Pipe
        Dream,*" *Steinbeck Newsletter,* 10:1 (Spring 1996), 24-25.

3057   Shone, Tom. "Love that Merits a Lynch Mob (*Of Mice and
        Men*)," *Mail on Sunday*, November 29, 1992, 38-39.

3058   Shuller, Barbara Rose. "Opera Season at Hidden Valley Takes
        Intriguing Turn Via Steinbeck Play," *Coasting* (Monterey-
        Carmel, California), January 23, 1985, 28.

3059   Simmons, Jerold L. "The Production Code and Precedent:
        How Hollywood's Censors Sought to Eliminate Brothels
        and Prostitutes in *From Here to Eternity* and *East of
        Eden,*" *Journal of Popular Film and Television,* 20 (Fall
        1992),70-80.

3060   Simmonds, Roy S. "The 1943 London Stage Production of
        The Moon Is Down," *The Steinbeck Newsletter,* 3:1
        (Winter, 1990), 8-9.

3061   Simon, John. "Oklahoma, Tennessee and Beyond," *New York,*
        23 (April 2, 1990), 93. (*The Grapes of Wrath*)

3062   Simpson, Emma. "American Players Celebrate Double First,"
        Festival Times, n.d.

3063   Singer, Karen. "*Burning Bright* Makes Opera Sizzle for Yale
        Premiere," *New Haven Register*, October 31, 1993, D1,
        D4.

3064   Slide, Anthony, ed. *Selected Film Criticism 1941-1950.*
        Metuchen, N. J.: Scarecrow Press, 1983. (pp. 119-121)
        (*Lifeboat*)

3065   Smith, Liz. "A Bunch of Praise for '*Grapes*,'" *New York Daily News,* March 27, 1990, n.p.

3066   Smith, Liz, "Gossip: MGM Hopes Name Change Means Success," (*Of Mice and Men*), *San Francisco Chronicle*, June 8, 1992, D1.

3067   Smith, Liz. "Gossip Column," *San Francisco Chronicle*, November 27, 1986, 86. (Elaine Steinbeck responds to a clipping that said her famous husband's life would be made into a mini-series.)

3068   Smith, Liz. "Heading to Battle," (Screenplay for *In Dubious Battle*) *Los Angeles Times*, Feburary 16, 1993, n.p.

3069   Steel, Mike. "Frost Writes Drama from Steinbeck's *The Pearl*," *Minneapolis Tribune*, October 27, 1974, 1, 4D.

3070   "Steinbeck on Stage," *Stratford Bard*, January 4, 1984, 9.

3071   "Steinbeck Show to Air Sunday," *Salinas Californian,* November 15, 1985, 13.

3072   "Steinbeck's 'Chrysanthemums' Bloom," *Salinas Californian*, March 22, 1990, n.p.

3073   "Steinbeck's Films Shown from December 5 to December 17, 1983 at the National Film Theatre in London," National Film Theatre (December 1983), 12-14. (Films shown included *Of Mice and Men, The Grapes of Wrath, Tortilla Flat, The Moon Is Down, Lifeboat, A Medal for Benny, The Pearl, The Red Pony, East of Eden* and *The Wayward Bus*).

3074   "Steinbeck's Words and Carlisle Floyd's Music Are
         Combined in Hidden Valley Opera," *Coasting* (Monterey,
         Carmel, California), January 16, 1985, 11.

3075   Stone, Judy. "Revival of *Pearl* — and It's a Gem," *San
         Francisco Chronicle*, May 21, 1986, 58.

3076   Sullivan, Dan. "The Taming of *Of Mice and Men*," *Los
         Angeles Times*, February 5, 1985, VI, 1, 4.

3077   Swartz, Joan. "Steinbeck Book Hits Musical High Note at the
         Forest Theatre," *Coasting* (Monterey, Carmel, California),
         August 6, 1986, 12.

3078   Swertlow, Frank. "Hollywood Freeway," *San Francisco
         Chronicle*, April 4, 1987, 33. (Reports on David Wolper
         and ABC and screenwriter James Lee, who plan to do a
         TV movie on the tales of King Arthur and the nights of the
         Round Table with the script based on Steinbeck's novel
         The Acts of King Arthur and His Noble Knights.)

3079   Takamura, Hiromasa. "Plays: Panel Discussion II: The Art of
         Steinbeck and Its Form," *John Steinbeck Society of Japan
         Newsletter*, 10 (April 1987), 6.

3080   Takamura, Hiromasa. "A Review of Steinbeck's Plays in
         Japan — 1994-1995," *Steinbeck Studies*, 19 (May 1996),
         21-26.

3081   Tenebaum, Joanne. "Hidden Valley Shines with *Of Mice and
         Men*," *Carmel Pine Cone*, January 24, 1985, 29.

3082   Thaxter, John. "From Big Top to High Seas in Minor Classic,"
         Wandsworth Borough News, September 30, 1994, n.p.
         (*Burning Bright*)

3083 "Theater: The Prime of Dame Maggie, the Cat's Meow, Steinbeck's Okie Classic," *Newsweek,* 115:14 (April 2, 1990), 54.

3084 "Theatre: Oklahoma, Tennessee, and Beyond," (*The Grapes of Wrath*), *New Yorker*, 23 (April 2, 1990), 93.

3085 "Three Wives," *The New York Post*, October 10, 1986. ("Barney Rosenzweig, the Emmy Award-Winning Producer of *Cagney and Lacey*, Is Laying the Groundwork for a Miniseries on the Life of Author and Journalist John Steinbeck.")

3086 Tinker, Jack. "The Still Small Voice of Perfection," *Daily Mail*, June 23, 1989, 5. (*The Grapes of Wrath*)

3087 "To the Heart of an American Classic (*Of Mice and Men*)," *Daily Telegraph*, November 26, 1992, 18.

3088 "*Tortilla Flat,*" *New Yorker,* 66 (April 2, 1990), 29.

3089 "*Tortilla Flat,*" *TV Times*, February 11-17, 1989, 39.

3090 Valadez, Eloise Marie. "*The Grapes of Wrath* Portrayed Realistically by Steppenwolf," *Daily Calumet and Pointer*, September 21, 1988, III, 1.

3091 Valadez, Eloise Marie. "The Joads Travel to the Stage," *Pulitzer Community Newspaper*, September 16, 1988, n.p.

3092 Valeo, Tom. "*The Grapes of Wrath* Accents Beauty of Steinbeck's Prose," *Chicago Daily Herald*, September 20, 1988, n.p.

3093 Van Gelder, Lawrence. "At the Movies: Horton Foote Screenplay (*Of Mice and Men*)," *New York Times*, November 29, 1991, 12.

3094 Van Gelder, Lawrence. "Lifeboat," (Video release of the film) *New York Times*, June 9, 1985, n.p.

3095 "Vintage Time," (*Grapes of Wrath* play), *Times* (London), October 26, 1962, 11.

3096 *"Viva Zapata!" Independent*, March 25, 1989, 53.

3097 *"Viva Zapata!" New Yorker,* 65 (January 8, 1990), 23.

3098 *"Viva Zapata!" Observer*, March 26, 1989, 52.

3099 *"Viva Zapata!" Sunday Times* (London) March 26, 1989, Screen sec., III.

3100 *"Viva Zapata!" TV Times*, March 25-31, 1989, 32, 79.

3101 "Vox Pop (*The Grapes of Wrath*)," *Festival Times*, No. 3, August 26-31, 1989, n.p.

3102 Walls, Trevor. "The Early Birds Home in on the Fringe," *Evening News*, April 25, 1987, n.p.

3103 Ward, Michael. "'*Grapes*' Bitter Taste: An Interview with Elaine Steinbeck," *Sunday Times*, June 25, 1989, B16.

3104 Wardle, Irving. "*Of Mice and Men*," *Times* (London), September 28, 1984, n.p.

3105   Warman, Christopher. "Of Mice, Men and Mills," *Times* (London), November 17-23, 1984, 20.

3106   Weales, Gerald. "American Theater Watch, 1989-1990," *Georgia Review,* XLIV (Fall 1990), 485-498. (*The Grapes of Wrath*)

3107   Weiss, Hedy, and Wynne Delacoma. "Steppenwolf Gathers Support for *The Grapes of Wrath* Staging," *Chicago Sun-Times,* August 9, 1988, 2, 30, 34.

3108   Weiss, Hedy. "Steppenwolf Offers a Flawless, Faithful *The Grapes of Wrath,*" *Chicago Sun-Times,* September 19, 1988, II, 1-2.

3109   Weiss, Hedy. "Steppenwolf to Pop Cork on Classic *Grapes,*" *Chicago Sun-Times,* September 11, 1988, 6-7.

3110   Whipp, Glenn. "Plays Echoes Riots: *Grapes of Wrath* Creates Ambrosia from Anger," *Pasadena Star News,* September 11, 1992 (n.p.).

3111   Whitebrook, Peter. "On Staging Steinbeck," *Scotsman,* July 27, 1987, n.p.

3112   Wickers, David. "Cruising the Pacific Highway," *Times* (London), March 19, 1989, H7.

3113   Williams, Albert. "Stage Notes: Two New Shows Put Musicians in the Spotlight," (Source Unknown), September 9, 1988, 7.

3114   Wilson, Lanford. "Grape Performances," *Mirabella* (April 1990), 48-50. (*The Grapes of Wrath*)

3115   Winn, Steven. "*Of Mice and Men* Brings Sinise Full Circle,"
        San Francisco Chronicle, October 10, 1992, C5.

3116   "Winner! Best Play 1990 Tony Award: *The Grapes of Wrath*,"
        New York Times, June 6, 1990, n.p.

3117   Witchel, Alex. "*The Grapes of Wrath*: Raves and a Tony Do
        Not Breed a Hit," *New York Times*, July 2, 1990, C11-12.

3118   Wolf, Matt. "London Critics Praise *Grapes of Wrath* Play
        (Steppenwolf)," *Monterey Herald*, June 24, 1989, 6.

3119   "Work in Progress: *East of Eden*," *Summerfest 1990*, (The
        Western Stage), 10.

3120   Wright, Allen. "Fringe (*The Grapes of Wrath*) Festival,"
        Scotsman, August 10, 1987, n.p.

3121   Yamada, Kozo. "*East of Eden* (Movie): As Popular as Ever,"
        Yomiuri (Tokyo), (February 18, 1988), XII-4.

3122   Yordon, Judy. "Review of Audio Version of *Sweet Thursday*
        by Jerry Farden," *Steinbeck Quarterly*, XXIV (3-4
        Summer/Fall 1991), 130-132.

3123   Young, Robert. "*Of Mice and Men* and Marketing," *Writers
        Digest*, 67 (August 1987), 54.

3124   Zaiser, Catherine. "*Of Mice and Men* Creates Memorable
        Steinbeck Characters," *Fargo Forum*, July 9, 1987, A8.

3125   Zeff, Dan. "*The Grapes of Wrath* Lives Up to Billing," *Daily Courier-News*, September 23, 1988, 19.

Reference

3126   Adelman, Irving. *The Contemporary Novel: A Checklist of Critical Literature on the British and American Novel Since 1945.* Metuchen, N. J.: Scarecrow Press, 1972.

3127   Adelman, Irving. *Modern Drama: A Checklist of Critical Literature on 20th Century Plays.* Metuchen, N. J.: Scarecrow Press, 1967.

3127A   Adelman, Irving, and Rita Dworkin. *The Contemporary Novel: A Checklist of Critical Literature on the English Language Novel Since 1945.* Second Edition. Lanham, Md.: Scarecrow Press, 1997.

3128   Astro, Richard. "Steinbeck" in *Fifty Western Writers: A Bio-Bibliographical Source Book.* ed. Richard W. Etulain and Fred Erisman. Westport, Conn.: Greenwood Press, 1982. (pp. 477-487)

3129   Barker, David, comp. *John Steinbeck: A Checklist.* Salem, Ore.: David and Judy Barker Booksellers, 1984.

3130   Beacham, Walton, et. al. *Research Guide to Biography and Criticism.* Vol. II. Washington, D.C.: Beacham, 1985. ("John Steinbeck" by Joseph Millichap on pp. 1115-1118)

3131   Beacham, Walton, et. al. *Research Guide to Biography and Criticism. 1990 Update.* Washington, D.C.: Beacham, 1990. ("John Steinbeck" by Joseph Millichap on pp. 478-480)

3132   Benson, Jackson J. "A Comprehensive Checklist of Criticism," in *The Short Novels of John Steinbeck.* Durham: Duke University Press, 1990. (pp. 315-346)

3133   "Book and Magazine Collectors' Review of Current Selling Prices: John Steinbeck, a Guide to the Current State of the

Market in First Editions by the Author of *East of Eden*," *Book and Magazine Collector*, 75 (June 1990), 42-47.

3134   Breed, Paul F. *Dramatic Criticism Index: A Bibliography of Commentaries on Playwrights from Ibsen to the Avant Garde.* Detroit: Gale Research, 1972.

3135   Bryer, Jackson R., ed. *Sixteen Modern American Authors: A Survey or Research and Criticism since 1972.* Vol. 2 of 2. Durham: Duke University Press, 1990. (contains John Steinbeck by Warren French, pp. 582-622)

3136   Busch, Chrisopher S. "A Historical, Bibliographical Survey of the *Steinbeck Monograph Series* (1971-1991) and the *Steinbeck Essay Series* (1986-1991)," *Steinbeck Quarterly*, XXVI:1-2 (Winter/Spring 1993), 23-37.

3137   Coers, Donald. "Selected Bibliography" in *John Steinbeck as Propagandist: 'The Moon Is Down' Goes To War.* Tuscaloosa, Ala.: University of Alabama Press, 1991. (pp. 157-165)

3138   Combs, Richard C., and Nancy R. Owen, eds. *Authors: Critical and Biographical References.* 2nd ed. Metuchen, N. J.: Scarecrow Press, 1993. (p. 236)

3139   Crystal, Bernard R. "Steinbeck Archives: Pt. II, John Steinbeck Letters and Manuscripts in the Columbia University Libraries," *Steinbeck Newsletter*, 6:1 (Winter 1993), 14-17.

3140   DeMott, Robert. *A Bibliography of Books by and about John Steinbeck.* San Jose, Calif.: San Jose State University, Steinbeck Research Center, 1985.

3141   DeMott, Robert. "*East of Eden*: A Bibliographical Checklist," *Steinbeck Quarterly,* XXV:1-2 (Winter/Spring 1992), 14-28. (a later version incorporated into "'One Book to a Man': Charting a Bibliographical Preface to *East of Eden*"

in DeMott's *Steinbeck's Typewriter: Essays On His Art.*
Troy, N.Y.: Whitston, 1996)

3142   DeMott, Robert. *John Steinbeck: A Checklist of Books by and
about.* Bradenton, Fla.: Opuscula Press, 1987. (also
incorporated into "A Bibliography of Books by and about
John Steinbeck" in DeMott's *Steinbeck's Typewriter:
Essays on His Art.* Troy, N.Y.: Whitston, 1996)

3143   DeMott, Robert, comp. "Tetsumaro Hayashi: A Checklist of
Scholarly Publications," in *After "The Grapes of Wrath":
Essays on John Steinbeck in Honor of Tetsumaro Hayashi.*
ed. Donald Coers, Paul Ruffin, and Robert DeMott.
Athens, Ohio: Ohio University Press, 1995. (pp. 274-288)

3144   DeMott, Robert. "The Steinbeck Research Center: A Checklist
of Autographed First Editions," *Steinbeck Newsletter*, 1:1
(Fall 1987), 1,3,4.

3145   DeMott, Robert. *Steinbeck's Reading: A Catalogue of Books
Owned and Borrowed.* New York: Garland, 1984.

3146   Eddelman, Floyd Eugene. *American Drama Criticism:
Interpretations, 1890-1977.* 2nd ed. Hamden, Conn.: Shoe
String Press, 1979.

3147   Erisman, Fred, and Richard W. Etulain, eds. *Fifty Western
Writers: A Bio-Bibliographical Source Book.* Westport,
Conn.: Greenwood Press, 1982. (contains Richard Astro's
"Steinbeck" on pp. 477-487)

3148   Etheridge, Charles L., Jr. "Changing Attitudes toward
Steinbeck's Naturalism and the Changing Reputation of
East of Eden: A Survey of Criticism Since 1974," in *The
Steinbeck Question: New Essays in Criticism.* Troy, N.Y.:
Whitston, 1993. (pp. 250-259)

3149   Etulain, Richard W., and Fred Erisman, eds. *Fifty Western
Writers: A Bio-Bibliographical Source Book.* Westport,
Conn.: Greenwood Press, 1982. See #3147.

3150   *Facts on File: Bibliography of American Fiction, 1919-1988.*
         New York: Facts on File, 1991. ("John Steinbeck," 476-
         81.)

3151   Fiorelli, Edward. "John Steinbeck," *Critical Survey of Short
         Fiction.* Revised Edition. Vol. 6. ed. Frank N. Magill.
         Englewood Cliffs, N. J.: Salem Press, 1993. (pp. 2205-
         2210)

3152   Folsom, James K. "John Steinbeck," *Critical Survey of Short
         Fiction.* Vol. 6. ed. Frank N. Magill. Englewood Cliffs,
         N. J.: Salem Press, 1981. (pp. 2274-2279)

3153   French, Warren, ed. *American Literary Scholarship 1983.*
         Durham: Duke University Press, 1984. (references to
         Steinbeck on pp. 260-263. 472, 482)

3154   French, Warren. "John Steinbeck," *Sixteen Modern American
         Authors: A Survey of Research and Criticism since 1972.*
         Vol. 2. ed. Jackson J. Bryer. Durham: Duke University
         Press, 1990. (pp. 582-622)

3155   French, Warren. "Selected Bibliography," in *John Steinbeck's
         Fiction Revisited.* New York: Twayne, 1994. (pp. 147-
         158)

3156   French, Warren. "Selected Bibliography," in *John Steinbeck's
         Nonfiction Revisited.* New York: Twayne, 1996. (pp. 138-
         142)

3157   Gladstein, Mimi Reisel. "Selected Bibliography," in *The
         Indestructible Woman in Faulkner, Hemingway, and
         Steinbeck.* Ann Arbor, Mich.: UMI Research Press, 1986.

3158   Harmon, Robert B. *"Cannery Row": A Selected Fifty Year
         Bibliographic Survey.* San Jose, Calif.: Dibco Press, 1995.

3159   Harmon, Robert B., and John F. Early, eds. *"The Grapes of
         Wrath": A Fifty Year Bibliographic Survey.* San Jose,

Calif.: Steinbeck Research Center, San Jose State University, 1990.

3160 Harmon, Robert B., comp. *A Collector's Guide to the First Editions of John Steinbeck.* Bradenton, Florida: Opuscula Press, 1985.

3161 Harmon, Robert B. *The Collectible John Steinbeck: A Practical Guide.* Jefferson, N.C.: McFarland, 1986.

3162 Harmon, Robert B., comp. *Index to the Steinbeck Research Center at San Jose State University: A Descriptive Catalogue by Robert H. Woodward.* San Jose, Calif.: Steinbeck Research Center, 1987.

3163 Harmon, Robert B., ed. *Steinbeck Bibliographies: An Annotated Guide.* Metuchen, N. J.: Scarecrow Press, 1987.

3164 Harmon, Robert B. *Steinbeck Editions: A Bibliographic Checklist.* San Jose, Calif.: Bibliographic Research Services, 1992.

3165 Harris, Richard Hough. *Modern Drama in America and England, 1950-1970: A Guide to Information Sources.* Detroit: Gale Research, 1982.

3166 Hashiguchi, Yasuo, and Koichi Kaido. *A Catalogue of the Maurice Dunbar John Steinbeck Collection at Fukuoka University.* See #294.

3167 Hayashi, Tetsumaro, ed. *A New Steinbeck Bibliography: 1971 -1981.* Metuchen, N. J.: Scarecrow Press, 1983.

3168 Hayashi, Tetsumaro. "The A-B-C's of Steinbeck Studies: A Bibliographic Guide for English Majors," *Steinbeck Quarterly,* XXVI:3-4 (Summer/Fall 1993), 117-126.

3169 Hayashi, Tetsumaro, Donald L. Siefker, and Thomas Y. Moore. *The "Steinbeck Quarterly": A Cumulative Index to Volumes XI-XX. (1978-87)* Steinbeck Bibliography Series,

No. 2. Muncie, Ind.: Steinbeck Research Institute, Ball
State University Press, 1989.

3170   Hayashi, Tetsumaro, and Beverly K. Simpson. *John
Steinbeck: Dissertations, Abstracts and Research
Opportunities*. Metuchen, N. J.: Scarecrow Press, 1995.

3171   Hayashi, Tetsumaro. *A Student's Guide to Steinbeck's
Literature: Primary and Secondary Sources*. Muncie, Ind.:
Steinbeck Research Institute, Department of English, Ball
State University, 1986.

3172   Hayashi, Tetsumaro. "Selected Bibliography," in *A New
Study Guide to Steinbeck's Major Works Complete with
Critical Explications*. Metuchen, N. J.: Scarecrow Press,
1993. (pp. 285-290)

3172A   Hearle, Kevin, and Peter Lisca. "Bibliography," in *The Grapes
of Wrath*. Viking Critical Edition. New York: Viking,
1997. (pp.701-712)

3173   Hughes, Robert J. "Selected Bibliography," in *Beyond "The
Red Pony": A Reader's Companion to Steinbeck's
Complete Short Stories*. Metuchen, N. J.: Scarecrow Press,
1987. (pp. 142-155)

3174   Hughes, Robert J. "Selected Bibliography," in *John Steinbeck:
A Study of the Short Fiction*. Boston: Twayne, 1989. (pp.
198-210)

3175   Kaido, Koichi, and Yasuo Hashiguchi. *A Catalogue of the
Maurice Dunbar John Steinbeck Collection at Fukuoka
University*. See #295.

3176   Kellman, Steven G. *The Modern American Novel*. Pasadena,
Calif.: Salem Press, 1991. (contains commentary on
Steinbeck on pp. 122-132 and entries on *Cannery Row,
East of Eden, The Grapes of Wrath, Of Mice and Men, The
Pearl* and *Tortilla Flat*)

3177 Kohn, Philip C., ed. *American Playwrights Since 1945: A Guide to Scholarship, Criticism and Performance.* Westport, Conn.: Greenwood, 1989.

3178 Koster, Donald N. *American Literature and Language: A Guide to Information Sources.* Detroit: Gale Research, 1982.

3178A Lisca, Peter and Kevin Hearle. "Bibliography," in *The Grapes of Wrath.* Viking Critical Edition. See 3172A.

3179 Magill, Frank N., ed. *Critical Survey of Long Fiction.* Vol. 6. Englewood Cliffs, N. J.: Salem Press, 1983. ("John Steinbeck," by Joseph Millichap on 2518-2528, also on pp. 1803, 3602)

3180 Magill, Frank N., ed. *Critical Survey of Long Fiction: English Language Series.* New York: Salem Press, 1991. ("John Steinbeck," 3151-62.)

3181 Magill, Frank N., ed. *Critical Survey of Short Fiction.* Vol. 6. Englewood Cliffs, N. J.: Salem Press, 1981. ("John Steinbeck," by James K. Folsom on 2274-2279)

3182 Magill, Frank N., ed. *Critical Survey of Short Fiction.* Revised Edition. Vol. 6. Englewood Cliffs, N. J.: Salem Press, 1981. ("John Steinbeck," by Edward Fiorelli on 2205-2210)

3183 Magill, Frank N. *Magill's Bibliography of Literary Criticism: Selected Sources for the Study of More Than 3500 Outstanding Works of Western Literature.* Englewood Cliffs, N. J.: Salem, 1979.

3184 Magill, Frank, ed. *Magill's Bibliography of Literary Criticism.* Vol. 4. Englewood Cliffs, N. J.: Salem Press, 1985. ("John Steinbeck" on pp. 1993-2005 and entries on *Cannery Row, East of Eden, The Grapes of Wrath, In Dubious Battle, Of Mice and Men, The Pearl, The Short Reign of Pippin IV, The Wayward Bus, The Winter of Our*

Discontent, Tortilla Flat, "The Chrysanthemums," *The Red Pony,* "The Leader of the People.")

3185   Millichap, Joseph. "John Steinbeck," in Walton Beacham, et. al. *Research Guide to Biography and Criticism.* Vol. II. Washington, D.C.: Beacham, 1985. (pp. 1115-1118)

3186   Millichap, Joseph. "John Steinbeck," *Research Guide to Biography and Criticism. 1990 Update.* ed. Walton Beacham, et al. Washington, D.C.: Beacham, 1990. (pp. 478-480)

3187   Millichap, Joseph. "John Steinbeck," *Critical Survey of Long Fiction.* Vol. 6. ed. Frank N. Magill. Englewood Cliffs, N. J.: Salem Press, 1983. (pp. 2518-2528, also on pp. 1803, 3602)

3188   Millichap, Joseph. "Selected Bibliography," in *Steinbeck and Film.* New York: Frederick Ungar, 1983. (pp. 191-194)

3189   Moore, Thomas Y., Tetsumaro Hayashi, and Donald L. Siefker. *The "Steinbeck Quarterly": A Cumulative Index to Volumes XI-XX. (1978-87).* Steinbeck Bibliography Series, No. 2. See #3169.

3190   Nakayama, Kiyoshi. "A Checklist of Steinbeck Bibliography in Japan: 1982," *The John Steinbeck Society of Japan Newsletter,* 6 (May 1, 1983), 6-7.

3191   Nakayama, Kiyoshi. "A Checklist of Steinbeck Bibliography in Japan: 1983," *The John Steinbeck Society of Japan Newsletter,* 7 (May 1, 1984), 8.

3192   Nakayama, Kiyoshi. "A Checklist of Steinbeck Bibliography in Japan: 1984," *The John Steinbeck Society of Japan Newsletter,* 8 (May 1, 1985), 6.

3193   Nakayama, Kiyoshi. "A Checklist of Steinbeck Bibliography in Japan: 1985," *The John Steinbeck Society of Japan Newsletter,* 9 (May 1, 1986), 5-6.

3194 Nakayama, Kiyoshi. "A Checklist of Steinbeck Bibliography in Japan: 1986," *The John Steinbeck Society of Japan Newsletter*, 10 (May 1, 1987), 6-7.

3195 Nakayama, Kiyoshi. "A Checklist of Steinbeck Bibliography in Japan: 1987," *The John Steinbeck Society of Japan Newsletter*, 11 (April 1988), 8-9.

3196 Nakayama, Kiyoshi. "A Checklist of Steinbeck Bibliography in Japan: 1988," *The John Steinbeck Society of Japan Newsletter*, 12 (April 1989), 9-10.

3197 Nakayama, Kiyoshi. "A Checklist of Steinbeck Bibliography in Japan: 1989," *The John Steinbeck Society of Japan Newsletter*, 13 (April 1990), 10.

3198 Nakayama, Kiyoshi. "A Checklist of Steinbeck Bibliography in Japan: 1990," *The John Steinbeck Society of Japan Newsletter*, 14 (April 1991), 9-11.

3199 Nakayama, Kiyoshi. "A Checklist of Steinbeck Bibliography in Japan: 1991," *The John Steinbeck Society of Japan Newsletter*, 6 (April 1992), 7-9.

3200 Nakayama, Kiyoshi, comp. *Nihon Ni okeru Sutainbekku Bunken Shoshi. (Steinbeck in Japan: A Bibliography.)* Osaka, Japan: Kansai University Press, 1992.

3201 Nevius, Blake. *The American Novel: Sinclair Lewis to the Present.* New York: Appleton Century Crofts, 1970.

3202 Nordloh, David J., ed. *American Literary Scholarship 1986.* Durham: Duke University Press, 1987. (references to Steinbeck on pp. 202, 234, 263, 382, 386, 406, 407)

3203 Nordloh, David J., ed. *American Literary Scholarship 1989.* Durham: Duke University Press, 1990. (references to Steinbeck on pp. 221, 225-229, 248, 355, 387-88, 407, 439, 446-447, 448)

3204   Nordloh, David J., ed. *American Literary Scholarship 1991*.
        Durham: Duke University Press, 1992. (references to
        Steinbeck on pp. 243, 245-251, 383, 453-454)

3205   Nordloh, David J., ed. *American Literary Scholarship 1992*.
        Durham: Duke University Press, 1994. (references to
        Steinbeck on pp. 148, 235, 249, 251-252)

3206   Nordloh, David J., ed. *American Literary Scholarship 1994*.
        Durham: Duke University Press, 1996. (references to
        Steinbeck on pp. 279-280)

3207   Owen, Nancy R., and Richard E. Combs, eds. *Authors:*
        Critical and Biographical References. 2nd ed.   See #3138.

3208   Owens, Louis. *American Literary Scholarship: An Annual,*
        1983. Durham: Duke University Press, 1992. (pp. 260-
        263)

3209   Owens, Louis, ed. *American Literary Scholarship 1990*.
        Durham: Duke University Press, 1991. (references to
        Steinbeck on pp. 267-273, 447, 464, 481)

3210   Owens, Louis. "Selected Bibliography," in *"The Grapes of*
        Wrath": Trouble in The Promised Land. New York:
        Twayne, 1989. (pp. 111-117)

3211   Parks, Robert E. "John Steinbeck in the Pierpont Morgan
        Library," *Steinbeck Newsletter*, 8 (1-2 Winter/Spring
        1995), 19-21.

3212   Pownall, David E. *Articles on Twentieth Century Literature:*
        An Annotated Bibliography, 1954-1970. New York:
        Kraus-Thompson Organization, Ltd., 1973.

3213   Railsback, Brian. "Selected Bibliography," in *Parallel*
        Expeditions: Charles Darwin and the Art of John
        Steinbeck. Moscow, Idaho: University of Idaho Press,
        1995. (pp. 141-147)

3214   Robbins, J. Albert, ed. *American Literary Scholarship 1982.*
        Durham: Duke University Press, 1983. (references to
        Steinbeck on pp. 252-255, 471, 494)

3215   Robbins, J. Albert, ed. *American Literary Scholarship 1984.*
        Durham: Duke University Press, 1985. (references to
        Steinbeck on pp. 267, 270-272, 482, 496, 549-550, 559)

3216   Robbins, J. Albert, ed. *American Literary Scholarship 1985.*
        Durham: Duke University Press, 1986. (references to
        Steinbeck on pp. 180, 255-257, 486)

3217   Robbins, J. Albert, ed. *American Literary Scholarship 1988.*
        Durham: Duke University Press, 1989. (references to
        Steinbeck on pp. 159, 259-262)

3218   Salem, James, ed. *Guide to Critical Reviews. Pt. I. American
        Drama, 1909-1982.* 3rd ed. Metuchen, N. J.: Scarecrow
        Press, 1971. (entries on *Burning Bright, The Long Valley,
        The Moon Is Down, Of Mice and Men)*

3219   Salem, James, ed. *Guide to Critical Reviews. Pt. IV.*
        Metuchen, N. J.: Scarecrow Press, 1971. (entries on *The
        Pearl, Viva Zapata!, The Forgotten Village, A Medal for
        Benny, The Red Pony, Lifeboat)*

3220   Salem, James, ed. *A Guide to Critical Reviews. Pt. II. The
        Musical, 1909-1989.* 3rd ed. Metuchen, N. J.: Scarecrow
        Press, 1991. (*Pipe Dream,* pp. 520-521)

3221   Scharnhorst, Gary, ed. *American Literary Scholarship 1993.*
        Durham: Duke University Press, 1995. (references to
        Steinbeck on pp. 233-35, 334, 359, 390)

3222   Seidel, Alison P. *Literary Criticism and Authors' Biographies:
        An Annotated Index.* Metuchen, N. J.: Scarecrow Press,
        1978.

3223   Shillinglaw, Susan. "John Steinbeck," *Facts on File:
        Bibliography of American Fiction, 1919-1988.* ed. Judith

S. Baughman and Matthew J. Bruccoli. New York: Facts on File, 1991. (pp. 476-481)

3224   Shillinglaw, Susan. "John Steinbeck," *Modern Classic Writers*. ed. Judith S. Baughman and Matthew J. Bruccoli. New York: Facts on File, 1994. (pp. 48-60)

3225   Siefker, Donald L., Tetsumaro Hayashi, and Thomas Y. Moore. *The "Steinbeck Quarterly": A Cumulative Index to Volumes XI-XX. (1978-87)* Steinbeck Bibliography Series, No. 2. See #3169.

3226   Simmonds, Roy. "Selected Bibliography," in *John Steinbeck: The War Years*. Lewisburg, Pa.: Bucknell, 1996. (pp. 327-334)

3227   Simpson, Beverly K., and Tetsumaro Hayashi. *Steinbeck: A Guide to Dissertations*. See #3170.

3228   "Steinbeck Centers and Collections in the U.S.A.," *International Studies Newsletter,* 1 (Spring 1983), 12-15.

3229   *The Steinbeck Research Center: A Checklist of Autographed Books*. San Jose State University: Wahlquist Library, 1985.

3230   Thurston, Jarvis. *Short Fiction Criticism: A Checklist of Interpretation since 1925 of Stories and Novellettes (American, British, Continental), 1800-1958*. Denver: Alan Swallow, 1960.

3231   Timmerman, John H. "Selected Bibliography," in *The Dramatic Landscape of John Steinbeck's Fiction*. Norman, Okla: University of Oklahoma Press, 1990. (pp. 317-329)

3232   Timmerman, John H. "Selected Bibliography," in *John Steinbeck: The Aesthetics of the Road Taken*. Norman, Okla: U Oklahoma Press, 1986. (pp. 297-307)

3233   Timmerman, John H. "John Steinbeck's Use of the Bible: A
        Descriptive Bibliography of the Critical Tradition,"
        Steinbeck Quarterly, 21:1-2 (Winter/Spring 1988), 24-39.

3234   Walker, Warren S. *Twentieth Century Short Story Explication.*
        3rd Ed. with five supplements. Hamden, Conn.: Shoestring
        Press, 1977, 1980, 1984, 1987, 1989, 1991.

3235   Weixlman, Joe. *American Short Fiction Criticism and
        Scholarship, 1959-1977: A Checklist.* Chicago: Swallow
        Press, 1982.

3236   Werlock, Abby, ed. *Reader's Companion to the American
        Short Story*. New York: Facts on File, forthcoming. (lists
        several Steinbeck short stories and suggested 3-4 relevant
        critics on each one)

3237   Werner, Alan R., and Spencer Means. *Literary Criticism
        Index.* Metuchen, N. J.: Scarecrow Press, 1984. (pp. 574-
        575)

3238   Woodress, James, ed. *American Literary Scholarship 1987.*
        Durham: Duke University Press, 1988. (references to
        Steinbeck on pp. 255-56, 368, 376, 377, 400)

3239   Woodward, Robert H. ed. *The Steinbeck Research Center at
        San Jose State University: A Descriptive Catalogue.* San
        Jose, Calif.: San Jose Studies, San Jose State University,
        1985.

Translations and Foreign Editions

3240   Akasofu, Tetsuji, ed. "How Mr. Hogan Robbed a Bank," in
        The Best Short Stories from Great American Authors.
        Tokyo: Eichosa, 1982. (pp. 10-24)

3241   Araki, Kazuo, et al., eds. "Hurricane Donna," in *The New Age
        Readers New Edition.* Tokyo: Kenkyusha, 1991. (pp. 56-
        63) (excerpts from *Travels with Charley*)

3242   Azuma, Yoshio, and Kuniyasu Tsuschida, eds. "The
        Harness," in *Californian Stories.* Tokyo: Gaku Shobo,
        1984. (pp. 20-45)

3243   Baturin, Sergei, trans. *Russkie dnevnik: Dzhon Steinbek*
        (Traditsii Amerikanskor Literatury) Moskow: Khudozh
        Lit-ra, 1984. (A translation of Steinbeck's *A Russian
        Journal*)

3244   Egusa, Hisashi, et al., ed. "The White Quail," in *Modern
        American Masterpieces.* Tokyo: Asahi Press, 1985. (pp.
        51-74)

3245   Fukuzawa, Toshio, ed. *The Pearl.* Tokyo: Homeros-sha, 1991.

3246   Furuya, Kazuko, trans. "*Koretsu no Umi: Dai Go Sho (Sea of
        Cortez: Chapter 5)*," *Shi to Shimbun (Poetry and Prose),*
        50 (Shi to Shimbun no Kai, August 1990), 67-69. (a
        translation of Chapter 5)

3247   Furuya, Kazuko, trans. "*Koretsu no Umi: Dai Nisho (Sea of
        Cortez: Chapter 2)*," *Shi to Shimbun (Poetry and Prose),*
        46 (Shi to Shimbun no Kai, July 1989), 38-41. (a
        translation of Chapter 2)

3248   Furuya, Kazuko, trans. "*Koretsu no Umi: Dai Yisho (Sea of
        Cortez: Chapter 1)*," *Shi to Shimbun (Poetry and Prose),*

45 (Shi to Shimbun no Kai, December 1988), 61-68. (a translation of Chapter 1)

3249   Furuya, Kazuko, trans. "*Koretsu no Umi: Dai Yisho (Sea of Cortez: Chapter 3*)," *Shi to Shimbun (Poetry and Prose)*, 47 (Shi to Shimbun no Kai, December 1989), 21-24. (a translation of Chapter 3)

3250   Furuya, Kazuko, trans. "*Koretsu no Umi: Dai Yon Sho (ni) (Sea of Cortez: Chapter 4)*," *Shi to Shimbun (Poetry and Prose)*, 49 (Shi to Shimbun no Kai, April 1991), 55-59. (a translation of the second half of Chapter 4)

3251   Furuya, Kazuko, trans. "*Koretsu no Umi: Dai Yon Sho (Sea of Cortez: Chapter 4)*," *Shi to Shimbun (Poetry and Prose)*, 48 (Shi to Shimbun no Kai, August 1990), 73-78. (a translation of the first half of Chapter 4)

3252   Furuya, Kazuko, trans. "*Koretsu no Umi: Joron (Sea of Cortez: Introduction)*," *Shi to Shimbun (Poetry and Prose)*, 44 (Shi to Shimbun no Kai, June 1988), 59-62.

3253   Hashiguchi, Yasuo, ed. *The Complete Works of John Steinbeck*. 20 volumes. Kyoto: Rinsen Book Co., 1985. Contents: Vol. I: *Cup of Gold: A Life of Henry Morgan, Buccaneer with Occasional References to History*. Vol. II: *The Pastures of Heaven; Nothing So Monstrous*. Vol. III: *To a God Unknown*. Vol. IV: *Tortilla Flat*. Vol. V: *In Dubious Battle*. Vol. VI: *St. Katy the Virgin; The Red Pony; The Long Valley; How Edith McGillicuddy Met Robert Louis Stevenson*. Vol. VII: *Of Mice and Men; Of Mice and Men, a Play in Three Acts*. Vol. VIII: *The Grapes of Wrath*. Vol. IX: *The Moon Is Down; The Moon Is Down, a Play in Two Parts; Viva Zapata!* Vol. X: *Cannery Row; Sweet Thursday*. Vol. XI: *The Wayward Bus; The Pearl*. Vol. XII: *Burning Bright, a Play in Story Form; Burning Bright, Acting Edition*. Vol. XIII: *East of Eden*. Vol. XIV: *The Short Reign of Pippin IV, a Fabrication; The Winter of Our Discontent*. Vol. XV: *The Acts of King Arthur and His Noble Knights, from the*

Winchester Manuscript of Thomas Malory and Other Sources ed. Chase Horton. Vol. XVI: *Their Blood is Strong; Vanderbilt Clinic; Travels with Charley in Search of America; America and Americans.* Vol. XVII: *The Forgotten Village; The Log from the Sea of Cortez.* Vol. XVIII: *Bombs Away; Once There Was a War.* Vol. XIX: *A Russian Journal; Positano; Speech Accepting the Nobel Prize for Literature; Journal of a Novel.* Vol. XX: Appendix and Essays on Steinbeck Research Libraries in the United States.

3254   Idei, Yasuko, and Keisuke Tanaka, eds. "The White Quail," in *Americans Eves in Short Stories.* Tokyo: Eihosha, 1988. (pp. 72-89)

3255   Imaizumi, Haruko, and Keiichi Okano, eds. "The Snake," in *British and American Short Stories of Living Creatures.* Tokyo: Asahi Press, 1989. (pp. 42-58)

3256   Inoue, Kenji, ed. *The Log from the Sea of Cortez: About Ed Ricketts.* Tokyo: Kenkyusha, 1983. (iv+68+19)

3257   Inoue, Kenji, trans. *Kyanari Rou (Cannery Row).* Tokyo: Fukutake Shoten, 1989.

3258   Ito, Yoshio, Chotshi Nishimura, Hisashi Egusa, and Mitsuo Kato, ed. "The White Quail," in *Modern American Masterpieces.* Tokyo: Asahi Press, 1985. (pp. 51-84)

3259   *Izbrannye Proisvedeniia*/Selected Works. Moscow: N.A., 1988. (Contains a translation of *Tortilla Flat, Of Mice and Men, The Pearl, Cannery Row,* and *The Wayward Bus* in Russian) (also contains an introduction "Realism i romantika prozy Dzhona Steinbeka," by Alexander Muliarchik)

3260   Kato, Mitsuo, Chotshi Nishimura, Hisashi Egusa, and Yoshio Ito, eds. "The White Quail," in *Modern American Masterpieces.* See #3244.

3261   Kobayshi, Hiroyuki, Hiromu Shimizu, and Kiyoshi
        Nakayama, trans. *Tanoshii Mokuyobi (Sweet Thursday)*
        Tokyo: Shimin Shobo, 1984.

3262   Nakachi, Akira, and Nobuyuki Takenouchi, eds. "The Snake,"
        in *A First Step in Appreciating American Literature.*
        Tokyo: Gaku Shobo, 1982. (pp. 35-50)

3263   Nakayama, Kiyoshi, ed. *Uncollected Stories of John
        Steinbeck.* Tokyo: Nan'undo, 1986. Contents: "His
        Father"; "The Summer Before"; "How Edith McGillcuddy
        Met Robert L. Stevenson"; "Reunion at the Quiet Hotel";
        "The Miracle at Tepayac"; "The Gifts of Iban"; "The Time
        The Wolves Ate the Vice-Principal."

3264   Nakayama, Kiyoshi, Hiromu Shimizu, and Hiroyuki
        Kobayshi, trans. *Tanoshii Mokuyobi (Sweet Thursday).*
        See #3261.

3265   Nguyen, Hien Le, trans. *Mua* (Literary Collections of de
        Maupassant, Maugham, Steinbeck, et al.) Los Angeles: T
        and T, 1989. (in Vietnamese, originally published Saigon:
        Tien Bo, 1969) (contains Johnny Gau ("Johnny Bear");
        Nguoi Chi Huy ("The Leader of The People"); and Mot
        cuoc rap ("The Raid"))

3266   Nishida, Mioko, and Noriko Yoshimura, trans. *Korutesu no
        Umi* (Sea of Cortez) Tokyo: Kosakusha, 1992. (translation
        of John Steinbeck's *The Log from the Sea of Cortez,*
        Viking 1951 with translators' postscript)

3267   Nishimae, Yakashi, and Mitsuaki Yamashita, eds. *The Gift
        and The Leader of the People.* Tokyo: Oshisha, 1987.

3268   Ogami. Seiji. "Yaku Chu — John Steinbeck No Saku Hin
        Yori — The Red Pony" Hoka Toku Shu Steinbeck no Hito
        to saru hin, *Eigo Kenkyu,* 45 (April 1956), 12-17. ("The
        Gift," "Johnny Bear") No Sho yaku, Chu

3269   Oguri, Takashi, and Kozo Yokohama, eds. "The
         Chrysanthemums," in *British and American Masterpieces*.
         Tokyo: Kinseido, 1988. (pp. 16-30)

3270   Okada, Haruma, ed. "The Raid," in *Five Short Stories*.
         Tokyo: Eichosha, 1983. (pp. 48-61)

3271   Okano, Keiichi, and Haruko Imaizumi, eds. "The Snake," in
         British and American Short Stories of Living Creatures.
         See #3255.

3272   Omae, Masaomi, trans. *Chari tono Tabi: Amerika o
         Motomete. (Travels with Charley in Search of America)*
         Tokyo: Saimuru Shuppankai, 1987.

3273   *Punno ui Podo.* (A Korean translation of *The Grapes of
         Wrath*) Seoul: Hongsin Munhwasa, 1993.

3274   Shibuya, Yazaburo, ed. "The Chrysanthemums," in *New
         American Models*. Tokyo: Kinseido, 1984. (pp. 170-183)

3275   Shimizu, Hiromu, Hiroyuki Kobayshi, and Kiyoshi
         Nakayama, trans. *Tanoshii Mokuyobi (Sweet Thursday)*.
         See #3261.

3276   Shiraki, Shigeru, trans. *Akai Kouma (The Red Pony), Sekai no
         Meisaku Bungaku 4 (Masterpieces of World Literature*,
         Vol. 4). Tokyo: Iwasaki Shoten, 1985. (contains *Akai
         Kouma* (*The Red Pony*). "Kiku'" ("The
         Chrysanthemums"), "Shiroi Uzura" ("The White Quail"),
         and "Tobo" ("Flight"))

3277   Steinbeck, John. *Al Este de Eden.* Barcelona: Biblioteca
         Universal Caralt, 1990.

3278   Steinbeck, John. *De Ratones y Hombres*. Barcelona: Edhasa,
         1986. (*OMM*)

3279   Steinbeck, John. *La Perla*. Barcelona: Biblioteca Universal
        Caralt, 1986. (*The Pearl*)

3280   Steinbeck, John. *Las Unas de la Ira*. ed. Juan Jose Coy.
        Madrid: Editiones Catedra, S.A., 1995. (*GOW*)

3281   Steinbeck, John. *Los Hechos del rey Arturo y Sus Nobles
        Caballeros*. Barcelona: Edhasa, 1986. (*AKA*)

3282   Sugiyama,Takahiko, ed. *The Harvest Gypsies: On the Road to
        "The Grapes of Wrath,"* Tokyo: Kenkyusha, 1992.
        (includes the author's essay "Kariforunia no Okizu 'Ikari
        no Budo' Rikai no Ichijo toshite 'Okies' in California:
        Toward an Appreciation of *The Grapes of Wrath*," (pp. xi-
        xx) preface (pp. v-viii) and Japanese annotation (pp. 59-
        90))

3283   Takahisa, Kyoko, ed. "The Chrysanthemums," in *Women: A
        Variety of Lives*. Shohaskusha, 1989. (pp. 16-32)

3284   Takamura, Hiromasa, and Kiyoshi Nakayama, eds. *Of Mice
        and Men: A Play in Three Acts*. Tokyo: Ohshisha, 1993.
        (Includes the editor's preface in English (pp. 3-6),
        introduction (pp. 97-104), and Japanese annotations (pp.
        105-157).)

3285   Takenouchi, Nobuyuki, and Akira Nakachi, eds. "The Snake,"
        in *A First Step in Appreciating American Short Stories*.
        See #3262.

3286   Tanaka, Keisuke, and Yasuko Idei, eds. "The White Quail," in
        Americans Eves in Short Stories. See #3254.

3287   Tanaka, Tamotsu, and Toshio Yamagata, eds. "Breakfast," in
        Famous Short Stories: Pulitzer Prize Writers. Tokyo:
        Asahi Press, 1987. (pp. 4-8)

3288   Tsuboi, Kiyohiko, and Kyoko Ariki, eds. *Viva Zapata!* Tokyo:
        Eihosha, 1985.

3289   Tsuchida, Kuniyasu, and Yoshio Azuma, eds. "The Harness," in *Californian Stories*. See #3242.

3290   Ueno, Naozo, ed. "The Chrysanthemums," in *Anthology of American Short Stories*. Tokyo: Nun'undo, 1983. (pp. 118-128)

3291   Yamagata, Toshio, and Tamotsu Tanaka, eds. "Breakfast," in *Famous Short Stories: Pulitzer Prize Writers*. See #3287.

3292   Yamaguchi, Kyuichi, ed. "The White Quail," in *Love and Its Trail.* Tokyo: Seibido, 1986. (pp. 39-58)

3293   Yamashita, Mitsuaki, and Yakashi Nishimae, eds. *The Gift and The Leader of the People.* See #3267.

3294   Yamashita, Mitsuaki, trans. "Jon Sutainbekku no Shirazaru Kami ni," (John Steinbeck's *To A God Unknown*), in *Notre Dame Seishin University Bulletin: Foreign Language Studies, Foreign Literature*, 9:1 (March 1985), 75-86. (A translation of Ch. 1-4 of the novel)

3295   Yasunaga, Yoshio, ed. "Breakfast," in *A Day's Wait and Other Charming Stories*. Tokyo: Kinseido, 1982. (pp. 6-10)

3296   Yokohama, Kozo, and Takashi Oguri, eds. "The Chrysanthemums," in *British and American Masterpieces*. See #3269.

3297   Yoshimura, Noriko, and Mioko Nishida, trans. *Korutesu no Umi* (Sea of Cortez). See #3266.

Foreign Language Articles
and Book Reviews

3298 Abad, Francisco. "Lecturas, I: A proposito de Carlos Garcia
Gual La secta del perro; II: Las estructuras novelisticas de
la picaresca y de *The Grapes of Wrath*, (The Picaresque
Structures of *The Grapes of Wrath*); III: Sobre el
leonesismo de Libro de Alexandre," *Epos: Revista de
Filologia, Madrid Spain,* 5 (1989), 479-485.

3299 Alvarez Ude Cotera, Carlos. "Recuperacion de Steinbeck
como '*Caballero del Rey Arturo,*'" (Steinbeck's
Reconstruction of *The Acts of King Arthur and His Noble
Knights*) *Insula: Revista des Letras y Ciencias Humanas,
Madrid Spain,* 35 (July/August 1980), 404-405.

3300 Ariki, Kyoko. "Eden no Higashi no Shudai no Kousou o
Megutte — Cathy no Yakuwari o chushin ni," (On the
Thematic Design of *East of Eden*: Centering on Cathy's
Role) *Persica,* 19 (Okayama English Literary Society),
(March 25, 1992), 33-45.

3301 Ariki, Kyoko. "*Eden no Higashi* to Kyashii," (*East of Eden*
and Cathy) *Persica* (Okayama English Literary Society),
12 (March 1985), 51-62.

3302 Ariki, Kyoko. "*Fookunaa, Heminguwei, Sutainbekku no
Fumetsu no Onna* ni Kansuru Mimi Raiseru Guraddostain
no Kenkyu," (Review of Mimi Reisel Gladstein's *The
Indestructible Woman in Faulkner, Hemingway, and
Steinbeck)* in *Nihon Sutainbekku Kyokai Jimu-kyoku
Dayori,* 4 (November 11, 1987), 4-5.

3303   Ariki, Kyoko. *"Kanzume yokocho," (Cannery Row* and
        Steinbeck), *Persica* (Okayama English Literary Society),
        16 (1989), 99-106.

3304   Ariki, Kyoko. *"Nezumi to Otokotachi* Kou — Ningen no
        Kongenteki Yokkyu wo Megutte," (Speculation on *Of
        Mice and Men* — Human's Basic Instinct), *Persica*
        (Okayama English Literary Society), 18 (April 1991), 75-
        84.

3305   Ariki, Kyoko. "Nihon ni Okeru Sutainbekku no Kenkyu no
        Keikou," (Trends of Steinbeck Studies in Japan), *Chu-
        Shikoku America Bungaku Kenkyu (Chu-Shikoku Studies
        in American Literature),* 27 (June 1, 1991), 90-99.

3306   Ariki, Kyoto. "'Omamori' ga nanio shocho suruka — kurai
        fuyu no nochino yoakeno toulai o shinjite," (What "The
        Talisman" Symbolizes — Believing in the Advent of
        Dawn after the Dark Winter) *Persica* (Okayama English
        Literary Society), 13 (March 1986), 21-32. (*The Winter of
        Our Discontent*)

3307   Ariki, Kyoto. *"Shinju* wa nani o kataruka — Fuana no sonzai
        o chushin ni," (What *The Pearl* Tells — Centering on
        Juana's Existence) *Persica* (Okayama English Literary
        Society), 15 (1988), 67-74.

3308   Ariki, Kyoko. "Sutainbekku no *Chali Tono Tabi* ni tsuite,"
        (On Steinbeck's *Travels with Charley*), *Chu-Shikoku
        Studies in American Literature,* 23 (June 1987), 27-38.

3309   Ariki, Kyoko. "Sutainbekku to America: Sutainbekku no
        Americasei no kenkyu," (Steinbeck and America: A
        Study of Steinbeck's Americanness) in *Sutainbekku
        Sakka Sakuhin Ron. (Steinbeck and His Works): A
        Festschrift in Honor of Dr. Tetsumaro Hayashi.* ed. Eiko

Shiraga and Yasuo Hashiguchi. Tokyo: Eihosha, 1995. (pp. 17-33)

3310 Ariki, Kyoko. "*Viva Zapata* ni gyoshuku sareteiru Sutainbekku no futatsu no shuyo tema," (Steinbeck's Two Cardinal Themes Condensed in *Viva Zapata!*), *Chu-Shikoku America Bungaku Kenkyu (Chu-Shikoku American Literature Bulletin)*, 21 (June 1985), 56-67.

3311 Ariki, Kyoko, Yasuo Hashiguchi, and Yoshifumi Kato, trans. "Futari No Jody — Steinbeck and Rawlings," (Two Jodys: Steinbeck and Rawlings) by Kiyohiko Tsuboi in *John Steinbeck — Salinas Kara Sekai Ni Mukete (John Steinbeck: From Salinas to the World)*. Tokyo: Gaku Shobo, 1992. (a translation of the author's original essay in *John Steinbeck: From Salinas to the World*. ed. Tetsumaro Hayashi, Richard Peterson, and Shigeharu Yano. Tokyo: Gaku Shobo, 1986)

3312 Ariki, Kyoko, Yasuo Hashiguchi, and Yoshifumi Kato, trans. "Gekisakka Sutaainbekku — Jyoron," (Steinbeck as Dramatist: A Preliminary Account) by John Ditsky in *John Steinbeck — Salinas Kara Sekai Ni Mukete (John Steinbeck: From Salinas to the World)*. Tokyo: Gaku Shobo, 1992. (a translation of the author's original essay in *John Steinbeck: From Salinas to the World*. ed. Tetsumaro Hayashi, Richard Peterson, and Shigeharu Yano. Tokyo: Gaku Shobo, 1986)

3313 Ariki, Kyoko, Yasuo Hashiguchi, and Yoshifumi Kato, trans. "John Steinbeck: Salinas Kara Sekai Ni Mukete," (John Steinbeck: From Salinas to the World) by Warren French in *John Steinbeck — Salinas Kara Sekai Ni Mukete (John Steinbeck: From Salinas to the World)*. Tokyo: Gaku Shobo, 1992. (a translation of the author's original essay in *John Steinbeck: From Salinas to the World*. ed. Tetsumaro Hayashi, Richard Peterson, and Shigeharu Yano. Tokyo: Gaku Shobo, 1986)

3314   Ariki, Kyoko, Yasuo Hashiguchi, and Yoshifumi Kato, trans.
         "John Steinbeck — Sosaku Ron," (John Steinbeck and
         His Concept of Writing) by Tetsumaro Hayashi in *John
         Steinbeck — Salinas Kara Sekai Ni Mukete (John
         Steinbeck: From Salinas to the World)*. Tokyo: Gaku
         Shobo, 1992. (a translation of the author's original essay
         in *John Steinbeck: From Salinas to the World*. ed.
         Tetsumaro Hayashi, Richard Peterson, and Shigeharu
         Yano. Tokyo: Gaku Shobo, 1986)

3315   Ariki, Kyoko, Yasuo Hashiguchi, and Yoshifumi Kato, trans.
         "John Steinbeck to Kawabata Yasunari," (John Steinbeck
         and Yusanari Kawabata) by Kiyoshi Nakayama in *John
         Steinbeck — Salinas Kara Sekai Ni Mukete (John
         Steinbeck: From Salinas to the World)*. Tokyo: Gaku
         Shobo, 1992. (a translation of the author's original essay
         in *John Steinbeck: From Salinas to the World*. ed.
         Tetsumaro Hayashi, Richard Peterson, and Shigeharu
         Yano. Tokyo: Gaku Shobo, 1986)

3316   Ariki, Kyoko, Yasuo Hashiguchi, and Yoshifumi Kato, trans.
         "Lady Brett Kara Ma Joad: Josei No Ijyo Na Sukanasa,"
         (From Lady Brett to Ma Joad: A Singular Scarcity) by
         Mimi Reisel Gladstein in *John Steinbeck — Salinas Kara
         Sekai Ni Mukete (John Steinbeck: From Salinas to the
         World)*. Tokyo: Gaku Shobo, 1992. (a translation of the
         author's original essay in *John Steinbeck: From Salinas
         to the World*. ed. Tetsumaro Hayashi, Richard Peterson,
         and Shigeharu Yano. Tokyo: Gaku Shobo, 1986)

3317   Ariki, Kyoko, Yasuo Hashiguchi, and Yoshifumi Kato, trans.
         "Nonsense No Heroine, Camille Oaks — *Kimagore Basu
         Wo Saihyoko Suru*," (Camille Oaks, A Heroine of
         Nonsense — A Reassessment of *The Wayward Bus*) by
         Takahiko Sugiyama *John Steinbeck — Salinas Kara
         Sekai Ni Mukete (John Steinbeck: From Salinas to the
         World)*. Tokyo: Gaku Shobo, 1992. (a translation of the
         author's original essay in *John Steinbeck: From Salinas*

to the World. ed. Tetsumaro Hayashi, Richard Peterson, and Shigeharu Yano. Tokyo: Gaku Shobo, 1986)

3318 Ariki, Kyoko, Yasuo Hashiguchi, and Yoshifumi Kato, trans. "Steinbeck, Faulkner Soshite Buddhism," (Steinbeck, Faulkner and Buddhism) by Kingo Hanamoto in *John Steinbeck — Salinas Kara Sekai Ni Mukete (John Steinbeck: From Salinas to the World).* Tokyo: Gaku Shobo, 1992. (a translation of the author's original essay in *John Steinbeck: From Salinas to the World.* ed. Tetsumaro Hayashi, Richard Peterson, and Shigeharu Yano. Tokyo: Gaku Shobo, 1986)

3319 Ariki, Kyoko, Yasuo Hashiguchi, and Yoshifumi Kato, trans. "Steinbeck No Eiga," (Steinbeck's Films) by Robert Morsberger in *John Steinbeck — Salinas Kara Sekai Ni Mukete (John Steinbeck: From Salinas to the World).* Tokyo: Gaku Shobo, 1992. (a translation of the author's original essay in *John Steinbeck: From Salinas to the World.* ed. Tetsumaro Hayashi, Richard Peterson, and Shigeharu Yano. Tokyo: Gaku Shobo, 1986)

3320 Ariki, Kyoko, Yasuo Hashiguchi, and Yoshifumi Kato, trans. "Steinbeck no Sakuhin Ni Okeru Indo Shiso," (Indian Thought in Steinbeck's Works) by M. R. Satyanarayana in *John Steinbeck — Salinas Kara Sekai Ni Mukete (John Steinbeck: From Salinas to the World).* Tokyo: Gaku Shobo, 1992. (a translation of the author's original essay in *John Steinbeck: From Salinas to the World.* ed. Tetsumaro Hayashi, Richard Peterson, and Shigeharu Yano. Tokyo: Gaku Shobo, 1986)

3321 Ariki, Kyoko, Yasuo Hashiguchi, and Yoshifumi Kato, trans. "Steinbeck to Monterey — 'Monterey Sanbusaku' ni Okeru Theme and Humor," (Steinbeck and Monterey: Theme and Humor in "The Monterey Trilogy") by Noburu Shimomura in *John Steinbeck — Salinas Kara Sekai Ni Mukete (John Steinbeck: From Salinas to the*

World). Tokyo: Gaku Shobo, 1992. (a translation of the
author's original essay in *John Steinbeck: From Salinas
to the World.* ed. Tetsumaro Hayashi, Richard Peterson,
and Shigeharu Yano. Tokyo: Gaku Shobo, 1986)

3322   Ariki, Kyoko, Yasuo Hashiguchi, and Yoshifumi Kato, trans.
        "Tortilla Flat — Saihoyo No Kokorami," (*Tortilla Flat*:
        A Re-Evaluation) by Rajul Bhargava in *John Steinbeck
        — Salinas Kara Sekai Ni Mukete (John Steinbeck: From
        Salinas to the World).* Tokyo: Gaku Shobo, 1992. (a
        translation of the author's original essay in *John
        Steinbeck: From Salinas to the World.* ed. Tetsumaro
        Hayashi, Richard Peterson, and Shigeharu Yano. Tokyo:
        Gaku Shobo, 1986)

3323   Ariki, Kyoko, Ikuko Kawata, and Wakako Kakegawa, trans.
        "Akai kouma: no monogatarigun ni okeru 'Dairenpo' no
        ichi to sono juyousei ni tsuite," (The Place and
        Importance of "The Great Mountains" in *The Red Pony*
        Cycle) by Roy Simmonds in *Sutainbekku Kenkyu:
        Atarashii Tanpen Shousetsushu (Steinbeck Studies: New
        Essays on Short Stories).* Osaka Japan: Osaka Educational
        Publishing Co., 1995. (pp. 61-82) (a reprint of the
        author's original essay of the same title which appeared in
        Steinbeck's "The Red Pony": Essays in Criticism. ed.
        Tetsumaro Hayashi and Thomas J. Moore. Steinbeck
        Monograph Series, No. 13. Muncie, Ind.: Steinbeck
        Research Institute, Ball State University Press, 1988. (pp.
        17-27))

3324   Ariki, Kyoko, Ikuko Kawata, and Wakako Kakegawa, trans.
        "Chiisana monogatari: Sutainbekku no 'Jikeidanin,'"
        ("The Little Bit of a Story": Steinbeck's "The Vigilante')
        by Louis Owens in *Sutainbekku Kenkyu: Atarashii
        Tanpen Shousetsushu* (*Steinbeck Studies: New Essays on
        Short Stories).* Osaka: Osaka Educational Publishing,
        1995. (pp. 251-262)) (reprinted from *Steinbeck's Short
        Stories* in *"The Long Valley": Essays in Criticism.* ed.

Tetsumaro Hayashi. Steinbeck Monograph Series, No. 15. Muncie, Ind.: Steinbeck Research Institute, Ball State University Press, 1991. (pp. 49-53))

3325 Ariki, Kyoko, Ikuko Kawata, and Wakako Kakegawa, trans. "Eriku Erikuson to Jon Sutainbekku no deai: 'Okurimono' ni okeru shinri shakai gakuteki hattatsu," (Erik Ericson Meets John Steinbeck: Psycho-Social Development in "The Gift") by Thom Tammaro in *Sutainbekku Kenkyu: Atarashii Tanpen Shousetsushu (Steinbeck Studies: New Essays on Short Stories).* Osaka Japan: Osaka Educational Publishing Co., 1995. (pp. 21-42) (a reprint of the author's original essay of the same title which appeared in *Steinbeck's "The Red Pony": Essays in Criticism.* ed. Tetsumaro Hayashi and Thomas J. Moore. Steinbeck Monograph Series, No. 13. Muncie, Ind.: Steinbeck Research Institute, Ball State University Press, 1988. (pp. 1-9))

3326 Ariki, Kyoko, Ikuko Kawata, and Wakako Kakegawa, trans. "'Hebi' to sono ijousei," ("The Snake" and Its Anomalous Nature) by Robert M. Benton in *Sutainbekku Kenkyu: Atarashii Tanpen Shousetsushu (Steinbeck Studies: New Essays on Short Stories).* Osaka: Osaka Educational Publishing, 1995. (pp. 195-211) (reprinted from *Steinbeck's Short Stories in "The Long Valley": Essays in Criticism.* ed. Tetsumaro Hayashi. Steinbeck Monograph Series, No. 15. Muncie, Ind.: Steinbeck Research Institute, Ball State University Press, 1991. (pp. 26-31))

3327 Ariki, Kyoko, Ikuko Kawata, and Wakako Kakegawa, trans. "Henja maegaki," (Preface) by Tetsumaro Hayashi in *Sutainbekku Kenkyu: Atarashii Tanpen Shousetsushu (Steinbeck Studies: New Essays on Short Stories).* Osaka: Osaka Educational Publishing, 1995. (pp. 115-118)) (reprinted from *Steinbeck's Short Stories in "The Long Valley": Essays in Criticism.* ed. Tetsumaro Hayashi. Steinbeck Monograph Series, No. 15. Muncie, Ind.:

Steinbeck Research Institute, Ball State University Press, 1991. (pp. ix-x))

3328   Ariki, Kyoko, Ikuko Kawata, and Wakako Kakegawa, trans. "Henja maegaki," (Preface) by Tetsumaro Hayashi in *Sutainbekku Kenkyu: Atarashii Tanpen Shousetsushu (Steinbeck Studies: New Essays on Short Stories).* Osaka Japan: Osaka Educational Publishing Co., 1995. (pp. 3-6) (a reprint of the author's original essay of the same title which appeared in *Steinbeck's "The Red Pony": Essays in Criticism.* ed. Tetsumaro Hayashi and Thomas J. Moore. Steinbeck Monograph Series, No. 13. Muncie, Ind.: Steinbeck Research Institute, Ball State University Press, 1988. (pp. vii-viii))

3329   Ariki, Kyoko, Ikuko Kawata, and Wakako Kakegawa, trans. "Hitobito o hikiiru mono: Shounen no 'Kokoro aru ningen' eno seihyo," ("The Leader of the People": A Boy Becomes a Mench) by Mimi Reisel Gladstein in *Sutainbekku Kenkyu: Atarashii Tanpen Shousetsushu (Steinbeck Studies: New Essays on Short Stories).* Osaka Japan: Osaka Educational Publishing Co., 1995. (pp. 83-112) (a reprint of the author's original essay of the same title which appeared in *Steinbeck's "The Red Pony": Essays in Criticism.* ed. Tetsumaro Hayashi and Thomas J. Moore. Steinbeck Monograph Series, No. 13. Muncie, Ind.: Steinbeck Research Institute, Ball State University Press, 1988. (pp. 27-37))

3330   Ariki, Kyoko, Ikuko Kawata, and Wakako Kakegawa, trans. "Jobun," (Introduction) by Warren French in *Sutainbekku Kenkyu: Atarashii Tanpen Shousetsushu (Steinbeck Studies: New Essays on Short Stories).* Osaka Japan: Osaka Educational Publishing Co., 1995. (pp. 7-20) (a reprint of the author's original essay of the same title which appeared in *Steinbeck's "The Red Pony": Essays in Criticism.* ed. Tetsumaro Hayashi and Thomas J. Moore. Steinbeck Monograph Series, No. 13. Muncie,

Ind.: Steinbeck Research Institute, Ball State University Press, 1988. (pp. ix-xiv))

3331 Ariki, Kyoko, Ikuko Kawata, and Wakako Kakegawa, trans. "Jobun," (Introduction) by Warren French in *Sutainbekku Kenkyu: Atarashii Tanpen Shousetsushu (Steinbeck Studies: New Essays on Short Stories).* Osaka: Osaka Educational Publishing, 1995. (pp. 119-134)) (reprinted from *Steinbeck's Short Stories in "The Long Valley":Essays in Criticism.* ed. Tetsumaro Hayashi. Steinbeck Monograph Series, No. 15. Muncie, Ind.: Steinbeck Research Institute, Ball State University Press, 1991. (pp. xi-xvii))

3331A Ariki, Kyoko, Ikuko Kawata, and Wakako Kakegawa, trans. "'Kaji' to sono ijousei," ("The Snake" and Its Anomalous Nature) by Robert M. Benton in *Sutainbekku Kenkyu: Atarashii Tanpen Shousetsushu (Steinbeck Studies: New Essays on Short Stories).* Osaka: Osaka Educational Publishing, 1995. (pp. 195-211) (reprinted from *Steinbeck's Short Stories in "The Long Valley": Essays in Criticism.* ed. Tetsumaro Hayashi. Steinbeck Monograph Series, No. 15. Muncie, Ind.: Steinbeck Research Institute, Ball State University Press, 1991. (pp. 26-31))

3332 Ariki, Kyoko, Ikuko Kawata, and Wakako Kakegawa, trans. "'Kiku': Sutainbekku no "Pigumarion," ("The Chrysanthemums": Steinbeck's *Pygmalion*) by Susan Shillinglaw in *Sutainbekku Kenkyu: Atarashii Tanpen Shousetsushu (Steinbeck Studies: New Essays on Short Stories).* Osaka: Osaka Educational Publishing, 1995. (pp. 135-157) (reprinted from *Steinbeck's Short Stories in "The Long Valley": Essays in Criticism.* ed. Tetsumaro Hayashi. Steinbeck Monograph Series, No. 15. Muncie, Ind.: Steinbeck Research Institute, Ball State University Press, 1991. (pp. 1-9))

3333 Ariki, Kyoko, Ikuko Kawata, and Wakako Kakegawa, trans. "Kotoba ni Kawaru shocho no kazukazu 'Chosuku' ni okeru Sutainbekku no mugon no messeji," ("Symbols for The Wordlessness": Steinbeck's Silent Message in "Breakfast") by Michael J. Meyer in *Sutainbekku Kenkyu: Atarashii Tanpen Shousetsushu (Steinbeck Studies: New Essays on Short Stories)*. Osaka: Osaka Educational Publishing, 1995. (pp. 211-224) (reprinted from *Steinbeck's Short Stories in "The Long Valley": Essays in Criticism*. ed. Tetsumaro Hayashi. Steinbeck Monograph Series, No. 15. Muncie, Ind.: Steinbeck Research Institute, Ball State University Press, 1991. (pp. 10-17))

3334 Ariki, Kyoko, Ikuko Kawata, and Wakako Kakegawa, trans. "'Kuko' no imino tsuikyuu," (A Search for Meaning in "Flight") by Robert M. Benton in *Sutainbekku Kenkyu: Atarashii Tanpen Shousetsushu (Steinbeck Studies: New Essays on Short Stories)*. Osaka: Osaka Educational Publishing, 1995. (pp. 177-194) (reprinted from *Steinbeck's Short Stories in "The Long Valley": Essays in Criticism*. ed. Tetsumaro Hayashi. Steinbeck Monograph Series, No. 15. Muncie, Ind.: Steinbeck Research Institute, Ball State University Press, 1991. (pp. 18-25))

3335 Ariki, Kyoko, Ikuko Kawata, and Wakako Kakegawa, trans. "Kuroi Itosugi to midori iro no oke: Sutainbekku no 'Yakusoku' ni okeru shi to seishoku," (The Black Cypress and the Green Tub: Death and Procreation in Steinbeck's "The Promise") by Robert S. Hughes in *Sutainbekku Kenkyu: Atarashii Tampen Shousetsushu (Steinbeck Studies: New Essays on Short Stories)*. Osaka Japan: Osaka Educational Publishing Co., 1995. (pp. 43-60) (a reprint of the author's original essay of the same title which appeared in *Steinbeck's "The Red Pony": Essays in Criticism*. ed. Tetsumaro Hayashi and Thomas J. Moore. Steinbeck Monograph Series, No. 13. Muncie, Ind.: Steinbeck Research Institute, Ball State University Press, 1988. (pp. 9-16))

3336 Ariki, Kyoko, Ikuko Kawata, and Wakako Kakegawa, trans.
"'Rakuen no genso' : Shougeki ni mirareru sekkyokuteki
kanyo no yukousei to gisei," ("The Illusion of Eden":
Efficacious Commitment and Sacrifice in "The Raid") by
Michael J. Meyer in *Sutainbekku Kenkyu: Atarashii
Tanpen Shousetsushu* (*Steinbeck Studies: New Essays on
Short Stories*). Osaka: Osaka Educational Publishing,
1995. (pp. 225-240) (reprinted from *Steinbeck's Short
Stories in "The Long Valley": Essays in Criticism*. ed.
Tetsumaro Hayashi. Steinbeck Monograph Series, No. 15.
Muncie, Ind.: Steinbeck Research Institute, Ball State
University Press, 1991. (pp. 32-37))

3337 Ariki, Kyoko, Ikuko Kawata, and Wakako Kakegawa, trans.
"Seisabetsu to Jinshu sabetsuka, soretomo Aironi ka
Sutainbekku no 'Satsujin,'" (Sexism and Racism, or
Irony? Steinbeck's "The Murder") by Patricia M. Mandia
in *Sutainbekku Kenkyu: Atarashii Tanpen Shousetsushu*
(*Steinbeck Studies: New Essays on Short Stories*). Osaka:
Osaka Educational Publishing, 1995. (pp. 283-298))
(reprinted from *Steinbeck's Short Stories in "The Long
Valley": Essays in Criticism*. ed. Tetsumaro Hayashi.
Steinbeck Monograph Series, No. 15. Muncie, Ind.:
Steinbeck Research Institute, Ball State University Press,
1991. (pp. 62-69))

3338 Ariki, Kyoko, Ikuko Kawata, and Wakako Kakegawa, trans.
"'Seishoujo Keiti': Sutainbekku no himerareta kokorono
kagi," ("Saint Katy the Virgin": The Key to Steinbeck's
Secret Heart) by Thom Tammaro in *Sutainbekku Kenyu:
Atarashii Tanpen Shousetsushu (Steinbeck Studies: New
Essays on Short Stories)*. Osaka Japan: Osaka Educational
Publishing Co., 1995. (pp. 299-318) (a reprint of the
author's original essay of the same title which appeared in
*Steinbeck's Short Stories in "The Long Valley": Essays in
Criticism*. ed. Tetsumaro Hayashi. Steinbeck Monograph
Series, No. 15. Muncie, Ind.: Steinbeck Research
Institute, Ball State University Press, 1991. (pp. 70-78))

3339   Ariki, Kyoko, Ikuko Kawata, and Wakako Kakegawa, trans.
        "'Shiroi uzura' no Eden no higashi ni okeru kosei to
        kyosei," (Pure and Corrupt: Agency and Communion in
        the Edenic Garden of "The White Quail") by Michael J.
        Meyer in *Sutainbekku Kenkyu: Atarashii Tanpen
        Shousetsushu (Steinbeck Studies: New Essays on Short
        Stories)*. Osaka: Osaka Educational Publishing, 1995. (pp.
        157-176)) (reprinted from *Steinbeck's Short Stories in
        "The Long Valley": Essays in Criticism*. ed. Tetsumaro
        Hayashi. Steinbeck Monograph Series, No. 15. Muncie,
        Ind.: Steinbeck Research Institute, Ball State University
        Press, 1991. (pp. 38- 44))

3340   Ariki, Kyoko, Ikuko Kawata, and Wakako Kakegawa, trans.
        "Sutainbekku 'Joni Bea' ni okeru Konton to Aku soshite
        shunsetsusen no wakisuji," (Chaos, Evil and the Dredger
        Subplot in Steinbeck's "Johnny Bear") by Patricia M.
        Mandia in *Sutainbekku Kenkyu: Atarashii Tanpen
        Shousetsushu (Steinbeck Studies: New Essays on Short
        Stories)*. Osaka: Osaka Educational Publishing, 1995. (pp.
        263-282)) (reprinted from *Steinbeck's Short Stories in
        "The Long Valley": Essays in Criticism*. ed. Tetsumaro
        Hayashi. Steinbeck Monograph Series, No. 15. Muncie,
        Ind.: Steinbeck Research Institute, Ball State University
        Press, 1991. (pp. 54-62))

3341   Ariki, Kyoko, Ikuko Kawata, and Wakako Kakegawa, trans.
        "Tanpen sakka Sutainbekku," (Steinbeck, the Short Story
        Writer) by Robert S. Hughes, Jr. in *Sutainbekku Kenkyu:
        Atarashii Tanpen Shousetsushu (Steinbeck Studies: New
        Essays on Short Stories)*. Osaka: Osaka Educational
        Publishing, 1995. (pp. 319-344)) (reprinted from
        *Steinbeck's Short Stories in "The Long Valley": Essays in
        Criticism*. ed. Tetsumaro Hayashi. Steinbeck Monograph
        Series, No. 15. Muncie, Ind.: Steinbeck Research
        Institute, Ball State University Press, 1991. (pp. 78-89))

3342 Ariki, Kyoko, Ikuko Kawata, and Wakako Kakegawa, trans. "Teichi to kouchi: Sutainbekku no 'Shimegu' no kintou no toreta otoko," ("Bottom and Upland": The Balanced Man in Steinbeck's "The Harness") by Louis Owens in *Sutainbekku Kenkyu: Atarashii Tanpen Shousetsushu* (*Steinbeck Studies: New Essays on Short Stories).* Osaka: Osaka Educational Publishing, 1995. (pp. 241-250)) (reprinted from *Steinbeck's Short Stories in "The Long Valley": Essays in Criticism.* ed. Tetsumaro Hayashi. Steinbeck Monograph Series, No. 15. Muncie, Ind.: Steinbeck Research Institute, Ball State University Press, 1991. (pp. 44-48))

3342A Ariki, Kyoko, Ikuko Kawata, and Wakako Kakegawa, trans. "'Touso' no imino tsuikyuu," (A Search for Meaning in "Flight") by Robert M. Benton in *Steinbekku Kenkyu: Atarashii Tanpen Shousetsushu* (*Steinbeck Studies: New Essays on Short Stories).* Osaka: Osaka Educational Publishing, 1995. (pp. 177-194) (reprinted from *Steinbeck's Short Stories in "The Long Valley": Essays in Criticism.* ed. Tetsumaro Hayashi. Steinbeck Monograph Series, No. 15. Muncie, Ind.: Steinbeck Research Institute, Ball State University Press, 1991. (pp. 18-25))

3343 Asano, Toshio. "Sutainbekku kenkyu-yowa futatsu," *Kyou-en,* 8 (Kirisutokyo tanki daigaku eibun gakkai, Spring 1982), 4-6.

3344 Belov, S. "Zima trevogi Dzhona Steinbeka," (John Steinbeck's *Winter of Discontent*) *Literaturnae Obozrenie, Moscow,* 11 (1982), 83-86.

3345 Bianchi, Ruggero. "Interfuit il testo imperfetto *Of Mice and Men* e il modello del play-novelette," (The Imperfect Text of *Of Mice and Men* as a Play/Novelette) *Letterature d'America Revista Trimestrale,* 4:17 (Spring 1983), 71-108.

3346   Bozzola, Sergio. "Note su Pavese e Vittorini traduttori di
        Steinbeck," (Note on Pavese and Vittorini, translators of
        Steinbeck) *Studi Novecenteschi Revista Semestrale di
        Storia della Letteratura Italiana Contemporanea, Agnano
        Pisano Italy,* 18:41 (June 1991), 63-101.

3347   Breines, Ron. "Steinbeck's Great Depressions: A Review of
        John Steinbeck, A Biography by Jay Parini," *The Daily
        Yomiuri,* May 15, 1994, 8(A).

3348   Calzone, Sergio. "Le traduzioni di Vittorini: Mediazione o
        riscrittura?" (The Translations of Vittorini: Mediation or
        Rewriting) *Iptotesi - 80; Riviste Quadrimestrale di
        Cultura Cosenza Italy,* 15-16 (1985-1986), 50-57.

3349   Chiba, Tsuyoshi. "*Of Mice and Men* to Baanzu no shi," (*Of
        Mice and Men* and Burns's Poem) in *Tokyo nogyodaigaku
        ippan Kyouikujutsu shuho* (*Tokyo Agricultural University
        General Education Bulletin),* 20 (March 1990), 16-22.

3350   Chida, Akio. "Sutainbekku no *Shirarezaru Kami e*: Sakuhin ni
        mirareru ikyouseishin," (Steinbeck's *To a God Unknown*:
        Paganism Seen in the Work) *Toho Gakuen Junior College
        Bulletin,* 2 (October 1983), 1-14.

3351   Chikamatsu, Junko. "Jon *Sutainbekku* no egaku josei-tachi,"
        (John Steinbeck's Portrayal of Females) *Kansai Eigo
        Eibungaku Kenkyu Kai* (*Kansai Review* — Kansai English
        Literature Study Society), 5 (November 1985), 65-73.

3352   Cruz, Adina. "Similitud y contraste en las novelas Huasipungo
        y *The Pearl*," (Similarities and Contrasts in the Novels of
        Huasipungo to *The Pearl*) *Kanina: Revista dee Artes y
        Letras de la Universidad da Costa Rica, San Jose Costa
        Rica,* 4:2 (July-December 1980), 109-115.

3353   Diankov, Krustan. "Viara v mazolestite rutse," *Literaturen Front: Organ na Suiuza na Bulgarskite Pisateli, Sofia Bulgaria,* 38 (March 18, 1882), 8, 11.

3354   Egusa, Hisachi. *"Akai Kouma," (The Red Pony)* in *Steinbeck Kenkyu: Tanpen Shosetsu Ron.* ed. Hisachi Egusa. Tokyo: Yashio Shuppan-sha, 1987. (pp. 186-193)

3355   Egusa, Hisachi. "Bunkaron Sutainbekku no *Akai Kouma,*" (Cultural Studies in Steinbeck's *The Red Pony*) *Hokkaidou Shinbun Yukan* (July 6, 1987), 4.

3356   Egusa, Hisachi. "Choshoko," (Breakfast) in *Steinbeck Kenkyu: Tanpen Shosetsu Ron.* ed. Hisachi Egusa. Tokyo: Yashio Shuppan-sha, 1987. (pp. 81-88)

3357   Egusa, Hisachi. "Kiku," (The Chrysanthemums) in *Steinbeck Kenkyu: Tanpen Shosetsu Ron.* ed. Hisachi Egusa. Tokyo: Yashio Shuppan-sha, 1987. (pp. 9-22)

3358   Egusa, Hisachi. "Maegaki," (Preface) in *Sutainbekku Kenkyu — Tanpen Shosetsu Ron.* ed. Hisachi Egusa. Tokyo: Yashio Shuppan-sha, 1987. (pp. i-iv)

3359   Egusa, Hisachi. "Nagai Bonchi," *(The Long Valley)* in *Steinbeck Kenkyu: Tanpen Shosetsu Ron.* ed. Hisachi Egusa. Tokyo: Yashio Shuppan-sha, 1987. (pp. 3-8)

3360   Egusa, Hisachi. *"The Red Pony* Saidoku shikai no ji," *Kaihou,* 5 (May 1982), 2.

3361   Egusa, Hisachi. "Review of Kiyoshi Nakayama's *Sutainbekku Bungaku no Kenkyu — Kariforunia Jidai,*" (*Steinbeck's Writing: The California Years* by Kiyoshi Nakayama) *America bungaku kenkyu —* Nihon America Bungaku kai, 27 (February 25, 1991), 150-155.

3362   Egusa, Hisachi. "Shiroi Uzura," (The White Quail) in *Sutainbekku Kenkyu: Tanpen Shosetsu Ron.* ed. Hisachi Egusa. Tokyo: Yashio Shuppan-sha, 1987. (pp. 23-45)

3363   Egusa, Hisachi. "Sutainbekku kenkyu no shinryoiki — Dai
        sankai Kokusai Sutainbekku gakkai kara," (A New Realm
        of the Steinbeck Studies: A Report of the Third
        International Steinbeck Conference) *Eigo Seinen*, 136: 6
        (September 1, 1990), 290-291.

3364   Egusa, Hisachi. "Sutainbekku no *Akai Kouma*," (Steinbeck's
        The Red Pony) *Hokkaido Shinbun* (The Evening Edition),
        July 6, 1987, 4.

3365   Egusa, Hisachi, and Mitsuo Kato. "Sutainbekku Nenpu,"
        (Steinbeck's Chronology) in *Sutainbekku Kenkyu —
        Tanpen shosetsu-ron*. ed. Hisachi Egusa. Tokyo: Yashio
        Shuppan-sha, 1987. (pp. 249-257)

3366   Frank, Arain Paul. "'Langsachsen': Ein in der Textlinguistik
        vernachlassigtes Problem der literarischen Ubersetzung;
        Akten des International ubersetsungswiss," in
        Textlinguistik und Fachsprache. ed. Reiner Arnst.
        Hildesheim: Olms, 1988. (pp. 485-497)

3367   Fujisaki, Matsuo. "Eimi wa nani o akirikani suruka: bunkaron
        ni okeru Sutainbekku no 'Joni Bea,'" (What Amy
        Reveals: Steinbeck's "Johnny Bear" in the Cultural
        Context) *Eigo Eibungaku Ronshuu - Kyushu Daigaku
        Eigo Eibungaku Kenkyukai* (*Studies in English Language
        and Literature - Kyushu University*), 41 (February 1991),
        73-82.

3368   Fujita, Eiichi. "Jon Sutainbekku no *"Ikari no Budou"* — Hito
        no Ronri to Kinson no Ronri," (John Steinbeck's *The
        Grapes of Wrath*: Man's Logic and the Logic of
        Capitalism) in *Amerikajin to Bunkateki Dento (Americans
        and the Cultural Tradition)*. Osaka: Sogensha, 1991. (pp.
        153-200)

3369   Fukazawa, Toshio. "*Akai Kouma* Ni Okeru Shudai Ni Tsuite,"
        (On the Theme of *The Red Pony*) *Tokyo Rissho Jyoshi*

Tanki Daigaku Kiyo (Tokyo Rissho Women's Junior College Bulletin), 10 (March 1982), 44-55.

3370   Fukazawa, Toshio. *"East of Eden* ni okeru zenaku to aizo ni tsuite: Adamu to Kyashii o chushin ni," (On the Good/Evil and Love/Hatred Dualities in *East of Eden*: Centering around Adam and Cathy) *Shotoku daigaku jimbungakubu Kenkyu Kiyo (Shotoku University, Faculty of Humanities Bulletin)*, 1 (December 15, 1990), 119-127.

3371   Fukazawa, Toshio. *"Ikari no Budo* ni okeru jinluishugi," (Humanism in *The Grapes of Wrath*) *Seitoku University Jimbun Gakubu Bulletin*, 3 (December 15, 1992), 127-37.

3372   Fukazawa, Toshio. *"Kanzume Yokocho* Ni Tsuite Doc to Mac No Ningenzo," (On *Cannery Row*: Portraits of Doc and Mac) *Tokyo Rissho Jyoshi Tanki Daigaku Kiyo (Tokyo Risho Women's Junior College Bulletin)*, 11 (February 28, 1983), 27-41.

3373   Fukazawa, Toshio. "On Paisanos in *Tortilla Flat*: What Danny Signifies," *Bulletin of the Faculty of Dentistry, Nippon University*, 9 (1981), 10-16.

3374   Fukazawa, Toshio. "Steinbeck to warai: *Tortilla Flat* ni Tsuite," (Steinbeck and Laughter: On *Tortilla Flat*) *Tokyo Rissho Jyoshi Tanki Daigaku Kiyo (Tokyo Risho Women's Junior College Bulletin)*, 15 (February 1987), 39-49.

3375   Fukuzawa, Toshio. "Sutainbekku no tanpenshu: 'Kiku' to 'Shiroi Uzura' ni okeru shujinkouzou," (On the Protagonists' Images in Steinbeck's Short Stories "The Chrysanthemums" and "The White Quail") *Journal of Tokyo English and American Literature Society*, 4 (June 20, 1993), 41-52.

3376   Fukazawa, Toshio. "*Tengoku no sougen* no kousei to buntai ni
        tsuite," (On the Structure and Style of *The Pastures of
        Heaven) Shotuku University, Faculty of Humanities
        Bulletin,* 5 (December 15, 1994), 153-159.

3377   Fukazawa, Toshio. "*Utagawashiki tatakai* ni okeru
        Sutainbekku no nerai," (Steinbeck's Aim in *In Dubious
        Battle) Tokyo Eibei Bungaku Kenkyu kai kiyou Bulletin,* 1
        (March 1987), 50-60.

3378   Furubeppu, Hizuru. "Jon Sutainbekku no yoru *Shinju* no
        kenkyu — Kino no tamashii no hensen ni miru shinju
        hoki no imi," (The Study of *The Pearl* by John Steinbeck
        — the Meaning of Abandonment of the Pearl in Kino's
        Change in His Soul) *Kagoshima Junshin Joshi Tanki
        Daigaku Kenkyu Kiyou (Kagoshima Junshin Women's
        Junior College Study Bulletin),* 16 (January 1986), 123-
        132.

3379   Furutani, Saburo. "Sutainbekku ni miru hiroin no keizu —
        Tanpen ni miru futa josei," (Genealogy of Steinbeck's
        Heroine — Two Females from the Short Stories) *Seitoku
        Gakuen Tanki Daigaku Kiyo (Bulletin of Seitoku Gakuen
        Junior College),* 18 (December 1985), 205-213.

3380   Furuya, Kazuko. "*Cotezukai no Sutainbekku* to no kenkyu,"
        (Review of *With Steinbeck in the Sea of Cortez* by Sparky
        Enea as told to Audry Lynch) *Jimukyoku Dayori
        (Steinbeck Newsletter in Japanese),* 14 (November 10,
        1992), 3-4.

3381   Furuya, Kazuko. "Steinbeck no *Charley tono tabi*,"
        (Steinbeck's *Travels with Charley) Shi to Sanbun no Kai
        (Poetry and Prose),* 51 (March 10, 1992), 45-54.

3382   Georgoudaki, Katia. "Chronologio John Steinbeck,"
        (Chronology of John Steinbeck) *Diavazo,* 173 (September
        2, 1987), 14-19.

3383   Georgoudaki, Katia. "John Steinbeck: Kiria logotechnica erga
        ke kritikes apopsis," (John Steinbeck: Main Critical
        Approaches) *Diavazo,* 173 (September 2, 1987), 20-28.

3384   Grojnowski, Daniel, et al. "Des enfants, Des souris et des
        hommes, ou l'utilisation en classe d'un texte de Steinbeck:
        Homage a Pierre Albuoy," (The Children, the Mice and the
        Men or the Utilization of Class in the Text of John
        Steinbeck: In Recognition of Pierre Albuoy) in *Recherches
        en sciences des textes.* ed. Yves Gohin and Robert Ricatte.
        Grenoble: University of Grenoble, 1977. (pp. 169-179)

3385   Hagenbuchle, Helen. "Die Kainsgeschichte in *East of Eden:*
        John Steinbeck's Pladoyer fur Selbstverantwortung und
        Selbstverwirklichung," (Cain's history in *East of Eden*:
        John Steinbeck's Speech for Self-Responsibility and Self-
        Worth) in *Paradigmata, Literarische Typologie des Alten
        Testaments.* ed. Franz Link. Berlin: Duncker and
        Humblot, 1989. (pp. 629-651)

3386   Hagiwara, Tsutomu. "Sutainbekku to warai — *Pippen Yonsei
        no tankeitouchi* o chushin ni," (Steinbeck and Laughter
        — Centering on *The Short Reign of Pippen IV*) *Senshu
        University of Humanities Bulletin*, 39 (February 1987),
        97-125.

3387   Hamaguchi, Osamu. "Review of *Sutainbekku Zen Tampen
        Ron: Akai Kouma wo Koete,"* (Essays on All of
        Steinbeck's Short Stories: Beyond "The Red Pony") trans.
        Kiyohiko Tsuboi and Fumio Momose in *Jimukyoku
        Dayori (Steinbeck Newsletter)*, 12 (November 15, 1991),
        4-5.

3388   Hamaguchi, Osamu. "Sutainbekku no 'Kiku' o yomu,"
        (Reading Steinbeck's 'The Chrysanthemums') *Hiroshima
        Daigaku Gakko Kyouiku Gakubu Kiyou (Hiroshima
        University School Education Department Bulletin)* Part II,
        9 (December 1985), 25-33.

3389   Hamaguchi, Osamu. "Sutainbekku no *Utagawashiki tatakai Kenkyu*," (Steinbeck's *In Dubious Battle* Study) *Chu-Shikoku Studies in American Literature*, 20 (June 20, 1984), 77-87.

3390   Hamaguchi, Osamu. "*Utagawashiki tatakai* ni okeru Sutainebekku no kenkyu," (A Study of Steinbeck's *In Dubious Battle*) *Chu-Shikoku Studies in American Literature*, 20 (March 1984), 77-87.

3391   Hamaguchi, Osamu. "Yakusha Atogaki," (Translator's Afterword) in *John Sutainbekku — Sariinasu kara Sekai ni mukete*. trans. Osamu Hamaguchi, Kyoko Ariki, and Yoshifumi Kato. Tokyo: Oushisha, 1992. (pp. 339-340)

3392   Hashiguchi, Yasuo. "'Boss wa shoyusha ka?' 'Iya, Kantokuda,'" ("Boss the Owner?"/ "Naw, Superintendent") *Studies in English Language and English and American Literature*, (Yasuda Women's University), 4 (February 1, 1995), 67-73.

3393   Hashiguchi, Yasuo. "Kenyu no Genkyu to Kadai: Steinbeck," (Steinbeck Studies in Japan: Present and Future) *Eigo Seinen* (*The Rising Generation*), 128:6 (September 1982), 354-56.

3394   Hashiguchi, Yasuo. "Review of *Steinbeck's Travel Literature*. (1985) ed. Tetsumaro Hayashi, trans. Mikio Inui," *Kyushu American Literature*, 27 (September 1986), 26-27.

3395   Hashiguchi, Yasuo. "Steinbeck and Three Japanese," in *Sutainnbekku Sakka Sakuhin Ron (Steinbeck and His Works: a Festschrift in Honor of Dr. Tetsumaro Hayashi)*. ed. Eiko Shiraga and Yasuo Hashiguchi. Tokyo: Eihosha, 1995. (pp. 141-154)

3396   Hashiguchi, Yasuo. "Steinbeck ni okeru Josei tachi: Uwaki
       onna ni tsuite," (Steinbeck's Women: On So Called
       "Flirts") *Studies in English and American Literature and
       Language* (Yasuda Women's University), 33 (February
       1994), 131-40.

3397   Hashiguchi, Yasuo. "Sutainbekku — Bungakuteki Kenkyu
       genjo to kadai," (Steinbeck — Literary Research: Status
       Quo and Future Problems Column) Special Number in
       Eigo Seinen (*The Rising Generation*), 130 (June 10,
       1984), 118-20.

3398   Hashiguchi, Yasuo, Kyoko Ariki, and Yoshifumi Kato, trans.
       "Futari No Jody — Steinbeck and Rawlings," (Two
       Jodys: Steinbeck and Rawlings) by Kiyohiko Tsuboi in
       *John Steinbeck — Salinas Kara Sekai Ni Mukete (John
       Steinbeck: From Salinas to the World).* See #3311.

3399   Hashiguchi, Yasuo, Kyoko Ariki, and Yoshifumi Kato, trans.
       "Gekisakka Steinbeck — Jyoron," (Steinbeck as
       Dramatist: A Preliminary Account) by John Ditsky in
       *John Steinbeck — Salinas Kara Sekai Ni Mukete (John
       Steinbeck: From Salinas to the World).* See #3312.

3400   Hashiguchi, Yasuo, Kyoko Ariki, and Yoshifumi Kato, trans.
       "John Steinbeck: Salinas Kara Sekai Ni Mukete," (John
       Steinbeck: From Salinas to the World). by Warren
       French in *John Steinbeck — Salinas Kara Sekai Ni
       Mukete (John Steinbeck: From Salinas to the World)* See
       #3313.

3401   Hashiguchi, Yasuo, Kyoko Ariki, and Yoshifumi Kato, trans.
       "John Steinbeck — Sosaku Ron," (John Steinbeck and
       His Concept of Writing) by Tetsumaro Hayashi in *John
       Steinbeck — Salinas Kara Sekai Ni Mukete (John
       Steinbeck: From Salinas to the World).* See #3314.

3402   Hashiguchi, Yasuo, Kyoko Ariki and Yoshifumi Kato, trans.
       "John Steinbeck to Kawabata Yasanari," (John Steinbeck
       and Yasanari Kawabata) by Kiyoshi Nakayama in *John*

Steinbeck — Salinas Kara Sekai Ni Mukete (John Steinbeck: From Salinas to the World). See #3315.

3403   Hashiguchi, Yasuo, Kyoko Ariki, and Yoshifumi Kato, trans. "Lady Brett Kara Ma Joad: Josei No Ijyo Na Sukanasa" (From Lady Brett to Ma Joad: A Singular Scarcity) by Mimi Reisel Gladstein in *John Steinbeck — Salinas Kara Sekai Ni Mukete (John Steinbeck: From Salinas to the World).* See #3316.

3404   Hashiguchi, Yasuo, Kyoko Ariki, and Yoshifumi Kato, trans. "Nonsense No Heroine, Camille Oaks — *Kimagore Basu* Wo Saihyoko Suru," (Camille Oaks, A Heroine of Nonsense — A Reassessment of *The Wayward Bus)* by Takahiko Sugiyama in *John Steinbeck — Salinas Kara Sekai Ni Mukete (John Steinbeck: From Salinas to the World).* See #3317.

3405   Hashiguchi, Yasuo, Kyoko Ariki, and Yoshifumi Kato, trans. "Steinbeck, Faulkner Soshite Buddhism," (Steinbeck, Faulkner and Buddhism) by Kingo Hanamoto in *John Steinbeck — Salinas Kara Sekai Ni Mukete (John Steinbeck: From Salinas to the World).* See #3318.

3406   Hashiguchi, Yasuo, Kyoko Ariki, and Yoshifumi Kato, trans. "Steinbeck No Eiga," (Steinbeck's Films) by Robert Morsberger in *John Steinbeck — Salinas Kara Sekai Ni Mukete (John Steinbeck: From Salinas to the World).* See #3319.

3407   Hashiguchi, Yasuo, Kyoko Ariki, and Yoshifumi Kato, trans. "Steinbeck no Sakuhin Ni Okeru Indo Shiso," (Indian Thought in Steinbeck's Works) by M. R. Satyanarayana in *John Steinbeck — Salinas Kara Sekai Ni Mukete (John Steinbeck: From Salinas to the World).* See #3320.

3408   Hashiguchi, Yasuo, Kyoko Ariki, and Yoshifumi Kato, trans. "Steinbeck to Monterey — 'Monterey Sanbusaku' ni Okeru Theme and Humor," (Steinbeck and Monterey:

Theme and Humor in "The Monterey Trilogy") by Noburu Shimomura in *John Steinbeck — Salinas Kara Sekai Ni Mukete (John Steinbeck: From Salinas to the World)*. See #3321.

3409　Hashiguchi, Yasuo, Kyoko Ariki, and Yoshifumi Kato, trans. "*Tortilla Flat* — Saihoyo No Kokorami," (*Tortilla Flat*: A Re-Evaluation) by Rajul Bhargava in *John Steinbeck — Salinas Kara Sekai Ni Mukete (John Steinbeck: From Salinas to the World)*. See #3322.

3410　Hashikura, Satoshi. "Kiku," (The Chrysanthemums) *Kaishi, Nagano-ken Eigo Kenkyu Kai (Nagano Pref. English Study Society)*, 11 (1985), 71-73.

3411　Hashimoto, Fukuo. "Futatabi daimei ni tsuite," (About the Title Once Again) in *Chosakushu Dai III kan Eibei Bungaku Ron*. Tokyo: Hayakawa Shobo, 1989. (pp. 137-144) (*In Dubious Battle*)

3412　Hashimoto, Fukuo. "Kaisetsu: Steinbeck," (Interpretation: Steinbeck) in *Chosakushu Dai III kan Eibei Bungaku Ron*. Tokyo: Hayakawa Shobo, 1989. (pp. 123-133)

3413　Hashimoto, Fukuo. "Steinbeck ron," (Theory of Steinbeck) in *Chosakushu Dai III kan Eibei Bungaku Ron*. Tokyo: Hayakawa Shobo, 1989. (pp. 114-122)

3414　Hashimoto, Fukuo. "*Utagawashii tatakai*, toiu Daimei," (The Title '*In Dubious Battle*') in *Chosakushu Dai III kan Eibei Bungaku Ron*. Tokyo: Hayakawa Shobo, 1989. (pp. 134-136)

3415　Hayashi, Tetsumaro. "Jobun," (Preface) in *Sutainbekku no Joseizo (Steinbeck's Women)* ed. Mitsuaski Yamashita. Tokyo: Oshisha, 1991. (pp. 7-11)

3416　Hayashi, Tetsumaro. "Kageki *Eden no Higashi* ni tsuite," (Some Thoughts on the Musical Play, *East of Eden*) Play

Programme, *East of Eden* and *Dandyism,* Takarazuka
Grand Theater, June 30, 1995, 53.

3417　　Hayashi, Tetsumaro. "Nippon no Dokushae," (To the
Japanese Readers) in *Sutainbekku no Joseizo (Steinbeck's
Women).* ed. Mitsuaski Yamashita. Tokyo: Oshisha, 1991.
(pp. 1-2)

3418　　Hayashi, Tetsumaro. "Shoshi," (A Selected Bibliography) in
Sutainbekku no Joseizo (Steinbeck's Women). ed.
Mitsuaski Yamashita. Tokyo: Oshisha, 1991. (pp. 165-
169)

3419　　Hayashida, Eiji. "*Eden no Higashi* ni Okeru Sutainbekku no
Ningenkan," (Steinbeck's Concept of Man in *East of
Eden*) *Utopian Wandering Fellow,* 1 (October 27, 1988),
12-39.

3420　　Hayashida, Eiji. "Louis Owens's *Ikari No Budou: Yakusoku
no chi deno Sainan* no Kenkyu," (Review of Louis
Owens's *The Grapes of Wrath: Trouble in the Promised
Land) Jimukyoku Dayori,* 9 (July 20, 1990), 6-7.

3421　　Hayashida, Eiji. "Steinbeck no Shinjyu ni Okeru Kino no
Ninshiki no Arikata ni tsuite," (On Kino's Way of
Recognition in Steinbeck's *The Pearl) Utopian
Wandering Fellow,* 2 (April 1989), 54-59.

3422　　Hirose, Hidekazu. "Steinbeck no Fukei Byosha," (Steinbeck's
Landscape Descriptions) in *Sutainnbekku Sakka Sakuhin
Ron (Steinbeck and His Works: a Festschrift in Honor of
Dr. Tetsumaro Hayashi).* ed. Eiko Shiraga and Yasuo
Hashiguchi. Tokyo: Eihosha, 1995. (pp. 3-16)

3423　　Hirose, Hidekazu. "Steinbeck to 1930 nendai," (Steinbeck and
the 1930s) in *Those Who Learned American Literature.*
Kyoto: Sekaishisosha, 1987. (pp. 131-34)

3424　　Horbacheva, I. I. "Melori i Steinbek: Spadkoimnist" siuzhetu
pro korolia Artura," (Malory and Steinbeck: For King

Arthur) *Radians' ke Literaturoznavstvo: Naukovo Teoretychnyi Zhurnal,* Kiev Ukraine, 8 (August 1986), 59-64. (*The Acts of King Arthur and His Noble Knights*)

3425   Horiuchi, Toshikazu. "*Of Mice and Men* ni okeru nichi jo eigo — Amerika-eigo no ichi tokucho," (Conventional English in *Of Mice and Men* — Uniquely Distinctive Features of American English) *Aichi Shukutoku Daigaku Ronshu (Aichi Women's University Collected Discourses*), 13 (February 1988), 43-54.

3426   Horiuchi, Toshikazu. "Steinbeck no 'Kiku' no Oboegaki – Hyogen Giho to Kaishakujo no Mondaiten," (Steinbeck's "The Chrysanthemums" Memo — Expression Technique and Problems of Interpretation) *Aichi Shuntoku Daigaku Ronshu (Aichi Shuntoku University Bulletin),* 11 (March 1985), 161-171.

3427   Hozumi, Ken. "John Sutainbekku Toshokan (John Steinbeck Library) *Hakyu,* (Ichimura Gakuen Tanki Daigaku Toshokanhou), 16 (November 1988), 4-5.

3428   Ichinose, Kazuo. "Kaigai Shinchoran 90nendai ni Mukete : '89-'90 no shizun kara," *Eigo Seinen,* 136:5 (August 1990), 248. (Steppenwolf ni yoru burou dowei no Cort Theatre ni okeru "The Grapes of Wrath" (Play) ni kansuru Kenkyu — A review of Steppenwolf's Theater's production of *The Grapes of Wrath* at the Cort Theater)

3429   Imamura, Tateo. "Jokyo no Hembo Sutainbekku: Hacho no Toropizumu," (Tropism of "Crack Up") in *Amerika Bungaku to Jidai Hembo (American Literature and Its Historical Changes).* ed. Shigeo Hammano. Tokyo: Kenkyusha, 1989. (pp. 234-238) (examines Hemingway, Steinbeck and Dos Passos).

3430   Inoue, Hirotsugu. "*Hatsuka Nezumi* ni Okeru Yume to Sono Hokai," (The Dream and its Collapse in *Of Mice and Men*) *Kobe Kaisei Joshi Gakuin Daigaku kenkyu kiyou*

*(Bulletin of Kobe Kaisei Women's University
Postgraduate School Study),* 23 (December 1984), 21-38.

3431   Inoue, Hirotsugu. "Henry Thoreau to John Steinbeck no
        Ningen Kousatsu ni tsuite," (Henry Thoreau and John
        Steinbeck: With Regard to Their Views of Man)
        Sapienta: Eichi University Bulletin, 27 (February 20,
        1993), 225-47.

3432   Inoue, Hirotsugu. "Huckleberry Finn to Tom Joad: Jiko Kaku
        Ritsu no tabi," (Huckleberry Finn and Tom Joad: Journey
        as Path to Self-Establishment) in *Sutainbekku Sakka
        Sakuhin Ron (Steinbeck and His Works: a Festschrift in
        Honor of Dr. Tetsumaro Hayashi).* ed. Eiko Shiraga and
        Yasuo Hashiguchi. Tokyo: Eihosha, 1995. (pp. 50-65)

3433   Inoue, Hirotsugu. *"Ikari No Budou* ni Okeru Josei kan —
        Bungakuteki Kanten ni tsuite," (The Female Image in *The
        Grapes of Wrath*: On the Characteristics of Its Literary
        Style) *Buntai-ron Kenkyu — Nihon Buntai-ron Gakkai
        (Studies in Stylistics),* 37 (March 25, 1991), 71-85.

3434   Inoue, Hirotsugu. "Steinbeck no *Hatsuka Nezumi to Ningen* ni
        Okeru Yume to Hokai," (The Dream and Its Collapse in
        Steinbeck's *Of Mice and Men*) in *The Dream and Its
        Collapse in American Literature.* Osaka: Sogensha, 1988.
        (pp. 128-141)

3435   Inoue, Hirotsugu. "John Steinbeck no 'The Snake': Phillips'
        hakasi ni tsuite no Ronshu," (John Steinbeck's "The
        Snake": Controversy on Dr. Phillips) *Amerika Bungaku
        Kenkyu (American Literature Studies),* 26 (1989), 31-43.

3436   Inoue, Kenji. "Curley no Tsuma ni Tsuite — 'Hatsuka-nezumi
        to Ningen' Kenkyu memo," (About Curley's Wife — *Of
        Mice and Men* Study Memo) *America Bungaku no Josei
        Tachi (Women in American Literature).* ed. Toshio

Kanezeki, Sumio Kanashimo, and Kazuko Kawachi. Tokyo: Nanundo, 1985. (pp. 257-264)

3437 Inoue, Kenji. "Gaikoku Bungaku-no Miryoku: Steinbeck-no Dokkai-to Kansho — *Ikari No Budou* no Teemato Giho," (Foreign Literature's Appeal: Comprehension and Appreciation of Steinbeck — Theme and Technique of *The Grapes of Wrath*) *Gekkan Kokugo Kyouiku Sangastu-go* (*Language Education Monthly* 4:12, Tokyo Horei Shuppan, (February 25, 1985), 16-20.

3438 Inoue, Kenji. "Gaikoku Bungaku-no Miryoku: Steinbeck-no Dokkai-to Kansho — Steinbeck-no Ningen-kan," (Foreign Literature's Appeal: Comprehension and Appreciation of Steinbeck — Steinbeck's view of Humanity) *Gekkan Kokugo Kyouiku Shigastu-go*, (*Language Education Monthly,* 4:13 (March 25, 1985), 12-17.

3439 Inoue, Kenji. "Gaikoku Bungaku-no Miryoku: Steinbeck-no Dokkai-to Kansho — Steinbeck-no Sosaku-no Giho," (Foreign Literature's Appeal: Comprehension and Appreciation of Steinbeck — Steinbeck's Way of Creation) *Gekkan Kokugo Kyouiku Gogastu-go* (*Language Education Monthly,* 4:14 (April 25, 1985), 12-17.

3440 Inoue, Kenji. "*Ikari no Budou* no Teema to Gihou," (The Theme and Technique of *The Grapes of Wrath*) in *America Dokusho Zakki (A Notebook of Readings of American Literature).* Tokyo: Nan' undo, 1993. (pp. 45-52)

3441 Inoue, Kenji. "Inyou Kenkyu: Steinbeck to Frank Norris, Shoshite Hemingway," (A Study on Borrowing: Steinbeck, Frank Norris, and Hemingway) *Bulletin of the Institute of Humanties, Meiji University,* 35 (1994), 306-317.

3442   Inoue, Kenji, trans. "Kin-No-Sakazuki," (*Cup of Gold*) in
                 Steinbeck Sakuhin-Ron II. Tokyo: Eihosha, 1982. (pp. 3-
                 27) (a translation of Martha Heasley Cox's Steinbeck's
                 Cup of Gold (1929) originally in *A Study Guide to*
                 Steinbeck Pt. II. ed. Tetsumaro Hayashi, Metuchen, N. J.:
                 Scarecrow Press, 1979, pp. 19-45)

3443   Inoue, Kenji. "*The Moon Is Down* ni tsuite," (On *The Moon Is*
                 Down) in *Amerika Dukosho Noto (Notes on American*
                 Literature). Tokyo: Nan'undo, 1991. (pp. 26-29)

3444   Inoue, Kenji. "Ningen no Minikui Genjitsu: John Steinbeck no
                 The Acts of King Arthur and His Noble Knights," (Men's
                 Ugly Reality: John Steinbeck's *The Acts of King Arthur*
                 and His Noble Knights) in *America Dokusho Zakki (A*
                 Notebook of Readings of American Literature). Tokyo:
                 Nan' undo, 1993. (pp. 71-73)

3445   Inoue, Kenji. "Review of *Sutainbekku to Engeki (Steinbeck*
                 and Drama) by Hiromasa Takamura," *Eigo Seinen,* 136:
                 10 (January 1, 1991), 59.

3446   Inoue, Kenji, trans. "*Run-Run to Moyuru*," in *Steinbeck*
                 Sakuhin-Ron II. Tokyo: Eihosha, 1982. (pp. 86-101). (a
                 translation of Martha Heasley Cox's essay, Steinbeck's
                 Burning Bright (1950) originally in *A Study Guide to*
                 Steinbeck Pt. II. ed. Tetsumaro Hayashi. Metuchen, N. J. :
                 Scarecrow Press, 1979, 46-62)

3447   Inoue, Kenji. "Steinbeck e no Tsuioku," (In Memory of
                 Steinbeck) in *Amerika Dukosho Noto (Notes on*
                 American Literature). Tokyo: Nan'undo, 1991. (pp. 30-
                 32)

3448   Inoue, Kenji. "Steinbeck Kenkyu: *Ikari no Budou*," (A Study
                 of Steinbeck: *The Grapes of Wrath*) in *Amerika Bungaku*
                 Tokuhon (An Introduction to American Literature). ed.

Kichinosuke Ohashi. Tokyo: Yuhikaku, 1982. (pp. 209-226)

3449   Inoue, Kenji. "Steinbeck Kenkyu no Oboegaki: Hemingway kara no Eikyo ni tsuite," (A Memorandum of Steinbeck Studies: On Hemingway's Influence) *Obirin Studies in English Language and Literature* (Obirin University), 33 (March 1, 1993), 149-53.

3450   Inoue, Kenji. "Steinbeck no Hyogenhou," (Steinbeck's Way of Writing) in *America Dokusho Zakki (A Notebook of Readings of American Literature).* Tokyo: Nan'undo, 1993. (pp. 62-70)

3451   Inoue, Kenji. "Steinbeck no Ningenkan," (Steinbeck's View of Men) in *America Dokusho Zakki (A Notebook of Readings of American Literature).* Tokyo: Nan'undo, 1993. (pp. 53-61)

3452   Inoue, Kenji. "Steinbeck to Jinshuteki Henken," (Steinbeck and Racial Prejudices) in *Bungaku to America: Ohashi Kenzaburo Kyoju Kanreki Kinen Ronbushu.* Tokyo: Nan'undo, 1980. (pp. 390-403)

3453   Inoue, Kenji. "Steinbeck to kageki na Henken," (Steinbeck and Racial Prejudices) in *Literature and America* (III). Tokyo: Nan'undo Press, 1980. (pp. 390-403)

3454   Inoue, Kenji. "Steinbeck Wo Yomu . . . *Ikari-No-Budou* Oboe-Gaki," (Reading Steinbeck: *The Grapes of Wrath* Notes) in *American Literature Reader (Amerika Bungaku Tokuhon).* ed. Kichinosude Ohashi. Tokyo: Yuhikaku Press, 1982. (pp. 209-226)

3455 Inoue, Kenji. "Sutainbekku shoshi," (Steinbeck Bibliography) in *Sutainbekku Sakuhin Ron II.* Tokyo, Eihou-sha, 1982. (210-221)

3456 Inoue, Kenji. "Thirties-nendai Bungaku Sai-hyoka," (Literature of '30s Re-evaluation) Tokushu: Sen-kyuhyaku-sanju nendai America bungaku sai-ko (Special edition: Reconsideration of 1930s American Literature). *Eigo Seinen (English Youth),* 130:1 (April 1, 1984), 10-11.

3457 Inoue, Kenji. "Yakusha Atogaki," (Translator's Afterword) in *Kyanarii Rou* (Fukumu Bunko). Tokyo: Fukumu shoten, 1989. (pp. 244-250)

3458 Inoue, Kenji. "Yakusha atogaki," (Translator's Afterword) in *Sutainbekku Sakuhin Ron II.* Tokyo: Eihousha, 1982. (pp. 222-224)

3459 Inoue, Kenji. "Yamamoto Shugoro — Anderson — Steinbeck," (Yamamoto Shugoro, Anderson, Steinbeck) *Bungaku Kukan* (Bungaku Kenkyukai, Soju-sha), II: 9 (July 1989), 91-99.

3460 Inoue, Mitsuharu. "*Ikari no Budou* — Sutainbekku," (*The Grapes of Wrath* and Steinbeck) in *Sekai Meisaku Bungakukan*, Mitsuharu Inoue. Tokyo: Kouzaidou, 1991. (pp. 74-77) (Shippitsu-sha Guruupu Bungakukan)

3461 Inoue, Toshihiro. "*Ikari no Budou* Shiron — 'The Joads' no Hi-Koseika" (*The Grapes of Wrath* Theory — The Un-individualization of "The Joads") *Touchstone (Kansai Gakuin Daigaku Eibunka Insei-kai),* 2 (July 1, 1991), 67-78.

3462 Inoue, Toshihiro. "*Tortilla Flat* — Pezano Shakai no Tokaika," (*Tortilla Flat*: The Urbanization of Paisano

Society) Kansai America Bungaku — Nihon America
Bungaku-kai Kansai Shibu *(Kansai American Literature)*,
27 (November 30, 1991), 41-51.

3463   Inui, Mikio, trans. "Steinbeck no *Travels with Charley*,"
       (Steinbeck's *Travels with Charley*) by John Ditsky in
       Steinbeck's Travel Literature. ed. Tetsumaro Hayashi.
       Tokyo, Japan: Kaibundo Press, 1986.

3464   Inui, Mikio, trans. "*The Wayward Bus:* Amerika deno Ai to
       Toki," *(The Wayward Bus*: Love and Time in America)
       by John Ditsky in *Steinbeck's Travel Literature*. ed.
       Tetsumaro Hayashi. Tokyo, Japan: Kaibundo Press, 1986.

3465   Ishii, Akio. "*Eden No Higashi* no Butai no Okeru Yonin no
       Yousei," (The Four Fairies on the Stage of *East of Eden)*
       Play Programme, *East of Eden* and *Dandyism,*
       Takarazuka Grand Theater, June 30, 1995, 56-57.

3466   Ishijima, Haruo. "Dai 1 sho Steinbeck no *Ogon no Sakazuki*,"
       (Ch. 1: Steinbeck's *Cup of Gold*) in *Karibu no Kaizoku,
       Henry Morgan* (*Henry Morgan, the Buccaneer*) in *Dai-
       Kokaisha no Sekai* (*The World of the Great Voyagers)*.
       Vol. V. Tokyo: Hara Shobo, 1992. (pp. 1-13)

3467   Ito, Yoshio. "Jonni Bea," (Johnny Bear) in *Steinbeck Kenkyu:
       Tanpen Shosetsu Ron.* ed. Hisachi Egusa. Tokyo: Yashio
       Shuppan-sha, 1987. (pp. 138-152)

3468   Ito, Yoshio. "*The Red Pony* no Kousei to Gihou ni Tsuite,"
       (The Design and Technique of *The Red Pony*) *Kaihou*, 5
       (1982), 3.

3469   Ito, Yoshio. "*The Red Pony* No Kousei to Giko," (On *The Red
       Pony*: Its Structure and Steinbeck's Technique) *Fuji
       Jyoshi Daigaku Kiyo Dai-ichi-bu* (*Fuji Women's College
       Bulletin)*, 19 (January 25, 1982), 79-94.

3470   Ito, Yoshio. "Nishimura Sennen "Sutainbekku Shoshi,"
        (Steinbeck Bibliography) in *Sutainbekku Kenkyu —
        Tanpen shosetsu-ron.* Tokyo: Yashio Shuppan-sha, 1987.
        (pp. 258-274)

3471   Ito, Yoshio. "Tousou," (Flight) in *Steinbeck Kenkyu: Tanpen
        Shosetsu Ron.* ed. Hisachi Egusa. Tokyo: Yashio
        Shuppan-sha, 1987. (pp. 46-59)

3472   Jou, Yuji. "Steinbeck no Shiseikan," (Steinbeck's View of
        Life and Death) *Eigo Eibungaku Kenkyu — Souka
        Daigaku Eibun Gakkai*) 28 (vol. 15, no. 2) (March 1991),
        83-100.

3473   Jou, Yuji. "*Ten no Bokujou* ni Okeru Hi-Mokuteki Ronteki
        Shikou no tenkai," (Development of Unintentional
        Thoughts in *The Pastures of Heaven*) *Eigo Eibungaku
        Kenkyu — Souka Daigaku Eibungakkai*), 29 (vol. 16, no.
        1) (December 1991), 81-99.

3474   Kagawa, Kazuko. "*Cannery Row* no sekai," (The World of
        Cannery Row) *Ebara Review* (Nomura Eibungaku
        Kenkyu kai — Nomura English Literature Study Society),
        2 (1986), 61-72.

3475   Kagawa, Kazuko. "*Of Mice and Men* no Curley no tsuma ni
        tsuite," (About the Wife of Curley in *Of Mice and Men*)
        *Eibei Bungaku Gogaku Ronsou Okamoto Seikei Kyoju
        Sanju Kinenron Bunshu (Anglo-American Literature/
        Language Study Bulletin; Professor Seikei Okamoto's
        Eightieth Calendar Year Commemoration Thesis
        Collection).* Tokyo: Kirihara Shoten, 1984. (pp. 189-198)

3476   Kaida, Kouichi. "*In Dubious Battle* ni okeru hito wo shimesu
        Rough Words ni tsui-te," (Rough Words That Indicate
        People in *In Dubious Battle*) *Kaihou,* 5 (1982), 1.

3477   Kaida, Kouichi. "*Of Mice and Men* (Play) o Chushin ni Shite,"
        (Focusing on *Of Mice and Men*) *Kaihou* 4 (May 1981), 3.

3478 Kakegawa, Wakako. *"Cannery Row* no sekai," (The World of *Cannery Row*) *Ebara Review*, 2 (1986), 61-72.

3479 Kakegawa, Wakako. *"Kyanarii-Rou* to *Korutesu no Umi Kokai Nisshi,"* (Cannery Row and The Log from the Sea of Cortez) *Ebara Review*, 3 (December 20, 1988), 55-64.

3480 Kakegawa, Wakako. *"Kyanarii-Rou* to *Korutesu no Umi Kokai Nisshi,"* (Cannery Row and The Log from the Sea of Cortez) in *Eibei bungaku to Gengo — Artarashii Kenkyu no Chihei wo motomete (English and American Literature and Language: Searching for a New Horizon of Research.* ed. Bibulos Society. Tokyo: Homerosu-sha, 1990. (pp. 355-65)

3481 Kakegawa, Wakako. "Lennie No Shi o Megutte," (On Lennie's Death) *Ebara Review*, Soukango (Nomura Eibungaku kenkyu Kai), (1983), 65-77.

3482 Kakegawa, Wakako. "Sononakade Ningen ga Tsugitsugito Yakarenakereba Naranai Honou," (The Flame in Which Human Beings Must Be Repeatedly Burnt) in *Sutainnbekku Sakka Sakuhin Ron (Steinbeck and His Works: a Festschrift in Honor of Dr. Tetsumaro Hayashi).* ed. Eiko Shiraga and Yasuo Hashiguchi. Tokyo: Eihosha, 1995. (pp. 259-271)

3483 Kakegawa, Wakako. "Sutainbekku no Haafu Witto ni Tsuite," (About Steinbeck's Half-wit) *Kaihou*, 5 (1982), 1.

3484 Kakegawa, Wakako. "Tsumi, Tsumi no Ishiki, Soshite Timusheru," (Crime, Sense of Crime, and Timshel) *Ebara Review,* 4 (July 1990), 39-46.

3485 Kakegawa, Wakako, Kyoko Ariki, and Ikuko Kawata, trans. *"Akai kouma:* no Monogatarigun ni Okeru 'Dairenpo' no Ichi to Sono juyousei ni tsuite," (The Place and

　　　　　Importance of "The Great Mountains" in *The Red Pony*
　　　　　Cycle) by Roy Simmonds. See #3323.

3486　　Kakegawa, Wakako, Kyoko Ariki, and Ikuko Kawata, trans.
　　　　　"Chiisana Monogatari: Sutainbekku no "Jikeidanin,"
　　　　　("The Little Bit of a Story": Steinbeck's "The Vigilante")
　　　　　by Louis Owens. See 3324.

3487　　Kakegawa, Wakako, Kyoko Ariki, and Ikuko Kawata, trans.
　　　　　"Eriku Erikuson to Jon Sutainbekku no Deai:
　　　　　'Okurimono' ni Okeru Shinri Shakai Gakuteki: Kannen
　　　　　Kara Mita Hattatsu," (Erik Ericson Meets John Steinbeck:
　　　　　Psycho-Social Development in "The Gift") by Thom
　　　　　Tammaro. See #3326.

3488　　Kakegawa, Wakako, Kyoko Ariki, and Ikuko Kawata, trans.
　　　　　"Henja maegaki," (Preface) by Tetsumaro Hayashi. See
　　　　　#3327.

3489　　Kakegawa, Wakako, Kyoko Ariki, and Ikuko Kawata, trans.
　　　　　"Henja maegaki," (Preface) by Tetsumaro Hayashi. See
　　　　　#3328.

3490　　Kakegawa, Wakako, Kyoko Ariki, and Ikuko Kawata, trans.
　　　　　"Hitobito o Hikiiru Mono: Shounen no 'Kokoro aru
　　　　　ningen' eno seihyo," ("The Leader of the People": A Boy
　　　　　Becomes a Mensch) by Mimi Reisel Gladstein. See
　　　　　#3329.

3491　　Kakegawa, Wakako, Kyoko Ariki, and Ikuko Kawata, trans.
　　　　　"Jobun," (Introduction) by Warren French. See #3330.

3492　　Kakegawa, Wakako, Kyoko Ariki, and Ikuko Kawata, trans.
　　　　　"Jobun," (Introduction) by Warren French. See #3331.

3493   Kakegawa, Wakako, Kyoko Ariki, and Ikuko Kawata, trans.
        "'Kaji' to sono ijousei," ("The Snake" and Its Anomalous
        Nature) by Robert M. Benton . See #3331A.

3494   Kakegawa, Wakako, Kyoko Ariki, and Ikuko Kawata, trans.
        "'Kiku': Sutainbekku no *Pigumarion*" ("The
        Chrysanthemums": Steinbeck's *Pygmalion*) by Susan
        Shillinglaw. See #3332

3495   Kakegawa, Wakako, Kyoko Ariki, and Ikuko Kawata, trans.
        "Kotoba ni Kawaru Shouchou no Kazukazu Asameshi ni
        Okeru Sutainbekku no Mugon no messeji," ("Symbols for
        The Wordlessness": Steinbeck's Silent Message in
        "Breakfast") by Michael J. Meyer. See #3333.

3495A   Kakegawa, Wakako, Kyoko Ariki, Ikuko Kawata, trans.
        "'Kuko' no imino tsuikyuu," (A Search for Meaning in
        "Flight") by Robert M. Benton. See #3334.

3496   Kakegawa, Wakako, Kyoko Ariki, and Ikuko Kawata, trans.
        "Kuroi Itosugi to Midori iro no Oke: Sutainbekku no
        'Yakusoku' ni Okeru Shi to Seishoku," (The Black
        Cypress and the Green Tub: Death and Procreation in
        Steinbeck's "The Promise") by Robert S. Hughes. See
        #3335.

3497   Kakegawa, Wakako, Kyoko Ariki, and Ikuko Kawata, trans.
        "'Rakuen no Genso': Shougeki ni Mirareru Sekkyokuteki
        kanyo no Yukousei to Gisei," ("The Illusion of Eden":
        Efficacious Commitment and Sacrifice in "The Raid") by
        Michael J. Meyer. See #3336.

3498   Kakegawa, Wakako, Kyoko Ariki, and Ikuko Kawata, trans.
        "Seisabetsu to Jinshusabetsu ka, Soretomo Hiniku ka:
        Sutainbekku no 'Satsujin,'" (Sexism and Racism, or
        Irony? Steinbeck's "The Murder") by Patricia M.
        Mandia. See #3337.

3499   Kakegawa, Wakako, Kyoko Ariki, and Ikuko Kawata, trans.
        "'Seishoujo Keitii' : Sutainbekku no Himerareta Kokro
        no Kagi," ("Saint Katy the Virgin": The Key to
        Steinbeck's Secret Heart) by Thom Tammaro. See #3338

3500   Kakegawa, Wakako, Kyoko Ariki, and Ikuko Kawata, trans.
        "'Shiroi Uzura' no Eden no Higashi ni Okeru Kosei to
        Kyosei," (Pure and Corrupt: Agency and Communion in
        the Edenic Garden of "The White Quail") by Michael J.
        Meyer. See #3339.

3501   Kakegawa, Wakako, Kyoko Ariki, and Ikuko Kawata, trans.
        "Sutainbekku 'Joni Bea' ni Okeru Konton to Aku Soshite
        Shunsetsusen no Wakisuji," (Chaos, Evil and the
        Dredger Subplot in Steinbeck's "Johnny Bear") by
        Patricia M. Mandia. See 3340.

3502   Kakegawa, Wakako, Kyoko Ariki, and Ikuko Kawata, trans.
        "Tanpen Sakka Sutainbekku," (Steinbeck, the Short Story
        Writer) by Robert S. Hughes, Jr. See #3341.

3503   Kakegawa, Wakako, Kyoko Ariki, and Ikuko Kawata, trans.
        "Teichi to Kouchi: Sutainbekku no 'Shimegu' no Kintou
        no Toreta Otoko," ("Bottom and Upland": The Balanced
        Man in Steinbeck's "The Harness") by Louis Owens. See
        #3342

3504   Kakegawa, Wakako, Kyoko Ariki, and Ikuko Kawata, trans.
        "'Tousou' no Imi no Tsuikyuu," (A Search for Meaning
        in "Flight") by Robert M. Benton. See #3342A.

3505   Kami, Yuji. "*Ikari no Budou* ni Okeru sei to shi," (Life and
        Death in *The Grapes of Wrath) Eigo Eibungaku Kenkyu
        (Studies in English Language and Literature),* English
        Literature Society of Souka University, 31 (Vol. 17, #1)
        (December 1992), 111-127.

3506   Kami, Yuji. "John Steinbeck no Seishikan," (John Steinbeck's View of Life and Death) *Eigo Eibungaku Kenkyu (Studies in English Language and Literature),* The English Literature Society of Souka University, 28 (March 1991), 83-100.

3507   Kami, Yuji. "*The Pastures of Heaven* ni Okeru Himokute kishikoo no Sokushin," (The Development of Non-Teleological Thinking in *The Pastures of Heaven*) *Eigo Eibungaku Kenkyu (Studies in English Language and Literature),* English Literature Society of Souka University, 28 (March 1991), 81-99.

3508   Kami, Yuji. "Review of *Sutainbekku Kenkyu: Nagai Tanima Ron,*" (*A Study of Steinbeck: Essays on "The Long Valley"*) trans. Hiromasa Takamura, T. J. O'Brien and Tatsuo Narita," in *Jimukyoku Dayori (Steinbeck Newsletter in Japanese),* 14 (November 10, 1992), 2-3.

3509   Kami, Yuji. "*Shirarezaru Kami* o Yomu: Nichijou Seikatsu Kara Shinwas no Sekai e," (A Reading of *To a God Unknown:* From Everyday Life to the World of Myth) *Studies in English Language and Literature* (The English Literature Society of Souka University), 36 (December 20, 1995), 33-46.

3510   Kami, Yuji. "Steinbeck Bungaku no Kaika no Daiichi Choukou: *Kinno Sakazuki* ni Okeru sei to shi o chusin ni," (The First Signs of Flowering Steinbeck Literature: Centering on Life and Death in *Cup of Gold*) *Studies in English Language and Literature* (The English Literature Society of Souka University), 32 (March 20, 1993), 57-75.

3511   Kami, Yuji. "Steinbeck no Ningenzou — Dantai to Kojin," (Steinbeck's View of Man — A Group and an Individual) *Eigo Eibungaku Kenkyu (English Language and*

Literature Studies — The English Literature Society of Souka University), 2 (November 1977), 77.

3512   Kami, Yuji. "Sutainbekku no Himokuteki ron no tsuite," (On Steinbeck's Non-Teleology) *Eigo Eibungaku Kenkyu* (*English Language and Literature Studies* — The English Literature Society of Souka University), 27 (December 1990), 45-74.

3513   Kami, Yuji. "*Tsukiwa Shizuminu* ni yoru sei to shi," (Life and Death in *The Moon is Down*) *Eigo Eibungaku Kenkyu* (*Studies in English Language and Literature*) English Literature Society of Souka University, 30 (Vol. 16, no. 2), (March 1992), 97-110.

3514   Kami, Yuji. "*The Winter of Our Discontent* no Okeru sei to shi," (Life and Death in *The Winter of Our Discontent*) *Eigo Eibungaku Kenkyu* (*Studies in English Language and Literature)* The English Literature Society of Souka University, 33 (March 20, 1993), 133-43.

3515   Kaname, Hiroshi. "Arukadia no saigo: *The Pastures of Heaven* ni tsuite," (The End of an Arcadia: On *The Pastures of Heaven*) *Studies in English and American Literature,* 38 (English and American Literature Society, University of Osaka Prefecture, 1990), 43-64.

3516   Kaname, Hiroshi. "Kyokou ni Okeru Henry Morgan," (Henry Morgan in Fiction) *Osaka Prefectural University, Faculty of Humanities and Social Sciences Bulletin,* 43 (1995), 65-75.

3517   Kaname, Hiroshi. "Steinbeck no 'Kiku' ni tsuite: Jikokaihou," (On Steinbeck's "The Chrysanthemums": The Self Liberation) in *American Short Stories.* ed. Hirotsugu Inoue. Osaka: Sogensha, 1994. (pp. 157-74)

3518   Kaneko, Mitsuo. "'Saint Katy the Virgin' ni Kansuru Ichi-
        Kousatsu," (A Consideration of "Saint Katy the Virgin")
        *Bunka to Gengo Sapporo Daigaku Gaikokugo Gakubu
        Kiyou (Culture and Language Sapporo University
        Foreign Language Department Bulletin),* 18:1 (March 25,
        1985), 1-16.

3519   Kaneko, Mitsushige. "John Steinbeck *Shinju"* — Guuwa
        Toshite no Sono Imi," (John Steinbeck's *The Pearl* — Its
        Meaning as a Fable) *Ohita Daigaku Kyouiku Gakubu
        Kenkyu Kiyou Jinmon-Shakai Kagaku (Ohita University
        Education Department Study Humanities and Social
        Science Bulletin),* 7:2 (October 31, 1985), 45-57.

3520   Kataoka, Sakie. "Sutainbekku no *Hatsuka Nezumi* to ningen,"
        (Steinbeck: *Of Mice and Men) Journal of Oubirin Junior
        College,* 25 (March 1989), 1-9.

3521   Kato, Hirofumi. "John Steinbeck no Koki Sakuhin ni Miru
        Kojinzou — *East of Eden* Kara *The Winter of Our
        Discontent,"* (Personal Image of John Steinbeck in His
        Later Works — From *East of Eden* to *The Winter of Our
        Discontent) Ehime Daigaku Kyouyoubu Kiyou (Ehime
        University Liberal Arts Department Bulletin),* 19:1
        (December 20, 1986), 113-137.

3522   Kato, Mitsuo. "*Akai Kouma,* no Kousou to Gikou," (The Idea
        and Technique of *The Red Pony*) in *Steinbeck Kenkyu:
        Tanpen Shosetsu Ron (Steinbeck Studies: New Essays on
        the Short Stories).* ed. Hisachi Egusa. Tokyo: Yashio
        Shuppan-sha, 1987. (pp. 222-247)

3523   Kato, Mitsuo. "Dai san-kai Sutainbekku Kokusai Taikai ni
        Sanka shite," (A Report on the Third International
        Steinbeck Congress, Honolulu, Hawaii, May 27-30,
        1990) *Nihon America Bungaku kai Hokkaidoushibu
        Newsletter (American Literature Society of Japan,
        Hokkaido Chapter Newsletter),* 6 (June 1990), 5-6.

3524   Kato, Mitsuo. "Dai Niwa Dai Yonwa no Shiten," *Kaihou*, 5
        (1982), 3.

3525   Kato, Mitsuo. "Dairenpo to Jinmin no Shidosha," ("The Great
        Mountains" and "The Leader of the People") in *Steinbeck
        Kenkyu: Tanpen Shosetsu Ron (Steinbeck Studies: New
        Essays on the Short Stories)*. ed. Hisachi Egusa. Tokyo:
        Yashio Shuppan-sha, 1987. (pp. 207-221)

3526   Kato, Mitsuo. "*Eden no Higashi* no Cathy/Kate no Jitsuzou,"
        (The Real Figure of Cathy/Kate in *East of Eden*) *Shiron
        Bunka To Gengo: Sapporo Daigaku Gaikukugo-Gakubu
        Kiyo (Culture and Language,* Sapporo University),
        (March 30, 1992), 1-23.

3527   Kato, Mitsuo. "*Eden no Higashi:* Kyashii no Shijitso-jou,"
        (East of Eden: Cathy's Real Figure) in *Sutainnbekku
        Sakka Sakuhin Ron (Steinbeck and His Works: A
        Festschrift in Honor of Dr. Tetsumaro Hayashi)*. ed. Eiko
        Shiraga and Yasuo Hashiguchi. Tokyo: Eihosha, 1995.
        (pp. 222-242)

3528   Kato, Mitsuo. "Hebi," ("The Snake") in *Steinbeck Kenkyu:
        Tanpen Shosetsu Ron (Steinbeck Studies: New Essays on
        the Short Stories)*. ed. Hisachi Egusa. Tokyo: Yashio
        Shuppan-sha, 1987. (pp. 60-80)

3529   Kato, Mitsuo. "J. Steinbeck: 'Hebi' (On John Steinbeck's
        "The Snake") *Shiron Bunka to Gengo: Sapporo Daigaku
        Gaikokugo-Gakubu Kiyo (Culture and Language,
        Sapporo University Dept. of Foreign Languages
        Bulletin)*, 15:2 (March 1982), 7-17.

3530   Kato, Mitsuo. "John Steinbeck 'Shi megu,'" (John Steinbeck:
        "The Harness" Essay) *Shiron Bunka To Gengo: Sapporo
        Daigaku Gaikukugo-Gakubu Kiyo (Culture and
        Language: Sapporo University Dept. of Foreign
        Languages Bulletin),* 17:1 (September 25, 1983), 1-17.

3531　Kato, Mitsuo. "Robert S. Hughes, Jr. no *Akai Kouma o Koete: Steinbeck no Kanzen Shousetsu no Dokusha no Tebiki* no Kousatsu," (Review of Robert S. Hughes, Jr.'s *Beyond the Red Pony: A Reader's Companion to Steinbeck's Complete Short Stories) Jimukyoku Dayori*, 6 (November 11, 1988), 4-5.

3532　Kato, Mitsuo. "Shi megu," ("The Harness") in *Steinbeck Kenkyu: Tanpen Shosetsu Ron (Steinbeck Studies: New Essays on the Short Stories).* ed. Hisachi Egusa. Tokyo: Yashio Shuppan-sha, 1987. (pp. 105-124)

3533　Kato, Mitsuo. "'Shojo Seijo Katy,'" ("St. Katy the Virgin") in *Steinbeck Kenkyu: Tanpen Shosetsu Ron (Steinbeck Studies: New Essays on the Short Stories).* ed. Hisachi Egusa. Tokyo: Yashio Shuppan-sha, 1987. (pp. 168-183)

3534　Kato, Mitsuo. "'Shojo Seijo Katy' no Kenkyu," (A Study of "Saint Katy the Virgin") *Culture & Language* (Sapporo University), 18:1 (March 1985), 1-16.

3535　Kato, Mitsuo. "Steinbeck *no Shitsumon*: Hihan ni Okeru Shinsakuhin no Kousatsu," (Review of *The Steinbeck Question: New Essays in Criticism.* ed. Donald Noble) *Japan Steinbeck Society Bulletin*, 17 (June 30, 1994), 3-4.

3536　Kato, Mitsuo. "A Study of *The Red Pony*: Chiefly on 'The Great Mountain' and 'The Leader of the People,'" *Culture and Language* (Sapporo University), 15:1 (1981), 39-48.

3537　Kato, Mitsuo. "Sutainbekku no Tegami wo Tazunete," (In Search of Steinbeck's Letters) *Nihon America Bungaku kai Hokkaidoushibu Newsletter*, 3 (December 16, 1988), 1.

3538   Kato, Toyoo. "John Steinbeck no 'Kiku,'" (John Steinbeck's
        'The Chrysanthemums') *Shouin Literary Review,* 15
        (1981), 21-38.

3539   Kato, Tsunehiko. "'America no Yume' to Sono Zasetsu —
        'Ikari no Budo' to *'America no Higeki'* wo Hikaku Suru,"
        ('American Dream' and its Breakdown — Comparing
        The Grapes of Wrath and *An American Tragedy) Gaikoku
        Bungaku Kenkyu (Foreign Literature Study),* Ritsumeikan
        Daigaku Gaikokugoka Renraku Kyogikai — Ritsumeikan
        University Foreign Language Department Liaison
        Council, 67 (August 31, 1985), 1-20.

3540   Kato, Yoshifumi. *"Eden No Higashi* ni Okeru Kageki na
        Ningensei no Tsuikyu," (The Search for Radical
        Humanities in *East of Eden) Oita University Economics
        Review,* 5 (January 1985), 275-97.

3541   Kato, Yoshifumi. *"Eden no Higashi* Saikou: Samuel Hamilton
        no Yuuki," (Reconsideration of *East of Eden:* Samuel
        Hamilton's Courage) *Faculty of Liberal Arts, Ehime
        University Bulletin,* 27 (December 21, 1994), 45-56.

3542   Kato, Yoshifumi. *"In Dubious Battle* Ni Okeru Kojin To
        Shudan," (The Individual and the Group in *In Dubious
        Battle) Ooita Daigaku Keizai Ronshu (Ooita University
        Economics Bulletin),* 34: 4-5-6 Soritsu 60 Shunen Kinen-
        go (January 1983), 441-454.

3543   Kato, Yoshifumi. "John H. Timmerman ni yoru *Steinbeck
        Tanpen ni Okeru Gekitekina Fukei,"* (Review of *The
        Dramatic Landscape of Steinbeck's Short Stories* by John
        H. Timmerman) *Jimukyoku Dayori (Steinbeck
        Newsletter),* 11 (June 20, 1991), 2-3.

3544   Kato, Yoshifumi. *"Of Mice and Men* ron — Ningen no Yume
        to Kodoku," (*Of Mice and Men* Study — Human's Dream
        and Solitude) *Ohita Daigaku Keizai-ronshyu (Ohita
        University Keizai Bulletin),* 35:4 (January 1984), 74-97.

3545   Kato, Yoshifumi. "Review of *Sutainbekku Kenkyu: Nagai
        Tanima Ron,*" *(A Study of Steinbeck: Essays on the Long
        Valley)* trans. Hiromasa Takamura, T. J. O'Brien, and
        Tatsuo Narita," *Shigaku (Otani Women's University)*, 24
        (December 1993), 152.

3546   Kato, Yoshifumi. "Steinbeck no Kuni no Kensetsu to
        Hikensetsu no Dorama," (A Drama of Construction and
        Deconstruction of Steinbeck Country) in *Festschrift in
        honor of Professor Michio Kawai: Studies in English
        Language and Literature. (Kawai Michio Sensei Taikan
        Kinen Rombunshu Kanko Iinkai.)* Tokyo: Eihosha, 1993.
        (pp. 547-554)

3547   Kato, Yoshifumi. "Steinbeck to Amerika Indian," (Steinbeck
        and American Indians) in *Sutainbekku Sakka Sakuhin Ron
        (Steinbeck and His Works: A Festschrift in Honor of Dr.
        Tetsumaro Hayashi).* ed. Eiko Shiraga and Yasuo
        Hashiguchi. Tokyo: Eihousha, 1995. (pp. 34-49)

3548   Kato, Yoshifumi. "Steinbeck to Riketsutu no Kankei (1) —
        Steinbeck no Sakuhin ni Miru Rikketsu-zo," (Steinbeck
        and Ricketts's Relationship (1) — Image of Ricketts in
        the Works of Steinbeck) *Ohita Daigaku Keizai Ronshu
        (Ohita University Keizai Bulletin),* 36:4 (January 1985),
        45-65.

3549   Kato, Yoshifumi. "Sutainbekku to Rikettsu no Kankei (2) —
        Rikettsu kara Sutainbekku," (The Relationship Between
        Steinbeck and Ricketts (2) — From Ricketts to Steinbeck)
        *Ehime Daigaku Kyouyoubu Kiyo (Ehime Liberal Arts
        Department Bulletin)* 21: 3 (December 1988), 15-27.

3550   Kato, Yoshifumi, Kyoko Ariki, and Yasuo Hashiguchi, trans.
        "Futari No Jody — Steinbeck and Rawlings," (Two
        Jodys: Steinbeck and Rawlings) by Kiyohiko Tsuboi in
        *John Steinbeck — Salinas Kara Sekai Ni Mukete (John
        Steinbeck: From Salinas to the World).* See #3311.

3551   Kato, Yoshifumi, Kyoko Ariki, and Yasuo Hashiguchi, trans.
        "Gekisakka Steinbeck — Jyoron," (Steinbeck as
        Dramatist: A Preliminary Account) by John Ditsky in
        *John Steinbeck — Salinas Kara Sekai Ni Mukete (John
        Steinbeck: From Salinas to the World)*. See #3312.

3552   Kato, Yoshifumi, Kyoko Ariki, and Yasuo Hashiguchi, trans.
        "John Steinbeck — Sosaku Ron," (John Steinbeck and
        His Concept of Writing) by Tetsumaro Hayashi in *John
        Steinbeck — Salinas Kara Sekai Ni Mukete (John
        Steinbeck: From Salinas to the World)*. See #3313.

3553   Kato, Yoshifumi, Kyoko Ariki, and Yasuo Hashiguchi, trans.
        "John Steinbeck: Salinas Kara Sekai Ni Mukete," (John
        Steinbeck: From Salinas to the World) by Warren French
        in *John Steinbeck — Salinas Kara Sekai Ni Mukete (John
        Steinbeck: From Salinas to the World)*. See #3314.

3554   Kato, Yoshifumi, Kyoko Ariki, and Yasuo Hashiguchi, trans.
        "John Steinbeck to Kawabata Yasunari," (John Steinbeck
        and Yusanari Kawabata) by Kiyoshi Nakayama in *John
        Steinbeck — Salinas Kara Sekai Ni Mukete (John
        Steinbeck: From Salinas to the World)*. See #3315.

3555   Kato, Yoshifumi, Kyoko Ariki, and Yasuo Hashiguchi, trans.
        "Lady Brett Kara Ma Joad: Josei No Ijyo Na Sukanasa"
        (From Lady Brett to Ma Joad: A Singular Scarcity) by
        Mimi Reisel Gladstein in *John Steinbeck — Salinas Kara
        Sekai Ni Mukete (John Steinbeck: From Salinas to the
        World)*. See #3316.

3556   Kato, Yoshifumi, Kyoko Ariki, and Yasuo Hashiguchi, trans.
        "Nonsense No Heroine, Camille Oaks — "*Kimagore
        Basu*" Wo Saihyoko Suru," (Camille Oaks, A Heroine of
        Nonsense — A Reassessment of *The Wayward Bus*) by
        Takahiko Sugiyama in *John Steinbeck — Salinas Kara*

Sekai Ni Mukete (John Steinbeck: From Salinas to the World). See #3317.

3557   Kato, Yoshifumi, Kyoko Ariki, and Yasuo Hashiguchi, trans. "Steinbeck, Faulkner Soshite Buddhism," (Steinbeck, Faulkner and Buddhism) by Kingo Hanamoto in *John Steinbeck — Salinas Kara Sekai Ni Mukete (John Steinbeck: From Salinas to the World).* See #3318.

3558   Kato, Yoshifumi, Kyoko Ariki, and Yasuo Hashiguchi, trans. "Steinbeck No Eiga," (Steinbeck's Films) by Robert Morsberger in *John Steinbeck — Salinas Kara Sekai Ni Mukete (John Steinbeck: From Salinas to the World).* See #3319.

3559   Kato, Yoshifumi, Kyoko Ariki, and Yasuo Hashiguchi, trans. "Steinbeck no Sakuhin Ni Okeru Indo Shiso," (Indian Thought in Steinbeck's Works) by M. R. Satyanarayana in *John Steinbeck — Salinas Kara Sekai Ni Mukete (John Steinbeck: From Salinas to the World).* See #3320.

3560   Kato, Yoshifumi, Kyoko Ariki, and Yasuo Hashiguchi, trans. "Steinbeck to Monterey — 'Monterey Sanbusaku' ni Okeru Theme and Humor," (Steinbeck and Monterey: Theme and Humor in The Monterey Trilogy) by Noboru Shimomura in *John Steinbeck — Salinas Kara Sekai Ni Mukete (John Steinbeck: From Salinas to the World).* See #3321.

3561   Kato, Yoshifumi, Kyoko Ariki, and Yasuo Hashiguchi, trans. "*Tortilla Flat* — Saihoyo No Kokorami," (*Tortilla Flat*: A Re-Evaluation) by Rajul Bhargava in *John Steinbeck — Salinas Kara Sekai Ni Mukete (John Steinbeck: From Salinas to the World).* See #3322.

3562   Kawata, Ikuko. "*Eden no Higashi* ni Okeru Kyashii Eimuzu ni Tsuite no ikkosatsu," (A Consideration of Cathy Ames in

East of Eden) Kobe Joshi Daigaku (Bungakubu) Kiyo (Kobe Women's University Literature Department Bulletin), 50:24 (November 15, 1990), 33-45.

3563   Kawata, Ikuko. *"Eden no Higashi* ni Okeru 'Timshel' ni Kansuru Ichi-Kousatsu (1)"* (Consideration of "Timshel" in *East of Eden I) Kobe Joshi Daigaku (Bungakubu) Kiyo, (Kobe Women's University Literature Department Bulletin),* 18:1 (March 20, 1985), 19-39.

3564   Kawata, Ikuko. *"Eden no Higashi* ni Okeru 'Timshel' ni Kansuru Ichi-Kousatsu (2)," (Consideration of "Timshel" in *East of Eden II) Kobe Joshi Daigaku (Bungakubu) Kiyou (Kobe Women's University Literature Department Bulletin),* 19:1 (March 20, 1986), 1-14.

3565   Kawata, Ikuko. *"Eden no Higashi* ni Okeru 'Timshel' ni Kansuru Ichi-Kousatsu (3)," (Consideration of "Timshel" in *East of Eden III) Kobe Joshi Daigaku (Bungakubu) Kiyo (Bulletin of Kobe Women's University)*, 21:1 (March 20, 1988), 1-20.

3566   Kawata, Ikuko. "Rose of Sharon no Shochotekina Imi," (The Meaning of the Name, "Rose of Sharon") *Kobe Joshi Daigaku (Bungakubu) Kiyo (Bulletin of Kobe Women's University),* 26 (March 10, 1993), 1-14.

3567   Kawata, Ikuko. "'Rose of Sharon' no Shochotekina Imi," (The Symbolic Meaning of Rose of Sharon) in *Sutainnbekku Sakka Sakuhin Ron (Steinbeck and His Works: A Festschrift in Honor of Dr. Tetsumaro Hayashi).* ed. Eiko Shiraga and Yasuo Hashiguchi. Tokyo: Eihosha, 1995. (pp. 203-221)

3568   Kawata, Ikuko, Kyoko Ariki, and Wakako Kakegawa, trans. *"Akai kouma:* no Monogatarigun ni Okeru 'Dairenpo' no Ichi to Sono Juyousei ni Tsuite," (The Place and Importance of "The Great Mountains" in *The Red Pony* Cycle) by Roy Simmonds. See #3323.

3569 Kawata, Ikuko, Kyoko Ariki, and Wakako Kakegawa, trans. "Chiisana Monogatari: Sutainbekku no "Jikeidanin," ("The Little Bit of a Story": Steinbeck's "The Vigilante") by Louis Owens. See #3324.

3570 Kawata, Ikuko, Kyoko Ariki, and Wakako Kakegawa, trans. "Eriku Erikuson to Jon Sutainbekku no Deai: 'Okurimono' ni Okeru Shinri Shakai-gakuteki: Kannen kara Mita Hattatsu," (Erik Ericson Meets John Steinbeck: Psycho-Social Development in "The Gift") by Thom Tammaro. See #3325.

3370A Kawata, Ikuko, Kyoko Ariki, and Wakako Kakegawa, trans. "'Hebi' to sono ijousei," ("The Snake" and Its Anomalous Nature) by Robert M. Benton. See #3326.

3571 Kawata, Ikuko, Kyoko Ariki, and Wakako Kakegawa, trans. "Henja Maegaki," (Preface) by Tetsumaro Hayashi. See #3327.

3572 Kawata, Ikuko, Kyoko Ariki, and Wakako Kakegawa, trans. "Henja Maegaki," (Preface) by Tetsumaro Hayashi. See #3328.

3573 Kawata, Ikuko, Kyoko Ariki, and Wakako Kakegawa, trans. "Hitobito no Hikiiru Mono: Shounen no 'Kokoroaru Ningen' eno seihyou," ("The Leader of The People": A Boy Becomes a Mensch) by Mimi Reisel Gladstein. See #3329.

3574 Kawata, Ikuko, Kyoko Ariki, and Wakako Kakegawa, trans. "Jobun," (Introduction) by Warren French. See #3330.

3575 Kawata, Ikuko, Kyoko Ariki, and Wakako Kakegawa, trans. "Jobun," (Introduction) by Warren French. See #3331.

3576   Kawata, Ikuko, Kyoko Ariki, and Wakako Kakegawa, trans.
        "'Kaji' to sono ijousei," ("The Snake" and Its Anomalous
        Nature) by Robert M. Benton. See #3331A.

3577   Kawata, Ikuko, Kyoko Ariki, and Wakako Kakegawa, trans.
        "'Kiku': Sutainbekku no *Pigumarion*," ("The
        Chrysanthemums": Steinbeck's *Pygmalion*) by Susan
        Shillinglaw. See #3332.

3578   Kawata, Ikuko, Kyoko Ariki, and Wakako Kakegawa, trans.
        "Kotoba ni Kawaru shouchou no kazukazu Asameshi ni
        okeru Sutainbekku no mugon no messeji," ("Symbols for
        The Wordlessness": Steinbeck's Silent Message in
        "Breakfast") by Michael J. Meyer. See #3333.

3578A   Kawata, Ikuko, Kyoko Ariki, and Wakako Kakegawa, trans.
        "'Kuko' no imino tsuikyuu," (A Search for Meaning in
        "Flight") by Robert M. Benton. See #3334.

3579   Kawata, Ikuko, Kyoko Ariki, and Wakako Kakegawa, trans.
        "Kuroi Itosugi to midori iro no oke: Sutainbekku no
        'Yakusoku' ni okeru shi to seishoku," (The Black
        Cypress and the Green Tub: Death and Procreation in
        Steinbeck's "The Promise") by Robert S. Hughes. See
        #3335.

3580   Kawata, Ikuko, Kyoko Ariki, and Wakako Kakegawa, trans.
        "'Rakuen no genso' : Shougeki ni mirareru sekkyokuteki
        kanyo no yukousei to gisei," ("The Illusion of Eden":
        Efficacious Commitment and Sacrifice in "The Raid") by
        Michael J. Meyer. See #3336.

3581   Kawata, Ikuko, Kyoko Ariki, and Wakako Kakegawa, trans.
        'Seisabetsu to Jinshu sabetsuka, soretomo Aironi ka
        Sutainbekku no 'Satsujin,'" (Sexism and Racism, or
        Irony? Steinbeck's "The Murder") by Patricia M.
        Mandia. See #3337

3582   Kawata, Ikuko, Kyoko Ariki, and Wakako Kakegawa, trans.
        "'Seishoujo Keti': Sutainbekku no himerareta kokrono
        kagi," ("Saint Katy the Virgin": The Key to Steinbeck's
        Secret Heart) by Thom Tammaro. See #3338.

3583   Kawata, Ikuko, Kyoko Ariki, and Wakako Kakegawa, trans.
        "'Shiroi uzura' no Eden no higashi ni okeru kosei to
        kyosei," (Pure and Corrupt: Agency and Communion in
        the Edenic Garden of "The White Quail") by Michael J.
        Meyer. See #3339.

3584   Kawata, Ikuko, Kyoko Ariki, and Wakako Kakegawa, trans.
        "Sutainbekku 'Joni Bea' ni okeru Konton to Aku soshite
        shunsetsusen no sabuprotto," (Chaos, Evil and the
        Dredger Subplot in Steinbeck's "Johnny Bear") by
        Patricia M. Mandia. See #3340.

3585   Kawata, Ikuko, Kyoko Ariki, and Wakako Kakegawa, trans.
        "Tanpen sakka Sutainbekku," (Steinbeck, the Short Story
        Writer) by Robert S. Hughes, Jr. See #3341.

3586   Kawata, Ikuko, Kyoko Ariki, and Wakako Kakegawa, trans.
        "Teichi to kouchi: Sutainbekku no 'Shimegu' ni okeru
        kintou no toreta otoko," ("Bottom and Upland": The
        Balanced Man in Steinbeck's "The Harness") by Louis
        Owens. See #3342.

3587   Kawata, Ikuki, Kyoko Ariki, and Wakako Kakegawa, trans.
        "'Touso' no imino tsuikyuu," (A Search for Meaning in
        "Flight") by Robert M. Benton. See #3342A.

3588   Kename, Hiroshi. "America Teki Higeki No Tankyu —
        Richard Wright to John Steinbeck No Baai," (A Search
        for American Tragedy: Richard Wright and John
        Steinbeck) in *Sagai to Amerika Shosetsu (Alienation and
        American Novels)*, ed. Mitsuru Mouri. Osaka: Book Loan
        Press, 1982. (pp. 140-150)

3589   Kename, Hiroshi. "Arukadia no Shimetsu — *The Pastures of Heaven* ni tsuite," (Extinction of Arcadia: On *The Pastures of Heaven*) *Eibei-Bungaku: kenkyu To Kansho, Dai-31-go, Osaka Furitsu Daigaku Eibei-Bungaku kenkyu Kai (English and American Literature — Study and Appreciation*, Osaka Prefectural University), 31 (1990), 33-45.

3590   Kename, Hiroshi. "John Steinbeck: Shisa to Kochiku — Eibei bungaku sotsugyo ronbun no te-ema," (John Steinbeck: Parallax and Construction — A Theme of Anglo-American Literature Graduation Thesis) ed. Tsuyoshi Uchida. Tokyo: Shinozaki Shorin, 1984. (pp. 343-356)

3591   Kename, Hiroshi. "*Of Mice and Men* Ron — Kozo Ni Mirareru Rakuen Kaifuku Ganbo," (Steinbeck's *Of Mice and Men*: The Structure and Desire for Paradise Regained) *Eibei-Bungaku: kenkyu To Kansho, Dai-31-go, Osaka Furitsu Daigaku Eibei-Bungaku kenkyu Kai (English and American Literature - Study and Appreciation*, Osaka Prefectural University), 31 (1983), 51-80.

3592   Kipnis, Gregorii. "Kak Dzhon Steinbek v Kiev priezzhal," (How John Steinbeck Came to Kiev) *Literaturnaia Gazeta, Moscow*, 30 (July 27, 1994), 5510.

3593   Kishi, Akio. "Steinbeck no tampenshu. *Nagai Tanima* no ipoen," (Steinbeck's Collected Short Stories: About *The Long Valley's* Other Land) 'Kiku' ni tsuite, ("The Chrysanthemums") *Biblia*, 9 (Yamagata Biblia no Kaim) (July 1987), 129-130.

3594   Kitsune. "Shinkansho o Yomu ni atatteno Jogen — John Steinbeck no Sea of Cortez no bunseki, Yoshimura Noriko to nishida Mioko, yaku," (Some Pointers on Reading New Books — A Review of John Steinbeck's *Sea of Cortez*. trans. Noriko Yoshimura and Mioko Nishida) *Nikkan Gendai*, 4985 (January 14, 1993), 13.

3595   Ko, Samyon. "'Joni Bea': Zoku Ikiru koto o mananda hon 30"
        ("'Johnny Bear': 30 Books I Learned to Live by,
        Continued) *Chikuma,* 227 (February 1, 1990), 36-37.

3595A   Kobe, Haruki. "Steinbeck saku *Ikari no Budo,*" in *Sekai
        Bungaku no Meisaku to Shujinko Soukaisetsu.*
        (Steinbeck's Work *The Grapes of Wrath* in *Literary
        Masterpieces and Heroes of the World).* Jiyu Kokumin-
        sha henshu bu hen. Tokyo: Jiyukoku-minsha, 1990. (pp.
        176-177)

3596   Kofujita, Chieko. "James Dean no Eiga, *Eden no Higashi,*"
        (James Dean's Movie, *East of Eden)* Play Programme,
        East of Eden and *Dandyism,* Takarazuka Grand Theater,
        June 30, 1995, 54-55.

3597   Konan, Shiho. "*Hatsuka Nezumi to Ningen*: Hare no tokusen
        sakuhin Dokusho kansou bun ken konkuru Koutou
        gakkou no bu Dai 1 rui," (*Of Mice and Men*: Work of
        Special Commendation: Category of Descriptions of
        Impressions on Reading by High School Students
        Section) *Mainichi Shinbun,* (Nara-ban, January 29,1984),
        20.

3598   Kotani, Kazuko. "Steinbeck no 'Hi-mokuteki ron-teki-shiko'
        to 'Phalanx ron' no tenkai," (A Consideration of
        Steinbeck's "Non-teleological theory" and an Explanation
        of the development of his "Phalanx theory") *Ronshu
        (Bulletin)* Aoyama Gakuin Daigaku Daigakuin bungaku
        kenkyu-ka Eibei bungaku senkoinsei-kai (Aoyama
        Gakuin University postgraduate school, postgraduate
        literature course, Society of Anglo-American literature
        major), 8 (March 1984), 1-13.

3599   Kozachenko, Vasyl. "My musymo zhyty my ne nozhemo
        vchynyty samohubstvo . . . : Pys' mennyts' I rozdumy pro
        zustrichi z Dzhonom Steinbekom,"(We Have to Live; We
        Cannot Commit Suicide: The Beliefs of John Steinbeck)
        Vsesvit: Zhurnal Inozemnoi Literatury, Literaturno

mystets'kyi ta Hromads' ko Politychnyi Misiachny,(The Congregation and The World; Journal of Earthly Literature Regarding the Elite of a City - Political) Kiev, Ukraine, 679 (July 7, 1985), 121-129.

3600   Kuramoto, Mamoru. "Kaigen monogatari toshite-no John Steinbeck no *The Red Pony* ni kansuru ichi kousatsu," (A Consideration of John Steinbeck's *The Red Pony* as a Story of Initiation) *Eibungaku Shicho (The Trend of English Literature)*, Aoyama Gakuin Daigaku Eibun Gakkai (Aoyama Gakuin University English Literature Society), 57 (1984), 57-83.

3601   Kuroda, Koichiro. "Steinbeck no 'Kiku' o Yomu: Tanpen Shosetsu no Tanoshimi," (A Reading of Steinbeck's "The Chrysanthemums": The Pleasure of the Short Story) *Nagoya Music College Bulletin,* 14 (March 1995), 1-20. 889.

3602   Kusubashi, Osamu. "*Cup of Gold* Saiko — 'jinbutsu byosha' to 'Shizen byosha' o toshite," (Reconsideration of *Cup of Gold* — Through "Character Description" and "Nature Description") *Matsuyama Tohun Tanki Daigaku Kenkyu Ronshu (Matsuyama Tohun Junior College Study Bulletin)*, 17 (December 1986), 37-52.

3603   Kusubashi, Osamu. "Steinbeck No Goi — Iro No Teema o Chushin To Shite," (Vocabulary of Steinbeck: Centering on the Theme of Color) *Mutsuyama Tohun Tanki Daigaku Kenkyu Ronshu (Matsuyama Tohun Junior College Study Bulletin),* 13 (December 1982), 15-27.

3604   Kusubashi, Osamu. "Sutainbekku no Sakuhin ni miru Sutiivunsun nohikari to kage," (Lights and Shadows of Stevenson As Seen in Steinbeck's Work) *Matsuyama higashikimoi tanki daigaku kenkyu ronshu (Matsuyama Higashikumo Junior College Research Collected Discourses)*, 20 (December 1989), 47-60.

3605 Kusubashi, Osamu. "Sutainbekku to Sutiivunsun — Monterey to futari no fusgina konen," (Steinbeck and Stevenson — Monterey and the Mysterious Troubled Connection Between the Two) *Matsuyama higashikimoi tanki daigaku kenkyu ronshu (Matsuyama Higashikumo Junior College Research Collected Discourses)*, 19 (December 1988), 35-46.

3606 Makino, Keiko. "*The Pastures of Heaven* Kenkyu: Kojin to Songan," (A Study of *The Pastures of Heaven*: Individuals and Respectability) *Konan Women's University Graduate School, English Literature Bulletin*, 9 (1991), 15-25.

3607 Makino, Keiko. "Review of *Jon Sutainbekku: Sarinasu kara Sekai ni Mukete (John Steinbeck: From Saliras to the World).* trans. Osamu Hamaguchi, Kyoko Ariki, and Yoshifumi Kato," *Jimukyoku Dayori (Steinbeck Newsletter in Japanese),* 13 (June 25, 1992), 3-4.

3608 Makino, Keiko. "'Ten no Bokujou'-Kou — Kojin to Respectability," (On *The Pastures of Heaven*: The Individual and Respectability) *Kounan Joshi Daigaku Daigakuin Eibungaku Ronshu — Konan Women's University Graduate School, English Literature Bulletin*, 9 (December 10, 1991), 15-25.

3609 Makino, Keiko. "*Utagawashii Tatakai* to *Ikari no Budou* — Futatsuno Tatakai," (The Two Battles: *In Dubious Battle* and *The Grapes of Wrath*) *Kounan Joshi Daigaku Daigakuin Eibungaku Ronshu — Konan Women's University Graduate School, English Literature Bulletin*, 8 (January 10, 1991), 11-21.

3610 Makino, Keiko. "Zenakuno Taritsu: Ethan Hawley no keisu," (Conflict between Good and Evil: The Case of Ethan Hawley) *Konan Woman's University Graduate School,*

English Literature Bulletin, 8 (March 31, 1994), 65-74.
(The Winter of Our Discontent)

3611 Masunaga, Toshikazu. "'Shiroi Uzura' to 'Touso': *Nagai Tanima* ni Okeru Nishumi no Ningen Kankei," ("The White Quail" and "Flight": Two Forms of Human Relationship in *The Long Valley*) *Journal of the Society of English and American Literature, Kwansei Gakuin University*, 26:1 (December 1981), 87-99.

3612 Materassi, Mario. "Il doppio paradigma idealogico di *The Pearl* di John Steinbeck," (The Double Ideological Paradigm of *The Pearl* by John Steinbeck) *Studi Americani*, (volume and date unavailable) 25-26.

3613 Meguro, Mitsuru. "*Eden No Higashi*: Sentaku No Sekai," (*East of Eden*: The World of Choice) *Higashi Nippon Gakuin Daigaku Kyoyo-Bu Ronshu* (*Bulletin of the Faculty of Liberal Arts, Higashi Nippon Gakuen University*), 8 (May 1, 1982), 55-65.

3614 Meguro, Mitsuru. "*Ikari no Budou*: Ishi no Sekai," (*The Grapes of Wrath*: The World of Will) *Higashi Nippon Gakuin Daigaku Kyoyo-Bu Ronshu* (*Higashi Nippon Gakuin Journal of Liberal Arts and Science*), 7 (1981), 53-62.

3615 Meguro, Mitsuru. "Monterey Sanbu Saku no Sekai," (The World of "The Monterey Trilogy") in *Eigo Eibungaku Shicho (New Currents in English Language and Literature) 1991-1992*. ed. Tsunehiko Kondo. Tokyo: New Current International, 1992. (pp. 208-216)

3616 Meguro, Mitsuru. "Ningen kyusai-no ryotei," (Journey in Search of Redemption of Man) *Higashi-Nihon Gakuen Daigaku Kyouyoubu Ronshu* (*Higashi-Nihon Gakuen University Liberal Arts Department Bulletin*), 11 (June 1, 1985), 7-15.

3617   Meguro, Mitsuru. "Sentaku-shiko no ishi-no Sekai," (The
            World of Choice-Oriented Will) *Higashi Nihon Gakuen
            Daigaku Kyouyoubu Ronshu (Higashi Nihon Gakuen
            University Liberal Arts Faculty Bulletin),* 10 (June 1,
            1984), 15-22.

3618   Meguro, Mitsuru. "Steinbeck no ai wo chukaku to suru
            Sekai," (The World of Love as a Nucleus in Steinbeck)
            Eibungaku (English Literature), Waseda Daigaku
            Eibungakukai (Waseda University English Literature
            Society), 62 (February 15, 1986), 222-233.

3619   Meguro, Mitsuru. "Steinbeck no Rinri teki na Sekai,"
            (Steinbeck's Ethical World) *Eibungaku (English
            Literature),* Waseda Daigaku Eibungakukai (Waseda
            University English Literature Society), 62 (March 1983),
            172-182.

3620   Meguro, Mitsuru. "Steinbeck to D.H. Lawrence: Ni Sakka no
            Sekai," (Steinbeck and D. H. Lawrence: The World of
            Two Writers) in *Sutainnbekku Sakka Sakuhin Ron
            (Steinbeck and His Works: a Festschrift in Honor of Dr.
            Tetsumaro Hayashi).* ed. Eiko Shiraga and Yasuo
            Hashiguchi. Tokyo: Eihosha, 1995. (pp. 107-123)

3621   Meguro, Mitsuru. "*Warera Ga Fuman no Fuyu:* Kurushimino
            Sekai," *(The Winter of Our Discontent*: The World of
            Distress) *Higashi-Nihon Gakuen Daigaku Kyouyoubu
            Ronshu (Bulletin of the Faculty of Liberal Arts, Higashi
            Nippon Gakuen University),* 9 (June 1983), 47-54.

3622   Meguro, Mitsuru. "Yume to genjitsu ni okeru no Soukotsu no
            Sekai," (Dream and Reality in the World of Soukotsu)
            *Higashi-Nihon Gakuen Daigaku Kyouyoubu Ronshu
            (Higashi-Nihon Gakuen University Bulletin),* 12 (May
            1986), 31-37.

3623   Meli, Franco. "Letteratura e/o Biologia? *The Log from the Sea
            of Cortez* di John Steinbeck," (John Steinbeck's *The Log*

from the Sea of Cortez: Literature or Biology?) *Lingua e letteratura*, 14-15 (1990), 25-40.

3624   Meyer, Matthew C. "*Of Mice and Men* ni Okeru Keishiki, Haikei to Teema no Mikata," (Aspects of Form, Setting and Theme in John Steinbeck's *Of Mice and Men) Studies in English Language and Literature* (Seinan Gakuin University), 33:1 (August 1992), 41-77.

3625   Mitsuwa, Hidehiko. "Steinbeck Moshikuwa Hininsho-Shosetsu No Genkai," (Steinbeck or the Limits of the Impersonal Novel) *America Shosetsu-Judai — Shosetsu to Eiga (American Literature Era: Novels and Films).* Tokyo: Film Art Sha, 1983. (pp. 175-191)

3626   Miura, Toshiaki. "Dai 4 sho: Steinbeck no '*Shinju*': Zenaku no Taritsu," (Chapter 4: Steinbeck's *The Pearl*: Conflicts Between Good and Evil) in *Gendai Sakka no Gobo to Buntai (Usage and Style of Modern Writers: Stevenson, Maugham, Hemingway and Steinbeck).* ed. Tsunehiko Kondo. Tokyo: Bunka Shobo Hakubunsha, 1992. (pp. 154-174)

3627   Miyagawa, Hiroyuki. "Steinbeck no Hironriteki Shiko to Phalanx ron ni tsuite," (On Steinbeck's Non-teleological Thinking and Phalanx Theory) *Chu-Shikoku Studies in American Literature*, 30 (June 1, 1994), 52-61.

3628   Miyagawa, Hiroyuki. "Steinbeck no *Tortilla Flat* ni tsuite," (On Steinbeck's *Tortilla Flat) Chu-Shikoku Studies in American Literature*, 20 (March 1984), 88-100.

3629   Miyoshi, Noriko. "*Cat in the Rain* to 'The Chrysanthemums' Ni Okeru tsuma Tachi No Jyokyo," (Kenkyu-Noto) (The Situation of Wives in *The Cat in the Rain* and "The Chrysanthemums" — Study Notes) *Arisu Eibei-Bungaku Kenkyu (Arisu English/American Literature Studies)* 4 (Arisu Jimukkyoku, 1983), 77-85.

3630   Momose, Fumio, trans. "*Eden-No-Higashi*," in *Steinbeck Sakuhin-Ron II.* Tokyo: Eihosha, 1982. (pp. 114-139) (a translation of Richard F. Peterson's Steinbeck's *East of Eden* (1952) in *A Study Guide to Steinbeck Pt. II,* ed. Tetsumaro Hayashi. Metuchen, N. J.: Scarecrow Press, 1979, pp. 63-86)

3631   Momose, Fumio. "*The Forgotten Village* no jyo-ei-kinshi wo megutte," (On the Banning of the Film, *The Forgotten Village) Kaihou,* 4 (1981) 2.

3632   Momose, Fumio. "*Ikari no Budou* to Kirisuto Kyoteki Humani Zumus," (*The Grapes of Wrath* and Christian Humanism) *Hosei University Quarterly of General Education,* 61 (January 1987), 1-16.

3633   Momose, Fumio, trans. "*Kimagure-Basu*," in *Steinbeck Sakuhin-Ron II.* Tokyo: Eihosha, 1982. (pp. 46-69) (a translation of Robert Morsberger's Steinbeck's *The Wayward Bus* (1947) in *A Study Guide to Steinbeck Pt. II,* ed. Tetsumaro Hayashi. Metuchen, N. J.: Scarecrow Press, 1979, pp. 210-231)

3634   Momose, Fumio, trans. "*Korutesu-No-Umi* Koukai-Nisshi," in *Steinbeck Sakuhin-Ron II.* Tokyo: Eihosha, 1982. (pp. 102-113) (a translation of Richard F. Peterson's Steinbeck's *The Log from the Sea of Cortez* (1951) in *A Study Guide to Steinbeck Pt. II,* ed. Tetsumaro Hayashi. Metuchen, N. J.: Scarecrow Press, 1979, pp. 87-99)

3635   Momose, Fumio. "Maccashi Senpu to Steinbeck no Yunjin," (McCarthyism and Steinbeck's Friends) *Bungaku Kukan* (20 Seiki Bungaku Kenkyukai, Sojusha), 3:8 (December 25, 1995), 7-22.

3636   Momose, Fumio, trans. "*Sapata Banzi*," in *Steinbeck Sakuhin-Ron II.* Tokyo: Eihosha, 1982. (pp. 191-209) (a translation of Robert M. Morsberger's Steinbeck's *Viva Zapata!* (screenplay 1952; published 1975) in *A Study*

Guide to Steinbeck Pt. II, ed. Tetsumaro Hayashi,
Metuchen, N. J.: Scarecrow Press, 1979, 191-209)

3637   Momose, Fumio. "Steinbeck to Arthur Miller: Maccashi
        Senpu Deno Konran," (Steinbeck and Arthur Miller: In
        the Turmoil of McCarthyism) in *Sutainnbekku Sakka
        Sakuhin Ron (Steinbeck and His Works: A Festschrift in
        Honor of Dr. Tetsumaro Hayashi).* ed. Eiko Shiraga and
        Yasuo Hashiguchi. Tokyo: Eihosha, 1995. (pp. 83-92)

3638   Momose, Fumio, and Hisachi Tsuboi. "Bunken Mokuroku
        sho," (Commentary Booklet) in *Sutainbekku zen tanpen
        ron — Akai Uma wo koete.* Tokyo: Eihousha, 1991. (pp.
        182-194)

3639   Momose, Fumio, and Kiyohiko Tsuboi. "Yakusha Atogaki,"
        (Translator's Afterword) in *Sutainbekku zen tanpen ron
        — Akai Uma wo koete.* Tokyo: Eihousha, 1991. (pp. 195-
        196)

3640   Morita, Shoji. "Hayashi no *Shin Steinbeck Den: 1971-1981* no
        Saikou," (A Review of Hayashi's *A New Steinbeck
        Bibliography: 1971-1981)* in *Chu-Shikoku Studies in
        American Literature,* 20 (March 1984), n.p.

3641   Morita, Shoji. "Review of Hisachi Egusa, ed. *Sutainbekku
        Kenkyu — Tanpen shosetsu-ron,*" (*Steinbeck Studies:
        Essays on the Short Stories) Jimukyoku Dayori,* 4
        (November 11, 1987), 2-3.

3642   Muliarchik, Alexander. "Introduction: Realism i romantika
        prozy Dzhona Steinbeka," (Realism or Romanticism in
        the Writing of John Steinbeck) in *Izbrannye
        Proisvedeniia/*Selected Works. Moscow: N.A., 1988.
        (Contains a translation of *Tortilla Flat, Of Mice and Men,
        The Pearl, Cannery Row,* and *The Wayward Bus* in
        Russian)

3643 Muraire, Andre. "Radicalisme et Subversion dans *The Grapes of Wrath* de John Ford," (Radicalism and Subversion in John Ford's film of *The Grapes of Wrath*) in *Hollywood: Reflections sur l'ecran.* Paris: Actes du Grena, 1984. (pp. 64-78)

3644 Nagahara, Makoto. "John Steinbeck's *Ikari no Budo*," (John Steinbeck's *The Grapes of Wrath*) *Eibei Bungaku — Meisaku-eno Sampo-michi America-hen. (Anglo-American Literature — A Stroll to the Masterpiece: America)* ed. Akio Ohura, Hidemitsu Togo, Astuhiko Murayama, Tadashi Yamamoto. Tokyo: Sanyu Sha, 1985. (pp. 200-210)

3645 Naka, Michiko. "Steinbeck, Sarinasu to Monteri," (Steinbeck, Salinas and Monterey) *The New English Classroom,* 319 (Sanyu-sha Shuppan), March 1996, 35-38.

3646 Nakachi, Akira. "*Akaruku Moeru* ni tsuite," (On *Burning Bright) Toyo Gakuen University Bulletin*, 2 (June 1994), 35-41.

3647 Nakachi, Akira. "Monterey No Omoide — *Kanzume Yokocho* ni Tsuite," (A Study of *Cannery Row) Toyo Jyoshi Tanki Daigaku Kiyo (The Toyo Review —* Toyo Women's Junior College Bulletin), 15 (March 1983), 1-9.

3648 Nakachi, Akira. "*Kimegaru Basu* no Shoukai," (An Introduction to *The Wayward Bus) Toyo Gakuen University Bulletin,* 1 (1993), 53-61.

3649 Nakachi, Akira. "Shinjyu no Kagayaki *The Pearl* Ron," (A Study of *The Pearl:* Its Brightness*) Toyo Jyoshi Tanki Daigaku Kiyo (The Toyo Review —* Toyo Women's Junior College), 14 (March 1982), 27-37.

3650 Nakachi, Akira. *"Shirarezaru Kami* no Saikou,*" (To a God Unknown*: Reconsideration) *Toyo Jyoshi Tanki Daigaku Kiyo* (*Toyo Review* — Toyo Women's Junior College),18 (1986), 1-7.

3651 Nakachi, Akira. "Steinbeck no Konran: *Tsukiwa Shizuminu* no Kenkyu," (Steinbeck's Confusion: A Study of *The Moon Is Down*) *Toyo Jyoshi Tanki Daigaku Kiyo* (*Toyo Review* — Toyo Women's Junior College) 23 (March 15, 1991), 1-11.

3652 Nakachi, Akira. "Sutainbekku Hihyo no Nagare," (A Current of Steinbeck Criticism) *Eigo Kyouiku (The English Teachers' Magazine)* Taishukan, 35:12 (February 1987), 44-47.

3653 Nakachi, Kozen. *"Eden no Higashi* ni okeru shudai to kosei," (Theme and Composition of *East of Eden*) *Ryukyu Daigaku Gogaku Bungaku Ronshu (Ryukyu Daigaku Language Literature Bulletin),* 30 (December, 1985), 129-155.

3654 Nakachi, Kozen. "John H. Timmerman no *John Steinbeck no Kyokou: Eranda Michi no Bigaku* no Saikou," (Review of John H. Timmerman's *John Steinbeck's Fiction: The Aesthetics of the Road Taken) Jimukyoku Dayori*, 5 (July 1, 1988), 5-6.

3655 Nakachi, Kozen. *"Kimagure Basu:* Gensou to Genjitsu,*" (The Wayward Bus:* Illusion and Reality) *Ryukyu Daigaku Gogaku Bungaku Ronso (Ryudai Review of Language and Literature)*, 32 (December 1987), 153-173.

3656 Nakachi, Kozen. "Samuel Hamilton ni tsuite," (On Samuel Hamilton) in *Sutainbekku Sakka Sakuhin Ron (Steinbeck and His Works: A Festschrift in Honor of Dr. Tetsumaro*

Hayashi). ed. Eiko Shiraga and Yasuo Hashiguchi.
Tokyo: Eihosha, 1995. (pp. 243-258)

3657   Nakachi, Kozen. "Steinbeck no *Kanzume Yokocho* o Yomu,"
        (A Reading of Steinbeck's *Cannery Row) Ryukyu
        Daigaku Gogaku Bungaku Ronso (Ryudai Review of
        Language and Literature* — College of Law and Letters,
        University of Ryukyus), 37 (December 1992), 45-63.

3658   Nakachi, Kozen. "Steinbeck to Seibu: Bensou no Kokufuku,"
        (Steinbeck and the West: The Overcoming of Illusions)
        *Amerika Bunmei to Chii ki no Yakawari (American
        Civilization and the Significance of Its Region) Bulletin of
        the University of the Ryukyus, American Studies Society,*
        1989-1991 (March 31, 1992), 11-25.

3659   Nakachi, Kozen. *"Ten no makiba* — yume (genso) kara
        samete" *(The Pastures of Heaven:* Awakening from
        Illusion) *Ryukyu Daigaku Gogaku Bungaku Ronso
        (Ryudai Review of Language & Literature* — College of
        Law and Letters, University of the Ryukyus), 34
        (December 1989), 167-88.

3660   Nakachi, Noboru. *"To a God Unknown* Saiko,"
        (Reconsideration of *To a God Unknown) Toyo Joshi
        Tanki Daigaku Kiyou (Toyo Women's Junior College
        Bulletin),* No.18 (1986), 1-7.

3661   Nakagawa, Yoko. "Kanojo wa naze Rouba no youni
        Nakunoka: 'Kiku' to Kagami ni Okeru Elisa," (Why Does
        She Cry "Like an Old Woman"?: Elisa in "The
        Chrysanthemums" and Mirrors) *Studies in American
        Literature* (The Japan American Literature Society), 30
        (February 25,1994), 75-87.

3662   Nakagawa, Yoko. "Kataritewa Nani o Kataruka: Steinbeck no
        'Shiroi Uzura' ni Okeru Fushinda to Shinjitsu," (What the

"Teller" Tells: The Depths/the Truth in Steinbeck's "The White Quail") *Aichi Kenritsu University, Faculty of Letters Bulletin*, 43 (1994), 63-76.

3663   Nakajima, Mokichi. "Hiromasa Takamura no *Steinbeck to Engeki* no Kenkyu," (Review of Hiromasa Takamura's *Sutainbekku to Engeki*) *America Bungaku Kenkyukai* (Nihon America Baungakukai), 28 (February 25, 1992), 179-183.

3664   Nakajima, Mokichi. "*Of Mice and Men* ni tsuite: Shosetsu kara Gekie," (On *Of Mice and Men*: Novel into Play) *Kara Gikyoku E Kumammoto Daigaku Kyoyo-Bu Kiyo: Gaikoku-go, Gaikoku-Bungaku Hen* (*Bulletin of the Faculty of Liberal Arts, Kumamoto University*), 17 (January 1982), 53-68.

3664A   Nakajima, Mokichi. "*The Pastures of Heaven* Shoron," Kumamoto Daigaku Kyoyo-bu Kiyo: Gaikokugo, Gaikoku — Bungaken hen, 18 (January 1983), 65-75.

3665   Nakajima, Mokichi. 'Shinpojiamu *Of Mice and Men* ni tsui-te — shikai no ji," (On the Symposium of *Of Mice and Men*) *Kaihou*, 4 (1981), 2-3.

3666   Nakamura, Masao. "John Steinbeck No 'Kiku' Ni Tsuite," (On John Steinbeck's "Chrysanthemums") *Nagasaki Daigaku Kyoyo-Bu Kiyo: Jinbun-Kagaku* (*Bulletin of The Faculty of Liberal Arts, Nagasaki University*), 22: 2 (February 1982), 49-62.

3667   Nakashima, Saikichi. "Hiromasa Takamura no *Steinbeck to Engeki* no Kenkyu," (Review of *Sutainbekku to Engeki (Steinbeck and Drama)* by Hiromasa Takamura) in *Studies in American Literature* (The American Literature Society of Japan), 28 (February 25, 1992), 179-183.

3668 Nakashima, Saikichi. *"The Pastures of Heaven* ni Tsuite," (On *The Pastures of Heaven*) *Bulletin of the Faculty of Liberal Arts, Kumamoto University,* 18 (1983), n.p.

3669 Nakata, Yuji. *"Ikari no Budo* — Shousetsu kara Eiga-e," (*The Grapes of Wrath*: From Novel into Film) *Konan Joshi Daigaku Eibungaku Kenkyu (Konan Women's University English Literature Study),* 20 (March 1984), 90-100.

3670 Nakata,Yuji. "Steinbeck no *Working Days* to *Ikari no Budo* ni tsuite," (On Steinbeck's *Working Days* and *The Grapes of Wrath) Konan Joshi Daigaku Eibungaku Kenkyu (Studies in English Literature Konan Women's University),* 31 (March 1995), 25-32.

3671 Nakayama, Kiyoshi. "'Aimani naniga Okoruka': *Tanoshii Makuyoubi* no Tekisuto," ("What Happens In-Between": The Typescripts and Text of *Sweet Thursday)* in *Sutainnbekku Sakka Sakuhin Ron (Steinbeck and His Works: A Festschrift in Honor of Dr. Tetsumaro Hayashi).* ed. Eiko Shiraga and Yasuo Hashiguchi. Tokyo: Eihosha, 1995. (pp. 272-288)

3672 Nakayama, Kiyoshi, trans. *"Charley Tono Tabi* — America Motomete,"* (Travels with Charley*: Towards America) in *Steinbeck Sakuhin-Ron II.* Tokyo: Eihosha, 1982. (pp. 165-190). (translation of Roy S. Simmonds' Steinbeck's *Travels with Charley in Search of America* (1962) in *A Study Guide to Steinbeck Pt. II,* ed. Tetsumaro Hayashi, Metuchen, N. J.: Scarecrow Press, 1979, pp. 165-190)

3673 Nakayama, Kiyoshi. "Edowaado F. Rikettsu (Dokku) ni tsuite," (About Ed Ricketts or Doc) in *Tanoshii Moku-yobi.* Tokyo: Shimin shobo, 1984. (pp. 215-220)

3674 Nakayama, Kiyoshi. "Hiromasa Takamura no *Steinbeck to Engeki* no Kousatsu," (Review of *Sutainbekku to Engeki*

(*Steinbeck and Drama*) by Hiromasa Takamura) *Shigaku* (*Otani Women's University*), 24 (December 1993), 150-51.

3675 Nakayama, Kiyoshi. "*Ikari no Budou* no Geijutsusei: Steinbeck no go Godankei no Shocho shugi," (The Artistic Design of *The Grapes of Wrath*: Steinbeck's Five Layers of Symbolism) *Essays and Studies, Kansai University*, 31 (March 1982), 117-125.

3676 Nakayama, Kiyoshi. "*Ikari no Budou* no Nihongo Hatsuyaku ni tsuite," (On the first Japanese translation of *The Grapes of Wrath*) *The Browser*, 36 (Osaka Yousho, April 1989), 6-10.

3677 Nakayama, Kiyoshi. "*Ikari no Budou* Saikou," (Reconsideration of *The Grapes of Wrath*) *Kaihou*, 5 (1982), 2.

3678 Nakayama, Kiyoshi. "Jackson J. Benson no *John Steinbeck no Shinjitsu no Bouken* no Kousatsu," (A Review of Jackson J. Benson's *The True Adventues of John Steinbeck, Writer*) *Eigo Seinen* (*The Rising Generation*), 130: 7 (October 1, 1984), 350-351.

3679 Nakayama, Kiyoshi. "John Sutainbekku," (John Steinbeck) in *Eigo Eibenbungaku Handobukka* (*A Handbook to English Language and English and American Literature*), ed. Tsuyoshi Uchida, et al. Osaka: Sogensha, 1988. (pp. 227-232)

3680 Nakayama, Kiyoshi. "John Sutainbekku Nenpu," (Chronology of John Steinbeck) in *Sutainbekku Bungaku no Kenkyu—Karuforunia Jidai.* Kansai: Kansai Daigaku Shuppanbu, 1989. (pp. 334-413)

3681 Nakayama, Kiyoshi. "Kaisetsu," (Interpretation) in *Tanoshii Moku-yobi.* Tokyo: Shimin shobo, 1984. (pp. 211-232)

3682   Nakayama, Kiyoshi. "Nihon ni okeru Sutainbekku Bunken
        shoshi — Kenkyu ronbunhen (1940-1991)," (A Checklist
        of Steinbeck Studies in Japan: Books and Articles 1940-
        1991) *Kansai Daigaku Eibungaku Ronshu (Kansai
        University Studies in English Literature Bulletin)*, 31
        (December 20, 1991), 74-130.

3683   Nakayama, Kiyoshi. "Nihon ni okeru Sutainbekku shoshi:
        1978-1980," (A Checklist of Steinbeck Studies in Japan:
        1978-1980) *Kaihou*, 4 (May 1981), 4-6. (bibliography)

3684   Nakayama, Kiyoshi. "1930 nendai no Steinbeck – Denkiteki
        Kenkyu," (Steinbeck's 1930's — Biographical Study)
        *Bungaku Ronshu Souritsu Hyaku shunen kinen tokushu
        go,* Kansai Daigaku Bungaku kai (*Literature Bulletin
        Hundredth Anniversary Special Edition,* Kansai
        University Literature Society), 36 (November 4, 1986),
        117- 141.

3685   Nakayama, Kiyoshi. "*Of Mice and Men*: Ichizuke, o-yobi
        haikei," (*Of Mice and Men*: Placement and Background)
        Kaihou, 4 (1981), 3.

3686   Nakayama, Kousuke. "Ohkubo Yasuo yaku Shincho bunko
        Sutainbekku Tanpenshu — Watashi ga kokoro arawareru
        it-satsu," (Review of Yasuo Ohkudo's translation of
        Steinbeck: The Work Which Captures the Heart)
        Mainichi Shinbun, 39039 (August 31, 1991), 13. (Hayase
        Keiichi ni yoru intabyu kiji)

3687   Nakayama, Kiyoshi. "Pari no Sheikusupia shoten de mitsuketa
        kikanbon," (A Rare Book Found at the Shakespeare and
        Company in Paris) *The Browser,* 44 (Osaka Yosho, June
        1990), 5-8.

3688   Nakayama, Kiyoshi. "Rejisutansu Shousetsu no Bungaku
        kachi no Saihyouka: Sendensha to shiteno John Steinbeck
        no Kousatsu; Donald Coers' no *Tsukiwa Shizuminu* ga
        sensou e iku," (Reappraisal of the Literary Value of a

Resistance Novel: A Review of *John Steinbeck As Propogandist: "The Moon Is Down" Goes to War* by Donald Coers) *Eigo Seinen (The Rising Generation)*, 138:2 (May 1, 1992), 89-91.

3689   Nakayama, Kiyoshi, ed. *Report of the Steinbeck Society of Japan — Executive Director's Office*, 3 (July 1, 1987), 1-6. (This report features two reviews: Minoru Sano's review of Louis D. Owens's *John Steinbeck's Re-Vision of America* (1985) and Hiromasa Takamura's review of Shigeharu Yano, et al. (eds.), *John Steinbeck: From Salinas to the World* (1986))

3690   Nakayama, Mokichi. "Review of Kiyoshi Nakayama's *Sutainbekku Bungaku no Kenkyu — Kariforunia Jidai,*" (Review of Steinbeck's Writings: The California Years) *Jimukyoku Dayori*, 10 (October 22, 1990), 3-4.

3691   Nakayama, Kiyoshi. "Sakuhin ni tsui-te," (On His Work) in *Tanoshii Moku-yobi.* Tokyo: Shimin shobo, 1984. (pp. 220-232)

3692   Nakayama, Kiyoshi. "*Sea of Cortez* kara *The Pearl* e: Hikaku Kousatsu," (From *Sea of Cortez* to *The Pearl:* A Comparative Study) *Studies and Essays, Faculty of Letters, Kansai University,* 43:1 (November 1993), 1-16.

3693   Nakayama, Kiyoshi, trans. "Soviet-Kikou," in *Steinbeck Sakuhin-Ron II.* Tokyo: Eihosha, 1982. (pp. 70-85) (a translation of Charles J. Clancy's Steinbeck's *A Russian Journal* (1948) in *A Study Guide to Steinbeck Pt. II,* ed. Tetsumaro Hayashi. Metuchen, N. J.: Scarecrow Press, 1979, pp. 122-138)

3694   Nakayama, Kiyoshi. "Steinbeck no *Cannery Row* ni tsuite," (On Steinbeck's *Cannery Row*) *Kansai Daigaku Ei-Bungaku Ronshu (Studies in English Literature, Kansai University)*, 23 (December 20, 1983), 79-114.

3695   Nakayama, Kiyoshi. "Steinbeck no 'Kiku' ni okeru josei shinri no Ryoumen kachi," (On Steinbeck's "The Chrysanthemums" — A Woman's Ambivalent Psychology) *Kansai Amerika Bungaku (Kansai American Literature)*, 25 (November 30, 1988), 32-47.

3696   Nakayama, Kiyoshi. "Steinbeck no 'Ohgon no Sakazuki' ni tsuite," (About Steinbeck's *Cup of Gold*) *Kansai Daigaku Eibungaku Ronshu (Kansai University English Literature Bulletin)*, 25 (December 20, 1985), 35-60.

3697   Nakayama, Kiyoshi. "Steinbeck no *Sea of Cortez*," (A Reading of Steinbeck's *Sea of Cortez*) *Kansai Daigaku Eibungaku Ronshu (Kansai University Studies in English Literature Bulletin),* 33 (January 30, 1994), 72-98.

3698   Nakayama, Kiyoshi. "Steinbeck no *Shirarezaru Kami ni* ni tsuite," (About Steinbeck's *To a God Unknown*) *Kansai Daigaku Kenkyu Kiyou (Kansai University Study Bulletin),* 26 (December 20, 1986), 84-121.

3699   Nakayama, Kiyoshi. "Steinbeck no *Ten no Bokujo* ni tsuite," (About Steinbeck's *Pastures of Heaven*) *Bungaku Ronshu (Literature Bulletin), Kansai Daigaku Bungaku kai (Kansai University Literature Society)*, 35:2 (January 31, 1986), 85-107.

3700   Nakayama, Kiyoshi. "Steinbeck no *Tsukiwa Shizuminu*: Engeki Shousetsu to Engekiban," (Steinbeck's *The Moon Is Down:* A Reading of Play Novelette and Play Versions), *Studies in English Literature* (Society of English Language and Literature, Kansai University), 34 (December 20, 1994), 151-182.

3701   Nakayama, Kiyoshi. "Steinbeck to Dai Niji Sekai Taisen," (Steinbeck and World War II) in *Pleasure of Studying English and American Literature: Festschrift in Honor of Professor Toshio Tada.* Osaka: Osaka Kyouikutosho, 1995. (pp. 134-150)

3702   Nakayama, Kiyoshi. "Sutainbekku no *Akai Kouma* ni tsuite,"
        (On Steinbeck's *The Red Pony*) *Kansai Daigaku Bungaku
        Ronshu (Studies in English Literature, Kansai
        University)*, 27 (December 1987), 70-87.

3703   Nakayama, Kiyoshi. "Sutainbekku no *Utawawashii Tatakai* ni
        tsuite," (On Steinbeck's *In Dubious Battle*), *Kansai
        Daigaku Eibungaku Ronshu (Studies in English
        Literature, Kansai University)*, 28 (December 1988), 75-
        105.

3704   Nakayama, Kiyoshi, trans. "Tanoshii Mokuyoubi," in
        Steinbeck Sakuhin-Ron II. Tokyo: Eihosha, 1982. (pp.
        140-164) (a translation of Roy S. Simmonds' Steinbeck's
        Sweet Thursday (1954) in *A Study Guide to Steinbeck Pt.
        II.* ed. Tetsumaro Hayashi. Metuchen, N. J.: Scarecrow
        Press, 1979, pp. 139-164)

3705   Nakayama, Kiyoshi, trans. "Tsuki Wa Sizuminu," in
        Steinbeck Sakuhin-Ron II. Tokyo: Eihosha, 1982. (pp. 28-
        45) (a translation of Charles J. Clancy's Steinbeck's *The
        Moon is Down* (1942) in *A Study Guide to Steinbeck Pt.
        II.* ed. Tetsumaro Hayashi. Metuchen, N. J.: Scarecrow
        Press, 1979, pp. 100-121)

3706   Nakayasu, Hironori. "*Nichiyo Kurabu* (Sunday Club): *Chikyu
        Kakueki Teisha* (The Local Train on Earth: A Walk
        through Masterpieces of the Movies): Monterey, Salinas:
        East of Eden: Shocking Adolescence and an After-
        image," *The Mainichi Shimbun*, 39368 (July 26, 1992), 7.

3707   Nakayata, Yuji. "66 Nenme no 66-Gousen," (66th Year of
        Route 66) *Studies in English Literature, Konan Women's
        University,* 29 (March 1993), 75-84.

3708   Nekrasov, Viktor. "Veselyi starik," (The Joyful Old Man)
        Literaturnaia Gazeta, Moscow, 30 (July 27, 1994), 5510.

3709   Niimura, Akio. "'The Chrysanthemums' Kenkyu," (Study of
        "The Chrysanthemums") *Kitakyushyu Daigaku
        Bungakubu Kiyou (Kita-kyushyu University Literature
        Bulletin),* 42 (March 1990), 45-67.

3710   Niimura, Akio. *"Akai Kouma* no 'Okurimono' — Shonen no
        yume to genjitsu," ("The Gift" in *The Red Pony* — The
        Boy's Dream and Reality) *Kita-Kyushu Daigaku
        Bungakubu Kiyou (Kita-Kyushu University Department of
        Literature Bulletin),* 34 (January 1985), 109-129.

3711   Nikolaeva, E.A. "Pozitsiya avtora v povesti. D Steinbeka
        Nebeskye Pastbishcha. K. vaprosu ob ideino
        Khudozhestvennoi Evolutsii pisatelya," (The Position of
        the Author in Steinbeck's *Pastures of Heaven:* Toward
        the Question of the Ideological and Artistic Evolution of
        the Author) in *Formy raskrytiya avtorskogo coznaniya
        (Forms of Disclosure of Authorial Consciousness)*
        Moscow: Voronezh, 1986. (pp. 121-129)

3712   Nishimura, Chitoshi. "J. Steinbeck No *Akai Kouma* Kenkyu
        'Okurimono' To 'Yakusoku' Chushin To Shite," (A
        Study on J. Steinbeck's *The Red Pony*: Chiefly on "The
        Gift" and "The Promise") *Otaru Jyoshi Tanki Daigaku
        Kenkyu Kiyo (Otaru Women's Junior College Bulletin),*
        13 (March 1982), 37-53.

3713   Nishimura, Chitoshi. "J. Steinbeck no 'The Murder' ni tsuite,"
        (About J. Steinbeck's "The Murder") *Kodaru Joshi Tanki
        Daigaku Kenkyu Kiyou (Otaru Women's Junior College
        Study Bulletin),* 16 (January 1986), 147-163.

3713A   Nishimura, Chitoshi. "J. Steinbeck no 'The Raid' ni Tsuite,"
        (About John Steinbeck's "The Raid") Hokkaido Eigo
        Eibun-gaku, 28 (1983), 39-48.

3714   Nishimura, Chitoshi. "Jikei danin," ("The Vigilante") in
        Steinbeck Kenkyu: Tanpen Shosetsu Ron. ed. Hisachi
        Egusa. Tokyo: Yashio Shuppan-sha, 1987. (pp. 125-137)

3715   Nishimura, Chitoshi. "'Okurimono' to 'Yakusoku,'" ("The
       Gift" and "The Promise") in *Steinbeck Kenkyu: Tanpen
       Shosetsu Ron.* ed. Hisachi Egusa. Tokyo: Yashio
       Shuppan-sha, 1987. (pp. 194-206)

3716   Nishimura, Chitoshi. "Satsuzin," ("The Murder") in *Steinbeck
       Kenkyu: Tanpen Shosetsu Ron.* ed. Hisachi Egusa. Tokyo:
       Yashio Shuppan-sha, 1987. (pp. 153-167)

3717   Nishimura, Chitoshi. "Shugeki," ("The Raid") in *Steinbeck
       Kenkyu: Tanpen Shosetsu Ron.* ed. Hisachi Egusa. Tokyo:
       Yashio Shuppan-sha, 1987. (pp. 89-104)

3718   Nishimura, Chitoshi. "Yamashita Mitsuaki no *Steinbeck
       Sakuhin* no bunseki," (Review of *Steinbeck's Novels* by
       Mitsuaki Yamashita) *Japan Steinbeck Society Bulletin*, 17
       (June 30, 1994), 6-7.

3719   Nishimura, Sennen. "Dai ichiwa Dai niwa ni okeru Jody no
       seicho," (Jody's Growth in Chapters 1 and 2 — *The Red
       Pony*) *Kaihou*, 5 (1982), 3.

3720   Nishimura, Sennen, and Yoshio Ito. "Sutainbekku Shoshi,"
       (Ridiculous Steinbeck) in *Sutainbekku Kenkyu — Tanpen
       shosetsu-ron.* Tokyo: Yashio Shuppan-sha, 1987. (pp.
       258-274) (zouho shinpan, June 1st 1991)

3721   Nishio, Iwao. "John Steinbeck: 'The Murder' shiron —
       Hemingway *Hi wa mata noburu (The Sun Also Rises)* no
       kozo hikaku wo chushin ni," (A Study of John
       Steinbeck's "The Murder": Focusing on the Structural
       Comparison with Hemingway's *The Sun Also Rises*)
       Kyoyo Shogaku Kenkyu (Waseda Daigaku Seiji Keizai
       Gakubu — Waseda University Faculty of Politics and
       Economics), 88 (March 31, 1990), 77-99.

3722   Nobuoka, Haruki. "*Ikari no Budo* Kenkyu," (A Study of *The
       Grapes of Wrath* I) *Studies in English and American*

Literature, (Kansai English and American Literature Society), 29 (November 25, 1991), 154-64.

3723 Nobuoka, Haruki. "*Ikari no Budo* Kenkyu," (A Study of *The Grapes of Wrath* II) *Studies in English and American Literature* (Kansai English and American Literature Society, 30 (December 29, 1992), 129-37.

3724 Ogawa, Takayoshi. "Phalanx no yukue — Steinbeck wa nani o mezashitaka," (The Trace of Phalanx — What Steinbeck Aimed For) *Yokohama-shiritsu Daigaku Ronsou (Jinbun Kagaku keiretsu), (Yokohama-shiritsu University Bulletin (Humanities affiliate)),* 37:1 (March 1986), 49-61.

3725 Ogawa, Takayoshi. "Sakka *Steinbeck no shin no bouken* no bunseki: *Eibungaku kyokai* ni okeru Jackson J. Benson no Denki," (Review of *The True Adventures of John Steinbeck, Writer: A Biography* by Jackson J. Benson in *Eibungaku Kyokai* (Nihon Eibungaku-kai), 63:2 (December 1, 1986), 370-373.

3726 Ohira, Kazuto. "Noberu-sho jushosha Steinbeck o sasaeru otokoto sanbon no ashi," (One Man and Three Legs Supporting the Nobel Laureate Steinbeck) *Ushio,* 410 (May 1993), 278-83. (an interview with Elaine Steinbeck)

3727 Ohmae, Masaomi. "Shin no America wo moto-mete — Yakusha maegaki," (Searching for the True America: Translator's foreword) in *Chahree to no Tabi — America wo moto-mete.* Tokyo: Saimaru Shuppankai, 1987. (pp. 1-5)

3728 Okoshi, Takashi. "Steinbeck Ni Okeru Sei E No Ai To Kurushimi Kiyo," (Suffering and Reverence for Life in the Novels of John Steinbeck) *Eigo Eibei Bungaku Kenkyu Oubirin Daigaku (Obirin Studies in English and American Literature),* 22 (March 1982), 91-102.

3728A   Ose, Eichi. "Steinbeck to '30s nendai Amerika Bungaku wo
        hagimeru hitobito no Tanae ni Iwayama Tajiro hen,"
        (Steinbeck in 1930s American Literature for beginning
        learners, version by Tajiro Iwayama) Kyoto: Sekai
        Shishosa, 1987. (pp. 131-134)

3729   Ota, Toshio. *"Shinbun Shoukairan John Steinbeck hyo* no
        bunseki," (Review of *Shinbun shoukairan John
        Sutainbekku-hyo.* ed. Han Shimizu, Hiroyuki Kobayashi,
        and Kiyoshi Nakayama. *Tanoshii Moku-yobi,* Shimin
        shobo), *Kansia Daigaku Tsushin,* 145 (April 8, 1985), 8.

3730   Ota, Toshio. "Shinkan shoukairan Bungakubu kyouju
        Nakayama Kiyoshi hyo *Sutainbekku Bungaku no
        Kenkyu,*" (Review of Kiyoshi Nakayama's *Sutainbekku
        Bungaku no Kenkyu) Kansia Daigaku Tsushin,* 188
        (February 1, 1990), 8.

3731   Ozawa, Akiko. "'The Chrysanthemums,' ('Kiku') ni o-keru
        shuhou wo show-chou," (Symbolism of Methods used in
        "The Chrysanthemums") *Kaihou,* 4 (1981), 2.

3732   Ozawa, Akiko. "Ishiki To Muishiki No Togo — Steinbeck
        Shinju To Taiyo-Shinwa Obei-Bungaku Koryu No
        Shooso," (Integration of Consciousness and
        Unconsciousness: Steinbeck's *The Pearl* and Solarism) in
        *Obei Bungaku Koryu no Shoyoso (Some Aspects of
        Literary Interchange between Europe and America)* ed.
        Hitoshi Toyota and Tsutomu Hasegawa. Tokyo:
        Sanshusha, 1983. (pp. 199-220)

3733   Ozawa, Akiko. "Jackson Benson hen no *John Steinbeck
        Tanpen: Steinbeck Hiyan no Chekkuristo o fukumu
        Hihyo,*" (Review of *The Short Novels of John Steinbeck:
        Critical Essays with a Checklist to Steinbeck Criticism* ed.
        Jackson J. Benson) *Jimukyoku Dayori (Steinbeck
        Newsletter),* 12 (November 15, 1991), 2-3.

3734 Ozawa, Akiko. "'Kiku' ni okeru higekisei: Hanshoku to Funin no Imeji o toshite," (The Tragical Theme in "The Chrysanthemums": Through the Images of Fertility and Sterility) *Gakuen (Campus) Showa Women's University*, 496 (April 1981), 65-75.

3735 Oziwara, Riki. "Steinbeck to Warai wo Chushin ni," (Focusing on Steinbeck and Jokes) *Senshu Jinbun Ronshu*, 39 (February 1987), 97-125. (*The Short Reign of Pippin IV*)

3736 Peterson, Richard F, "Shogen," (Introduction) in *Sutainbekku no Joseizo (Steinbeck's Women)*. ed. Mitsuaski Yamashita. Tokyo: Oshisha, 1991. (pp. 12-19)

3737 Pugh, Scott. "Steinbeck Sakuhin: Computer ni yoru keishikiteki buntai no kanousei," (Steinbeck's Novels: Possibilities for Stylistic Analysis by Computer) in *Eigo Eibungaku Kenkyu to Computer (Studies in English Language and Literature and the Computer)*. ed. Toshio Saito. Tokyo: Eichosha, 1992. (pp. 52-71)

3738 Pugh, Scott. "Steinbeck no Shousetsu — Computer ni yoru buntaibunseki no kanousei," (Steinbeck's Novels: Possibility of Stage Analysis by Computer) in *Eigo-eibungaku kenkyu to computer*. ed. Toshio Saito. Tokyo: Eishosha, 1992. (pp. 29-48)

3739 Renaux, Sigrid. "Antropomorfismo e Zoomorfismo no Conto 'Fuga' de John Steinbeck," (Anthropomorphism and Zoomorphism in the Short Story "Flight," by John Steinbeck) *Revista Letras Curitiba, Parana Brazil*, 32 (1983), 138-151.

3740 "Review of *Conversations with John Steinbeck*. Edited by Thomas Fensch. Literary Conversations Series," *Jimukyoku Dayori*, 8 (1990), 4-5.

3741   "Review of *Sutainbekku Sakuhin (Steinbeck's Novels)* by
         Mitsuaki Yamashita," *Sanyo Shimbun* (March 21, 1994),
         8.

3742   Rolli, Doris. "The Theme of History in *The Grapes of Wrath*,"
         in "Chronique Annuelle de la Faculté des Lettres: Année
         académique 1983/1984," *Etudes de Lettres* (Revue de la
         Faculté des Lettres, Université de Lausanne),
         (Janvier/Mars 1985), 131.

3742A   Rucklin-Banderier, Christine. "John Steinbeck as a Reader of
         Frazer in *The Grapes of Wrath*," *Mythes, Croyances et
         Religions dans le Monde Anglo-Saxon (Myths Beliefs and
         Religions in the Anglo-Saxon World)* 13, 1995.

3742B   Rucklin-Banderier, Christine. "Steinbeck lecteur de Sophocle
         dans le *Raisins de la Colere*," (Steinbeck's Reading of
         Sophocles in *The Grapes of Wrath*) *Revue
         Luxembourgeoise de Literature Generale et Conparee*,
         (Luxembourg Review of General and Comparative
         Literature), 1995.

3743   Saima, Yumiko. "*The Pastures of Heaven* ni okeru 'noroi' ni
         tsuite," (On the 'Curses' in *The Pastures of Heaven*)
         Jissen English Literature (Jissen Women's University) 41
         (July 20, 1992), 145-155.

3744   Sakai, Yasuhiro. "Sutainbekku no 'The Chrysanthemums' ni
         mirareru ishiki to muishiki — Elisa ga shitta mono," (The
         Conscious and the Unconscious in Steinbeck's "The
         Chrysanthemums": What Elisa Knew) *Chu-Shikoku
         Studies in American Literature* (The Chu-Shikoku
         American Literature Society), 26 (June 1990), 54-66.

3745   Sakai, Yasuhiro. "Sutainbekku *The Pearl* Kenkyu Buntai kara
         mita sakuhin no kaishaku," (A Study of Steinbeck's *The*

Pearl: An Interpretation from the Stylistic Viewpoint) *Yonago Technical College Bulletin*, 23 (1987), 49-58.

3746 Sakai, Yasuhiro. "Tuleracito ni mirareru muishiki no kozo," (The Structure of the Unconscious in Tularecito) *Chu-Shikoku American Literature Bulletin*, 23 (June 1987), 39-48.

3747 Sakai, Yasuhiro. "Seiyou geki no atarashii kokoromi: *Eden no Higashi* kanatsu," (The Western Stage's New Attempts: A Viewing of *East of Eden*) *Japan Steinbeck Society Bulletin*, 18 (November 10, 1994), 6.

3748 Sano, Makoto. "Louis D. Owens ni yoru *John Steinbeck no Amerikae no Atarashii mikata*," (Review of Louis D. Owens' *John Steinbeck's Re-Vision of America*) *Jimukyoku Dayori*, 3 (July 1, 1987), 2-3.

3749 Sano, Minoru. "*Akai Kouma* ron," (On *The Red Pony*) *Tokiwa Gakuen Daigaku Kenkyu Kiyo (Tokoha Gakuen University Bulletin)*, 4 (December 25, 1987), 1-12.

3750 Sano, Tomoko. "*The Pastures of Heaven* ni okeru Haha to msume," (Mothers and Daughters in *The Pastures Of Heaven*) *Jissen Eibungaku (English Literature Society, Jissen Women's University)*, 44 (January 30, 1994), 1-15.

3751 Sasakura, Hiroko. "Steinbeck *ni okeru Dainiji Sekai Taisen Fikushon 'The Moon Is Down': Mittsuno Kaishau* no bunseki," (Review of *Steinbeck's World War II Fiction, "The Moon Is Down": Three Explications*. ed. Tetsumaro Hayashi. trans. Eiko Shiraga) *Japan Steinbeck Society Bulletin*, 17 (June 30, 1994), 4-5.

3752 Sasakura, Hiroko. "Sutainbekku josei no nimen to sono yugo," (Steinbeck: The Two Sides of Women and Their Fusion) *Persica* (Okayama English Anglo American Cultural Studies Assn.), 116 (March 1989), 115-125.

3753   Sato, Yoshitaka. *"Ikari no Budo* no Hih," (On the Criticism of *The Grapes of Wrath) Gifu Women's University Bulletin,* 21 (January 31, 1993), 47-53.

3754   Sawada, Suketaro. "Dai-ichiwa: *Ikari no Budo,"* (Chapter 1: *The Grapes of Wrath*) in *Amerika Bungaku to Kyuyaku Seisho: Sutainbekku, Heminguuei, Fokuna, Forusuto, Meruviru (American Literature and the Old Testament: Steinbeck, Hemingway, Faulkner, Frost and Melville)* Tokyo: Kindai Bungeisha, 1993. (pp. 11-22)

3755   Sawada, Suketaro. "Dai-niwa: *Eden no Higashi,"* (Chapter 2: *East of Eden*) in *Amerika Bungaku to Kyuyaku Seisho: Sutainbekku, Heminguuei, Fokuna, Forusuto, Meruviru (American Literature and the Old Testament: Steinbeck, Hemingway, Faulkner, Frost and Melville)* Tokyo: Kindai Bungeisha, 1993. (pp. 23-35)

3756   Sawada, Suketaro. "Steinbeck no *Ikari no Budo* to Kyuyaku Seisho," (Steinbeck's *The Grapes Of Wrath* and the Old Testament) *Gifu Women's University Bulletin,* 22 (February 27, 1993), 37-43.

3757   Senda, Akio. "Steinbeck No *To a God Unknown* Sakuhin Ni Mirareru Ikyo-sei Ni Tsuite," (Steinbeck's *To a God Unknown*: Heathenism in His Novel) *Toho Gakuen Daigaku Tanki Daigaku-bu Kiyo (Toho Gakuen Junior College Bulletin),* 2 (October 1983), 1-14.

3758   Setogawa, Takeshi. "Shizen to Bunmei no Kankei ni tsuite: John Steinbeck no *Sea of Cortez* no bunseki," (Insight on the Relation Between Nature and Civilization: A Review of John Steinbeck's *Sea of Cortez,* trans. Noriko Yoshimura and Mioko Nishida) *Mainichi Shimbun,* 39557 (February 1, 1993), 11.

3759   Shikii, Kumiko. "Shinjyu Nidai: chusei to Gendai," (The Two "Pearls": Medieval and Modern) *Sendai Shirayuri Gakuen Bulletin*, 15 (1987), 115-127.

3760   Shima, Ryotaro. "Jikan no Sayou no Sugomi — *Ikari no Budou* no machi," (The Gruesomeness of Times's Work: The Cities of *The Grapes of Wrath*) America Subyou Dai 1 bu 6, *Yomiuri Shinbun,* 11662 (April 6, 1985), 1. (also *America Su-byo.* Tokyo, Yomiuri Shinbunsha (April 11 1986), 53-62 ni sairoku)

3760A   Shimada, Saburo. "J. Steinbeck Kenkyu (iii): *Ikari No Budo* no Guayule no Gomu no ki ni Tsuite," (John Steinbeck study (Pt. III): *The Grapes of Wrath* Criticism) *Kenmei Joshi Gakuin Tanki Daigaku Kenkyo Kiyo* (*Kenmei Women's Junior College Bulletin*), 18 (March 1983), 35-48.

3761   Shimada, Saburo. "J. Steinbeck to shokubutsu no byosha," (John Steinbeck and the Description of Plants) *Kaihou,* 3 (1980), 2.

3762   Shimada, Saburo. "John Steinbeck: *East of Eden* No Kenkyu (ii) — Futatsu No Hihyo Ni Tsuite," (A Study Note on John Steinbeck (Pt. II): Two Ways of Criticism of *East of Eden)* *Kenmei Jyoshi Gakuin Tanki Daigaku Kenkyu Kiyo* (*Kenmei Women's Junior College Bulletin*), 17 (March 1982), 1-15.

3763   Shimada, Saburo. "Mini-nyuzu-ran California Poppy Hanabishisou . . . keshi no it-shu," (Orchids, California Poppy and Hanbishou . . . Poppy's Life Cycle) *Kaihou,* 4 (1981), 6.

3764   Shimada, Saburo. "Mini-nyuzu-ran Rose of Sharon no koto," (About Rose of Sharon) *Kaihou,* 3 (1980), 5.

3765   Shimada, Saburo. "Mini Nyuzu ran Futatabi Rose of Sharon ni tsui-te," (Once Again about Rose of Sharon) *Kaihou*, 5 (1982), 6.

3766   Shimada, Saburo. "Steinbeck to Shokubutsu Toro Ni Kakete,"
        (Steinbeck and Plants) *Kenmei Jyoshi Gakuin Tanki
        Daigaku DoSoukai (Kenmei Women's Junior College
        Bulletin),* December 1982, pp. 46-76.

3767   Shimizu, Han. "Atogaki," (Afterword) in *Tanoshii Moku-yobi
        (Sweet Thursday).* Tokyo: Shimin shobo, 1984. (pp. 233-
        238)

3768   Shimizu, Han. "Gaka no dentou ni okeru Sutainbekku,"
        (Steinbeck from the Tradition of Artists) *Kaihou,* 3
        (1980), 1.

3769   Shimizu, Han. "Seisho Kaishaku kara Bungaku Kanshou e –
        Shousetsu no Daimei o Megutte," (From Bible
        Interpretation to Literature Appreciation — Concerning
        the Title of Novels) *Shingaku to Jinmon-Osaka
        Kirisutokyou Tandai Kiyou (Theology and Humanity
        Osaka Christianity Junior College Bulletin),* 25 (October
        1985), 83-93.

3770   Shimomura, Noboru. "Kenkyu Happyo Shikai no Ji,"
        (Research Publications — Address of the Chairperson)
        Kaihou, 4 (1981), 1.

3771   Shimomura, Noboru. "Sutainbekku no zentaizou syposium —
        shukyouteki shinpishugi-teki Sokumen," (Steinbeck's
        Overall Symposium: Religious and Mystical Aspects)
        Kaihou, 3 (1980), 3.

3772   Shinmura, Akio. "'The Chrysanthemums' Kenkyu,"
        (Research on "The Chrysanthemums") *Kitakyushu
        Daigaku Bungakubu Kiyo (Journal of the Faculty of
        Literature — Kitakyushu University),* 42 (March 1990),
        45-67.

3773   Shinmura, Akio. "*Akai Kouma* ni okeru 'okurimono' —
        Shonen no Yume to genjitsu," ("The Gift" in *The Red
        Pony* — Dream and Reality of a Boy) *Kitakyushu*

Daigaku Bungakubu Kiyo (Journal of The Faculty of Literature — Kitakyushu University), 34 (1985), 109-129.

3774   Shinmura, Akio. "'The Great Mountains' to 'Kogane no ken' ni okeru chusei dansetsu," (Medieval Legends in "The Great Mountains" and "The Golden Sword") *Kitakyushu Daigaku Bungakubu Kiyo (Kitakyushu University Faculty of Literature Bulletin)*, 38 (October 1987), 17-36.

3775   Shinmura, Akio. "'The Promise' — Nyukai monogatari no kansei," (Steinbeck on "The Promise" — the Finish of an Initiation Story) *Kitakyushu Daigaku Bungakubu Kiyo (Kitakyushu University Faculty of Literature Bulletin)*, 40 (October 1989), 27-43.

3776   Shiraga, Eiko. "Of Mice and Men Hatsuka Nezumi to Ningen ni Okeru Curley no tsuma no yaku," (The Role of Curley's Wife in Steinbeck's *Of Mice and Men*) in *Sutainnbekku Sakka Sakuhin Ron (Steinbeck and His Works: A Festschrift in Honor of Dr. Tetsumaro Hayashi).* ed. Eiko Shiraga and Yasuo Hashiguchi. Tokyo: Eihosha, 1995. (155-170)

3777   Shiraga, Eiko, trans. "Steinbeck to Gengo Dentatsu," (Steinbeck and Speech Communication) *Shujitsu Women's University Bulletin*, 10 (March 20, 1992), 207-230. (a translation of Tetsumaro Hayashi's 1990 lecture entitled "John Steinbeck on Speech Communication")

3778   Shirakami, Shigeko. "Steinbeck no 'Satsujin' Kousatsu," (A Consideration of "The Murder") *Narima Eigaku Ronshu (Narima English Collective Discourse, Narima Women's University English Assn.)*, 7 (March 20, 1988), 17-33.

3779   Silhol, Robert. "*Les Raisins de la Colere* et l'histoire: Conditions sociologiques de production," (*The Grapes of Wrath* and History: Sociological Conditions of Its

Composition) *Revue Francaise d'Etudes Americaines,*
Paris, France, 53 (August 1992), 281-292.

3780   Silhol, Robert. *"Les Raisins de la Colere* et la crise de 1929:
        Actes du Groupe de Recherche et d'Etudes Nord
        Americaines," (*The Grapes of Wrath* and the 1929 Crisis:
        Acts of the Research Group of North America Studies) in
        The Twenties. ed. Barbara Smith Lemeunier. Aix-en
        Provence: Université de Provence, 1982. (pp. 121-128)

3781   Sogabu, Manabu. "Steinbeck *Kanzume Yokocho* ni taisuru
        Hihyo wo Megutte: Suzki Yukio Sensei Kinen Ron bushu
        Kanko IIkai," (On the Criticism of Steinbeck's *Cannery
        Row*: Mr. Yukio Suzuki's Memorial Essay Publishing
        Committee) and *Kimegure Basu: Phoenix o Motomete*
        (Steinbeck's *The Wayward Bus*: Seeking for the Phoenix)
        in *Sensei Kinen Ronbu-shu Kanko Iiin-kai: Eibei Shosetsu
        no Yukue.* ed. Yukio Suzuki *(The Search for the Phoenix:
        The Future of American/British Novels).* Tokyo: Nanundo,
        1982. (pp. 325-338)

3782   "Steinbeck no Dokurha," (Steinbeck's Reading Public)
        *Fukuoka University General Education Research Institute
        Bulletin (Fukuoka Daigaku Sogo Kenkyusho Hokoku),* 8
        (April 1984), 2-3.

3783   "Steinbeck-sai ni sankashite I," (Participating in the
        Steinbeck Festival I) *Kyouiku Gakujutsu Shimbun* (Tokyo),
        (October 5, 1983), 3.

3784   "Steinbeck-sai ni sankashite I," (Participating in the Steinbeck
        Festival I) *Kyouiku Gakujutsu Shimbun* (Tokyo), (October
        12, 1983), 4.

3785   "Steinbeck tono Kaiwa no bunseki," (Review of
        Conversations with John Steinbeck. ed. Thomas Fensch.

Literary Conversations Series) *Jimukyoku Dayori*, 8 (1990), 4-5.

3786   Sugiura, Ginsaku. "Shimomura Noboru ni okeru *John Steinbeck Kenkyu: Shosetsu ni okeru Shinpisei*," (Review of *A Study of John Steinbeck: Mysticism in His Novels* by Noboru Shimomura) *America Bungaku Kenkyu* (Nihon America Bungakukai), 20 (1983), 106-112.

3787   Sugiyama, Takahiko. "Bokka no Byourigaku *The Pastures of Heaven*," (Pastoral Pathology: *The Pastures of Heaven*) *Kaihou*, 3 (1980), 3.

3788   Sugiyama, Takahiko. "Bokka Hougaku no Kenshou Kiyo — 'Akai Kouma' to *Nagai Tani*," (A Pastoral Verification – "The Red Pony" and *The Long Valley*) *Seijo Hogaku Kiyo Ronshu* (*Seijo Law Liberal Arts Bulletin*), 4 (March, 1984), 123-138.

3789   Sugiyama, Takahiko. "Bokka no Fukken — "S*hirerazaru Kami ni'* to *Tortilla Flat*," (Pastoral Reinstatement — *To a God Unknown* and *Tortilla Flat*) *Seijo hogaku Kyoyo Ronshu (Seijo Jurisprudence Liberal Arts Bulletin)*, 6 (May 1986), 3-26.

3790   Sugiyama, Takahiko. "Choryu no ecoroji: Steinbeck no Shizen Kanten," (Ecology of the Tide Pools: Steinbeck's View of Nature) *Seijo Hogaku Kyoyo Ronshu* (*Seijo Law Liberal Arts Bulletin*), 10 (January 1993), 5-33.

3791   Sugiyama, Takahiko. "Chuken-geki to Camera no Me o 'Modus Operandi' to shite: Steinbeck to Hemingway," (Play-Novelette and Camera Eye as Modus Operandi: Steinbeck and Hemingway," in *Sutainnbekku Sakka Sakuhin Ron (Steinbeck and His Works: A Festschrift in Honor of Dr. Tetsumaro Hayashi).* ed. Eiko Shiraga and Yasuo Hashiguchi. Tokyo: Eihosha, 1995. (66-82)

3792 Sugiyama, Takahiko. "Daigo Steinbeck-sai ni Sanka Shite - Dai-ni kai Steinbeck Kokusai Kaigi," (On Steinbeck Festival V — International Steinbeck Congress II) *Eigo Hyogen Kenkyu* (*Bulletin of the Japan Society of English Usage and Style)*, 5 (November 10, 1984), 10-11.

3793 Sugiyama, Takahiko. "Gendaijin Sutainbekku: Makuro-bungaku — sona-ei," (Modernist Steinbeck: Macro-Literature II) *Seijo Hougaku Kyouiku Ronshu (Liberal Arts Review, Seijo University Faculty of Law)*, 8 (December 1990), 5-41.

3794 Sugiyama, Takahiko. "John Steinbeck bunseki: Rodo no Hibi," (Review of John Steinbeck: *Working Days: The Journal of "The Grapes of Wrath,"* ed. Robert DeMott) *Jimukyoku Dayori*, 8 (1990), 6-7.

3795 Sugiyama, Takahiko. "Sarinasu kara Sekai-e Mukete — Dai-ni kai Sutainbekku Kokusai Kaigi," (From Salinas to the World: Second International Steinbeck Congress) *Eigo Seinen* (*The Rising Generation*), 130:8 (November 1, 1984), 395.

3796 Sugiyama, Takahiko. "Steinbeck Kenkyu — Tanpen Shosetsu ron ni Okeru Egusa Hisaji ni yoru shinkansho kanran," (Review of Newly Published Articles by Hisaji Egusa in Steinbeck Studies — Essays on the Short Stories) *Eigo Seinen*, 133:7 (October 1, 1987), 351.

3797 Sugiyama, Takahiko. "Sutainbekku Bungaku Jiten eno Kokoromi — Kenkyu Noto," (Work in Progress — Steinbeck Dictionary) *Seijo Hougaku Kyouiku Ronshu (Liberal Arts Review, Seijo University Faculty of Law)*, 7 (April 1988), 93-130.

3798 Sumikawa, Sho. "Inoue Hirotsugu hen no *America Bungaku ni okeru Yume to Houkai* bunseki," (Review of *The Dream*

and Its Destruction in American Literature, ed. Hirotsugu
Inoue) Eibungaku Shichou (Aoyama Gakuin Daigaku
Eibungakukai), 61 (December 20, 1988), 115-117.

3799   Suzue, Akiko. "Cathy ni tsuite: Eden no Higashi Kenkyu II,"
(On Cathy: A Study of East of Eden II), Hinchou
Eibungaku, Jissen Eibungakkai (Jissen English Literature,
Jissen Women's University), 39 (July 10, 1991), 1-12.

3800   Suzue, Akiko. "Henshii to Jobun o fukumu Harold Bloom no
John Steinbeck, Gendai Hihan Ron no bunseki," (Review
of Harold Bloom's (ed. with introduction) John Steinbeck,
Modern Critical Views) Jimukyoku Dayori, 5 (July 1,
1988), 2-4.

3801   Suzue, Akiko. "Kagamino no naka no Cathy: Eden no
Higashi Kenkyu," (Cathy in The Mirror: A Study of East
of Eden (III)) Hinchou Eibungaku, Jissen Eibungakkai
(Jissen English Literature, Jissen Women's University), 39
(March 20, 1993), 135-146.

3802   Suzue, Akiko. "Sutainbekku no Sekai — Eden no Higashi wo
Yomu," (Steinbeck's World: On Reading East of Eden)
Hinchou Eibungaku, Jissen Eibungakkai (Jissen English
Literature, Jissen Women's University), (October 1989),
75-123.

3803   Suzuki, Reiko. "Steinbeck Ikari no budo ni tsuite no ichi
kenkyu," (A Research of Steinbeck's Grapes of Wrath)
Tohoku Fukushi Daigaku Kiyou (Tohoku Fukushi
University Bulletin), 11 (1986), 101-109.

3804   Suzuki, Yoshio. "Steinbeck No Shinwa Gendai Eibei-
Bungaku No Isho" (The Legend of Steinbeck: The Master
of Contemporary English American Literature). Tokyo:
Tokyo-do Shuppan, 1982. (pp. 203-214)

3805   Tada, Toshio. "John Steinbeck: Asia teki Kanten no bunseki,"
(Review of John Steinbeck: Asian Perspectives. ed.

Kiyoshi Nakayama, et al.) *Kansai Daigaku Tsushin (Kansai University News)*, 214 (January 11, 1993), 8.

3806   Tada, Toshio. "Review of *Sutainbekku Bungaku no Kenkyu: Kariforunia Jidai* by Kiyoshi Nakayama," *(Steinbeck's Writings: The California Years) Kansai University Newsletter,* 188 (February 1990), 8.

3807   Tagaya, Satoru. "Kuso ni okeru Steinbeck no Jikken: *King Arthur to Kare no Kedakai Kishi Tachi* no todo," (John Steinbeck's Experiment in Fabulation: *The Acts of King Arthur and His Noble Knights*) *Baika Joshi Daigaku Eibei Bungaku Gakkai (Baika Review,* Baika Women's University), 24 (March 20, 1991), 31-41.

3808   Tagaya, Satoru. "Steinbeck and Vonnegut: Guwa kara Kuso e," (Steinbeck and Vonnegut: From Fable to Fabulation) in *Sutainnbekku Sakka Sakuhin Ron (Steinbeck and His Works: A Festschrift in Honor of Dr. Tetsumaro Hayashi).* ed. Eiko Shiraga and Yasuo Hashiguchi. Tokyo: Eihosha, 1995. (pp. 93-106)

3809   Takahashi, Sakae. "Steinbeck no Kankyouteki Kanten," (Steinbeck's Ecological Viewpoint) *Danwa Amerika Bungaku Matsue* (Matsue American Literature Society), 2 (June 1994), 36-41.

3810   Takamura, Hiromasa. "*Akaruku Moeru* o Opera: Souzou e no Michi," *(Burning Bright* as Opera: The Path of Creation) *Ohtani Joshi Daigaku Eibungaku Kaishi (Studies in English Literature Ohtani Women's University),* 22 (March 10, 1995), 115-132.

3811   Takamura, Hiromasa. "Atogaki" (Afterword) in *Sutainbekku Tanpen Kenkyu — "Nagai Tanima" Ron (Steinbeck's: Short Stories in "The Long Valley": Essays in Criticism.* ed. Tetsumaro Hayashi). trans. Hiromasa Takamura, T. J.

O'Brien, and Tatsuo Narita. Kyoto: Aporon-sha, 1992.
(pp. 217-218)

3812   Takamura, Hiromasa. "Gigyoku "Hatsuka nezumi to ningen"
        no ichi-kousatsu," (Consideration of the Play *Of Mice and
        Men*) *Ohtani Joshi Daigaku Eibungaku Kaishi* (*Ohtani
        Women's University English Literature Bulletin*), 12
        (March, 1985), 1-14.

3813   Takamura, Hiromasa. "*Ikari no Budou*," *(The Grapes Of
        Wrath) Japan Steinbeck Society Bulletin*, 18 (November
        10, 1994), 8.

3814   Takamura, Hiromasa. "*Of Mice and Men*: Opera no Kenkyu,"
        (A Study of *Of Mice and Men* as Opera) in *Sutainnbekku
        Sakka Sakuhin Ron (Steinbeck and His Works: A
        Festschrift in Honor of Dr. Tetsumaro Hayashi)*. ed. Eiko
        Shiraga and Yasuo Hashiguchi. Tokyo: Eihosha, 1995.
        (pp. 171-188)

3815   Takamura, Hiromasa. "Review of Shigeharu Yano,
        Tetsumaro Hayashi, Richard F. Peterson and Yasuo
        Hashiguchi, eds. *John Steinbeck : From Salinas to the
        World*," *Jimukyoku Dayori*, 3 (July 1, 1987), 2-3.

3816   Takamura, Hiromasa. "Steinbeck — Himokutekishikoo to
        Ikinukuchikara," (Steinbeck — Non-teleological Thinking
        and Power of Survival) in *Kawa no America Bungaku*. ed
        Tajiro Iwayama and Beppu Keiko. Tokyo: Nan' undo,
        1992. (pp. 203-214)

3817   Takanori, Kinoshita, trans. "R. W. B. Lewis's "John
        Steinbeck" in *The Young Rebel in American Literature,*"
        ed. Carl Bode. Tokyo: Nanundo Press, 1984. (pp. 185-212)

3818   Tanaka, Keisuke. "Dantai to Kojin to shi te no George,
        Lennie," (George and Lennie and the Concept of Group-
        Man) *Kaihou*, 4 (1981), 3. (*Of Mice and Men*)

3819   Tanaka, Keisuke. "*John Steinbeck Kenkyu: Eikou no Toki,*
        1936-1939, Tetsumaro Hayashi, Henshusha," (Review of
        John Steinbeck: The Years Of Greatness, 1936-1939, ed.
        Tetsumaro Hayashi) *Japan Steinbeck Society Bulletin,* 17
        (June 30, 1994), 2-3.

3820   Taniguchi, Yoshiro. "*Nihon ni Okeru Steinbeck no Kenkyu:*
        Denki, Kiyoshi Nakayama, Henshusah," (Review of
        Steinbeck in Japan: A Bibliography, ed. Kiyoshi
        Nakayama) *Kansai Daigaku Tsushin* (Kansai University
        News), 215 (February 1, 1993), 8.

3821   "Theater ran Butai no Yomi gaetta *Ikari no Budou,"*
        Newsweek (April 19, 1990), 69. (Steppenwolf's
        production of *The Grapes of Wrath*)

3822   Tomiyama, Takao. "Mikainarumono to Gusnshin —
        California Kara Mexico," (Primitiveness and the War-God:
        From California to Mexico," *Shisho (Thought),* 688
        (October 1981), 165-177.

3823   Tomiyama, Takao. "Mikainarumono to Gusnshin —
        California Kara Mexico," (Primitiveness and the War-God
        (*To a God Unknown):* from California to Mexico) in
        Tekisuto no Kigo-Ron (Symbolism in the Text). Tokyo:
        Nan' undo, 1982. (pp. 78-97)

3824   Toyonaga, Akira. "Hashiguchi Yasuo to Koichi Kaida no
        Ikari no Budou, Eichosha Buraken Mokuroku Sho no
        Saikou," (Review of Yasuo Hashiguchi and Koichi
        Kaida's *The Grapes of Wrath, Eichosha Commentary
        Booklet*) *Jimukyoku Dayori,* 6 (November 11, 1988), 2-3.

3825   Tsuboi, Hisaji, and Fumio Momose. "Bunken Mokuroku
        sho," (Commentary Booklet) in *Sutainbekku zen tanpen
        ron — Akai Uma wo koete* (Steinbeck's *The Red Pony*).
        Tokyo: Eihousha, 1991. (pp. 182-194)

3826 Tsuboi, Kiyohiko. "Nihon Sutainbekku Kyokai," (Japan
Steinbeck Society) *Nihon America Bungaku Kaihou ALSJ,*
xxiii (1985), 21, 27.

3827 Tsuboi, Kiyohiko. "Nihon Sutainbekku Kyoukai (katsudou
jyokyo)," (Japan Steinbeck Society Bulletin), *Tokyo
Daigaku America Kenkyu Shiryo Sentah Nenpo,* Dai 5 go,
(March 1982), 99-100.

3828 Tsuboi, Kiyohiko. "Review of Robert DeMott's *Steinbeck's
Reading: A Catalogue of Books Owned and Borrowed,*
(1984)," *Persica* (Okayama Eigo Eibei Bungaku Kenkyu
kai — Okayama English Literary Society), 12 (March 1,
1985), 67.

3829 Tsuboi, Kiyohiko. "Review of *Steinbekku Sakuhinron (II).*
trans. Kenji Inoue, Kiyoshi Nakayama, and Fumio
Momose." Tokyo, Japan: Eihosha Press, 1982. (a
translation of Tetsumaro Hayashi, ed. *A Study Guide to
Steinbeck (II)* (Metuchen, N. J.: Scarecrow Press, 1979))

3830 Tsuboi, Kiyohiko. "Review of *Sutainbekku Bungaku no
Kenkyu: Kariforunia Jidai* by Kiyoshi Nakayama,"
*(Steinbeck's Writings: The California Years) Eigo Seinen
(The Rising Generation),* 136:2 (May 1, 1990), 43.

3831 Tsuboi, Kiyohiko. "Review of *Sutainbekku no Joseizo
(Steinbeck's Women),* trans. Mitsuaki Yamashita," (a
translation of Tetsumaro Hayashi's *Steinbeck's Women:
Essays in Criticism) Jimukyoku Dayori (Steinbeck
Newsletter),* 11 (June 20, 1991), 4.

3832 Tsuboi, Kiyohiko. "Steinbeck *Kenkyu* no Saikou —
Tetsumaro Hayashi, henshusha, Mikio Inui, Yakusha no
Kikou Bungaku-ronshu to John Ditsky no *John Steinbeck:
Sinsei to Shigato Sorekara Hihan,*" (Review of
Sutainbekku Kenkyu — Kikou Bungakuron-shu, ed.
Tetsumaro Hayashi and trans. Mikio Inui. (Mikio Inui's

translation of *Steinbeck's Travel Literature* (SMS, No. 10,
1980)) and John Ditsky's *John Steinbeck: Life Work, and
Criticism*) *Persica* (Okayama Eigoeibun gakkai —
Okayama English Literary Society), 13 (March 1986),
109-111.)

3833   Tsuboi, Kiyohiko, and Fumio Momose. "Yakusha Atogaki,"
(Translator's Afterword) in *Sutainbekku zen tanpen ron* —
Akai Uma wo koete (Steinbeck's *The Red Pony*). Tokyo:
Eihousha, 1991. (pp. 195-196)

3834   Tsuboyama, Mariko. "John Steinbeck no *Ikari no Budou* no
Kenkyu," (A Study of John Steinbeck's *The Grapes of
Wrath)* Otsuma Review* (Otsuma Women's University
English Literature Society), 25 (July 15, 1992), 141-49.

3835   Tsuji, Takeo. "Hieiyu jidai no hiiroo Sutainbekku no 'Jinmin
no Shidousha' ni tsuite," (Hero in Unheroic Times — On
Steinbeck's "The Leader of the People"*) Nagasaki
Daigaku Kyouikugakuku Jimbun Kagaku Kenkyu Kihoku
(Humanities Research Bulletin, Nagasaki University
Faculty of Education)*, 37 (March 1988), 45-50.

3836   Tsuji, Takeo. "Kino to Juana no kikan — 'Shinju' ni okeru
Steinbeck no seishin-shugi," (Kino and Juana's Return —
Steinbeck's Spiritual Principle in *The Pearl*) *Nagasaki
Daigaku Kyouiku Gakubu Jimbun-kagaku Kenkyu Hokoku
(Nagasaki University Education Department Humanities
Study Report)*, 34 (March 1985), 1-14.

3837   Tsuji, Takeo. "Kino to Juana no kikan — 'Shinju' ni okeru
Steinbeck no seishin-shugi," (Kino and Juana's Return —
Steinbeck's Spiritual Principle in *The Pearl*) *Bulletin of
the Faculty of General Education, Nagasaki University*, 12
(March 1985), 51-57.

3838   Tsuji, Takeo. "Mary Teller No Niwa: Steinbeck No 'Shiroi
Uzura' Ni Tsuite," (Mary Teller's Garden: About
Steinbeck's "The White Quail") *Nagasaki Daigaku*

Kyouiku-Gakubu Jinbun-Kagaku Kenkyu Hokoku (*Nagasaki University Education Department Humanity Study Report*), 31 (March 1983), 17-27.

3839 Tsuji, Takeo. "Steinbeck no *Kanzume Yokocho* — Sonzai no hiai no kenkyu," (Steinbeck's *Cannery Row* — Existence of Sorrow Study) *Nagasaki Daigaku Kyouiku Gakubu Jinbun Kagaku Kenkyu Hokoku (Nagasaki University Education Department Humanity Study Report)*, 35 (March 1986), 63-73.

3840 Tsuji, Takeo. "Steinbeck no 'Kiku' — Futrkigou na Fufu no Monogatari," (Steinbeck's "The Chrysanthemums"): A Story of a Mismatched Couple) *Nagasaki Daigaku Kyouiku gakubu Jinbunkagaku Kenkyu Houkoku (Nagasaki University Faculty of Education and Humanities Bulletin)*, 42 (March 1991), 43-50.

3841 Uza, Tokumitsu. "*Charley tono Tabi* ni okeru Steinbeck no Jigazo to Shite," (*Travels with Charley* as Steinbeck's Self-Portrait) *Nagasaki Kenritsu Kokusai Keizai Daigaku Ronshu* (Journal of Liberal Arts and Economics, University of International Economics, Sasebo, Nagasaki, Japan), 17:1 (August 1983), 1-26.

3842 Uza, Tokumitsu. "Kobayashi to Steinbeck no Hikaku Kenkyu: Tohashin ni Tsuite," (A Comparative Approach to Kobayashi and Steinbeck: In Light of Partisanship) *Nagasaki Kenritsu Kokusai Keizai Daigaku Onshu* (Journal of Liberal Arts and Economics, University of International Economics, Sasebo, Nagasaki, Japan), 15 (August 1981), 99-120.

3843 Uza, Tokumitsu. "*Shugoteki Seikaku Byosha* ni Okeru Kanibune to *Utagawahii Tatakai* no Hikaku," (*A Crab-Packing Vessel* vs. *In Dubious Battle* in Collective Characterization) *Nagasaki Kenritsu Kokusai Keizai*

Daigaku Onshu (Journal of Liberal Arts and Economics, University of International Economics, Sasebo, Nagasaki, Japan), 15 (November 1981), 91-108.

3843A   Wada, Tesuya. "John Steinbeck no *Of Mice and Men* ni Tsuite," (A Study of John Steinbeck's *Of Mice and Men*) *Jyoshi Daigaku Kiyo: Bungaku-bu en*, 31 (1983), 21-29.

3844   Watanabe, Kazukiyo. *"Eden no Higashi* to California*,"* *(East of Eden* and California) *Japan Steinbeck Society Bulletin*, 18 (November 10, 1994), 6.

3845   Watanabe, Kazukiyo. *"Tortilla Flat* ni Okeru John Steinbeck no Saikuru," (John Steinbeck's "Cycle" in *Tortilla Flat*) in *Amerika Gendai Shosetsu Ron: Andason, Heminguwei, Sutainbekku (Studies in Modern American Novels: Anderson, Hemingway, and Steinbeck).* Osaka: Osaka Kyouiku Tosho, 1994. (pp. 135-55)

3846   Watanabe, Kazukiyo. *"Tortilla Flat* ni Okeru John Steinbeck no saikuru ni tsuite," (On John Steinbeck's Cycle in *Tortilla Flat) Osaka Gakuin University Foreign Languages Bulletin,* 20 (October 1989), 22-41.

3847   Watanabe, Kazukiyo. "John Steinbeck no *Utagawashii Tatakai* no Kousei," (The Structure of John Steinbeck's *In Dubious Battle) Osaka Gakuin University Studies in Foreign Language,* 27 (March 25, 1993), 19-46. (reprinted in *America Gendai Shosetsu Ron: Anderson, Heminguwei, Sutainbekku (Studies in Modern American Novels: Anderson, Hemingway, and Steinbeck).* Osaka: Osaka Kyouiku Tosho, 1994. (pp. 169-198).

3848   Watanabe, Kazukiyo. "Steinbeck mo 'Kiku' ni oite Shizen Shugisha Eliza ga Nanio Shitte Itaka," (What the Naturalist Eliza Knew in Steinbeck's "The Chrysanthemums") *Osaka Gakuin University Tsushin,* 24:2 (May 1993), 95-107.

(reprinted in *Amerika Gendai Shosetsu Ron: Andason, Heminguwei, Sutainbekku (Studies in Modern American Novels: Anderson, Hemingway, and Steinbeck)*. Osaka: Osaka Kyouiku Tosho,1994. (pp. 156-68))

3849   Weiss, Jonathan M. "Une Lecture americaine de Volkswagen Blues," (One American Speech about the Volkswagen Blues) *Etudes Francaise, Montreal,* 21:3 (Winter 1985-1986), 89-96.

3850   Yagyu, Nozomu. "Steinbeck ni miru Seisho no inyu," (Biblical Metaphor in Steinbeck) *Yiyama Ronso (Yiyama Polemic), Tokyo Kogei Daigaku Joshi Tandaibu (Tokyo Kogei University Women Junior College Section),* 2:1 (March 1985), 105-123.

3851   Yagyu, Nozomu. "Yakusoku no Chi Canaan no Yume-wo Otte — Steinbeck's *Ikari no Budo,*" (The Trail of the Promised Land, Canaan's Dream — Steinbeck's *The Grapes of Wrath*), *Eibei bungaku ni Miru Gendaijin-no Ishiki-no Henyo (Change of Consciousness in Men of Today As Seen in Anglo-American Literature).* Tokyo: Jordan sha, 1985. (pp. 85-101) (a revised version of "Kami-huzai-no Bungaku" / "Literature with absence of God")

3852   Yamaguchi, Kuyichi. "*East of Eden* ni okeru Timshel ni tsuite," (On Timshel in regard to *East of Eden*) *Toita Women's Junior College Anglo American Cultural Studies,* 46 (December 1989), 27-38.

3853   Yamaguchi, Kuyichi. "Steinbeck Bungaku no Honshitsu: 'Kiku' ni Okeru Eiyu Shinrigaku," (Essence of Steinbeck's Literature: The Heroine Psychology in "The Chrysanthemums") *Kobe Yamate Women's Junior College Annual Report,* 26 (1981), 1-11.

3854   Yamaguchi, Kuyichi. "Sutainbekku 'Shiroi Usura' ronko —
        fumo no niwa no narushishizumu," (A Study of
        Steinbeck's "The White Quail" — Narcissism of the
        Barren Garden) *Kobe Yamate Women's Junior College
        Bulletin*, 30 (December 1987), 85-96.

3855   Yamashita, Mitsuaki. "*Eden no Higashi* ni okeru aizo," (Love
        and Hatred in *East of Eden*) *Saikoanaritikaru Eibungaku
        Ronso (Collection of Psycho-Analytical English Literaure,
        Psycho-Analytical English Literature Assn.)*, 10 (February
        15, 1987), 61-76.

3856   Yamashita, Mitsuaki. "*Ikari no Budou* ni Okeru Teema," (The
        Themes of *The Grapes of Wrath)* in *Sutainnbekku Sakka
        Sakuhin Ron (Steinbeck and His Works: A Festschrift in
        Honor of Dr. Tetsumaro Hayashi)*. ed. Eiko Shiraga and
        Yasuo Hashiguchi. Tokyo: Eihosha, 1995. (pp. 189-202)

3857   Yamashita, Mitsuaki. "*The Long Valley* Ni Okeru Seisho Teki
        Imeigi," (Biblical Images in *The Long Valley)* *Notre Dame
        Seishin Jyoshi Daigaku Kiyo (Notre Dame Seishin
        University Bulletin)*, 6:1 (March 1982), 61-71.

3858   Yamashita, Mitsuaki. "Kenji Inoue Honyaku no Yoru
        Cannery Row no Saikou," (Review of Kenji Inoue's
        translation of *Kyanarii Rou (Kanzume Yokocho)*, (Fukumy
        bunko) *Jimukyoku Dayori*, 9 (July 20, 1990), 4.

3859   Yamashita, Mitsuaki. "*The Pastures of Heaven* ni okeru
        Steinbeck no joeizou," (Steinbeck's Women Figures in *The
        Pastures of Heaven)* *Notre Dame Sacred Heart University
        Bulletin (Foreign Languages and Literature)*, 17:1 (1993),
        67-73.

3860   Yamashita, Mitsuaki. "Review of *Nihon ni okeru Sutainbekku
        Bunkenshoshi (Steinbeck in Japan: A Bibliography)*, comp.

by Kiyoshi Nakayama," *The Browser* (Osaka Yosho), 72 (February/March 1994), 10-12.

3861 Yamashita, Mitsuaki. "Steinbeck no Sekai," (Steinbeck's World) *Notre Dame Seishen Jyoshi Daigaku Kiyo — Gaikok-go, Gaikoku Bungaku hen (Notre Dame Sacred Heart University Bulletin — Foreign Languages and Literature),* 7 (March 1983), 51-61.

3862 Yamashita, Mitsuaki. "Sutainbekku no Sekai," (Steinbeck's World — Pt. I) *Notre Dame Seishen Jyoshi Daigaku Kiyo — Gaikok-go, Gaikoku Bungaku hen (Notre Dame Sacred Heart University Bulletin — Foreign Languages and Literature),* 12: 1 (March 1, 1988), 1-10.

3863 Yamashita, Mitsuaki, trans. "Steinbeck no Josei no Toujou Jinbutsu Tachi — Fukujiteki Jinbutsu wa Jyuyou de Aruka?" in *Sutainbekku no Joseizo (Steinbeck's Women).* Tokyo: Oshisha, 1991. (pp. 63-86) (A translation of Mimi Reisel Gladstein's "Female Characters in Steinbeck: Minor Characters of Major Importance?" in *Steinbeck's Women: Essays in Criticism.* ed. Tetsumaro Hayashi. Steinbeck Monograph Series #9 (Muncie, Ind.: Ball State University, 1979))

3864 Yamashita, Mitsuaki, trans. "Steinbeck no Juana — Kachi Aru Josei," in *Sutainbekku no Joseizo (Steinbeck's Women).* Tokyo: Oshisha, 1991. (pp. 153-163) (A translation of Mimi Reisel Gladstein's "Steinbeck's Juana: A Woman of Worth," in *Steinbeck's Women: Essays in Criticism.* ed. Tetsumaro Hayashi. Steinbeck Monograph Series #9 (Muncie, Ind.: Ball State University, 1979))

3865 Yamashita, Mitsuaki, trans. "Steinbeck no Onna no Asobinin Tachi — *Hatsuka Nezumi to Ningen, Run-run to Moyuru, Tsukiwa Shizuminu,* and *Sapata Banzai!* no Kenkyu," in *Sutainbekku no Joseizo (Steinbeck's Women)* Tokyo: Oshisha, 1991. (pp. 37-62) (A translation of Sandra Beatty's "Steinbeck's Play-Women: A Study of Female

Presence in *Of Mice and Men, Burning Bright, The Moon Is Down,* and *Viva Zapata!*" in *Steinbeck's Women: Essays in Criticism.* ed. Tetsumaro Hayashi. Steinbeck Monograph Series #9 (Muncie, Ind.: Ball State University, 1979))

3866   Yamashita, Mitsuaki, trans. "Steinbeck no Shiawase na Baishunfu Tachi," in *Sutainbekku no Joseizo (Steinbeck's Women)* Tokyo: Oshisha, 1991. (pp. 115-152) (A translation of Robert E. Morsberger's "Steinbeck's Happy Hookers," in *Steinbeck's Women: Essays in Criticism,* ed. Tetsumaro Hayashi. Steinbeck Monograph Series #9 (Muncie, Ind.: Ball State University, 1979))

3867   Yamashita, Mitsuaki, trans. "Steinbeck no Shousetsu ni Okeru Josei no Seikaku Byousha no Kenkyu," in *Sutainbekku no Joseizo (Steinbeck's Women).* Tokyo: Oshisha, 1991. (pp. 21-36) (A translation of Sandra Beatty's "A Study of Female Characterization in Steinbeck's Fiction," in *Steinbeck's Women: Essays in Criticism.* ed. Tetsumaro Hayashi. Steinbeck Monograph Series #9 (Muncie, Ind.: Ball State University, 1979))

3868   Yamashita, Mitsuaki, trans. "Steinbeck no Tsuyoi Josei Tachi — Tanpen ni Okeru josei no Dokujisei," in *Sutainbekku no Joseizo (Steinbeck's Women).* Tokyo: Oshisha, 1991. (pp. 87-114) (A translation of Marilyn L. Mitchell's "Steinbeck's Strong Women: Feminine Identity in the Short Stories," in *Steinbeck's Women: Essays in Criticism.* ed. Tetsumaro Hayashi. Steinbeck Monograph Series #9 (Muncie, Ind.: Ball State University, 1979))

3869   Yamashita, Mitsuaki. "Yakusha Atogaki," (Translator's Afterword) in *Sutainbekku no Joseizou.* Tokyo: Oushisha, 1991. (pp. 172-178)

3870   Yamauchi, Kiyoshi. "*Akai Kouma* ni Okeru John Steinbeck no Me no Byosha," (John Steinbeck's Description of Eyes in *The Red Pony*) *Touchstone* (Touchstone Dojinkai), 3 (December 1992), 1-18.

3871 Yamauchi, Kiyoshi. "John Steinbeck no Ningen Byosha," (John Steinbeck's Descriptions of Men) *Journal of the Faculty of General Education, Azabu University,* 26 (March 1993), 31-47.

3872 Yamauchi, Kiyoshi. "Steinbeck no Kuni e no Saihoumon," (Re-Visit to Steinbeck Country) *Forum* (Tokyo: International Essayist Association), 8 (June 30, 1995), 33-37.

3873 Yanagi, Masami. "John Steinbeck no *Ikari no Budou* ni okeru Ningen Ai," (Love for Humanity in John Steinbeck's *The Grapes of Wrath*) *Evergreen* (The Society for English Literature, Aichi Shukutoku College), 8 (1985), 53-65.

3874 Yano, Shigeharu. "Bunkaron Kokusai Stainbekku kaigi no koto," (On the International Steinbeck Congress) *Sankei Shimbun* (November 17, 1984), 5.

3875 Yano, Shigeharu. "Dai 11 kai Nihon Sutainbekku Gakkai — Inshouki," (Impressions of the 11th Conference of the John Steinbeck Society of Japan) *Kyouiku Gakujutsu Shinbun* (*Education and Academy News),* 1432 (July 1, 1987), 1, 4.

3876 Yano, Shigeharu. "Dai 12 kai Nihon Sutainbekku Gakkai — Inshouki," (Impressions of the 12th National Meeting of the John Steinbeck Society of Japan) *Kyouiku Gakujyutsu Shinbun* (*Education and Academy News),* 1477 (August 3, 1988), 4.

3877 Yano, Shigeharu. "Dai 13 kai Nihon Sutainbekku Gakkai — Inshouki," (Impressions of the 13th National Meeting of the John Steinbeck Society of Japan) *Kyouiku Gakujyutsu Shinbun* (*Education and Academy News),* 1514 (June 21, 1989), 4.

3878   Yano, Shigeharu. "Dai 14 kai Nihon Sutainbekku Gakkai —
        Inshouki," (Impressions of the 14th National Meeting of
        the John Steinbeck Society of Japan) *Kyouiku Gakujyutsu
        Shinbun* (*Education and Academy News*), 1573 (November
        14, 1990), 3.

3879   Yano, Shigeharu. "Dai 15 kai Nihon Sutainbekku Gakkai —
        Inshouki" (Impressions of the 15th National Meeting of the
        John Steinbeck Society of Japan) *Kyouiku Gakujyutsu
        Shinbun* (*Education and Academy News*), 1619 (June 12,
        1991), 4.

3880   Yano, Shigeharu. "Dai 15 kai Nihon Sutainbekku Gakkai —
        Inshouki" (Impressions of the 15th National Meeting of the
        John Steinbeck Society of Japan) *Kyouiku Gakujutsu
        Shimbun* (*Education and Academy News*), n. v. (November
        14, 1991), 3.

3881   Yano, Shigeharu. "Dai 16 kai Nihon Sutainbekku Gakkai —
        Inshouki" (Impressions of the 16th National Meeting of the
        John Steinbeck Society of Japan) *Kyouiku Gakujutsu
        Shimbun (Education and Academy News*), 1642 (July 1,
        1992), 4.

3882   Yano, Shigeharu. "Dai ni Bunkaron Kokusai Steinbeck Kaigi:
        Inshou," (The Second International Steinbeck Congress:
        The Impressions) *Kado Wafu,* n. v. (November 1984), 4.

3883   Yano, Shigeharu, trans. "*Eden No Higashi* ni Okeri Higashi,"
        (The "East" in *East of Eden*) by John Ditsky in *John
        Steinbeck: East and West,* ed. Tetsumaro Hayashi, Yasuo
        Hashiguchi and Richard F. Peterson. Tokyo: Hokuseido
        Press, 1982. (pp. 111-26)

3884   Yano, Shigeharu. "Sariinasu kara Sekai e mukete: Dai ni
        Bunkaron Kokusai Steinbeck Kaigi no Inshouki (I),"
        (From Salinas to the World: Second International
        Steinbeck Congress — Impressions Part I) *Kyouiku*

Gakujutsu Shimbun (Educational and Scholarly News)
n. v. (September 5, 1984), 4.

3885　Yano, Shigeharu. "Sariinasu kara Sekai e mukete: Dai ni
Bunkaron Kokusai Steinbeck Kaigi no Inshouki (II),"
(From Salinas to the World: Second International
Steinbeck Congress — Impressions Part II) *Kyouiku
Gakujutsu Shimbun* (Educational and Scholarly News)
n. v. (September 12, 1984), 4.

3886　Yano, Shigeharu. "Sariinasu kara Sekai e mukete: Dai ni
Bunkaron Kokusai Steinbeck Kaigi no Inshouki (III),"
(From Salinas to the World: Second International
Steinbeck Congress — Impressions Part III) *Kyouiku
Gakujutsu Shimbun* (Educational and Scholarly News)
n. v. (September 19, 1984), 4.

3887　Yano, Shigeharu. "Jyodo-ke wo Sasa-eta Haha-oya no Ai,
meisaku ni miru jyoseizou dai ikkai," (The Love of Ma
Joad Who Supported the Joad Family, Women in Classics,
Pt. I) *Reirou (Retro)*, Hiroike Gaukuen shuppanbu,
(January 1982), 64-67.

3888　Yano, Shigeharu. "Kokusai Gakkai no Tanoshimi" (Pleasure
of Participating in an International Conference) *Kado Wafu*
(Juridicial Foundation of Wafu School), 8 (August 25,
1990), 4.

3889　Yano, Shigeharu. "Nihon Sutainbekku Kyokai Dai 10 kai
Kinen Taikai wo Muka-e-te (jyo)," (Celebrating the 10th
Annual Conference of the Japan Steinbeck Society, Pt. I)
Kyouiku Gakujyutsu Shinbun, 1395 (July 23, 1986), 4.

3890　Yano, Shigeharu. "Nihon Sutainbekku Kyokai Dai 10 kai
Kinen Taikai wo Muka-e-te (ge)," (Celebrating the 10th
Annual Conference of the Japan Steinbeck Society, Pt. II)
Kyouiku Gakujyutsu Shinbun, 1396 (August 6, 1986), 4.

3891   Yano, Shigeharu. "Steinbeck Matsuri (3) Sanka Shite," (On
        Participating in Steinbeck Festival III (1982)) *Eigo Seinen*
        (The Rising Generation), 128 (December 1, 1982), 582.

3892   Yano, Shigeharu. "Shinri-gaku to shakai-gaku no kan-ten kara
        mita *The Winter of Our Discontent*," (Psychological and
        Sociological View to *The Winter of Our Discontent*)
        Kaihou, 3 (1980), 3.

3893   Yano, Shigeharu. "Steinbeck: Seiyou to Touyou no
        Kakehashi," (Steinbeck: The Bridge Between East and
        West) in *Sutainnbekku Sakka Sakuhin Ron (Steinbeck and
        His Works: A Festschrift in Honor of Dr. Tetsumaro
        Hayashi)*. ed. Eiko Shiraga and Yasuo Hashiguchi. Tokyo:
        Eihosha, 1995. (pp. 124-140)

3894   Yokozawa, Shiro. "John Steinbeck: Amerika Bungaku no
        Jiko-tenkai: 20-seiki no Amerika Bungaku II," *(Self-
        Development in 20th Century American Literature*) in
        America Bungaku Kenkyu Sosho 3. ed. Toshihiko Ogata.
        Kyoto: Yamaguchi Shoten Press, 1982. (pp. 125-154)

3895   Yoshikawa, Reizo. "Kaibutsuteki Kusouka to Nami no
        Hitobito: *The Pastures of Heaven* ni Okeru Tojo-jinbutsu
        ni tsuite," (Monstrous Dreamers and Mediocre People: On
        the Characters in *The Pastures of Heaven*) *Satientia* (Eichi
        University Bulletin), 29 (February 28, 1995), 151-178.

3896   Yoshikawa, Reizo. "1940 Nendai no Steinbeck: Tassei e no
        Kanawanu Yume," (Steinbeck in 1940's: Lost Dreams of
        Achievement) *Tezukayama Junior College Bulletin,* 29
        (March 1, 1992), 77-91.

3897   Yoshikawa, Reizo. "Shudan no Hitobito: *Of Mice and Men* no
        Kenkyu," (Those Who Are Outside of the Group: A Study
        of *Of Mice and Men*) *Tezukayama Junior College
        Bulletin,* 30 (March 1, 1993), 87-102.

3898   Yoshikawa, Reizo. "Steinbeck no Kobai: *Nagai Tanima* ni
        Okeru shi ni tsuite," (Steinbeck's Bewilderment: With
        Regard to Death in *The Long Valley) Tezukayama Junior
        College Bulletin,* 28 (February 10, 1991), 72-89.

3899   Yoshikawa, Reizo. "Steinbeck to Eiga: *Viva Sapata!* o
        Chushin ni," (Steinbeck and Film: Centering on *Viva
        Zapata!) Helicon,* 16 (September 30, 1991), 3-20.

3900   Yoshizawa, Eijiro. "'The Harness' shoron," (A Brief
        Discussion of "The Harness") *Komazawa Tanki Daigaku
        Kenkyu Kiyou (Komazawa Junior College Study Bulletin),*
        19 (March 1990), 1-6.

3901   Yoshizawa, Eijiro. "Hatsuka-Nezumi to Ningen ni Okeru
        Kojinteki Kenkai," (Personal Opinion Concerning *Of Mice
        and Men) Komazawa Tanki Daigaku Kenkyu Kiyou
        (Komazawa Junior College Study Bulletin),* n. v. (March
        1985), 15-22.

3902   Yoshizawa, Eijiro. "Review of *Steinbeck Kenkyu, Steinbeck's
        Travel Literature,* ed. Tetsumaro Hayashi, trans. Mikio
        Inui," *Toshi Shimbun* (September 7, 1985), 5.

3903   Yuhara, Tsuyoshi or (Takashi). "Kozui to Jonu no imeeji ni
        tsuite — Steinbeck *Ikari no Budo* Ron," (About the
        Images of Flood and Nursing — Steinbeck's *The Grapes
        of Wrath* Study) *Chiba Review, (Chiba Daigaku),* 6
        (November 11, 1984), 75-92.

3904   Yuji, Kami. "Review of *Sutainbekku Kenkyu: Nagai Tanima
        Ron,* trans. Hiromasa Takamura, et al.," (*A Study of
        Steinbeck: Essays on "The Long Valley")* *Jimukyoku
        Dayori (Steinbeck Newsletter in Japanese)*, 14 (November
        10, 1992), 2-3.

3905   Yuki, Kyoko. "Cathy Ames-wa nazo-no kaibutsu ka — *Eden-
        no Higashi* ni okeru Cathy to shudai tono kakawari ni
        tsuite-no ichi-kousatsu," (Is Cathy Ames a Mysterious

Monster? — A Consideration of the Relationship between Cathy and the Theme in *East of Eden*) *Persica* (Okayama English Literary Society), 12 (March 1985), 51- 61.

3906   Yuki, Kyoko. "*Viva Zapata!* ni shuyaku saleta Steinbeck-no nidai teema," (Two Major Themes of Steinbeck Intensified in *Viva Zapata!*) *Chu-Shikoku America Bungaku Kenkyu (Chu-Shikoku American Literature Study),* 21 (June, 1985), 56-67.

Foreign Language Books

3907   *Amerika Bungaku to Kyuyaku Seisho: Sutainbekku, Heminguuei, Fokuna, Forusuto, Meruviru (American Literature and the Old Testament: Steinbeck, Hemingway, Faulkner, Frost and Melville).* Tokyo: Kindai Bungeisha, 1993. (contains Ch. 1: *The Grapes of Wrath* by Suketaro Sawada on pp. 11-22 and Ch. 2: *East of Eden* by the same author on pp. 23-35)

3908   *Amerika Dokusho Noto* (*Notes on American Literature*). Tokyo: Nan - Un-Do Press 1991. (contains "In Memory of Steinbeck," by Kenji Inoue (pp. 30-32); "On *The Moon Is Down*," by Kenji Inoue (pp. 26-29))

3909   *Amerika Dokusho Zakki (A Notebook of Readings of American Literature).* Tokyo: Nan" undo, 1993. (contains "Men's Ugly Reality: John Steinbeck's *The Acts of King Arthur and His Noble Knights*," by Kenji Inoue on pp. 71-73; "Steinbeck's View of Men," by Kenji Inoue on pp. 53-61; "Steinbeck's Way of Writing," by Kenji Inoue on pp. 62-70; "The Theme and Technique of *The Grapes of Wrath*," by Kenji Inoue on pp. 45-52)

3910   *America Gendai Shosetsu Ron: Anderson, Heminguwei, Sutainbekku. (Studies in Modern American Novels: Anderson, Hemingway, and Steinbeck).* Osaka: Osaka Kyoiku Tosho, 1994. (contains "The Structure of John Steinbeck's *In Dubious Battle*," by Kazukiyo Watanabe on pp. 156-168)

3911   *Amerikajin to Bunkateki Dento (Americans and the Cultural
        Tradition).* Osaka: Sogensha, 1991. (contains "John
        Steinbeck's *The Grapes of Wrath*: Man's Logic and
        Capital's Logic," by Eiichi Fujita on pp. 153-200)

3912   *Amerikanskaya Literatura v russkoi kritike.
        Bibliograpficheskii ukazatel 1981-1985. (American
        Literature in Russian Criticism: A Bibliographical List
        1981-1985).* Moscow: Institut Nauchnoi Informatsii po
        Obshchestvennym. Moscow: Naukam, 1989. (20 entries on
        Steinbeck)

3912A   Araki, Kazuo, et al. eds. "Hurricane Donna," in *The New Age
        Readers New Edition.* Tokyo: Kenkyusha, 1991. (contains
        excerpts from *Travels with Charley in Search of America*)

3913   Ariki, Kyoko, Yasuo Hashaguchi, and Yoshifumo Kato, trans.
        *Jon Sutainbekku: Sarinasu kara Sekai ni Mukete (John
        Steinbeck: From Salinas to the World).* Tokyo: Oshisha,
        1992. (a translation of *John Steinbeck: From Salinas to
        the World*, ed. Shigeharu Yano, et al.) See Books in
        English (Entry 558) for a complete list of essays in this
        translation.

3914   Ariki, Kyoko, Ikuko Kawata, and Wakako Kakegawa, trans.
        *Steinbekku Kenkyu: Atarashii Tanpen Shosetsushu
        (Steinbeck Studies: New Essays on Short Stories).* Osaka:
        Osaka Educational Publishing, 1995. (A reprint in
        Japanese of *Steinbeck Monograph Series*, No. 13 (1988)
        and No. 15 (1991)) (See these entries in the Foreign
        Articles Section as well as Books in English (entries 308-
        309) for a complete citation of the translated essays)

3915   Arnst, Reiner, ed. *Textlinguistik und Fachsprache (Textual
        Lunguistics and Technical Language),* Hildesheim: Olms,
        1988. (contains "'Langsachsen': Ein in der Textlinguistik
        vernachlassigtes Problem der literarischen Ubersetzung;

Akten des International ubersetsungswiss," by Arain Paul
Frank on pp. 485-497)

3916   Asano, Toshio, trans. *Sutainbekku no Sosaku-ron (Steinbeck:
On Creative Writing)*. Tokyo: Shimbisha, 1992. (a
translation of *John Steinbeck: On Writing*. ed. Tetsumaro
Hayashi. Steinbeck Essay series #2 — see English Entry
302 for details)

3917   Baturin, Sergei S. *Dzhon Steinbek i traditisii Amerikanskoi
literatury (John Steinbeck and the Tradition of American
Literature)*. Moscow: Khudozhestvennaya Literatura,
1984.

3918   Bibulos Society, ed. *English and American Literature and
Language: Searching for a New Horizon of Research*.
Tokyo: Homerosu-sha, 1990. (contains *"Cannery Row* and
The Log from the Sea of Cortez," by Wakako Kakegawa
on pp. 355-65)

3919   *Bungaku to America: Ohashi Kenzaburo Kyoju Kanreki Kinen
Ronbushu*. Tokyo: Nan' undo, 1980. (contains "Steinbeck
to Jinshuteki Henken," by Kenji Inoue on pp. 390-403)

3920   *Dai-Kokaisha no Sekai (The World of the Great Voyagers)*,
Vol. V. Tokyo: Hara Shobo, 1992. (contains Haruo
Ishijima's "Chapter 1: Steinbeck's *Cup of Gold*," Karibu
no Kaizoku: Henry Morgan (Henry Morgan, the
Buccaneer) on pp. 1-13)

3921   *The Dream and Its Collapse in American Literature*. Osaka:
Sogensha, 1988. (contains "The Dream and Its Collapse in
Of Mice and Men," by Hirotsugu Inoue on pp. 128-141)

3922   Egusa, Hisashi, ed. *Sutainbekku Kenkyu — Tanpen Shosetsu
Ron (A Study of Steinbeck: Essay on Short Stories)*. Tokyo:

Yashio Shuppan-sha, 1987. (revised 1991 with a
bibliography of Japanese scholarship on pp. 258-278)
Contents: "Maesaki" (Introduction) i-iv; "*Nagai Bonchi,*"
(*The Long Valley*) by Hisachi Egusa, 3-8; "Kiku," ("The
Chrysanthemums") by Hisachi Egusa, 9-22; "Shiroi
Uzura," ("The White Quail") by Hisachi Egusa, 23-45;
"Toubou," ("Flight") by Yoshio Ito, 46-59; "Hebi," ("The
Snake") by Mitsuo Kato, 60-80; "Cho Shoku,"
("Breakfast") by Hisachi Egusa, 81-88; "Shugeki," ("The
Raid") by Nishimura, 89-104; "Shimegu," ("The Harness")
by Mitsuo Kato, 105-124; "Jikeidanin," ("The Vigilante")
by Chitoshi Nishimura, 125-137; "Johnny Bear," by
Yoshio Ito, 138-152; "Satsuzin," ("The Murder") by
Chitoshi Nishimura, 153-167; "Seisho Ixo Katy," ("St.
Katy the Virgin") by Mitsuo Kato, 168-185; "*Akai
Kouma,*" (*The Red Pony*) by Hisachi Egusa, 186-193;
"Okurimona" and "Yakusoku," ("The Gift" and "The
Promise") by Chitoshi Nishimura, 194-206; "Dairenkai"
and "Shidosha," ("The Great Mountains" and "The Leader
of the People"), by Mitsuo Kato, 207-221; "*Akai kouma,
no koso to gikou,*" (*The Red Pony*) by Mitsuo Kato, 222-
247.)

3923   Fingerhuth, Frank. *John Steinbeck and John Dos Passos:
American Tradition and Gesellschaftliche Wertlichkeit.*
(American Tradition and Social Values). Hamburg,
Germany: Hamburger Buchagentur, 1981.

3924   *Formy raskrytiya avtorskogo coznaniya (Forms of Disclosure
of Authorial Consciousness).* Moscow: Voronezh, 1986.
(Contains "Pozitsiya avtora v povesti. D Steinbeka
Nebeskye Pastbishcha. K. vaprosu ob ideino
Khudozhestvennoi Evolutsii pisatelya," (The Position of
the Author in Steinbeck's *Pastures of Heaven:* Toward the
Question of the Ideological and Artistic Evolution of the
Author) by E. A. Nikolaeva on pp. 121-129)

3925   *Gendai Sakka no Gobo to Buntai (Usage and Style of Modern*
        Writers: Stevenson, Maugham, Hemingway and
        Steinbeck). Tokyo: Bunka Shobo Hakubunsha, 1992.
        (Contains Toshiaki Miura's "Chapter 4: Steinbeck's *The*
        Pearl: Conflicts between Good and Evil," on pp. 154-174)

3926   Gohin, Yves, and Robert Ricatte. *Recherches en sciences des*
        textes(Research in the Science of Texts). Grenoble:
        University of Grenoble, 1977. (contains "Des enfants, Des
        souris et des hommes, ou l'utilisation en classe d'un texte
        de Steinbeck; Homage a Pierre Albuoy," (Of the Children
        and *Of Mice and Men* or the Utilization in Class of the text
        of John Steinbeck: In Recognition of Pierre Albuoy) by
        Daniel Grojnowski, et al., 169-179)

3927   No entry

3928   Hammano, Shigeo. *Amerika Bungaku to Jidai Hembo*
        (American Literature and Its Historical Changes). ed.
        Shigeo Hammano. Tokyo: Kenkyusha, 1989. (pp. 221-
        228) (Contains "Tropism of 'Crack Up'" by Tateo
        Imamura and examines Hemingway, Steinbeck and Dos
        Passos)

3929   Hashiguchi, Yasuo, and Koichi Kaida, eds. John Steinbeck,
        The Grapes of Wrath (Eihosha Commentary Booklet
        Series), annotated, with an introduction by the editors.
        Tokyo: Eichosha, 1989.

3930   Hashiguchi, Yasuo, Kyoko Ariki, and Yoshifumi Kato, trans.
        'John Steinbeck — Salinas Kara Sekai Ni Mukete (John
        Steinbeck: From Salinas to the World). Tokyo: Gaku
        Shobo, 1992. (a translation of *John Steinbeck: From*
        Salinas to the World, ed. Shigeharu Yano, et al.) See
        Books in English (Entry 558) for a complete list of essays
        in this translation.

3931   Hashiguchi,Yasuo, and Eiko Shiraga, eds. *Sutainnbekku Sakka Sakuhin Ron (Steinbeck and His Works: A Festschrift in Honor of Dr. Tetsumaro Hayashi).* Tokyo: Eihosha, 1995. Contents: Hirose, Hidekazu. "Steinbeck no Fukei Byosha," (Steinbeck's Landscape Descriptions) by Hisekazu Hirose, 3-16; "Sutainbekku to America; Sutainbekku no Americasei no kenkyu," (Steinbeck and America: A Study of Steinbeck's Americanness) by Kyoko Ariki, 17-33; "Steinbeck to Amerika Indian," (Steinbeck and American Indians) by Yoshifumi Kato, 34-49; "Huckleberry Finn to Tom Joad: Jiko Kaku Ritsu no tabi," (Huckleberry Finn and Tom Joad: Journey as Path to Self-Establishment) by Hitorsugu Inoue, 50-65; "Chuken-geki to Camera no Me o 'Modus Operandi' to shite: Steinbeck to Hemingway," (Play-Novelette and Camera Eye as Modus Operandi: Steinbeck and Hemingway) by Takahiko Sugiyama, 66-82; "Steinbeck to Arthur Miller: Maccashi Senpu Deno Konran," (Steinbeck and Arthur Miller: In the Turmoil of McCarthyism) by Fumio Momose, 83-92; "Steinbeck and Vonnegut: Guwa kara Kuso e," (Steinbeck and Vonnegut: From Fable to Fabulation) by Satoru Tagaya, 93-106; "Steinbeck to D.H. Lawrence: Ni Sakka no Sekai," (Steinbeck and D. H. Lawrence: The World of Two Writers) by Mitsuru Meguro, 107-123; "Steinbeck: Seiyou to Touyou no Kakehashi," (Steinbeck: The Bridge Between East and West) by Shigeharu Yano, 124-140; "Steinbeck and Three Japanese," by Yasuo Hashiguchi, 141-154; "*Hatsuka Nezumi to Ningen* ni Okeru Curley no tsuma no yaku," (The Role of Curley's Wife in *Of Mice and Men*) by Eiko Shiraga, 155-170; "*Of Mice and Men*: Opera no Kenkyu," (A Study of *Of Mice and Men* as Opera) by Hiromasa Takamura, 171-188; "*Ikari no Budou* ni Okeru Teema," (The Themes of *The Grapes of Wrath)* by Mitusaki Yamashita, 189-202; "'Rose of Sharon' no Shochotekina Imi," (The Symbolic Meaning of Rose of Sharon) by Ikuko Kawata, 203-221; "*Eden no Higashi:* Kyashii no Shijitso-jou," *(East of Eden:* Cathy's Real Figure) by Mitsuo Kato, 222-242; "Samuel Hamilton ni tsuite," (On Samuel Hamilton) by Kozen Nakachi, 243-258; "Sononakade Ningen ga Tsugitsugito Yakarenakereba

Naranai Honou," (The Flame in Which Human Beings
Must Be Repeatedly Burnt) by Wakako Kakegawa, 259-
271; "'Aimani naniga Okoruka': *Tanoshii Makuyoubi* no
Tekisuto," ("What Happens In-Between": The Typescripts
and Text of *Sweet Thursday)* by Kiyoshi Nakayama, 272-
288.

3932   Hayashi, Tetsumaro, and Eiko Shiraga, trans. *Steinbeck's
        World War II Fiction, "The Moon Is Down": Three
        Explications/Sutainbekku no Hansen Shosetsu: Tsuki wa
        Shizuminu Ronko (Steinbeck's Resistance Novel: "The
        Moon Is Down").* Okayama: Daigaku Kyoiku Shuppan,
        1993. (See English Entry 311 for details)

3933   Hiromu, Shimizu, Hiroyuki Kobayashi, and Kiyoshi
        Nakayama, trans. *Tanoshii Mokuyobi,* a Japanese
        translation of Steinbeck's *Sweet Thursday.* Tokyo: Shimin
        Shobo Press, 1985.

3934   Inoue, Kenji, Kiyoshi Nakayama, and Fumio Momose, trans.
        Steinbeku Sakuhinron (II). Tokyo, Japan: Eihosha Press,
        1982. (a translation of Tetsumaro Hayashi, ed. *A Study
        Guide to Steinbeck (II)* (Metuchen, N. J.: Scarecrow Press,
        1979) Contents: Tetsumaro Hayashi, "Preface"; Reloy
        Garcia, "Introduction"; Tetsumaro Hayashi, "Preface to the
        Japanese translation"; Martha Heasley Cox, "Kin-No-
        Sakazuki," (Steinbeck's *Cup of Gold* (1929)); Charles J.
        Clancy, "Tsuki Wa Sizuminu," (Steinbeck's *The Moon is
        Down* (1942)); Robert Morsberger, "Kimagure-Basu,"
        (Steinbeck's *The Wayward Bus* (1947)); Charles J. Clancy,
        "Soviet-Kikou," (Steinbeck's *A Russian Journal* (1948));
        Martha H. Cox, "Run-Run to Moyuru," (Steinbeck's
        Burning Bright (1950)); Richard Peterson, "Korutesu-No-
        Umi Koukai-Nisshi," (Steinbeck's *The Log from the Sea of
        Cortez* (1951)); Richard Peterson, "Eden-No-Higashi,"
        (Steinbeck's *East of Eden* (1952)); Roy Simmonds,
        "Tanoshii Mokuyo-Bi," (Steinbeck's *Sweet Thursday*
        (1954)); Roy Simmonds, "Charley Tono Tabi — America

Wo Motowete," *(*Steinbeck's *Travels with Charley in Search of America* (1962)); Robert Morsberger, "Sapata Banzi," (Steinbeck's *Viva Zapata!* (screenplay 1952: published 1975))

3935   Inui, Mikio, trans. *Sutainbekku Kenkyu-Kikobungaku Ronshu (A Study of John Steinbeck: Essays on Travel Literature).* Tokyo: Kaibunsha Shuppan, 1985. (a translation of *Steinbeck's Travel Literature: Essays in Critisism,* ed. Tetsumaro Hayashi. *Steinbeck Monograph Series,* No. 10, 1980) Contents: Preface, 1-2; Preface and Acknowledgements, 7-11; "Sutainbekku to tabashiki; shiko nohosoku to jibutsu no housaku," (Richard Astro's "Travels with Steinbeck: The Laws of Thought and the Laws of Things") 13-33; "Waga sokoku — tohou mo naku itoshiku katsu uruwashi: Sutainbekku *Amerika to Amerikajin,*" (Roy Simmonds's "Our Land — 'Incredibly Dear and Beautiful' — Steinbeck's *America and Americans*") 35-48; Kaizoku o Hatarakini dekake Spain no machi o nottoru: *Ogon no sakazuki* no ikutsukano jushichiseikiteki shiten," (Darlene Eddy's "To Go A-Buccaneering and Take a Spanish Town: Some Seventeenth-Century Aspects of *A Cup of Gold*") 49-72; "*Koretsu no Umi* no monogatari bubun no keishiki: genjitsu kara atsumerareta hyohon," (Betty Perez's "The Form of the Narrative Section of *Sea of Cortez*: A Specimen Collected from Reality") 73-91; "Sutainbekku no *Chaarii tono Tabi*: Shippai shita tankyu," (John Ditsky's *Travels with Charley*: The Quest That Failed") 93-104; "*Kimegure Basu*: Amerika ni Okeru Ai to Jidai," (John Ditsky's "*The Wayward Bus*: Love and Time in America") 105-137.

3936   Kaida, Koichi, and Yasuo Hashiguchi, eds. John Steinbeck, *The Grapes of Wrath* (Eichosha Commentary Booklet Series), annotated, with an introduction by the editors. Tokyo: Eichosha, 1985.

3937   Kakegawa, Wakako, Kyoko Ariki, and Ikuko Kawata, trans.
        Steinbekku Kenkyu: Atarashii Tanpen Shosetsushu
        (*Steinbeck Studies: New Essays on Short Stories*). Osaka:
        Osaka Educational Publishing, 1995. A reprint in Japanese
        of *Steinbeck Monograph Series*, No. 13 (1988) and No. 15
        (1991). (See these entries in the Foreign Articles Section as
        well as Books in English (entries 308-309) for a complete
        citation of the translated essays)

3938   Kanazeki, Toshio, and Kazuko Kawachi, eds. *Women in
        English and American Literature*. Tokyo: Nan-un-do,
        1986. (contains "On Curley's Wife: A Study Note on *Of
        Mice and Men*," by Kenji Inoue on pp. 257-264)

3939   Kato, Yoshifumo, Yasuo Hashaguchi, and Kyoko Ariki, trans.
        *Jon Sutainbekku: Sarinasu kara Sekai ni Mukete (John
        Steinbeck: From Salinas to the World)*. Tokyo: Oshisha,
        1992. (a translation of *John Steinbeck: From Salinas to the
        World*, ed. Shigeharu Yano, et al.) See Books in English
        (Entry 558) for a complete list of essays in this translation.

3940   Kawachi, Kazuko, and Toshio Kanazeki, eds. *Women in
        English and American Literature*. Tokyo: Nan-un-do,
        1986. (contains "On Curley's Wife: A Study Note on *Of
        Mice and Men*," by Kenji Inoue on pp. 257-264)

3941   *Kawai Michio Sensei Taikan Kinen Rombunshu Kanko Iinkai.
        (Festschrift in Honor of Professor Michio Kawai: Studies
        in English Language and Literature)*. Tokyo: Eihosha,
        1993. (contains "A Drama of Construction and
        Deconstruction of Steinbeck Country," by Yoshifumi Kato
        on pp. 547-554)

3942   Kawata, Ikuko, Kyoko Ariki, and Wakako Kakegawa, trans.
        Steinbeku Kenkyu: Atarashii Tanpen Shosetsushu
        (*Steinbeck Studies: New Essays on Short Stories*). Osaka:
        Osaka Educational Publishing, 1995. A reprint in Japanese

of *Steinbeck Monograph Series*, No. 13 (1988) and No. 15
(1991). (See these entries in the Foreign Articles Section as
well as Books in English (entries 308-309) for a complete
citation of the translated essays)

3943   Kinoshita, Takanori, and Haruki Kobe. trans. *Jon Sutainbekku
          No Shousetku: Sono Shudai to Kousatu* (*Thematic Design
          in the Novels of John Steinbeck* by Lester Jay Marks).
          Tokyo, Japan: Hokuseido Press, 1984. (The original was
          published in 1971 by Mouton in The Hague) Contents:
          Shaji (Acknowledgements), 5; Jobun (Preface), 6; Dai Ishi:
          Shudai ni Okeru Mittsu no Kata (Ch. 1: Three Thematic
          Patterns), 9-29; Dai Ni-sho: *Kin no Sakazuki* (Ch. 2: *Cup
          of Gold*), 30-38; Dai San-sho: *Shirarezaru Kamini* —
          Gishiki e no Doukei (Ch. 3: *To a God Unknown*: The
          Yearning for Ritual), 39-58; Dai Yon-sho: *Utagawashiki
          Tatakai* — Himokuteki Ron to Shudan Shinri (Ch. 4: *In
          Dubious Battle*: Non-teleology and the Psychology), 59-
          73; Dai Go-sho: "Aru Dekigoto" ni Tsuite no Tansho (Ch.
          5: A Few Words about "Something That Happened"), 74-
          84; Dai Roku-sho: *Ikari no Budo* (Ch. 6: *The Grapes of
          Wrath*), 85-111; Dai Nana-sho: Sensou to Sereni Tsuzuku
          Sunen (Ch. 7: The War and a Few Years After), 112-156;
          Dai Hachi-sho: *Eden no Higashi* — "Nanji — Surukoto
          Aru Beshi" (Ch. 8: *East of Eden*: "Thou Mayest"), 157-
          183; Dai Kyu-sho: Musubi — San-pen no Shosetsu to
          Hitotsu no sho (Ch. 9: Conclusion: Three Novels and a
          Prize), 184-192; Yakusha Atogaki (Translator's
          Afterword), 193-199; Shuyou Sankou Bunken (Selected
          Bibliography), 199-206.

3944   Kobe, Haruki, and Takanori Kinoshita, trans. *Jon
          Sutainbekku No Shousetku: Sono Shudai to Kousatu* (a
          translation of *Thematic Design in the Novels of John
          Steinbeck* by Lester Jay Marks). Tokyo, Japan: Hokuseido
          Press, 1984. See 3943.

3945 Kondo, Tsunehiko, ed. *Eigo Eibungaku Shicho* (*New Currents in English Language and Literature*): *1991-1992.* Tokyo: New Current International, 1992. (contains Mitsuru Meguro's "The World of The Monterey Trilogy," on pp. 208-216)

3946 Kondo, Tsunehiko, ed. *Gendai Sakka no Gobo to Buntai* (*Usage and Style of Modern Writers: Stevenson, Maugham, Hemingway and Steinbeck).* Tokyo: Bunka Shobo Hakubunsha, 1992. (contains "Chapter 4: Steinbeck's *The Pearl*: Conflicts between Good and Evil," by Toshiaki Miura on pp. 154-174)

3947 Lemardeley-Cunci, Christine. *Des Souris et des Hommes de John Steinbeck* (*About the Mice and Men of John Steinbeck*). Paris: Gallimard, 1992.

3948 Lemeunier, Barbara Smith, ed. *The Twenties.* Aix-en Provence: Université de Provence, 1982. (contains *"Les Raisins de la Colere* et la crise de 1929: Actes du Groupe de Recherche et d'Etudes Nord Americaines," (*The Grapes of Wrath* and the 1929 crash: Proceedings of the Research Group of North America Studies) by Robert Silhol on pp. 121-128)

3949 Link, Franz. *Geschichte du Amerika-nischen Erzahlkunst, 1900-1950* (*The History of the American Art of Prose, 1900-1950*), Stuttgart: Kalbhammer, 1983.

3950 Link, Franz, ed. *Paradigmata, Literarische Typologie des Alten Testaments.* Berlin: Duncker and Humblot, 1989. (contains "Die Kainsgeschichte in *East of Eden:* John Steinbeck's Pladoyer fur Selbstverantwortung und Selbstvertwirklichung," (Cain's History in *East of Eden*: John Steinbeck's Speech for Self-Responsibility and Self-Worth) by Helen Haegenbuchle on pp. 629-651)

3951   *Literature and America* (III). Tokyo: Nan-undo Press, 1980.
        (contains "Steinbeck and the Racial Prejudices," by Kenji
        Inoue on pp. 390-403)

3952   Lombardo, Giuseppe. *Ombre sui Pascoli del Cielo: Utopia e
        realta nei Romanzi di John Steinbeck* (*Shadows on The
        Pastures of Heaven: Utopia and Reality in the Novels of
        John Steinbeck*). Roma: Herder, 1990. (discusses *East of
        Eden, To a God Unknown, In Dubious Battle, Of Mice and
        Men, The Grapes of Wrath*)

3953   Maier, Wolfgang Christian. *Die Grundformen den
        menschlischen Existenz in den Romanen von John
        Steinbeck.* (*The Basic Forms of Human Existence in the
        Novels of John Steinbeck*). Munchen: Uni-Druck, 1960.

3954   Marin, Armel, *Recontre avec Steinbeck* (*Meeting With
        Steinbeck*). Paris: Editions de l'Ecole, 1974.

3955   Mohri, Itaru, ed. *Sagai to Amerika Shosetsu (Alienation and
        American Novels).* Osaka: Book Loan Press, 1982.
        (contains "A Search for American Tragedy: Richard
        Wright and John Steinbeck" on pp. 140-150)

3956   Momose, Fumio, and Kiyohiko Tsuboi, trans. *Sutainbekku
        Zen Tampen Ron: Akai Kouma wo Koete (Essays on All of
        Steinbeck's Short Stories: Beyond "The Red Pony").*
        Tokyo: Eihosha, 1991. (a translation of *Beyond "The Red
        Pony": A Reader's Companion to Steinbeck's Complete
        Short Stories* by Robert S. Hughes, Jr. (Metuchen, N. J.:
        Scarecrow Press, 1987 — see Books in English (326) for
        full table of contents)

3957   Momose, Fumio, Kiyoshi Nakayama, and Kenji Inoue, trans.
        Steinbeku Sakuhinron (II). Tokyo, Japan: Eihosha Press,
        1982. (a translation of Tetsumaro Hayashi, ed. *A Study*

Guide to Steinbeck (II). (Metuchen, N. J.: Scarecrow Press, 1979). See #3934.

3958   Muraire, Andre. "Radicalisme et Subversion dans *The Grapes of Wrath* de John Ford," (Radicalism and Subversion in John Ford's Film of *The Grapes of Wrath*) in *Hollywood: Reflections sur l'ecran*. Paris: Actes du Grena, 1984. (pp. 64-78)

3959   Nakayama, Kiyoshi, and Hiromasa Takamura, eds. *Of Mice and Men: A Play in Three Acts*. Tokyo: Ohshisha, 1993. (Includes the editor's preface in English (pp. 3-6), introduction (pp. 97-104) and Japanese annotations (pp. 105-157))

3960   Nakayama, Kiyoshi, and Yoshimitsu Nakayama, trans. *John Steinbeck. Ikari No Budo O Yomu: Amerika No Eden No Hate* (Louis Owens's *"The Grapes of Wrath": Trouble In the Promised Land*, (1989)). Osaka, Japan: Kansai University Press, 1993. (See English Book Entry 428 for further details on this citation)

3961   Nakayama, Kiyoshi, comp. *Nihon Niokeru Sutainbekku Bunkenshoshi.* (*Steinbeck in Japan: A Bibliography*). Osaka, Japan: Kansai University Press, 1992.

3962   Nakayama, Kiyoshi, Kenji Inoue, and Fumio Momose, trans. *Steinbeku Sakuhinron (II)*. Tokyo, Japan: Eihosha Press, 1982. (a translation of Tetsumaro Hayashi, ed. *A Study Guide to Steinbeck (II)*. (Metuchen, N. J.: Scarecrow Press, 1979). See #3934.

3963   Nakayama, Kiyoshi. *Sutainbekku Bungaku no Kenkyu: Cariforunia Jidai* (*Steinbeck's Writings: The California Years*). Osaka: Kansai University Press, 1989. Contents: Ch. 1: Ogon no Sakazuki. Ch. 2: Shirarezaru kami ni. Ch. 3: Ten no bokujyo. Ch. 4: *Akai kouma* (*The Red Pony*).

Ch. 5: *Totiiya Furatto* (*Tortilla Flat*). Ch. 6: *Utagawashiki tatakai* (*In Dubious Battle*). Ch. 7: *Hatsuka nezumi to ningen* (*Of Mice and Men*). Ch. 8: *Nagai Tanima* (*The Long Valley*). Ch. 9: *Ikari no budo* (*The Grapes of Wrath*). Ch. 10: John Steinbeck nempu. Inshobunken Steinbeck shoshi sakuin.

3964   Nakayama, Yoshimitsu, and Kiyoshi Nakayama, trans. *John Steinbeck. Ikari No Budo O Yomu: Amerika No Eden No Hate* (Louis Owens's *The Grapes of Wrath: Trouble in the Promised Land*, 1989). Osaka, Japan: Kansai University Press, 1993. See Books in English (Entry 428) for a complete breakdown of this text.

3965   Narita, Tatsuo, Hiromasa Takamura, and T. J. O'Brien, trans. *Sutainbekku Kenkyu: Nagai Tanima Ron* (*A Study of Steinbeck: Essays on "The Long Valley"*). Koto: Apollon-sha, 1992. (A translation of *A Study Guide to Steinbeck's "The Long Valley,"* ed. Tetsumaro Hayashi. Ann Arbor: Pierian Press, 1976) Contents: "Maegaki," (foreward); "Nihongo-ban Jobun," (Preface to the Japanese Version) by Tetsumaro Hayashi, i-v; "'Kiku' — Seiteki, Seishinteki, Aimaisei," (Sexual and Spiritual Ambiguity in "The Chrysanthemums") by William V. Miller, 3-20; "'Shiroi Uzura' — Aru Geijutsuka no Shouzou," ("The White Quail":A Portrait of an Artist) by Arthur L. Simpson, 21-29; "'Tousou' — Otokorashisa no Aimaisa," (Steinbeck's "Flight": Ambiguity of Manhood) by John Ditsky, 30-41; "'Hebi' — Aru Kaishaku," (Steinbeck's "The Snake": An Explication) 42-54; "'Asameshi' — I to II," ("Breakfast I and II") by Robert M. Benton, 55-66; "'Shugeki' to *Utagawshiki Tatakai*," ("The Raid" and *In Dubious Battle*) by Peter Lisca, 67-75; "'Shimegu,'" ("The Harness") by Joseph Fontenrose, 76-85; "'Jeikei Danin' — Aru Jikeidanin no Gensou," (A Vigilante's Fantasy) by Franklin E. Court, 86-92; "'Johnny Bear' — Steinbeck no 'Yellow Peril' Monogatari," ("Johnny Bear" — Steinbeck's "Yellow Peril" Story) by Warren French, 95-107; "'Satsujin' — Realism ka Ritual ka?," ('The Murder'

— Realism or Ritual?) by Robert E. Morsberger, 108-120; "'Seishojo Katy' no Himerareta Setsuyu," (The Cryptic Raillery of "Saint Katy the Virgin") by Sanford E. Marovitz, 121-134; "'Okurimono' no Realism to seicho to Taisho," (Realism, Growth and Contrast in "The Gift") by Robert M. Benton, 135-151; "'Dairenpo' — Seihai Densetsu o Megutte," (The Grail Legend and Steinbeck's "The Great Mountains") by Richard F. Peterson, 152-163; "'Yakusoku' — Yakusoku towa," (The Promise of Steinbeck's "The Promise") by Robert H. Woodward, 164-174; "'Shidousha' — Hi-mokiteki Ronteki Approach," (Something That Happened: A Non-teleological Approach to "The Leader of the People") by Richard Astro, 175-184; "Tanpen Sakka to Shiteno Steinbeck," (Steinbeck as a Short Story Writer) by Brian Barbour, 185-216; "Atogaki," (Afterword) 217-218; "Shippitsusha, Henja, Yakusha Shoukai," (Introduction of the Author, Editor and Translator), 219-211.

3966   *Obei Bungaku Koryu no Shoyoso (Some Aspects of Literary Interchange between Europe and America).* Tokyo: Sanshusha, 1983. (contains "Integration of Consciousness and Unconsciousness: Steinbeck's *The Pearl* and Solarism," by Akiko Ozawa on pp. 199-220)

3967   O'Brien, T. J., Hiromasa Takamura, and Tatsuo Narita, trans. *Sutainbekku Kenkyu: Nagai Tanima Ron (A Study of Steinbeck: Essays on "The Long Valley").* Koto: Apollon-sha, 1992. (A translation of *A Study Guide to Steinbeck's "The Long Valley,"* ed. Tetsumaro Hayashi. Ann Arbor: Pierian Press, 1976) See #3965.

3968   Ohashi, Kichinosuke, ed. *Amerika Bungaku Tokuhon (American Literature Reader).* Tokyo: Yuhikaku Press, 1982. (contains "Reading Steinbeck," by Kenji Inoue on pp. 209-226; "A Study of Steinbeck: *The Grapes of Wrath*," by Kenji Inoue on pp. 209-226)

3969   Ogata, Toshihiko, ed. *Amerika Bungaku no Jikotenkai: 20-
        seiki no Amerika Bungaku II (Self-Development in
        American Literature)*. Kyoto: Yamaguchi Shoten Press,
        1982. (contains "John Steinbeck," by Shiro Yokozawa on
        pp. 125-154)

3970   Olson, Ake. *Route 66: Med Vredons Druvor i 30-tal och 80-
        tal (Route 66: With "The Grapes of Wrath" in the 1930s
        and the 1980s)*. Stockholm: Forfattarforlaget, 1983.

3971   Oura, Akio, ed. *Promenade to Masterpieces of English and
        American Literature*. Tokyo: Sanyusha, 1995. (contains
        "Steinbeck's *The Grapes of Wrath*," by Makoto Nagahara
        on pp. 200-10).

3972   *Phoenix o Motomete: Eibei Shosetsu no Yukue (The Search
        for the Phoenix: The Future of American/British Novels)*.
        Tokyo: Nun'undo, 1982. (contains Manubu Sogabu,
        "Steinbeck *Kanzume Yokocho* ni taisuru Hihyo o Megutte;
        Suzuki Yukio Sensei Kinen Ronbushu Kanko Iinkai," (On
        the Criticism of Steinbeck's *Cannery Row*: Mr. Yukio
        Suzuki's Memorial Essay Publishing Committee) and
        Kimegure Basu: Phoenix o Motomete (Steinbeck's *The
        Wayward Bus*: Seeking for the Phoenix) on pp. 325-338)

3973   Ricatte, Robert, and Yves Gohin. *Recherches en sciences des
        textes (Research in the Science of Texts)*. Grenoble:
        University of Grenoble, 1977. See #3926.

3974   Saito, Toshio, ed. *Eigo Eibungaku Kenkyu to Computer
        (Studies in English Language and Literature and the
        Computer)*. Tokyo: Eichosha, 1992. (contains Scott Pugh's
        "Steinbeck's Novels: Possibilities for Stylistic Analysis by
        Computer," on pp. 52-71)

3975   Sano, Minoru, trans. *J. Suttainbekku: Henreki-no Kishi (John
        Steinbeck: The Errant Knight* by Nelson Valjean). Kyoto,

Japan: Yamaguchi Shoten, 1981. (See Books in English of the previous bibliography for a complete citation of this entry)

3976   Shiraga, Eiko and Yasuo Hashiguchi, eds. *Sutainnbekku Sakka Sakuhin Ron (Steinbeck and His Works: A Festschrift in Honor of Dr. Tetsumaro Hayashi)*. Tokyo: Eihosha, 1995. See #3931.

3977   Shiraga, Eiko, and Tetsumaro Hayashi, trans. *Steinbeck's World War II Fiction, "The Moon Is Down": Three Explications/Sutainbekku no Hansen Shosetsu: Tsuki wa Shizuminu Ronko (Steinbeck's Resistance Novel: "The Moon Is Down")*. Okayama: Daigaku Kyoiku Shuppan, 1993. (See Books in English (Entry 310) for a complete citation of contents)

3978   Takamura, Hiromasa. *Sutainbekku to Engeki (Steinbeck and Drama)*. Kyoto: Apolonsha Press, 1990. Contents: Ch. 1: Shosetsuka Steinbeck no gikyoku. Ch. 2: *Hatsuka Nezumi to Ningen* (Gikyoku). (*Of Mice and Men*) Ch. 3: Tsukiwa Shizuminu (Gikyoku). (*The Moon Is Down*) Ch. 4: Run run to Moyuru (Gikyoku). (*Burning Bright*) Ch. 5: Sapata bansai (Eiga Kyakuhon) (*Viva Zapata!*).

3979   Takamura, Hiromasa, T. J. O'Brien, and Tatsuo Narita, trans. *Sutainbekku Kenkyu: Nagai Tanima Ron (A Study of Steinbeck: Essays on "The Long Valley")*. Koto: Apollonsha, 1992. (A translation of *A Study Guide to Steinbeck's "The Long Valley,"* ed. Tetsumaro Hayashi. Ann Arbor: Pierian Press, 1976) See #3965.

3980   Theodorake, Despoina. *Mia Matia ste Sovietske Henose meso tessaron syngrapheon (A Glance at the Soviet Union through Literary Works)*. Herakleion Kretes: Demos Herakleiou, 1988.

3981   Tsuboi, Kiyohiko, and Fumio Momose, trans. *Sutainbekku*
        Zen Tampen Ron: Akai Kouma wo Koete (Essays on All of
        Steinbeck's Short Stories: Beyond "The Red Pony").
        Tokyo: Eihosha, 1991. (a translation of *Beyond "The Red*
        Pony": A Reader's Companion to Steinbeck's Complete
        Short Stories by Robert S. Hughes, Jr. (Metuchen, N. J.:
        Scarecrow Press, 1987) - See Books in English entry (326)
        for full table of contents.

3982   No entry.

3983   Yamashita, Mitsuaki, ed. John Steinbeck's "The Gift" and
        "The Leader of the People." Tokyo: Oshisha Press, 1987.
        Introduction and annotations in Japanese.

3984   Yamashita, Mitsuaki, trans. *Sutainbekku no Joseizo*
        (Steinbeck's Women). Tokyo: Oshisha, 1991. (a translation
        of *Steinbeck's Women: Essays in Criticism.* ed. Tetsumaro
        Hayashi. Steinbeck Monograph Series #9 (Muncie, Ind.:
        Ball State University, 1979)) Contents: Tetsumaro
        Hatyashi, "Nippon no Dokushae," (To the Japanese
        Readers) 1-2; Tetsumaro Hayashi, "Jobun," (Preface) 7-11;
        Richard F. Peterson, "Shogen," (Introduction) 12-19;
        "Steinbeck no Shousetsu ni Okeru Josei no Seikaku
        Byousha no Kenkyu," (A translation of Sandra Beatty's "A
        Study of Female Characterization in Steinbeck's Fiction")
        21-36; "Steinbeck no Onna no Asobinin Tachi — *Hatsuka*
        Nezumi to Ningen, Run-run to Moyuru, Tsuki wa
        Shizuminu, and *Sapata Banzai!* no Kenkyu," (a translation
        of Sandra Beatty's "Steinbeck's Play-Women: A Study of
        Female Presence in *Of Mice and Men, Burning Bright, The*
        Moon is Down, and *Viva Zapata!")* 37-62; "Steinbeck no
        Josei no Toujou Jinbutsu Tachi — Fukujiteki Jinbutsu wa
        Jyuyou de Aruka?" (A translation of Mimi Reisel
        Gladstein's "Female Characters in Steinbeck: Minor
        Characters of Major Importance?") 63-86; "Steinbeck no
        Tsuyoi Josei Tachi — Tanpen ni Okeru josei no
        Dokujisei," (A translation of Marilyn L. Mitchell's

"Steinbeck's Strong Women: Feminine Identity in the Short Stories") 87-114; "Steinbeck no Shiawase na Baishunfu Tachi," (A translation of Robert E. Morsberger's "Steinbeck's Happy Hookers") 115-152; "Steinbeck no Juana — Kachi Aru Josei," (A translation of Mimi Resiel Gladstein's "Steinbeck's Juana: A Woman of Worth") 153-163; Tetsumaro Hayashi, 'Shoshi," (A Selected Bibliography) 165-169; "Kikousha; Hensha Shoukai," (Introduction of writers and Editors), 170-172; "Yakusha Atogaki," (Notes by the Translator), 173-178.

3985 Yamashita, Mitsuaki. *Sutainbekku no Shosetsu* (Steinbeck's Novels). Osaka: Osaka Kyoiku Tosho, 1994. (Includes Dr. Tetsumaro Hayashi's "Introduction," Steinbeck Chronology, Book Reviews, Two Selected Bibliographies, and Index)

3986 Yano, Shigeharu, trans. *Jon Sutainbekku: Toyou to Seiyou* (*John Steinbeck: East and West*). Tokyo: Hokuseido, 1982. (a translation of *John Steinbeck: East and West*. (Steinbeck Monograph Series #8), ed. Tetsumaro Hayashi, Yasuo Hashiguchi, and Richard F. Peterson) Contents: Tetsumaro Hayashi, "Jobun to Shaji" (Preface and Acknowledgements), 7-10; Warren French, "Joron" (Introduction), 11-14; Dai Ichi-bu: Steinbeck Hihyo (Pt I: Steinbeck Criticism) Takahiko Sugiyama, "Steinbeck Hihyo: Genzai to Mirai" (Steinbeck Criticism: Present and Future), 15-23; Hidekazu Hirose, "Doc Burton kara Jim Casy e — 1930 nendai ni okeru Steinbeck" (From Doc Burton to Jim Casy: Steinbeck in the Latter Half of the 1930's), 24-32; Martha Heasley Cox, "*Ikari no Budo* ni okeru Jijitsu Kara Shosetsu e" (Fact into Fiction in *The Grapes of Wrath*: The Weedpatch and Arvin Camps), 33-49; Richard Astro, "Mizuumi Damari kara Hoshi e — Steinbeck no Basho Kankaku (From Tidepool to the Stars: Steinbeck's Sense of Place), 50-58; Dai Ni-bu: Steinbeck — Hikaku Kenkyu (Pt. II: Steinbeck: Comparative Studies) Tetsumaro Hayashi, "*Julius Caesar* to *Sapata Banzai!* ni okeru kakumei no Shudai" (The Theme of

Revolution in *Julius Caesar* and *Viva Zapata!*), 59-78; Kiyohiko Tsuboi, "Steinbeck no *Ogon no Sakazuki* to Fitzgerald no *Idai Naru Gatsby*" (Steinbeck's *Cup of Gold* and Fitzgerald's *The Great Gatsby*), 79-90; Dai San-bu: Steinbeck no Josei (Pt. III: Steinbeck's Women) Fusae Matsumoto, "*Nagai Tani* ni Okeru Steinbeck no Josei" (Steinbeck's Women in *The Long Valley*), 91-99; Sigeharu Yano, "*Nagai Tani* ni Okeru Steinbeck no Josei no shinri Gakuteki Kaishaku" (Psychological Interpretations of Steinbeck's Women in *The Long Valley*), 100-110; Dai Yonbu Steinbeck: Touyou to Seiyou (Pt. IV: Steinbeck: East and West) John Ditsky, "*Eden no Higashi* ni okeru 'higashi'" (The 'East' in *East of Eden*), 111-126; Kiyoshi Nakayama, "Steinbeck no Bungaku to Shishou to Touyou teki Ichi Kaishaku" (An Oriental Interpretation of Steinbeck's Literature and Thought), 127-147; Noburu Shimomura, "John Steinbeck no Shosetsu ni okeru Shinpi Shugi" (Mysticism in John Steinbeck's Novels), 148-160; Shippitsusha Oyobi Henshusha ni tsuite no shokai (Introduction to the Writer and Editor), 161-164.

3987   Zlobin, Georgii Pavlovich. *Po tu storunu mechty. Stranitsy Amerikanskoi literatury XX veka (On This Side of the Dream: Pages of 20th Century American Literature).* Moscow: Khudozhestvennaya Literatura, 1985. (*The Grapes of Wrath*)

Addenda

The following theatrical and movie reviews did not appear in the original bibliographies issued in 1973 and 1983.

Reviews of *Pipe Dream* (musical), an adaptation of Steinbeck's *Sweet Thursday* by Rogers and Hammerstein, may be found in:

America, 94 (January 7, 1956), 417-418.

Catholic World, 182 (February 1956), 388.

Commonweal, 63 (December 30, 1955), 331.

Nation, 181 (December 17, 1955), 544.

New York Theater Critics' Reviews (1955), 544.

New York Times (December 1, 1955), 44.

New Yorker (December 10, 1955), 104.

Newsweek (December 12, 1955), 110.

Saturday Review, 38 (December 18, 1955), 24.

Saturday Review, 39 (September 15, 1956), 13.

Theatre Arts, 40 (February 1956), 12-13.

Time, 66 (December 12, 1955), 67.

Reviews of *Forgotten Village* (screenplay) can be found in:

New York Times (January 26, 1941), Sec. IX: 5.

Saturday Review, 35 (April 12, 1952), 58.

Reviews of *The Red Pony* (screenplay) may be found in:

Photoplay, 35 (May 1949), 32.

Scholastic, 54 (April 6, 1949), 30.

Reviews of *Lifeboat* (screenplay) may be found in:

Cosmopolitan, 116 (February 1944), 92.

New York Times (February 1944), 92.

Theatre Arts, 33 (May 1949), 36.

Reviews of *Viva Zapata!* (screenplay) may be found in:

Catholic World, 174 (March 1952), 459.

Christian Century, 69 (April 23, 1952), 510.

Commonweal, 55 (February 29, 1952), 517.

Holiday, 11 (May 1952), 105.

Library Journal, 77 (February 15, 1952), 311.

Life, 32 (February 25, 1952), 59-61.

New Republic, 126 (February 25, 1952), 21.

New York Times (June 17, 1951), Sec. II: 5.

New York Times (February 3, 1952), Sec. IV: 46.

New York Times (February 3, 1952), Sec. VI: 47.

New York Times (February 8, 1952), 19.

New York Times (February 17, 1952), Sec. II: 1.

New Yorker, 27 (February 16, 1952), 105.

Newsweek, 39 (February 4, 1952), 78.

Saturday Review, 35 (February 9, 1952), 25.

Saturday Review, 35 (February 16, 1952), 6.

Scholastic, 60 (March 5, 1952), 26.

Time, 59 (February 11, 1952), 92.

Reviews of *The Pearl* (screenplay) may be found in:

New York Times (January 19, 1947), Sec. II: 5.

New York Times (February 18, 1948), 36.

Reviews of *A Medal for Benny* (screenplay) may be found in:

New York Times (May 24, 1945), 15.

New York Times (May 27, 1945), Sec. II: 1.

Index

Boldface type indicates the entry is written in a foreign language

About the Author

Michael J. Meyer acquired his keen interest in John Steinbeck while studying at Loyola University Chicago (Ph. D., 1985). Since then he has published chapters on the author in *The Short Novels of John Steinbeck* (Duke University Press, 1990), *The Steinbeck Question* (Whitston, 1993) and *After the "Grapes of Wrath": A Festschrift in Honor of Tetsumaro Hayashi* (Ohio University, 1995). He has also served as assistant editor of *The Steinbeck Quarterly* from 1990-1993 and contributed articles to the International John Steinbeck Society's monograph on *The Long Valley* (Ball State University Press, 1991). Other contributions to Steinbeck scholarship include articles on *Cannery Row* and *The Winter of Our Discontent* in Tetsumaro Hayashi's *A New Study Guide to Steinbeck's Major Works* (Scarecrow Press, 1993) and on *The Pastures of Heaven* and *The Grapes of Wrath* in Brian Railsback's *Steinbeck Encyclopaedia* (Greenwood, forthcoming). Other chapters on Steinbeck have appeared in *Literature and the Bible* and *Literature and Myth* published by Rodopi (Amsterdam/Atlanta, 1993) a press where Meyer also serves as a contributing editor for the Perspectives of Modern Literature series, having edited *Literature and the Grotesque* (1995) and *Literature and Ethnic Discrimination* (1997). An independent scholar, he is now at work on *Cain Sign: The Betrayal of Brotherhood in the Work of John Steinbeck*, a collection of essays tracing the use of the biblical myth in the Steinbeck canon and on *Literature and Homosexuality* for Rodopi.